Principles of Computer System Design

An Introduction

Principles of Computer System Design

An Introduction

Jerome H. Saltzer

M. Frans Kaashoek

Massachusetts Institute of Technology

AMSTERDAM • BOSTON • HEIDELBERG • LONDON
NEW YORK • OXFORD • PARIS • SAN DIEGO
SAN FRANCISCO • SINGAPORE • SYDNEY • TOKYO
Morgan Kaufmann is an imprint of Elsevier

Morgan Kaufmann Publishers is an imprint of Elsevier.
30 Corporate Drive, Suite 400,
Burlington, MA 01803, USA

This book is printed on acid-free paper. ♾

Suggestions, comments, and corrections: Please send correspondence by e-mail to Saltzer@mit.edu and kaashoek@mit.edu

Library of Congress Cataloging-in-Publication Data
Application Submitted

ISBN: 978-0-12-374957-4

For information on all Morgan Kaufmann publications,
visit our Web site at *www.mkp.com* or *www.elsevierdirect.com*

Printed in the United States of America
09 10 11 12 13 10 9 8 7 6 5 4 3 2 1

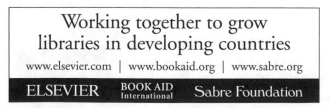

Typeset by: diacriTech, Chennai, India

To Marlys and Mathilda

Contents

PART I

PART II [ON-LINE]

List of Sidebars

Part I

Preface

To the best of our knowledge this textbook is unique in its scope and approach. It provides a broad and in-depth introduction to the main principles and abstractions for engineering computer systems, be it an operating system, a client/service application, a database system, a secure Web site, or a fault-tolerant disk cluster. These principles and abstractions are timeless and are of value to any student or professional reader, whether or not specializing in computer systems. The principles and abstractions derive from insights that have proven to work over generations of computer systems, the authors' own experience with building computer systems, and teaching about them for several decades.

The book teaches a broad set of principles and abstractions, yet it explores them in depth. It captures the core of a concept using pseudocode so that readers can test their understanding of a concrete instance of the concept. Using pseudocode, the book carefully documents the essence of client/service computing, remote procedure calls, files, threads, address spaces, best-effort networks, atomicity, authenticated messages, and so on. This approach continues in the problem sets, where readers can explore the design of a wide range of systems by studying their pseudocode.

This printed textbook is Part I of a two-part publication, containing just the first six chapters. Part II, consisting of Chapters 7–11 and additional supporting materials, is posted on-line as an open educational resource. For details of how and where to find Part II on-line, see "Where to find Part II and other on-line materials" on page xxix.

WHY THIS TEXTBOOK?

Many fundamental ideas concerning computer systems, such as design principles, modularity, naming, abstraction, concurrency, communications, fault tolerance, and atomicity, are common to several of the upper-division electives of the Computer Science and Engineering (CSE) curriculum. A typical CSE curriculum starts with two beginning courses, one on programming and one on hardware. It then branches out, with one of the main branches consisting of systems-oriented electives that carry labels such as

- Operating systems
- Networks
- Database systems
- Distributed systems
- Programming languages
- Software engineering
- Security
- Fault tolerance
- Concurrency
- Architecture

The primary problem with this list is that it has grown over the last three decades, and most students interested in systems do not have the time to take all or even several of those courses. The typical response is for the CSE curriculum to require either "choose three" or "take Operating Systems plus two more". The result is that most students end up with no background at all in the remaining topics. In addition, none of the electives can assume that any of the other electives have preceded it, so common material ends up being repeated several times. Finally, students who are not planning to specialize in systems but want to have some background have little choice but to go into depth in one or two specialized areas.

This book cuts across all of these courses, identifying common mechanisms and design principles, and explaining in depth a carefully chosen set of cross-cutting ideas. This approach provides an opportunity to teach a core undergraduate course that is accessible to all Computer Science and Engineering students, whether or not they intend to specialize in systems. On the one hand, students who will just be users of systems will take away a solid grounding, while on the other hand those who plan to plan to make a career out of designing systems can learn more advanced material more effectively through electives that have the same names as in the list above but with more depth and less duplication. Both groups will acquire a broad base of what the authors hope are timeless concepts rather than current and possibly short-lived techniques. We have found this course structure to be effective at M.I.T.

The book achieves its extensive range of coverage without sacrificing intellectual depth by focusing on underlying and timeless concepts that will serve the student over an entire professional career, rather than providing detailed expositions of the mechanics of operation of current systems that will soon become obsolete. A pervading philosophy of the book is that pedagogy takes precedence over job training. For example, the text does not teach a particular operating system or rely on a single computer architecture. Instead it introduces models that exhibit the main ideas found in contemporary systems, but in forms less cluttered with evolutionary vestiges. The pedagogical model is that for someone who understands the concepts, the detailed mechanics of operation of any particular system can easily and quickly be acquired from other books or from the documentation of the system itself. At the same time, the text makes concepts concrete using pseudocode fragments, so that students have something specific to examine and to test their understanding of the concepts.

FOR WHOM IS THIS BOOK INTENDED?

The authors intend the book for students and professionals who will

- Design computer systems.
- Supervise the design of computer systems.
- Engineer applications of computer systems to information management.
- Direct the integration of computer systems within an organization.
- Evaluate performance of computer systems.

- Keep computer systems technologically up to date.
- Go on to study individual topics such as networks, security, or transaction management in greater depth.
- Work in other areas of computer science and engineering, but would like to have a basic understanding of the main ideas about computer systems.

Level: This book provides an *introduction* to computer systems. It does not attempt to explore every issue or get to the bottom of those issues it does explore. Instead, its goal is for the reader to acquire insight into the complexities of the systems he or she will be depending on for the remainder of a career as well as the concepts needed to interact with system designers. It provides a solid foundation about the mechanisms that underlie operating systems, database systems, data networks, computer security, distributed systems, fault tolerant computing, and concurrency. By the end of the book, the reader should in principle be able to follow the detailed engineering of many aspects of computer systems, be prepared to read and understand current professional literature about systems, and know what questions to ask and where to find the answers.

The book can be used in several ways. It can be the basis for a one-semester, two-quarter, or three-quarter series on computer systems. Or one or two selected chapters can be an introduction of a traditional undergraduate elective or a graduate course in operating systems, networks, database systems, distributed systems, security, fault tolerance, or concurrency. Used in this way, a single book can serve a student several times. Another possibility is that the text can be the basis for a graduate course in systems in which students review those areas they learned as undergraduates and fill in the areas they missed.

Prerequisites: The book carefully limits its prerequisites. When used as a textbook, it is intended for juniors and seniors who have taken introductory courses on software design and on computer hardware organization, but it does not require any more advanced computer science or engineering background. It defines new terms as it goes, and it avoids jargon, but nevertheless it also assumes that the reader has acquired some practical experience with computer systems from a summer job or two or from laboratory work in the prerequisite courses. It does not require that the reader be fluent in any particular computer language, but rather be able to transfer general knowledge about computer programming languages to the varied and sometimes *ad hoc* programming language used in pseudocode examples.

Other Readers: Professionals should also find this book useful. It provides a modern and forward-looking perspective on computer system design, based on enforcing modularity. This perspective recognizes that over the last decade or two, the primary design challenge has become that of keeping complexity under control rather than fighting resource constraints. In addition, professionals who in college took only a subset of the classes in computer systems or an operating systems class that focused on resource management will find that this text refreshes them with a modern and broader perspective.

HOW TO USE THIS BOOK

Exercises and Problem Sets: Each chapter of the textbook ends with a few short-answer exercises intended to test understanding of some of the concepts in that chapter. At the end of the book is a much longer collection of problem sets that challenge the reader to apply the concepts to new and different problems similar to those that might be encountered in the real world. In most cases, the problem sets require concepts from several chapters. Each problem set identifies the chapter or chapters on which it is focused, but later problem sets typically draw concepts from all earlier chapters. Answers to the exercises and solutions for the problem sets are available from the publisher in a separate book for instructors.

The exercises and problem sets can be used in several ways:

- *As tools for learning.* In this mode, the answers and solutions are available to the student, who is encouraged to work the exercises and problem sets and come up with answers and solutions on his or her own. By comparing those answers and solutions with the expected ones, the student receives immediate feedback that can correct misconceptions and can raise questions about ambiguities or misunderstandings. One technique to encourage study of the exercises and solutions is to announce that questions identical to or based on one or more of the problem sets will appear on a forthcoming examination.
- *As homework or examination material.* In this mode, exercises and problem sets are assigned as homework, and the student hands in answers that are evaluated and handed back together with copies of the answers and solutions.
- *As the source of ideas for new exercises and problem sets.*

Case Studies and Readings: To complement the text, the reader should supplement it with readings from the professional technical literature and with case studies. Following the last chapter is a selected bibliography of books and papers that offer wisdom, system design principles, and case studies surrounding the study of systems. By varying the pace of introduction and the number and intellectual depth of the readings, the text can be the basis for a one-term undergraduate core course, a two-term or three-quarter undergraduate sequence, or a graduate-level introduction to computer systems.

Projects: Our experience is that for a course that touches many aspects of computer systems, a combination of several lightweight hands-on assignments (for example, experimentally determine the size of the caches of a personal computer or trace asymmetrical routes through the Internet), plus one or two larger paper projects that involve having a small team do a high-level system design (for example, in a 10-page report design a reliable digital storage system for the Library of Congress), make an excellent adjunct to the text. On the other hand, substantial programming projects that require learning the insides of a particular system take so much homework time that when combined with a broad concepts course they create an overload. Courses with programming projects do work well in follow-on specialized electives, for example, on operating systems, networks, databases, or distributed systems. For this reason, at M.I.T. we assign programming projects in several advanced electives but not in the systems course that is based on this textbook.

Support: Several on-line resources provide support for this textbook. The first of these resources is a set of course syllabi, reading lists, problem sets, videotaped lectures, quizzes, and quiz solutions. A second resource is a Web site of the publisher that is devoted to collecting resources and links of interest to students, professional readers, and instructors. A third resource is a mostly open Web site for communication between instructors of M.I.T. course 6.033, which uses this text, and their current students. It contains announcements, readings, and problem assignments for the current or most recent teaching term. In addition to current class communications, this Web site also holds an archive going back to 1995 that includes

- Design project assignments
- Hands-on assignments
- Examinations and solutions (These overlap the exercises and problem sets of the textbook but they also include exam questions and answers about the outside readings.)
- Lecture and recitation schedules
- Reading assignments and essay questions about the readings

Instructions for finding all of these on-line resources are in the section "Where to find Part II and other on-line materials".

HOW THE BOOK IS ORGANIZED

Because not every instructor may want to use every chapter of the textbook, it is presented in what, at least at the time of publication, may be viewed as a somewhat novel way: The first six chapters, which the authors consider to be the core materials for almost any course about computer systems, appear in this printed book. The remaining five chapters are available on-line from the authors and M.I.T. under a Creative Commons license that permits free, unlimited non-commercial use and remixing. The on-line chapters are also available on the Web site of the publisher of this textbook. There are many forward cross-references from the core chapters to the later chapters. Those cross-references are identified as in this example: "This topic is explored in more detail in Section 7.4.1 [on-line]".

Themes: Three themes run through this textbook. First, as suggested by its title, the text emphasizes the importance of systematic design principles. As each design principle is encountered for the first time, it appears in display form with a label and a mnemonic catchphrase. When that design principle is encountered again, it is identified by its name and highlighted with a distinctive print format as a reminder of its wide applicability. The design principles are also summarized on the inside front cover of this book. A second theme is that the text is network-centered, introducing communication and networks in the beginning chapters and building on that base in the succeeding chapters. A third theme is that it is security-centered, introducing enforced modularity in early chapters and adding successively more stringent enforcement methods in succeeding chapters. The security chapter ends the book, not because it is an afterthought, but because it is the logical culmination of a development based on enforced modularity. Traditional texts and courses teach about threads and virtual memory primarily as a resource allocation problem. This text approaches those topics primarily as ways of providing and enforcing modularity, while at the same time taking advantage of multiple processors and large address spaces.

Terminology and examples: The text identifies and develops concepts and design principles that are common to several specialty fields: software engineering, programming languages, operating systems, distributed systems, networking, database systems, and machine architecture. Experienced computer professionals are likely to find that at least some parts of this text use examples, ways of thinking, and terminology that seem unusual, even foreign to their traditional ways of explaining their favorite topics. But workers from these different specialties will compile different lists of what seems foreign. The reason is that, historically, workers within these specialties have identified what turn out to be identical underlying concepts and design principles, but they have used different language, different perspectives, different examples, and different terminology to explain them.

This text chooses, for each concept, what the authors believe is the most pedagogically effective explanation and examples, adopting widely used terminology wherever possible. In cases where different specialty areas use conflicting terms, glossaries and sidebars provide bridges and discuss terminology collisions. The result is a novel, but in our experience effective, way of teaching new generations of Computer Science and Engineering students what is fundamental about computer system design. With this starting point, when the student reads an advanced book or paper or takes an advanced elective course, he or she should be able to immediately recognize familiar concepts cloaked in the terminology of the specialty. A scientist would explain this approach by saying "The physics is independent of the units of measurement." A similar principle applies to the engineering of computer systems: "The concepts are independent of the terminology".

Citations: The text does not use citations as a scholarly method of identifying the originators of each concept or idea; if it did, the book would be twice as thick. Instead the citations that do appear are pointers to related materials that the authors think are worth knowing about. There is one exception: certain sections are devoted to war stories, which may have been distorted by generations of retelling. These stories include citations intended to identify the known sources of each story, so that the reader has a way to assess their validity.

CHAPTER CONTENT

Relation to ACM/IEEE recommendations: The ACM/IEEE Computer Science and Engineering recommendations of 2001 and 2004 describe two layers. The first layer is a set of modules that constitute an appropriate CSE education. The second layer consists of several suggested packagings of those modules into term-sized courses. This book may be best viewed as a distinct, modern packaging of the modules, somewhat resembling the ACM/IEEE Computer Science 2001 recommendation CS226c, Operating Systems and Networking (compressed), but with the additional scope of naming, fault tolerance, atomicity, and both system and network security. It also somewhat resembles the ACM/IEEE Computer engineering 2004 recommendation CPE_D203, Operating Systems and Net-Centric computing, with the additional scope of naming, fault tolerance, atomicity, and cryptographic protocols.

Chapter 1: Systems. This chapter lays out the general philosophy of the authors on ways to think about systems, with examples illustrating how computer systems are similar to, and different from, other engineering systems. It also introduces three main ideas: (1) the importance of systematic design principles, (2) the role of modularity in controlling complexity of large systems, and (3) methods of enforcing modularity.

Chapter 2: Elements of Computer System Organization. This chapter introduces three key methods of achieving and taking advantage of modularity in computer systems: abstraction, naming, and layers. The discussion of abstraction lightly reviews computer architecture from a systems perspective, creating a platform on which the rest of the book builds, but without simple repetition of material that readers probably already know. The naming model is fundamental to how computer systems are modularized, yet it is a subject usually left to advanced texts on programming language design. The chapter ends with a case study of the way in which naming, layering, and abstraction are applied in the UNIX file system. Because the case study develops as a series of pseudocode fragments, it provides both a concrete example of the concepts of the chapter and a basis for reference in later chapters.

Chapter 3: Design of Naming Schemes. This chapter continues the discussion of naming in system design by introducing pragmatic engineering considerations and reinforcing the role that names play in organizing a system as a collection of modules. The chapter ends with a case study and a collection of war stories. The case study uses the Uniform Resource Locator (URL) of the World Wide Web to show an example of nearly every naming scheme design consideration. The war stories are examples of failures of real-world naming systems, illustrating what goes wrong when a designer ignores or is unaware of design considerations.

Chapter 4: Enforcing Modularity with Clients and Services. The first three chapters developed the importance of modularity in system design. This chapter begins the theme of enforcing that modularity by introducing the client/service model, which is a powerful and widely used method of allowing modules to interact without interfering with one another. This chapter also begins the network-centric perspective that pervades the rest of the book. At this point, we view the network only as an abstract communication system that provides a strong boundary between client and service. Two case studies again help nail down the concepts. The first is of the Internet Domain Name System (DNS), which provides a concrete illustration of the concepts of both Chapters 3 and 4. The second case study, that of the Sun Network

File System (NFS), builds on the case study of the UNIX file system in Chapter 2 and illustrates the impact of remote service on the semantics of application programming interfaces.

Chapter 5: Enforcing Modularity with Virtualization. This chapter switches attention to enforcing modularity within a computer by introducing virtual memory and virtual processors, commonly called threads. For both memory and threads, the discussion begins with an environment that has unlimited resources. The virtual memory discussion starts with an assumption of many threads operating in an unlimited address space and then adds mechanisms to prevent threads from unintentionally interfering with one another's data—addressing domains and the user/kernel mode distinction. Finally, the text examines limited address spaces, which require introducing virtual addresses and address translation, along with the inter-address-space communication problems that they create.

Similarly, the discussion of threads starts with the assumption that there are as many processors as threads, and concentrates on coordinating their concurrent activities. It then moves to the case where a limited number of real processors are available, so thread management is also required. The discussion of thread coordination uses eventcounts and sequencers, a set of mechanisms that are not often seen in practice but that fit the examples in a natural way. Traditionally, thread coordination is among the hardest concepts for the first-time reader to absorb. Problem sets then invite readers to test their understanding of the principles with semaphores and condition variables.

The chapter explains the concepts of virtual memory and threads both in words and in pseudocode that help clarify how the abstract ideas actually work, using familiar real-world problems. In addition, the discussion of thread coordination is viewed as the first step in understanding atomicity, which is the subject of Chapter 9 [on-line].

The chapter ends with a case study and an application. The case study explores how enforced modularity has evolved over the years in the Intel x86 processor family. The application is the use of virtualization to create virtual machines. The overall perspective of this chapter is to focus on enforcing modularity rather than on resource management, taking maximum advantage of contemporary hardware technology, in which processor chips are multicore, address spaces are 64 bits wide, and the amount of directly addressable memory is measured in gigabytes.

Chapter 6: Performance. This chapter focuses on intrinsic performance bottlenecks that are found in common across many kinds of computer systems, including operating systems, databases, networks, and large applications. It explores two of the traditional topics of operating systems books—resource scheduling and multilevel memory management—but in a context that emphasizes the importance of maintaining perspective on performance optimization in a world where each decade brings a thousand-fold improvement in some underlying hardware capabilities while barely affecting other performance metrics. As an indication of this different perspective, scheduling is illustrated with a disk arm scheduling problem rather than the usual time-sharing processor scheduler.

Chapters 7 through 11 are on-line, in Part II of the book. Their contents are described in the section titled "About Part II" on page 369, and information on how to locate them can be found in "Where to find Part II and other on-line materials".

Suggestions for Further Reading. A selected reading list includes commentary on why each selection is worth reading. The selection emphasis is on books and papers that provide insight rather than materials that provide details.

Problem Sets. The authors use examinations not just as a method of assessment, but also as a method of teaching. Therefore, some of the exercises at the end of each chapter and the problem sets at the end of the book (all of which are derived from examinations administered over the years while teaching the material of this textbook) go well beyond simple practice with the concepts. In working the problems out, the student explores alternative designs, learns about variations of techniques seen in the textbook, and becomes familiar with interesting, sometimes exotic, ideas and methods that have been proposed for or used in real system designs. The problem sets generally have significant setup, and they ask questions that require applying concepts creatively, with the goal of understanding the trade-offs that arise in using these methods.

Glossary. As mentioned earlier, the literature of computer systems derives from several different specialties that have each developed their own dictionaries of system-related concepts. This textbook adopts a uniform terminology throughout, and the Glossary offers definitions of each significant term of art, indicates which chapter introduces the term, and in many cases explains different terms used by different workers in different specialties. For completeness and for easy reference, the Glossary in this book includes terms introduced in Part II.

Index of Concepts. The index tells where to find the defining discussion of every concept. In addition, it lists every application of each of the design principles. (For completeness, it includes concepts that are introduced in Part II, listing just the chapter number.)

Where to find Part II and other On-line Materials

1. Professors Saltzer and Kaashoek and MIT OpenCourseWare* provide, free of charge, on-line versions of Chapters 7 through 11, additional problem sets, a copy of the glossary, and a comprehensive index in the form of one Portable Document Format (PDF) file per chapter or section and also a single PDF file containing the entire set. Those materials can be found at

   `http://ocw.mit.edu/Saltzer-Kaashoek`

2. The publisher of this printed book also maintains a set of on-line resources at

   `www.ElsevierDirect.com/9780123749574`

   Click on the link "Companion Materials" where you will find Part II of the book as well as other resources, including figures from the text in several formats. Additional materials for instructors (registration required) can be found by clicking the "Manual" link.

3. Teaching and support materials can be found at

   `http://ocw.mit.edu/6-033`

4. The Web site for the current MIT class that uses this textbook, including the archives of older teaching materials, is at

   `http://mit.edu/6.033`

   (Some copyrighted or privacy-sensitive materials on that Web site are restricted to current MIT students.)

---

*The M.I.T. OpenCourseWare initiative places on-line, for non-commercial free access, teaching materials from many M.I.T. courses, and thus is helping set a standard for curricula in science and engineering. In addition to Chapters 7 through 11, OpenCourseWare publishes on-line materials for the M.I.T. course that uses these materials, 6.033. Thus, an instructor interested in making use of the textbook can find in one place course syllabi, reading lists, problem sets, videotaped lectures, quizzes, and solutions.

Acknowledgments

This textbook began as a set of notes for the advanced undergraduate course Engineering of Computer Systems (6.033, originally 6.233), offered by the Department of Electrical Engineering and Computer Science of the Massachusetts Institute of Technology starting in 1968. The text has benefited from four decades of comments and suggestions by many faculty members, visitors, recitation instructors, teaching assistants, and students. Over 5,000 students have used (and suffered through) draft versions, and observations of their learning experiences (as well as frequent confusion caused by the text) have informed the writing. We are grateful for those many contributions. In addition, certain aspects deserve specific acknowledgment.

1. Naming (Section 2.2 and Chapter 3)

The concept and organization of the materials on naming grew out of extensive discussions with Michael D. Schroeder. The naming model (and part of our development) follows closely the one developed by D. Austin Henderson in his Ph.D. thesis. Stephen A. Ward suggested some useful generalizations of the naming model, and Roger Needham suggested several concepts in response to an earlier version of this material. That earlier version, including in-depth examples of the naming model applied to addressing architectures and file systems, and an historical bibliography, was published as Chapter 3 in Rudolf Bayer et al., editors, *Operating Systems: An Advanced Course, Lecture Notes in Computer Science 60*, pages 99–208. Springer-Verlag, 1978, reprinted 1984. Additional ideas have been contributed by many others, including Ion Stoica, Karen Sollins, Daniel Jackson, Butler Lampson, David Karger, and Hari Balakrishnan.

2. Enforced Modularity and Virtualization (Chapters 4 and 5)

Chapter 4 was heavily influenced by lectures on the same topic by David L. Tennenhouse. Both chapters have been improved by substantial feedback from Hari Balakrishnan, Russ Cox, Michael Ernst, Eddie Kohler, Chris Laas, Barbara H. Liskov, Nancy Lynch, Samuel Madden, Robert T. Morris, Max Poletto, Martin Rinard, Susan Ruff, Gerald Jay Sussman, Julie Sussman, and Michael Walfish.

3. Networks (Chapter 7 [on-line])

Conversations with David D. Clark and David L. Tennenhouse were instrumental in laying out the organization of this chapter, and lectures by Clark were the basis for part of the presentation. Robert H. Halstead Jr. wrote an early draft set of notes about networking, and some of his ideas have also been borrowed. Hari Balakrishnan provided many suggestions and corrections and helped sort out muddled explanations, and Julie Sussman and Susan Ruff pointed out many opportunities to improve the presentation. The material on congestion control was developed with the help of extensive discussions with Hari Balakrishnan and Robert T. Morris, and is based in part on ideas from Raj Jain.

4. Fault Tolerance (Chapter 8 [on-line])

Most of the concepts and examples in this chapter were originally articulated by Claude Shannon, Edward F. Moore, David Huffman, Edward J. McCluskey, Butler W. Lampson, Daniel P. Siewiorek, and Jim N. Gray.

5. Transactions and Consistency (Chapters 9 [on-line] and 10 [on-line])

The material of the transactions and consistency chapters has been developed over the course of four decades with aid and ideas from many sources. The concept of version histories is due to Jack Dennis, and the particular form of all-or-nothing and before-or-after atomicity with version histories developed here is due to David P. Reed. Jim N. Gray not only came up with many of the ideas described in these two chapters, he also provided extensive comments. (That doesn't imply endorsement—he disagreed strongly about the importance of some of the ideas!) Other helpful comments and suggestions were made by Hari Balakrishnan, Andrew Herbert, Butler W. Lampson, Barbara H. Liskov, Samuel R. Madden, Larry Rudolph, Gerald Jay Sussman, and Julie Sussman.

6. Computer Security (Chapter 11 [on-line])

Sections 11.1 and 11.6 draw heavily from the paper "The protection of information in computer systems" by Jerome H. Saltzer and Michael D. Schroeder, *Proceedings of the IEEE 63,* 9 (September, 1975), pages 1278–1308. Ronald Rivest, David Mazières, and Robert T. Morris made significant contributions to material presented throughout the chapter. Brad Chen, Michael Ernst, Kevin Fu, Charles Leiserson, Susan Ruff, and Seth Teller made numerous suggestions for improving the text.

7. Suggested Outside Readings

Ideas for suggested readings have come from many sources. Particular thanks must go to Michael D. Schroeder, who uncovered several of the classic systems papers in places outside computer science where nobody else would have thought to look; Edward D. Lazowska, who provided an extensive reading list used at the University of Washington; and Butler W. Lampson, who provided a thoughtful review of the list.

8. The Exercises and Problem Sets

The exercises at the end of each chapter and the problem sets at the end of the book have been collected, suggested, tried, debugged, and revised by many different faculty members, instructors, teaching assistants, and undergraduate students over a period of 40 years in the process of constructing quizzes and examinations while teaching the material of the text.

Certain of the longer exercises and most of the problem sets, which are based on lead-in stories and include several related questions, represent a substantial effort by a single individual. For those problem sets not developed by one of the authors, a credit line appears in a footnote on the first page of the problem set.

Following each problem or problem set is an identifier of the form "*1978-3-14*". This identifier reports the year, examination number, and problem number of the examination in which some version of that problem first appeared.

Jerome H. Saltzer
M. Frans Kaashoek
2009

CHAPTER

Systems

1

CHAPTER CONTENTS

Principles of Computer System Design: An Introduction

DOI: 10.1016/B978-0-12-374957-4.00009-8

OVERVIEW

This book is about computer systems, and this chapter introduces some of the vocabulary and concepts used in designing computer systems. It also introduces "systems perspective", a way of thinking about systems that is global and encompassing rather than focused on particular issues. A full appreciation of this way of thinking can't really be captured in a short summary, so this chapter is actually just a preview of ideas that will be developed in depth in succeeding chapters.

The usual course of study of computer science and engineering begins with linguistic constructs for describing computations (software) and physical constructs for realizing computations (hardware). It then branches, focusing, for example, on the theory of computation, artificial intelligence, or the design of systems, which itself is usually divided into specialities: operating systems, transaction and database systems, computer architecture, software engineering, compilers, computer networks, security, and reliability. Rather than immediately tackling one of those specialties, we assume that the reader has completed the introductory courses on software and hardware, and we begin a broad study of computer systems that supports the entire range of systems specialties.

Many interesting applications of computers require

- fault tolerance
- coordination of concurrent activities
- geographically separated but linked data
- vast quantities of stored information
- protection from mistakes and intentional attacks
- interactions with many people

To develop applications that have these requirements, the designer must look beyond the software and hardware and view the computer system as a whole. In doing so, the designer encounters many new problems—so many that the limit on the scope of computer systems generally arises neither from laws of physics nor from theoretical impossibility, but rather from limitations of human understanding.

Some of these same problems have counterparts, or at least analogs, in other systems that have, at most, only incidental involvement of computers. The study of systems is one place where computer engineering can take advantage of knowledge from other engineering areas: civil engineering (bridges and skyscrapers), urban planning (the

Much wisdom about systems that has accumulated over the centuries is passed along in the form of folklore, maxims, aphorisms and quotations. Some of that wisdom is captured in the boxes at the bottom of these pages.

Everything should be made as simple as possible, but no simpler.

> **— commonly attributed to Albert Einstein; it is actually a paraphrase of a comment he made in a 1933 lecture at Oxford.**

design of cities), mechanical engineering (automobiles and air conditioning), aviation and space flight, electrical engineering, and even ecology and political science. We start by looking at some of those common problems. Then we will examine two ways in which computer systems pose problems that are quite different. Don't worry if some of the examples are of things you have never encountered or are only dimly aware of. The sole purpose of the examples is to illustrate the range of considerations and similarities across different kinds of systems.

As we proceed in this chapter and throughout the book, we shall point out a series of *system design principles*, which are rules of thumb that usually apply to a diverse range of situations. Design principles are not immutable laws, but rather guidelines that capture wisdom and experience and that can help a designer avoid making mistakes. The astute reader will quickly realize that sometimes a tension, even to the point of contradiction, exists between different design principles. Nevertheless, if a designer finds that he or she is violating a design principle, it is a good idea to review the situation carefully.

At the first encounter of a design principle, the text displays it prominently. Here is an example, found on page 16.

Avoid excessive generality

If it's good for everything, it's good for nothing.

Each design principle thus has a formal title ("Avoid excessive generality") and a brief informal description ("If it's good for . . ."), which are intended to help recall the principle. Most design principles will show up several times, in different contexts, which is one reason why they are useful. The text highlights later encounters of a principle such as: *avoid excessive generality*. A list of all of the design principles in the book can be found on the inside front cover and also in the index, under "Design principles".

The remaining sections of this chapter discuss common problems of systems, the sources of those problems, and techniques for coping with them.

1.1 SYSTEMS AND COMPLEXITY

1.1.1 Common Problems of Systems in Many Fields

The problems one encounters in these many kinds of systems can usefully be divided into four categories: *emergent properties, propagation of effects, incommensurate scaling*, and *trade-offs*.

> Seek simplicity and distrust it.
>
> — **Alfred North Whitehead, *The Concept of Nature* (1920)**

1.1.1.1 Emergent Properties

Emergent properties are properties that are not evident in the individual components of a system, but show up when combining those components, so they might also be called surprises. Emergent properties abound in most systems, although there can always be a (fruitless) argument about whether or not careful enough prior analysis of the components might have allowed prediction of the surprise. It is wise to avoid this argument and instead focus on an unalterable fact of life: some things turn up only when a system is built.

Some examples of emergent properties are well known. The behavior of a committee or a jury often surprises outside observers. The group develops a way of thinking that could not have been predicted from knowledge about the individuals. (The concept of—and the label for—emergent properties originated in sociology.) When the Millennium Bridge for pedestrians over the River Thames in London opened, its designers had to close it after only a few days. They were surprised to discover that pedestrians synchronize their footsteps when the bridge sways, causing it to sway even more. Interconnection of several electric power companies to allow load sharing helps reduce the frequency of power failures, but when a failure finally occurs it may take down the entire interconnected structure. The political surprise is that the number of customers affected may be large enough to attract the unwanted attention of government regulators.

1.1.1.2 Propagation of Effects

The electric power inter-tie also illustrates the second category of system problems—*propagation of effects*—when a tree falling on a power line in Oregon leads to the lights going out in New Mexico, 1000 miles away. What looks at first to be a small disruption or a local change can have effects that reach from one end of a system to the other. An important requirement in most system designs is to limit the impact of failures. As another example of propagation of effects, consider an automobile designer's decision to change the tire size on a production model car from 13 to 15 inches. The reason for making the change might have been to improve the ride. On further analysis, this change leads to many other changes: redesigning the wheel wells, enlarging the spare tire space, rearranging the trunk that holds the spare tire, and moving the back seat forward slightly to accommodate the trunk redesign. The seat change makes knee room in the back seat too small, so the backs of the seats must be made thinner, which in turn reduces the comfort that was the original reason for changing the tire size, and it may also reduce safety in a collision. The extra weight of the trunk and rear seat design means that stiffer rear springs are now needed. The rear axle ratio must be modified to keep the force delivered to the road by the wheels correct, and the speedometer gearing must be changed to agree with the new tire size and axle ratio.

Those effects are the obvious ones. In complicated systems, as the analysis continues, more distant and subtle effects normally appear. As a typical example, the

> Our life is frittered away by detail . . . simplicity, simplicity, simplicity!
>
> **— Henry David Thoreau, *Walden; or, Life in the Woods* (1854)**

automobile manufacturer may find that the statewide purchasing office for Texas does not currently have a certified supplier for replacement tires of the larger size. Thus there will probably be no sales of cars to the Texas government for two years, which is the length of time it takes to add a supplier onto the certified list. Folk wisdom characterizes propagation of effects as: "There are no small changes in a large system".

1.1.1.3 Incommensurate Scaling

The third characteristic problem encountered in the study of systems is *incommensurate scaling*: as a system increases in size or speed, not all parts of it follow the same scaling rules, so things stop working. The mathematical description of this problem is that different parts of the system exhibit different orders of growth. Some examples:

- Galileo observed that "nature cannot produce a ... giant ten times taller than an ordinary man unless by ... greatly altering the proportions of his limbs and especially of his bones, which would have to be considerably enlarged over the ordinary" [*Discourses and Mathematical Demonstrations on Two New Sciences*, second day, Leiden, 1638]. In a classic 1928 paper, "On being the right size" [see Suggestions for Further Reading 1.4.1], J. B. S. Haldane uses the example of a mouse, which, if scaled up to the size of an elephant, would collapse of its own weight. For both examples, the reason is that weight grows with volume, which is proportional to the cube of linear size, but bone strength, which depends primarily on cross-sectional area, grows only with the square of linear size. Thus a real elephant requires a skeletal arrangement that is quite different from that of a scaled-up mouse.
- The Egyptian architect Sneferu tried to build larger and larger pyramids. Unfortunately, the facing fell off the pyramid at Meidum, and the ceiling of the burial chamber of the pyramid at Dashur cracked. He later figured out that he could escalate a pyramid to the size of the pyramids at Giza by lowering the ratio of the pyramid's height to its width. The reason this solution worked has apparently never been completely analyzed, but it seems likely that incommensurate scaling was involved—the weight of a pyramid increases with the cube of its linear size, while the strength of the rock used to create the ceiling of a burial chamber increases only with the area of its cross-section, which grows with the square.
- The captain of a modern oil supertanker finds that the ship is so massive that when underway at full speed it takes 12 miles to bring it to a straight line stop—but 12 miles is beyond the horizon as viewed from the ship's bridge (see Sidebar 1.1 for the details).
- The height of a skyscraper is limited by the area of lower floors that must be devoted to providing access to the floors above. The amount of access area

> By undue profundity we perplex and enfeeble thought.
>
> — **Edgar Allan Poe, "The Murders in the Rue Morgue" (1841)**

Sidebar 1.1 Stopping a Supertanker A little geometry reveals that the distance to the visual horizon is proportional to the square root of the height of the bridge. That height (presumably) grows with the first power of the supertanker's linear dimension. The energy required to stop or turn a supertanker is proportional to its mass, which grows with the third power of its linear dimensions. The time required to deliver the stopping or turning energy is less clear, but pushing on the rudder and reversing the propellers are the only tools available, and both of those have surface area that grows with the square of the linear dimension.

Here is the bottom line: if we double the tanker's linear dimensions, the momentum goes up by a factor of 8, and the ability to deliver stopping or turning energy goes up by only a factor of 4, so we need to see twice as far ahead. Unfortunately, the horizon will be only 1.414 times as far away. Inevitably, there is some size for which visual navigation must fail.

required (for example, for elevators and stairs) is proportional to the number of people who have offices on higher floors. That number is in turn proportional to the number of higher floors multiplied by the usable area of each floor. If all floors have the same area, and the number of floors increases, at some point the bottom floor will be completely used up providing access to higher floors, so the bottom floor provides no added value (apart from being able to brag about the building's height). In practice, the economics of office real estate dictate that no more than 25% of the lowest floor be devoted to access.

Incommensurate scaling shows up in most systems. It is usually the factor that limits the size or speed range that a single system design can handle. On the other hand, one must be cautious with scaling arguments. They were used at the beginning of the twentieth century to support the claim that it was a waste of time to build airplanes (see Sidebar 1.2).

1.1.1.4 Trade-offs

The fourth problem of system design is that many constraints present themselves as *trade-offs*. The general model of a trade-off begins with the observation that there is a limited amount of some form of goodness in the universe, and the design challenge is first to maximize that goodness, second to avoid wasting it, and third to allocate it to the places where it will help the most. One common form of trade-off is sometimes called the *waterbed effect*: pushing down on a problem at one point causes another problem to pop up somewhere else. For example, one can typically push a hardware circuit to run at a higher clock rate, but that change increases both power consumption and the risk of timing errors. It may be possible to reduce the risk of timing errors by making the circuit physically smaller, but then less area will be available to dissipate the heat caused

KISS: Keep It Simple, Stupid.

— traditional management folklore; source lost in the mists of time

Sidebar 1.2 Why Airplanes can't Fly The weight of an airplane grows with the third power of its linear dimension, but the lift, which is proportional to surface area, can grow only with the second power. Even if a small plane can be built, a larger one will never get off the ground.

This line of reasoning was used around 1900 by both physicists and engineers to argue that it was a waste of time to build heavier-than-air machines. Alexander Graham Bell proved that this argument wasn't the whole story by flying box kites in Maine in the summer of 1902. In his experiments he attached two box kites side by side, a configuration that doubled the lifting surface area, but also allowed removal of the redundant material and supports where the two kites touched. Thus, the lift-to-weight ratio actually improved as the scale increased. Bell published his results in "The tetrahedral principle in kite structure" [see Suggestions for Further Reading 1.4.2].

by the increased power consumption. Another common form of trade-off appears in *binary classification*, which arises, for example, in the design of smoke detectors, spam (unwanted commercial e-mail message) filters, database queries, and authentication devices. The general model of binary classification is that we wish to classify a set of things into two categories based on the presence or absence of some property, but we lack a direct measure of that property. We therefore instead identify and use some indirect measure, known as a *proxy*. Occasionally, this scheme misclassifies something. By adjusting parameters of the proxy, the designer may be able to reduce one class of mistakes (in the case of a smoke detector, unnoticed fires; for a spam filter, legitimate messages marked as spam), but only at the cost of increasing some other class of mistakes (for the smoke detector, false alarms; for the spam filter, spam marked as legitimate messages). Appendix A explores the binary classification trade-off in more detail. Much of a system designer's intellectual effort goes into evaluating various kinds of trade-offs.

Emergent properties, propagation of effects, incommensurate scaling, and trade-offs are issues that the designer must deal with in every system. The question is how to build useful computer systems in the face of such problems. Ideally, we would like to describe a constructive theory, one that allows the designer systematically to synthesize a system from its specifications and to make necessary trade-offs with precision, just as there are constructive theories in such fields as communications systems, linear control systems, and (to a certain extent) the design of bridges and skyscrapers. Unfortunately, in the case of computer systems, we find that we were apparently born too soon. Although our early arrival on the scene offers the challenge to develop the missing theory, the problem is quickly apparent—we work almost entirely by analyzing *ad hoc* examples rather than by synthesizing.

Fools ignore complexity. Pragmatists suffer it. Some can avoid it. Geniuses remove it.

— Alan J. Perlis, "Epigrams in Programming" (1982)

So, in place of a well-organized theory, we use case studies. For each subtopic in this book, we shall begin by identifying requirements with the apparent intent of deriving the system structure from the requirements. Then, almost immediately we switch to case studies and work backwards to see how real, in-the-field systems meet the requirements that we have set. Along the way we point out where systematic approaches to synthesizing a system from its requirements are beginning to emerge, and we introduce representations, abstractions, and design principles that have proven useful in describing and building systems. The intended result of this study is insight into how designers create real systems.

1.1.2 Systems, Components, Interfaces, and Environments

Webster's Third New International Dictionary, Unabridged, defines a system as "a complex unity formed of many often diverse parts subject to a common plan or serving a common purpose." Although this definition will do for casual use of the word, engineers usually prefer something a bit more concrete. We identify the "many often diverse parts" by naming them *components*. We identify the "unity" and "common plan" with the *interconnections* of the components, and we perceive the "common purpose" of a system to be to exhibit a certain behavior across its *interface* to an *environment*. Thus we formulate our technical definition: **A *system* is a set of interconnected components that has an expected behavior observed at the interface with its environment**.

The underlying idea of the concept of system is to divide all the things in the world into two groups: those under discussion and those not under discussion. Those things under discussion are part of the system—those that are not are part of the *environment*. For example, we might define the solar system as consisting of the sun, planets, asteroids, and comets. The environment of the solar system is the rest of the universe. (Indeed, the word "universe" is a synonym for environment.)

There are always interactions between a system and its environment; these interactions are the *interface* between the system and the environment. The interface between the solar system and the rest of the universe includes gravitational attraction for the nearest stars and the exchange of electromagnetic radiation. The primary interfaces of a personal computer typically include things such as a display, keyboard, speaker, network connection, and power cord, but there are also less obvious interfaces such as the atmospheric pressure, ambient temperature and humidity, and the electromagnetic noise environment.

One studies a system to predict its overall behavior, based on information about its components, their interconnections, and their individual behaviors. Identifying the components, however, depends on one's point of view, which has two aspects, *purpose* and *granularity*. One may, with different purposes in mind, look at a system quite

> And simplicity is the unavoidable price we must pay for reliability.
>
> — **Charles Anthony Richard Hoare, "Data Reliability" (1975)**

Sidebar 1.3 Terminology: Words used to Describe System Composition Since systems can contain component subsystems that are themselves systems from a different point of view, decomposition of systems is recursive. To avoid recursion in their writing, authors and designers have come up with a long list of synonyms, all trying to capture this same concept: *systems*, *subsystems*, *components*, *elements*, *constituents*, *objects*, *modules*, *submodules*, *assemblies*, *subassemblies*, and so on.

differently. One may also choose any of several different granularities. These choices affect one's identification of the components of the system in important ways.

To see how point of view can depend on purpose, consider two points of view of a jet aircraft as a system. The first looks at the aircraft as a flying object, in which the components of the system include the body, wings, control surfaces, and engines. The environment is the atmosphere and the earth, with interfaces consisting of gravity, engine thrust, and air drag. A second point of view looks at the aircraft as a passenger-handling system. Now, the components include seats, flight attendants, the air conditioning system, and the galley. The environment is the set of passengers, and the interfaces are the softness of the seats, the meals, and the air flowing from the air conditioning system.

In the first point of view, the aircraft as a flying object, the seats, flight attendants, and galley were present, but the designer considers them primarily as contributors of weight. Conversely, in the second point of view, as a passenger-handling system, the designer considers the engine as a source of noise and perhaps also exhaust fumes, and probably ignores the control surfaces on the wings. Thus, depending on point of view, we may choose to ignore or consolidate certain system components or interfaces.

The ability to choose granularity means that a component in one context may be an entire system in another. From an aircraft designer's point of view, a jet engine is a component that contributes weight, thrust, and perhaps drag. On the other hand, the manufacturer of the engine views it as a system in its own right, with many components—turbines, hydraulic pumps, bearings, afterburners, all of which interact in diverse ways to produce thrust—one interface with the environment of the engine. The airplane wing that supports the engine is a component of the aircraft system, but it is part of the environment of the engine system.

When a system in one context is a component in another, it is usually called a *subsystem* (but see Sidebar 1.3). The composition of systems from subsystems or decomposition of systems into subsystems can be carried on to as many levels as is useful.

In summary, then, to analyze a system one must establish a point of view to determine which things to consider as components, what the granularity of those

Pluralitas non est ponenda sine neccesitate. (Plurality should not be assumed without necessity.)

— **William of Ockham (14th century. Popularly known as "Occam's razor," though the idea itself is said to appear in writings of greater antiquity.)**

components should be, where the boundary of the system lies, and which interfaces between the system and its environment are of interest.

As we use the term, a *computer system* or an *information system* is a system intended to store, process, or communicate information under automatic control. Further, we are interested in systems that are predominantly digital. Here are some examples:

- a personal computer
- the onboard engine controller of an automobile
- the telephone system
- the Internet
- an airline ticket reservation system
- the space shuttle ground control system
- a World Wide Web site

At the same time we will sometimes find it useful to look at examples of nondigital and nonautomated information handling systems, such as the post office or library, for ideas and guidance.

1.1.3 Complexity

Webster's definition of "system" used the word "complex". Looking up that term, we find that *complex* means "difficult to understand". Lack of systematic understanding is the underlying feature of complexity. It follows that complexity is both a subjective and a relative concept. That is, one can argue that one system is more complex than another, but even though one can count up various things that seem to contribute to complexity, there is no unified measure. Even the argument that one system is more complex than another can be difficult to make compelling—again because of the lack of a unified measure. In place of such a measure, we can borrow a technique from medicine: describe a set of *signs* of complexity that can help confirm a diagnosis. As a corollary, we abandon hope of producing a definitive description of complexity. We must instead look for its signs, and if enough appear, argue that complexity is present. To that end, here are five signs of complexity:

1. **Large number of components.** Sheer size certainly affects our view of whether or not a system rates the description "complex".
2. **Large number of interconnections.** Even a few components may be interconnected in an unmanageably large number of ways. For example, the Sun and the known planets comprise only a few components, but every one has gravitational

> Il semble que la perfection soit atteinte non quand il n'y a plus rien à ajouter, mais quand il n'y a plus rien à retrancher. (It is as if perfection be attained not when there is nothing more to add, but when there is nothing more to take away.)
>
> **— Antoine de Saint-Exupéry, *Terre des Hommes* (1939)**

attraction for every other, which leads to a set of equations that are unsolvable (in closed form) with present mathematical techniques. Worse, a small disturbance can, after a while, lead to dramatically different orbits. Because of this sensitivity to disturbance, the solar system is technically *chaotic*. Although there is no formal definition of chaos for computer systems, that term is often informally applied.

3. **Many irregularities.** By themselves, a large number of components and interconnections may still represent a simple system, if the components are repetitive and the interconnections are regular. However, a lack of regularity, as shown by the number of exceptions or by non-repetitive interconnection arrangements, strongly suggests complexity. Put another way, exceptions complicate understanding.

4. **A long description.** Looking at the best available description of the system one finds that it consists of a long laundry list of properties rather than a short, systematic specification that explains every aspect. Theoreticians formalize this idea by measuring what they call the "Kolmogorov complexity" of a computational object as the length of its shortest specification. To a certain extent, this sign may be merely a reflection of the previous three, although it emphasizes an important aspect of complexity: it is relative to understanding. On the other hand, lack of a methodical description may also indicate that the system is constructed of ill-fitting components, is poorly organized, or may have unpredictable behavior, any of which add complexity to both design and use.

5. **A team of designers, implementers, or maintainers.** Several people are required to understand, construct, or maintain the system. A fundamental issue in any system is whether or not it is simple enough for a single person to understand all of it. If not, it is a complex system because its description, construction, or maintenance will require not just technical expertise but also coordination and communication across a team.

Again, an example can illustrate: contrast a small-town library with a large university library. There is obviously a difference in scale: the university has more books, so the first sign is present. The second sign is more subtle: where the small library may have a catalog to guide the user, the university library may have not only a catalog,

'Tis the gift to be simple, 'tis the gift to be free,
'Tis the gift to come down where we ought to be;
And when we find ourselves in the place just right,
'Twill be in the valley of love and delight.
When true simplicity is gained
To bow and to bend we shan't be ashamed;
To turn, turn will be our delight,
Till by turning, turning we come round right.

— ***Simple Gifts*, traditional Shaker hymn**

but also finding aids, readers' guides, abstracting services, journal indexes, and so on. Although these elaborations make the large library more useful (at least to the experienced user), they also complicate the task of adding a new item to the library: someone must add many interconnections (in this case, cross-references) so that the new item can be found in all the intended ways. The third sign, a large number of exceptions, is also apparent. Where the small library has only a few classifications (fiction, biography, nonfiction, and magazines) and a few exceptions (oversized books are kept over the newspaper rack), the university library is plagued with exceptions. Some books are oversized, others come on microfilm or on digital media, some books are rare or valuable and must be protected, the books that explain how to build a hydrogen bomb can be loaned only to certain patrons, some defy cataloging in any standard classification system. As for the fourth sign, any user of a large university library will confirm that there are no methodical rules for locating a piece of information and that library usage is an art, not a science.

Finally, the fifth sign of complexity, a staff of more than one person, is evident in the university library. Where many small towns do in fact have just one librarian—typically an energetic person who knows each book because at one time or another he or she has had occasion to touch it—the university library has not only many personnel, but even specialists who are familiar with only one facet of library operations, such as the microform collection.

The university library exhibits all five signs of complexity, but unanimity is not essential. On the other hand, the presence of only one or two of the signs may not make a compelling case for complexity. Systems considered in thermodynamics contain an unthinkably large number of components (elementary particles) and interactions, yet from the right point of view they do not qualify as complex because there is a simple, methodical description of their behavior. It is exactly when we lack such a simple, methodical description that we have complexity.

One objection to conceiving complexity as being based on the five signs is that all systems are indefinitely, perhaps infinitely, complex because the deeper one digs the more signs of complexity turn up. Thus, even the simplest digital computer is made of gates, which are made with transistors, which are made of silicon, which is composed of protons, neutrons, and electrons, which are composed of quarks, which some physicists suggest are describable as vibrating strings, and so on. We shall address this objection in a moment by limiting the depth of digging, a technique known as *abstraction*. The complexity that we are interested in and worried about is the complexity that remains despite the use of abstraction.

> Whatever man builds . . . all of man's . . . efforts . . . invariably culminate in . . . a thing whose sole and guiding principle is . . . simplicity . . . perfection of invention touches hands with absence of invention, as if . . . [there] were a line that had not been invented but . . . [was] in the beginning . . . hidden by nature and in the end . . . found by the engineer.
>
> — **Antoine de Saint-Exupéry, *Terre des Hommes* (1939)**

1.2 SOURCES OF COMPLEXITY

There are many sources of complexity, but two merit special mention. The first is in the number of requirements that the designer expects a system to meet. The second is one particular requirement: maintaining high utilization.

1.2.1 Cascading and Interacting Requirements

A primary source of complexity is just the list of requirements for a system. Each requirement, viewed by itself, may seem straightforward. Any particular requirement may even appear to add only easily tolerable complexity to an existing list of requirements. The problem is that the accumulation of many requirements adds not only their individual complexities but also complexities from their interactions. This interaction complexity arises from pressure for generality and exceptions that add complications, and it is made worse by change in individual requirements over time.

Most users of a personal computer have by now encountered some version of the following scenario: The vendor announces a new release of the program you use to manage your checkbook, and the new release has some feature that seems important or useful (e.g., it handles the latest on-line banking systems), so you order the program. Upon trying to install it, you discover that this new release requires a newer version of some shared library package. You track down that newer version and install it, only to find that the library package requires a newer version of the operating system, which you had not previously had any reason to install. Biting the bullet, you install the latest release of the operating system, and now the checkbook program works, but your add-on hard disk begins to act flaky. On investigation it turns out that the disk vendor's proprietary software is incompatible with the new operating system release. Unfortunately, the disk vendor is still debugging an update for the disk software, and the best thing available is a beta test version that will expire at the end of the month.

The underlying cause of this scenario is that the personal computer has been designed to meet many requirements: a well-organized file system, expandability of storage, ability to attach a variety of I/O devices, connection to a network, protection from malevolent persons elsewhere in the network, usability, reliability, low cost—the list goes on and on. Each of these requirements adds complexity of its own, and the interactions among them add still more complexity.

Similarly, the telephone system has, over the years, acquired a large number of line customizing features—call waiting, call return, call forwarding, originating and terminating call blocking, reverse billing, caller ID, caller ID blocking, anonymous call

> When in doubt, make it stout, and of things you know about.
> When in doubt, leave it out.
>
> — **folklore sayings from the automobile industry**

Sidebar 1.4 The Cast of Characters and Organizations In concrete examples throughout this book, the reader will encounter a standard cast of characters named Alice, Bob, Charles, Dawn, Ella, and Felipe. Alice is usually the sender of a message, and Bob is its recipient. Charles is sometimes a mutual acquaintance of Alice and Bob. The others play various supporting roles, depending on the example. When we come to security, an adversarial character named Lucifer will appear. Lucifer's role is to crack the security measures and perhaps interfere with the presumably useful work of the other characters.

The book also introduces a few fictional organizations. There are two universities: Pedantic University, on the Internet at Pedantic.edu, and The Institute of Scholarly Studies, at Scholarly.edu. There are also four mythical commercial organizations on the Internet at TrustUs.com, ShopWithUs.com, Awesome.net, and Awful.net.

M.I.T. Professor Ronald Rivest introduced Alice and Bob to the literature of computer science in Suggestions for Further Reading 11.5.1. Any other resemblance to persons living or dead or organizations real or imaginary is purely coincidental.

rejection, do not disturb, vacation protection—again, the list goes on and on. These features interact in so many ways that there is a whole field of study of "feature interaction" in telephone systems. The study begins with debates over what *should* happen. For example, so-called 900 numbers have the feature called reverse billing—the called party can place a charge on the caller's bill. Alice (Alice is the first character we have encountered in our cast of characters, described in Sidebar 1.4) has a feature that blocks outgoing calls to reverse billing numbers. Alice calls Bob, whose phone is forwarded to a 900 number. Should the call go through, and if so, which party should pay for it, Bob or Alice? There are three interacting features, and at least four different possibilities: block the call, allow the call and charge it to Bob, ring Bob's phone, or add yet another feature that (for a monthly fee) lets Bob choose the outcome.

The examples suggest that there is an underlying principle at work. We call it the:

Principle of escalating complexity

Adding a requirement increases complexity out of proportion.

The principle is subjective because complexity itself is subjective—its magnitude is in the mind of the beholder. Figure 1.1 provides a graphical interpretation of the

> Perfection must be reached by degrees; she requires the slow hand of time.
>
> — **attributed to François-Marie Arouet (Voltaire)**

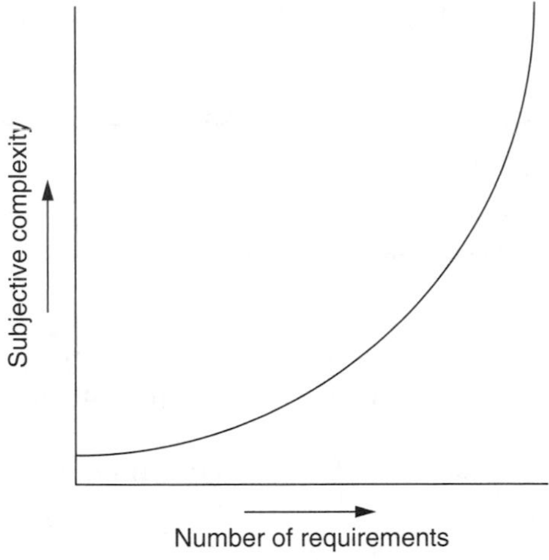

FIGURE 1.1

The principle of escalating complexity.

principle. Perhaps the most important thing to recognize in studying this figure is that the complexity barrier is soft: as you add features and requirements, you don't hit a solid roadblock to warn you to stop adding. It just gets worse.

As the number of requirements grows, so can the number of exceptions and thus the complications. It is the incredible number of special cases in the United States tax code that makes filling out an income tax return a complex job. The impact of any one exception may be minor, but the cumulative impact of many interacting exceptions can make a system so complex that no one can understand it. Complications also can arise from outside requirements such as insistence that a certain component must come from a particular supplier. That component may be less durable, heavier, or not as available as one from another supplier. Those properties may not prevent its use, but they add complexity to other parts of the system that have to be designed to compensate.

Meeting many requirements with a single design is sometimes expressed as a need for *generality*. Generality may be loosely defined as "applying to a variety of circumstances." Unfortunately, generality contributes to complexity, so it comes with a trade-off, and the designer must use good judgment to decide how much of the generality is actually *wanted*. As an extreme example, an automobile with four independent steering wheels, each controlling one tire, offers some kind of ultimate in generality, almost all of which is unwanted. Here, both the aspect of unwantedness and the resulting complexity of guidance of the auto are obvious enough, but in many cases both of these aspects are more difficult to assess: How much does a proposed form of generality complicate the system, and to what extent is that generality really useful? Unwanted generality also contributes to complexity indirectly: users of a system with excessive generality will adopt styles of usage that simplify and suppress generality that they do not need. Different users may adopt different styles and then discover that they cannot easily exchange ideas with one another. Anyone who tries to use a personal computer customized by someone else will notice this problem.

Periodically, someone tries to design a vehicle that one can drive on the highway, fly, and use as a boat, but the result of such a general design does not seem to work

> The best is the enemy of the good.
>
> — **François-Marie Arouet (Voltaire), *Dictionnaire Philosophique* (1764)**

well in any of the intended modes of transport. To help counter excessive generality, experience suggests another design principle:*

Avoid excessive generality

If it is good for everything, it is good for nothing.

There is a tension between exceptions and generality. Part of the art of designing a subsystem is to make its features general enough to minimize the number of exceptions that must be handled as special cases. This area is one where the judgment of the system designer is most evident.

Counteracting the effects of incommensurate scaling can be an additional source of complexity. Haldane, in his essay "On being the right size", points out that small organisms such as insects absorb enough oxygen to survive through their skins, but larger organisms, which require an amount of oxygen proportional to the cube of their linear size, don't have enough surface area. To compensate for this incommensurate scaling, they add complexity in the form of lungs and blood vessels to absorb and deliver oxygen throughout their bodies. In the case of computers, the programmer of a 4-bit microprocessor to control a toaster can in a few days successfully write the needed code entirely with binary numbers, while the programmer of a video game with a 64-bit processor and 40 gigabytes of supporting data requires an extensive array of tools—compilers, image or video editors, special effects generators, and the like, as well as an operating system, to be able to get the job done within a lifetime. Incommensurate scaling has required employment of a far more complex set of tools.

Finally, a major source of complexity is that requirements *change*. System designs that are successful usually remain in use for a long time, during which the environment of the system changes. Improvements in hardware technology may lead the system maintainers to want to upgrade to faster, cheaper, or more reliable equipment. Meanwhile, knowledge of how to maintain the older equipment (and the supply of spare parts) may be disappearing. As users accumulate experience with the system, it becomes clearer that some additional requirements should have been part of the design and that some of the original requirements were less important than originally thought. Often a system will expand in scale, sometimes far beyond the vision of its original designers.

In each of these cases, the ground rules and assumptions that the original designers used to develop the system begin to lose their relevance. The system designers

---

*Computer industry consultant (and erstwhile instructor of the course for which this textbook was written) Michael Hammer suggested the informal version of this design principle.

> A complex system that works is invariably found to have evolved from a simple system that works.
>
> — **John Gall, *Systemantics* (1975)**

may have foreseen some environmental changes, but there were other changes they probably did not anticipate. As changes to meet unforeseen requirements occur, they usually add complexity. Because it can be difficult to change the architecture of a deployed system (Section 1.3 explains why), there is a powerful incentive to make changes within the existing architecture, whether or not that is the best thing to do. Propagation of effects can amplify the problems caused by change because more distant effects of a change may not be noticed until someone invokes some rarely used feature. When those distant effects finally do surface, the maintainer may again find it easiest to deal with them locally, perhaps by adding exceptions. Incommensurate scaling effects begin to dominate behavior when a later maintainer scales a system up in size or replaces the underpinnings with faster hardware. Again, the first response to these effects is usually to make local changes (sometimes called *patches*) to counteract them rather than to make fundamental changes in design that would require changing several modules or changing interfaces between modules.

A closely related problem is that as systems grow in complexity with the passage of time, even the simplest change, such as to repair a bug, has an increasing risk of introducing another bug because complexity tends to obscure the full impact of the repair. A common phenomenon in older systems is that the number of bugs introduced by a bug fix release may exceed the number of bugs fixed by that release.*

The bottom line is that as systems age, they tend to accumulate changes that make them more complex. The lifetime of a system is usually limited by the complexity that accumulates as it evolves farther and farther from its original design.

1.2.2 Maintaining High Utilization

One requirement by itself is frequently a specific source of complexity. It starts with a desire for high performance or high efficiency. Whenever a scarce resource is involved, an effort arises to keep its *utilization* high.

Consider, for example, a single-track railroad line running through a long, narrow canyon.† To improve the utilization of the single track, and push more traffic through, one might allow trains to run both ways at the same time by installing a switch and a short side track in a wide spot about halfway through the canyon. Then, if one is careful in scheduling, trains going in opposite directions will meet at the side track, where

*This phenomenon was documented by Laszlo A. Belady and Meir M. Lehman in "A model of large program development", *IBM Systems Journal 15*, 3 (1976), pages 225–252.

†Michael D. Schroeder suggested this example of a railroad line in a canyon.

> Een schip op't droogh gezeylt, dat is een seeker baken. (A ship, sailed on to dry land, that is a certain beacon. Learn from the mistakes of others.)
>
> **— Jacob Cats, *Mirror on Old and New Times* (1632), based on a Dutch proverb**

they can pass each other, effectively doubling the number of trains that the track can carry each day. However, the train operations are now much more complex than they used to be. If either train is delayed, the schedules of both are disrupted. A signaling system needs to be installed because human schedulers or operators may make mistakes. And—an emergent property—the trains now have a limit on their length. If two trains are to pass in the middle, at least one of them must be short enough to pull completely onto the side track.

The train in the canyon is a good illustration of how efforts to increase utilization can increase complexity. When striving for higher utilization, one usually encounters a general design principle that economists call

---

The law of diminishing returns

The more one improves some measure of goodness, the more effort the next improvement will require.

This phenomenon is particularly noticeable in attempts to use resources more efficiently: the more completely one tries to use a scarce resource, the greater the complexity of the strategies for use, allocation, and distribution. Thus a rarely used street intersection requires no traffic control beyond a rule that the car on the right has the right-of-way. As usage increases, one must apply progressively more complex measures: stop signs, then traffic lights, then marked turning lanes with multiphase lights, then vehicle sensors to control the lights. As traffic in and out of an airport nears the airport's capacity, measures such as stacking planes, holding them on the ground at distant airports, or coordinated scheduling among several airlines must be taken. As a general rule, the more one tries to increase utilization of a limited resource, the greater the complexity (see Figure 1.2).

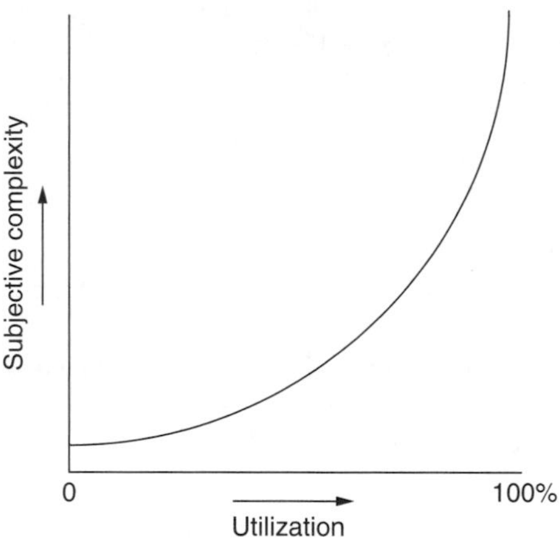

FIGURE 1.2

An example of diminishing returns: complexity grows with increasing utilization.

The perceptive reader will notice that Figures 1.1 and 1.2 are identical. It would

> It is impossible to foresee the consequences of being clever.
>
> — **Christopher Strachey, as reported by Roger Needham**

be useful to memorize this figure because some version of it can be used to describe many different things about systems.

1.3 COPING WITH COMPLEXITY I

As one might expect, with many fields contributing examples of systems with common problems and sources of complexity, some common techniques for coping with complexity have emerged. These techniques can be loosely divided into four general categories: *modularity, abstraction, layering,* and *hierarchy.* The following sections sketch the general method of each of the techniques. In later chapters many examples of each technique will emerge. It is only by studying those examples that their value will become clear.

1.3.1 Modularity

The simplest, most important tool for reducing complexity is the divide-and-conquer technique: analyze or design the system as a collection of interacting subsystems, called *modules*. The power of this technique lies primarily in being able to consider interactions among the components within a module without simultaneously thinking about the components that are inside other modules.

To see the impact of reducing interactions, consider the debugging of a large program with, say, N statements. Assume that the number of bugs in the program is proportional to its size and the bugs are randomly distributed throughout the code. The programmer compiles the program, runs it, notices a bug, finds and fixes the bug, and recompiles before looking for the next bug. Assume also that the time it takes to find a bug in a program is roughly proportional to the size of the program. We can then model the time spent debugging:

$$\begin{aligned} BugCount &\sim N \\ DebugTime &\sim N \times BugCount \\ &\sim N^2 \end{aligned}$$

Unfortunately, the debugging time grows proportional to the square of the program size.

Now suppose that the programmer divides the program into K modules, each of roughly equal size, so that each module contains N/K statements. To the extent that the modules implement independent features, one hopes that discovery of a bug usually will require examining only one module. The time required to debug any one module is thus reduced in two ways: the smaller module can be debugged faster, and

> Plan to throw one away; you will, anyhow.
>
> — **Frederick P. Brooks, *The Mythical Man Month* (1974)**

since there are fewer bugs in smaller programs, any one module will not need to be debugged as many times. These two effects are partially offset by the need to debug all K modules. Thus our model of the time required to debug the system of K modules becomes

$$\begin{aligned} \textit{DebugTime} &\sim \left(\frac{N}{K}\right)^2 \times K \\ &\sim \frac{N^2}{K} \end{aligned}$$

Modularization into K components thus reduces debugging time by a factor of K. Although the detailed mechanism by which modularity reduces effort differs from system to system, this property of modularity is universal. For this reason, one finds modularity in every large system.

The feature of modularity that we are taking advantage of here is that it is easy to replace an inferior module with an improved one, thus allowing incremental improvement of a system without completely rebuilding it. Modularity thus helps control the complexity caused by change. This feature applies not only to debugging but to all aspects of system improvement and evolution. At the same time, it is important to recognize a design principle associated with modularity, which we may call

---

The unyielding foundations rule

It is easier to change a module than to change the modularity.

The reason is that once an interface has been used by another module, changing the interface requires replacing at least two modules. If an interface is used by many modules, changing it requires replacing all of those modules simultaneously. For this reason, it is particularly important to get the modularity right.

Whole books have been written about modularity and the good things it brings. Sidebar 1.5 describes one of those books.

1.3.2 Abstraction

An important assumption in the numerical example of the effect of modularity on debugging time may not hold up in practice: that discovery of a bug should usually lead to examining just one module. For that assumption to hold true, there is a further requirement: there must be little or no propagation of effects from one module to

> The purpose of computing is insight, not numbers.
>
> — **Richard W. Hamming, *Numerical Methods for Scientists and Engineers* (1962)**

Sidebar 1.5 How Modularity Reshaped the Computer Industry Two Harvard Business School professors, Carliss Baldwin and Kim Clark, have written a whole book about modularity.* It discusses many things, but one of the most interesting is its explanation of a major transition in the computer business. In the 1960s, computer systems were a vertically integrated industry. That is, IBM, Burroughs, Honeywell, and several others each provided top-to-bottom systems and support, offering processors, memory, storage, operating systems, applications, sales, and maintenance; IBM even manufactured its own chips. By the 1990s, the industry had transformed into a horizontally organized one in which Intel sells processors, Micron sells memory, Seagate sells disks, Microsoft sells operating systems, Adobe sells text and image applications, Oracle sells database systems, and Gateway and Dell assemble boxes called "computers" out of components provided by the other players.

Carliss Baldwin and Kim Clark explain this transition as an example of modularity in action. The companies that created vertically integrated product lines immediately found complexity running amok, and they concluded that the only effective way to control it was to modularize their products. After a few experiments with wrong modularities (IBM originally designed different computers for business and for scientific applications), they eventually hit on effective ways of splitting things up and thereby keeping their development costs and delivery schedules under control:

- IBM developed the System/360 architecture specification, which could apply to machines of widely ranging performance. This modularity allowed any software to run on any size processor. IBM also developed a standard I/O bus and disk interface, so that any I/O device or disk manufactured by IBM could be attached to any IBM computer.
- Digital Equipment Corporation developed the PDP-11 family, which, with improving technology, could simultaneously be driven down in price toward the PDP-11/03 and up in function toward the PDP-11/70. A hardware-assisted emulation strategy for missing hardware instructions on the smaller machines allowed applications written for any machine to run on any other machine in the family. Digital also developed an I/O architecture, the UNIBUS®, that allowed any I/O device to attach to any PDP-11 model.

The long-range result was that once this modularity was defined and proven to be effective, other vendors were able to jump in and turn each module into a distinct business. The result is the computer industry since the 1990s, which is remarkably horizontal, especially considering its rather different shape only 20 years earlier.

(Sidebar continues)

*Carliss Y. Baldwin and Kim B. Clark. *Design Rules: The Power of Modularity* [see Suggestions for Further Reading 1.3.7]. Warning: the authors use the word "modularity" to mean all of modularity, abstraction, layering, and hierarchy.

Carliss Baldwin and Kim Clark also observe, more generally, that a market economy is characterized by modularity. Rather than having a self-supporting farm family that does everything for itself, a market economy has coopers, tinkers, blacksmiths, stables, dressmakers, and so on, each being more productive in a modular specialty, all selling things to one another using a universal interface—money.

another. Although there are lots of ways of dividing a system up into modules, some of these ways will prove to be better than others—"according to the natural formation, where the joint is, not breaking any part as a bad carver might" (Plato, *Phaedrus* 265e, Benjamin Jowett translation).

Thus the best divisions usually follow natural or effective boundaries. They are characterized by fewer interactions among modules and by less propagation of effects from one module to another. More generally, they are characterized by the ability of any module to treat all the others entirely on the basis of their external specifications, without need for knowledge about what goes on inside. This additional requirement on modularity is called *abstraction*. Abstraction is separation of interface from internals, of specification from implementation. Because abstraction nearly always accompanies modularity, some authors do not make any distinction between the two ideas. One sometimes sees the term *functional modularity* used to mean modularity with abstraction.

Thus one purchases a DVD player planning to view it as a device with a dozen or so buttons on the front panel and hoping never to look inside. If one had to know the details of the internal design of a television set in order to choose a compatible DVD player, no one would ever buy the player. Similarly, one turns a package over to an overnight delivery service without feeling a need to know anything about the particular kinds of vehicles or routes the service will use. Confidence that the package will be delivered tomorrow is the only concern.

In the computer world, abstraction appears in countless ways. The general ability of sequential circuits to remember state is abstracted into particular, easy-to-describe modules called *registers*. Programs are designed to hide details of their representation of complex data structures and details of which other programs they call. Users expect easy-to-use, button-pushing application interfaces such as computer

It must be remembered that there is nothing more difficult to plan, more doubtful of success, nor more dangerous to manage than the creation of a new system. For the initiator has the enmity of all who would profit by the preservation of the old institutions and merely lukewarm defenders in those who would gain by the new ones.

— Niccolò Machiavelli, *The Prince* (1513, published 1532; Tr. by Thomas G. Bergin, Appleton-Century-Crofts, 1947)

games, spreadsheet programs, or Web browsers that abstract incredibly complex underpinnings of memory, processor, communication, and display management.

The goal of minimizing interconnections among modules may be defeated if unintentional or accidental interconnections occur as a result of implementation errors or even well-meaning design attempts to sneak past modular boundaries in order to improve performance or meet some other requirement. Software is particularly subject to this problem because the modular boundaries provided by separately compiled subprograms are somewhat soft and easily penetrated by errors in using pointers, filling buffers, or calculating array indices. For this reason, system designers prefer techniques that enforce modularity by interposing impenetrable walls between modules. These techniques ensure that there can be no unintentional or hidden interconnections. Chapters 4 and 5 develop some of these techniques for enforcing modularity.

Well-designed and properly enforced modular abstractions are especially important in limiting the impact of faults because they control propagation of effects. As we shall see when we study fault tolerance in Chapter 8 [on-line], modules are the units of fault containment, and the definition of a failure is that a module does not meet its abstract interface specifications.

Closely related to abstraction is an important design rule that makes modularity work in practice:

The robustness principle

Be tolerant of inputs and strict on outputs.

This principle means that a module should be designed to be liberal in its interpretation of its input values, accepting them even if they are not within specified ranges, if it is still apparent how to sensibly interpret them. On the other hand, the module should construct its outputs conservatively in accordance with its specification—if possible making them even more accurate or more constrained than the specification requires. The effect of the robustness principle is to tend to suppress, rather than propagate or even amplify, noise or errors that show up in the interfaces between modules.

The robustness principle is one of the key ideas underlying modern mass production. Historically, machinists made components that were intended to mate by machining one of the components and then machining a second component to exactly fit against or into the first one, a technique known as *fitting*. The breakthrough came with the realization that if one specified *tolerances* for components and designed

> We are faced with an insurmountable opportunity.
>
> — **Pogo (Walt Kelley)**

each component to mate with any other component that was within its specified tolerance, then it would be possible to modularize and speed up manufacturing by having interchangeable parts. Apparently, this concept was first successfully applied in an 1822 contract to deliver rifles to the United States Army. By the time production lines for the Model T automobile were created, Henry Ford captured the concept in the aphorism, "In mass production there are no fitters."

The robustness principle plays a major role in computer systems. It is particularly important in human interfaces, network protocols, and fault tolerance, and, as Section 1.4 of this chapter explains, it forms the basis for digital logic. At the same time, a tension exists between the robustness principle and another important design principle:

The safety margin principle

Keep track of the distance to the cliff, or you may fall over the edge.

When inputs are not close to their specified values, that is usually an indication that something is starting to go wrong. The sooner that something going wrong can be noticed, the sooner it can be fixed. For this reason, it is important to track and report out-of-tolerance inputs, even if the robustness principle would allow them to be interpreted successfully.

Some systems implement the safety margin principle by providing two modes of operation, which might be called "shake-out" and "production". In shake-out mode, modules check every input carefully and refuse to accept anything that is even slightly out of specification, thus allowing immediate discovery of problems and of programming errors near their source. In production mode, modules accept any input that they can reasonably interpret, in accordance with the robustness principle. Carefully designed systems blend the two ideas: accept any reasonable input but report any input that is beginning to drift out of tolerance so that it may be repaired before it becomes completely unusable.

1.3.3 Layering

Systems that are designed using good abstractions tend to minimize the number of interconnections among their component modules. One powerful way to reduce module interconnections is to employ a particular method of module organization known as *layering*. In designing with layers, one builds on a set of mechanisms that is already complete (a lower layer) and uses them to create a different complete set of mechanisms (an upper layer). A layer may itself be implemented as several modules,

There is no such thing as a small change to a large system.

— systems folklore, source lost in the mists of time

but as a general rule, a module of a given layer interacts only with its peers in the same layer and with the modules of the next higher and next lower layers. That restriction can significantly reduce the number of potential intermodule interactions in a big system.

Some of the best examples of this approach are found in computer systems: an interpreter for a high-level language is implemented using a lower-level, more machine-oriented, language. Although the higher-level language doesn't allow any new programs to be expressed, it is easier to use, at least for the application for which it was designed.

Thus, nearly every computer system comprises several layers. The lowest layer consists of gates and memory cells, upon which is built a layer consisting of a processor and memory. On top of this layer is built an operating system layer, which acts as an augmentation of the processor and memory layer. Finally, an application program executes on this augmented processor and memory layer. In each layer, the functions provided by the layer below are rearranged, repackaged, reabstracted, and reinterpreted as appropriate for the convenience of the layer above. As will be seen in Chapter 7 [on-line], layers are also the primary organizing technique of data communication networks.

Layered design is not unique to computer systems and communications. A house has an inner structural layer of studs, joists, and rafters to provide shape and strength, a layer of sheathing and drywall to keep the wind out, a layer of siding, flooring and roof tiles to make it watertight, and a cosmetic layer of paint to make it look good. Much of mathematics, particularly algebra, is elegantly organized in layers (in the case of algebra, integers, rationals, complex numbers, polynomials, and polynomials with polynomial coefficients), and that organization provides a key to deep understanding.

1.3.4 Hierarchy

The final major technique for coping with complexity also reduces interconnections among modules but in a different, specialized way. Start with a small group of modules, and assemble them into a stable, self-contained subsystem that has a well-defined interface. Next, assemble a small group of subsystems to produce a larger subsystem. This process continues until the final system has been constructed from a small number of relatively large subsystems. The result is a tree-like structure known as a *hierarchy*. Large organizations such as corporations are nearly always set up this way, with a manager responsible for only five to ten employees, a higher-level manager responsible for five to ten managers, on up to the president of the company, who may

> The first 80 percent of a project takes 80 percent of the effort.
> The last 20 percent takes another 80.
>
> **— source unknown**

supervise five to ten vice presidents. The same thinking applies to armies. Even layers can be thought of as a kind of degenerate one-dimensional hierarchy.

There are many other striking examples of hierarchy, ranging from microscopic biological systems to the assembly of Alexander's empire. A classic paper by Herbert Simon, "The architecture of complexity" [Suggestions for Further Reading 1.4.3], contains an amazing range of such examples and offers compelling arguments that, under evolution, hierarchical designs have a better chance of survival. The reason is that hierarchy constrains interactions by permitting them only among the components of a subsystem. Hierarchy constrains a system of N components, which in the worst case might exhibit $N \times (N - 1)$ interactions, so that each component can interact only with members of its own subsystem, except for an interface component that also interacts with other members of the subsystem at the next higher level of hierarchy. (The interface component in a corporation is called a "manager"; in an army it is called the "commanding officer"; for a program it is called the "application programming interface".) If subsystems have a limit of, say, 10 components, this number remains constant no matter how large the system grows. There will be $N/10$ lowest level subsystems, $N/100$ next higher level subsystems, and so on, but the total number of subsystems, and thus the number of interactions, remains proportional to N. Analogous to the way that modularity reduces the effort of debugging, hierarchy reduces the number of potential interactions among modules from square-law to linear.

This effect is most strongly noticed by the designer of an individual module. If there are no constraints, each module should in principle be prepared to interact with every other module of the system. The advantage of a hierarchy is that the module designer can focus just on interactions with the interfaces of other members of its immediate subsystem.

1.3.5 Putting it Back Together: Names Make Connections

The four techniques for coping with complexity—modularity, abstraction, layering, and hierarchy—provide ways of dividing things up and placing the resulting modules in suitable relation one to another. However, we still need a way of connecting those modules. In digital systems, the primary connection method is that one module *names* another module that it intends to use. Names allow postponing of decisions, easy replacement of one module with a better one, and sharing of modules. Software uses names in an obvious way. Less obviously, hardware modules connected to a bus also use names for interconnection—addresses, including bus addresses, are a kind of name.

> Hofstadter's Law: It always takes longer than you expect, even when you take into account Hofstadter's Law.
>
> — **Douglas Hofstadter: *Gödel, Escher, Bach: An Eternal Golden Braid* (1979)**

In a modular system, one can usually find several ways to combine modules to implement a desired feature. The designer must at some point choose a specific implementation from among many that are available. Making this choice is called *binding*. Recalling that the power of modularity comes from the ability to replace an implementation with a better one, the designer usually tries to maintain maximum flexibility by delaying binding until the last possible instant, perhaps even until the first instant that the feature is actually needed.

One way to delay binding is just to name a feature rather than implementing it. Using a name allows one to design a module as if a feature of another module exists, even if that feature has not yet been implemented, and it also makes it mechanically easy to later choose a different implementation. By the time the feature is actually invoked, the name must, of course, be bound to a real implementation of the other module. Using a name to delay or allow changing a binding is called *indirection*, and it is the basis of a design principle:

Decouple modules with indirection

Indirection supports replaceability.

A folk wisdom version of this principle, attributed to computer scientist David Wheeler of the University of Cambridge, exaggerates the power of indirection by suggesting that "any problem in a computer system can be solved by adding a layer of indirection." A somewhat more plausible counterpart of this folk wisdom is the observation that any computer system can be made faster by removing a layer of indirection.

When a module has a name, several other modules can make use of it by name, thereby sharing the design effort, cost, or information contained in the first module. Because names are a cornerstone element of modularity in digital systems, Chapters 2 and 3 are largely about the design of naming schemes.

1.4 COMPUTER SYSTEMS ARE THE SAME BUT DIFFERENT

As we have repeatedly suggested, there is an important lesson to be drawn from the wide range of examples used up to this point to illustrate system problems. Certain common problems show up in all complex systems, whatever their field. Emergent properties, propagation of effects, incommensurate scaling, and trade-offs are considerations in activities as diverse as space station design, management of the economy,

> A system is never finished being developed until it ceases to be used.
>
> — **attributed to Gerald M. Weinberg**

the building of skyscrapers, gene-splicing, petroleum refineries, communication satellite networks, and the governing of India, as well as in the design of computer systems. Furthermore, the techniques that have been devised for coping with complexity are universal. Modularity, abstraction, layering, and hierarchy are used as tools in most fields that deal with complex systems. It is therefore useful for the computer system designer to investigate systems from other fields, both to gain additional perspective on how system problems arise and to discover specific techniques from other fields that may also apply to computer systems. Stated briefly, we conclude that *computer systems are the same as all other systems*.

But there is one problem with that conclusion: it is wrong. There are at least two significant ways in which computer systems differ from every other kind of system with which designers have experience:

- *The complexity of a computer system is not limited by physical laws.*
- *The rate of change of computer system technology is unprecedented.*

These two differences have an enormous impact on complexity and on ways of coping with it.

1.4.1 Computer Systems have no Nearby Bounds on Composition

Computer systems are mostly digital, and they are controlled by software. Each of these two properties separately leads to relaxations of what, in other systems, would be limits on complexity arising from physical laws.

Consider first the difference between analog and digital systems. All analog systems have the engineering limitation that each component of the system contributes noise. This noise may come from the environment in the form of, for example, vibration or electromagnetic radiation. Noise may also appear because the component's physical behavior does not precisely follow any tractable model of operation: the pile of rocks that a civil engineer specifies to go under a bridge abutment does not obey a simple deformation model; a resistor in an electronic circuit generates random noise whose level depends on the temperature. When analog components are composed into systems, the noise from individual components accumulates (if the noise sources are statistically independent, the noise may accumulate only slowly but it still accumulates). As the number of components increases, noise will at some point dominate the behavior of the system. (This analysis applies to systems designed by human engineers.

> I was to learn later in life that we tend to meet any new situation by reorganisation; and what a wonderful method it can be for creating the illusion of progress while producing confusion, inefficiency and demoralisation.
>
> — **shortened version of an observation by Charlton Ogburn, "Merrill's Marauders: The truth about an incredible adventure", *Harper's Magazine* (January 1957). Widely but improbably misattributed to Petronius Arbiter (ca. A.D. 60)**

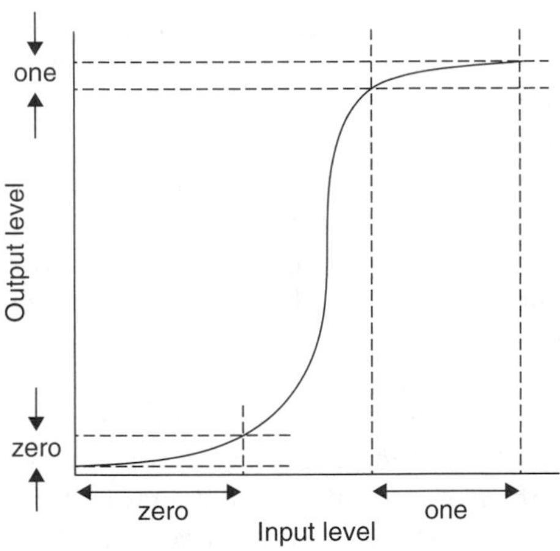

FIGURE 1.3

How gain and non-linearity of a digital component restore levels. The input level and output level span the same range of values, but the range of accepted inputs is much wider than the range of generated outputs.

Natural biological, thermodynamic, and macroeconomic systems, composed of billions of analog components, somehow use hierarchy, layering, abstraction, and modularity to operate despite noise, but they are so complex that we do not understand them well enough to adopt the same techniques.)

Noise thus provides a limit on the number of analog components that a designer can usefully compose or on the number of stages that a designer can usefully cascade. This argument applies to any engineered analog system: a bridge across a river, a stereo, or an airliner. It is the reason a photocopy of a photocopy is harder to read than the original. There may also be other limits on size (arising from the strength of materials, for example), but noise is always a limit on the complexity of analog systems.

In contrast, digital systems are noise-free; complexity can therefore grow without any constraint of a bound arising from noise. The designers of digital logic use a version of the *robustness principle* known as the *static discipline*. This discipline is the primary source of the magic that seems to surround digital systems. The static discipline requires that the range of analog values that a device accepts as meaning the digital value ONE (or ZERO) be wider than the range of analog values that the device puts out when it means digital ONE (or ZERO). This discipline is an example of being tolerant of inputs and strict on outputs.

Digital systems are, at some lower level, constructed of analog components. The analog components chosen for this purpose are non-linear, and they have gain between input and output. When used appropriately, non-linearity allows inputs to have a wide tolerance, and gain ensures that outputs stay within narrow specifications, as shown in Figure 1.3. Together they produce the property of digital circuits called level restoration or regeneration. Regenerated signal levels appear at the output of every digital component, whatever their level of granularity: a gate, a flip-flop, a memory chip, a processor, or a complete computer system. Regenerated levels create clean interfaces that allow one subsystem to be connected to the next with

> The probability of failure of a system tends to be proportional to the confidence that its designer has in its reliability.
>
> — **systems folklore, source lost**

confidence. Unlike the civil engineer's pile of rocks, a logic gate performs exactly as its designer intends.

The static discipline and level restoration do *not* guarantee that devices with digital inputs and outputs never make mistakes. Any component can fail. Or an input signal that is intended to be a ONE may be so far out of tolerance that the receiving component accepts it as a ZERO. When that happens, the output of the component that accepted that value incorrectly is likely to be wrong, too. The important consequence is that digital components make big mistakes, not little ones, and as we shall see when we reach the chapter on fault tolerance, big mistakes are relatively easy to detect and handle.

If a signal does not accumulate noise as it goes through a string of devices, then noise does not limit the number of devices one can string together. In other words, noise does not constrain the maximum depth of composition for digital systems. Unlike analog systems, digital systems can grow in complexity until they exceed the ability of their designers to understand them. As of 2009, processor chips contain over two billion transistors, far more than any analog chip. No airliner has nearly that many components—except in its on-board computers.

The second reason composition has no nearby bounds is that computer systems are controlled by software. Bad as the contribution to complexity from the static discipline may be, the contribution from software turns out to be worse. Hardware is at least subject to *some* physical limits—the speed of light, the rate of settling of signals in real semiconductor materials, unwanted electrical coupling between adjacent components, the rate at which heat can be removed, and the space that it occupies. Software appears to have no physical limits whatever beyond the availability of memory to store it and processors to execute it. As a result, composition of software can go on as fast as people can create it. Thus one routinely hears of operating systems, database systems, and even word processors consisting of more than 10 million program statements.

In principle, abstraction can help control software composition by hiding implementation beneath module interfaces. The problem is that most abstractions are, in reality, slightly "leaky" in that they don't perfectly conceal the underlying implementation. A simple example of leakiness is addition of integers: in most implementations, the addition operation perfectly matches the mathematical specification as long as the result fits in the available word size, but if the result is larger than that, the resulting overflow becomes a complication for the programmer. Leakiness, like noise in analog systems, accumulates as the number of software modules grows. Unlike noise, it accumulates in the form of complexity, so the lack of physical constraints on

> The major difference between a thing that might go wrong and a thing that cannot possibly go wrong is that when a thing that cannot possibly go wrong goes wrong it usually turns out to be impossible to get at or repair.
>
> — **Douglas Adams, *Mostly Harmless (Hitchhiker's Guide to the Galaxy V)* (1993)**

software composition remains a fundamental problem. It is, therefore, mechanically easy to create a system with complexity that is far beyond the ability of its designers to understand. And since it is easy, it happens often, and sometimes with disastrous results.*

Between the absence of a noise-imposed limit on composition of digital hardware and very distant physical limits on composition of software, it is too easy for an unwary designer to misuse the tools of modularity, abstraction, layering, and hierarchy to include still more complexity. This phenomenon is quite unknown in the design of bridges and airliners. *In contrast with other systems, computer systems allow composition to a depth whose first limit is the designer's ability to understand.* Unfortunately, this lack of nearby natural, physical bounds on depth of composition tempts designers to build more complex systems. If nature does not impose a nearby limit on composition, the designer must self-impose a limit. Since it can be hard to say no to a reasonable-sounding feature, features keep getting added. Therein lies the fate of too many computer system designs.

1.4.2 d(technology)/dt is Unprecedented

For reasons partly explained by Sidebar 1.6, during the last 35 years the cost of the digital hardware used for computation and communication has dropped an average of about 30% each year. This rate of change means that just two years' passage of time has been enough to allow technology to cut prices in half, and in seven or eight years it has led to a drop in prices by a factor of 10. Some components have experienced even greater rates of improvement. Figure 1.4 shows the cost of magnetic disk storage over a 25-year span. During that time, disk prices have actually dropped by a factor of 10 roughly every five years, so disk prices have dropped nearly 60% each year. Disk experts project a similar rate of improvement for at least another few years. Their projection seems relatively safe, since no major roadblocks have been reported by development laboratories that are already working on the next rounds of magnetic recording technology. Similar charts apply to random access memory, processor cost, and the speed of optical fiber transmission.

This rapid change of technology has created a substantial difference between computer systems and other engineering systems. Since complex systems can take several years to build, by the time a computer system is ready for delivery, the

*The terminology "leaky" is apparently due to software developer Joel Spolsky.

> Structural engineering is the art of modeling materials we do not wholly understand, into shapes we cannot precisely analyse so as to withstand forces we cannot properly assess, in such a way that the public has no reason to suspect the extent of our ignorance.
>
> **— A. R. Dykes, Scottish Branch, Institution of Structural Engineers (1946)**

Sidebar 1.6 Why Computer Technology has Improved Exponentially with Time Popular media frequently use the term "exponential" to describe the explosive rate of improvement of computer technology. Stephen Ward has pointed out that there is a good reason this adjective is appropriate: computer technology appears to be the rare engineering discipline in which the technology being improved is routinely employed to improve the technology. People building airplanes, bridges, skyscrapers, and chemical plants rarely, if ever, have this opportunity.

For example, the performance of a microprocessor is determined at least in part by the cleverness of its layout, which in turn is limited by the time available to use computer-assisted layout tools that can take advantage of lithography advances. If Intel, through improved layout, makes a version of the Pentium that is twice as fast, as soon as that new Pentium is available, it will be used as the processor to make the layout tools for the next Pentium run twice as fast; the next design can benefit from twice as much computation in its layout. This effect is probably one of the drivers of Moore's law, which predicts an exponential increase in component count on chips with a doubling time of 18 months [Suggestions for Further Reading 1.6.1].

If indeed the rate at which we can improve our technology is proportional to the quality of the technology itself, we can express this idea as

$$\frac{d(technology)}{dt} = K \times technology$$

which has an exponential solution,

$$technology = e^{K \cdot t}$$

The actual situation is, of course, far more complicated than that equation suggests, but all equations that even remotely resemble that form, in which technology's rate of growth is some positive function of its current state, have growing exponentials in their solution.

In the real world, exponentials must eventually hit some limit. In hardware there are fairly clear fundamental physical limits to exponential growth, such as the uncertainty principle, the minimum energy required to switch a gate, and the rate at which heat can be removed from a device. The interesting part is that it isn't obvious which one is going to become the roadblock, or when. Thus far, engineering ingenuity in exploiting trade-offs has postponed the day of reckoning. For software, similar limits on exponential growth must exist, but their nature is not at all clear.

More to the immediate point, virtually every improvement in computer and communications technology—whether faster chips, better Internet routing algorithms, more effective prototyping languages, better browser interfaces, faster compilers, bigger disks, or larger RAM—is immediately put to work by everyone who is working on faster chips, better Internet routing algorithms, more effective prototyping languages, better browser interfaces, faster compilers, bigger disks, or larger RAM. Computer system designers live inside a giant feedback system that, at least for the moment, is enjoying exponential solutions.

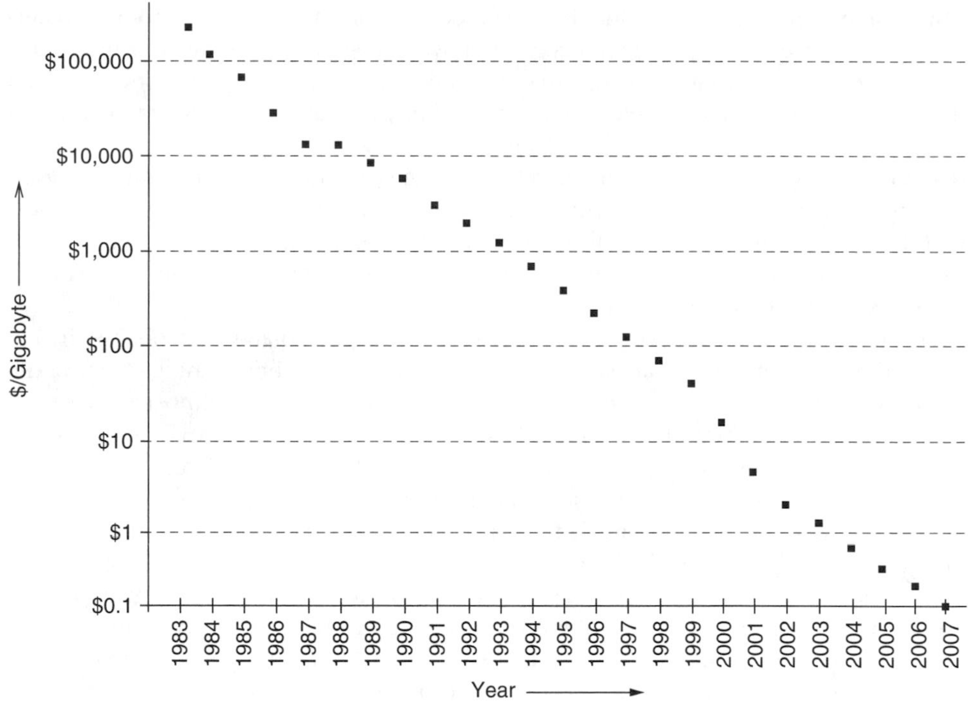

FIGURE 1.4

Magnetic disk price history and projection, 1983–2007.

ground rules under which it was originally designed have shifted. Incommensurate scaling typically means that the designer must adjust for strains when any system parameter changes by a factor of 2, because not all of the components scale up (or down) by the same proportion. More to the point, a whole new design is usually needed when any system parameter changes by a (decimal) order of magnitude. This rule of thumb about strains caused by parameter changes gives us our next design principle:

The incommensurate scaling rule

Changing any system parameter by a factor of 10 usually requires a new design.

> If you design it so that it can be assembled wrong, someone will assemble it wrong.
>
> — **Edward A. Murphy, Jr. (paraphrase of the original Murphy's law, 1949; see sidebar 2.5)**

This rule, when combined with the observed rate of change of technology, means that by the time a newly designed computer system is ready for delivery it may have already needed two rounds of adjustment and be ready for a complete redesign. Even if the designer has tried to predict the impact of technology change, crystal balls are at best cloudy. Worse, during the development of the system, things may run an order of magnitude slower than they will when the system is finished, the code and data don't fit in the available address space, or perhaps the data has to be partitioned across several hard disks instead of nicely fitting on one. One can compensate for each of these problems, but each such compensation absorbs intellectual resources and contributes complexity to the development process.

Even without those adjustments or redesign, the original plan was probably already a new design. A bridge (or airplane) may have a modest number of things that are different from the previous one, but a civil (or aeronautical) engineer almost always ends up designing something that is only a little different from some previous bridge (or airplane). In the case of computer systems, ideas that were completely unrealistic a year or two ago can become mainstream in no time, so the computer system designer almost always ends up designing something that is significantly different from the previous computer system. This difference makes deep analysis of previous designs more rewarding for civil and aeronautical engineers than for computer system designers, and also usually means that in computer systems there hasn't been time to discover and iron out most of the mistakes of the previous design before going on to the next major revision. Those mistakes can contribute strongly to complexity.

Because technology has improved so rapidly, the field of computer system design tends to place much less emphasis on detailed performance analysis and fine-tuning than do most other engineering endeavors. Where an electric power generation system may benefit dramatically from a new steam turbine that improves energy transfer by 1%, a needed 20% improvement in performance of a computer system can usually be obtained just by waiting four months for the next round of hardware product announcements. If a proposal to rewrite an application to obtain that same improvement would require a year of work, it is probably more cost-effective to just wait for technology change to solve the problem. Put another way, rapidly improving technology means that brute-force solutions (buy more memory, wait for a faster processor, use a simpler algorithm) are often the right approach in computer systems, whereas in other systems they may be unthinkable. The owner of the railroad through the canyon probably would not view as economically reasonable a proposal to blast the canyon wider and install a second track. Even if the resources were available, the environmental impact would be a deterrent.

> This "telephone" has too many shortcomings to be seriously considered as a means of communication. The device is inherently of no value to us.
>
> **— frequently attributed to an 1876 Western Union internal memo, but there is no evidence of this memo and it is probably a myth.**

A second major consequence of the rapid rate of change of technology in computer systems is that usability, and related qualities that go under the label "human engineering", of computer systems is always ragged. It takes years of trial and error to make systems usable, friendly, and forgiving, but by the time one level of computer technology has been tamed, a new level of computer technology opens the possibilities of many new features at the same cost, or of providing the previous features more cheaply to a vast new audience of unprepared users.

Similarly, legal and judicial processes take decades to come to grips with new issues, as people debate the wisdom of various policies, discover abuses, and explore alternative remedies. In the face of rapidly changing computer system technology, these processes fall far behind, delaying resolution of such concerns as how to reward innovative software ideas, or what rules should protect information stored in computers, and adding uncertainty of requirements to the burden of the computer system designer.*

Finally, modern high-speed communications with global reach have greatly accelerated the rate at which people discover that a new technology is useful and adopt it. Where it took several decades for electricity and the telephone to move from curiosities to widespread use, recent innovations such as digital cameras and DVDs have swept their markets in less than a decade, and a single mention of a previously obscure World Wide Web site on CNN or in *Newsweek* magazine can cause that site to be suddenly overwhelmed with millions of hits per day. More generally, newly viable applications, such as peer-to-peer file sharing, can change the shape of the workload on existing systems practically overnight.

Thus, the study of computer systems involves telescoping of the usual processes of planning, examining requirements, tailoring details, and integrating with users and society. This telescoping leads to the delivery of systems that have rough edges and without the benefit of the cleverest thought. People who build airplanes and bridges do not have to face these problems. Such problems can be viewed either as a frustrating difficulty or as an exciting challenge, depending on one's perspective.

1.5 COPING WITH COMPLEXITY II

Modest physical limits in hardware and very distant physical limits in software together give us the opportunity to create systems of unimaginable—and unmanageable—complexity, and the rapid pace of technology change tempts designers to deliver

*Lawrence Lessig provides a good analysis of the interactions of law, society, and computer technology in *Code: and Other Laws of Cyberspace* [Suggestions for Further Reading 1.1.4].

> Books will soon be obsolete in the public schools. . . . It is possible to teach every branch of human knowledge with the motion picture. Our school system will be completely changed inside of ten years.
>
> **— Thomas A. Edison, as quoted in the *New York Dramatic Mirror* (July 9, 1913)**

systems using new and untested ground rules. These two effects amplify the complexity of computer systems when compared with systems from other engineering areas. Thus, computer system designers need some additional tools to cope with complexity.

1.5.1 Why Modularity, Abstraction, Layering, and Hierarchy aren't Enough

Modularity, abstraction, layering, and hierarchy are a major help, but by themselves they aren't enough to keep the resulting complexity under control. The reason is that all four of those techniques assume that the designer understands the system being designed. In the real, fast-changing world of computer systems, it is hard to choose

- the *right* modularity from a sea of plausible alternative modularities.
- the *right* abstraction from a sea of plausible alternative abstractions.
- the *right* layering from a sea of plausible alternative layerings.
- the *right* hierarchy from a sea of plausible alternative hierarchies.

Although some design principles are available, they are far too few, and the only real guidance comes from experience with previous systems.

As might be expected, designers of computer systems have developed and refined at least one additional technique to cope with complexity. Designers of other kinds of systems use this technique as well, but they usually do not consider it to be so fundamental to success as it is for computer systems, probably because the technique is particularly feasible with software. It is a development process called *iteration*.

1.5.2 Iteration

The essence of iteration is to start by building a simple, working system that meets only a modest subset of the requirements and then evolve that system in small steps to gradually encompass more and more of the full set of requirements. The idea is that small steps can help reduce the risk that complexity will overwhelm a system design. Having a working system available at all times helps provide assurance that something can be built and provides on-going experience with the current technology ground rules as well as an opportunity to discover and fix bugs. Finally, adjustments for technology changes that arrive during the system development are easier to incorporate as part of one or more of the iterations. When you see a piece of software identified as "release 5.4", that is usually an indication that the vendor is using iteration.

Successful iteration requires considerable foresight. That foresight involves several elements, two of which we identify as design principles:

> I think there is a world market for maybe five computers.
>
> — **Frequently claimed to be said by Thomas J. Watson, Sr., chairman of IBM, in a 1943 talk, but there is little evidence that it is anything but a legend.**

- First of all,

Design for iteration

You won't get it right the first time, so make it easy to change.

Document the assumptions behind the design so that when the time comes to change the design you can more easily figure out what else has to change. Expect not only to modify and replace modules, but also to remodularize as the system and its requirements become better understood.

- *Take small steps.* The purpose is to allow discovery of both design mistakes and bad ideas quickly, so that they can be changed or removed with small effort and before other parts of the system in later iterations start to depend on them and they effectively become unchangeable. Systems under active development may be subjected to a complete system rebuild every day because the rebuilding process invokes a large number of checks and tests that can reveal implementation mistakes, while the changes that caused the mistakes are fresh in the minds of the implementers.
- *Don't rush.* Even though individual steps may be small, they must still be well planned. In most projects, the temptation is to rush to implementation. With iterative design, that temptation can be stronger, and the designer must make sure that the design is ready for the next step.
- *Plan for feedback.* Include as part of the design both feedback paths and positive incentives to provide feedback. Testers, installers, maintainers, and users of the system can provide much of the information needed to refine it. Alpha testing ("we're not at all sure this even works") and beta testing ("seems to work, use at your own risk") are common examples, and many vendors encourage users to report details of problems and transcripts of failures by e-mail. A well-designed system will provide many such feedback schemes at all levels.
- *Study failures.* An important goal is to learn from failures rather than assign blame for them. Incentives must be carefully designed to ensure that feedback about failures is not ignored or even suppressed by people fearful of being blamed. Then, having found the apparent cause of a failure,

---

Keep digging

Complex systems fail for complex reasons.

Computers in the future may weigh no more than 1.5 tons.

— ***Popular Mechanics*** **(March 1949)**

> Continue looking for other contributing or more basic causes. Working systems often work for reasons that aren't well understood. It is common to find that a new release of a system reveals a bug that has actually been in the system for a long time but has never mattered until now. Much can be learned by figuring out why it never mattered. It can also be useful to explore the mindset of the designers to understand what allowed them to design a system that could fail in this way.* Similarly, don't ignore unexplained behavior. If the feedback reports something that now seems not to be a problem or to have gone away, it is probably a sign that something is wrong rather than that the system magically fixed itself.

Iteration sounds like a straightforward technique, but several obstacles tend to interfere with it. The main obstacle is that as a design evolves through a series of iterations, a risk of losing conceptual integrity arises. That risk suggests that the overall plan for the initial, simplest version of the system must accommodate all of the iterations needed to reach the final version (thus the need for foresight). Someone must constantly be on guard to make sure that the overall design rationale remains clear despite changes made during iteration.

In most organizations, good news (e.g., a major piece of the system is working ahead of schedule) flows rapidly throughout the organization, but bad news (e.g., an important module isn't working yet) often gets confined to the part of the organization that discovers it, at least until it can fix the problem and report good news. This phenomenon, the *bad-news diode*, can prevent realization that changing a different part of the system is more appropriate.

A related problem is that when someone finally realizes that the modularity is wrong, it can be hard to change, for two reasons. First, the *unyielding foundations rule* (see page 20) comes into play. Changing modularity by definition involves changing more than one module, and sometimes several. Second, designers who have invested time and effort in developing a module that, from their point of view, is doing what was intended can be reluctant to see this time and effort lost in a rework. Simply put, to change modularity one must deal with both committed components and committed designers.

---

*The idea of learning from failure and the observation that complex systems fail for complex reasons are the themes of a fascinating book by Henry Petroski, *Design Paradigms: Case Histories of Error and Judgment in Engineering* [Suggestions for Further Reading 1.2.3].

> Based on extensive financial and market analysis, it's projected that no more than five thousand of the new Haloid machines will sell. . . . Model 914, has no future in the office copying market.
>
> **— Consulting firm Arthur D. Little's report to IBM on the prospects for xerographic copying machines (1959)**

A longer-term risk of iteration sometimes shows up when the initial design is both simple and successful. Success can lead designers to be overconfident and to be too ambitious on a later iteration. Technology has improved in the time since deployment of the initial version of the system and feedback has suggested lots of new features. Each suggested feature looks straightforward by itself, and it is difficult to judge how they might interact. The result is often a disastrous overreaching and consequent failure that is so common that it has a name: the *second-system effect*.

Iteration can be thought of as applying modularity to the management of the system design and implementation process. It thus takes us into the realm of management techniques, which are not directly addressed in this book.*

1.5.3 Keep it Simple

Remarkably, one of the most effective techniques in coping with complexity is also one that is most difficult to apply: *simplicity*. As Section 1.4.1 explained, computer systems lack natural physical limits to curb their complexity, so the designer must impose limits; otherwise the designer risks being overwhelmed.

The problem with the apparently obvious advice to keep it simple is that

- previous systems give a taste of how great things could be if more features were added.
- the technology has improved so much that cost and performance are not constraints.
- each of the suggested new features has been successfully demonstrated somewhere.
- none of the exceptions or other complications seems by itself to be especially hard to deal with.
- there is fear that a competitor will market a system that has even more features.
- among system designers, arrogance, pride, and overconfidence are more common than clear awareness of the dangers of complexity.

These considerations make it hard to say "no" to any one requirement, feature, exception, or complication. It is their cumulative impact that produces the complexity explosion illustrated in Figure 1.1. The system designer must keep this cumulative

*An excellent book on the subject of system development, by a veteran designer, is Frederick P. Brooks Jr., *The Mythical Man-Month* [Suggestions for Further Reading 1.1.3]. Another highly recommended reading is the Alan Turing Award lecture by Fernando J. Corbató, "On building systems that will fail" [Suggestions for Further Reading 1.5.3].

> There is no reason anyone would want a computer in their home.
>
> — **Kenneth Olsen, president of Digital Equipment Corporation (1977)**

impact in mind at all times. The bottom line is that a computer system designer's most potent weapon against complexity is the ability to say, "No. This will make it too complicated."

As we proceed to study specific computer system engineering topics, we shall make much use of a particular kind of simplicity, to the extent that it is yet another design principle:

Adopt sweeping simplifications

So you can see what you are doing.

Each topic area will explicitly introduce one or more sweeping simplifications. The reason is that they allow the designer to make compelling arguments for correctness, they make detail irrelevant, and they make clear to all participants exactly what is going on. They will turn out to be one of our best hopes for keeping control of complexity.

WHAT THE REST OF THIS BOOK IS ABOUT

This chapter has introduced some basic ideas that underlie the study of computer systems. In the course of building on these basic ideas, the ensuing chapters explore a series of system engineering topics in the light of three recurring themes:

- The pervasive importance of modularity
- Principle-based system design
- Making systems robust and resilient

Modularity appears in each engineering topic either as one of the goals of that topic or as one of its design cornerstones. Words from chapter titles suggest this theme. *Abstractions and layering* are particular ways to build on modularity. *Naming* is a fundamental mechanism for interconnecting and replacing modules. *Clients and services* and *virtualization* are two ways of enforcing modularity. *Networks* are built on a foundation of modularity. In *fault tolerance*, the module is the unit that limits the extent of failure. A*tomicity* is an exceptionally robust form of modularity that the designer can exploit to obtain *consistency*. Finally, *protection of information* involves further strengthening of modular walls.

The second theme, principle-based system design, has already emerged, both in explicit mention of several principles and in the list of *design principles* on the inside front cover. These principles capture, in brief phrases, widely applicable nuggets of wisdom that have been developed by generations of computer system designers. Later chapters apply these general principles and also introduce additional design principles that are more specific to particular engineering areas. Even with these principles in mind, it is often difficult to offer a precise recipe for design. Therefore throughout the text the reader will find a second form of captured wisdom in the form of several design *hints* that encode rationales for making trade-offs.* Together, the principles and hints suggest that computer system design, though for the most part not based on mathematical theories, is also not completely *ad hoc*: it is actually based on sound principles derived from experience and analysis of both successful and failed systems. The reader who understands and absorbs these principles and hints will have learned much of what this book has to say.

The third theme, making systems robust and resilient, has also already emerged, both in the statement of the *robustness principle* and with the idea that modularity, by limiting interconnections, can help control propagation of effects. The terms *robustness* and *resilience* are informal and overlapping descriptions of a general goal of design: that a system should not be sensitive to modest, long-term shifts in its environment (usually called robustness) and that it should continue operating correctly in the face of transient adversity (usually called resilience). Each succeeding chapter introduces at least one progressively stronger way to make a system more robust and resilient. Thus, the chapter on naming shows how indirection of names can make systems less fragile. Then, the chapters on clients and services and on virtualization demonstrate how to enforce modularity to limit the effects of mistakes and accidents. The chapter on networks introduces techniques that provide reliable communications despite communication failures. The chapter on fault tolerance then generalizes those techniques to make entire systems resilient, even though they contain faulty components. The chapters on atomicity and consistency apply fault tolerance techniques to the particular problem of maintaining the integrity of stored data, despite concurrent activity and in the face of software and hardware failures. Finally, the chapter on protecting information introduces techniques to limit the impact of malicious adversaries who would deliberately steal, modify, or deny access to information.

EXERCISES

1.1 True or false? Explain: modularity reduces complexity because

A. It reduces the effect of incommensurate scaling.

B. It helps control propagation of effects.

1994-1-3d and 1995-1-1e

1.2 True or false? Explain: hierarchy reduces complexity because

A. It reduces the size of individual modules.

B. It cuts down on the number of interconnections between elements.

C. It assembles a number of smaller elements into a single larger element.

D. It enforces a structure on the interconnections between elements.

E. All of the above.

1994-1-3c and 1999-1-02

*Many, if not all, of the hints were originally described by Butler Lampson in his paper "Hints for computer system design" [Suggestions for Further Reading 1.5.4].

1.3 If one created a graph of personal friendships, one would have a hierarchy. True or false?

1995–1–1b

1.4 Which of the following is usually observed in a complex computer system?

A. The underlying technology has a high rate of change.

B. It is easy to write a succinct description of the behavior of the system.

C. It has a large number of interacting features.

D. It exhibits emergent properties that make the system perform better than envisioned by the system's designers.

2005-1-1

1.5 Ben Bitdiddle has written a program with 16 major modules of code. Each module contains several procedures. In the first implementation of his program, he finds that each module contains at least one call to every other module. Each module contains 100 lines of code.

1.5a How long is Ben's program in lines of code?

1.5b How many module interconnections are there in his implementation? (Each call from one module to another is an interconnection.)

Ben decides to change the implementation. Now there are four main modules, each containing four submodules in a one-level hierarchy. The four main modules each have calls to all the other main modules, and within each main module, the four submodules each have calls to one another. There are still 100 lines of code per submodule, but each main module needs 100 lines of management code.

1.5c How long is Ben's program now?

1.5d How many interconnections are there now? Include module-to-module and submodule-to-submodule interconnections.

1.5e Was using hierarchy a good decision? Why or why not?

1996–1–2a…e

Additional exercises relating to Chapter 1 can be found in the problem sets beginning on page 425.

CHAPTER

Elements of Computer System Organization

2

CHAPTER CONTENTS

Principles of Computer System Design: An Introduction

DOI: 10.1016/B978-0-12-374957-4.00010-4

OVERVIEW

Although the number of potential abstractions for computer system components is unlimited, remarkably the vast majority that actually appear in practice fall into one of three well-defined classes: *the memory, the interpreter*, and *the communication link*. These three abstractions are so fundamental that theoreticians compare computer algorithms in terms of the number of data items they must remember, the number of steps their interpreter must execute, and the number of messages they must communicate.

Designers use these three abstractions to organize physical hardware structures, not because they are the only ways to interconnect gates, but rather because

- they supply fundamental functions of recall, processing, and communication,
- so far, these are the only hardware abstractions that have proven both to be widely useful and to have understandably simple interface semantics.

To meet the many requirements of different applications, system designers build layers on this fundamental base, but in doing so they do not routinely create completely different abstractions. Instead, they elaborate the same three abstractions, rearranging and repackaging them to create features that are useful and interfaces that are convenient for each application. Thus, for example, the designer of a general-purpose system such as a personal computer or a network server develops interfaces that exhibit highly refined forms of the same three abstractions. The user, in turn, may see the memory in the form of an organized file or database system, the interpreter in the form of a word processor, a game-playing system, or a high-level programming language, and the communication link in the form of instant messaging or the World Wide Web. On examination, underneath each of these abstractions is a series of layers built on the basic hardware versions of those same abstractions.

A primary method by which the abstract components of a computer system interact is *reference*. What that means is that the usual way for one component to connect to another is by *name*. Names appear in the interfaces of all three of the fundamental abstractions as well as the interfaces of their more elaborate higher-layer counterparts. The memory stores and retrieves objects by name, the interpreter manipulates named objects, and names identify communication links. Names are thus the glue that interconnects the abstractions. Named interconnections can, with proper design, be easy to change. Names also allow the sharing of objects, and they permit finding previously created objects at a later time.

This chapter briefly reviews the architecture and organization of computer systems in the light of abstraction, naming, and layering. Some parts of this review will be familiar to the reader with a background in computer software or hardware, but the systems perspective may provide some new insights into those familiar concepts and it lays the foundation for coming chapters. Section 2.1 describes the three fundamental abstractions, Section 2.2 presents a model for naming and explains how names are used in computer systems, and Section 2.3 discusses how a designer combines the abstractions, using names and layers, to create a typical computer system, presenting the file system as a concrete example of the use of naming and layering for the memory abstraction. Section 2.4 looks at how the rest of this book will consist of designing some higher-level version of one or more of the three fundamental abstractions, using names for interconnection and built up in layers. Section 2.5 is a case study showing how abstractions, naming, and layering are applied in a real file system.

2.1 THE THREE FUNDAMENTAL ABSTRACTIONS

We begin by examining, for each of the three fundamental abstractions, what the abstraction does, how it does it, its interfaces, and the ways it uses names for interconnection.

2.1.1 Memory

Memory, sometimes called *storage*, is the system component that remembers data values for use in computation. Although memory technology is wide-ranging, as suggested by the list of examples in Figure 2.1, all memory devices fit a simple abstract model that has two operations, named WRITE and READ:

WRITE (*name, value*)
value ← READ (*name*)

The WRITE operation specifies in *value* a value to be remembered and in *name* a name by which one can recall that value in the future. The READ operation specifies in *name* the name of some previously remembered value, and the memory device returns that value. A later call to WRITE that specifies the same name updates the value associated with that name.

Hardware memory devices:
- RAM chip
- Flash memory
- Magnetic tape
- Magnetic disk
- CD-R and DVD-R

Higher level memory systems:
- RAID
- File system
- Database management system

FIGURE 2.1

Some examples of memory devices that may be familiar.

Memories can be either volatile or non-volatile. A *volatile* memory is one whose mechanism of retaining information consumes energy; if its power supply is interrupted for some reason, it forgets its information content. When one turns off the power to a *non-volatile* memory (sometimes called "stable storage"), it retains its content, and when power is again available, READ operations return the same values as before. By connecting a volatile memory to a battery or an

Sidebar 2.1 Terminology: Durability, Stability, and Persistence Both in common English usage and in the professional literature, the terms *durability, stability,* and *persistence* overlap in various ways and are sometimes used almost interchangeably. In this text, we define and use them in a way that emphasizes certain distinctions.

Durability A property of a storage medium: the length of time it remembers.
Stability A property of an object: it is unchanging.
Persistence A property of an active agent: it keeps trying.

Thus, the current chapter suggests that files be placed in a durable storage medium—that is, they should survive system shutdown and remain intact for as long as they are needed. Chapter 8 [on-line] revisits durability specifications and classifies applications according to their durability requirements.

This chapter introduces the concept of stable bindings for names, which, once determined, never again change.

Chapter 7 [on-line] introduces the concept of a persistent sender, a participant in a message exchange who keeps retransmitting a message until it gets confirmation that the message was successfully received, and Chapter 8 [on-line] describes persistent faults, which keep causing a system to fail.

uninterruptible power supply, it can be made *durable*, which means that it is designed to remember things for at least some specified period, known as its *durability*. Even non-volatile memory devices are subject to eventual deterioration, known as *decay*, so they usually also have a specified durability, perhaps measured in years. We will revisit durability in Chapters 8 [on-line] and 10 [on-line], where we will see methods of obtaining different levels of durability. Sidebar 2.1 compares the meaning of durability with two other, related words.

At the physical level, a memory system does not normally name, READ, or WRITE values of arbitrary size. Instead, hardware layer memory devices READ and WRITE contiguous arrays of bits, usually fixed in length, known by various terms such as *bytes* (usually 8 bits, but one sometimes encounters architectures with 6-, 7-, or 9-bit bytes), *words* (a small integer number of bytes, typically 2, 4, or 8), *lines* (several words), and *blocks* (a number of bytes, usually a power of 2, that can measure in the thousands). Whatever the size of the array, the unit of physical layer memory written or read is known as a memory (or storage) *cell*. In most cases, the *name* argument in the READ and WRITE calls is actually the name of a cell. Higher-layer memory systems also READ and WRITE contiguous arrays of bits, but these arrays usually can be of any convenient length, and are called by terms such as *record*, *segment*, or *file*.

2.1.1.1 Read/Write Coherence and Atomicity

Two useful properties for a memory are *read/write coherence* and *before-or-after atomicity*. Read/write coherence means that the result of the READ of a named cell is always the same as the most recent WRITE to that cell. Before-or-after atomicity means that the result of every READ or WRITE is as if that READ or WRITE occurred either completely before or completely after any other READ or WRITE. Although it might seem that a designer should be able simply to assume these two properties, that assumption is risky and often wrong. There are a surprising number of threats to read/write coherence and before-or-after atomicity:

- *Concurrency.* In systems where different actors can perform READ and WRITE operations concurrently, they may initiate two such operations on the same named cell at about the same time. There needs to be some kind of arbitration that decides which one goes first and to ensure that one operation completes before the other begins.
- *Remote storage.* When the memory device is physically distant, the same concerns arise, but they are amplified by delays, which make the question of "which WRITE was most recent?" problematic and by additional forms of failure introduced by communication links. Section 4.5 introduces remote storage, and Chapter 10 [on-line] explores solutions to before-or-after atomicity and read/write coherence problems that arise with remote storage systems.
- *Performance enhancements.* Optimizing compilers and high-performance processors may rearrange the order of memory operations, possibly changing the very meaning of "the most recent WRITE to that cell" and thereby destroying read/write coherence for concurrent READ and WRITE operations. For example, a compiler might delay the WRITE operation implied by an assignment statement until the register holding the value to be written is needed for some other purpose. If someone else performs a READ of that variable, they may receive an old value. Some programming languages and high-performance processor architectures provide special programming directives to allow a programmer to restore read/write coherence on a case-by-case basis. For example, the Java language has a SYNCHRONIZED declaration that protects a block of code from read/write incoherence, and Hewlett-Packard's Alpha processor architecture (among others) includes a *memory barrier* (MB) instruction that forces all preceding READs and WRITEs to complete before going on to the next instruction. Unfortunately, both of these constructs create opportunities for programmers to make subtle mistakes.
- *Cell size incommensurate with value size.* A large value may occupy multiple memory cells, in which case before-or-after atomicity requires special attention. The problem is that both reading and writing of a multiple-cell value is usually done one cell at a time. A reader running concurrently with a writer that is updating the same multiple-cell value may end up with a mixed bag of cells, only some of which have been updated. Computer architects call this hazard *write tearing.* Failures that occur in the middle of writing multiple-cell values can further complicate the situation. To restore before-or-after atomicity, concurrent readers and writers must somehow be coordinated, and a failure in the middle of an update must leave either all or none of the intended update intact. When these conditions are met, the READ or WRITE is said to be *atomic.* A closely related

risk arises when a small value shares a memory cell with other small values. The risk is that if two writers concurrently update different values that share the same cell, one may overwrite the other's update. Atomicity can also solve this problem. Chapter 5 begins the study of atomicity by exploring methods of coordinating concurrent activities. Chapter 9 [on-line] expands the study of atomicity to also encompass failures.

- *Replicated storage.* As Chapter 8 [on-line] will explore in detail, reliability of storage can be increased by making multiple copies of values and placing those copies in distinct storage cells. Storage may also be replicated for increased performance, so that several readers can operate concurrently. But replication increases the number of ways in which concurrent READ and WRITE operations can interact and possibly lose either read/write coherence or before-or-after atomicity. During the time it takes a writer to update several replicas, readers of an updated replica can get different answers from readers of a replica that the writer hasn't gotten to yet. Chapter 10 [on-line] discusses techniques to ensure read/write coherence and before-or-after atomicity for replicated storage.

Often, the designer of a system must cope with not just one but several of these threats simultaneously. The combination of replication and remoteness is particularly challenging. It can be surprisingly difficult to design memories that are both efficient and also read/write coherent and atomic. To simplify the design or achieve higher performance, designers sometimes build memory systems that have weaker coherence specifications. For example, a multiple processor system might specify: "The result of a READ will be the value of the latest WRITE if that WRITE was performed by the same processor." There is an entire literature of "data consistency models" that explores the detailed properties of different memory coherence specifications. In a layered memory system, it is essential that the designer of a layer know precisely the coherence and atomicity specifications of any lower layer memory that it uses. In turn, if the layer being designed provides memory for higher layers, the designer must specify precisely these two properties that higher layers can expect and depend on. Unless otherwise mentioned, we will assume that physical memory devices provide read/write coherence for individual cells, but that before-or-after atomicity for multicell values (for example, files) is separately provided by the layer that implements them.

2.1.1.2 Memory Latency

An important property of a memory is the time it takes for a READ or a WRITE to complete, which is known as its *latency* (often called *access time*, though that term has a more precise definition that will be explained in Sidebar 6.4). In the magnetic disk memory (described in Sidebar 2.2) the latency of a particular sector depends on the mechanical state of the device at the instant the user requests access. Having read a sector, one may measure the time required to also read a different but nearby sector in microseconds—but only if the user anticipates the second read and requests it before the disk rotates past that second sector. A request just a few microseconds late may encounter

Sidebar 2.2 How Magnetic Disks Work Magnetic disks consist of rotating circular platters coated on both sides with a magnetic material such as ferric oxide. An electromagnet called a *disk head* records information by aligning the magnetic field of the particles in a small region on the platter's surface. The same disk head reads the data by sensing the polarity of the aligned particles as the platter spins by. The disk spins continuously at a constant rate, and the disk head actually floats just a few nanometers above the disk surface on an air cushion created by the rotation of the platter.

From a single position above a platter, a disk head can read or write a set of bits, called a *track*, located a constant distance from the center. In the top view below, the shaded region identifies a track. Tracks are formatted into equal-sized blocks, called *sectors*, by writing separation marks periodically around the track. Because all sectors are the same size, the outer tracks have more sectors than the inner ones.

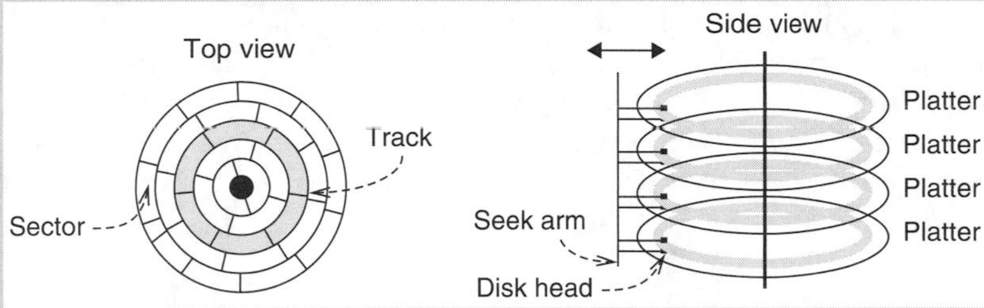

A typical modern disk module, known as a "hard drive" because its platters are made of a rigid material, contains several platters spinning on a common axis called a *spindle*, as in the side view above. One disk head per platter surface is mounted on a comb-like structure that moves the heads in unison across the platters. Movement to a specific track is called *seeking*, and the comb-like structure is known as a *seek arm*. The set of tracks that can be read or written when the seek arm is in one position (for example, the shaded regions of the side view) is called a *cylinder*. Tracks, platters, and sectors are each numbered. A sector is thus addressed by geometric coordinates: track number, platter number, and rotational position. Modern disk controllers typically do the geometric mapping internally and present their clients with an address space consisting of consecutively numbered sectors.

To read or write a particular sector, the disk controller first seeks the desired track. Once the seek arm is in position, the controller waits for the beginning of the desired sector to rotate under the disk head, and then it activates the head on the desired platter. Physically encoding digital data in analog magnetic domains usually requires that the controller write complete sectors.

The time required for disk access is called *latency*, a term defined more precisely in Chapter 6. Moving a seek arm takes time. Vendors quote seek times of 5 to 10 milliseconds, but that is an average over all possible seek arm moves. A move from one

(Sidebar continues)

cylinder to the next may require only 1/20 of the time of a move from the innermost to the outermost track. It also takes time for a particular sector to rotate under the disk head. A typical disk rotation rate is 7200 rpm, for which the platter rotates once in 8.3 milliseconds. The time to transfer the data depends on the magnetic recording density, the rotation rate, the cylinder number (outer cylinders may transfer at higher rates), and the number of bits read or written. A platter that holds 40 gigabytes transfers data at rates between 300 and 600 megabits per second; thus a 1-kilobyte sector transfers in a microsecond or two. Seek time and rotation delay are limited by mechanical engineering considerations and tend to improve only slowly, but magnetic recording density depends on materials technology, which has improved both steadily and rapidly for many years.

Early disk systems stored between 20 and 80 megabytes. In the 1970s Kenneth Haughton, an IBM inventor, described a new technique of placing disk platters in a sealed enclosure to avoid contamination. The initial implementation stored 30 megabytes on each of two spindles, in a configuration known as a 30–30 drive. Haughton nicknamed it the "Winchester", after the Winchester 30-30 rifle. The code name stuck, and for many years hard drives were known as Winchester drives. Over the years, Winchester drives have gotten physically smaller while simultaneously evolving to larger capacities.

a delay that is a thousand times longer, waiting for that second sector to again rotate under the read head. Thus the maximum rate at which one can transfer data to or from a disk is dramatically larger than the rate one would achieve when choosing sectors at random. A *random access memory (RAM)* is one for which the latency for memory cells chosen at random is approximately the same as the latency for cells chosen in the pattern best suited for that memory device. An electronic memory chip is usually configured for random access. Memory devices that involve mechanical movement, such as optical disks (CDs and DVDs) and magnetic tapes and disks, are not.

For devices that do not provide random access, it is usually a good idea, having paid the cost in delay of moving the mechanical components into position, to READ or WRITE a large block of data. Large-block READ and WRITE operations are sometimes relabeled GET and PUT, respectively, and this book uses that convention. Traditionally, the unqualified term *memory* meant random-access volatile memory and the term *storage* was used for non-volatile memory that is read and written in large blocks with GET and PUT. In practice, there are enough exceptions to this naming rule that the words "memory" and "storage" have become almost interchangeable.

2.1.1.3 Memory Names and Addresses

Physical implementations of memory devices nearly always name a memory cell by the geometric coordinates of its physical storage location. Thus, for example, an electronic memory chip is organized as a two-dimensional array of flip-flops, each holding one named bit. The access mechanism splits the bit name into two parts, which in turn go to a pair of multiplexers. One multiplexer selects an x-coordinate, the other a y-coordinate, and the two coordinates in turn select the particular flip-flop that holds that bit. Similarly, in a magnetic disk memory, one component of the name electrically selects one of the recording platters, while a distinct component of the name selects the position of the seek arm, thereby choosing a specific track on that platter. A third name component selects a particular sector on that track, which may be identified by counting sectors as they pass under the read head, starting from an index mark that identifies the first sector.

It is easy to design hardware that maps geometric coordinates to and from sets of names consisting of consecutive integers (0, 1, 2, etc.). These consecutive integer names are called *addresses*, and they form the *address space* of the memory device. A memory system that uses names that are sets of consecutive integers is called a *location-addressed memory*. Because the addresses are consecutive, the size of the memory cell that is named does not have to be the same as the size of the cell that is read or written. In some memory architectures each byte has a distinct address, but reads and writes can (and in some cases must always) occur in larger units, such as a word or a line.

For most applications, consecutive integers are not exactly the names that one would choose for recalling data. One would usually prefer to be allowed to choose less constrained names. A memory system that accepts unconstrained names is called an *associative memory*. Since physical memories are generally location-addressed, a designer creates an associative memory by interposing an associativity layer, which may be implemented either with hardware or software, that maps unconstrained higher-level names to the constrained integer names of an underlying location-addressed memory, as in Figure 2.2. Examples of software associative memories, constructed on top of one or more underlying location-addressed memories, include personal telephone directories, file systems, and corporate database systems. A *cache*, a device that remembers the result of an expensive computation in the hope of not redoing that computation if it is needed again soon, is sometimes implemented as an

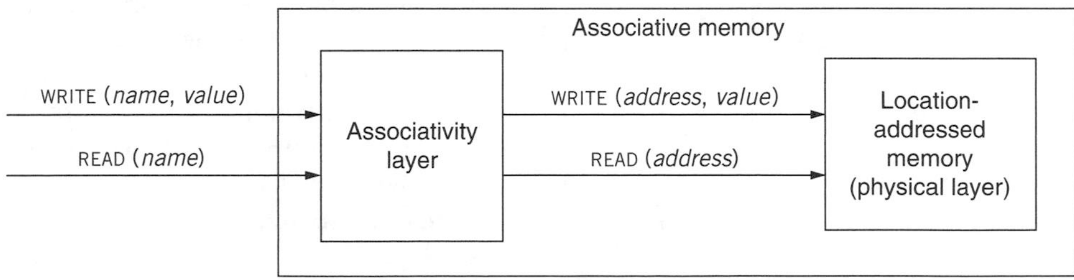

FIGURE 2.2

An associative memory implemented in two layers. The associativity layer maps the unconstrained names of its arguments to the consecutive integer addresses required by the physical layer location-addressed memory.

associative memory, either in software or hardware. (The design of caches is discussed in Section 6.2.)

Layers that provide associativity and name mapping figure strongly in the design of all memory and storage systems. For example, Table 2.2 on page 93 lists the layers of the UNIX file system. For another example of layering of memory abstractions, Chapter 5 explains how memory can be virtualized by adding a name-mapping layer.

2.1.1.4 Exploiting the Memory Abstraction: RAID

Returning to the subject of abstraction, a system known as RAID provides an illustration of the power of modularity and of how the storage abstraction can be applied to good effect. RAID is an acronym for Redundant Array of Independent (or Inexpensive) Disks. A RAID system consists of a set of disk drives and a controller configured with an electrical and programming interface that is identical to the interface of a single disk drive, as shown in Figure 2.3. The RAID controller intercepts READ and WRITE requests coming across its interface, and it directs them to one or more of the disks. RAID has two distinct goals:

- Improved performance, by reading or writing disks concurrently
- Improved durability, by writing information on more than one disk

Different RAID configurations offer different trade-offs between these goals. Whatever trade-off the designer chooses, because the interface abstraction is that of a single disk, the programmer can take advantage of the improvements in performance and durability without reprogramming.

Certain useful RAID configurations are traditionally identified by (somewhat arbitrary) numbers. In later chapters, we will encounter several of these numbered configurations. The configuration known as RAID 0 (in Section 6.1.5) provides increased performance by allowing concurrent reading and writing. The configuration known as RAID 4 (shown in Figure 8.6 [on-line]) improves disk reliability by applying error-correction codes. Yet another configuration known as RAID 1 (in Section 8.5.4.6 [on-line]) provides high durability by

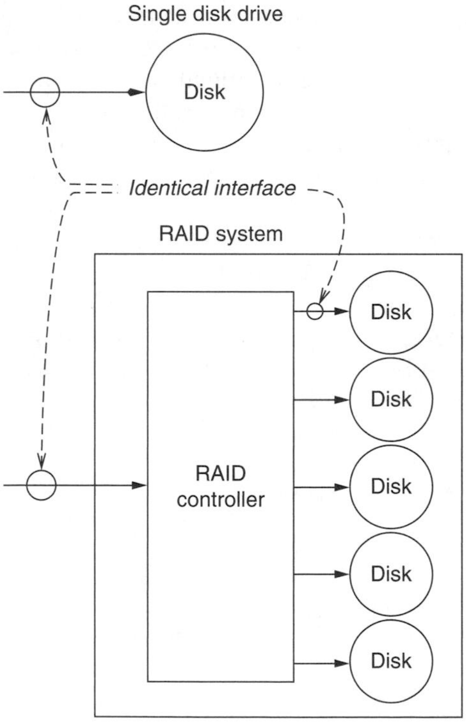

FIGURE 2.3

Abstraction in RAID. The READ/WRITE electrical and programming interface of the RAID system, represented by the solid arrow, is identical to that of a single disk.

making identical copies of the data on different disks. Exercise 8.8 [on-line] explores a simple but elegant performance optimization known as RAID 5. These and several other RAID configurations were originally described in depth in a paper by Randy Katz, Garth Gibson, and David Patterson, who also assigned the traditional numbers to the different configurations [see Suggestions for Further Reading 10.2.2].

2.1.2 Interpreters

Interpreters are the active elements of a computer system; they perform the *actions* that constitute computations. Figure 2.4 lists some examples of interpreters that may be familiar. As with memory, interpreters also come in a wide range of physical manifestations. However, they too can be described with a simple abstraction, consisting of just three components:

1. An *instruction reference*, which tells the interpreter where to find its next instruction
2. A *repertoire*, which defines the set of actions the interpreter is prepared to perform when it retrieves an instruction from the location named by the instruction reference
3. An *environment reference*, which tells the interpreter where to find its *environment*, the current state on which the interpreter should perform the action of the current instruction

The normal operation of an interpreter is to proceed sequentially through some program, as suggested by the diagram and pseudocode of Figure 2.5. Using the environment reference to find the current environment, the interpreter retrieves from that environment the program instruction indicated in the instruction reference. Again using the environment reference, the interpreter performs the action directed by the program instruction. That action typically involves using and perhaps changing data in the environment, and also an appropriate update of the instruction reference. When it finishes performing the instruction, the interpreter moves on, taking as its next instruction the one now named by the instruction reference. Certain events, called *interrupts*, may catch the attention of the interpreter, causing it, rather than the program, to supply the next instruction. The original program no longer controls the interpreter; instead, a different program, the interrupt handler, takes control and handles the event. The interpreter may also change the environment reference to one that is appropriate for the interrupt handler.

Hardware:
- Pentium 4, PowerPC 970, UltraSPARC T1
- disk controller
- display controller

Software:
- Alice, AppleScript, Perl, Tcl, Scheme
- LISP, Python, Forth, Java bytecode
- JavaScript, Smalltalk
- TeX, LaTeX
- Safari, Internet Explorer, Firefox

FIGURE 2.4

Some common examples of interpreters. The disk controller example is explained in Section 2.3 and the Web browser examples are the subject of Exercise 4.5.

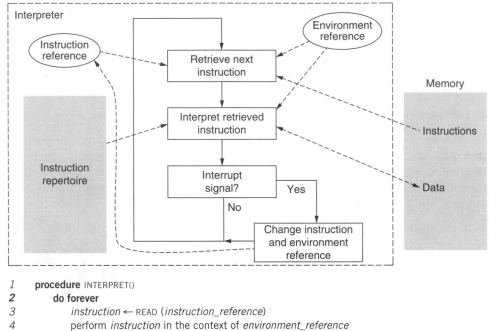

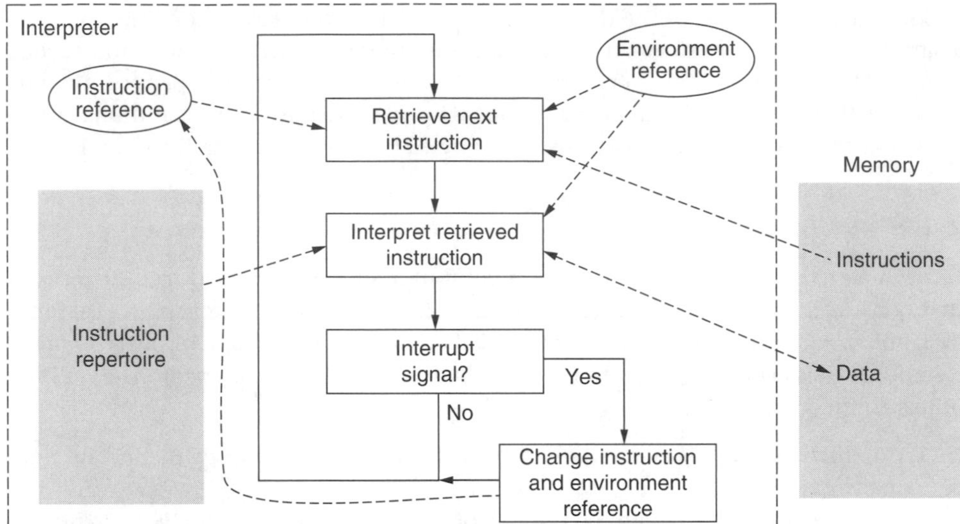


```
procedure INTERPRET()
    do forever
        instruction ← READ (instruction_reference)
        perform instruction in the context of environment_reference
        if interrupt_signal = TRUE then
            instruction_reference ← entry point of INTERRUPT_HANDLER
            environment_reference ← environment ref of INTERRUPT_HANDLER
```

FIGURE 2.5

Structure of, and pseudocode for, an abstract interpreter. Solid arrows show control flow, and dashed arrows suggest information flow. Sidebar 2.3 describes this book's conventions for expressing pseudocode.

Sidebar 2.3 Representation: Pseudocode and Messages This book presents many examples of program fragments. Most of them are represented in pseudocode, an imaginary programming language that adopts familiar features from different existing programming languages as needed and that occasionally intersperses English text to characterize some step whose exact detail is unimportant. The pseudocode has some standard features, several of which this brief example shows.

```
1   procedure SUM (a, b)     // Add two numbers.
2       total ← a + b
3       return total
```

The line numbers on the left are not part of the pseudocode; they are there simply to allow the text to refer to lines in the program. Procedures are explicitly declared

(*Sidebar continues*)

(as in line *1*), and indentation groups blocks of statements together. Program variables are set in *italic*, program key words in **bold**, and literals such as the names of procedures and built-in constants in SMALL CAPS. The left arrow denotes substitution or assignment (line *2*) and the symbol "=" denotes equality in conditional expressions. The double slash precedes comments that are not part of the pseudocode. Various forms of iteration (**while**, **until**, **for each**, **do occasionally**), conditionals (**if**), set operations (**is in**), and case statements (**do case**) appear when they are helpful in expressing an example. The construction **for** *j* **from** 0 **to** 3 iterates four times; array indices start at 0 unless otherwise mentioned. The construction *y.x* means the element named *x* in the structure named *y*. To minimize clutter, the pseudocode omits declarations wherever the meaning is reasonably apparent from the context. Procedure parameters are passed by value unless the declaration **reference** appears. Section 2.2.1 of this chapter discusses the distinction between use by value and use by reference. When more than one variable uses the same structure, the declaration *structure_name* **instance** *variable_name* may be used.

The notation *a*(11. . .15) denotes extraction of bits 11 through 15 from the string *a* (or from the variable *a* considered as a string). Bits are numbered left to right starting with zero, with the most significant bit of integers first (using big-endian notation, as described in Sidebar 4.3). The + operator, when applied to strings, concatenates the strings.

Some examples are represented in the instruction repertoire of an imaginary reduced instruction set computer (RISC). Because such programs are cumbersome, they appear only when it is essential to show how software interacts with hardware.

In describing and using communication links, the notation

$$x \Rightarrow y: \{M\}$$

represents a message with contents M from sender x to recipient y. The notation {*a*, *b*, *c*} represents a message that contains the three named fields marshaled in some way that the recipient presumably understands how to unmarshal.

Many systems have more than one interpreter. Multiple interpreters are usually *asynchronous*, which means that they run on separate, uncoordinated, clocks. As a result, they may progress at different rates, even if they are nominally identical and running the same program. In designing algorithms that coordinate the work of multiple interpreters, one usually assumes that there is no fixed relation among their progress rates and therefore that there is no way to predict the relative timing, for example, of the LOAD and STORE instructions that they issue. The assumption of interpreter asynchrony is one of the reasons memory read/write coherence and before-or-after atomicity can be challenging design problems.

2.1.2.1 Processors

A general-purpose processor is an implementation of an interpreter. For purposes of concrete discussion throughout this book, we use a typical reduced instruction set processor. The processor's instruction reference is a *program counter*, stored in a fast memory register inside the processor. The program counter contains the address of the memory location that stores the next instruction of the current program. The environment reference of the processor consists in part of a small amount of built-in location-addressed memory in the form of named (by number) registers for fast access to temporary results of computations.

Our general-purpose processor may be directly wired to a memory, which is also part of its environment. The addresses in the program counter and in instructions are then names in the address space of that memory, so this part of the environment reference is wired in and unchangeable. When we discuss virtualization in Chapter 5, we will extend the processor to refer to memory indirectly via one or more registers. With that change, the environment reference is maintained in those registers, thus allowing addresses issued by the processor to map to different names in the address space of the memory.

The repertoire of our general-purpose processor includes instructions for expressing computations such as adding two numbers (ADD), subtracting one number from another (SUB), comparing two numbers (CMP), and changing the program counter to the address of another instruction (JMP). These instructions operate on values stored in the named registers of the processor, which is why they are colloquially called "op-codes".

The repertoire also includes instructions to move data between processor registers and memory. To distinguish program instructions from memory operations, we use the name LOAD for the instruction that READs a value from a named memory cell into a register of the processor and STORE for the instruction that WRITEs the value from a register into a named memory cell. These instructions take two integer arguments, the name of a memory cell and the name of a processor register.

The general-purpose processor provides a *stack*, a push-down data structure that is stored in memory and used to implement procedure calls. When calling a procedure, the caller pushes arguments of the called procedure (the callee) on the stack. When the callee returns, the caller pops the stack back to its previous size. This implementation of procedures supports recursive calls because every invocation of a procedure always finds its arguments at the top of the stack. We dedicate one register for implementing stack operations efficiently. This register, known as the *stack pointer*, holds the memory address of the top of the stack.

As part of interpreting an instruction, the processor increments the program counter so that, when that instruction is complete, the program counter contains the address of the next instruction of the program. If the instruction being interpreted is a JMP, that instruction loads a new value into the program counter. In both cases, the flow of instruction interpretation is under control of the running program.

The processor also implements interrupts. An interrupt can occur because the processor has detected some problem with the running program (e.g., the program attempted to execute an instruction that the interpreter does not or cannot implement, such as dividing by zero). An interrupt can also occur because a signal arrives from outside the processor, indicating that some external device needs attention (e.g., the keyboard signals that a key press is available). In the first case, the interrupt mechanism may transfer control to an *exception* handler elsewhere in the program. In the second case, the interrupt handler may do some work and then return control to the original program. We shall return to the subject of interrupts and the distinction between interrupt handlers and exception handlers in the discussion of threads in Chapter 5.

In addition to general-purpose processors, computer systems typically also have special-purpose processors, which have a limited repertoire. For example, a clock chip is a simple, hard-wired interpreter that just counts: at some specified frequency, it executes an ADD instruction, which adds 1 to the contents of a register or memory location that corresponds to the clock. All processors, whether general-purpose or specialized, are examples of interpreters. However, they may differ substantially in the repertoire they provide. One must consult the device manufacturer's manual to learn the repertoire.

2.1.2.2 Interpreter Layers

Interpreters are nearly always organized in layers. The lowest layer is usually a hardware engine that has a fairly primitive repertoire of instructions, and successive layers provide an increasingly rich or specialized repertoire. A full-blown application system may involve four or five distinct layers of interpretation. Across any given layer interface, the lower layer presents some repertoire of possible instructions to the upper layer. Figure 2.6 illustrates this model.

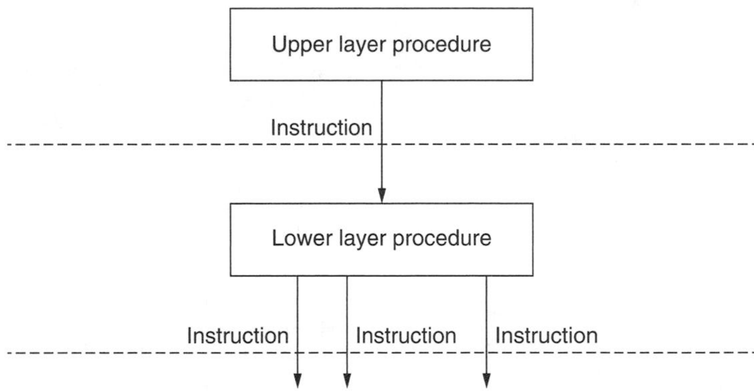

FIGURE 2.6

The model for a layered interpreter. Each layer interface, shown as a dashed line, represents an abstraction barrier, across which an upper layer procedure requests execution of instructions from the repertoire of the lower layer. The lower layer procedure typically implements an instruction by performing several instructions from the repertoire of a next lower layer interface.

Consider, for example, a calendar management program. The person making requests by moving and clicking a mouse views the calendar program as an interpreter of the mouse gestures. The instruction reference tells the interpreter to obtain its next instruction from the keyboard and mouse. The repertoire of instructions is the set of available requests—to add a new event, to insert some descriptive text, to change the hour, or to print a list of the day's events. The environment is a set of files that remembers the calendar from day to day.

The calendar program implements each action requested by the user by invoking statements in some programming language such as Java. These statements—such as iteration statements, conditional statements, substitution statements, procedure calls—constitute the instruction repertoire of the next lower layer. The instruction reference keeps track of which statement is to be executed next, and the environment is the collection of named variables used by the program. (We are assuming here that the Java language program has not been compiled directly to machine language. If a compiler is used, there would be one less layer.)

The actions of the programming language are in turn implemented by hardware machine language instructions of some general-purpose processor, with its own instruction reference, repertoire, and environment reference.

Figure 2.7 illustrates the three layers just described. In practice, the layered structure may be deeper—the calendar program is likely to be organized with an internal upper layer that interprets the graphical gestures and a lower layer that manipulates the calendar data, the Java interpreter may have an intermediate byte-code interpreter layer, and some machine languages are implemented with a microcode interpreter layer on top of a layer of hardware gates.

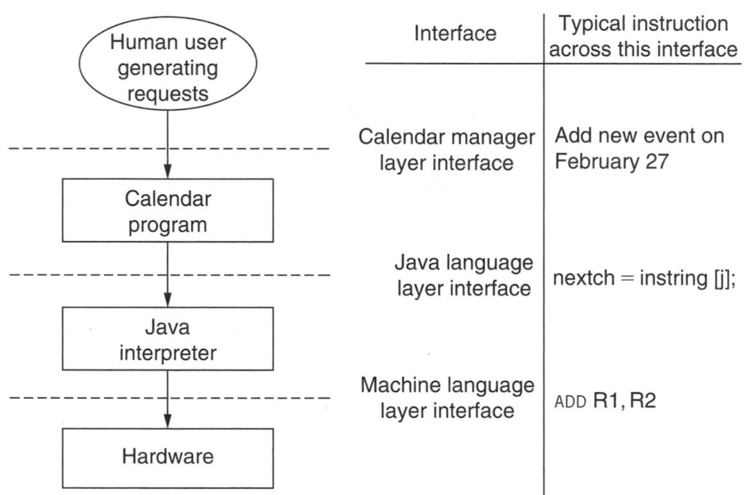

FIGURE 2.7

An application system that has three layers of interpretation, each with its own repertoire of instructions.

One goal in the design of a layered interpreter is to ensure that the designer of each layer can be confident that the layer below either completes each instruction successfully or does nothing at all. Half-finished instructions should never be a concern, even if there is a catastrophic failure. That goal is another example of atomicity, and achieving it is relatively difficult. For the moment, we simply assume that interpreters are atomic, and we defer the discussion of how to achieve atomicity to Chapter 9 [on-line].

2.1.3 Communication Links

A *communication link* provides a way for information to move between physically separated components. Communication links, of which a few examples are listed in Figure 2.8, come in a wide range of technologies, but, like memories and interpreters, they can be described with a simple abstraction. The communication link abstraction has two operations:

SEND (*link_name, outgoing_message_buffer*)
RECEIVE (*link_name, incoming_message_buffer*)

The SEND operation specifies an array of bits, called a *message,* to be sent over the communication link identified by *link_name* (for example, a wire). The argument *outgoing_message_buffer* identifies the message to be sent, usually by giving the address and size of a buffer in memory that contains the message. The RECEIVE operation accepts an incoming message, again usually by designating the address and size of a buffer in memory to hold the incoming message. Once the lowest layer of a system has received a message, higher layers may acquire the message by calling a RECEIVE interface of the lower layer, or the lower layer may "upcall" to the higher layer, in which case the interface might be better characterized as DELIVER (*incoming_message*).

Names connect systems to communication links in two different ways. First, the *link_name* arguments of SEND and RECEIVE identify one of possibly several available communication links attached to the system. Second, some communication links are actually multiply-attached networks of links, and some additional method is needed to name which of several possible recipients should receive the message. The name of the intended recipient is typically one of the components of the message.

At first glance, it might appear that sending and receiving a message is just an example of copying an array of bits from one memory to another memory over a wire using a sequence of READ and WRITE operations,

Hardware technology:
- twisted pair
- coaxial cable
- optical fiber

Higher level
- Ethernet
- Universal Serial Bus (USB)
- the Internet
- the telephone system
- a UNIX pipe

FIGURE 2.8

Some examples of communication links.

so there is no need for a third abstraction. However, communication links involve more than simple copying—they have many complications, such as a wide range of operating parameters that makes the time to complete a SEND or RECEIVE operation unpredictable, a hostile environment that threatens integrity of the data transfer, asynchronous operation that leads to the arrival of messages whose size and time of delivery can not be known in advance, and most significant, the message may not even be delivered. Because of these complications, the semantics of SEND and RECEIVE are typically quite different from those associated with READ and WRITE. Programs that invoke SEND and RECEIVE must take these different semantics explicitly into account. On the other hand, some communication link implementations do provide a layer that does its best to hide a SEND/RECEIVE interface behind a READ/WRITE interface.

Just as with memory and interpreters, designers organize and implement communication links in layers. Rather than continuing a detailed discussion of communication links here, we defer that discussion to Section 7.2 [on-line], which describes a three-layer model that organizes communication links into systems called *networks*. Figure 7.18 [on-line] illustrates this three-layer network model, which comprises a link layer, a network layer, and an end-to-end layer.

2.2 NAMING IN COMPUTER SYSTEMS

Computer systems use names in many ways in their construction, configuration, and operation. The previous section mentioned memory addresses, processor registers, and link names, and Figure 2.9 lists several additional examples, some of which are probably familiar, others of which will turn up in later chapters. Some system names resemble those of a programming language, whereas others are quite different. When building systems out of subsystems, it is essential to be able to use a subsystem without having to know details of how that subsystem refers to its components. Names are thus used to achieve modularity, and at the same time, modularity must sometimes hide names.

We approach names from an object point of view: the computer system manipulates *objects*. An interpreter performs the manipulation under control of a program or perhaps under the direction of a human user. An object may be structured, which means that it uses other objects as components. In a direct analogy with two ways in which procedures can pass arguments, there are two ways to arrange for one object to use another as a component:

- create a copy of the component object and include the copy in the using object (use by *value*), or
- choose a name for the component object and include just that name in the using object (use by *reference*). The component object is said to *export* the name.

When passing arguments to procedures, use by value enhances modularity, because if the callee accidentally modifies the argument it does not affect the original. But use by value can be problematic because it does not easily permit two or more objects to *share* a component object whose value changes. If both object A

R5	(processor register)
$174FFF_{hex}$	(memory address)
`pedantic.edu`	(network attachment point name)
18.72.0.151	(network attachment point address)
alice	(user name)
`alice@pedantic.edu`	(e-mail address)
/u/alice/startup_plan.doc	(file name)
`http://pedantic.edu/alice/home.html`	(WWW URL)

FIGURE 2.9

Examples of names used in systems.

and B use object C by value, then changing the value of C is a concept that is either meaningless or difficult to implement—it could require tracking down the two copies of C included in A and B to update them. Similarly, in procedure calls it is sometimes useful to give the callee the ability to modify the original object, so most programming languages provide some way to pass the name (pseudocode in this text uses the **reference** declaration for that purpose) rather than the value. One purpose of names, then, is to allow use by reference and thus simplify the sharing of changeable objects.

Sharing illustrates one fundamental purpose for names: as a communication and an organizing tool. Because two uses of the same name can refer to the same object, whether those uses are by different users or by the same user at different times, names are invaluable both for communication and for organization of things so that one can find them later.

A second fundamental purpose for a name is to allow a system designer to defer to a later time an important decision: to which object should this name refer? A name also makes it easy to change that decision later. For example, an application program may refer to a table of data by name. There may be several versions of that table, and the decision about which version to use can wait until the program actually needs the table.

Decoupling one object from another by using a name as an intermediary is known as *indirection*. Deciding on the correspondence between a name and an object is an example of *binding*. Changing a binding is a mechanically easy way to replace one object with another. Modules are objects, so naming is a cornerstone of modularity.

This section introduces a general model for the use of names in computer systems. Some parts of this model should be familiar; the discussion of the three fundamental abstractions in the previous section introduced names and some naming terminology. The model is only one part of the story. Chapter 3 discusses in more depth the many decisions that arise in the design of naming schemes.

2.2.1 The Naming Model

It is helpful to have a model of how names are associated with specific objects. A system designer creates a *naming scheme*, which consists of three elements. The first element is a *name space*, which comprises an alphabet of symbols together with syntax rules that specify which names are acceptable. The second element is a *name-mapping algorithm*, which associates some (not necessarily all) names of the name space with some (again, not necessarily all) values in a *universe of values*, which is the third and final element of the naming scheme. A *value* may be an object, or it may be another name from either the original name space or from a different name space. A name-to-value mapping is an example of a *binding*, and when such a mapping exists, the name is said to be *bound* to the value. Figure 2.10 illustrates.

In most systems, typically several distinct naming schemes are in operation simultaneously. For example, a system may be using one naming scheme for e-mail mailbox names, a second naming scheme for Internet hosts, a third for files, and a fourth for virtual memory addresses. When a program interpreter encounters a name, it must know which naming scheme to invoke. The environment surrounding use of the name usually provides enough information to identify the naming scheme. For example, in an application program, the author of that program knows that the program should expect file names to be interpreted only by the file system and Internet host names to be interpreted only by some network service.

The interpreter that encounters the name runs the name-mapping algorithm of the appropriate naming scheme. The name-mapping algorithm *resolves* the name, which means that it discovers and returns the associated value (for this reason, the name-mapping algorithm is also called a *resolver*). The name-mapping algorithm is usually controlled by an additional parameter, known as a *context*. For a given naming scheme, there can be many different contexts, and a single name of the name space may map to different values when the resolver uses different contexts. For example, in ordinary discourse when a person refers to the names "you", "here", or "Alice", the meaning of each of those names depends on the context in which the person utters it. On the other hand, some naming schemes have only one context. Such naming schemes provide what are called *universal name spaces*, and they have the nice property that a name always has the same meaning within that naming scheme, no matter who uses it. For example, in the United States, social security numbers, which identify government pension and tax accounts, constitute a universal name space.

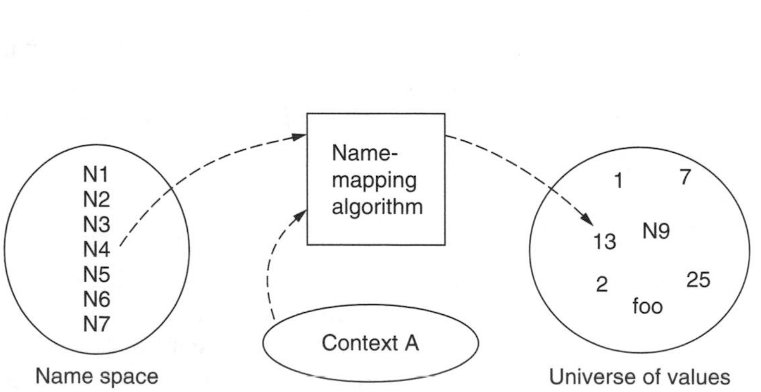

FIGURE 2.10

General model of the operation of a naming scheme. The name-mapping algorithm takes in a name and a context, and it returns an element from the universe of values. The arrows indicate that, using context "A", the algorithm resolves the name "N4" to the value "13".

When there is more than one context, the interpreter may tell the resolver which one it should use or the resolver may use a default context.

We can summarize the naming model by defining the following conceptual operation on names:

value ← RESOLVE (*name*, *context*)

When an interpreter encounters a name in an object, it first figures out what naming scheme is involved and thus which version of RESOLVE it should invoke. It then identifies an appropriate context, resolves the name in that context, and replaces the name with the resolved value as it continues interpretation. The variable *context* tells RESOLVE which context to use. That variable contains a name known as a ***context reference***.

In a processor, register numbers are names. In a simple processor, the set of register names, and the registers those names are bound to, are both fixed at design time. In most other systems that use names (including the register naming scheme of some high-performance processors), it is possible to create new bindings and delete old ones, ***enumerate*** the name space to obtain a list of existing bindings, and compare two names. For these purposes we define four more conceptual operations:

status ← BIND (*name*, *value*, *context*)
status ← UNBIND (*name*, *context*)
list ← ENUMERATE (*context*)
result ← COMPARE (*name1*, *name2*)

The first operation changes *context* by adding a new binding; the *status* result reports whether or not the change succeeded (it might fail if the proposed *name* violates the syntax rules of the name space). After a successful call to BIND, RESOLVE will return the new *value* for *name*.* The second operation, UNBIND, removes an existing binding from *context*, with *status* again reporting success or failure (perhaps because there was no such existing binding). After a successful call to UNBIND, RESOLVE will no longer return that *value* for *name*. The BIND and UNBIND operations allow the use of names to make connections between objects and change those connections later. A designer of an object can, by using a name to refer to a component object, choose the object to which that name is bound either then or at a later time by invoking BIND, and eliminate a binding that is no longer appropriate by invoking UNBIND, all without modifying the object that uses the name. This ability to delay and change bindings is a powerful tool used in the design of nearly all systems. Some naming implementations provide an ENUMERATE operation, which returns a list of all the names that can be resolved in *context*. Some implementations of ENUMERATE can also return a list of all values currently bound in *context*. Finally, the COMPARE operation reports (TRUE or FALSE) whether or not *name1* is the same as *name2*. The meaning of "same" is an interesting question addressed in Section 2.2.5, and it may require supplying additional context arguments.

---

*The WRITE operation of the memory abstraction creates a name-value association, so it can be viewed as a specialized instance of BIND. Similarly, the READ operation can be viewed as a specialized instance of RESOLVE.

Different naming schemes have different rules about the uniqueness of name-to-value mappings. Some naming schemes have a rule that a name must map to exactly one value in a given context and a value must have only one name, while in other naming schemes one name may map to several values, or one value may have several names, even in the same context. Another kind of uniqueness rule is that of a ***unique identifier name space***, which provides a set of names that will never be reused for the lifetime of the name space and, once bound, will always remain bound to the same value. Such a name is said to have a ***stable binding***. If a unique identifier name space also has the rule that a value can have only one name, the unique names become useful for keeping track of objects over a long period of time, for comparing references to see if they are to the same object, and for coordination of multiple copies in systems where objects are replicated for performance or reliability. For example, the customer account number of most billing systems constitutes a unique identifier name space. The account number will always refer to the same customer's account as long as that account exists, despite changes in the customer's address, telephone number, or even personal name. If a customer's account is deleted, that customer's account number will not someday be reused for a different customer's account. Named fields within the account, such as the balance due, may change from time to time, but the binding between the customer account number and the account itself is stable.

The name-mapping algorithm plus a single context do not necessarily map all names of the name space to values. Thus, a possible outcome of performing RESOLVE can be a *not-found* result, which RESOLVE may communicate to the caller either as a reserved value or as an exception. On the other hand, if the naming scheme allows one name to map to several values, a possible outcome can be a list of values. In that case, the UNBIND operation may require an additional argument that specifies which value to unbind. Finally, some naming schemes provide *reverse lookup*, which means that a caller can supply a value as an argument to the name-mapping algorithm, and find out what name or names are bound to that value.

Figure 2.10 illustrates the naming model, showing a name space, the corresponding universe of values, a name-mapping algorithm, and a context that controls the name-mapping algorithm.

In practice, one encounters three frequently used name-mapping algorithms:

- Table lookup
- Recursive lookup
- Multiple lookup

The most common implementation of a context is a table of {*name*, *value*} pairs. When the implementation of a context is a table, the name-mapping algorithm is just a lookup of the name in that table. The table itself may be complex, involving hashing or B-trees, but the basic idea is still the same. Binding a new name to a value consists of adding that {*name*, *value*} pair to the table. Figure 2.11 illustrates this common implementation of the naming model. There is one such table for each context, and different contexts may contain different bindings for the same name.

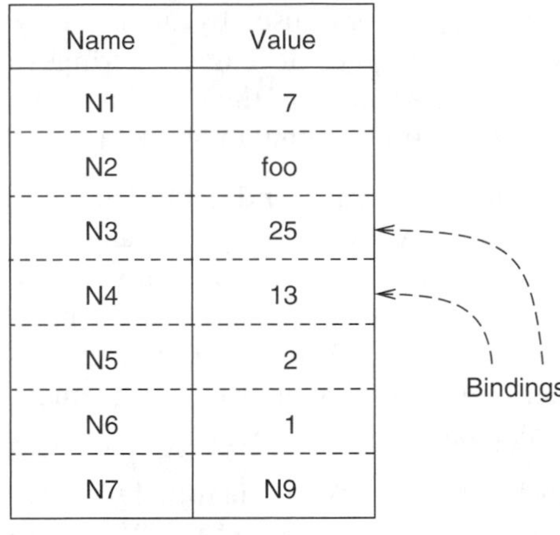

Name
Value
N1
7
N2
foo
N3
25
N4
13
N5
2
N6
1
N7
N9
Bindings
Context A

FIGURE 2.11

A system that uses table lookup as the name-mapping algorithm. As in the example of Figure 2.10, this system also resolves the name "N4" to the value "13".

Real-world examples of both the general naming model and the table-lookup implementation abound:

1. A telephone book is a table-lookup context that binds names of people and organizations to telephone numbers. As in the data communication network example, telephone numbers are themselves names that the telephone company resolves into physical line appearances, using a name-mapping algorithm that involves area codes, exchanges, and physical switchgear. The telephone books for Boston and for San Francisco are two contexts of the same naming scheme; any particular name may appear in both telephone books, but if so, it is probably bound to different telephone numbers.

2. Small integers name the registers of a processor. The value is the register itself, and the mapping from name to value is accomplished by wiring.

3. Memory cells are similarly named with the numbers called addresses, and the name-to-value mapping is again accomplished by wiring. Chapter 5 describes an address-renaming mechanism known as virtual memory, which binds blocks of virtual addresses to blocks of contiguous memory cells. When a system implements multiple virtual memories, each virtual memory is a distinct context; a given address can refer to a different memory cell in each virtual memory. Memory cells can also be shared among virtual memories, in which case the same memory cell may have the same (or different) addresses in different virtual memories, as determined by the bindings.

4. A typical computer file system uses several layers of names and contexts: disk sectors, disk partitions, files, and directories are all named objects. Directories are examples of table-lookup contexts. A particular file name may appear in several different directories, bound to either the same or different files. Section 2.5 presents a case study of naming in the UNIX file system.

5. Computers connect to data communication networks at places known as *network attachment points.* Network attachment points are usually named with two distinct naming schemes. The first one, used inside the network, involves a name space consisting of numbers in a fixed-length field. These names are bound, sometimes permanently and sometimes only briefly, to physical entrance

and exit points of the network. A second naming scheme, used by clients of the network, maps a more user-friendly universal name space of character strings to names of the first name space. Section 4.4 is a case study of the Domain Name System, which provides user-friendly attachment point naming for the Internet.

6. A programmer identifies procedure variables by names, and each activation of the procedure provides a distinct context in which most such names are resolved. Some names, identified as "static" or "global names", may instead be resolved in a context that is shared among activations or among different procedures. When a procedure is compiled, some of the original user-friendly names of variables may be replaced with integer identifiers that are more convenient for a machine to manipulate, but the naming model still holds.

7. A Uniform Resource Locator (URL) of the World Wide Web is mapped to a specific Web page by a relatively complicated algorithm that breaks the URL up into several constituent parts and resolves the parts using different naming schemes; the result eventually identifies a particular Web page. Section 3.2 is a case study of this naming scheme.

8. A customer billing system typically maintains at least two kinds of names for each customer account. The account number names the account in a unique identifier name space, but there is also a distinct name space of personal names that can also be used to identify the account. Both of these names are typically mapped to account records by a database system, so that accounts can be retrieved either by account number or by personal name.

These examples also highlight a distinction between "naming" and binding. Some, but not all, contexts "name" things, in the sense that they map a name to an object that is commonly thought of as having that name. Thus, the telephone directory does not "name" either people or telephone lines. Somewhere else there are contexts that bind names to people and that bind telephone numbers to particular physical phones. The telephone directory binds the names of people to the names of telephones.

For each of these examples a context reference must identify the context in which the name-mapping algorithm should resolve the name. Next, we explore where context references come from.

2.2.2 Default and Explicit Context References

When a program interpreter encounters a name in an object, someone must supply a context reference so that the name-mapping algorithm can know which context it should use to resolve the name. Many apparently puzzling problems in naming can be simply diagnosed: the name-mapping algorithm, for whatever reason, used the wrong context reference.

There are two ways to come up with a context with which to resolve the names found in an object: default and explicit. A *default context reference* is one that the resolver supplies, whereas an *explicit context reference* is one that comes packaged

Context references for names found in an object

- Default: supplied by the resolver
  - Constant built in to the resolver
  - Variable from the current environment
- Explicit: supplied by the object
  - Per object
  - Per name (qualified name)

FIGURE 2.12

Taxonomy of context references.

with the name-using object. Sometimes a naming scheme allows for use of both explicit and default methods: it uses an explicit context reference if the object or name provides one; if not, it uses a default context. Figure 2.12 outlines the taxonomy of context references described in the next two paragraphs.

A default context reference can be a constant that is built in to the resolver as part of its design. Since a constant allows for just one context, the resulting name space is universal. Alternatively, a default context reference can be a variable that the resolver obtains from its current execution environment. That variable may be set by some context assignment rule. For example, in most multiple-user systems, each user's execution environment contains a state variable called the *working directory*. The working directory acts as the default context for resolving file names. Similarly, the system may assign a default context for each distinct activity of a user or even, as will be seen in Chapter 3 (Figures 3.2 and 3.3), for each major subsystem of a system.

In contrast, an explicit context reference commonly comes in one of two forms: a single-context reference intended to be used for all the names that an object uses, or a distinct context reference associated with each name in the object. The second form, in which each name is packaged with its own context reference, is known as a *qualified name*.

A context reference is itself a name (it names the context), which leads some writers to describe it as a *base name*. The name resolver must thus resolve the name represented by the context reference before it can proceed with the original name resolution. This recursion may be repeated several times, but it must terminate somewhere, with the invocation of a name resolver that has a single built-in context. This built-in context contains the bindings that permit the recursion to be unraveled.

That description is quite abstract. To make it concrete, let's revisit the previous real-world examples of names, in each case looking for the context reference the resolver uses:

1. When looking up a number in a telephone book, you must provide the context reference: you need to know whether to pick up the Boston or the San Francisco telephone book. If you call Directory Assistance to ask for a number, the operator will immediately ask you for the context reference by saying, "What city, please?" If you got the name from a personal letter, that letter may mention the city—an example of an explicit context reference. If not, you may have to guess, or undertake a search of the directories of several different cities.

2. In a processor, there is usually only one set of numbered registers; they comprise a default context that is built-in using wires. Some processors have multiple

register sets, in which case there is an additional register, usually hidden from the application programmer, that determines which register set is currently in use. The processor uses the contents of that register, which is a component of the current interpretation environment, as a default context reference. It resolves that number with a built-in context that binds register set numbers to physical register sets by interpreting the register set number as an address that locates the correct bank of registers.

3. In a system that implements multiple virtual memories, the interpretation environment includes a processor register (the page-map address register of Chapter 5) that names the currently active page table; that register contains a reference to the default context. Some virtual memory systems provide a feature known as *segments*. In those systems, a program may issue addresses that contain an explicit context reference known as a *segment number*. Segments are discussed in Section 5.4.5.

4. In a file system with many directories, when a program refers to a file using an unqualified or incompletely qualified file name, the file system uses the working directory as a default context reference. Alternatively, a program may use an *absolute path name*, an example of a fully qualified name that we will discuss in depth in just a moment. The path name contains its own explicit context reference. In both the working directory and the absolute path name, the context reference is itself a name that the resolver must resolve before it can proceed with the original name resolution. This need leads to recursive name resolution, which is discussed in Section 2.2.3.

5. In the Internet, names of network attachment points may be qualified (e.g., `ginger.pedantic.edu`) or unqualified (e.g., `ginger`). When the network name resolver encounters an unqualified name, it qualifies that name with a default context reference, sometimes called the default domain. However it materializes, a qualified name is an absolute path name that still needs to be resolved. A different default—usually a configuration parameter of the name resolver—supplies the context for resolution of that absolute path name in the universal name space of Internet domain names. Section 4.4 describes in detail the rather elaborate mechanism that resolves Internet domain names.

6. The programming language community uses its own terminology to describe default and explicit context references. When implementing *dynamic scope*, the resolver uses the current naming environment as a default context for resolving names. When implementing *static* (also called *lexical*) *scope*, the creator of an object (usually a procedure object) associates the object with an explicit context reference—the naming environment at that instant. The language community calls this combination of an object and its context reference a *closure*.

7. For resolution of a URL for the World Wide Web, the name resolver is distributed, and different contexts are used for different components of the URL. Section 3.2 provides details.

8. Database systems provide the contexts for resolution of both account numbers and personal names in a billing system. If the billing system has a graphical user interface, it may offer a lookup form with blank fields for both account number and personal name. A customer service representative chooses the context reference by typing in one of the two fields and hitting a "find" button, which invokes the resolver. Each of the fields corresponds to a different context.

A context reference can be dynamic, meaning that it changes from time to time. An example is when the user clicks on a menu button labeled "Help". Although the button may always appear in the same place on the screen, the context in which the name "Help" is resolved (and thus the particular help screen that appears in response) is likely to depend on which application program, or even which part of that program, is running at the instant that the user clicks on the button.

A common problem is that the object that uses a name does not provide an explicit context, and the name resolver chooses the wrong default context. For example, a file system typically resolves a file name relative to a current working directory, even though this working directory may be unrelated to the identity of the program or data object making the reference. Compared with the name resolution environment of a programming system, most file systems provide a rather primitive name resolution mechanism.

An electronic mail system provides an example of the problem of making sure that names are interpreted in the intended context. Consider the e-mail message of Figure 2.13, which originated at Pedantic University. In this message, `Alice`, `Bob`, and `Dawn` are names from the local name space of e-mailboxes at Pedantic University, and `Charles@cse.Scholarly.edu` is a qualified name of an e-mailbox managed by a mail service named `cse.Scholarly.edu` at the Institute of Scholarly Studies. The name `Charles` is of a particular mailbox at that mail service, and the @-sign is conventionally used to separate the name of the mailbox from the name of the mail service.

As it stands, if user `Charles` tries to reply to the sender of this message, the response will be addressed to `Bob`. Since the first name resolver to encounter the reply message is probably inside the system named `cse.Scholarly.edu`, that resolver would in the normal course of events use as a default context reference the name of the local mail service. That is, it would try to send the message to `Bob@cse.Scholarly.edu`. That isn't the mailbox address of the user who sent the original message. Worse, it might be someone else's mailbox address.

```
To: Bob
Cc: Charles@cse.Scholarly.edu
From: Alice
------
Based on Dawn's suggestions, this chapter has
experienced a major overhaul this year. If you
like it, send your compliments to Dawn (her e-mail
address is "Dawn"); if you do not like it, send your
complaints to me.
```

FIGURE 2.13

An e-mail message that uses default contexts.

```
To: Bob@Pedantic.edu
cc: Charles@cse.Scholarly.edu
From: Alice@Pedantic.edu
------
Based on Dawn's suggestions, this chapter has
experienced a major overhaul this year. If you
like it, send your compliments to Dawn (her e-mail
address is "Dawn"); if you do not like it, send
your complaints to me.
```

FIGURE 2.14

The e-mail message of Figure 2.13 after the mail system expands every unqualified address in the headers to include an explicit context reference.

When constructing the e-mail message, Alice intended local names such as `Bob` to be resolved in her own context. Most mail sending systems know that a local name is not useful to anyone outside the local context, so it is conventional for the mail system to tinker with unqualified names found in the address fields by automatically rewriting them as qualified names, thus adding an explicit context reference to the names `Bob` and `Alice`, as shown in Figure 2.14.

Unfortunately, the mail system can perform this address rewriting only for the headers because that is the only part of the message format it fully understands. If an e-mail address is embedded in the text of the message (as in the example, the mailbox name `Dawn`), the mail system has no way to distinguish it from the other text. If the recipient of the message wishes to make use of an e-mail address found in the text of the message, that recipient is going to have to figure out what context reference is needed. Sometimes it is easy to figure out what to do, but if a message has been forwarded a few times, or the recipient is unaware of the problem, a mistake is likely.

A partial solution could be to tag the e-mail message with an explicit context reference, using an extra header, as in Figure 2.15. With this addition, a recipient of this message could select either `Alice` in the header or `Dawn` in the text and ask the mail system to send a reply. The mail system could, by examining the `Context:` header, determine how to resolve any unqualified e-mail address associated with this message, whether found in the original headers or extracted from the text of the message. This scheme is quite *ad hoc*; if user `Bob` forwards the message of Figure 2.15 with an added note to someone in yet another naming context, any unqualified addresses in the added note would need a different explicit context reference. Although this scheme is not actually used in any e-mail system that the authors are aware of, it has been used in other naming systems. An example is the base element of HTML, the display language of the World Wide Web, described briefly in Section 3.2.2.

A closely related problem is that different contexts may bind different names for the same object. For example, to call a certain telephone, it may be that a person in the same organization dials 2-7104, a second person across the city dials 312-7104, a third who is a little farther away dials (517) 312-7104, and a person in another country may have to dial 001 (517) 312-7104. When the same object has different names in different contexts, passing a name from one user to another is awkward because, as with the e-mail message example, someone must translate the name before the other user can use it. As with the e-mail address, if someone hands you a scrap of paper on

```
To: Bob
cc: Charlies@cse.Scholarly.edu
From: Alice
Context: Pedantic.edu
------
Based on Dawn's suggestions, this chapter has
experienced a major overhaul this year. If you
like it, send your compliments to Dawn (her e-mail
address is "Dawn"); if you do not like it, send your
complaints to me.
```

FIGURE 2.15

An e-mail message that provides an explicit context reference as one of its headers.

which is written the telephone number 312-7104, simply dialing that number may or may not ring the intended telephone. Even though the several names are related, some effort may be required to figure out just what translation is required.

2.2.3 Path Names, Naming Networks, and Recursive Name Resolution

The second of the three common name-mapping algorithms listed on page 64 is *recursive name resolution*. A path name can be thought of as a name that explicitly includes a reference to the context in which it should be resolved. In some naming schemes, path names are written with the context reference first, in others with the context reference last. Some examples of path names are:

```
ginger.pedantic.edu.
/usr/bin/emacs
Macintosh HD:projects:CSE 496:problem set 1
```
Chapter 2, section 2, part 3, first paragraph
Paragraph 1 of part 3 of section 2 of chapter 2

As these examples suggest, a path name involves multiple components and some syntax that permits a name resolver to parse the components. The last two examples illustrate that different naming schemes place the component names in opposite orders, and indeed the other examples also demonstrate both orders. The order of the components must be known to the user of the name and to the name resolver, but either way interpretation of the path name is most easily explained recursively by borrowing terminology from the representation of numbers: all but the least significant component of a path name is an explicit context reference that identifies the context to be used to resolve that least significant component. In the above examples, the least significant components and their explicit context references are, respectively,

Least significant component	Explicit context reference
`ginger`	`pedantic.edu.`
`emacs`	`/usr/bin`
`problem set 1`	`Macintosh hd:projects:CSE 491`
first paragraph	Chapter 2, section 2, part 3
Paragraph 1	part 3 of section 2 of chapter 2

The recursive aspect of this description is that the explicit context reference is itself a path name that must be resolved. So we repeat the analysis as many times as needed until what was originally the most significant component of the path name is also the least significant component, at which point the resolver can do an ordinary table lookup using some context. In the choice of this context, the previous discussion of default and explicit context references again applies. In a typical design, the resolver uses one of two default context references:

- A special context reference, known as the *root,* that is built in to the resolver. The root is an example of a universal name space. A path name that the resolver can resolve with recursion that ends at the root context is known as an *absolute path name*.
- The path name of yet another default context. To avoid circularity, this path name must be an absolute path name. A path name that is resolved by looking up its most significant component in yet another context is known as a *relative path name*. (In a file system, the path name of this default context is what example 4 on page 68 identified as the working directory.) Thus in the UNIX file system, for example, if the working directory is `/usr/Alice`, the relative path name `plans/Monday` would resolve to the same file as the absolute path name `/usr/Alice/plans/Monday`.

If a single name resolver is prepared to resolve both relative and absolute path names, some scheme such as a syntactic flag (e.g., the initial `"/"` in `/usr/bin/emacs` and the terminal `"."` in `ginger.pedantic.edu.`) may distinguish one from the other, or perhaps the name resolver will try both ways in some order, using the first one that seems to work. Trying two schemes in order is a simple form of multiple name lookup, about which we will have more to say in the next subsection.

Path names can also be thought of as identifying objects that are organized in what is called a *naming network*. In a naming network, contexts are treated as objects, and any context may contain a name-to-object binding for any other object, including another context. The name resolver somehow chooses one context to use as the root (perhaps by having a lower-level name for that context wired into the resolver), and it then resolves all absolute path names by tracing a path from the chosen root to the first named context in the path name, then the next, continuing until it reaches the object that was named by the original path name. It similarly resolves relative path names starting with a default context found in a variable in its environment. That variable contains the absolute path name of the default context. Since there can be many paths from one place to another, there can be many different path names for the same object or context. Multiple names for the same object are known as *synonyms* or *aliases*. (This text avoids the word "alias" because different systems use it in quite different ways.) On the other hand, since the root provides a universal name space, every object that uses the same absolute path name is referring to the same exporting object.

Sharing names of a naming network can be a problem because each user may express path names relative to a different starting point. As a result, it may not be obvious how to translate a path name when passing it from one user to another. One standard solution to this problem is to require that users share only absolute path names, all of which begin with the root.

The file system of a computer operating system is usually organized as a naming network, with directories acting as contexts. It is common in file systems to encounter implementation-driven restrictions on the shape of the naming network, for example, requiring that the contexts be organized in a *naming hierarchy* with the root acting as the base of the tree. A true naming hierarchy is so constraining that it is rarely found in practice; real systems, even if superficially hierarchical, usually provide some way of adding cross-hierarchy *links*. The simplest kind of link is just a synonym: a single object may be bound in more than one context. Some systems allow a more sophisticated kind of link, known as an *indirect name*. An indirect name is one that a context binds to another name in the same name space rather than to an object. Because many designers have independently realized that indirect names are useful, they have come to be called by many different labels, including *symbolic link*, *soft link, alias,* and *shortcut*. The UNIX file system described in Section 2.5 includes a naming hierarchy, links, and indirect names called soft links.

A path name has internal structure, so a naming scheme that supports path names usually has rules regarding construction of allowable path names. Path names may have a maximum length, and certain symbols may be restricted for use only as structural separators.

2.2.4 Multiple Lookup: Searching through Layered Contexts

Returning to the topic of default contexts (in the taxonomy of Figure 2.12), context assignment rules are a blunt tool. For example, a directory containing library programs may need to be shared among different users; no single assignment rule can suffice. This inflexibility leads to the third, more elaborate name resolution scheme, *multiple lookup*.* The idea of multiple lookup is to abandon the notion of a single, default context and instead resolve the name by systematically trying several different contexts. Since a name may be bound in more than one context, multiple lookup can produce multiple resolutions, so some scheme is needed to decide which resolution to use.

A common such scheme is called the *search path*, which is nothing more than a specific list of contexts to be tried, in order. The name resolver tries to resolve the name using the first context in the list. If it gets a not-found result, it tries the next context, and so on. If the name is bound in more than one of the listed contexts, the one earliest in the list wins and the resolver returns the value associated with that binding.

A search path is often used in programming systems that have libraries. Suppose, for example, a library procedure that calculates the square root math function exports

*The operating system community traditionally uses the word "search" for multiple lookup, but the advent of "search engines" on both the Internet and the desktop has rendered that usage ambiguous. The last paragraph of Section 2.2.4, on page 75, discusses this topic.

a procedure interface named SQRT. After compiling this function, the writer places a copy of the binary program in a math library. A prospective user of the square root function writes the statement

$x \leftarrow$ SQRT(y)

in a program, and the compiler generates code that uses the procedure named SQRT. The next step is that the compiler (or in some systems a later loader) undertakes a series of lookups in various public and private libraries that it knows about. Each library is a context, and the search path is a list of the library contexts. Each step of the multiple lookup involves an invocation of a simpler, single-context name resolver. Some of these attempted resolutions will probably return a not-found result. The first resolution attempt that finds a program named SQRT will return that program as the result of the lookup.

A search path is usually implemented as a per-user list, some or all of whose elements the user can set. By placing a library that contains personally supplied programs early in the search path, an individual user can effectively replace a library program with another that has the same name, thereby providing a *user-dependent binding*. This replace-by-name feature can be useful, but it can also be hazardous because one may unintentionally choose a name for a program that is also exported by some completely unrelated library program. When some other application tries to call that unrelated program, the ensuing multiple lookup may find the wrong one. As the number of libraries and names in the search path increases, the chance increases that two libraries will accidentally contain two unrelated programs that happen to export the same name.

Despite the hazards, search paths are a widely used mechanism. In addition to loaders using search paths to locate library procedures, user interfaces use search paths to locate commands whose names the user typed, compilers use search paths to locate interfaces, documentation systems use search paths to find cited documents, and word processing systems use search paths to locate text fragments to be included in the current document.

Some naming schemes use a more restricted multiple lookup method. For example, rather than allowing an arbitrary list of contexts, a naming scheme may require that contexts be arranged in nested layers. Whenever a resolution returns not-found in some layer, the resolver retries in the enclosing layer. Layered contexts were at one time popular in programming languages, where programs define and call on subprograms, because it can be convenient (to the point of being undisciplined, which is why it is no longer so popular) to allow a subprogram access by name to the variables of the defining or calling program. For another example, the scheme for numbering Internet network attachment points has an outer public layer and an inner private layer. Certain Internet address ranges (e.g., all addresses with a first byte of 10) are reserved for use in private networks; those address ranges constitute an inner private layer. These network addresses may be bound to different network attachment points in different private contexts without risk of conflict. Internet addresses that are outside the ranges reserved for private contexts should not be bound in any private context; they are instead resolved in the public context.

In a set of layered contexts, the *scope* of a name is the range of layers in which the name is bound to the same object. A name that is bound only in the outermost layer, and is always bound to the same object, independent of the current context layer, is known as a *global name*. The outermost layer that resolves global names is an example of a universal name space.

Incidentally, we have now used the term *path* as both an adjective qualifier and a noun, but with quite different meanings. A *path name* is a name that carries its own explicit context, while a *search path* is a context that consists of a list of contexts. Thus each element of a search path may be a path name.

The word "search" also has another, related but somewhat different, meaning. Internet search engines such as Google and AltaVista take as input a query consisting of one or more key words, and they return a list of World Wide Web pages that contain those key words. Multiple results (known as "hits") are the common case, and Google, for example, implements a sophisticated system for ranking the hits. Google also offers the user the choice of receiving just the highest-ranked hit ("I'm feeling lucky") or receiving a rank-ordered list of hits. Most modern desktop computer systems also provide some form of key word search for local files. When one encounters the unqualified word "search", it is a good idea to pause and figure out whether it refers to multiple lookup or to key word query.

2.2.5 Comparing Names

As mentioned earlier, one more operation is sometimes applied to names:

result ← COMPARE(*name1*, *name2*)

where *result* is a binary value, TRUE or FALSE. The meaning of name comparison requires some thought because the invoker might have one of three different questions in mind:

1. Are the two names the same?
2. Are the two names bound to the same value?
3. If the value or values are actually the identifiers of storage containers, such as memory cells or disk sectors, are the contents of the storage containers the same?

The first question is mechanically easiest to answer because it simply involves comparing the representations of the two names ("Is Jim Smith the same as Jim Smith?"), and it is exactly what a name resolver does when it looks things up in a table-lookup context: look through the context for a name that is the same as the one being resolved. On the other hand, in many situations the answer is not useful, since the same name may be bound to different values in different contexts and two different names may be synonyms that are bound to the same value. All one learns from the first question is whether or not the name strings have the same bit pattern.

For that reason, the answer to the second question is often more interesting. ("Is the Jim Smith who just received the Nobel prize the same Jim Smith I knew in high school?") Getting that answer requires supplying the contexts for the two names as additional arguments to COMPARE, so that it can resolve the names and compare the results. Thus, for example, resolving the variable name *A* and the variable name *B* may reveal that they are both bound to the same storage cell address. Even this answer may still not reveal as much as expected because the two names may resolve to two names of a different, lower-layer naming scheme, in which case the same questions need to be asked recursively about the lower-layer names. For example, variable names *A* and *B* may be bound to different storage cell addresses, but if a virtual memory is in use those different virtual storage cell addresses might map to the same physical cell address. (This example will make more sense when we reach Chapter 5.)

Even after reaching the bottom of that recursion, the result may be the names of two different physical storage containers that contain identical copies of data, or it may be two different lower-layer names (that is, synonyms) for the same storage container. ("This biography file on Jim Smith is identical to that biography file on Jim Smith. Are there one or two biography files?" "This biography about Edwin Aldrin is identical to that biography about Buzz Aldrin. Are those two names for the same person?") Thus the third question arises, along with a need to understand what it means to be the "same". Unless one has some specific understanding of the underlying physical representation, the only way to distinguish the two cases may be to change the contents of one of the named storage containers and see if that causes the contents of the other one to change. ("Kick this one and see if that one squeals.")

In practice, systems (and some programming languages) typically provide several COMPARE operators that have different semantics designed to help answer these different questions, and the programmer or user must understand which COMPARE operation is appropriate for the task at hand. For example, the LISP language provides three comparison operators, named EQ (which compares the bindings of its named arguments), EQU (which compares the values of its named arguments), and EQUALS (which recursively compares entire data structures.)

2.2.6 Name Discovery

Underlying all name reference is a recursive protocol that answers the question, "How did you know to use this name?" This *name discovery protocol* informs an object's prospective user of the name that the object exports. Name discovery involves two basic elements: the exporter *advertises* the existence of the name, while the prospective user *searches* for an appropriate advertisement. The thing that makes name discovery recursive is that the name user must first know the name of a place to search for the advertisement. This recursion must terminate somewhere, perhaps in a direct, outside-the-computer communication between some name user and some name exporter.

The simplest case is a programmer who writes a program consisting of two procedures, one of which refers to the other by name. Since the same programmer wrote both, name discovery is explicit and no recursion is necessary. Next, suppose the two programs are written by two different programmers. The programmer who wants to use a procedure by name must somehow discover the exported name. One possibility is that the second programmer performs the advertisement by shouting the procedure's name down the hall. Another possibility is that the using programmer looks in a shared directory in which everyone agrees to place shared procedures. How does that programmer know the name of that shared directory? Perhaps someone shouted that name down the hall. Or perhaps it is a standard library directory whose name is listed in the programmers' reference manual, in which case that manual terminates the recursive protocol. Although program library names don't usually appear in magazine advertisements or on billboards, it has become commonplace to discover the name of a World Wide Web site in such places. Name discovery can take several forms:

- *Well-known name:* A name (such as "Google" or "Yahoo!") that has been advertised so widely that one can depend on it being stable for at least as long as the thing it names. Running across a well-known name is a method of name discovery.
- *Broadcast:* A way of advertising a name, for example by wearing a badge that says "Hello, my name is . . . ", posting the name on a bulletin board, or sending it to a mailing list. Broadcast is used by automatic configuration protocols sometimes called "plug-and-play" or "zero configuration". It may even be used on a point-to-point communication link in the hope that there is someone listening at the other end who will reply. Listening for broadcasts is a method of name discovery.
- *Query* (also called *search*): Present one or more key words to, for example, a search engine such as Google. Query is a widely used method of name discovery.
- *Broadcast query:* A generalized form of key word query. Ask everyone within hearing distance "does anyone know a name for. . . ?" (sometimes confusingly called "reverse broadcast").
- *Resolving a name of one name space to a name of a different name space:* Looking up a name in the telephone book leads to discovery of a telephone number. The Internet Domain Name System, described in Section 4.4, performs a similar service, looking up a domain name and returning a network attachment point address.
- *Introduction:* What happens at parties and in on-line dating services. Some entity that you already know knows a name and gives that name to you. In a computer system, a friend may send you an e-mail message that mentions the name of an interesting Web site or the e-mail address of another friend. For another example, each World Wide Web page typically contains introductions (technically known as hypertext links) to other Web pages.
- *Physical rendezvous:* A meeting held outside the computer. It requires somehow making prior arrangements concerning time and place, which implies prior communication, which implies prior knowledge of some names. Once set up, physical rendezvous can be used for discovering other names as well as for verifying authenticity. Many organizations require that setting up a new account on a company computer system must involve a physical rendezvous with the system administrator to exchange names and choose a password.

Any of the above methods of name discovery may require first discovering some other name, such as the name of the reference source for well-known names, the name of the bulletin board on which broadcasts are placed, the name of the name resolver, the name of the party host, and so on. The method of discovering this other name may be the same as the method first invoked, or it may be different. The important thing the designer must keep in mind is that the recursion must terminate somewhere—it can't be circular.

Some method of name discovery is required wherever a name is needed. An interesting exercise is to analyze some of the examples of names mentioned in earlier parts of this chapter, tracing the name discovery recursion to see how it terminates, because in many cases that termination is so distant from the event of name usage and resolution that it has long since been forgotten. Many additional examples of name discovery will show up in later chapters: names used for clients and services, where a client needs to discover the name of an appropriate service; data communication networks, where routing provides a particularly explicit example of name discovery; and security, where it is critical to establish the integrity of the terminating step.

2.3 ORGANIZING COMPUTER SYSTEMS WITH NAMES AND LAYERS

Section 2.1 demonstrated how computer system designers use layers to implement more elaborate versions of the three fundamental abstractions, and Section 2.2 explained how names are used to connect system components. Designers also use layers and names in many other ways in computer systems. Figure 2.16 shows the typical organization of a computer system as three distinct layers. The bottom layer consists of hardware components, such as processors, memories, and communication links. The middle layer consists of a collection of software modules, called the *operating system* (see Sidebar 2.4), that abstract these hardware resources into a convenient *application programming interface (API)*. The top layer consists of software that implements application-specific functions, such as a word processor, payroll program, computer game, or Web

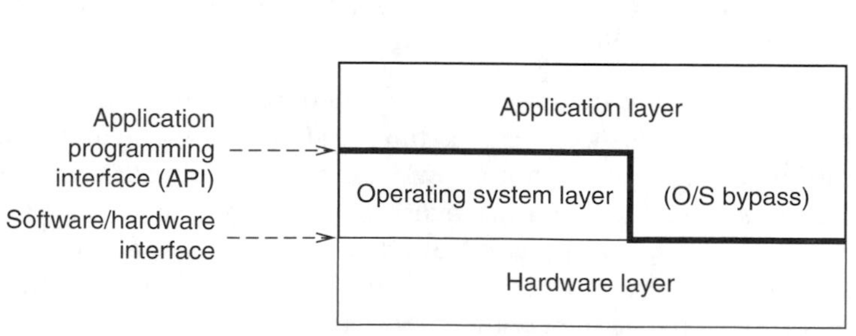

FIGURE 2.16

A typical computer system organized in three layers. The operating system layer allows bypass, so the application layer can directly invoke many features of the hardware layer. However, the operating system layer hides certain dangerous features of the hardware layer.

Sidebar 2.4 What is an Operating System? An *operating system* is a set of programs and libraries that make it easy for computer users and programmers to do their job. In the early days of computers, operating systems were simple programs that assisted operators of computers (at that time the only users who interacted with a computer directly), which is why they are called operating systems.

Today operating systems come in many flavors and differ in the functions they provide. The operating system for the simplest computers, such as that for a microwave oven, may comprise just a library that hides hardware details in order to make it easier for application programmers to develop applications. Personal computers, on the other hand, ship with operating systems that contain tens of millions of lines of code. These operating systems allow several people to use the same computer; permit users to control which information is shared and with whom; can run many programs at the same time while keeping them from interfering with one another; provide sophisticated user interfaces, Internet access, file systems, backup and archive applications, device drivers for the many possible hardware gadgets on a personal computer, and a wide range of abstractions to simplify the job of application programmers, and so on.

Operating systems also offer an interesting case study of system design. They are evolving rapidly because of new requirements. Their designers face a continuous struggle to control their complexity. Some modern operating systems have interfaces consisting of thousands of procedures, and their implementations are so complex that it is a challenge to make them work reliably.

This book has much more to say about operating systems, starting in Section 5.1.1, where it begins development of a minimal model operating system.

browser. If we examine each layer in detail, we are likely to find that it is itself organized in layers. For example, the hardware layer may comprise a lower layer of gates, flip-flops, and wires, and an upper layer of registers, memory cells, and finite-state machines.

The exact division of labor between the hardware layer and the software layers is an engineering trade-off and a topic of considerable debate between hardware and software designers. In principle, every software module can be implemented in hardware. Similarly, most hardware modules can also be implemented in software, except for a few foundational components such as transistors and wires. It is surprisingly difficult to state a generic principle for how to decide between an implementation in hardware or software. Cost, performance, flexibility, convenience, and usage patterns are among the factors that are part of the trade-off, but for each individual function they may be weighted differently. Rather than trying to invent a principle, we discuss the trade-off between hardware and software in the context of specific functions as they come up.

The operating system layer usually exhibits an interesting phenomenon that we might call *layer bypass*. Rather than completely hiding the lower, hardware layer, an operating system usually hides only a few features of the hardware layer, such as particularly dangerous instructions. The remaining features of the hardware layer (in particular, most of the instruction repertoire of the underlying processor) pass through the operating system layer for use directly by the application layer, as in Figure 2.16. Thus, the dangerous instructions can be used only by the operating system layer, while all of the remaining instructions can be used by both the operating system and application layers. Conceptually, a designer could set things up so that the operating system layer intercepts every invocation of the hardware layer by the application layer and then explicitly invokes the hardware layer. That design would slow a heavily used interface down unacceptably, so in the usual implementation the application layer directly invokes the hardware layer, completely bypassing the operating system layer. Operating systems provide bypass for performance reasons, but bypass is not unique to operating systems, nor is it used only to gain performance. For example, the Internet is a layered communication system that permits bypass of most features of most of its layers, to achieve flexibility.

In this section we examine two examples of layered computer system organization: the hardware layer at the bottom of a typical computer system and one part of the operating system layer that creates the typical application programming interface known as the file system.

2.3.1 A Hardware Layer: The Bus

The hardware layer of a typical computer is constructed of modules that directly implement low-level versions of the three fundamental abstractions. In the example of Figure 2.17, the processor modules interpret programs, the random access memory modules store both programs and data, and the input/output (I/O) modules implement communication links to the world outside the computer.

There may be several examples of each kind of hardware module—multiple processors (perhaps several on one chip, an organization that goes by the buzzword name *multicore*), multiple memories, and several kinds of I/O modules. On closer inspection the I/O modules turn out to be specialized interpreters that implement I/O programs. Thus, the disk controller is an interpreter of disk I/O programs. Among its duties are mapping disk addresses to track and sector numbers and moving data from the disk to the memory. The network controller is an interpreter that talks on its other side to one or more real communication links. The display controller interprets display lists that it finds in memory, lighting pixels on the display as it goes. The keyboard controller interprets keystrokes and places the result in memory. The clock may be nothing but a minuscule interpreter that continually updates a single register with the time of day.

The various modules plug into the shared *bus*, which is a highly specialized communication link used to SEND messages to other modules. There are numerous bus designs, but they have some common features. One such common feature is a set of wires*

*This description in terms of several parallel wires is of a structure called a *parallel bus*. A more thorough discussion of link communication protocols in Section 7.3 [on-line] shows how a bus can also be implemented by sending coded signals down just a few wires, a scheme called a *serial bus*.

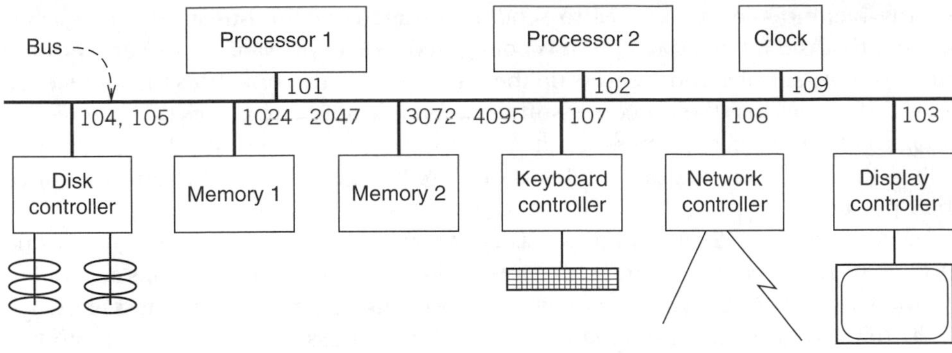

FIGURE 2.17

A computer with several modules connected by a shared bus. The numbers are the bus addresses to which the attached module responds.

comprising address, data, and control lines that connect to a *bus interface* on each module. Because the bus is shared, a second common feature is a set of rules, called the *bus arbitration protocol,* for deciding which module may send or receive a message at any particular time. Some buses have an additional module, the *bus arbiter*, a circuit or a tiny interpreter that chooses which of several competing modules can use the bus. In other designs, bus arbitration is a function distributed among the bus interfaces. Just as there are many bus designs, there are also many bus arbitration protocols. A particularly influential example of a bus is the UNIBUS®, introduced in the 1970s by Digital Equipment Corporation. The modularity provided by a shared bus with a standard arbitration protocol helped to reshape the computer industry, as was described in Sidebar 1.5.

A third common feature of bus designs is that a bus is a *broadcast* link, which means that every module attached to the bus hears every message. Since most messages are actually intended for just one module, a field of the message called the *bus address* identifies the intended recipient. The bus interface of each module is configured to respond to a particular set of bus addresses. Each module examines the bus address field (which in a parallel bus is usually carried on a set of wires separate from the rest of the message) of every message and ignores any message not intended for it. The bus addresses thus define an address space. Figure 2.17 shows that the two processors might accept messages at bus addresses 101 and 102, respectively; the display controller at bus address 103; the disk controller at bus addresses 104 and 105 (using two addresses makes it convenient to distinguish requests for its two disks); the network at bus address 106; the keyboard at bus address 107; and the clock at bus address 109. For speed, memory modules typically are configured with a range of bus addresses, one bus address per memory address. Thus, if in Figure 2.17 the two memory modules each implement an address space of 1,024 memory addresses, they might be configured with bus addresses 1024–2047 and 3072–4095, respectively.*

*These bus addresses are chosen for convenience of the illustration. In practice, a memory module is more likely to be configured with enough bus addresses to accommodate several gigabytes.

Any bus module that wishes to send a message over the bus must know a bus address that the intended recipient is configured to accept. Name discovery in some buses is quite simple: whoever sets up the system explicitly configures the knowledge of bus addresses into the processor software, and that software passes this knowledge along to other modules in messages it sends over the bus. Other bus designs dynamically assign bus addresses to modules as they are plugged in to the bus and announce their presence.

A common bus design is known as *split-transaction*. In this design, when one module wants to communicate with another, the first module uses the bus arbitration protocol on the control wires to request exclusive use of the bus for a message. Once it has that exclusive use, the module places a bus address of the destination module on the address wires and the remainder of the message on the data wires. Assuming a design in which the bus and the modules attached to it run on uncoordinated clocks (that is, they are asynchronous), it then signals on one of the control wires (called READY) to alert the other modules that there is a message on the bus. When the receiving module notices that one of its addresses is on the address lines of the bus, it copies that address and the rest of the message on the data wires into its local registers and signals on another control line (called ACKNOWLEDGE) to tell the sender that it is safe to release the bus so that other modules can use it. (If the bus and the modules are all running with a common clock, the READY and ACKNOWLEDGE lines are not needed; instead, each module checks the address lines on each clock cycle.) Then, the receiver inspects the address and message and performs the requested operation, which may involve sending one or more messages back to the original requesting module or, in some cases, even to other modules.

For example, suppose that processor #2, while interpreting a running application program, encounters the instruction

```
LOAD        1742, R1
```

which means "load the contents of memory address 1742 into processor register R1". In the simplest scheme, the processor just translates addresses it finds in instructions directly to bus addresses without change. It thus sends this message across the bus:

processor #2 ⇒ *all bus modules*: {1742, READ, 102}

The message contains three fields. The first message field (1742) is one of the bus addresses to which memory #1 responds; the second message field requests the recipient to perform a READ operation; and the third indicates that the recipient should send the resulting value back across the bus, using the bus address 102. The memory addresses recognized by each memory module are based on powers of two, so the memory modules can recognize all of the addresses in their own range by examining just a few high-order address bits. In this case, the bus address is within the range recognized by memory module 1, so that module responds by copying the message into its own registers. It acknowledges the request, the processor releases the bus, and the memory module then performs the internal operation

value ← READ (1742)

With *value* in hand, the memory module now itself acquires the bus and sends the result back to processor #2 by performing the bus operation

memory #1 ⇒ *all bus modules*: {102, *value*}

where 102 is the bus address of the processor as supplied in the original READ request message. The processor, which is probably waiting for this result, notices that the bus address lines now contain its own bus address 102. It therefore copies the value from the data lines into its register R1, as the original program instruction requested. It acknowledges receipt of the message, and the memory module releases the bus for use by other modules.

Simple I/O devices, such as keyboards, operate in a similar fashion. At system initialization time, one of the processors SENDs a message to the keyboard controller telling it to SEND all keystrokes to that processor. Each time that the user depresses a key, the keyboard controller SENDs a message to the processor containing as data the name of the key that was depressed. In this case, the processor is probably *not* waiting for this message, but its bus interface (which is in effect a separate interpreter running concurrently with the processor) notices that a message with its bus address has appeared. The bus interface copies the data from the bus into a temporary register, acknowledges the message, and sends a signal to the processor that will cause the processor to perform an interrupt on its next instruction cycle. The interrupt handler then transfers the data from the temporary register to some place that holds keyboard input, perhaps by SENDing yet another message over the bus to one of the memory modules.

One potential problem of this design is that the interrupt handler must respond and read the keystroke data from the temporary register before the keyboard handler SENDS another keystroke message. Since keyboard typing is slow compared with computer speeds, there is a good chance that the interrupt handler will be there in time to read the data before the next keystroke overwrites it. However, faster devices such as a hard disk might overwrite the temporary register. One solution would be to write a processor program that runs in a tight loop, waiting for data that the disk controller sends over the bus and immediately SENDing that data again over the bus to a memory module.

Some low-end computer designs do exactly that, but a designer can obtain substantially higher performance by upgrading the disk controller to use a technique called *direct memory access*, or DMA. With this technique, when a processor SENDs a request to a disk controller to READ a block of data from the disk, it includes the address of a buffer in memory as a field of the request message. Then, as data streams in from the disk, the disk controller SENDs it directly to the memory module, incrementing the memory address appropriately between SENDs. In addition to relieving the load on the processor, DMA also reduces the load on the shared bus because it transfers each piece of data across the bus just once (from the disk controller to the memory) rather than twice (first from the disk controller to the processor and then from the processor to the memory). Also, if the bus allows long messages, the DMA controller may be able to take better advantage of that feature than the processor, which is usually designed to SEND and RECEIVE bus data in units that are the same size as its own registers. By SENDing longer messages, the DMA controller increases performance because it amortizes the overhead of the bus arbitration protocol, which it must perform once per message. Finally, DMA allows the processor to execute some other program at the same time that the disk controller is transferring data. Because concurrent operation can hide the latency of the disk transfer, it can provide an additional performance enhancement. The idea of enhancing performance by hiding latency is discussed further in Chapter 6.

A convenient interface to I/O and other bus-attached modules is to assign bus addresses to the control registers and buffers of the module. Since each processor maps bus addresses directly into its own memory address space, LOAD and STORE instructions executed in the processor can in effect address the registers and buffers of the I/O module as if they were locations in memory. The technique is known as *memory-mapped I/O*.

Memory-mapped I/O can be combined with DMA. For example, suppose that a disk controller designed for memory-mapped I/O assigns bus addresses to four of its control registers as follows:

bus address	control register
121	*sector_number*
122	*DMA_start_address*
123	*DMA_count*
124	*control*

To do disk I/O, the processor uses STORE instructions to SEND appropriate initialization values to the first three disk controller registers and a final STORE instruction to SEND a value that sets a bit in the *control* register that the disk controller interprets as the signal to start. A program to GET a 256-byte disk sector currently stored at sector number 11742 and transfer the data into memory starting at location 3328 starts by loading four registers with these values and then issuing STOREs of the registers to the appropriate bus addresses:

```
R1 ← 11742; R2 ← 3328; R3 ← 256; R4 ← 1;
STORE 121,R1                          // set sector number
STORE 122,R2                          // set memory address register
STORE 123,R3                          // set byte count
STORE 124,R4                          // start disk controller running
```

Upon completion of the bus SEND generated by the last STORE instruction, the disk controller, which was previously idle, leaps into action, reads the requested sector from the disk into an internal buffer, and begins using DMA to transfer the contents of the buffer to memory one block at a time. If the bus can handle blocks that are 8 bytes long, the disk controller would SEND a series of bus messages such as

disk controller #1 ⇒ *all bus modules*: {3328, *block*[1]}
disk controller #1 ⇒ *all bus modules*: {3336, *block*[2]}
etc . . .

Memory-mapped I/O is a popular interface because it provides a uniform memory-like LOAD and STORE interface to every bus module that implements it. On the other hand, the designer must be cautious in trying to extend the memory-mapped model too far. For example, trying to arrange so the processor can directly address individual bytes or words on a magnetic disk could be problematic in a system with a 32-bit address space because a disk as small as 4 gigabytes would use up the entire address space. More important, the latency of a disk is extremely large compared with the cycle time of a processor. For the STORE instruction to sometimes operate in a few nanoseconds (when the address is in electronic memory) and other times require 10 milliseconds to complete (when the address is on the disk) would be quite unexpected and would make it difficult to write programs that have predictable performance. In addition, it would violate a fundamental rule of human engineering, the *principle of least astonishment* (see Sidebar 2.5). The bottom line is that the physical properties of the magnetic disk make the DMA access model more appropriate than the memory-mapped I/O model.

Sidebar 2.5 Human Engineering and the Principle of Least Astonishment An important principle of human engineering for usability, which for computer systems means designing to make them easy to set up, easy to use, easy to program, and easy to maintain, is the principle of least astonishment.

The principle of least astonishment

People are part of the system. The design should match the user's experience, expectations, and mental models.

Human beings make mental models of the behavior of everything they encounter: components, interfaces, and systems. If the actual component, interface, or system follows that mental model, there is a better chance that it will be used as intended and less chance that misuse or misunderstanding will lead to a mistake or disappointment. Since complexity is relative to understanding, the principle also tends to help reduce complexity.

For this reason, when choosing among design alternatives, it is usually better to choose one that is most likely to match the expectations of those who will have to use, apply, or maintain the system. The principle should also be a factor when evaluating trade-offs. It applies to all aspects of system design, especially to the design of human interfaces and to computer security.

Some corollaries are to be noted: Be consistent. Be predictable. Minimize side-effects. Use names that describe. Do the obvious thing. Provide sensible interpretations for all reasonable inputs. Avoid unnecessary variations.

Some authors prefer the words "principle of least surprise" to "principle of least astonishment". When Bayesian statisticians invoke the principle of least surprise, they usually mean "choose the mostly likely explanation", a version of the closely related Occam's razor. (See the aphorism at the bottom of page 9.)

(Sidebar continues)

Human Engineering and the Original Murphy's Law. If you ask a group of people "What is Murphy's law?" most responses will be some variation of "If anything can go wrong, it will", followed by innumerable equivalents, such as the toast always falls butter side down.

In fact, Murphy originally said something quite different. Rather than a comment on the innate perversity of inanimate objects (sometimes known as *Finagle's law*, from a science fiction story), Murphy was commenting on a property of human nature that one must take into account when designing complex systems: *If you design it so that it can be assembled wrong, someone will assemble it wrong*. Murphy was pointing out the wisdom of good human engineering of things that are to be assembled: design them so that the only way to assemble them is the right way.

Edward A. Murphy, Jr., was an engineer working on United States Air Force rocket sled experiments at Edwards Air Force Base in 1949, in which Major John Paul Stapp volunteered to be subjected to extreme decelerations (40 Gs) to determine the limits of human tolerance for ejection seat design. On one of the experiments, someone wired up all of the strain gauges incorrectly, so at the end of Stapp's (painful) ride there was no usable data. Murphy said, in exasperation at the technician who wired up the strain gauges, "if that guy can find a way to do it wrong, he will." Stapp, who as a hobby made up laws at every opportunity, christened this observation "Murphy's law," and almost immediately began telling it to others in the different and now widely known form "If anything can go wrong, it will."

A good example of Murphy's original observation in action showed up in an incident on a Convair 580 cargo plane in 1997. Two identical control cables ran from a cockpit control to the elevator trim tab, a small movable surface on the rear stabilizing wing that, when adjusted up or down, forces the nose of the plane to rise or drop, respectively. Upon take-off on the first flight after maintenance, the pilots found that the plane was pitching nose-up. They tried adjusting the trim tab to maximum nose-down position, but the problem just got worse. With much effort they managed to land the plane safely. When mechanics examined the plane, they discovered that the two cables to the trim tab had been interchanged, so that moving the control up caused the trim tab to go down and vice versa*.

A similar series of incidents in 1988 and 1989 involved crossed connections in cargo area smoke alarm signal wires and fire extinguisher control wires in the Boeing 737, 757, and 767 aircraft†.

---

*Transportation Safety Board of Canada, *Report A97O0077*, January 13, 2000, updated October 6, 2002.

†Karen Fitzgerald, "Boeing's crossed connections", *IEEE Spectrum 26*, 5 (May 1989), pages 30–35.

2.3.2 A Software Layer: The File Abstraction

The middle and higher layers of a computer system are usually implemented as software modules. To make this layered organization concrete, consider the *file*, a high-level version of the memory abstraction. A file holds an array of bits or bytes, the number of which the application chooses. A file has two key properties:

- *It is durable.* Information, once stored, will remain intact through system shutdowns and can be retrieved later, perhaps weeks or months later. Applications use files to durably store documents, payroll data, e-mail messages, programs, and anything else they do not want to be lost.
- *It has a name.* The name of a file allows users and programs to store information in such a way that they can find and use it again at a later time. File names also make it possible for users to share information. One can WRITE a named file and tell a friend the file name, and then the friend can use the name to READ the file.

Taken together, these two features mean that if, for example, Alice creates a new file named "strategic plan", WRITES some information in it, shuts down the computer, and the next day turns it on again, she will then be able to READ the file named "strategic plan" and get back its content. Furthermore, she can tell Bob to look at the file named "strategic plan". When Bob asks the system to READ a file with that name, he will read the file that she created. Most file systems also provide other additional properties for files, such as timestamps to determine when they were created, last modified, or last used, assurances about their durability (a topic that Chapter 10 [on-line] revisits), and the ability to control who may share them (one of the topics of Chapter 11 [on-line]).

The system layer implements files using modules from the hardware layer. Figure 2.18 shows the pseudocode of a simple application that reads input from a keyboard device, writes that input to a file, and also displays it on the display device.

```
character buf                                   // buffer for input character
file ← OPEN ("strategic plan", READWRITE)       // open file for reading and writing
input ← OPEN ("keyboard", READONLY)             // open keyboard device for reading
display ← OPEN ("display", WRITEONLY)           // open display device for writing

while not END_OF_FILE (input) do
    READ (input, buf, 1)                        // read 1 character from keyboard
    WRITE (file, buf, 1)                        // store input into file
    WRITE (display, buf, 1)                     // display input

CLOSE (file)
CLOSE (input)
CLOSE (display)
```

FIGURE 2.18

Using the file abstraction to implement a display program, which also writes the keyboard input in a file. For clarity, this program ignores the possibility that any of the abstract file primitives may return an error status.

A typical API for the file abstraction contains calls to OPEN a file, to READ and WRITE parts of the file, and to CLOSE the file. The OPEN call translates the file name into a temporary name in a local name space to be used by the READ and WRITE operations. Also, OPEN usually checks whether this user is permitted access to the file. As its last step, OPEN sets a *cursor*, sometimes called a *file pointer*, to zero. The cursor records an offset from the beginning of the file to be used as the starting point for READs and WRITEs. Some file system designs provide a separate cursor for READs and WRITEs, in which case OPEN may initialize the WRITE cursor to the number of bytes in the file.

A call to READ delivers to the caller a specified number of bytes from the file, starting from the READ cursor. It also adds to the READ cursor the number of bytes read so that the next READ proceeds where the previous READ left off. If the program asks to read bytes beyond the end of the file, READ returns some kind of end-of-file status indicator.

Similarly, the WRITE operation takes as arguments a buffer with bytes and a length, stores those bytes in the file starting at the offset indicated by the WRITE cursor (if the WRITE cursor starts at or reaches the end of the file, WRITE usually implies extending the size of the file), and adds to the WRITE cursor the number of bytes written so that the next WRITE can continue from there. If there is not enough space on the device to write that many bytes, the WRITE procedure fails by returning some kind of device-full error status or exception.

Finally, when the program is finished reading and writing, it calls the CLOSE procedure. CLOSE frees up any internal state that the file system maintains for the file (for example, the cursors and the record of the temporary file name, which is no longer meaningful). Some file systems also ensure that, when CLOSE returns, all parts of the modified file have been stored durably on a non-volatile memory device. Other file systems perform this operation in the background after CLOSE returns.

The file system module implements the file API by mapping bytes of the file to disk sectors. For each file the file system creates a record of the name of the file and the disk sectors in which it has stored the file. The file system also stores this record on the disk. When the computer restarts, the file system must somehow discover the place where it left these records so that it can again find the files. A typical procedure for name discovery is for the file system to reserve one, well-known, disk sector such as sector number 1, and use that well-known disk sector as a toehold to locate the sectors where it left the rest of the file system information. A detailed description of the UNIX file system API and its implementation is in Section 2.5.

One might wonder why the file API supports OPEN and CLOSE in addition to READ and WRITE; after all, one could ask the programmer to pass the file name and a file position offset on each READ and WRITE call. The reason is that the OPEN and CLOSE procedures mark the beginning and the end of a sequence of related READ and WRITE operations so that the file system knows which reads and writes belong together as a group. There are several good reasons for grouping and for the use of a temporary file name within the grouping. Originally, performance and resource management concerns motivated the introduction of OPEN and CLOSE, but later implementations of the interface exploited the existence of OPEN and CLOSE to provide clean semantics under concurrent file access and failures.

Early file systems introduced OPEN to amortize the cost of resolving a file name. A file name is a path name that may contain several components. By resolving the file name once on OPEN and giving the result a simple name, READ and WRITE avoid having to resolve the name on each invocation. Similarly, OPEN amortizes the cost of checking whether the user has the appropriate permissions to use the file.

CLOSE was introduced to simplify resource management: when an application invokes CLOSE, the file system knows that the application doesn't need the resources (e.g., the cursor) that the file system maintains internally. Even if a second application removes a file before a first application is finished reading and writing the file, the file system can implement READ and WRITE procedures for the first application sensibly (for example, discard the contents of the file only after everyone that OPENed the file has called CLOSE).

More recent file systems use OPEN and CLOSE to mark the beginning and end of an *atomic* action. The file system can treat all intervening READ and WRITE calls as a single indivisible operation, even in the face of concurrent access to the file or a system crash after some but not all of the WRITEs have completed. Two opportunities ensue:

1. The file system can use the OPEN and CLOSE operations to coordinate concurrent access to a file: if one program has a file open and another program tries to OPEN that same file, the file system can make the second program wait until the first one has CLOSEd the file. This coordination is an example of *before-or-after atomicity*, a topic that Section 5.2.4 explores in depth.

2. If the file system crashes (for example, because of a power failure) before the application CLOSEs the file, none of the WRITEs will be in the file when the system comes back up. If it crashes after the application CLOSEd the file, all of the WRITES will be in the file. Not all file systems provide this guarantee, known as *all-or-nothing atomicity*, since it is not easy to implement correctly and efficiently, as Chapter 9 [on-line] explains.

There is a cost to the OPEN/CLOSE model: the file system must maintain per-client state in the form of the resolved file name and the cursor(s). It is possible to design a completely stateless file interface. An example is the Network File System, described in Section 4.5.

The file is such a convenient memory abstraction that in some systems (for example, the UNIX system and its derivatives) *every* input/output device in a computer system provides a file interface (see Figure 2.19). In such systems, files not only are an abstraction for non-volatile memories (e.g., magnetic disks), but they are also a convenient interface to the keyboard device, the display, communication links, and so on. In such systems, each I/O device has a name in the file naming scheme. A program OPENs the keyboard device, READs bytes from the keyboard device, and then CLOSEs the keyboard device, without having to know any details about the keyboard management procedure, what type of keyboard it is, and the like. Similarly, to interact with the display, a program can OPEN the display device, WRITE to it, and CLOSE it. The program need not know any details about the display. In accordance with the *principle of least astonishment*, each device management procedure provides some reasonable interpretation for every file system method. The pseudocode of Figure 2.18 exemplifies the benefit of this kind of design uniformity.

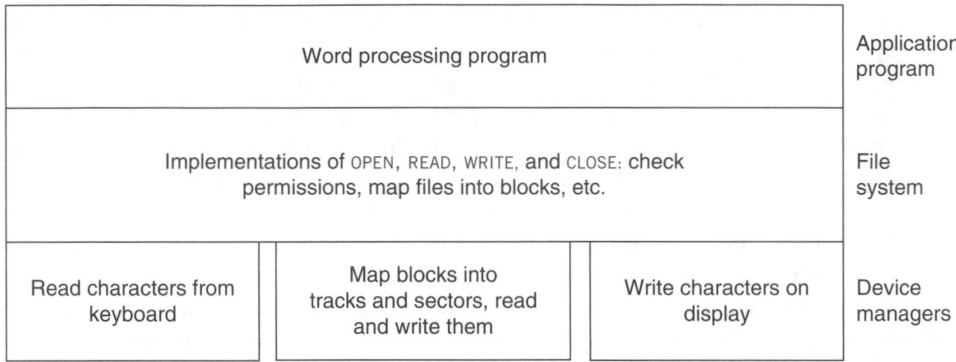

FIGURE 2.19

Using the file abstraction and layering to integrate different kinds of input and output devices. The file system acts as an intermediary that provides a uniform, abstract interface, and the various device managers are programs that translate that abstract interface into the operational requirements for different devices.

One feature of such a uniform interface is that in many situations one can, by simply rebinding the name, replace an I/O device with a file, or vice versa, without modifying the application program in any way. This use of naming in support of modularity is especially helpful when debugging an application program. For example, one can easily test a program that expects keyboard input by slipping a file filled with text in the place of the keyboard device. Because of such examples, the file system abstraction has proven to be very successful.

2.4 LOOKING BACK AND AHEAD

This chapter has developed several ideas and concepts that provide useful background for the study of computer system design. First, it described the three major abstractions used in designing computer systems—memory, interpreters, and communication links. Then it presented a model of how names are used to glue together modules based on those abstractions to create useful systems. Finally, it described some parts of a typical modern layered computer system in terms of the three major abstractions. With this background, we are now prepared to undertake a series of more in-depth discussions of specific computer system design topics. The first such in-depth discussion, in Chapter 3, is of the several engineering problems surrounding the use of names. Each of the remaining chapters undertakes a similar in-depth discussion of a different system design topic.

Before moving on to those in-depth discussions, the last section of this chapter is a case study of how abstraction, naming, and layers appear in practice. The case study uses those three concepts to describe the UNIX system.

2.5 CASE STUDY: UNIX® FILE SYSTEM LAYERING AND NAMING

The UNIX family of operating systems can trace its lineage back to the UNIX operating system that was developed by Bell Telephone Laboratories for the Digital Equipment Corporation PDP line of minicomputers in the late 1960s and early 1970s [Suggestions for Further Reading 2.2], and before that to the Multics* operating system in the early 1960s [Suggestions for Further Reading 1.7.5 and 3.1.4]. Today there are many flavors of UNIX systems with complex historical relationships; a few examples include GNU/Linux, versions of GNU/Linux distributed by different organizations (e.g., Red Hat, Ubuntu), Darwin (a UNIX operating system that is part of Apple's operating system Mac OS X), and several flavors of BSD operating systems. Some of these are directly derived from the early UNIX operating system; others provide similar interfaces but have been implemented from scratch. Some are the result of an effort by a small group of programmers, and others are the result of an effort by many. In the latter case, it is even unclear how to exactly name the operating system because substantial parts come from different teams.† The collective result of all these efforts is that operating systems of the UNIX family run on a wide range of computers, including personal computers, server computers, parallel computers, and embedded computers. Most of the UNIX interface is an official standard,‡ and non-UNIX operating systems often support this standard too. Because the source code of some versions is available to the public, one can easily study the UNIX system.

This case study examines the various ways in which the UNIX file system uses names in its design. In the course of examining how it implements its naming scheme, we will also incidentally get a first-level overview of how the UNIX file system is organized.

2.5.1 Application Programming Interface for the UNIX File System

A program can create a file with a user-chosen name, read and write the file's content, and set and get a file's metadata. Example metadata include the time of last modification, the user ID of the file's owner, and access permissions for other users. (For a full discussion of metadata see Section 3.1.2.) To organize their files, users can group them in directories with user-chosen names, creating a naming network. Users can also graft a naming network stored on a storage device onto an existing naming network, allowing naming networks for different devices to be incorporated into a single large nam-

---

*The name UNIX evolved from Unics, which was a word joke on Multics.

†We use "Linux" for the Linux kernel, while we use "GNU/Linux" for the complete system, recognizing that this naming convention is not perfect either because there are pieces of the system that are neither GNU software nor part of the kernel (e.g., the X Window System; see Sidebar 4.4).

‡POSIX® (Portable Operating System Interface), Federal Information Processing Standards (FIPS) 151-2. FIPS 151-2 adopts ISO/IEC 9945-1: 2003 (IEEE Std. 1003.1: 2001) Information Technology-Portable Operating System Interface (POSIX)-Part 1: System Application: Program Interface (API) [C Language].

Table 2.1 UNIX File System Application Programming Interface

Procedure	Brief Description
OPEN (*name, flags, mode*)	Open file *name*. If the file doesn't exist and *flags* is set, create file with permissions *mode*. Set the file cursor to 0. Returns a file descriptor.
READ (*fd, buf, n*)	Read *n* bytes from the file at the current cursor and increase the cursor by the number of bytes read.
WRITE (*fd, buf, n*)	Write *n* bytes at the current cursor and increase the cursor by the bytes written.
SEEK (*fd, offset, whence*)	Set the cursor to *offset* bytes from beginning, end, or current position.
CLOSE (*fd*)	Delete file descriptor. If this is the last reference to the file, delete the file.
FSYNC (*fd*)	Make all changes to the file durable.
STAT (*name*)	Read metadata of file.
CHMOD, CHOWN, etc.	Various procedures to set specific metadata.
RENAME (*from_name, to_name*)	Change name from *from_name* to *to_name*
LINK (*name, link_name*)	Create a hard link *link_name* to the file *name*.
UNLINK (*name*)	Remove *name* from its directory. If *name* is the last name for a file, remove file.
SYMLINK (*name, link_name*)	Create a symbolic name *link_name* for the file *name*.
MKDIR (*name*)	Create a new directory named *name*.
CHDIR (*name*)	Change current working directory to *name*.
CHROOT (*name*)	Change the default root directory to *name*.
MOUNT (*name, device*)	Graft the file system on *device* onto the name space at *name*.
UNMOUNT (*name*)	Unmount the file system at *name*.

ing network. To support these operations, the UNIX file system provides the application programming interface (API) shown in Table 2.1.

To tackle the problem of implementing this API, the UNIX file system employs a divide-and-conquer strategy. The UNIX file system makes use of several hidden layers of machine-oriented names (that is, addresses), one on top of another, to implement files. It then applies the UNIX durable object naming scheme to map user-friendly names to these files. Table 2.2 illustrates this structure.

In the rest of this section we work our way up from the bottom layer of Table 2.2 to the top layer, proceeding from the lowest layer of the system up toward

Table 2.2 The Naming Layers of the UNIX File System

Layer	Purpose	
Symbolic link layer	Integrate multiple file systems with symbolic links.	↑
Absolute path name layer	Provide a root for the naming hierarchies.	user-oriented names
Path name layer	Organize files into naming hierarchies.	↓
File name layer	Provide human-oriented names for files.	machine-user interface
Inode number layer	Provide machine-oriented names for files.	↑
File layer	Organize blocks into files.	machine-oriented names
Block layer	Identify disk blocks.	↓

the user. This description corresponds closely to the implementation of Version 6 of the UNIX system, which dates back to the early 1970s. Version 6 is well documented [Suggestions for Further Reading 2.2.2] and captures the important ideas that are found in many modern UNIX file systems, but modern versions are more complex; they provide better robustness and handle large files, many files, and so on, more efficiently. In a few places we will point out some of these differences, but the reader is encouraged to consult papers in the file system literature to find out how modern UNIX file systems work and are evolving.

2.5.2 The Block Layer

At the bottom layer the UNIX file system names some physical device such as a magnetic disk, flash disk, or magnetic tape that can store data durably. The storage on such a device is divided into fixed-size units, called *blocks*. For a magnetic disk (see Sidebar 2.2), a block corresponds to a small number of disk sectors. A block is the smallest allocation unit of disk space, and its size is a trade-off between several goals. A small block reduces the amount of disk wasted for small files; if many files are smaller than 4 kilobytes, a 16-kilobyte block size wastes space. On the other hand, a very small block size may incur large data structures to keep track of free and allocated blocks. In addition, there are performance considerations that impact the block size, some of which we discuss in Chapter 6. In version 6, the UNIX file system used 512-byte blocks, but modern UNIX file systems often use 8-kilobyte blocks.

The names of these blocks are numbers, which typically correspond to the offset of the block from the beginning of the device. In the bottom naming layer, a storage device can be viewed as a context that binds block numbers to physical blocks. The name-mapping algorithm for a block device is simple: it takes as input a block number and returns the block. Actually, we don't really want the block itself—that would be a pile of iron oxide. What we want is the *contents* of the block, so the algorithm actually implements a fixed mapping between block name and block contents. If we represent the storage device as a linear array of blocks, then the following code fragment implements the name-mapping algorithm:

```
procedure BLOCK_NUMBER_TO_BLOCK (integer b) returns block
    return device[b]
```

In this simple algorithm the variable name *device* refers to some particular physical device. In many devices the mapping is more complicated. For example, a hard drive might keep a set of spare blocks at the end and rebind the block numbers of any blocks that go bad to spares. The hard drive may itself be implemented in layers, as will be seen in Section 8.5.4 [on-line]. The value returned by BLOCK_NUMBER_TO_BLOCK is the contents of block *b*.

Name discovery: The names of blocks are integers from a compact set, but the block layer must keep track of which blocks are in use and which are available for assignment. As we will see, the file system in general has a need for a description of the layout of the file system on disk. As an anchor for this information, the UNIX file system starts with a *super block*, which has a well-known name (e.g., 1). The super block contains, for example, the size of the file system's disk in blocks. (Block 0 typically stores a small program that starts the operating system; see Sidebar 5.3.)

Different implementations of the UNIX file system use different representations for the list of free blocks. The version 6 implementation keeps a list of block numbers of unused blocks in a linked list that is stored in some of the unused blocks. The block number of the first block of this list is stored in the super block. A call to allocate a block leads to a procedure in the block layer that searches the list array for a free block, removes it from the list, and returns that block's block number.

Modern UNIX file systems often use a bitmap for keeping track of free blocks. Bit *i* in the bitmap records whether block *i* is free or allocated. The bitmap itself is stored at a well-known location on the disk (e.g., right after the super block). Figure 2.20 shows a possible disk layout for a simple file system. It starts with the super block, followed by a bitmap that records which disk blocks are in use. After the bitmap comes the inode table, which has one entry for each file (as explained next), followed by blocks that are either free or allocated to some file. The super block contains the size of the bitmap and inode table in blocks.

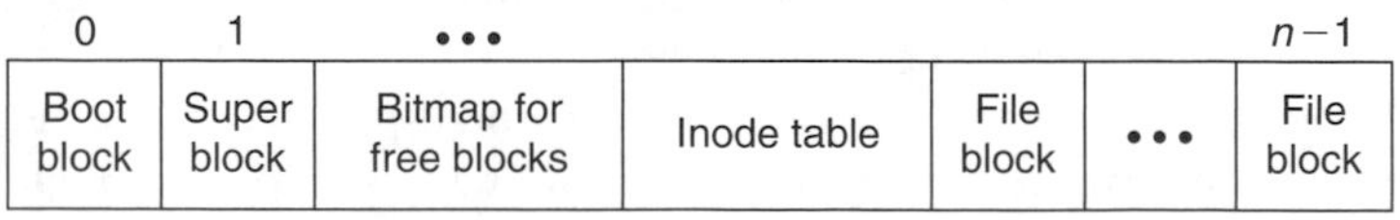

0	1	•••				$n-1$
Boot block	Super block	Bitmap for free blocks	Inode table	File block	•••	File block

FIGURE 2.20

Possible disk layout for a simple file system.

2.5.3 The File Layer

Users need to store items that are larger than one block in size and that may grow or shrink over time. To support such items, the UNIX file system introduces a next naming layer for *files*. A file is a linear array of bytes of arbitrary length. The file system needs to record in some way which blocks belong to each file. To support this requirement, the UNIX file system creates an index node, or ***inode*** for short, as a container for metadata about the file. Our initial declaration of an inode is:

```
structure inode
    integer block_numbers[N]    // the numbers of the blocks that constitute the file
    integer size                // the size of the file in bytes
```

The inode for a file is thus a context in which the various blocks of the file are named by integer block numbers. With this structure, a simplified name-mapping algorithm for resolving the name of a block in a file is as follows:

```
procedure INDEX_TO_BLOCK_NUMBER (inode instance i, integer index) returns integer
    return i.block_numbers[index]
```

The version 6 UNIX file system uses this algorithm for small files, which are limited to $N = 8$ blocks. For large files, version 6 uses a more sophisticated algorithm for mapping the *index*-th block of an inode to a block number. The first seven entries in *i.block_numbers* are ***indirect blocks***. Indirect blocks do not contain data, but block numbers. For example, with a block size of 512 bytes and an *index* of 2 bytes (as in Version 6), an indirect block can contain 256 2-byte block numbers. The eighth entry is a doubly indirect block (blocks that contain block numbers of indirect blocks). This design with indirect and doubly indirect blocks allows for $(N - 1) \times 256 + 1 \times 256 \times 256 = 67{,}329$ blocks when $N = 8$, about 32 megabytes.* Problem set *1* explores some design trade-offs to allow the file system to support large files. Some modern UNIX file systems use different representations or more sophisticated data structures, such as B+ trees, to implement files.

The UNIX file system allows users to name any particular byte in a file by layering the previous two naming schemes and specifying the byte number as an offset from the beginning of the file:

```
procedure INODE_TO_BLOCK (integer offset, inode instance i) returns block
    o ← offset / BLOCKSIZE
    b ← INDEX_TO_BLOCK_NUMBER (i, o)
    return BLOCK_NUMBER_TO_BLOCK (b)
```

The value returned is the entire block that holds the value of the byte at *offset*. Version 6 used for *offset* a 3-byte number, which limits the maximum file size to 2^{24} bytes. Modern UNIX file systems use a 64-bit number. The procedure returns the

*The implementation of Version 6, however, restricts the maximum number of blocks per file to 2^{15}.

entire block that contains the named byte. As we will see in Section 2.5.11, READ uses this procedure to return the requested bytes.

2.5.4 The Inode Number Layer

Instead of passing inodes themselves around, it would be more convenient to name them and pass their names around. To support this feature, the UNIX file system provides another naming layer that names inodes by an inode number. A convenient way to implement this naming layer is to employ a table that directly contains all inodes, indexed by inode number. Here is the naming algorithm:

```
procedure INODE_NUMBER_TO_INODE (integer inode_number) returns inode
    return inode_table[inode_number]
```

where *inode_table* is an object that is stored at a fixed location on the storage device (e.g., at the beginning). The name-mapping algorithm for *inode_table* just returns the starting block number of the table.

Name discovery: inode numbers, like disk block numbers, are a compact set of integers, and again the inode number layer must keep track of which inode numbers are in use and which are free to be assigned. As with block number assignment, different implementations use various representations for a list of free inodes and provide calls to allocate and deallocate inodes. In the simplest implementation, the inode contains a field recording whether or not it is free.

By putting these three layers together, we obtain the following procedure:

```
procedure INODE_NUMBER_TO_BLOCK (integer offset, integer inode_number)
                                                        returns block
    inode instance i ← INODE_NUMBER_TO_INODE (inode_number)
    o ← offset / BLOCKSIZE
    b ← INDEX_TO_BLOCK_NUMBER (i, o)
    return BLOCK_NUMBER_TO_BLOCK (b)
```

This procedure returns the block that contains the byte at *offset* in the file named by *inode_number*. This procedure traverses three layers of naming. There are numbers for storage blocks, numbered indexes for blocks belonging to an inode, and numbers for inodes.

2.5.5 The File Name Layer

Numbers are convenient names for use by a computer (numbers can be stored in fixed-length fields that simplify storage allocation) but are inconvenient names for use by people (numbers have little mnemonic value). In addition, block and inode numbers specify a location, so if it becomes necessary to rearrange the physical storage, the numbers must change, which is again inconvenient for people. The UNIX file system deals with this problem by inserting a naming layer whose sole purpose is

File name	Inode number
program	10
paper	12

FIGURE 2.21

A directory.

to hide the metadata of file management. Above this layer is a user-friendly naming scheme for durable objects—files and input/output devices. This naming scheme again has several layers. The most visible component of the durable object naming scheme is the *directory*. In the UNIX file system, a directory is a context containing a set of bindings between character-string names and inode numbers.

To create a file, the UNIX file system allocates an inode, initializes its metadata, and binds the proposed name to that inode in some directory. As the file is written, the file system allocates blocks to the inode.

By default, the UNIX file system adds the file to the current working directory. The current working directory is a context reference to the directory in which the active application is working. The form of the context reference is just another inode number. If *wd* is the name of the state variable that contains the working directory for a running program (called a *process* in the UNIX system), one can look up the inode number of the just-created file by supplying *wd* as the second argument to a procedure such as:

```
procedure NAME_TO_INODE_NUMBER (character string filename, integer dir) returns integer
    return LOOKUP (filename, dir)
```

The procedure CHDIR, whose implementation we describe later, allows a process to set *wd*.

To represent a directory, the UNIX file system reuses the mechanisms developed so far: it represents directories as files. By convention, a file that represents a directory contains a table that maps file names to inode numbers. For example, Figure 2.21 is a directory with two file names ("program" and "paper"), which are mapped to inode numbers 10 and 12, respectively. In Version 6, the maximum length of a name is 14 bytes, and the entries in the table have a fixed length of 16 bytes (14 for the name and 2 for the inode number). Modern UNIX file systems allow for variable-length names, and the table representation is more sophisticated.

To record whether an inode is for a directory or a file, the UNIX file system extends the inode with a type field:

```
structure inode
    integer block_numbers[N]    // the numbers of the blocks that constitute the file
    integer size                // the size of the file in bytes
    integer type                // type of file: regular file, directory, . . .
```

MKDIR creates a zero-length file (directory) and sets *type* to DIRECTORY. Extensions introduced later will add additional values for *type*.

With this representation of directories and inodes, LOOKUP is as follows:

```
1   procedure LOOKUP (character string filename, integer dir) returns integer
2       block instance b
3       inode instance i ← INODE_NUMBER_TO_INODE (dir)
4       if i.type ≠ DIRECTORY then return FAILURE
5       for offset from 0 to i.size – 1 do
6           b ← INODE_NUMBER_TO_BLOCK (offset, dir)
7           if STRING_MATCH (filename, b) then
8               return INODE_NUMBER (filename, b)
9           offset ← offset + BLOCKSIZE
10      return FAILURE
```

LOOKUP reads the blocks that contain the data for the directory *dir* and searches for the string *filename* in the directory's data. It computes the block number for the first block of the directory (line *6*) and the procedure STRING_MATCH (no code shown) searches that block for an entry for the name *filename*. If there is an entry, INODE_NUMBER (no code shown) returns the inode number in the entry (line *8*). If there is no entry, LOOKUP computes the block number for the second block, and so on, until all blocks of the directory have been searched. If none of the blocks contain an entry for *filename*, LOOKUP returns an error (line *10*). As an example, an invocation of LOOKUP ("program", *dir*), where *dir* is the inode number for the directory of Figure 2.21, would return the inode number 10.

2.5.6 The Path Name Layer

Having all files in a single directory makes it hard for users to keep track of large numbers of files. Enumerating the contents of a large directory would generate a long list that is organized simply (e.g., alphabetically) at best. To allow arbitrary groupings of user files, the UNIX file system permits users to create named directories.

A directory can be named just like a file, but the user also needs a way of naming the files in that directory. The solution is to add some structure to file names: for example, "projects/paper", in which "projects" names a directory and "paper" names a file in that directory. Structured names such as these are examples of path names. The UNIX file system uses a virgule (forward slash) as a separator of the components of a path name; other systems choose different separator characters such as period, back slash, or colon. With these tools, users can create a hierarchy of directories and files.

The name-resolving algorithm for path names can be implemented by layering a recursive procedure over the previous directory lookup procedure:

```
procedure PATH_TO_INODE_NUMBER (character string path, integer dir) returns integer
    if (PLAIN_NAME (path)) return NAME_TO_INODE_NUMBER (path, dir)
    else
        dir ← LOOKUP (FIRST (path), dir)
        path ← REST (path)
        return PATH_TO_INODE_NUMBER (path, dir)
```

The function PLAIN_NAME (*path*) scans its argument for the UNIX standard path name separator (forward slash) and returns TRUE if it does not find one. If there is no separator, the program resolves the simple name to an inode number in the requested directory (line *2*). If there is a separator in *path*, the program takes it to be a path name and goes to work on it (lines *4* through *6*). The function FIRST peels off the first component name from the path, and REST returns the remainder of the path name. Thus, for example, the call PATH_TO_NAME ("projects/paper", *wd*) results in the recursive call PATH_TO_NAME ("paper", *dir*), where *dir* is the inode number for the directory "projects".

With path names, one often has to type names with many components. To address this annoyance, the UNIX file system supports a change directory procedure, CHDIR, allowing a process to set its working directory:

```
procedure CHDIR (path character string)
    wd ← PATH_TO_INODE_NUMBER (path, wd)
```

When a process starts, it inherits the working directory from the parent process that created this process.

2.5.7 Links

To refer to files in directories other than the current working directory still requires typing long names. For example, while we are working in the directory "projects"—after calling CHDIR ("projects")—we might have to refer often to the file "Mail/inbox/new-assignment". To address this annoyance, the UNIX file system supports synonyms known as ***links***. In the example, we might want to create a link for this file in the current working directory, "projects". Invoking the LINK procedure with the following arguments:

```
LINK ("Mail/inbox/new-assignment", "assignment")
```

makes "assignment" a synonym for "Mail/inbox/new-assignment" in "projects", if "assignment" doesn't exist yet. (If it does, LINK will return an error saying "assignment" already exists.) With links, the directory hierarchy turns from a strict hierarchy into a directed graph. (The UNIX file system allows links only to files, not to directories, so the graph is not only directed but acyclic. We will see why in a moment.)

The UNIX file system implements links simply as bindings in different contexts that map different file names to the same inode number; thus, links don't require any extension to the naming scheme developed so far. For example, if the inode number for "new-assignment" is 481, then the directory "Mail/inbox" contains an entry {"new-assignment", 481} and after the above command is executed the directory "projects" contains an entry {"assignment", 481}. In UNIX system jargon, "projects/assignment" is now linked to "Mail/inbox/new-assignment".

When a file is no longer needed, a process can remove a file using UNLINK (*filename*), indicating to the file system that the name *filename* is no longer in use. UNLINK removes the binding of *filename* to its inode number from the directory that contains *filename*. The file system also puts *filename*'s inode and the blocks of *filename*'s inode on the free list if this binding is the last one containing the inode's number.

Before we added links, a file was bound to a name in only one directory, so if a process asks to delete the name from that directory, the file system can also delete the file. But now that links have been added, when a process asks to delete a name, there may still be names in other directories bound to the file, in which case the file shouldn't be deleted. This raises the question, when should a file be deleted? The UNIX file system deletes a file when a process removes the last binding for a file. The UNIX file system implements this policy by keeping a reference count in the inode:

```
structure inode
    integer block_numbers[N]
    integer size
    integer type
    integer refcnt
```

Whenever it makes a binding to an inode, the file system increases the reference count of that inode. To delete a file, the UNIX file system provides an UNLINK(*filename*) procedure, which deletes the binding specified by *filename*. At the same time the file system decreases the reference count in the corresponding inode by one. If the decrease causes the reference count to go to zero, that means there are no more bindings to this inode, so the file system can free the inode and its corresponding blocks. For example, UNLINK ("Mail/inbox/new-assignment") removes the directory entry "new-assignment" in the directory "Mail/inbox", but not "assignment", because after the unlink the *refcnt* in inode 481 will be 1. Only after calling UNLINK ("assignment") will the inode 481 and its blocks be freed.

Using reference counts works only if there are no cycles in the naming graph. To ensure that the UNIX naming network is a directed graph without cycles, the UNIX file system forbids links to directories. To see why cycles are avoided, consider a directory "a", which contains a directory "b". If a program invokes LINK ("a/b/c", "a") in the directory that contains "a", then the system would return an error and not perform the operation. If the system had performed this operation, it would have created a cycle from "c" to "a" and would have increased the reference count in the inode of "a" by one. If a program then invokes UNLINK ("a"), the name "a" is removed, but the inode and the blocks of "a" wouldn't be removed because the reference count in the inode of "a" is still positive (because of the link from "c" to "a"). But once the name "a" would be removed, a user would no longer be able to name the directory "a" and wouldn't be able to remove it either. In that case, the directory "a" and its subdirectories would be disconnected from the naming graph, but the system would not remove it because the reference count in the inode of "a" is still positive. It is possible to detect this situation, for example by using garbage collection, but it is expensive to do so. Instead, the designers chose a simpler solution: don't allow links to directories, which rules out the possibility of cycles.

There are two special cases, however. First, by default each directory contains a link to itself; the UNIX file system reserves the string "." (a single dot) for this purpose. The name "." thus allows a process to name the current directory without knowing which the directory it is. When a directory is created, the directory's inode has a reference count of two: one for the inode of the directory and one for the link ".", because it points to itself. Because "." introduces a cycle of length 0, there is no risk that part of the naming network will become disconnected when removing a directory. When unlinking a directory, the file system just decreases the reference count of the directory's inode by 2.

Second, by default, each directory also contains a link to a parent directory; the file system reserves the string ".." (two consecutive dots) for this purpose. The name ".." allows a process to name a parent directory and, for example, move up the file hierarchy by invoking CHDIR (".."). The link doesn't create problems. Only when a directory has no other entries than "." and ".." can it be removed. If a user wants to remove a directory "a", which contains a directory "b", then the file system refuses to do so until the user first has removed "b". This rule ensures that the naming network cannot become disconnected.

2.5.8 Renaming

Using LINK and UNLINK, Version 6 implemented RENAME (*from_name*, *to_name*) as follows:

```
1   UNLINK (to_name)
2   LINK (from_name, to_name)
3   UNLINK (from_name)
```

This implementation, however, has an undesirable property. Programs often use RENAME to change a working copy of a file into the official version; for example, a user may be editing a file "x". The text editor actually makes all changes to a temporary file "#x". When the user saves the file, the editor renames the temporary file "#x" to "x".

The problem with implementing RENAME using LINK and UNLINK is that if the computer fails between steps 1 and 2 and then restarts, the name *to_name* ("x" in this case) will be lost, which is likely to surprise the user, who is unlikely to know that the file still exists but under the name "#x". What is really needed is that "#x" be renamed to "x" in a single, atomic operation, but that requires atomic actions, which are the topic of Chapter 9 [on-line].

Without atomic actions, it is possible to implement the following slightly weaker specification for RENAME: if *to_name* already exists, an instance of *to_name* will always exist, even if the system should fail in the middle of RENAME. This specification is good enough for the editor to do the right thing and is what modern versions provide.

Modern versions implement this specification in essence as follows:

```
1   LINK (from_name, to_name)
2   UNLINK (from_name)
```

Because one cannot link to a name that already exists, RENAME implements the effects of these two calls by manipulating the file system structures directly. RENAME first changes the inode number in the directory entry for *to_name* to the inode number for *from_name* on disk. Then, RENAME removes the directory entry for *from_name*. If the file system fails between these two steps, then on recovery the file system must increase the reference count in *from_name*'s inode because both *from_name* and *to_name* are pointing to the inode. This implementation ensures that if *to_name* exists before the call to RENAME, it will continue to exist, even if the computer fails during RENAME.

2.5.9 The Absolute Path Name Layer

The UNIX system provides each user with a personal directory, called a user's *home directory*. When a user logs on to a UNIX system, it starts a command interpreter (known as the *shell*) through which a user can interact with the system. The shell starts with the working directory (*wd*) set to the inode number of the user's home directory. With the above procedures, users can create personal directory trees to organize the files in their home directory.

But having several personal directory trees does not allow one user to share files with another. To do that, one user needs a way of referring to the names of files that belong to another user. The easiest way to accomplish that is to bind a name for each user to that user's top-level directory, in some context that is available to every user. But then there is a requirement to name this systemwide context. Typically, there are needs for other systemwide contexts, such as a directory containing shared program libraries. To address these needs with a minimum of additional mechanisms, the file system provides a universal context, known as the *root* directory. The root directory contains bindings for the directory of users, the directory containing program libraries, and any other widely shared directories. The result is that all files of the system are integrated into a single directory tree (with restricted cross-links) based on the root.

This design leaves a name discovery question: how can a user name the root directory? Recall that name lookup requires a context reference—the name of a directory inode—and until now that directory inode has been supplied by the working directory state variable. To implement the root, the file system simply declares inode number 1 to be the inode for the root directory. This *well-known name* can then be used by any user as the starting context in which to look up the name of a shared context, or another user (or even to look up one's own name, to set the working directory when logging in).

The file system actually provides two ways to refer to things in the root directory. Starting from any directory in the system, one can use the name ".." to name that directory's parent, "../.." to name the directory above that, and so on until the root directory is reached. A user can tell that the root directory is reached, because ".." in the root directory names the root directory. That is, in the root directory, both "." and ".." are links to the root directory. The other way is with absolute path names, which in the UNIX file system are names that start with a "/", for example, "/Alice/Mail/inbox/new-assignment".

To support absolute path names as well as relative path names, we need one more layer in the naming scheme:

```
procedure GENERALPATH_TO_INODE_NUMBER (character string path) returns integer
    if (path[0] = "/") return PATH_TO_INODE_NUMBER(path, 1)
    else return PATH_TO_INODE_NUMBER(path, wd)
```

At this point we have completed a naming scheme that allows us to name and share durable storage on a single disk. For example, to find the blocks corresponding to the file "/programs/pong.c" with the information in Figure 2.22, we start by finding the inode table, which starts at a block number (block 4 in our example) stored in the super block (not shown in this figure, but see Figure 2.20). From there we locate the root inode (which is known to be inode number 1). The root inode contains the block numbers that in turn contain the blocks of the root directory; in the figure the root starts in block number 14. Block 14 lists the entries in the root directory: "programs" is named by inode number 7. The inode table says that data for inode number 7 starts in block number 23, which contains the contents of the "programs" directory. The file "pong.c" is named by inode number 9. Referring once more to the inode table, to see where inode 9 is stored, we see that the data corresponding to inode 9 starts in block number 61. In short, directories and files are carefully laid out so that all information can be found by starting from the well-known location of the root inode.

The default root directory in Version 6 is inode 1. Version 7 added a call, CHROOT, to change the root directory for a process. For example, a Web server can be run in the corner of the UNIX name space by changing its root directory to, for example, "/tmp". After this call, the root directory for the Web server corresponds to the inode number of the directory "/tmp" and ".." in "/tmp" is a link to "/tmp". Thus, the server can name only directories and files below "/tmp".

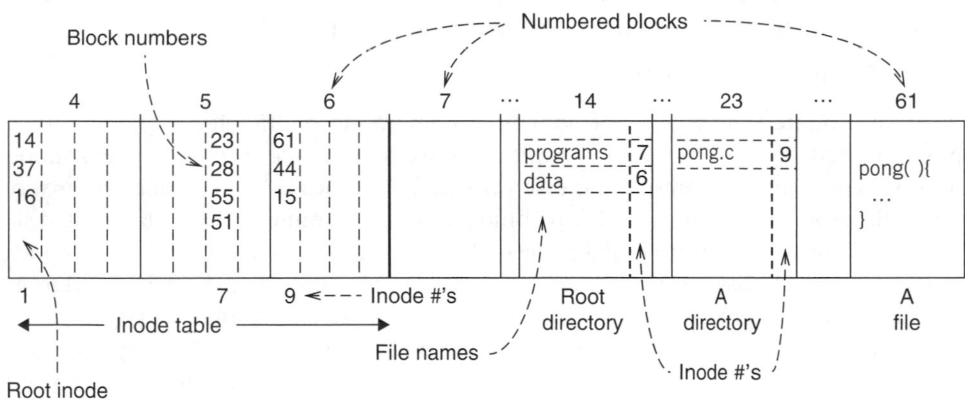

FIGURE 2.22

Example disk layout for a UNIX file system, refining Figure 2.20 by focusing on the inode table and data blocks. The inode table is a group of contiguous blocks starting at a well-known address, found in the super block (not shown). In this example, blocks 4, 5, and 6 contain the inode table, while blocks 7–61 contain directories and files. The root inode is by convention the well-known inode #1. Typically, inodes are smaller than a block, so in this example there are four inodes in each block. Blocks #14, #37, and #16 constitute the root directory, while block #23 is the first of four blocks of the directory named "/programs", and block #61 is the first block of the three-block file "/programs/pong.c".

2.5.10 The Symbolic Link Layer

To allow users to name files on other disks, the UNIX file system supports an operation to attach new disks to the name space. A user can choose the name under which each device is attached: for example, the procedure

```
MOUNT ("/dev/fd1", "/flash")
```

grafts the directory tree stored on the physical device named "/dev/fd1" onto the directory "/flash". (This command demonstrates that each device also has a name in the same object name space we have been describing; the file corresponding to a device typically contains information about the device itself.) Typically mounts do not survive a shutdown: after a reboot, the user has to explicitly remount the devices. It is interesting to contrast the elegant UNIX approach with the DOS approach, in which devices are named by fixed one-character names (e.g., "C:").

The UNIX file system implements MOUNT by recording in the in-memory inode for "flash" that a file system has been mounted on it and keeps this inode in memory until at least the corresponding UNMOUNT. In memory, the system also records the device and the root inode number of the file system that has been mounted on it. In addition, it records in the in-memory version of the inode for "/dev/fd1" what its parent inode is.

The information for mount points is all recorded in volatile memory instead of on disk and doesn't survive a computer failure. After a failure, the system administrator or a program must invoke MOUNT again. Supporting MOUNT also requires a change to the file name layer: if LOOKUP runs into an inode on which a file system is mounted, it uses the root inode of the mounted file system for the lookup.

UNMOUNT undoes the mount.

With mounted file systems, synonyms become a more difficult problem because per mounted file system there is an address space of inode numbers. Every inode number has a default context: the disk on which it is located. Thus, there is no way for a directory entry on one disk to bind to an inode number on a different disk. This problem can be approached in several ways, two of which are: (1) make inodes unique across all disks or (2) create synonyms for files on other disks in a different way. The UNIX system chooses the second approach by using indirect names called *symbolic* or *soft* links, which bind a file name to another file name. Most systems use method (2) because of the complications that would be involved in trying to keep inode numbers universally unique, small in size, and fast to resolve.

Using the procedure SYMLINK, users can create synonyms for files in the same file system or for files in mounted file systems. The file system implements the procedure SYMLINK by allowing the type field of an inode to be a SYMLINK, which tells whether the blocks associated with the inode contain data or a path name:

```
structure inode
    integer block_numbers[N]
    integer size
    integer type        // Type of inode: regular file, directory, symbolic link, . . .
    integer refcnt
```

If the *type* field has value SYMLINK, then the data in the array *blocks*[*i*] actually contains the characters of a path name rather than a set of inode numbers.

Soft links can be implemented by layering them over GENERALPATH_TO_NODE_NUMBER:

```
procedure PATHNAME_TO_INODE (character string filename) returns inode
    inode instance i
    inode_number ← GENERALPATH_TO_INODE_NUMBER (filename)
    i ← INODE_NUMBER_TO_INODE (inode_number)
    if i.type = SYMBOLIC then
        i = GENERALPATH_TO_INODE_NUMBER (COERCE_TO_STRING (i.block_numbers))
    return i
```

The value returned by PATHNAME_TO_INODE is the contents of the inode for the file named by *filename*. The procedure first looks up the inode number for *filename*. Then, it looks up the the inode using INODE_NUMBER_TO_INODE. If the inode indicates that this file is a symbolic link, the procedure interprets the contents of data of the file as a path name and invokes GENERALPATH_TO_INODE_NUMBER again.

We now have two types of synonyms. A direct binding to an inode number is called a ***hard link***, to distinguish it from a soft link. Continuing an earlier example, a soft link to "Mail/inbox/new-assignment" would contain the string "Mail/inbox/new-assignment", rather than the inode number 481. A soft link is an example of an indirect name: it binds a name to another name in the same name space, while a hard link binds a name to an inode number, which is a name in a lower-layer name space. As a result, the soft link depends on the file name "Mail/inbox/new-assignment"; if the user changes the file's name or deletes the file, then "projects/assignment", the link, will end up as a dangling reference (Section 3.1.6 discusses dangling references). But because it links by name rather than by inode number, a soft link can point to a file on a different disk.

Recall that the UNIX system forbids cycles of hard links, so that it can use reference counts to detect when it is safe to reclaim the disk space for a file. However, you can still form cycles with soft links: a name deep down in the tree can, for example, name a directory high up in the tree. The resulting structure is no longer a directed acyclic graph, but a fully general naming network. Using soft links, a program can even invoke SYMLINK ("cycle", "cycle"), creating a synonym for a file name that doesn't have a file associated with it! If a process opens such a file, it will follow the link chain only a certain number of steps before reporting an error such as "Too many levels of soft links".

Soft links have another interesting behavior. Suppose that the working directory is "/Scholarly/programs/www" and that this working directory contains a symbolic link named "CSE499-web" to "/Scholarly/CSE499/www". The following calls

```
CHDIR ("CSE499-web")
CHDIR ("..")
```

leave the caller in "/Scholarly/CSE499" rather than back where the user started. The reason is that ".." is resolved in the new default context, "/Scholarly/CSE499/www", rather than what might have been the intended context, "/Scholarly/programs/www". This behavior may be desirable or not, but it is a direct consequence of the UNIX

Table 2.3 The UNIX Naming Layers, with Details of the Naming Scheme of Each Layer

Layer	Names	Values	Context	Name-Mapping Algorithm	
Symbolic link	Path names	Path names	The directory hierarchy	PATHNAME_TO_GENERAL_PATH	↑
Absolute path name	Absolute path names	Inode numbers	The root directory	GENERALPATH_TO_INODE_NUMBER	user-oriented names
Path name	Relative path names	Inode numbers	The working directory	PATH_TO_INODE_NUMBER	↓
File name	File names	Inode numbers	A directory	NAME_TO_INODE_NUMBER	machine-user interface
Inode number	Inode numbers	Inodes	The inode table	INODE_NUMBER_TO_INODE	↑
File	Index numbers	Block numbers	An inode	INDEX_TO_BLOCK_NUMBER	machine-oriented names
Block	Block numbers	Blocks	The disk drive	BLOCK_NUMBER_TO_BLOCK	↓

naming semantics; the Plan 9 system has a different plan,* which is also explored in exercises 3.2 and 3.3.

In summary, much of the power of the UNIX object naming scheme comes from its layers of naming. Table 2.3 reprises Table 2.2, this time showing the name, value, context, and pseudocode procedure used at each layer interface. (Although we have examined each of the layers in this table, the algorithms we have demonstrated have in some cases bridged across layers in ways not suggested by the table.) The general design technique has been to introduce for each problem another layer of naming, an application of the principle *decouple modules with indirection*.

2.5.11 Implementing the File System API

In the process of describing how the UNIX file system is structured, we saw how it implements CHDIR, MKDIR, LINK, UNLINK, RENAME, SYMLINK, MOUNT, and UNMOUNT. We complete the description of the file system API by describing the implementation of OPEN, READ, WRITE, and CLOSE. Before describing their implementation, we describe what features they must support.

*Rob Pike. Lexical File Names in Plan 9 or Getting Dot-Dot Right. *Proceedings of the 2000 USENIX Technical Conference* (2000), San Diego, pages 85–92.

The file system allows users to control who has access to their files. An owner of a file can specify with what permissions other users can make accesses to the file. For example, the owner may specify that other users have permission only to read a file but not to write it. OPEN must check whether the caller has the appropriate permissions. As a sophistication, a file can be owned by a group of users. Chapter 11 [on-line] discusses security in detail, so we will skip the details here.

The file system records timestamps that capture the date and time of the last access, last modification to a file, and last change to a file's inode. This information is important for programs such as incremental backup, which must determine which files have changed since the last time backup ran. The file system procedures must update these values. For example, READ updates last access time, WRITE updates last modification time and change time, and LINK updates last change time.

OPEN returns a short name for a file, called a file descriptor (*fd*), which READ, WRITE, and CLOSE use to name the file. Each process starts with three open files: "standard in" (file descriptor 0), "standard out" (file descriptor 1), and "standard error" (file descriptor 2). A file descriptor may name a keyboard device, a display device, or a file on disk; a program doesn't need to know. This setup allows a designer to develop a program without having to worry about where the program's input is coming from and where the program's output is going to; the program just reads from file descriptor 0 and writes to file descriptor 1.

Several processes can use a file concurrently (e.g., several processes might write to the display device). If several processes open the same file, their READ and WRITE operations have their own file cursor for that file. If one process opens a file, and then passes the file descriptor for that file to another process, then the two processes share the cursor of the file. This latter case is common because in the UNIX system when one process (the *parent*) starts another process (the *child*), the child inherits all open file descriptors from the parent. This design allows the parent and child, for instance, to share a common output file correctly. If the child writes to the output file, for example, after the parent has written to it, the output of the child appears after the output of the parent because they share the cursor.

If one process has a file open and another process removes the last name pointing to that file, the inode isn't freed until the first process calls CLOSE.

To support these features, the inode is extended as follows:

```
structure inode
    integer block_numbers[N]    // the number of blocks that constitute the file
    integer size                // the size of the file in bytes
    integer type                // type of file: regular file, directory, symbolic link
    integer refcnt              // count of the number of names for this inode
    integer userid              // the user ID that owns this inode
    integer groupid             // the group ID that owns this inode
    integer mode                // inode's permissions
    integer atime               // time of last access (READ, WRITE, . . . )
    integer mtime               // time of last modification
    integer ctime               // time of last change of inode
```

To implement OPEN, READ, WRITE, and CLOSE, the file system keeps in memory several tables: one file table (*file_table*) and for each process a file descriptor table (*fd_table*). The file table records information for the files that processes have open (i.e., files for which OPEN was successful, but for which CLOSE hasn't been called yet). For each open file, this information includes the inode number of the file, its file cursor, and a reference count recording how many processes have the file open. The file descriptor table records for each file descriptor the index into the file table. Because a file's cursor is stored in the *file_table* instead of the *fd_table*, children can share the cursor for an inherited file with their parent.

With this information, OPEN is implemented as follows:

```
1   procedure OPEN (character string filename, flags, mode)
2       inode_number ← PATH_TO_INODE_NUMBER (filename, wd)
3       if inode_number = FAILURE and flags = O_CREATE then          // Create the file?
4           inode_number ← CREATE (filename, mode)                  // Yes, create it.
5       if inode_number = FAILURE then
6           return FAILURE
7       inode ← INODE_NUMBER_TO_INODE (inode_number)
8       if PERMITTED (inode, flags) then  // Does this user have the required permissions
9           file_index ← INSERT (file_table, inode_number)
10          fd ← FIND_UNUSED_ENTRY (fd_table)   // Find entry in file descriptor table
11          fd_table[fd] ← file_index           // Record file index for file descriptor
12          return fd                           // Return fd
13      else return FAILURE                     // No, return a failure
```

Line *2* finds the inode number for the file *filename*. If the file doesn't exist, but the caller wants to create the file as indicated by the flag O_CREATE (line *3*), OPEN calls CREATE, which allocates an inode, initializes it, and returns its inode number (line *4*). If the file doesn't exist (even after trying to create it), OPEN returns a value indicating a failure (line *6*). Line *7* locates the inode. Line *8* uses the information in the inode to check if the caller has permission to open the file; the check is described in detail in Section 11.6.3.4 [on-line]. If so, line *9* creates a new entry for the inode number in the file table and sets the entry's file cursor to zero and reference count to 1. Line *10* finds the first unused file descriptor, records its file index, and returns the file descriptor to the caller (lines *10* through *12*). Otherwise, it returns a value indicating a failure (line *13*).

If a process starts another process, the child process inherits the open file descriptors of the parent. That is, the information in every used entry in the parent's *fd_table* is copied to the same numbered entry in the child's *fd_table*. As a result, the parent and child entries in the *fd_table* will point to the same entry in the *file_table*, resulting in the cursor being shared between parent and child.

READ is implemented as follows:

```
1   procedure READ (fd, character array reference buf, n)
2       file_index ← fd_table[fd]
3       cursor ← file_table[file_index].cursor
4       inode ← INODE_NUMBER_TO_INODE (file_table[file_index].inode_number)
5       m = MINIMUM (inode.size – cursor, n)
6       atime of inode ← NOW ()
7       if m = 0 then return END_OF_FILE
8       for i from 0 to m – 1 do {
9           b ← INODE_NUMBER_TO_BLOCK (i, inode_number)
10          COPY (b, buf, MINIMUM (m – i, BLOCKSIZE))
11          i ← i + MINIMUM (m – i, BLOCKSIZE)
12      file_table[file_index].cursor ← cursor + m
13      return m
```

Lines *2* and *3* use the file index to find the cursor for the file. Line *4* locates the inode. Line *5* and *6* compute how many bytes READ can read and updates the last access time. If there are no bytes left in the file, READ returns a value indicating end of file. Lines *8* through *12* copy the bytes from the file's blocks into the caller's *buf*. Line *13* updates the cursor.

One could design a more sophisticated naming scheme for READ that, for example, allowed naming by keywords rather than by offsets. Database systems typically implement such naming schemes by representing the data as structured records that are indexed by keywords. But in order to keep its design simple, the UNIX file system restricts its representation of a file to a linear array of bytes.

The implementation of WRITE is similar to READ. The major differences are that it copies *buf* into the blocks of the inode, allocating new blocks as necessary, and that it updates the inode's *size* and *mtime*.

CLOSE frees the entry in the file descriptor table and decreases the reference count in entry in the file table. If no other processes are sharing this entry (i.e., the reference count has reached zero), it also frees the entry in the file table. If there are no other entries in the file table using this file and the reference count in the file's inode has reached zero (because another process unlinked it), then CLOSE frees the inode.

Like RENAME, some of these operations require several disk writes to complete. If the file system fails (e.g., because the power goes off) in the middle of one of the operations, then some of the disk writes may have completed and some may not. Such a failure can cause inconsistencies among the on-disk data structures. For example, the on-disk free list may show that a block is allocated, but no on-disk inode records that block in its index. If nothing is done about this inconsistency, then that block is effectively lost. Problem set *8* explores this problem and a simple, special-case solution. Chapter 9 [on-line] explores systematic solutions.

Version 6 (and all modern implementations) maintain an in-memory cache of recently used disk blocks. When the file system needs a block, it first checks the cache for the block. If the block is present, it uses the block from the cache; otherwise, it reads it from the storage device. With the cache, even if the file system needs to read a particular block several times, it reads that block from the storage device only once. Since reading from a disk device is often an expensive operation, the cache can improve the performance of the file system substantially. Chapter 6 discusses the implementation of caches in detail and how they can be used to improve the performance of a file system.

Similarly, to achieve high performance on operations that modify a file (e.g., WRITE), the file system will update the file's blocks in the cache, but will not force the file's modified inode and blocks to the storage device immediately. The file system delays the writes until later so that if a block is updated several times, it will write the block only once. Thus, it can coalesce many updates in one write (see Section 6.1.8).

If a process wants to ensure that the results of a write and inode changes are propagated to the device that stores the file system, it must call FSYNC; the UNIX specification requires that if an invocation of FSYNC for a file returns, all changes to the file must have been written to the storage device.

2.5.12 The Shell and Implied Contexts, Search Paths, and Name Discovery

Using the file system API, the UNIX system implements programs for users to manipulate files and name spaces. These programs include text editors (such as `ed`, `vi`, and `emacs`), `rm` (to remove a file), `ls` (to list a directory's content), `mkdir` (to make a new directory), `rmdir` (to remove a directory), `ln` (to make link names), `cd` (to change the working directory), and `find` (to search for a file in a directory tree).

One of the more interesting UNIX programs is its command interpreter, known as the "shell". The shell illustrates a number of other UNIX naming schemes. Say a user wants to compile the C source file named "x.c". The UNIX convention is to overload a file name by appending a suffix indicating the type of the file, such as ".c" for C source files. (A full discussion of overloading can be found in Section 3.1.2.) The user types this command to the shell:

```
cc x.c
```

This command consists of two names: the name of a program (the compiler "cc") and the name of a file containing source code ("x.c") for the compiler to compile. The first thing the shell must do is find the program we want to run, "cc". To do that, the UNIX command interpreter uses a default context reference contained in an environment variable named PATH. That environment variable contains a list of contexts (in this case directories) in which to perform a multiple lookup for the thing named "cc". Assuming the lookup is successful, the shell launches the program, calling it with the argument "x.c".

The first thing the compiler does is try to resolve the name "x.c". This time it uses a different default context reference: the working directory. Once the compilation is underway, the file "x.c" may contain references to other named files, for example, statements such as

```
#include <stdio.h>
```

This statement tells the compiler to include all definitions in the file "stdio.h" in the file "x.c". To resolve "stdio.h", the compiler needs a context in which to resolve it. For this purpose, the compiler consults another variable (typically passed as an argument when invoking the compiler), which contains a default context to be used as a search path where include files may be found. The variables used by the shell and by the compiler each consist of a series of path names to be used as the basis for an ordered multiple lookup just as was described in Section 2.2.4.

Many other UNIX programs, such as the documentation package, `man`, also do multiple lookups for files using search paths found in environment variables.

The shell resolves names for commands using the PATH variable, but sometimes it is convenient to be able to say "I want to run the program located in the current working directory". For example, a user may be developing a new version of the C compiler, which is also called "cc". If the user types "`cc`", the shell will look up the C compiler using the PATH variable and find the standard one instead of the new one in the current working directory.

For these cases, users can type the following command:

```
./cc x.c
```

which bypasses the PATH variable and invokes the program named "cc" in the current working directory (".").

Of course, the user could insert "." at the beginning of the PATH variable, so that all programs in the user's working directory will take precedence over the corresponding standard program. That practice, however, may create some surprises. Suppose "." is first entry in the PATH variable, and a user issues the following command sequence to the shell:

```
cd /usr/potluck
ls
```

intending to list the contents of the directory named `potluck`. If that directory contained a program named `ls` that did something different from the standard `ls` command, something surprising might happen (e.g., the program named `ls` could remove all private files)! For this reason, it is not a good idea to include names that are context-dependent, such as "." or ".." in a search path. It is better to include the absolute path name of the desired directory to the front of PATH.

Another command interpreter extension is that names can be descriptive rather than simple names. For example, the descriptive name "*.c", matches all file names that end with ".c". To provide this extension, the command interpreter transforms the single argument into a list of arguments (with the help of a more complicated lookup operation on the entries in the context) before it calls the specified command program. In the UNIX shell, users can use full-blown regular expressions in descriptive names.

As a final note, in practice, the UNIX object naming space has quite a bit of conventional structure. In particular, there are several directories with well-known names. For example, "/bin" names programs, "/etc" names configuration files, "/dev" names input/output devices, and "/usr" (rather than the root itself) names user directories. Over time these conventions have become so ingrained both in programmers' minds and in programs that much UNIX software will not install correctly, and a UNIX wizard will become badly confused, when confronted with a system that does not follow these conventions.

2.5.13 Suggestions for Further Reading

For a detailed description of a more modern UNIX operating system, see the book describing the BSD operating system [Suggestions for Further Reading 1.3.4]. A descendant of the original UNIX system is Plan 9 [Suggestions for Further Reading 3.2.2], which contains a number of novel naming abstractions, some of which are finding their way back into newer UNIX implementations. A rich literature exists describing file system implementations and their trade-offs. A good starting point are the papers on FFS [Suggestions for Further Reading 6.3.2], LFS [Suggestions for Further Reading 9.3.1], and soft updates [Suggestions for Further Reading 6.3.3].

EXERCISES

2.1 Ben Bitdiddle has accepted a job with the telephone company and has been asked to implement call forwarding. He has been pondering what to do if someone forwards calls to some number and then the owner of that number forwards calls to a third number. So far, Ben has thought of two possibilities for his implementation:

a. *Follow me.* Bob is going to a party at Mary's home for the evening, so he forwards his telephone to Mary. Ann is baby-sitting for Bob, so she forwards her telephone to Bob. Jim calls Ann's number, Bob's telephone rings, and Ann answers it.

b. *Delegation.* Bob is going to a party at Mary's home for the evening, so he forwards his telephone to Mary. Ann is gone for the week and has forwarded her telephone to Bob so that he can take her calls. Jim calls Ann's number, Mary's telephone rings, and Mary hands the phone to Bob to take the call.

2.1a Using the terminology of the naming section of this chapter, explain these two possibilities.

2.1b What might go wrong if Bob has already forwarded his telephone to Mary before Ann forwards her telephone to him?

2.1c The telephone company usually provides *Delegation* rather than *Follow me*. Why?

2.2 Consider the part of the file system naming hierarchy illustrated in the following:

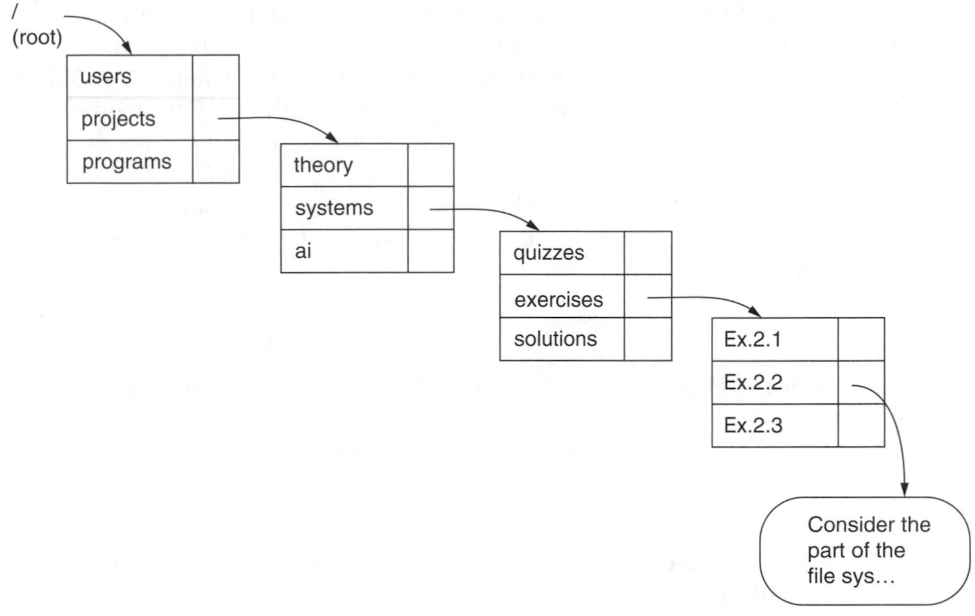

You have been handed the following path name:

`/projects/systems/exercises/Ex.2.2`

and you are about to resolve the third component of that path name, the name `exercises`.

2.2a In the path name and in the figure, identify the context that you should use for that resolution and the context reference that allows locating that context.

2.2b Which of the terms *default*, *explicit*, *built-in*, *per-object*, and *per-name* apply to this context reference?

1995–2–1a

2.3 One way to speed up the resolving of names is to implement a cache that remembers recently looked-up {name, object} pairs.

2.3a What problems do synonyms pose for cache designers, as compared with caches that don't support synonyms?

1994–2–3

2.3b Propose a way of solving the problems if every object has a unique ID.

1994–2–3a

2.4 Louis Reasoner has become concerned about the efficiency of the search rule implementation in the Eunuchs system (an emasculated version of the UNIX system). He proposes to add a *referenced object table* (ROT), which the system will maintain for each session of each user, set to be empty when the user logs in. Whenever the system resolves a name through of use a search path, it makes an entry in the ROT consisting of the name and the path name of that object. The "already referenced" search rule simply searches the ROT to determine if the name in question appears there. If it finds a match, then the resolver will use the associated path name from the ROT. Louis proposes to always use the "already referenced" rule first, followed by the traditional search path mechanism. He claims that the user will detect no difference, except for faster name resolution. Is Louis right?

1985-2-2

2.5 The last line of Figure 2.4 names three Web browsers as examples of interpreters. Explain how a Web browser is an interpreter by identifying its instruction reference, its repertoire, and its environment reference.

2009-0-1

Additional exercises relating to Chapter 2 can be found in the problem sets beginning on page 425.

CHAPTER

The Design of Naming Schemes

3

CHAPTER CONTENTS

OVERVIEW

In the previous chapter we developed an abstract model of naming schemes. When the time comes to design a practical naming scheme, many engineering considerations—constraints, additional requirements or desiderata, and environmental pressures—shape

Principles of Computer System Design: An Introduction

DOI: 10.1016/B978-0-12-374957-4.00011-6

the design. One of the main ways in which users interact with a computer system is through names, and the quality of the user experience can be greatly influenced by the quality of the system's naming schemes. Similarly, since names are the glue that connects modules, the properties of the naming schemes can significantly affect the impact of modularity on a system.

This chapter explores the engineering considerations involved in designing naming schemes. The main text introduces a wide range of naming considerations that affect modularity and usability. A case study of the World Wide Web Uniform Resource Locator (URL) illustrates both the naming model and some problems that arise in the design of naming schemes. Finally, a war stories section explores some pathological problems of real naming schemes.

3.1 CONSIDERATIONS IN THE DESIGN OF NAMING SCHEMES

We begin with a discussion of an interaction between naming and modularity.

3.1.1 Modular Sharing

Connecting modules by name provides great flexibility, but it introduces a hazard: the designer sometimes has to deal with preexisting names, perhaps chosen by someone else over whom the designer has no control. This hazard can arise whenever modules are designed independently. If, in order to use a module, the designer must know about and avoid the names used within that module for its components, we have failed to achieve one of the primary goals of modularity, called *modular sharing*. Modular sharing means that one can use a shared module by name without knowing the names of the modules it uses.

Lack of modular sharing shows up in the form of *name conflict*, in which for some reason two or more different values compete for the binding of the same name in the same context. Name conflict can arise when integrating two (or more) independently conceived sets of programs, sets of documents, file systems, databases, or indeed any collection of components that use the same naming scheme for internal interconnection as for integration. Name conflict can be a serious problem because fixing it requires changing some of the uses of the conflicting names. Making such changes can be awkward or difficult, for the authors of the original subsystems are not necessarily available to help locate, understand, and change the uses of the conflicting names.

The obvious way to implement modular sharing is to provide each subsystem with its own naming context, and then work out some method of cross-reference between the contexts. Getting the cross-reference to work properly turns out to be the challenge.

Consider, for example, the two sets of programs shown in Figure 3.1—a word processor and a spelling checker—each of which comprises modules linked by name and each of which has a component named INITIALIZE. The designer of the procedure WORD_PROCESSOR wants to use SPELL_CHECK as a component. If the designer tries to combine the two sets of programs by simply binding all of their names in one naming context, as in the figure (where the arrows show the binding of each name), there are two modules competing for binding of the name INITIALIZE. We have a name conflict.

So the designer instead tries to create a separate context for each set of programs, as in Figure 3.2. That step by itself doesn't completely address the problem because the program interpreter now needs some rule to determine which context to use

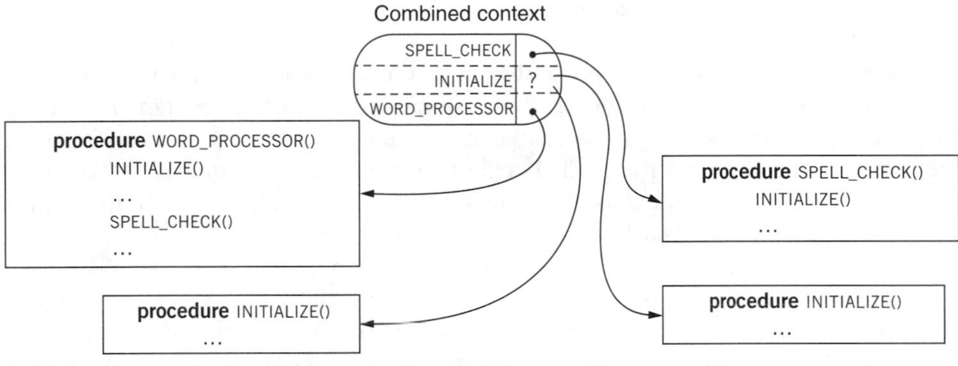

FIGURE 3.1

Too-simple integration of two independently written sets of programs by just merging their contexts. Procedure WORD_PROCESSOR calls SPELL_CHECK, but SPELL_CHECK has a component that has the same name as a component of WORD_PROCESSOR. No single set of bindings can do the right thing.

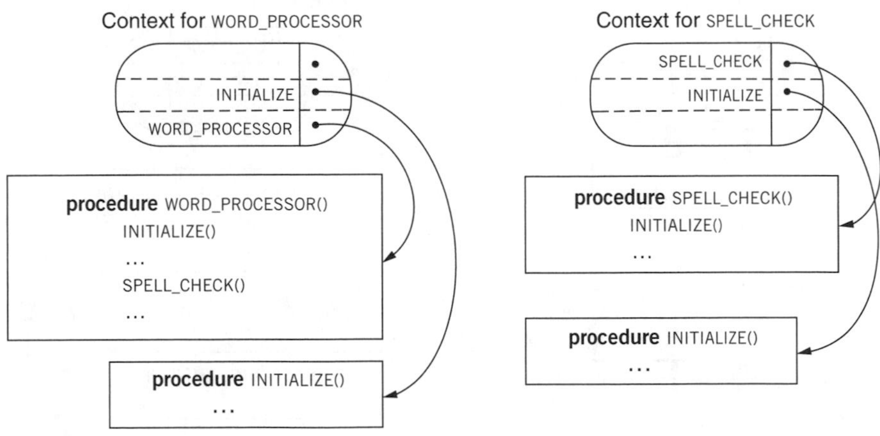

FIGURE 3.2

Integration of the same two programs but using separate contexts. Having a separate context for SPELL_CHECK eliminates the name conflict, but the program interpreter now needs some basis for choosing one context over the other.

for each use of a name. Suppose, for example, it is running WORD_PROCESSOR, and it encounters the name INITIALIZE. How does it know that it should resolve this name in the context of WORD_PROCESSOR rather than the context of SPELL_CHECK?

Following the naming model of Chapter 2, and the example of the e-mail system, a direct solution to this problem would be to add a binding for SPELL_CHECK in the WORD_PROCESSOR context and attach to every module an explicit context reference, as in Figure 3.3. This addition would require tinkering with the representation of the modules, an alternative that may not be convenient or even not allowed if some of the modules belong to someone else.

Figure 3.4 suggests another possibility: augment the program interpreter to keep track of the context in which it originally found each program. The program interpreter would use that context for resolving all names found in that program. Then, to allow the word processor to call the spell checker by name, place a binding for SPELL_CHECK in the WORD_PROCESSOR context as shown by the solid arrow numbered *1* in that figure. (imagine that the contexts are now file system directories).

That extra binding creates a subtle problem that may produce a later surprise. Because the program interpreter found SPELL_CHECK in the word processor's context, its context selection rule tells it (incorrectly) to use that context for the names it finds inside of SPELL_CHECK, so SPELL_CHECK will call the wrong version of INITIALIZE. A solution is to place an indirect name (the dashed arrow numbered *2* in Figure 3.2) in the word processor's context, bound to the name of SPELL_CHECK in SPELL_CHECK's own context. Then, the interpreter (assuming it keeps track of the context where it actually found each program) will correctly resolve names found in both groups of programs.

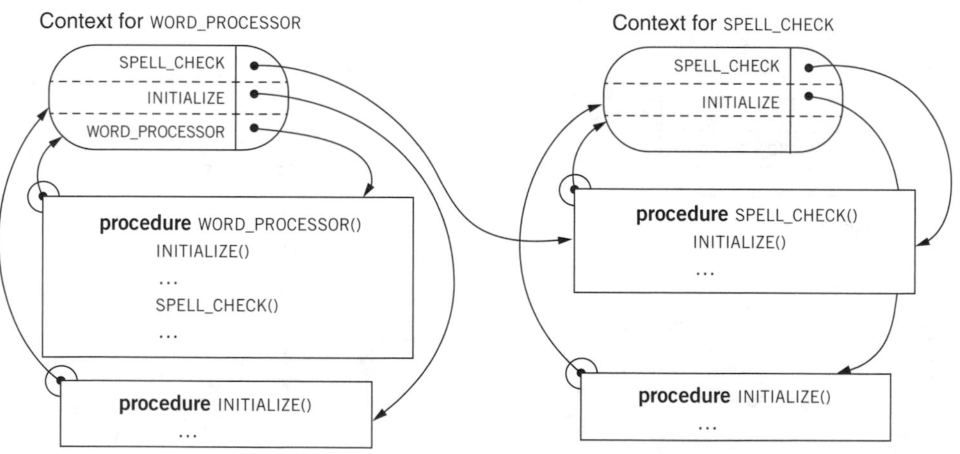

FIGURE 3.3

Modular sharing with explicit context references. The small circles added to each program module are context references that tell the name interpreter which context to use for names found in that module.

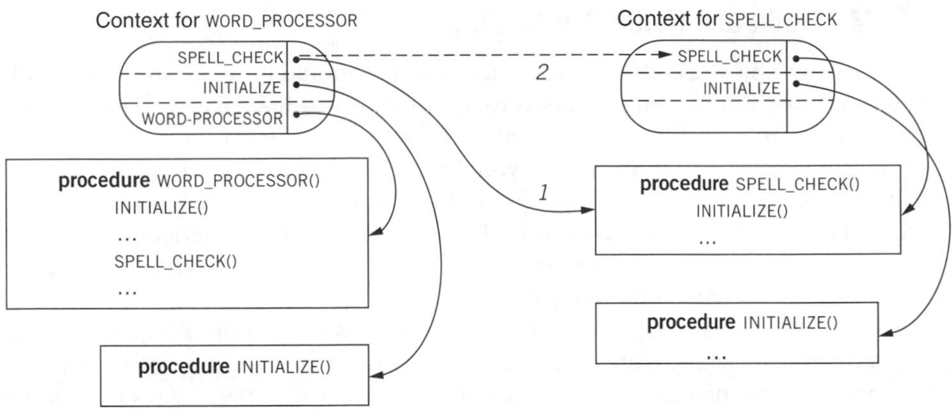

FIGURE 3.4

Integration with the help of separate contexts. Having a separate context for spell-check eliminates the name conflict, but the program interpreter still needs some basis for choosing one context over the other. Adding the solid arrow numbered *1* doesn't quite work, but the dashed arrow numbered *2*, an indirect name, does.

Keeping track of contexts and using indirect references (perhaps by using file system directories as contexts) is commonplace, but it is a bit *ad hoc*. Another, more graceful, way of attaching a context reference to an object without modifying its representation is to associate the name of an object not directly with the object itself but instead with a structure that consists of the original object plus its context reference. Some programming languages implement just such a structure for procedure definitions, known as a "closure", which connects each procedure definition with the naming context in which it was defined. Programming languages that use static scope and closures provide a much more systematic scheme for modular sharing of named objects within the different parts of a large application program, but comparable mechanisms are rarely found* in file systems or in merging applications such as the word processing and spell-checking systems of the previous example. One reason for the difference is that a program usually contains many references to lots of named objects, so it is important to be well organized. On the other hand, merging applications involves a small number of large components with only a few cross-references, so *ad hoc* schemes for modular sharing may seem to suffice.

*An ambitious attempt to design a naming architecture with all of these concepts wired into the hardware was undertaken by IBM in the 1970s, documented in a technical report by George Radin and Peter R. Schneider: *An architecture for an extended machine with protected addressing*, IBM Poughkeepsie Laboratory Technical Report TR 00.2757, May, 1976. Although the architecture itself never made it to the market, some of the ideas later appeared in the IBM System/38 and AS/400 computer systems.

3.1.2 Metadata and Name Overloading

The name of an object and the context reference that should be associated with it are two examples of a class of information called *metadata*—information that is useful to know about an object but that cannot be found inside the object itself (or if it is inside may not be easy to find). A library bibliographic record is a collection of metadata, including title, author, publisher, publication date, date of acquisition, and shelf location of a book, all in a standard format. Libraries have a lot of experience in dealing with metadata, but failure to systematically organize metadata is a design shortcoming frequently encountered in computer systems.

Some common examples of metadata associated with an object in a computer system are a user-friendly name, a unique identifier, the type of the object (executable program, word processing text, video stream, etc.), the dates it was created, last modified, and last backed up, the location of backup copies, the name of its owner, the program that created it, a cryptographic quality checksum (known as a *witness*—see Sidebar 7.1 [on-line]) to verify its integrity, the list of names of who is permitted to read or update the object, and the physical location of the representation of the object. A common, though not universal, property of metadata is that it is information about an object that may be changed without changing the object itself.

One strategy for maintaining metadata in a file system is to reserve storage for the metadata in the same file system structure that keeps track of the physical location of the file and to provide methods for reading and updating the metadata. This strategy is attractive because it allows applications that do not care about the metadata to easily ignore it. Thus, a compiler can read an input file without having to explicitly identify and ignore the file owner's name or the date on which the file was last backed up, whereas an automatic backup application can use the metadata access method to check those two fields. The UNIX file system, described in Section 2.5.1, uses this strategy by storing metadata in inodes.

Computer file systems nearly always provide for management of specialized metadata about each file such as its physical location, size, and access permissions, but they rarely have any provision for user-supplied metadata other than the file name. Because of this limitation, it is common to discover that file names are *overloaded* with metadata that has little or nothing to do with the use of the name as a reference.* The naming scheme may even impose syntax rules on allowable names to support overloading with metadata. A typical example of name overloading is a file name that ends with an extension that identifies the type of the file, such as text, word processing document, spreadsheet, binary application program, or movie. Other examples are illustrated in Figure 3.5. A physical address is another example of name overloading that is so common that the next section explores its special properties. Names that have no overloading whatever are known as *pure names*. The only operations it makes sense to apply to a pure name are COMPARE, RESOLVE, BIND, and UNBIND; one cannot

*Use of the word "overloading" to describe names that carry metadata is similar to, but distinct from, the use of the same word to describe symbols that stand for several different operators in a programming language.

Name	Some of the things that overload this name
solutions.txt	solutions = file content; txt = file format
solutions.txt.backup 2	backup 2 = this is the second backup copy
businessplan 10 26-2007.doc	10-26-2007 = when file was created
executive summary v4	v4 = version number
image079.large.jpg	079 = where file fits in a sequence; large = image size
/disk-07/archives/Alice/	disk-07 = physical device that holds file; Alice = user id
OSX.10.5.2.dmg	OSX = program name; 10.5.2 = program version
IPCC_report_TR-4	IPCC = author; TR-4 = technical report series identifier
cse.pedantic.edu	cse = department name; pedantic = university name; edu = registrar name
ax539&ttiejh!90rrwl	no (apparent) overloading

FIGURE 3.5

Some examples of overloaded names and a pure name.

extract metadata from it by applying a parsing operation. An overloaded name, on the other hand, can be used in two distinct ways:

1. As an identifier, using COMPARE, RESOLVE, BIND, and UNBIND.
2. As a source from which to extract the overloaded metadata.

Path names are especially susceptible to overloading. Because they describe a path through a series of contexts, the temptation is to overload them with information about the route to the physical location of the object.

Overloading of a name can be harmless, but it can also lead to violation of the principles of modular design and abstraction. The problem usually shows up in the form of a *fragile name*. Name fragility appears, for example, when it is necessary to change the name of a file that moves to a new physical location, even though the identity and content of the file have not changed. For example, suppose that a library program that calculates square roots and that happens to be stored on disk05 is named /disk05/library/sqrt. If disk05 later becomes too full and that library has to be moved to disk06, the path name of the program changes to /disk06/library/sqrt, and someone has to track down and modify every use of the old name. Name fragility is one of the reasons that World Wide Web addresses stop working. The case study in Section 3.2 explores that problem in more detail.

The general version of this observation is that overloading creates a tension between the goal of keeping names unchanged and the need to modify the overloaded information. Typically, a module that uses a name needs the name to remain unchanged for at least as long as that module exists. For this reason, overloading must be used with caution and with understanding of how the name will be used.

Finally, in a modular system, an overloaded name may be passed through several modules before reaching the module that actually knows how to interpret the overloading. A name is said to be *opaque* to a module if the name has no overloading that the module knows how to interpret. A pure name can be thought of as being opaque to all modules except RESOLVE.

There are also more subtle forms of metadata overloading. Overloading can be less obvious if the user's mind, rather than the computer system, performs the metadata extraction. For example, in the Internet host name "CityClerk.Reston.VA.US", the identifier of the context, "Reston.VA.US", is also recognizable as the identifier of a real place, a town named Reston, Virginia, in the United States. Each component of this name is being used to name two different real-world things: the name "Reston" identifies both a town and a table of name/value pairs that acts as a context in which the name of a municipal department may be looked up. Because it has mnemonic value, people find this reuse by overloading helpful—assuming that it is done accurately and consistently. (On the other hand, if someone names a World Wide Web service in Chicago "SaltLakeCity.net" people seeing that name are likely to assume—incorrectly—that it is actually located in Salt Lake City.)

3.1.3 Addresses: Names that Locate Objects

In a computer system, an *address* is the name of a physical location or of a virtual location that maps to a physical location. Computer systems are constructed of real physical objects, so they abound in examples of addresses: register numbers, physical and virtual memory addresses, processor numbers, disk sector numbers, removable media volume numbers, I/O channel numbers, communication link identifiers, network attachment point addresses, pixel positions on a display—the list seems endless.

Addresses are not pure names. The thing that characterizes an address is that it is overloaded in such a way that parsing the address provides a guide to the location of the named object in some virtual or real coordinate system. As with other overloaded names, addresses can be used in two ways, in this case:

1. As an identifier with the usual naming operations.
2. As a locator.

Thus, "Leonardo da Vinci" is an identifier that was once bound to a physical person and is now bound to the memory of that Leonardo. This identifier could have been used in comparisons to avoid confusion with Leonardo di Pisa when both of them were visiting Florence.* Today, the identifier helps avoid mixing up their writings. At the same time, "Leonardo da Vinci" is also a locator; it indicates that if you want to examine the birth record of that Leonardo, you should look in the archives of the town named Vinci.

Since access to many physical devices is geometric, addresses are often chosen from compact sets of integers in such a way that address adjacency corresponds to physical adjacency, and arithmetic operations such as "add 1" or subtracting one

*Actually, they could not have both visited Florence at the same time. The mathematician Leonardo di Pisa (also known as Fibonacci) lived three centuries before the artist Leonardo da Vinci.

address from another have a useful, physical meaning. For example, a seek arm finds track #1079 on a magnetic disk by counting the number of tracks it passes, and a disk arm scheduler looks at differences in track addresses to decide the best order in which to perform seeks. For another example, a memory chip contains an array of bits, each of which has a unique integer address. When a read or write request for a particular address arrives at the chip, the chip routes individual bits of that address to selectors that guide the flow of information to and from the intended bit of storage.

Sometimes it is inappropriate to apply arithmetic operations to addresses, even when they are chosen from compact sets of integers. For example, telephone numbers (known technically as "directory numbers") are integers that are overloaded with routing information in their area and exchange codes, but there is no necessary physical adjacency of two area codes that have consecutive addresses. Similarly, there is no necessary physical adjacency of two telephones that have consecutive directory numbers. (In decades past, there was physical adjacency of consecutive directory numbers inside the telephone switching equipment, but that adjacency was so constraining that it was abandoned by introducing a layer of indirection as part of the telephone switch gear.)

The overloaded location information found in addresses can cause name fragility. When an object moves, its address, and thus its name, changes. For this reason, system designers usually follow the example of telephone switching systems: they apply the design principle *decouple modules with indirection* to hide addresses. Adding a layer of indirection provides a binding from some externally visible, but stable, name to an address that can easily be changed when the object moves to a new location. Ideally, addresses never need to be exposed above the layer of interpretation that directly manipulates the objects. Thus, for example, the user of a personal computer that has a communication port may be able to write programs using a name such as `COM1` for the port, rather than a hexadecimal address such as $4D7C_{hex}$, which may change to $4D7E_{hex}$ when the port card is replaced.

When a name must be changed because it is being used as an address that is not hidden by a layer of indirection, things become more complicated and they may start to go wrong. At least four alternatives have been used in naming schemes:

- Search for and change all uses of the old address. At best, this alternative is a nuisance. In a large or geographically distributed system, it can be quite painful. The search typically misses some uses of the name, and those users, on their next attempted use of the name, either receive a puzzling not-found response for an object that still exists or, worse, discover that the old address now leads to a different object. For that reason, this scheme may be combined with the next one.

- Plan that users of the name must undertake an attribute-based search for the object if they receive a not-found response or detect that the address has been rebound to a different object. If the search finds the correct object, its new address can replace the old one, at least for that user. A different user will have to do another search.

- If the naming scheme provides either synonyms or indirect names, add bindings so that both the old and new addresses continue to identify the object. If addresses are scarce and must be reused, this alternative is not attractive.
- If the name is bound to an active agent, such as a post office service that accepts mail, place an active intermediary, such as a mail forwarder, at the old address.

None of these alternatives may be attractive. The better method is nearly always for the designer to hide addresses behind a layer of indirection. Section 3.3.2 provides an example of this problem and the solution using indirection. Exercise 2.1 explores some interesting indirection-related naming problems in the telephone system related to the feature known as call forwarding.

One might suggest avoiding the name fragility problem by using only pure names, that is, names with no overloading. The trouble with that approach is that it makes it difficult to locate the object. When the lowest-layer name carries no overloaded addressing metadata, the only way to resolve that name to a physical object is by searching through an enumeration of all the names. If the context is small and local, that technique may be acceptable. If the context is universal and widely distributed, name resolution becomes quite problematic. Consider, for example, the problem of locating a railway car, given only a unique serial number painted on its side. If for some reason you know that the car is on a particular siding, searching may be straightforward, but if the car can be anywhere on the continent, searching is a daunting prospect.

3.1.4 Generating Unique Names

In a unique identifier name space, some protocol is needed to ensure that all of the names actually are unique. The usual approach is for the naming scheme to *generate* a name for a newly created object, rather than relying on the creator to propose a unique name. One simple scheme for generating unique names is to dole out consecutive integers or sufficiently fine timestamp values. Sidebar 3.1 shows an example. Another scheme for generating unique names is to choose them at random from a sufficiently large name space. The idea is to make the probability of accidentally choosing the same name twice (a form of name conflict called a *collision*) negligibly small. The trouble with this scheme is that it is hard for a finite-state machine to create genuine randomness, so the chance of accidentally creating a name collision may be much higher than one would predict from the size of the name space. One must apply careful design, for example, by using a high-quality pseudorandom number generator and seeding it with a unique input such as a timestamp that was created when the system started. An example of such a design is the naming system used inside the Apollo DOMAIN operating system, which provided unique identifiers for all objects across a local-area network to provide a high-degree of transparency to users of the system; for more detail, see Suggestions for Further Reading 3.2.1.

Yet another way to avoid generated name collisions, for an object that has a binary representation and that already exists when it is being named, is to choose as its unique name the contents of the object. This approach assigns two objects with the same content the same name. In some applications, however, that may be a feature—it provides

Sidebar 3.1 Generating a Unique Name from a Timestamp Some banking systems generate a unique character-string name for each transaction. A typical name generation scheme is to read a digital clock to obtain a timestamp and convert the timestamp to a character string. A typical timestamp might contain the number of microseconds since January 1, 2000. A 50-bit timestamp would repeat after about 35 years, which may be sufficient for the bank's purpose. Suppose the timestamp at 1:35 P.M. on April 1, 2007, is

00010111110110101101001100111001100010111010011001

To convert this string of bits to a character string, divide it into five-bit chunks and interpret each chunk as an index into a table of 32 alphanumeric characters. The five-bit chunks are:

00010-11111-01101-01101-00110-01110-01100-01011-10100-11001

Next, reinterpret the chunks as index numbers:

2 31 13 13 6 16 12 11 20 25

Then look those numbers up in this table of 32 alphanumeric characters:

0	1	2	3	4	5	6	7	8	9	10	11	12	13	14	15	16	17	18	19	20	21	22	23	24	25	26	27	28	29	30	31
B	C	D	F	G	H	J	K	L	M	N	P	Q	R	S	T	U	V	W	X	Y	Z	1	2	3	4	5	6	7	8	9	0

The result is the 10-character unique name `"D9RRJ-UQTYP"`. You may have seen similar unique names in transactions performed with an on-line banking system.

a way of discovering the existence of unwanted duplicate copies. That name is likely to be fairly long, so a more practical approach is to use as the name a shorter version of its contents, known as a *hash*. For example, one might run the contents of a stored file through a cryptographic transformation function whose output is a bit string of modest, fixed length, and use that bit string as the name. One version of the Secure Hash Algorithm (SHA, described in Sidebar 11.8 [on-line]) produces, for any size of input, an output that is 160 bits in length. If the transforming function is of sufficiently high quality, two different files will almost certainly end up with different names.

The main problem with any naming scheme that is based on the contents of the named object is that the name is overloaded. When someone modifies an object whose name was constructed from its original contents, the question that arises is whether to change its name. This question does not come up in preservation storage systems that do not allow objects to be modified, so hash-generated unique names are sometimes used in those systems.

Unique identifiers and generated names can also be used in places other than unique identifier name spaces. For example, when a program needs a name for a temporary file, it may assign a generated name and place the file in the user's working directory. In this case, the design challenge for the name generator is to come up with an algorithm that will not collide with the names of already existing names chosen by people or generated by other automated name generators. Section 3.3.1 gives an example of a system that failed to meet this challenge.

Providing unique names in a large, geographically distributed system requires careful design. One approach is to create a hierarchical naming scheme. This idea takes advantage of an important feature of hierarchy: delegation. For example, a goal of the Internet is to allow creation of several hundred million different, unique names in a universal name space for attachment points for computers. If one tried to meet that goal by having someone at the International Telecommunications Union coordinating name assignment, the immense number of name assignments would almost certainly lead to long delays as well as mistakes in the form of accidental name collisions. Instead, some central authority assigns the name "edu" or "uk" and delegates the responsibility for naming things ending with that suffix to someone else—in the case of "edu", a specialist in assigning university names. That specialist accepts requests from educational institutions and, for example, assigns the name "pedantic" and thereby delegates the responsibility for names ending with the suffix ".pedantic.edu" to the Pedantic University network staff. That staff assigns the name "cse" to the Computer Science and Engineering Department, further delegating responsibility for names ending with the suffix ".cse.pedantic.edu" to someone in that department. The network manager inside the department can, with the help of a list posted on the wall or a small on-line database, assign a name such as "ginger" that is locally unique and at the same time can be confident that the fully qualified name "ginger.cse.pedantic.edu" is also globally unique.

A different example of a unique identifier name space is the addressing plan for the commercial Ethernet. Every Ethernet interface has a unique 48-bit *media access control* (MAC) *address*, typically set into the hardware by the manufacturer. To allow this assignment to be made uniquely, but without a single central registry for the whole world, there is a shallow hierarchy of MAC addresses. A standards-setting authority allocates to each Ethernet interface manufacturer a block of MAC addresses, all of which start with the same prefix. The manufacturer is then free to allocate MAC addresses within that block in any way that is convenient. If a manufacturer uses up all the MAC addresses in a block, it applies to the central authority for another block, which may have a prefix that has no relation to the previous prefix used by that same manufacturer.

One consequence of this strategy, especially noticeable in a large network, is that the MAC address of an Ethernet interface does not provide any overloading information that is useful for physically locating the interface card. Even though the MAC address is assigned hierarchically, the hierarchy is used only to delegate and thus decentralize address assignment, and it has no assured relation to any property (such as the physical place where the card attaches to the network) that would help locate it. Just as in locating a railway car knowing only its unique identifier, resolving a MAC address to the particular physical device that carries it is difficult unless one already has a good idea where to start looking.

People struggling to figure out how to tie a software license to a particular computer sometimes propose to associate the license with the Ethernet MAC address of that computer because that address is globally unique. Apart from the problem that some computers have no Ethernet interface and others have more than one, a trouble with this approach is that if an Ethernet interface card on the computer fails and needs to be replaced, the new card will have a different MAC address, even though the location of the system, the software, and its owner are unchanged. Furthermore, if the card that failed is later repaired and reinstalled in another system, that other system will now have the MAC address that was previously associated with the first system. The MAC address is thus properly viewed only as the unique name of a specific hardware component, not of the system in which it is embedded.

Deciding what constitutes the unique identity of a system that is constructed of replaceable components is ultimately a convention that requires an arbitrary choice by the designer of the naming scheme. This choice is similar to the question of establishing the identity of wooden ships. If, over the course of 300 years, every piece of wood in the ship has been replaced, is it still the same ship? Apparently, ship registries say "yes". They do not associate the name of the ship with any single component; the name is instead associated with the ship as a whole. Answering this identity question can clarify which of the three meanings of the COMPARE operation that was discussed in Section 2.2.5 is most appropriate for a particular design.

3.1.5 Intended Audience and User-Friendly Names

Some naming schemes are intended to be used by people. Names in such a name space are typically user-chosen and user-friendly strings of characters with mnemonic value such as "economics report", "shopping list", or "Joe.Smith" and are widely used as names of files and e-mailboxes. Ambiguity (that is, non-uniqueness) in resolving user-friendly names may be acceptable because in interactive systems the person using the name can be asked to resolve the ambiguity.

Other naming schemes are intended primarily for use by machines. In these schemes, the names need not have mnemonic value, so they are typically integers, often of fixed width designed to fit into a register and to allow fast and unambiguous resolution. Memory addresses and disk sector addresses are examples. Sometimes the term *identifier* is used for a name that is not intended to be intelligible to people, but this usage is by no means universal. Names intended for use by machines are usually chosen mechanically.

When a name is intended to be user-friendly, a tension arises between a need for it to be a unique, easily resolvable identifier and a need to respect other, non-technical values such as being easy to remember or being the same as some existing place or personal name. This tension may be resolved by maintaining a second, machine-oriented identifier, in addition to the user-friendly name—thus billing systems for large companies usually have both an account name and an account number. The second identifier can be unique and thus resolve ambiguities and avoid problems related to overloading of the account name. For example, personal names are usually overloaded with family history metadata (such as the surname, a given middle name that is the same as a mother's surname, or an appended "Jr." or "III"), and they are frequently not unique. Proposals to require that personal names be chosen uniquely always founder on cultural and personal identity objections. To avoid these problems, most systems that maintain personal records assign distinct unique identifiers to people, and include both the user-friendly name and the unique identifier in their metadata.

Another example of tension in the choice of user-friendly names is found in the use of capital and small letters. Up through the mid-1960s, computer systems used only capital letters, and printed computer output always seemed to be shouting. There were a few terminals and printers that had lower-case letters, but one had to write a device-dependent application to make use of that feature, just as today one has to write a device-dependent application to use a virtual reality helmet. In 1965, the designers of the Multics time-sharing system introduced lower-case alphabetics to names of the file system. This being the first time anyone had tried it, they got it wrong. The designers of the UNIX file system copied the mistake. In turn, many modern file systems copy the UNIX design in order to avoid changing a widely used interface. The mistake is that the names "Court docket 5" and "Court Docket 5" can be bound to different files. The resulting violation of the <u>*principle of least astonishment*</u> can lead to significant confusion, since the computer rigidly enforces a distinction that most people are accustomed to overlooking on paper. Systems that enforce this distinction are called *case-sensitive*.

A more user-friendly way to allow upper- and lower-case letters in names is to permit the user to specify a preferred combination of upper- and lower-case letters for storage and display of a name, but coerce all alphabetic characters to the same case when doing name comparisons. Thus, when another person types the name, the case does not have to precisely match the display form. Systems that operate this way are called *case-preserving*. Both the Internet Domain Name System (described in Section 4.4) and the Macintosh file system provide this more user-friendly naming interface. A less satisfactory way to reduce case confusion is *case-coercing*, in which all names are both coerced to and stored in one case. A case-coercing system constrains the appearance of names in a way that can interfere with good human engineering.

The case studies in Section 3.2 and the war stories in Section 3.3 describe some unusual results when a system design mixes case-sensitive and case-preserving naming systems.

User-friendly names are not always strings of characters. In a graphical user interface (GUI), the shape (and sometimes the position) of an icon on the display is an identifier that acts exactly like a name, even if a character string is not associated with it. What action the system undertakes when the user clicks the mouse depends on where the mouse cursor was at that instant, and in a video game the action may depend on what else is happening at the same time. The identifier is thus bound to a time and a position on the screen, and that combination of values is in turn an identifier that is bound to some action.

Another, similar example of a user-friendly name that does not take the form of a string of characters is the cross-linking system developed by the M.I.T. Shakespeare Project. In that system, hypertext links say where they are coming from rather than where they are going to. Resolution starts by looking up the identifier of the place where the link was found. The principle is identical to that of the GUI/mouse example, and the system is described in Sidebar 3.2.

Sidebar 3.2 Hypertext Links in the Shakespeare Electronic Archive There are many representations of all of Shakespeare's plays: a modern text, the sixteenth-century folios, and several movies. In addition, a huge amount of metadata is available about each play: commentaries, stage directions, photographs and sketches of sets, directors' notes, and so on. In the study of a play, it would be helpful if these various representations could be linked together, so that, for example, if one were interested in the line "Alas, poor Yorick! I knew him, Horatio" from *Hamlet*, one could quickly check the wording in the several editions, compare different movie clips of the presentation of that line, and examine commentaries and stage directions that pertain to that line.

The M.I.T. Shakespeare Project has developed a system intended to make this kind of cross-reference easy. The basic scheme is first to assign a line number to every line in the play and then index every representation of the play by line number. A user displays one representation, for example, the text of a modern edition, and selects a line. Because the edition is indexed by line number, that selection is a reference that is bound to the line number. The user then clicks on the selection, causing the system to look up the associated line number in one of several contexts, each context corresponding to one of the other representations. The user selects a context, and the system can immediately resolve the line number in that context and display that representation in a different window on the user's screen.

3.1.6 Relative Lifetimes of Names, Values, and Bindings

If names must be chosen from a name space of short, fixed-length strings of bits or characters, they are by nature *limited* in number. The designer may permanently bind the names of a limited name space, as in the case of the registers of a simple processor, which may, for example, run from zero to 31. If the names of a limited name space can be dynamically bound, they must be reused. Therefore, the naming scheme usually replaces the BIND and UNBIND operations with some kind of name allocation/deallocation procedure. In addition, the naming scheme for a limited name space typically assigns the names, rather than letting the user choose them. On the other hand, if the name space is *unlimited*, meaning that it does not significantly constrain name lengths, it is usually possible to allow the user to choose arbitrary names. Thus, the telephone system in North America uses a naming scheme with short, fixed-length names such as 208-555-0175 for telephone numbers, and the telephone company nearly always assigns the numbers. (Section 3.3.5 describes some of the resulting problems.) On the other hand, names in most modern computer file systems are for practical purposes unlimited, and the user gets to choose them.

A naming scheme, a name, the binding of that name to a value, and the value to which the name is bound can all have different lifetimes. Often, both names and values are themselves quite long-lived, but the bindings that relate one to the other are somewhat more transient. Thus, both personal names and telephone numbers are typically long-lived, but when a person moves to a different city, the telephone company will usually bind that personal name to a new telephone number and, after some delay, bind a new personal name to the old telephone number. In the same way, an application program and the operating system interfaces it uses may both be long-lived, but the binding that connects them may be established anew every time the program runs. Renewing the bindings each time the program is launched makes it possible to update the application program and the operating system independently. For another example, a named network service, such as `PostOffice.gov`, and a network attachment point, such as the Internet address 10.72.43.131, may both be long-lived, but the binding between them may change when the Post Office discovers that it needs to move that service to a different, more reliable computer, and it reassigns the old computer to a less important service.

When a name outlives its binding, any user of that name that still tries to resolve it will encounter a *dangling reference*, which is a use of a previously bound name that resolves either to a not-found result or to an irrelevant value. Thus, an old telephone number that rings in the wrong house or leads to a message saying "that number has been disconnected" is an example of a dangling reference. Dangling references are nearly always a concern when the name space is limited because names from limited name spaces must be reused. An object that incorrectly uses old names may make serious mistakes and even cause damage to an unrelated object that now has that name (for example, if the name is a physical memory address). In some cases, it may be possible to deal with dangling references by considering names to be simply hints that require verification. Thus when looking up the telephone number of a long-lost friend in a distant city, the first question when someone answers the phone at that number is something such as "are you the James Wilson who attended high school in . . . ?"

When a name space is unlimited and names are never reused, dangling references affect only the users of names that have for some reason been unbound from their former values. These dangling references can be less disruptive. For example, in a file system, an indirect name is one that is bound to some other (target) file system name. The indirect name becomes a dangling reference if someone removes the target name. Because an unbound indirect name simply produces a not-found result, it is more likely to be a nuisance than a source of damage. However, if someone accidentally or maliciously reuses the target name for a completely different file, the user of the indirect name could be in for a surprise.

When systems are large or distributed, however, a name, once bound and exported, tends to be discovered and remembered in widely dispersed places. That dispersion creates a need for stable bindings. This effect has been particularly noticed in the World Wide Web, whose design encourages the creation of cross-references to documents whose names are under someone else's control, with the result that cross-references often evolve into dangling references.

There is a converse to the dangling reference: when an object outlives every binding of a name to it, that object becomes what is known as an *orphan* or a *lost object* because no one can ever refer to it by name again. Lost objects can be a serious problem because there may be no good way to reclaim the physical storage they occupy. A system that regularly loses track of objects in this way is said to have a *storage leak*. To avoid lost objects, some naming schemes keep track of the number of bindings to each object, and, when an UNBIND operation causes that number to reach zero, the system takes the opportunity to reclaim the storage occupied by the object. We saw this reference counting scheme used for links in the case study in Section 2.5. It contrasts with *tracing garbage collection*, an alternative technique used in some programming languages that involves occasional exploration of the named connections among objects to see which objects can and cannot be reached. The UNIX file system, described in Section 2.5, uses reference counting for file objects.

3.1.7 Looking Back and Ahead: Names are a Basic System Component

In this and the previous chapter, we have explored both the underlying principles of, and many engineering considerations surrounding, the use of names, but we have only lightly touched on the applications of names in systems. Names are a fundamental building block in all system areas. Looking ahead, almost every chapter will develop techniques and methods that depend on the use of names, name spaces, and binding:

- In modularizing systems with clients and services (Chapter 4), clients need a way to name services.
- In modularizing systems with virtualization (Chapter 5), virtual memory is an address naming system.
- In enhancing performance (Chapter 6), caches are renaming devices.
- Data communication networks (Chapter 7 [on-line]) use names to identify nodes and to route data to them.
- In transactions (Chapter 9 [on-line]) it is frequently necessary to modify several distinct objects "at the same time", meaning that all the changes appear to happen in a single program step, an example of atomicity. One way to obtain this form of atomicity is by temporarily grouping copies of all the objects that are to be changed into a composite object that has a temporary, hidden name, modifying the copies, and then rebinding the composite object to a visible name. In this way, all of the changed components are revealed simultaneously.
- In security (Chapter 11 [on-line]), designers use *keys*, which are names chosen randomly from a very large and sparsely populated address space. The underlying idea is that if the only way to ask for something is by name, and you don't know and can't guess its name, you can't ask for it, so it is protected.

Name discovery, which was introduced in the preceding chapter, will reappear when we discuss information protection and security. When one user either tries to identify or grant permission to another named user, it is essential to know the authentic name of that other user. If someone can trick you into using the wrong name, you may grant permission to a user who shouldn't have it. That requirement in turn means that one needs to be able to trace the name discovery procedure back to some terminating direct communication step, verify that the direct communication took place in a credible fashion (such as examining a driver's license), and also evaluate the amount of trust to place in each of the other steps in the recursive name discovery protocol. Chapter 11 [on-line] describes this concern as the *name-to-key binding problem*.

Discovery of user names is one example in which authenticity is clearly of concern, but a similar authenticity concern can apply to any name binding, especially in systems shared by many users or attached to a network. If anyone can tinker with a binding, a user of that binding may make a mistake, such as sending something confidential to a hostile party. Chapter 11 [on-line] addresses in depth techniques of achieving authenticity. The User Internet Architecture research project uses such techniques to provide a secure, global naming system for mobile devices based on physical rendezvous and the trust found in social networks. For more detail, see Suggestions for Further Reading 3.2.5.

There is also a relation between uniqueness of names and security: If someone can trick you into using the same supposedly unique name for two different things, you may make a mistake that compromises security. The Host Identity Protocol addresses this problem by creating a name space of Internet hosts that is protected by cryptographic techniques similar to those described in Chapter 11 [on-line]. For more detail, see Internet Engineering Task Force *Request for Comments RFC 4423*.

This look ahead completes our introduction of concepts related to the design of naming systems. The next two sections of this chapter provide a case study of the relatively complex naming scheme used for pages of the World Wide Web, and a collection of war stories that illustrate what can go wrong when naming concepts fail to receive sufficient design consideration.

3.2 CASE STUDY: THE UNIFORM RESOURCE LOCATOR (URL)

The World Wide Web [see Suggestions for Further Reading 3.2.3] is a naming network with no unique root, potentially many different names for the same object, and complex context references. Its name-mapping algorithm is a conglomeration of several different component name-mapping algorithms. Let's fit it into the naming model.*

3.2.1 Surfing as a Referential Experience; Name Discovery

The Web has two layers of naming: an upper layer that is user-friendly, and a lower layer, which is also based on character strings, but is nevertheless substantially more mechanical.

*This case study informally introduces three message-related concepts that succeeding chapters will define more carefully: *client* (an entity that originates a request message); *server* (an entity that responds to a client's request); and *protocol* (an agreement on what messages to send and how to interpret their contents.) Chapter 4 expands on the client/service model, and Chapter 7 [on-line] expands the discussion of protocols.

At the upper layer, a Web page looks like any other page of illustrated text, except that one may notice what seem to be an unusually large number of underlined words, for example, Alice's page. These underlined pieces of text, as well as certain icons and regions within graphics, are labels for ***hyperlinks*** to other Web pages. If you click on a hyperlink, the browser will retrieve and display that other Web page. That is the user's view. The browser's view of a hyperlink is that it is a string in the current Web page written in HyperText Markup Language (HTML). Here is an example of a text hyperlink:

```
<a href="http://web.pedantic.edu/Alice/www/home.html">Alice's page</a>
```

Nestled inside this hyperlink, between the quotation marks, is a *Uniform Resource Locator* or, in Webspeak, a *URL*, which in the example is the name of another Web page at the lower naming layer. We can think of a hyperlink as binding a name (the underlined label) to a value (the URL) that is itself a name in URL name space. Since a context is a set of bindings of names to values, any page that contains hyperlinks can be thought of as a context, albeit not of the simple table-lookup variety. Instead, the name-mapping algorithm is one carried on in the mind of the user, matching ideas and concepts to the various hyperlink labels, icons, and graphics. The user does not usually traverse this naming network by typing path names, but rather by clicking on selected objects. In this naming network, a URL plays the role of a context reference for the links in the page fetched by the URL.

In order to retrieve a page in the World Wide Web, you need its URL. Many URLs can be found in hyperlinks on other Web pages, which helps if you happen to know the URL of one of those Web pages, but somewhere there must be a starting place. Most Web browsers come with one or more built-in Web pages that contain the URL of the browser maker plus a few other useful starting points in the Web. This is one way to get started on name discovery. Another form of name discovery is to see a URL mentioned in a newspaper advertisement.

3.2.2 Interpretation of the URL

In the example hyperlink above, we have an absolute URL, which means that the URL carries its own complete, explicit context reference:

```
http://web.pedantic.edu/Alice/www/home.html
```

The name-mapping algorithm for a URL works in several steps, as follows.

1. The browser extracts the part before the colon (here, `http`), considers it to be the name of a network protocol to use, and resolves that name to a protocol handler using a table-lookup context stored in the browser. The name of that context is built in to the browser. The interpretation of the rest of the URL depends on the protocol handler. The remaining steps describe the interpretation for the case of the hypertext transfer protocol (http) handler.

2. The browser takes the part between the // and the following / (in our example, that would be `web.pedantic.edu`) and asks the Internet Domain Name System (DNS) to resolve it. The value that DNS returns is an Internet address. Section 4.4

is a case study of DNS that describes in detail how this resolution works.

3. The browser opens a connection to the server at that Internet address, using the protocol found in step 1, and as one of the first steps of that protocol it sends the remaining part of the URL, `/Alice/www/home.html`, to the server.

4. The server looks for a file in its file system that has that path name.

5. If the name resolution of step 4 is successful, the server sends the file with that path name to the client. The client transforms the file into a page suitable for display.

(Some Web servers perform additional name resolution steps. The discussion in Section 3.3.4 describes an example.)

The page sent by the server might contain a hyperlink of its own such as the following:

```
<a href="contacts.html">How to contact Alice.</a>
```

In this case the URL (again, the part between the quotation marks) does not carry its own context. This abbreviated URL is called a *relative* or *partial* URL. The browser has been asked to interpret this name, and in order to proceed it must supply a default context. The URL specification says to derive a context from the URL of the page in which the browser found this hyperlink, assuming somewhat plausibly that this hypertext link should be interpreted in the same context as the page in which it was found. Thus it takes the original URL and replaces its last component (`home.html`) with the partial URL, obtaining

```
http://web.pedantic.edu/Alice/www/contacts.html
```

It then performs the standard name-mapping algorithm on this newly fabricated absolute URL, and it should expect to find the desired page in Alice's `www` directory.

A page can override this default context by providing something called a *base element* (e.g., `<base href="some absolute URL">`). The absolute URL in the base element is a context reference to use in resolving any partial URL found on the page that contains the base element.

3.2.3 URL Case Sensitivity

Multiple naming schemes are involved in the Web naming algorithm, as is clear by noticing that some parts of a URL are case sensitive and other parts are not. The result can be quite puzzling. The host name part of a Uniform Resource Locator (URL) is interpreted by the Internet Domain Name System, which is case-insensitive. The rest of the URL is a different matter. The protocol name part is interpreted by the client browser, and case sensitivity depends on its implementation. (Check to see if a URL starting with `"HTTP://"` works with your favorite Web browser.) The Macintosh implementation of Firefox treats the protocol name in a case-preserving fashion, but the now-obsolete Macintosh implementation of Internet Explorer is case-coercing.

The more interesting case-sensitivity questions come after the host name. The Web specifies that the server should interpret this part of the URL using a scheme that depends on the protocol. In the case of the HTTP protocol, the URL specification is insistent that this string is *not* a UNIX file name, but it is silent on case sensitivity. In practice, most systems interpret this string as a path name in their file system, so case-sensitivity depends on the file system of the server. Thus if the server is running a standard UNIX system, the path name is case-sensitive, while if the server is a standard Macintosh, the path name is case-preserving. There are examples that mix things up even further; Section 3.3.4 describes one such example.

3.2.4 Wrong Context References for a Partial URL

The practice of interpreting URL path names as path names of the server's file system can result in unexpected surprises. As described earlier, the Web browser supplies a default context reference for relative names (that is, partial URLs) found in Web pages. The default context reference it supplies is simply the URL that the browser used to retrieve the page that contained the relative name, truncated back to the last slash character. This context reference is the name of a directory at the server that should be used to resolve the (first component of) the relative name.

Some servers provide a URL name space by simply using the local (for example, UNIX) file system name space. When the local file system name space allows synonyms (symbolic links and the Network File System mounts described in Section 4.5 are two examples) for directory names, the mapping of local file system name space to the URL name space is not unique. Thus, several different URLs can have different path names for the same object. For example, suppose that there is a UNIX file system with a symbolic link named `/alice/home.html` that is actually an indirect reference to the file named `/alice/www/home.html`. In that case, the URLs

1 `<http://web.pedantic.edu/alice/home.html>`

and

2 `<http://web.pedantic.edu/alice/www/home.html>`

refer to the same file. Trouble can arise when the object that has multiple URLs is a directory whose name is used as a context reference. Continuing the example, suppose that file `home.html` contains the hyperlink `<a href = "contacts.html">`. Both `home.html` and `contacts.html` are stored in the directory `/alice/www`. Suppose further that the browser obtained `home.html` by using the URL *1* above.

Now, the user clicks on the hyperlink containing the partial URL `contacts.html`, asking the browser to resolve it. Following the usual procedure, the browser materializes a default context reference by truncating the original URL to obtain:

```
http://web.pedantic.edu/alice/
```

and then uses this name as a context by concatenating the partial URL:

```
http://web.pedantic.edu/alice/contacts.html
```

This URL will probably produce a not-found response because the file we are looking for actually has the path name `/alice/www/contacts.html`. Or worse, this request could return a different file that happens to be named `contacts.html` in the directory `/alice`. The confusion may be compounded if the different file with the same name turns out to be an out-of-date copy of the current `contacts.html`. On the other hand, if the user originally used URL *2*, the browser would retrieve the file named `/alice/www/contacts.html`, as the Web page designer expected.

A similar problem can arise when interpreting the relative name "..". This name is, conventionally, the name for the parent directory of the current directory. The UNIX system provides a semantic interpretation: look up the name ".." in the current directory, where by convention it evaluates (in inode name space) to the parent directory. In contrast, the Web specifies that ".." is a syntactic signal that means "modify the default context reference by discarding the least significant component of the path name." Despite these drastically different interpretations of "..", the result is usually the same because the parent of an object is usually the thing named by the next-earlier component of that object's path name. The exception (and the problem) arises when the Web's syntactic modification rule is applied to a path name with a component that is an indirect name for a directory. If the path name in the URL does not traverse the directory's parent, syntactic interpretation of ".." creates a default context reference different from the one that would be supplied by semantic interpretation.

Suppose, in our example, that the file `home.html` contains the hyperlink `<a href="../phone.html">`. If the user who reached home.html via URL *1* clicks on this hyperlink, the browser will truncate that URL and concatenate it with the partial URL, to obtain

```
http://web.pedantic.edu/alice/../phone.html
```

and then use the syntactic interpretation of `".."` to produce the URL

```
http://web.pedantic.edu/phone.html
```

another non-existent file. Again, if the user had started with URL *2*, the result of syntactic interpretation of `".."` would be to request the file

```
http://web.pedantic.edu/alice/phone.html
```

as originally intended.

This problem could be fixed in at least three different ways:

1. Arrange things so that the default context reference always works.
   a. Always install a UNIX link to the referenced page in the directory that held the referring page. (Or never use UNIX links at all.)
   b. Never use ".." in hyperlinks.

2. Do a better of job of choosing a default context reference.
   a. The client sends the original URL plus the Web link to the server and lets the server figure out what context to use.
3. Provide an explicit context reference.
   a. The server places an absolute URL in a location field of the protocol header.
   b. The client uses that URL as the context reference.

One might suggest that the implementer of the server (or the writer of the pages containing the relative links) failed to heed the following warning in the Web URL specification* for path names: "The similarity to unix and other disk operating system filename conventions should be taken as purely coincidental, and should not be taken to indicate that URIs should be interpreted as file names."

This warning is technically correct, but the suggestion is misleading. Unfortunately, the problem is built in to the Web naming specifications. Those specifications require that relative names be interpreted syntactically, yet they do not require that every object have a unique URL. Unambiguous syntactic interpretation of relative names requires that the context reference be a unique path name. Since the browser derives the context reference from the path name of the object that contained the relative name, and that object's path name does not have to be unique, it follows that syntactic interpretation of relative names will intrinsically be ambiguous. When servers try to map URL path names to UNIX path names, which are not unique, they are better characterized as exposing, rather than causing, the problem.

That analysis suggests that one way to conquer the problem is to change the way in which the browser acquires the context reference. If the browser could somehow obtain a canonical path name for the context reference, the same canonical path name that the UNIX system uses to reach the directory from the root, the problem would vanish.

3.2.5 Overloading of Names in URLs

Occasionally, one will encounter a URL that looks something like

```
http://www.amazon.com/exec/obidos/ASIN/0670672262/o/qid=
  921285151/sr=2-2/002-7663546-7016232
```

or perhaps

```
http://www.google.com/search?hl=en&q=books+about+systems&btnG=
  Google+Search&aq=f&oq=
```

Here we have two splendid examples of overloading of names. The first example is of a shopping service. Because the server cannot depend on the client to maintain any state about this shopping session other than the URL of the Web page currently being displayed, the server has encoded the state of the shopping session, in the form of an identifier of a state-maintaining file at the server, in the path name part of the URL.

*Tim Berners-Lee, *Universal Resource Identifiers: Recommendations*.

The second example is of a search service; the browser has encoded the user's search query into the path name part of the URL it has submitted. The tip-off here is the question mark in the middle of the name, which is a syntactic trick to alert the server that the string up to the question mark is the name of a program to be launched, while the string after the question mark is an argument to be given to that program. To see what processing www.google.com does to respond to such a query, see Suggestions for Further Reading 3.2.4.

There is another form of overloading in many URLs: they concatenate the name of a computer site with a path name of a file, neither of which is a particularly stable identifier. Consider the following name for an earthquake information service:

```
http://HPserver14.pedantic.edu/disk05/science/geophysics/
  quakes.html
```

This name is at risk of change if the HP computer is replaced by a Sun server, if the file server is moved to `disk04`, if the geophysics department is renamed "geology" or moves out of the school of science, or if the responsibility for the earthquake server moves to the Institute for Scholarly Studies. A URL such as this example frequently turns out to be unresolvable, even though the page it originally pointed to is still out there somewhere, perhaps having moved to a different site or simply to a different directory at the original site.

One way to avoid trapping the name of a site in the URLs that point to it is to choose a service name and arrange for DNS to bind that service name as an indirect name for the site. Then, if it becomes necessary to move the Web site to a different computer, a change to the binding of the service name is all that is needed for the old URLs to continue working. Similarly, one can avoid trapping an overloaded path name in a URL by judicious use of indirect file names. Thus the name

```
http://quake.org/library/quakes.html
```

could refer to the same Web page, yet it can remain stable through a wide variety of changes.

Considerable intellectual energy has been devoted to inventing a replacement for the URL that has less overloading and is thus more robust in the face of changes of server site and file system structure. Several systems have been proposed: *Permanent URL* (PURL), *Universal Resource Name* (URN), *Digital Object Identifier* (DOI)®, and *handle*. To date, none of these proposals has yet achieved wide enough adoption to replace the URL.

3.3 WAR STORIES: PATHOLOGIES IN THE USE OF NAMES

Although designing a naming scheme seems to be a straightforward exercise, it is surprisingly difficult to meet all of the necessary requirements simultaneously. The following are several examples of strange and sometimes surprising results that have been noticed in deployed naming schemes.

3.3.1 A Name Collision Eliminates Smiling Faces

A west coast university provides a "visual class list" Web interface that instructors can use to obtain the names and photos of all the students enrolled in a particular section of a class. At the beginning of the fall 2004 teaching term, instructors noticed that their classes had several photographs of the same individual. One might believe a section includes a set of triplets, but not triskaidekatuplets.

What went wrong: When there is no picture available for a student, the system inserts an image of a smiley face with the words "No picture available". The system designer stored the image in a file named "smiley.jpg". That fall a new freshman whose last name was Smiley registered the user name "smiley". As one might expect, the freshman's photograph was named "smiley.jpg", and it became the "No picture available" image.

3.3.2 Fragile Names from Overloading, and a Market Solution

Internet mailbox names such as `Alice@Awesome.net` can be viewed as two-component addresses. The component before the @-sign identifies a particular mailbox, and the component after the @-sign is an Internet domain name that identifies the Internet service provider (ISP) that provides that mailbox. When two ISPs (say, `Awesome.net` and `Awful.net`) merge, the customers of one of them (and sometimes both) typically receive a letter telling them that their mailbox address, which contained some representation of the name of their former ISP, will have to change. The new ISP may automatically forward mail addressed to the old address, or it may require that the user notify all of his or her correspondents of the new mailbox address. The reason for the change is that the second component of the old mailbox name was overloaded with a trademark. The new provider does not want to continue using that old trademark, and the old provider may not want to see the trademark used by the new provider.

Alice may also find, to her disappointment, that not only does the domain name of her mailbox change from `Awesome.net` to `Awful.net`, but that in `Awful.net`'s mailbox name space, another customer has already captured the personal mailbox name `Alice`, so she may even have to choose a new personal mailbox name, such as `Alice24`.

As the Internet grows, some ISPs have prospered and others have not, so there have been many mergers and buyouts. The resulting fragility of e-mail service provider names has created a market for indirect domain names. The customers in this market are users who require a stable e-mail address, such as people who run private businesses or who have a large number of correspondents. For an annual fee, an indirect name provider will register a new domain name, such as `Alice.com`, and configure a DNS name server so that the mailbox name `Alice@Alice.com` becomes a synonym for `Alice@Awesome.Net`. Then, upon being notified of the ISP merger, Alice simply asks the indirect name provider to rebind the mailbox name `Alice@Alice.com` to `Alice24@Awful.net`, and her correspondents don't have to know that anything happened.

3.3.3 More Fragile Names from Overloading, with Market Disruption

The United States Post Office assigns postal delivery codes, called Zip codes, hierarchically, so that it can take advantage of the hierarchy in routing mail. Zip codes have five digits. The first digit identifies one of 10 national areas; New England is area 0 and California, Washington, and Oregon comprise area 9. The next two digits identify a section. The South Station Postal Annex in Boston, Massachusetts, is the headquarters of section 021. All Zip codes beginning with those three digits have their mail sorted at that sectional center. Zip codes beginning with 024 identify the Waltham, Massachusetts, section. The last two digits of the Zip code identify a specific post office (known as a station), such as Waban, Massachusetts, 02468. Zip codes can also have four appended digits (called Zip + 4) that are used to sort mail into delivery order for each mail carrier. Although they are numerical, adjacent zip codes are not necessarily assigned to adjacent stations or adjacent sections, so they are really names rather than physical addresses. Despite not being interpretable as physical addresses, these names are overloaded with routing information.

Although routing is hierarchical, apparently the 10 national areas have no routing significance; everything is done by section. It is reported that if you walk into the South Station Postal Annex in Boston, you will find that outgoing mail is being sorted into 999 bins, one for each sectional center, nationwide. In addition, for mail addressed with Zip codes beginning with 021 (that is, within the South Station section) there are 99 bins, one for each station within the section. The mail in the outgoing bins goes into bags, with each bag containing mail for one section. Then all the bags for Southern California sections, for example, go into the same truck to the airport, where they go onto a plane to Los Angeles. As they come off the plane in Los Angeles, they are loaded onto different trucks that go to the various Southern California sections. The mail in the 99 bins for section 021 also goes into bags, with each bag destined for a different post office within the 021 section.

Mail that originates at a post office and is destined for the same post office still goes to the sectional center for sorting because individual post offices don't have the automatic sorting machines that can put things into delivery order. There used to be many exceptions to the rule that all mail goes to a sectional center, but the number of exceptions has been gradually reduced over the years.

When the volume of mail handled by the South Station Postal Annex began to exceed its capacity in the late 1990s, the Post Office decided to transfer part of that section's work to the newer Waltham, Massachusetts, section. Since the first three digits of the Zip code are overloaded with routing information, to accomplish this change it announced that about half of the Zip codes that began with 021 would, on July 1, 1998, change to 024. The result, as one might expect, was rather chaotic. The Post Office tried to work with large mailers to have them automatically update their address records, but loose ends soon appeared.

For example, American Express, a credit card company, installed a Zip code translator in its mail label printing system, so that its billing statements would go directly to the Waltham section, but it did not change its internal customer address records because its computer system flags all address changes as "moves", which affect verification procedures as well as credit ratings. So everything that American Express mailed was addressed properly, but their internal records retained the old Zip codes.

Now comes the problem: some Internet vendors will not accept a credit card unless the shipping address is identical to the credit card address. Customers began to encounter situations in which the Internet vendor rejected the Zip code 02168 as being an invalid delivery address, and American Express rejected the Zip code 02468 because it did not match its customer record. When this situation arose, it was not possible to complete a purchase without human intervention.

Despite the vendor check that identifies 02168 as invalid, mail addressed with that Zip code continued to be correctly delivered to addresses in Waban for several years. It just took an extra day to be delivered because it went first to the South Station Postal Annex, which simply forwarded it to the Waltham sectional center. The renaming was done not because the post office was running out of Zip codes, but rather because the sorting capacity of one of its sectional centers was exceeded.

3.3.4 Case-Sensitivity in User-Friendly Names

Even though, as described on page 128, the UNIX system propagated case-sensitive file names to many other file systems, not all widely used naming schemes are case-sensitive. The Internet generally is case-preserving. For example, in the Internet Domain Name System described in Section 4.4, one can open a network connection to `cse.pedantic.edu` or to `CSE.Pedantic.edu`; both refer to the same destination. The Internet mail system is also specified to be case-preserving, so you can send mail to `alice@pedantic.edu`, `Alice@pedantic.edu`, and `aLiCe@pedantic.edu`, and all three messages should go to the same mailbox.

In contrast, the Kerberos authentication system (described in Sidebar 11.6 [on-line]) is case-sensitive, so the names "alice" and "Alice" can identify different users. The rationale for this decision is muddy. Requiring that the case accurately match makes it harder for an intruder to guess a user's name, so one can argue that this decision enhances security. But allowing "alice" and "Alice" to identify different users can lead to serious mistakes in setting up permissions, so one can also argue that this decision weakens security. This decision comes to a head, for example, in the implementation of a mail delivery service with Kerberos authentication. It is not possible to correctly do a direct mapping of Kerberos user names to mailbox names because the necessary coercion might merge the identities of two distinct users.

A mixed example is a service-naming service developed at M.I.T. and called Hesiod, which uses the Internet Domain Name System (DNS) as a subsystem. One of the kinds of services Hesiod can name is a remote file system. DNS (and thus Hesiod) is case-insensitive, while file system names in UNIX systems are case-sensitive. This difference leads to another example of a user interface glitch. If a user asks to attach a remote file system, specifying its Hesiod name, Hesiod will locate the file system using whatever case the user typed, but the UNIX `mount` command mounts the file system using the name coerced to lower case. Thus if the user says, for example, to mount the remote file system named `CSE`, Hesiod will locate that remote file system, but the UNIX system will mount it using the name `cse`. To use this directory in a file name, the user must then type its name in lower case, which may come as a surprise.

Hesiod is used as a subsystem in larger systems, so the mixing of case-sensitive and case-insensitive names can become worse. For example, the current official M.I.T. Web server responds to the URL

```
http://web.mit.edu/Alice/www/home.html
```

by first trying a simple path name resolution of the string `/Alice/www/home.html`. If it gets a NOT-FOUND result from the resolution of that path name, it extracts the first component of the path name (`Alice`) and presents it to the Hesiod service naming system, with a request to interpret it as a remote file system name. Since Hesiod is case-insensitive, it doesn't matter whether the presented name is `Alice`, `alice`, or `aLiCe`. Whatever the case of the name presented, Hesiod coerces it to a standard case, and then it returns the standard file system path name of the corresponding remote file system directory, which for this example might be

```
/afs/athena/user/alice
```

The Web server then replaces the original first component (`Alice`) with this path name and attempts to resolve the path name:

```
/afs/athena/user/alice/www/home.html
```

Thus for the current M.I.T. Web server, the first component name after the host name in a URL is case-insensitive, while the rest of the name is case-sensitive.

3.3.5 Running Out of Telephone Numbers

"Nynex is Proposing New '646' Area Code for Manhattan Lines"

— headline, *Wall Street Journal,* March 3, 1997

The North American telephone numbering plan name space is nicely hierarchical, which would seem to make it easy to add phone numbers. Although this appears to be an example of an unlimited name space, it is not. It is hierarchical, but the hierarchy is rigid—there is a fixed number of levels, and each level has a fixed size.

Much of Europe does it the other way. In some countries it seems that every phone number has a different number of digits. A variable-length numbering plan has a downside. The telephone numbers are longest in the places that grew the most and thus have the most telephone calls. In addition, because the central exchange can't find the end of a variable-length telephone number by counting digits, some other scheme is necessary, such as noticing that the user has stopped dialing for a while.

A European-style solution to the shortage of phone numbers in Manhattan would be to simply announce that from now on, all numbers in Manhattan will be 11 digits long. But since the entire American telephone system assumes that telephone numbers are exactly 10 digits long, the American solution is to introduce a new area code.

A new area code can be introduced in one of two ways: *splitting* and *overlay*. Traditionally, the phone companies have used only splitting, but overlay is beginning to receive wider attention.

Splitting (sometimes called partition) is done by drawing a geographical line across the middle of the old area code—say 84th street in Manhattan—and declaring that everyone north of that line is now in code 646 and everyone south of that line will remain in code 212. When splitting is used, no one "changes" their seven-digit number, but many people must learn a new number when calling someone else. For example,

- Callers from Los Angeles who used to dial (212)-xxx-xxxx must now dial (646)-xxx-xxxx if they are calling to a phone north of 84th street, but they must use the old area code for phones located south of 84th street.
- Calling from one side of 84th street to the other now requires adding an area code, where previously a seven-digit number was all one had to dial.

In the alternative scheme, overlay, area code 212 would continue to cover all of Manhattan, but when there weren't any phone numbers left in that area code, the telephone companies would simply start assigning new numbers with area code 646. Overlay places a burden on the switching system, and it wouldn't have worked with the step-by-step switches developed in the 1920s, in which the telephone number described the route to that telephone. When the Bell System started to design the crossbar switches introduced in the 1940s, it realized that this inflexibility was a killer problem, so it introduced a number-to-route lookup—a name-resolving system called a *translator*—as part of switch design. With modern computer-based switches, translation is easy. So there is now nothing (but old software) to prevent two phones served by the same switch from having numbers with different area codes.

Overlay sounds like a great idea because it means that callers from Los Angeles continue to dial the same numbers they have always dialed. However, as in most engineering trade-offs, someone loses. Everyone in Manhattan now has to dial a 10-digit number to reach other places in Manhattan. One no longer can tell what the area code is by the geographic location of the phone. One also can't pinpoint the location of the target by its area code because the area code has lost its status as geographic metadata. This could be a concern if people become confused as to whether or not they were making a toll call.

Another possibility would be to use as a default context the area code of the originating phone. If calling from a 212 phone, one wouldn't have to dial an area code to call another 212 number. The prevailing opinion—which may be wrong—is that people can't handle the resulting confusion. Two phones on the same desk, or two adjacent pay phones, may have different area codes, and thus to call someone in the next office one might have to dial different numbers from the two phones.

Here is one way of coping: BankBoston (long since merged into larger banks) once arranged that the telephone number 788-5000 ring its customer service center from every area code in the state of Massachusetts. The nationwide toll-free number (800) 788-5000 also rang there. Although that arrangement did not completely eliminate name translation, it reduced it significantly and made the remaining name translation simple enough that people could actually remember how to do it.

Requiring that all numbers be dialed with all 10 digits encourages a more coherent model: the number you dial to reach a particular target phone does not depend on the number from which you are calling. The trade-off is that every North American number dialed would require 10 digits, even when calling the phone next door. The North American telephone system has been gradually moving in this direction for a long time. In many areas, it was once possible to call people in the same exchange simply by dialing just the last four digits of their number. Then it took five digits. Then seven. The jump to 10 would thus be another step in the sequence.

The newspaper also reports that at the rate telephone numbers are being used up in Manhattan, another area code will be needed within a few years. That observation would seem to affect the decision. Splitting is disruptive every time, but overlay is disruptive only the first time it is done. If there is going to be another area code needed that soon, it might be better to use overlay at the earliest opportunity, since adding still more area codes with overlay will cause no disruption at all.

Overlay is already widely used. Manhattan cell phones and beepers have long used area code 917, and little confusion resulted. Also, in response to an outcry over "yet another number change", in 1997 the Commonwealth of Massachusetts began requiring that future changes to its telephone numbering plan be done with overlay.

EXERCISES

3.1 Alyssa asks you for some help in understanding how metadata is handled in the UNIX file system, as described in Section 2.5.

3.1a Where does the UNIX system store system metadata about a file?

3.1b Where does it store user metadata about the file?

3.1c Where does it store system metadata about a file system?

2008-0-1

3.2 Bob and Alice are using a UNIX file system as described in Section 2.5. The file system has two disks, mounted as `/disk1` and `/disk2`. A system administrator creates a "home" directory containing symbolic links to the home directories of Bob and Alice via the commands:

```
mkdir /home
ln -s /disk1/alice /home/alice
ln -s /disk2/bob /home/bob
```

Subsequently, Bob types the following to his shell:

```
cd /home/alice
cd ../bob
```

and receives an error.

Which of the following best explains the problem?

A. The UNIX file system forbids the use of ".." in a cd command when the current working directory contains a symbolic link.

B. Since Alice's home directory now has two parents, the system complains that ".." is ambiguous in that directory.

C. In Alice's home directory, ".." is a link to `/disk1`, while the directory "bob" is in `/disk2`.

D. Symbolic links to directories on other disks are not supported in the UNIX file system; their call-by-name semantics allows their creation but causes an error when they are used.

2007-1-7

3.3 We can label the path names in the previous question as *semantic* path names. If Bob types `"cd .."` while in working directory `d`, the command changes the working directory to the directory in which `d` was created. To make the behavior of `".."` more intuitive, Alice proposes that `".."` should behave in path names *syntactically*. That is, the parent of a directory `d`, `d/..` is the same directory that would obtain if we instead referred to that directory by removing the last path name component of `d`. For example, if Bob's current working directory is `/a/b/c` and Bob types `"cd .."`, the result is exactly as if Bob had executed `"cd /a/b"`

3.3a If the UNIX file system were to implement syntactic path names, in which directory would Bob end up after typing the following two commands?

```
cd /home/alice
cd ../bob
```

3.3b Under what circumstances do semantic path names and syntactic path names provide the same behavior?

A. When the name space of the file system forms an undirected graph.

B. When the name space of the file system forms a tree rooted at "/".

C. When there are no synonyms for directories.

D. When symbolic links, like hard links, can be used as synonyms only for files.

3.3c Bob proposes the following implementation of syntactic names. He will first rewrite a path name syntactically to eliminate the "..", and then resolve the rewritten path name forward from the root. Compared to the implementation of semantic path names as described in Section 2.5, what is a disadvantage of this syntactic implementation?

A. The syntactic implementation may require many more disk accesses than for semantic path names.

B. This cost of the syntactic implementation scales linearly with the number of path name components.

C. The syntactic implementation doesn't work correctly in the presence of hard links.

D. The syntactic implementation doesn't resolve "." correctly in the current working directory.

2007-0-1

3.4 The inode of a file plays an important role in the UNIX file system. Which of these statements is true of the inode data structure, as described in Section 2.5?

A. The inode of a file contains a reference count.

B. The reference count of the inode of a directory should not be larger than 1.

C. The inode of a directory contains the inodes of the files in the directory.

D. The inode of a symbolic link contains the inode number of the target of the link.

E. The inode of a directory contains the inode numbers of the files in the directory.

F. The inode number is a disk address.

G. A file's inode is stored in the first 64 bytes of the file.

2005-1-4, 2006-1-1, and 2008-1-3

3.5 Section 3.3.1 describes a name collision problem. What could the designer of that system have done differently to eliminate (or reduce to a negligible probability) the possibility of this problem arising?

2008-0-2

Additional exercises relating to Chapter 3 can be found in the problem sets beginning on page 425.

CHAPTER

Enforcing Modularity with Clients and Services

4

CHAPTER CONTENTS

Principles of Computer System Design: An Introduction

DOI: 10.1016/B978-0-12-374957-4.00012-8

OVERVIEW

The previous chapters established that dividing a system into modules is good and showed how to connect modules using names. If all of the modules were correctly implemented, the job would be finished. In practice, however, programmers make errors, and without extra thought, errors in implementation may too easily propagate from one module to another. To avoid that problem, we need to strengthen the modularity. This chapter introduces a stronger form of modularity, called *enforced modularity*, that helps limit the propagation of errors from one module to another. In this chapter we focus on software modules. In Chapter 8 [on-line] we develop techniques to handle hardware modules.

One way to limit interactions between software modules is to organize systems as clients and services. In the client/service organization, modules interact only by sending messages. This organization has three main benefits:

- Messages are the only way for a programmer to request that a module provide a service. Limiting interactions to messages makes it more difficult for programmers to violate the modularity conventions.
- Messages are the only way for errors to propagate between modules. If clients and services fail independently and if the client and the service check messages, they may be able to limit the propagation of errors.
- Messages are the only way for an attacker to penetrate a module. If clients and services carefully check the messages before they act on them, they can block attacks.

Because of these three benefits, system designers use the client/service organization as a starting point for building modular, fault tolerant, and secure systems.

Designers use the client/service model to separate larger software modules, rather than, say, individual procedures. For example, a database system might be organized as clients that send messages with queries to a service that implements a complete database management system. As another example, an e-mail application might be organized into readers—the clients—that collect e-mail from a service that stores mailboxes.

One effective way to implement the client/service model is to run each client and service module in its own computer and set up a communication path over a wire between the computers. If each module has its own computer, then if one computer (module) fails, the other computer (module) can continue to operate. Since the only communication path is that wire, that is also the only path by which errors can propagate.

Section 4.1 of this chapter shows how the client/service model can enforce modularity between modules. Section 4.2 presents two styles of sending and receiving messages: remote procedure call and publish/subscribe. Section 4.3 summarizes the major issues identified in this chapter but not addressed, and presents a road map for addressing them. Finally, there are detailed case studies of two widely used client/service applications, the Internet Domain Name System and the Network File System.

4.1 CLIENT/SERVICE ORGANIZATION

A standard way to create modularity in a large program is to divide it up into named procedures that call one another. Although the resulting structure can be called modular, implementation errors can propagate from caller to callee and vice versa, and not just through their specified interfaces. For example, if a programmer makes a mistake and introduces an infinite loop in a called procedure and the procedure never returns, then the callee will never receive control again. Or since the caller and callee are in the same address space and use the same stack, either one can accidentally store something in a space allocated to the other. For this reason, we identify this kind of modularity as *soft*. Soft modularity limits interactions of correctly implemented modules to their specified interfaces, but implementation errors can cause interactions that go outside the specified interfaces.

To enforce modularity, we need hard boundaries between modules so that errors cannot easily propagate from one module to another. Just as buildings have firewalls to contain fires within one section of the building and keep them from propagating to other sections, so we need an organization that limits the interaction between modules to their defined interfaces.

This section introduces the client/service organization as one approach to structuring systems that limit the interfaces through which errors can propagate to the specified messages. This organization has two benefits: first, errors can propagate only with messages. Second, clients can check for certain errors by just considering the messages. Although this approach doesn't limit the propagation of all errors, it provides a *sweeping simplification* in terms of reasoning about the interactions between modules.

4.1.1 From Soft Modularity to Enforced Modularity

As a more concrete example of how modules interact, suppose we are writing a simple program that measures how long a function runs. We might want to split it into two modules: (1) one system module that provides an interface to obtain the time in units specified by the caller and (2) one application module that measures the running time of a function by asking for time from the clock device, running the function, and requesting the time from the clock device after the function completes. The purpose of this split is to separate the measurement program from the details of the clock device:

```
procedure MEASURE (func)
    start ← GET_TIME (SECONDS)
    func () // invoke the function
    end ← GET_TIME (SECONDS)
    return end – start
```

```
procedure GET_TIME (units)
    time ← CLOCK
    time ← CONVERT_TO_UNITS (time, units)
    return time
```

The procedure MEASURE takes a function *func* as argument and measures its running time. The procedure GET_TIME returns the time measured in the units specified by the caller. We may desire this clear separation in modules because, for example, we don't want every function that needs the time to know the physical address of the clock (CLOCK in line *2* of GETTIME) in all application programs, such as MEASURE, that use the clock. On one computer, the clock is at physical address $17E5_{hex}$, but on the next computer it is at $24FFF2_{hex}$. Or some clocks return microseconds, and others return sixtieths of a second. By putting the clock's specific properties into GET_TIME, the callers of GET_TIME do not have to be changed when a program is moved to another computer; only GET_TIME must be changed.

This boundary between GET_TIME and its caller, is soft, however. Although procedure call is a primary tool for modularity, errors can still leak too easily from one module to another. It is obvious that if GET_TIME returns a wrong answer, the caller has a problem. It is less obvious that programming errors in GET_TIME can cause trouble for the caller even if GET_TIME returns a correct answer. This section explains why procedure call allows propagation of a wide variety of errors and will introduce an alternative that resembles procedure call but that more strongly limits propagation of errors.

To see why procedure calls allow propagation of many kinds of errors, one must look at the detail of how procedure calls work and at the processor instructions that implement procedure calls. There are many ways to compile the procedures and the call from MEASURE to GET_TIME into processor instructions. For concreteness we pick one procedure call convention. Others differ in the details but exhibit the same issues that we want to explore.

We implement the call to GET_TIME with a stack, so that GET_TIME could call other procedures (although in this example it does not do so). In general, a called procedure may call another procedure or even call itself recursively. To allow for calls to other procedures, the implementation must adhere to the ***stack discipline***: each invocation of a procedure must leave the stack as it found it.

To adhere to this discipline, there must be a convention for who saves what registers, who puts the arguments on the stack, who removes them, and who allocates space on the stack for temporary variables. The particular convention used by a system is called the ***procedure calling convention***. We use the convention shown in Figure 4.1. Each procedure call results in a new stack frame, which has space for saved registers, the arguments for the callee, the address where the callee should return, and local variables of the callee.

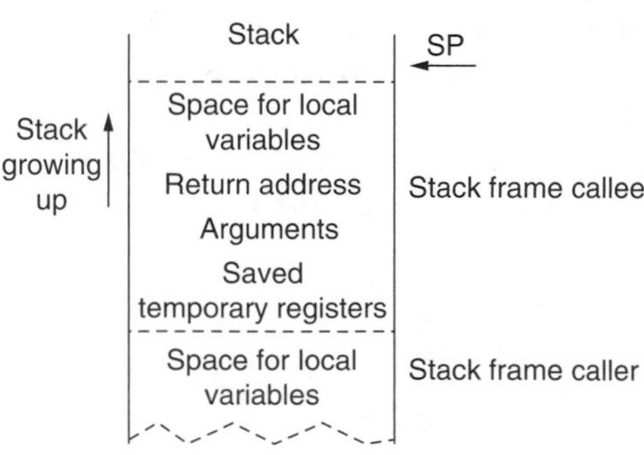

FIGURE 4.1

Procedure call convention.

Given this calling convention, the processor instructions for these two modules are shown in Figure 4.2. In this example, the instructions of the caller (MEASURE) start at address 100, the instructions of the callee (GET_TIME) start at address 200. The stack grows up, from a low address to a high address. The return value of a procedure is passed through register R0. For simplicity, assume that instructions, memory locations, and addresses are all 4 bytes wide. For our example, MEASURE invokes GETTIME as follows:

1. The caller saves content of temporary registers (R1 and R2) at addresses 100 through 112.
2. The caller stores the arguments on the stack (address 116 through 124) so that the callee can find them. (GET_TIME takes one argument: *unit*.)
3. The caller stores a return address on the stack (address 128 through 136) so that the callee can know where the caller should resume execution. (The return address is 148.)

Machine code for MEASURE:

```
100: STORE R1, SP          // save content of R1
104: ADD 4, SP             // adjust stack
108: STORE R2, SP          // save content of R2
112: ADD 4, SP             // adjust stack
116: MOV SECONDS, R1       // move argument to GET_TIME in R1
120: STORE R1, SP          // store argument in R1 on stack
124: ADD 4, SP             // adjust stack
128: MOV 148, R1           // place return address in R1
132: STORE R1, SP          // store return address in R1 on stack
136: ADD 4, SP             // adjust stack
140: STORE 200, R1         // load address of GET_TIME into R1
144: JMP R1                // jump to it
148: SUB 8, SP             // adjust top of stack
152: MOV SP, R2            // restore R2's content
156: SUB 4, SP             // adjust stack
160: MOV SP, R1            // restore R1's content
164: SUB 4, SP             // adjust stack
168: MOV R0, start         // store result in local stack variable start
172: .....                 // invoke func and GET_TIME again
```

Machine code for GET_TIME:

```
200: MOV SP, R1            // move stack pointer into R1
204: SUB 8, R1             // subtract 8 from SP in R1
208: LOAD R1, R2           // load argument from stack into R2
212: ....                  // instructions for body of GET_TIME
220: MOV time, R0          // move return value in R0
224: MOV SP, R1            // move stack pointer in R1
228: SUB 4, R1             // subtract 4 from SP in R1
232: LOAD R1, PC           // load return address from stack into PC
```

FIGURE 4.2

The procedure MEASURE (located at address 100) calls GET_TIME (located at address 200).

4. The caller transfers control to the callee by jumping to the address of its first instruction (address 140 and 144). (The callee, GET_TIME, is located at address 200.) The stack for our example looks now as in the following figure.

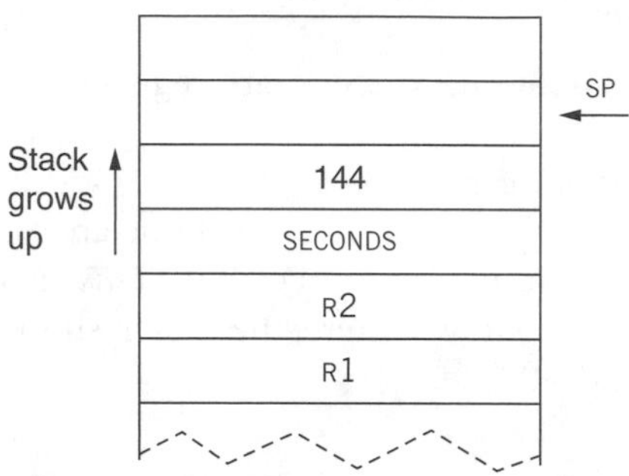

5. The callee loads its argument from the stack into R2 (address 200 through 208).
6. The callee computes with the arguments, perhaps calling other functions (address 212).
7. The callee loads the return value of GET_TIME into R0, the register the implementation reserves for returning values (address 220).
8. The callee loads the return address from the stack into PC (address 224 through 232), which causes the caller to resume control at address 148.
9. The caller adjusts the stack (address 148).
10. The caller restores content of R1 and R2 (addresses 152 through 164).

We use the low-level instructions of the processor for the specific example in Figure 4.2 because it exposes the fine print of the contract between the caller and the callee, and shows how errors can propagate. In the MEASURE example, the contract specifies that the callee returns the current time in some agreed-upon representation to the caller. If we look under the covers, however, we see that this functional specification is not the full contract and that the contract doesn't have a good way of limiting the propagation of errors. To uncover the fine print of the contract between modules, we need to inspect how the stack from Figure 4.2 is used to transfer control from one module to another. The contract between caller and callee contains several subtle potential problems:

- By contract, the caller and callee modify only shared arguments and their own variables in the stack. The callee leaves the stack pointer and the stack the way the caller has set it up. If there is a problem in the callee that corrupts the caller's area of the stack, then the caller might later compute incorrect results or fail.

- By contract, the callee returns where the caller told it to. If by mistake the callee returns somewhere else, then the caller probably performs an incorrect computation or loses control completely and fails.

- By contract, the callee stores return values in register R0. If by mistake the callee stores the return value somewhere else, then the caller will read whatever value is in register R0 and probably perform an incorrect computation.
- By contract, the caller saves the values in the temporary registers (R1, R2, etc.) on the stack before the call to the callee and restores them when it receives control back. If the caller doesn't follow the contract, the callee may have changed the content of the temporary registers when the caller receives control back, and the caller probably performs an incorrect computation.
- Disasters in the callee can have side effects in the caller. For example, if the callee divides by zero and, as a result, terminates, the caller may terminate too. This effect is known colloquially as *fate sharing*.
- If the caller and callee share global variables, then by contract, the caller and callee modify only those global variables that are shared between them. Again, if the caller or callee modifies some other global variable, they (or other modules) might compute incorrectly or fail altogether.

Thus, the procedure call contract provides us with what might be labeled *soft modularity*. If a programmer makes an error or there is an error in the implementation of the procedure call convention, these errors can easily propagate from the callee to the caller. Soft modularity is usually attained through specifications, but nothing forces the interactions among modules to their defined interfaces. If the callee doesn't adhere (intentionally or unintentionally) to the contract, the caller has a serious problem. We have modularity that is not enforced.

There are also other possibilities for propagation of errors. The procedures share the same address space, and, if a defective procedure incorrectly smashes a global variable, even a procedure that did not call the defective one may be affected. Any procedure that doesn't adhere, either intentionally or unintentionally, to the contract may cause trouble for other modules.

Using a constrained and type-safe implementation language such as Java can beef up soft modularity to a certain extent (see Sidebar 4.1) but is insufficient for complete systems. For one, it is uncommon that all modules in a system are implemented in type-safe language. Often some modules of a system are for performance reasons written in a programming language that doesn't enforce modularity, such C, C++, or processor instructions. But even if the whole system is developed in a type-safe language like Java, we have a need for stronger modularity. If any of the Java modules raises an error (because the interpreter raises a type violation, the module allocated more memory than available, the module couldn't open a file, etc.) or has a programming error (e.g., an infinite loop), we would like to ensure that other modules don't immediately fail too. Even if a called procedure doesn't return, we would like to ensure that the caller has a controlled problem.

What we desire in systems is *enforced modularity*: modularity that is enforced by some external mechanism. This external mechanism limits the interaction among modules to the ones we desire. Such a limit on interactions reduces the number of

Sidebar 4.1 Enforcing Modularity with a High-Level Languages A high-level language is helpful in enforcing modularity because its compiler and runtime system perform all stack and register manipulation, presumably accurately and in accordance with the procedure calling convention. Furthermore, if the programming language enforces a restriction that programs write only to memory locations that correspond to variables managed by the language and in accordance with their type, then programs cannot overwrite arbitrary memory locations and, for example, corrupt the stack. That is, a program cannot use the value of a variable of type integer as an address of a memory location and then store to that memory location. Such languages are called *strongly typed* and, if a program cannot avoid the type system in any way, *type safe*. Modern examples of strongly typed languages include Java and C#.

But even with strongly typed languages, modularity through procedure calls doesn't limit the interactions between modules to their defined interfaces. For example, if the callee has a programming error and allocates all of the available memory space, then the caller may be unable to proceed. Also, strongly typed languages allow the programmer to escape the type system of the language to obtain direct access to memory or to processor registers and to exercise system features that the language does not support (e.g., reading and writing memory locations that correspond to the control registers and state of a device). But this access opens a path for the programmer to make mistakes that violate the procedure call contract.

Another concern is that in many computer systems different modules are written in different programming languages, perhaps because an existing, older module is being reused, even though its implementation language does not provide the type-safety features, or because a lower-level language fragment is essential for achieving maximum performance. Even when the caller and callee are written in two different, strongly typed languages, unexpected interactions can occur at their interface because their conventions do not match.

Another source of errors, which in practice seem to occur much less often, is an implementation error in the interpreter of the application (though with increasing complexity of compilers, runtime support systems, and processor designs, this source may yet become significant). The compiler may have a programming error, the runtime support system may have set up the stack incorrectly, the processor or operating system may save and restore registers incorrectly on an interrupt, a memory error causes a LOAD instruction to return an incorrect value, and so on. Although these sources are less likely to occur than programming errors, it is good to contain the resulting errors so that they don't propagate to other modules.

For all these reasons, designers use the client/service organization. Combining the client/service organization with writing a system in a strongly typed language offers additional opportunities for enforcing modularity; see, for example, the design of the Singularity operating system [Suggestions for Further Reading 5.2.3].

opportunities for propagation of errors. It also allows verification that a user uses a module correctly, and it helps prevent an attacker from penetrating the security of a module.

4.1.2 Client/Service Organization

One good way to enforce modularity is to limit the interactions among modules to explicit messages. It is convenient to impose some structure on this organization by identifying participants in a communication as clients or services.

Figure 4.3 shows a common interaction between client and service. The *client* is the module that initiates a request: it builds a message containing all the data necessary for the service to carry out its job and sends it to a service. The *service* is the module that responds: it extracts the arguments from the request message, executes the requested operations, builds a response message, sends the response message back to the client, and waits for the next request. The client extracts the results from the response message. For convenience, the message from the client to the service is called the *request*, and the message is called the *response* or *reply*.

Figure 4.3 shows one common way in which a client and a service interact: a request is always followed by a response. Since a client and a service can interact using many other sequences of messages, designers often represent the interactions using *message timing diagrams* (see Sidebar 4.2). Figure 4.3 is an instance of a simple timing diagram.

Conceptually, the client/service model runs client and services on separate computers, connected by a wire. This implementation also allows client and service to be separated geographically (which can be good because it reduces the risk that both fail owing to a common fault such as a power outage) and restricts all interactions to well-defined messages sent across a wire.

The disadvantage of this implementation is that it requires one computer per module, which may be costly in equipment. It may also have a performance cost because it may take a substantial amount of time to send a message from one computer to another, in particular if the computers are far away geographically. In some cases these disadvantages are unimportant; for cases in which it does matter, Chapter 5 will explain how to implement the client/service model within a single computer using

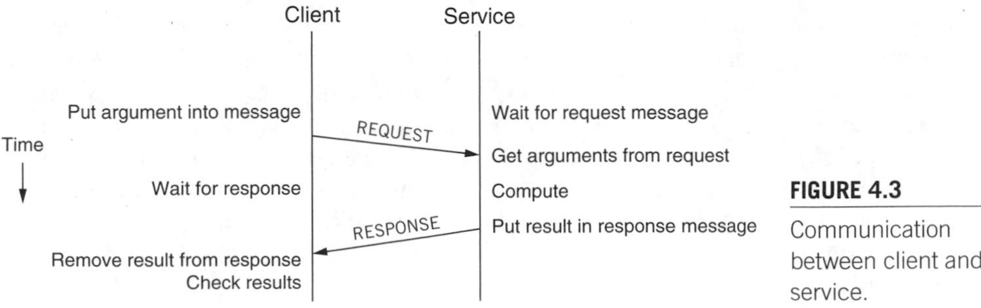

FIGURE 4.3
Communication between client and service.

Sidebar 4.2 Representation: Timing Diagrams A *timing diagram* is a convenient representation of the interaction between modules. When the system is organized in a client/service style, this presentation is particularly convenient, because the interactions between modules are limited to messages. In a timing diagram, the lifetime of a module is represented by a vertical line, with time increasing down the vertical axis. The following example illustrates the use of a timing diagram for a sewage pumping system. The label at the top of a timeline names the module (pump controller, sensor service, and pump service). The physical separation between modules is represented horizontally. Since it takes time for a message to get from one point to another, a message going from the pump controller to the pump service is represented by an arrow that slopes downward to the right.

The modules perform actions, and send and receive messages. The labels next to the time indicate actions taken by the module at a certain time. Modules can take actions at the same time, for example, if they are running on different processors.

The arrows indicate messages. The start of the arrow indicates the time the message is sent by the sending module, and the point of an arrow indicates the time the message is received at the destination module. The content of a message is described by the label associated with the arrow. In some examples, messages can be reordered (arrows cross) or lost (arrows terminate midflight before reaching a module).

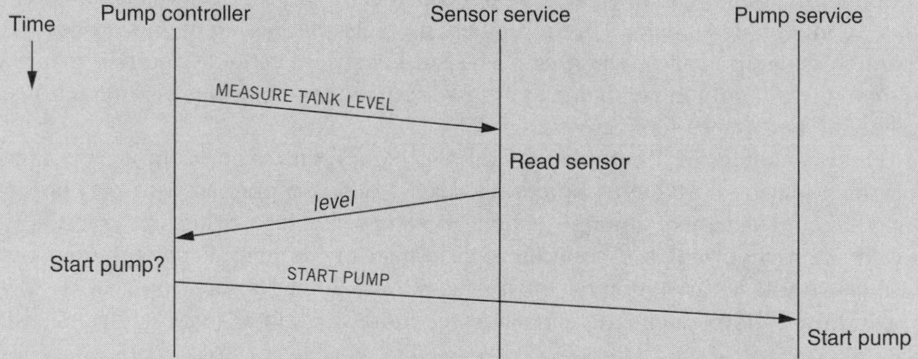

The simple timing diagram shown in this sidebar describes the interaction between a pump controller and two services: a sensor service and a pump service. There is a request containing the message "measure tank level" from the client to the sensor service, and a response reports the level read by the sensor. There is a third message, "start pump", which the client sends to the pump service when the level is too high. The second message has no response. The diagram shows three actions: reading the sensor, deciding whether the pump must be started, and starting the pump. Figure 7.7 [on-line] shows a timing diagram with a lost message, and Figure 7.9 [on-line] shows one with a delayed message.

an operating system. For the rest of this chapter we will assume that the client and the service each have their own computer.

To achieve high availability or handle big workloads, a designer may choose to implement a service using multiple computers. For instance, a file service might use several computers to achieve a high degree of fault tolerance; if one computer fails, another one can take over its role. An instance of a service running on a single computer is called a *server*.

To make the client/service model more concrete, let's rearrange our MEASURE program into a simple client/service organization (see Figure 4.4). To get a time from the service, the client procedure builds a request message that names the service and specifies the requested operation and arguments (lines *2* and *6*). The requested operation and arguments must be converted to a representation that is suitable for transmission. For example, the client computer may be a big-endian computer (see Sidebar 4.3), while the service computer may be a little-endian computer. Thus, the client must convert arguments into a canonical representation so that the service can interpret the arguments.

This conversion is called *marshaling*. We use the notation {*a*, *b*} to denote a marshaled message that contains the fields *a* and *b*. Marshaling typically involves converting an object into an array of bytes with enough annotation so that the

```
Client program

1   procedure MEASURE (func)
2       SEND_MESSAGE (NameForTimeService, {"Get time", CONVERT2EXTERNAL(SECONDS)})
3       response ← RECEIVE_MESSAGE (NameForClient)
4       start ← CONVERT2INTERNAL (response)
5       func ()     // invoke the function
6       SEND_MESSAGE (NameForTimeService, {"Get time", CONVERT2EXTERNAL(SECONDS)})
7       response ← RECEIVE_MESSAGE (NameForClient)
8       end ← CONVERT2INTERNAL (response)
9       return end – start

Service program

10  procedure TIME_SERVICE ()
11      do forever
12          request ← RECEIVE_MESSAGE (NameForTimeService)
13          opcode ← GET_OPCODE (request)
14          unit ← CONVERT2INTERNAL(GET_ARGUMENT (request))
15          if opcode = "Get time" and (unit = SECONDS or unit = MINUTES) then
16              time ← CONVERT_TO_UNITS (CLOCK, unit)
17              response ← {"OK", CONVERT2EXTERNAL (time)}
18          else
19              response ←{"Bad request"}
20          SEND_MESSAGE (NameForClient, response)
```

FIGURE 4.4

Example client/service application: time service.

Sidebar 4.3 Representation: Big-Endian or Little-Endian? Two common conventions exist for numbering bits within a byte, bytes within a word, words within a page, and the like. One convention is called *big-endian*, and the other *little-endian*.* In big-endian the most significant bit, byte, or word is numbered 0, and the significance of bits *decreases* as the address of the bit increases:

Words	0				1			
Bytes	0	1	...	7	0	1	...	7
Bits	$2^0\,2^1\,2^2\ldots$			$\ldots 2^{63}$	$2^0\,2^1\,2^2\ldots$			$\ldots 2^{63}$

In big-endian the hex number $ABCD_{hex}$ would be stored in memory, so that if you read from memory in increasing memory address order, you would see A-B-C-D. The string "john" would be stored in memory as john.

In little-endian, the other convention, the least significant bit, byte, or word is numbered 0, and the significance of bits *increases* as the address of the bit increases:

Words	*n*				*n*−1			
Bytes	7	...	1	0	7	...	1	0
Bits	$2^{63}\ldots$			$\ldots 2^2\,2^1\,2^0$	$2^{63}\ldots$			$\ldots 2^2\,2^1\,2^0$

In little-endian, the hex number $ABCD_{hex}$ would be stored in memory, so that if you read from memory in increasing memory address order, you see D-C-B-A. The string "john" would still be stored in memory as john. Thus, code that extracts bytes from character strings transports between architectures, but code that extracts bytes from integers does not transport.

Some processors, such as the Intel x86 family, use the little-endian convention, but others, such as the IBM PowerPC family, use the big-endian convention. As Danny Cohen pointed out in a frequently cited article "*On holy wars and a plea for peace*" [Suggestions for Further Reading 7.2.4], it doesn't matter which convention a designer uses as long as it is the *same* one when communicating between two processors. The processors must agree on the convention for numbering the bits sent over the wire (that is, send the most significant bit first or send the least significant bit first). Thus, if the communication standard is big-endian (as it is in the Internet protocols), then a client running on a little-endian processor must marshal data in big-endian order. This book uses the big-endian convention.

This book also follows the convention that bit numbers start with zero. This choice is independent of the big-endian convention; we could have chosen to use 1 instead, as some processors do.

---

*The labels "big-endian" and "little-endian" were coined by Jonathan Swift in Chapter 4 of *Gulliver's Travels*, to identify two quarreling factions that differed over which end of an egg it was best to open.

unmarshal procedure can convert it back into a language object. In this example, we show the marshal and unmarshal operations explicitly (e.g., the procedure calls starting with CONVERT), but in many future examples these operations will be implicit to avoid clutter.

After constructing the request, the client sends it (*2* and *6*), waits for a response (line *3* and *7*), and unmarshals the time (*4* and *8*).

The service procedure waits for a request (line *12*) and unmarshals the request (lines *13* and *14*). Then, it checks the request (line *15*), processes it (lines *16* through *19*), and sends back a marshaled response (line *20*).

The *client/service organization* not only separates functions (abstraction), it also enforces that separation (enforced modularity). Compared to modularity using procedure calls, the client/service organization has the following advantages:

- The client and service don't rely on shared state other than the messages. Therefore, errors can propagate from the client to the service, and vice versa, in only one way. If the services (as in line *15*) and the clients check the validity of the request and response messages, then they can control the ways in which errors propagate. Since the client and service don't rely on global, shared data structures such as a stack, a failure in the client cannot directly corrupt data in the service, and vice versa.

- The transaction between a client and a service is an arm's-length transaction. Many errors cannot propagate from one to the other. For instance, the client does not have to trust the service to return to the appropriate return address, as it does using procedure calls. As another example, arguments and results are marshaled and unmarshaled, allowing the client and service to check them.

- The client can protect itself even against a service that fails to return because the client can put an upper limit on the time it waits for a response. As a result, if the service gets into an infinite loop, or fails and forgets about the request, the client can detect that something has gone wrong and undertake some recovery procedure, such as trying a different service. On the other hand, setting timers can create new problems because it can be difficult to predict how long a wait is reasonable. The problem of setting timers for service requests is discussed in detail in Section 7.5.2 [on-line]. In our example, the client isn't defensive against service errors; providing these defenses will make the program slightly more complex but can help eliminate fate sharing.

- Client/Service organization encourages explicit, well-defined interfaces. Because the client and service can interact only through messages, the messages that a service is willing to receive provide a well-defined interface for the service. If those messages are well specified and their specification is public, a programmer can implement a new client or service without having to understand the internals of another client or the service. Clear specification allows clients and service to be implemented by different programmers, and can encourage competition for the best implementation.

Separating state and passing well-defined messages reduce the number of potential interactions, which helps contain errors. If the programmer who developed the service introduces an error and the service has a disaster, the client has only a *controlled* problem. The client's only concern is that the service didn't deliver its part of the contract; apart from this wrong or missing value, the client has no concern for its own integrity. The client is less vulnerable from faults in the service, or, in slightly different words, fate sharing can be reduced. Clients can be mostly independent of service failures, and vice versa.

The client/service organization is an example of a *sweeping simplification* because the model eliminates all forms of interaction other than messages. By separating the client and the service from each other using message passing, we have created a firewall between them. As with firewalls in buildings, if there is a fire in the service, it will be contained in the service, and, assuming the client can check for flames in the response, it will not propagate to the client. If the client and service are well implemented, then the only way to go from the client to the service and back is through well-defined messages.

Of course, the client/service organization is not a panacea. If a service returns an incorrect result, then the client has a problem. This client can check for certain problems (e.g., syntactic ones) but not all semantic errors. The client/service organization reduces fate sharing but doesn't eliminate it. The degree to which the client/service organization reduces fate sharing is also dependent on the interface between the client and service. As an extreme example, if the client/service interface has a message that allows a client to write any value to any address in the service's address space, then it is easy for errors to propagate from the client to the service. It is the job of the system designer to define a good interface between client and service so that errors cannot propagate easily. In this chapter and later chapters, we will see examples of good message interfaces.

For ease of understanding, most of the examples in this chapter exhibit modules consisting of a single procedure. In the real world, designers usually apply the client/service organization between software modules of a larger granularity. The tendency toward larger granularity arises because the procedures within an application typically need to be tightly coupled for some practical reason, such as they all operate on the same shared data structure. Placing every procedure in a separate client or service would make it difficult to manipulate the shared data. The designer thus faces a trade-off between ease of accessing the data that a module needs and ease of error propagation within a module. A designer makes this trade-off by deciding which data and procedures to group into a coherent unit with the data that they manipulate. That coherent unit then becomes a separate service, and errors are contained within the unit. The client and service units are often complete application programs or similarly large subsystems.

Another factor in whether or not to apply the client/service organization to two modules is the plan for recovery when the service module fails. For example, in a simulator program that uses a function to compute the square root of its argument, it makes little sense to put that function into a separate service because it doesn't reduce fate sharing. If the square-root function fails, the simulator program cannot proceed. Furthermore, a good recovery plan is for the programmer to reimplement the function correctly, as opposed to running two square-root servers, and failing over to the second one when the first one fails. In this example, the square-root function might as well be part of the simulator program because the client/service organization doesn't reduce fate sharing for the simulator program and thus there is no reason use it.

A nice example of a widely used system that is organized in a client/service style, with the client and service typically running on separate computers, is the World Wide Web. The Web browser is a client, and a Web site is a service. The browser and the site communicate through well-defined messages and are typically geographically separated. As long as the client and service check the validity of messages, a failure of a service results in a controlled problem for the browser, and vice versa. The World Wide Web provides enforced modularity.

In Figures 4.3 and 4.4, the service always responds with a reply, but that is not a requirement. Figure 4.5 shows the pseudocode for a pump controller for the sewage pumping system in Sidebar 4.2. In this example, there is no need for the pump service to send a reply acknowledging that the pump was turned off. What the client cares about is a confirmation from an independent sensor service that the level in the tank is going down. Waiting for a reply from the pump service, even for a short time, would just delay sounding the alarm if the pump failed.

Client program: pump controller

```
procedure PUMP_CONTROLLER ()
    do forever
        SEND_MESSAGE (NameForSensor, "measure tank level")
        level ← RECEIVE_MESSAGE (NameForClient)
        if level > UpperPumpLimit then SEND_MESSAGE (NameForPump, "turn on pump")
        if level < LowerPumpLimit then SEND_MESSAGE (NameForPump, "turn pump off")
        if level > OverflowLimit then SOUND_ALARM ()
```

Pump service

```
procedure PUMP_SERVICE ()
    do forever
        request ← RECEIVE_MESSAGE (NameForPump)
        if request = "Turn on pump" then SET_PUMP (on)
        else if request = "Turn off pump" then SET_PUMP (off)
```

Sensor service

```
procedure SENSOR_SERVICE ()
    do forever
        request ← RECEIVE_MESSAGE (NameForSensor)
        if request = "Measure tank level" then
            response ← READ_SENSOR ()
            SEND_MESSAGE (NameForClient, response)
```

FIGURE 4.5

Example client/service application: controller for a sewage pump.

Sidebar 4.4 The X Window System The X Window System [Suggestions for Further Reading 4.2.2] is the window system of choice on practically every engineering workstation and many personal computers. It provides a good example of using the client/service organization to achieve modularity. One of the main contributions of the X Window System is that it remedied a defect that had crept into the UNIX system when displays replaced typewriters: the display and keyboard were the only hardware-dependent parts of the UNIX application programming interface. The X Window System allowed display-oriented UNIX applications to be completely independent of the underlying hardware.

The X Window System achieved this property by separating the service program that manipulates the display device from the client programs that use the display. The service module provides an interface to manage windows, fonts, mouse cursors, and images. Clients can request services for these resources through high-level operations; for example, clients perform graphics operations in terms of lines, rectangles, curves, and the like. The advantage of this split is that the client programs are device independent. The addition of a new display type may require a new service implementation, but no application changes are required.

Another advantage of a client/service organization is that an application running on one machine can use the display on some other machine. This organization allows, for example, a computing-intensive program to run on a high-performance supercomputer, while displaying the results on a user's personal computer.

It is important that the service be robust to client failures because otherwise a buggy client could cause the entire display to freeze. The X Window system achieves this property by having client and service communicate through carefully designed remote procedure calls, a mechanism described in Section 4.2. The remote procedure calls have the property that the service never has to trust the clients to provide correct data and that the service can process other client requests if it has to wait for a client.

The service allows clients to send multiple requests back to back without waiting for individual responses because the rate at which data can be displayed on a local display is often higher than the network data rate between a client and service. If the client had to wait for a response on each request, then the user-perceived performance would be unacceptable. For example, at 80 characters per request (one line of text on a typical display) and a 5-millisecond round-trip time between client and service, only 16,000 characters per second can be drawn, while typical hardware devices are capable of displaying an order of magnitude faster.

Other systems avoid response messages for performance reasons. For example, the popular X Window System (see Sidebar 4.4) sends a series of requests that ask the service to draw something on a screen and that individually have no need for a response.

4.1.3 Multiple Clients and Services

In the examples so far, we have seen one client and one service, but the client/service model is much more flexible:

- One service can work for multiple clients. A printer service might work for many clients so that the cost of maintaining the printer can be shared. A file service might store files for many clients so that the information in the files can be shared.
- One client can use several services, as in the sewage pump controller (see Figure 4.5), which uses both a pump service and a sensor service.
- A single module can take on the roles of both client and service. A printer service might temporarily store documents on a file service until the printer is ready to print. In this case, the print service functions as a service for printing requests, but it is also a client of the file service.

4.1.4 Trusted Intermediaries

A single service that has multiple clients brings up another technique for enforcing modularity: the *trusted intermediary*, a service that functions as the trusted third party among multiple, perhaps mutually suspicious, clients. The trusted intermediary can control shared resources in a careful manner. For example, a file service might store files for multiple clients, some of which are mutually suspicious; the clients, however, trust the service to keep their affairs distinct. The file service could ensure that a client cannot have access to files not owned by that client, or it could, based on instructions from the clients, allow certain clients to share files.

The trusted intermediary enforces modularity among multiple clients and ensures that a fault in one client has limited (or perhaps no) effect on another client. If the trusted intermediary provides sharing of resources among multiple clients, then it has to be carefully designed and implemented to ensure that the failures of one client don't affect another client. For example, an incorrect update made by one client to its private files shouldn't affect the private files of another client.

A file service is only one example of a trusted intermediary. Many services in client/service applications are trusted intermediaries. E-mail services store mailboxes for many users so that individual users don't have to worry about losing their e-mail. As another example, instant message services provide private buddy lists. It is usually the clients that need some form of controlled sharing, and trusted intermediaries can provide that.

There are also situations in which intermediaries that do not have to be trusted are useful. For example, Section 4.2.3 describes how an untrusted intermediary can be used to buffer and deliver messages to multiple recipients. This use allows communication patterns other than request/response.

Another common use of trusted intermediaries is to simplify clients by having the trusted intermediary provide most functions. The buzzword in trade magazines for

Sidebar 4.5 Peer-to-peer: Computing without Trusted Intermediaries Peer-to-peer is a decentralized design that lacks trusted intermediaries. It is one of the oldest designs and has been used by, for example, the Internet e-mail system, the Internet news bulletin service, Internet service providers to route Internet packets, and IBM's Systems Network Architecture. Recently, it has received much attention in the popular press because file-sharing applications have rediscovered some of its advantages.

In a peer-to-peer application, every computer participating in the application is a peer and is equal in function (but perhaps not in capacity) to any other computer. That is, no peer is more important than any other peer; if one peer fails, then this failure may degrade the performance of the application, but it won't fail the application. The client/service organization doesn't have this property: if the service fails, the application fails, even if all client computers are operational.

UsenetNews is a good example of an older peer-to-peer application. UsenetNews, an on-line news bulletin, is one of the first peer-to-peer applications and has been operational since the 1980s. Users post to a newsgroup, from which other users read articles and respond. Nodes in UsenetNews propagate newsgroups to peers and serve articles to clients. An administrator of a node decides with which nodes the administrator's node peers. Because most nodes interconnect with several other nodes, the system is fault tolerant, and the failure of one node leads at most to a performance degradation rather than to a complete failure. Because the nodes are spread across the world in different jurisdictions, it is difficult for any one central authority to censor content (but an administrator of a node can decide not to carry a group). Because of these properties, designers have proposed organizing other applications in a peer-to-peer style. For example, LOCKSS [Suggestions for Further Reading 10.2.3] has built a robust digital library in that style.

Recently, music-sharing applications and improvements in technology have brought peer-to-peer designs into the spotlight. Today, client computers are as powerful as yesterday's computers for services and are connected with high data-rate links to the Internet. In music-sharing applications the clients are peers, and they serve and store music for one another. This organization aggregates the disk space and network links of all clients to provide a tremendous amount of storage and network capacity, allowing many songs to be stored and served. As often happens in the history of computer systems, the first version of this application was developed not by a computer scientist but by an 18-year-old, Shawn Fanning, who developed Napster. It (and its successors) has changed the characteristics of network traffic on the Internet and has raised legal questions as well.

In Napster, clients serve and store songs, but a trusted intermediary stores the location of a song. Because Napster was used for illegal music sharing, the Recording Industry Association of America (RIAA) sued the operators of the intermediary and was able to shut it down. In more recent peer-to-peer designs, developers adopted the design of censor-resistant applications and avoided the use of a trusted intermediary to locate

(Sidebar continues)

songs. In these successors to Napster, the peers locate music by querying other peers; if any individual node is shut down, it will not render the service unavailable. The RIAA must now sue individual users.

Accurately and quickly finding information in a large network of peers without a trusted intermediary is a difficult problem. Without an intermediary there is no central, well-known computer to track the locations of songs. A distributed algorithm is necessary to find a song. A simple algorithm is to send a query for a song to all neighbor peers; if they don't have a copy, the peers forward the query to their neighbors, and so on. This algorithm works, but it is inefficient because it sends a query to every node in the network. To avoid flooding the network of peers on each query, one can stop forwarding the query after it has been forwarded a number of times. Bounding a search in this way may cause some queries to return no answer, even though the song is somewhere in the network.

This problem has sparked interest in the research community, leading to the invention of better algorithms for decentralized search services and resulting in a range of new peer-to-peer applications. Some of these topics are covered in problem sets; see, for example, problem sets *20* [on-line] and *23* [on-line].

this use is "thin-client computing". In this use, only the trusted intermediary must run on a powerful computer (or a collection of computers connected by a high-speed network) because the clients don't run complex functions. Because in most applications there are a few trusted intermediaries (compared to the number of clients), they can be managed by a professional staff and located in a secure machine room. Trusted intermediaries of this type may be expensive to design, build, and run because they may need many resources to support the clients. If one isn't careful, the trusted intermediary can become a choke point during a flash crowd when many clients ask for the service at the same time. At the cost of additional complexity, this problem can be avoided by carefully dividing the work between clients and the trusted intermediary and replicating services using the techniques described in Chapters 8 [on-line] through 10 [on-line].

Designs that have trusted intermediaries also have some general downsides. The trusted intermediary may be vulnerable to failures or attacks that knock out the service. Users must trust the intermediary, but what if it is compromised or is subjected to censorship? Fortunately, there are alternative architectures; see Sidebar 4.5.

4.1.5 A Simple Example Service

Figure 4.6 shows the file system example of Figure 2.18 organized in a client/service style, along with the messages between the clients and services. The editor is a client of the file service, which in turn is a client of the block-storage service. The figure shows the message interaction among these three modules using a message timing diagram.

In the depicted example, the client constructs an OPEN message, specifying the name of the file to be opened. The service checks permissions and, if the user is allowed access, sends a response back indicating success (OK) and the value of the file pointer (0) (see Section 2.3.2 for an explanation of a file pointer). The client writes text to the file, which results in a WRITE request that specifies the text and the number of bytes to be written. The service writes the file by allocating blocks on the block service, copies the specified bytes into them, and returns a message stating the number of bytes written (16). After receiving a response from the block service, it constructs a response for the client, indicating success and informing the client of the new value of the file pointer. When the client is done editing, the client sends a CLOSE message, telling the service that the client is finished with this file.

This message sequence is too simple for use in practice because it doesn't deal with failures (e.g., what happens if the service fails while processing a write request), concurrency (e.g., what happens if multiple clients update a shared file), or security (e.g., how to ensure that a malicious person cannot write the business plan). A file service that is almost this simple is the Woodstock File System (WFS), designed by researchers at the Xerox Palo Alto Research Center [Suggestions for Further Reading 4.2.1]. Section 4.5 is a case study of a widely used successor, the Network File System (NFS), which is organized as a client/service application, and summarizes how NFS handles failures and concurrency. Handling concurrency, failures, and security in general are topics we explore in a systematic way in later chapters.

The file service is a trusted intermediary because it protects the content of files. It must check whether the messages came from a legitimate client (and not from an attacker), it decides whether the client has permission to perform the requested operation, and, if so, it performs the operation. Thus, as long as the file service does its job correctly, clients can share files (and thus also the block-storage service) in a protected manner.

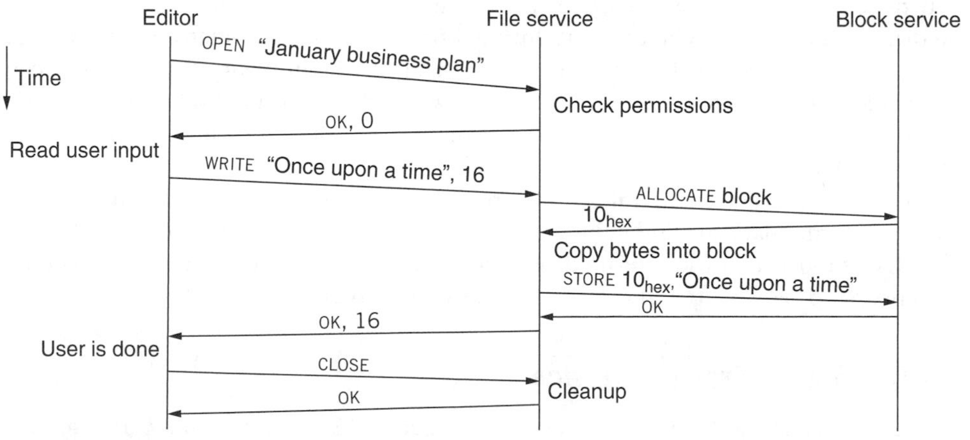

FIGURE 4.6

File service using message timing diagram.

4.2 COMMUNICATION BETWEEN CLIENT AND SERVICE

This section describes two extensions to sending and receiving messages. First, it introduces *remote procedure call (RPC)*, a stylized form of client/service interaction in which each request is followed by a response. The goal of RPC systems is to make a remote procedure call look like an ordinary procedure call. Because a service fails independently from a client, however, a remote procedure call can generally not offer identical semantics to procedure calls. As explained in the next subsection, some RPC systems provide various alternative semantics and the programmer must be aware of the details.

Second, in some applications it is desirable to be able to send messages to a recipient that is not on-line and to receive messages from a sender that is not on-line. For example, electronic mail allows users to send e-mail without requiring the recipient to be on-line. Using an intermediary for communication, we can implement these applications.

4.2.1 Remote Procedure Call (RPC)

In many of the examples in the previous section, the client and service interact in a stylized fashion: the client sends a request, and the service replies with a response after processing the client's request. This style is so common that it has received its own name: *remote procedure call*, or RPC for short.

RPCs come in many varieties, adding features to the basic request/response style of interaction. Some RPC systems, for example, simplify the programming of clients and services by hiding many the details of constructing and formatting messages. In the time service example above, the programmer must call SEND_MESSAGE and RECEIVE_MESSAGE, and convert results into numbers, and so on. Similarly, in the file service example, the client and service have to construct messages and convert numbers into bit strings and the like. Programming these conversions is tedious and error prone.

Stubs remove this burden from the programmer (see Figure 4.7). A stub is a procedure that hides the marshaling and communication details from the caller and callee. An RPC system can use stubs as follows. The client module invokes a remote procedure, say GET_TIME, in the same way that it would call any other procedure. However, GET_TIME is actually just the name of a stub procedure that runs inside the client module (see Figure 4.8). The stub marshals the arguments of a call into a message, sends the message, and waits for a response. On arrival of the response, the client stub unmarshals the response and returns to the caller.

Similarly, a service stub waits for a message, unmarshals the arguments, and calls the procedure that the client requests (GET_TIME in the example). After the procedure returns, the service stub marshals the results of the procedure call into a message and sends it in a response to the client stub.

Writing stubs that convert more complex objects into an appropriate on-wire representation becomes quite tedious. Some high-level programming languages

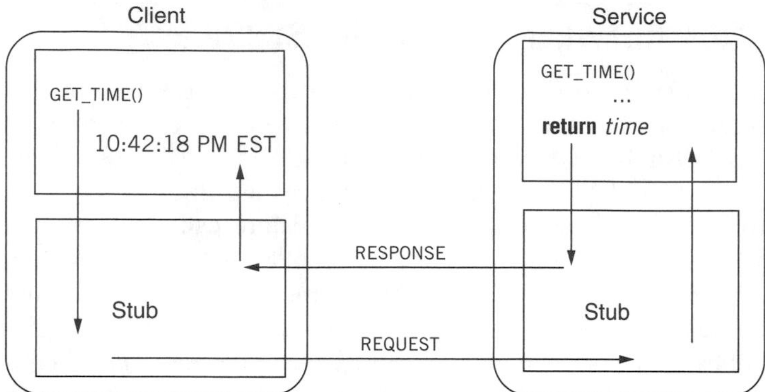

FIGURE 4.7

Implementation of a remote procedure call using stubs. The stubs hide all remote communication from the caller and callee.

Client program

```
procedure MEASURE (func)
    start ← GET_TIME (SECONDS)
    func ()        // invoke the function
    end ← GET_TIME (SECONDS)
    return end – start

procedure GET_TIME (unit)        // the client stub for GET_TIME
    SEND_MESSAGE (NameForTimeService, {"Get time", unit})
    response ← RECEIVE_MESSAGE (NameForClient)
    return CONVERT2INTERNAL (response)
```

Service program

```
procedure TIME_SERVICE ()        // the service stub for GET_TIME
    do forever
        request ← RECEIVE_MESSAGE (NameForTimeService)
        opcode ← GET_OPCODE (request)
        unit ← GET_ARGUMENT (request)
        if opcode = "Get time" and (unit = SECONDS or unit = MINUTES) then
            response ← {"ok", GET_TIME (unit)}
        else
            response ← {"Bad request"}
        SEND_MESSAGE (NameForClient, response)
```

FIGURE 4.8

GET_TIME client and service using stubs.

such as Java can generate these stubs automatically from an interface specification [Suggestions for Further Reading 4.1.3], simplifying client/service programming even further. Figure 4.9 shows the client for such an RPC system. The RPC system would generate a procedure similar to the GET_TIME stub in Figure 4.8. The client program of Figure 4.9 looks almost identical to the one using a local procedure call on page 149,

The client program

```
procedure MEASURE (func)
    try
        start ← GET_TIME (SECONDS)
    catch (signal servicefailed)
        return servicefailed
    func ()        // invoke the function
    try
        end ← GET_TIME (SECONDS)
    catch (signal servicefailed)
        return servicefailed
    return end – start
```

FIGURE 4.9

GET_TIME client using a system that generates RPC stubs automatically.

except that it handles an additional error because remote procedure calls are not identical to procedure calls (as discussed below).The procedure that the service calls on line 7 is just the original procedure GET_TIME on page 149.

Whether a system uses RPC with automatic stub generation is up to the implementers. For example, some implementations of Sun's Network File System (see Section 4.5) use automatic stub generation, but others do not.

4.2.2 RPCs are not Identical to Procedure Calls

It is tempting to think that by using stubs one can make a remote procedure call behave exactly the same as an ordinary procedure call, so that a programmer doesn't have to think about whether the procedure runs locally or remotely. In fact, this goal was a primary one when RPC was originally proposed—hence the name remote "procedure call". However, RPCs are different from ordinary procedure calls in three important ways: First, RPCs can reduce fate sharing between caller and callee by exposing the failures of the callee to the caller so that the caller can recover. Second, RPCs introduce new failures that don't appear in procedure calls. These two differences change the semantics of remote procedure calls as compared with ordinary procedure calls, and the changes usually require the programmer to make adjustments to the surrounding code.Third, remote procedure calls take more time than procedure calls; the number of instructions to invoke a procedure (see Figure 4.2) is much less than the cost of invoking a stub, marshaling arguments, sending a request over a network, invoking a service stub, unmarshaling arguments, marshaling the response, receiving the response over the network, and unmarshaling the response.

To illustrate the first difference, consider writing a procedure call to the library program SQRT, which computes the square root of its argument x. A careful programmer would plan for the case that SQRT (x) will fail when x is negative by providing an explicit exception handler for that case. However, the programmer using ordinary procedure calls almost certainly doesn't go to the trouble of planning for certain possible failures because they have negligible probability. For example, the programmer probably would not think of setting an interval timer when invoking SQRT (x), even though SQRT internally has a successive-approximation loop that, if programmed wrong, might not terminate.

But now consider calling SQRT with an RPC. An interval timer suddenly becomes essential because the network between client and service can lose a message, or the other computer can crash independently. To avoid fate sharing, the RPC programmer must adjust the code to prepare for and handle this failure. When the client receives a "service failure" signal, the client may be able to recover by, for example, trying a different service or choosing an alternative algorithm that doesn't use a remote service.

The second difference between ordinary procedure calls and RPCs is that RPCs introduce a new failure mode, the "no response" failure. When there is no response from a service, the client cannot tell which of two things went wrong: (1) some failure occurred before the service had a chance to perform the requested action, or (2) the service performed the action and then a failure occurred, causing just the response to be lost.

Most RPC designs handle the no-response case by choosing one of three implementation strategies:

- *At-least-once* RPC. If the client stub doesn't receive a response within some specific time, the stub resends the request as many times as necessary until it receives a response from the service. This implementation may cause the service to execute a request more than once. For applications that call SQRT, executing the request more than once is harmless because with the same argument SQRT should always produce the same answer. In programming language terms, the SQRT service has no side effects. Such side-effect-free operations are also *idempotent*: repeating the same request or sequence of requests several times has the same effect as doing it just once. An at-least-once implementation does not provide the guarantee implied by its name. For example, if the service was located in a building that has been blown away by a hurricane, retrying doesn't help. To handle such cases, an at-least-once RPC implementation will give up after some number of retries. When that happens, the request may have been executed more than once or not at all.

- *At-most-once* RPC. If the client stub doesn't receive a response within some specific time, then the client stub returns an error to the caller, indicating that the service may or may not have processed the request. At-most-once semantics may be more appropriate for requests that do have side effects. For example, in a banking application, using at-least-once semantics for a request to transfer \$100 from one account to another could result in multiple \$100 transfers. Using at-most-once semantics assures that either zero or one transfers take place, a somewhat more controlled outcome. Implementing at-most-once RPC is harder than it sounds because the underlying network may duplicate the request message without the client stub's knowledge. Chapter 7 [on-line] describes an at-most-once implementation, and Birrell and Nelson's paper gives a nice, complete description of an RPC system that implements at-most-once [Suggestions for Further Reading 4.1.1].

- *Exactly-once* RPC. These semantics are the ideal, but because the client and service are independent it is in principle impossible to guarantee. As in the case of at-least-once, if the service is in a building that was blown away by a hurricane, the best the client stub can do is return error status. On the other hand, by adding the complexity of extra message exchanges and careful record-keeping, one can approach exactly-once semantics closely enough to satisfy some applications. The general idea is that, if the RPC requesting transfer of $100 from account A to B produces a "no response" failure, the client stub sends a separate RPC request to the service to ask about the status of the request that got no response. This solution requires that both the client and the service stubs keep careful records of each remote procedure call request and response. These records must be fault tolerant because the computer running the service might fail and lose its state between the original RPC and the inquiry to check on the RPC's status. Chapters 8 [on-line] through 10 [on-line] introduce the necessary techniques.

The programmer must be aware that RPC semantics differ from those of ordinary procedure calls, and because different RPC systems handle the no-response case in different ways, it is important to understand just which semantics any particular RPC system tries to provide. Even if the name of the implementation implies a guarantee (e.g., at-least-once), we have seen that there are cases in which the implementation cannot deliver it. One cannot simply take a collection of legacy programs and arbitrarily separate the modules with RPC. Some thought and reprogramming is inevitably required. Problem set *2* explores the effects of different RPC semantics in the context of a simple client/service application.

The third difference is that calling a local procedure takes typically much less time than calling a remote procedure call. For example, invoking a remote SQRT is likely to be more expensive than the computation for SQRT itself because the overhead of a remote procedure call is much higher than the overhead of following the procedure calling conventions. To hide the cost of a remote procedure call, a client stub may deploy various performance-enhancing techniques (see Chapter 6), such as caching results and pipelining requests (as is done in the X Window System of Sidebar 4.4). These techniques increase complexity and can introduce new problems (e.g., how to ensure that the cache at the client stays consistent with the one at the service). The performance difference between procedure calls and remote procedure calls requires the designer to consider carefully what procedure calls should be remote ones and which ones should be ordinary, local procedure calls.

A final difference between procedure calls and RPCs is that some programming language features don't combine well with RPC. For example, a procedure that communicates with another procedure through global variables cannot typically be executed remotely because separate computers usually have separate address spaces. Similarly, other language constructs that use explicit addresses won't work. Arguments consisting of data structures that contain pointers, for example, are a problem because pointers to objects in the client computer are local addresses that have different bindings when resolved in the service computer. It is possible to design systems that use global references for objects that are passed by reference to remote procedure calls but require significant additional machinery and introduce new problems. For example, a new plan is needed for determining whether an object can be deleted locally because a remote computer might still have a reference to the object. Solutions exist, however; see, for example, the article on Network Objects [Suggestions for Further Reading 4.1.2].

Since RPCs don't provide the same semantics as procedure calls, the word "procedure" in "remote procedure call" can be misleading. Over the years the concept of RPC has evolved from its original interpretation as an exact simulation of an ordinary procedure call to instead mean any client/service interaction in which the request is followed by a response. This text uses this modern interpretation.

4.2.3 Communicating through an Intermediary

Sending a message from a sender to a receiver requires that both parties be available at the same time. In many applications this requirement is too strict. For example, in electronic mail we desire that a user be able to send an e-mail to a recipient even if the recipient is not on-line at the time. The sender sends the message and the recipient receives the message some time later, perhaps when the sender is not on-line. We can implement such applications using an intermediary. In the case of communication, this intermediary doesn't have to be trusted because communication applications often consider the intermediary to be part of an untrusted network and have a separate plan for securing messages (as we will see in Chapter 11 [on-line]).

The primary purpose of the e-mail intermediary is to implement *buffered* communication. Buffered communication provides the SEND/RECEIVE abstraction but avoids the requirement that the sender and receiver be present simultaneously. It allows the delivery of a message to be shifted in time. The intermediary can hold messages until the recipient comes on-line. The intermediary might buffer messages in volatile memory or in non-volatile memory, such as a file system. The latter design allows the intermediary to buffer messages across power failures.

Once we have an intermediary, three interesting design opportunities arise. First, the sender and receiver may make different choices of whether to *push* or *pull* messages. Push is when the initiator of a data movement sends the data. Pull is when the initiator of a data movement asks the other end to send it the data. These definitions are independent of whether or not the system uses an intermediary, but in systems with intermediaries it is not uncommon to find both in a single system. For example, the sender in the Internet's e-mail system, Simple Mail Transfer Protocol (SMTP), pushes the mail to the service that holds the recipient's mailbox. On the other hand, the receiving client pulls messages to fetch mail from a mailbox: the user hits the

"Get new mail" button, which causes the mail client to contact the mailbox service and ask it for any new mail.

Second, the existence of an intermediary opens an opportunity to apply the design principle *decouple modules with indirection* by having the intermediary, rather than the originator, determine to whom a message is delivered. For example, an Internet user can send a message to `president@whitehouse.gov`. The intermediary that forwards the message will deliver it to whoever happens to be the President. As another example, users should be able to send an e-mail to a mailing list or to post a message to a bulletin board without knowing exactly who is on the mailing list or subscribed to the bulletin board.

Third, when indirection through an intermediary is available, the designer has a choice of when and where to duplicate messages. In the mailing list example, the intermediary sends a copy of the e-mail to each member of the list. In the bulletin board example, an intermediary may group messages and send them as a group to other intermediaries. When a user fetches the bulletin article from its local intermediary, the local intermediary makes a final copy for delivery to the user.

Publish/subscribe is a general style of communication that takes advantage of the three design opportunities of communication through an intermediary. In this communication model, the sender is called the publisher and notifies an event service that it has produced a new message on a certain topic. Recipients subscribe to the event service and express their interest in certain topics. If multiple recipients are interested in the same topic, all of them receive a copy of the message. Popular usages of publish/subscribe are electronic mailing lists and instant messaging services that provide chat rooms. A user might join a chat room on a certain topic. When another user publishes a message in the room, all the members of that room receive it. Another publish/subscribe application is Usenet News, a bulletin board service (described in Sidebar 4.5 on peer-to-peer computing).

4.3 SUMMARY AND THE ROAD AHEAD

The client/service model enforces modularity and is the basic approach to organizing complex computer systems. The rest of the book works out major issues in building computer systems that this chapter has identified but has not addressed:

- *Enforcing modularity within a computer* (Chapter 5). Restricting the implementation of client/service systems to one computer per module can be too expensive. Chapter 5 shows how an operating system can use a technique called virtualization to create many virtual computers out of one physical computer. The operating system can enforce modularity between each client and each service by giving each client and each service a separate virtual computer.

- *Performance* (Chapter 6). Computer systems have implicit or explicit performance goals. If services are not carefully designed, it is possible that the slowest service in the system becomes a performance bottleneck, which causes the complete system to operate at the performance of the slowest service. Identifying performance bottlenecks and avoiding them is a challenge that a designer faces in most computer systems.

- *Networking* (Chapter 7 [on-line]). The client/service model must have a way to send the request message from the client to the service, and the response message back. Implementing SEND_MESSAGE and RECEIVE_MESSAGE is a challenging problem, since networks may lose, reorder, or duplicate messages while routing them between the client and the service. Furthermore, networks exhibit a wide range of performance properties, making straightforward solutions inadequate.
- *Fault tolerance* (Chapter 8 [on-line]). We may need for a service to continue to operate even if some of the hardware and software modules fail. For example, we may want to construct a fault tolerant date-and-time service that runs on several computers so that if one of the computers fails, another computer can still deliver a response to requests for the date and time. In systems that harness a large number of computers to deliver a single service, it is unavoidable that at any instant of time some of the computers will have failed. For example, Google, which indexes the Web, reportedly uses more than 100,000 computers to deliver the service. (A description of the systems Google has designed can be found in Suggestions for Further Reading 3.2.4 and 10.1.10.) With so many computers, some of them are certain to be unavailable. Techniques for fault tolerance allow designers to implement reliable services out of unreliable components. These techniques involve detecting failures, containing them, and recovering from them.
- *Atomicity* (Chapter 9 [on-line]). The file service described in this chapter (Figure 4.6 in Section 4.1.6) must work correctly in the face of concurrent access and failures, and use OPEN and CLOSE calls to mark related READ and WRITE operations. Chapter 9 [on-line] introduces a single framework called atomicity that addresses both issues. This framework allows the operations between an OPEN and CLOSE call to be executed as an atomic, indivisible action. As we saw in Section 4.2.2, exactly-once RPC is ideal for implementing a banking application. Chapter 9 [on-line] introduces the necessary tools for exactly-once RPC and building such applications.
- *Consistency* (Chapter 10 [on-line]). This chapter uses messages to implement various protocols to ensure consistency of data stores on different computers.
- *Security* (Chapter 11 [on-line]). The client/service model protects against accidental errors propagating from one module to another module. Some services may need to protect against malicious attacks. This requirement arises, for example, when a file service is storing sensitive data and needs to ensure that malicious users cannot read the sensitive data. Such protection requires that the service reliably identify users so that it can make an authorization decision. The design of systems in the face of malicious users is a topic known as *security*.

The subsystems that address these topics are interesting systems in their own right and are case studies of managing complexity. Typically, these subsystems are internally structured as client/service systems, applying the concept of this chapter recursively. The next two sections provide two case studies of real-world client/service systems and also illustrate the need for the topics addressed in the subsequent chapters.

4.4 CASE STUDY: THE INTERNET DOMAIN NAME SYSTEM (DNS)

The Internet Domain Name System (DNS) provides an excellent case study of both a client/service application and a successful implementation of a naming scheme, in this case for naming of Internet computers and services. Although designed for that specific application, DNS is actually a general-purpose name management and name resolution system that hierarchically distributes the management of names among different naming authorities and also hierarchically distributes the job of resolving names to different name servers. Its design allows it to respond rapidly to requests for name resolution and to scale up to extremely large numbers of stored records and numbers of requests. It is also quite resilient, in the sense that it provides continued, accurate responses in the face of many kinds of network and server failures.

The primary use for DNS is to associate user-friendly character-string names, called *domain names*, with machine-oriented binary identifiers for network attachment points, called *Internet addresses*. Domain names are hierarchically structured, the term *domain* being used in a general way in DNS: it is simply a set of one or more names that have the same hierarchical ancestor. This convention means that hierarchical regions can be domains, but it also means that the personal computer on your desk is a domain with just one member. In consequence, although the phrase "domain name" suggests the name of a hierarchical region, every name resolved by DNS is called a domain name, whether it is the name of a hierarchical region or the name of a single attachment point. Because domains typically correspond to administrative organizations, they also are the unit of delegation of name assignment, using exactly the hierarchical naming scheme described in Section 3.1.4.

For our purposes, the basic interface to DNS is quite simple:

value ← DNS_RESOLVE (*domain_name*)

This interface omits the context argument from the standard name-resolving interface of the naming model of Section 2.2.1 because there is just a single, universal, default context for resolving all Internet domain names, and the reference to that one context is built into DNS_RESOLVE as a configuration parameter.

In the usual DNS implementation, binding is not accomplished by invoking BIND and UNBIND procedures as suggested by our naming model, but rather by using a text editor or database generator to create and manage tables of bindings. These tables are then loaded into DNS servers by some behind-the-scenes method as often as their managers deem necessary. One consequence of this design is that changes to DNS bindings don't often occur within seconds of the time you request them; instead, they typically take hours.

Domain names are path names, with components separated by periods (called *dots,* particularly when reading domain names aloud) and with the least significant component coming first. Three typical domain names are

```
ginger.cse.pedantic.edu    ginger.scholarly.edu    ginger.com
```

DNS allows both relative and absolute path names. Absolute path names are supposed to be distinguished by the presence of a trailing dot. In human interfaces the trailing dot rarely appears; instead, DNS_RESOLVE applies a simple form of multiple lookup. When presented with a relative path name, DNS_RESOLVE first tries appending a default context, supplied by a locally set configuration parameter. If the resulting extended name fails to resolve, DNS_RESOLVE tries again, this time appending just a trailing dot to the originally presented name. Thus, for example, if one presents DNS_RESOLVE with the apparently relative path name "ginger.com", and the default context is "pedantic.edu.", DNS_RESOLVE will first try to resolve the absolute path name "ginger.com.pedantic.edu.". If that attempt leads to a NOT-FOUND result, it will then try to resolve the absolute path name "ginger.com."

4.4.1 Name Resolution in DNS

DNS name resolution might have been designed in at least three ways:

1. *The telephone book model:* Give each network user a copy of a file that contains a list of every domain name and its associated Internet address. This scheme has a severe problem: to cover the entire Internet, the size of the file would be proportional to the number of network users, and updating it would require delivering a new copy to every user. Because the frequency of update tends to be proportional to the number of domain names listed in the file, the volume of network traffic required to keep it up to date would grow with the cube of the number of domain names. This scheme was used for nearly 20 years in the Internet, was found wanting, and was replaced with DNS in the late 1980s.

2. *The central directory service model:* Place the file on a single well-connected server somewhere in the network and provide a protocol to ask it to resolve names. This scheme would make update easy, but with growth in the number of users its designer would have to adopt increasingly complex strategies to keep it from becoming both a performance bottleneck and a potential source of massive failure. There is yet another problem: whoever controls the central server is by default in charge of all name assignment. This design does not cater well to delegation of responsibility in assignment of domain names.

3. *The distributed directory service model.* The idea is to have many servers, each of which is responsible for resolving some subset of domain names, and a protocol for finding a server that can resolve any particular name. As we shall see in the following descriptions, this model can provide delegation and respond

to increases in scale while maintaining reliability and performance. For those reasons, DNS uses this model.

With the distributed directory service model, the operation of every name server is the same: a server maintains a set of name records, each of which binds a domain name to an Internet address. When a client sends a request for a name resolution, the name server looks through the collection of domain names for which it is responsible, and if it finds a name record, it returns that record as its response. If it does not find the requested name, it looks through a separate set of referral records. Each referral record binds a hierarchical region of the DNS name space to some other name server that can help resolve names in that region of the naming hierarchy. Starting with the most significant component of the requested domain name, the server searches through referral records for the one that matches the most components, and it returns that referral record. If nothing matches, DNS cannot resolve the original name, so it returns a "no such domain" response.

The referral architecture of DNS, though conceptually simple, has a number of elaborations that enhance its performance, scalability, and robustness. We begin with an example of its operation in a simple case, and we later add some of the enhancements. The dashed lines in Figure 4.10 illustrate the operation of DNS when the client computer named `ginger.cse.pedantic.edu`, in the lower left corner, tries to resolve the domain name `ginger.Scholarly.edu.` The first step, shown as request #1, is that DNS_RESOLVE sends that domain name to a *root name server*, whose Internet address it somehow knows. Section 4.4.4 explains how DNS_RESOLVE discovers that address.

The root name server matches the name in the request with the subset of domain names it knows about, starting with the most significant component of the requested domain name (in this example, `edu`). In this example, the root name server discovers that it has a referral record for the domain `edu`, so it responds with a referral, saying, in this example, "There is a name server for a domain named `edu`. The name record for that name server binds the name `names.edu.` to Internet address 192.14.71.191." This response illustrates that name servers, like any other servers, have both domain names and Internet addresses. Usually, the domain name of a name server gives some clue about what domain names it serves, but there is no necessary correspondence. Responding with a complete name record provides more information than the client really needs (the client usually doesn't care about the name of the name server), but it allows all responses from a name server to be uniform. Because the name server's domain name isn't significant and to reduce clutter in Figure 4.10, that figure omits it in the illustrated response.

When the client's DNS_RESOLVE receives this response, it immediately resends the same name resolution request, but this time it directs the request (request 2 in the figure) to the name server located at the Internet address mentioned in response number 1. That name server matches the requested path name with the set of domain names it knows about, again starting with the most significant component. In this case, it finds a match for the name `Scholarly.edu.` in a referral record. It thus sends back a response saying, "There is a name server for a domain named `Scholarly.edu.` The

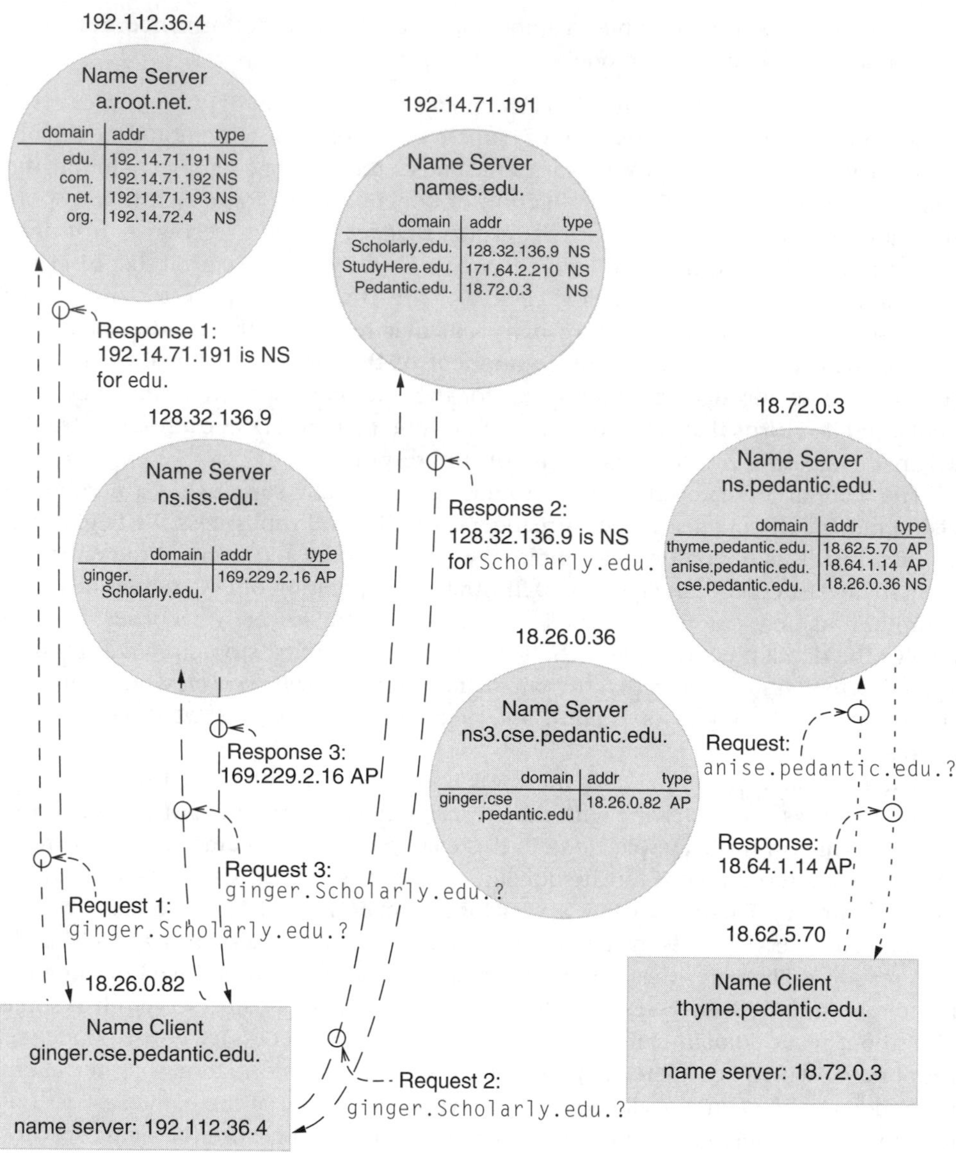

FIGURE 4.10

Structure and operation of the Internet Domain Name System. In this figure, each circle represents a name server, and each rectangle is a name client. The type NS in a table or in a response means that this is a referral to another name server, while the type AP in a table or a response means that this is an Internet address. The dashed lines show the paths of the three requests made by the name client in the lower left corner to resolve the name `ginger.Scholarly.edu`, starting with the root name server. The dotted lines show resolution of a request of the name client in the lower right corner to resolve `anise.pedantic.edu` starting with a local name server.

name record for that name server binds the name `ns.iss.edu.` to Internet address 128.32.136.9." The illustration again omits the domain name of the name server.

This sequence repeats for each component of the original path name, until DNS_RESOLVE finally reaches a name server that has the name record for `ginger.Scholarly.edu`. That name server sends back a response saying, "The name record for `ginger.Scholarly.edu.` binds that name to Internet address 169.229.2.16." This being the answer to the original query, DNS_RESOLVE returns this result to its caller, which can go on to initiate an exchange of messages with its intended target.

The server that holds either a name record or a referral record for a domain name is known as the *authoritative name server* for that domain name. In our example, the name server `ns3.cse.pedantic.edu.` is authoritative for the `ginger.cse.pedantic.edu.` domain, as well as all other domain names that end with `cse.pedantic.edu.`, and `ns.iss.edu.` is authoritative for the `Scholarly.edu.` domain. Since a name server does not hold the name record for its own name, a name server cannot be the authoritative name server for its own name. Instead, for example, the root name server is authoritative for the domain name `edu.`, while the `names.edu.` name server is authoritative for all domain names that end in `edu.`

That is the basic model of DNS operation. Here are some elaborations in its operation, each of which helps make the system fast-responding, robust, and capable of growing to a large scale.

1. It is not actually necessary to send the initial request to the root name server. DNS_RESOLVE can send the request to *any* convenient name server whose Internet address it knows. The name server doesn't care where the request came from; it simply compares the requested domain name with the list of domain names for which it is responsible in order to see if it holds a record that can help. If it does, it answers the request. If it doesn't, it answers by returning a referral to a root name server. The ability to send any request to a local name server means that the common case in which the client, the name server, and the target domain name are all three in the same domain (e.g., `pedantic.edu`) can be handled swiftly with a single request/response interaction. (The dotted lines in the lower right corner of Figure 4.10 show an example, in which `thyme.pedantic.edu.` asks the name server for the `pedantic.edu` domain for the address of `anise.pedantic.edu.`) This feature also simplifies name discovery because all a client needs to know is the Internet address of any nearby name server. The first request to that nearby server for a distant name (in the current example, `ginger.scholarly.edu`) will return a referral to the Internet address of a root name server.

2. Some domain name servers offer what is (perhaps misleadingly) called *recursive* name service. If the name server does not hold a record for the requested name, rather than sending a referral response, the name server takes on the responsibility for resolving the name itself. It forwards the initial request to a root name server, then continues to follow the chain of responses to resolve the complete path name, and finally returns the desired name record to its client. By

itself, this feature seems merely to simplify life for the client, but in conjunction with the next feature it provides a major performance enhancement.

3. Every name server is expected to maintain, in addition to its authoritative records, a cache of all name records it has heard about from other name servers. A server that provides recursive name service thus collects records that can greatly speed up future name resolution requests. If, for example, the name server for `cse.pedantic.edu` offers recursive service and it is asked to resolve the name `flower.cs.scholarly.edu`, in the course of doing so (assuming that it does not in turn request recursive service), its cache might acquire the following records:

```
edu                      refer to names.edu at 198.41.0.4
Scholarly.edu            refer to ns.iss.edu at 128.32.25.19
cs.Scholarly.edu         refer to cs.Scholarly.edu at 128.32.247.24
flower.cs.Scholarly.edu        Internet address is 128.32.247.29
```

Now, when this name server receives, for example, the request to resolve the name `psych.Scholarly.edu`, it will discover the record for the domain `Scholarly.edu` in the cache and it will be able to quickly resolve the name by forwarding the initial request directly to the corresponding name server.

A cache holds a duplicate copy, which may go out of date if someone changes the authoritative name record. On the basis that changes of existing name bindings are relatively infrequent in the Domain Name System and that it is hard to keep track of all the caches to which a domain name record may have propagated, the DNS design does not call for explicit invalidation of changed entries. Instead, it uses expiration. That is, the naming authority for a DNS record marks each record that it sends out with an expiration period, which may range from seconds to months. A DNS cache manager is expected to discard entries that have passed their expiration period. The DNS cache manager provides a memory model that is called *eventual consistency,* a topic taken up in Chapter 10 [on-line].

4.4.2 Hierarchical Name Management

Domain names form a hierarchy, and the arrangement of name servers described above matches that hierarchy, thereby distributing the job of name resolution. The same hierarchy also distributes the job of managing the handing out of names, by distributing the responsibility of operating name servers. Distributing responsibility is one of the main virtues of the distributed directory service model.

The way this works is actually quite simple: whoever operates a name server can be a *naming authority,* which means that he or she may add authoritative records to that name server. Thus, at some point early in the evolution of the Internet, some Pedantic University network administrator deployed a name server for the domain `pedantic.edu` and convinced the administrator of the `edu` domain to install a binding for the domain name `pedantic.edu.` associated with the name and Internet address of the `pedantic.edu` name server. Now, if Pedantic University wants to add a record, for example, for an Internet address that it wishes to name `archimedes.pedantic.edu`, its administrator can do so without asking permission of anyone else. A request to resolve the name `archimedes.pedantic.edu` can arrive at any domain name server in the Internet; that request will eventually arrive at the name server for the `pedantic.edu` domain, where it can be answered correctly. Similarly, a network administrator at the Institute for Scholarly Studies can install a name record for an Internet address named `archimedes.Scholarly.edu` on its own authority. Although both institutions have chosen the name `archimedes` for one of their computers, because the path names of the domains are distinct there was no need for their administrators to coordinate their name assignments. Put another way, their naming authorities can act independently.

Continuing this method of decentralization, any organization that manages a name server can create lower-level naming domains. For example, the Computer Science and Engineering Department of Pedantic University may have so many computers that it is convenient for the department to manage the names of those computers itself. All that is necessary is for the department to deploy a name server for a lower-level domain (named, for example, `cse.pedantic.edu`) and convince the administrator of the `pedantic.edu` domain to install a referral record for that name in its name server.

4.4.3 Other Features of DNS

To ensure high availability of name service, the DNS specification calls on every organization that runs a name service to arrange that there be at least two identical replica servers. This specification is important, especially at higher levels of the domain naming hierarchy, because most Internet activity uses domain names and inability to resolve a name component blocks reachability to all sites below that name component. Many organizations have three or four replicas of their name servers, and as of 2008 there were about 80 replicas of the root name server. Ideally, replicas should be attached to the network at places that are widely separated, so that there is some protection against local network and electric power outages. Again, the importance of separated attachment increases at higher levels of the naming hierarchy. Thus, the 80 replicas of the root name server are scattered around the world, but the three or four replicas of a typical organization's name server are more likely to be located within the campus of that organization. This arrangement ensures that, even if the campus is disconnected from the outside world, communication by name within the organization can still work. On the other hand, during such a disconnection, correspondents outside the organization cannot even verify that a name exists, for example, to validate an e-mail address. Therefore, a better arrangement might be to attach at least one of the organization's multiple replica name servers to another part of the Internet.

For the same reason that name servers need to be replicated, many network services also need to be replicated, so DNS allows the same name to be bound to several Internet addresses. In consequence, the *value* returned by DNS_RESOLVE can be a list of (presumably) equivalent Internet addresses. The client can choose which

Internet address to contact, based on order in the list, previous response times, a guess as to the distance to the attachment point, or any other criterion it might have available.

The design of DNS allows name service to be quite robust. In principle, the job of a DNS server is extremely simple: accept a request packet, search a table, and send a response packet. Its interface specification does not require it to maintain any connection state, or any other durable, changeable state; its only public interface is idempotent. The consequence is that a small, inexpensive personal computer can provide name service for a large organization, which encourages dedicating a computer to this service. A dedicated computer, in turn, tends to be more robust than one that supplies several diverse and unrelated network services. In addition a server with small, read-only tables can be designed so that when something such as a power failure happens, it can return to service quickly, perhaps even automatically. (Chapters 8 [on-line] and 9 [on-line] discuss how to design such a system.)

DNS also allows synonyms, in the form of indirect names. Synonyms are used conventionally to solve two distinct problems. For an example of the first problem, suppose that the Pedantic University Computer Science and Engineering Department has a computer whose Internet address is named `minehaha.cse.pedantic.edu`. This is a somewhat older and slower machine, but it is known to be very reliable. The department runs a World Wide Web server on this computer, but as its load increases the department knows that it will someday be necessary to move the Web server to a faster machine named `mississippi.cse.pedantic.edu`. Without synonyms, when the server moves, it would be necessary to inform everyone that there is a new name for the department's World Wide Web service. With synonyms, the laboratory can bind the indirect name `www.cse.pedantic.edu` to `minehaha.cse.pedantic.edu` and publicize the indirect name as the name of its Web site. When the time comes for `mississippi.cse.pedantic.edu` to take over the service, it can do so by simply having the manager of the `cse.pedantic.edu` domain change the binding of the indirect name. All those customers who have been using the name `www.cse.pedantic.edu` to get to the Web site will find that name continues to work correctly; they don't care that a different computer is now handling the job. As a general rule, the names of services can be expected to outlive their bindings to particular Internet addresses, and synonyms cater to this difference in lifetimes.

The second problem that synonyms can handle is to allow a single computer to appear to be in two widely different naming domains. For example, suppose that a geophysics group at the Institute of Scholarly Studies has developed a service to predict volcano eruptions but that organization doesn't actually have a computer suitable for running that service. It could arrange with a commercial vendor to run the service on a machine named, perhaps, `service-bureau.com` and then ask the manager of the Institute's name server to bind the indirect name `volcano.iss.edu` to `service-bureau.com`. The Institute could then advertise its service under the indirect name. If the commercial vendor raises its prices, it would be possible to move the service to a different vendor by simply rebinding the indirect name.

Because resolving a synonym requires an extra round-trip through DNS, and the basic name-to-Internet-address binding of DNS already provides a level of indirection, some network specialists recommend just manipulating name-to-Internet-address bindings to get the effect of synonyms.

4.4.4 Name Discovery in DNS

Name discovery comes up in at least three places in the Domain Name System: a client must discover the name of a nearby name server, a user must discover the domain name of a desired service, and the resolving system must discover an extension for unqualified domain names.

First, in order for DNS_RESOLVE to send a request to a name server, it needs to know the Internet address of that name server. DNS_RESOLVE finds this address in a configuration table. The real name-discovery question is how this address gets into the configuration table. In principle, this address would be the address of a root server, but as we have seen it can be the address of any existing name server. The most widely used approach is that when a computer first connects to a network it performs a name discovery broadcast to which the Internet service provider (ISP) responds by assigning the attacher an Internet address and also telling the attacher the Internet address of one or more name servers operated by or for the ISP. Another way to terminate name discovery is by direct communication with a local network manager, to obtain the address of a suitable name server, followed by configuring the answer into DNS_RESOLVE.

The second form of name discovery involves domain names themselves. If you wish to use the volcano prediction service at the Institute for Scholarly Studies, you need to know its name. Some chain of events that began with direct communication must occur. Typically, people learn of domain names via other network services, such as by e-mail, querying a search engine, reading postings in newsgroups or while surfing the Web, so the original direct communication may be long forgotten. But using each of those services requires knowing a domain name, so there must have been a direct communication at some earlier time. The purchaser of a personal computer is likely to find that it comes with a Web browser that has been preconfigured with domain names of the manufacturer's suggested World Wide Web query and directory services (as well as domain names of the manufacturer's support sites and other advertisers). Similarly, a new customer of an Internet service provider typically may, upon registering for service, be told the domain name of that ISP's Web site, which can then be used to discover names for many other services.

The third instance of name discovery concerns the extension that is used for unqualified domain names. Recall that the Domain Name System uses absolute path names, so if DNS_RESOLVE is presented with an unqualified name such as `library` it must somehow extend it, for example, to `library.pedantic.edu`. The default context used for extension is usually a configuration parameter of DNS_RESOLVE. The value of this parameter is typically chosen by the human user when initially setting up a computer, with an eye to minimizing typing for the most frequently used domain names.

4.4.5 Trustworthiness of DNS responses

A shortcoming of DNS is that, although it purports to provide authoritative name resolutions in its responses, it does not use protocols that allow authentication of those responses. As a result, it is possible (and, unfortunately, relatively easy) for an intruder to masquerade as a DNS server and send out mischievous or malevolent responses to name resolution requests.

Currently, the primary way of dealing with this problem is for the user of DNS to treat all of its responses as potentially unreliable hints and independently verify (using the terminology of Chapters 7 [on-line] and 11 [on-line] we would say "perform end-to-end authentication of") the identity of any system with which that user communicates. An alternative would be for DNS servers to use authentication protocols in communication with their clients. However, even if a DNS response is assuredly authentic, it still might not be accurate (for example, a DNS cache may hold out-of-date information, or a DNS administrator may have configured an incorrect name-to-address binding), so a careful user would still want to independently authenticate the identity of its correspondents.

Chapter 11 [on-line] describes protocols that can be used for authentication; there is an ongoing debate among network experts as to whether or how DNS should be upgraded to use such protocols.

The reader interested in learning more about DNS should explore the documents in the readings for DNS [Suggestions for Further Reading 4.3].

4.5 CASE STUDY: THE NETWORK FILE SYSTEM (NFS)

The Network File System (NFS), designed by Sun Microsystems, Inc. in the 1980s, is a client/service application that provides shared file storage for clients across a network. An NFS client grafts a remote file system onto the client's local file system name space and makes it behave like a local UNIX file system (see Section 2.5). Multiple clients can mount the same remote file system so that users can share files.

The need for NFS arose because of technology improvements. Before the 1980s, computers were so expensive that each one had to be shared among multiple users and each computer had a single file system. But a benefit of the economic pressure was that it allowed for easy collaboration because users could share files easily. In the early 1980s, it became economically feasible to build workstations, which allowed each engineer to have a private computer. But users still desired to have a shared file system for ease of collaboration. NFS provides exactly that: it allows a user at any workstation to use files stored on a shared server, a powerful workstation with local disks but often without a graphical display.

NFS also simplifies the management of a collection of workstations. Without NFS, a system administrator must manage each workstation and, for example, arrange for backups of each workstation's local disk. NFS allows for centralized management; for example, a system administrator needs to back up only the server's disks to archive the file system. In the 1980s, the setup also had a cost benefit: NFS allowed organizations to buy workstations without disks, saving the cost of a disk interface on every workstation and the cost of unused disk space on each workstation.

The designers of NFS had four major goals. NFS should work with existing applications, which means NFS should provide the same semantics as a local UNIX file system. NFS should be deployable easily, which means its implementation should be able to retrofit into existing UNIX systems. The client should be implementable in other operating systems such as Microsoft's DOS, so that a user on a personal computer can have access to the files on an NFS server; this goal implies that the client/service messages cannot be too UNIX system-specific. Finally, NFS should be efficient enough to be tolerable to users, but it doesn't have to provide as high performance as local file systems. NFS only partially achieves these goals because achieving them all is difficult. The designers made a trade-off: simplify the design and lose some of the UNIX semantics.

This section describes version 2 of NFS. Version 1 was never deployed outside of Sun Microsystems, while version 2 has been in use since 1987. The case study concludes with a brief summary of the changes in versions 3 (1990s) and 4 (early 2000s), which address weaknesses in version 2. Problem set *3* explores an NFS-inspired design to reinforce the ideas in NFS.

4.5.1 Naming Remote Files and Directories

To programs, NFS appears as a UNIX file system providing the file interface presented in Section 2.5. User programs can name remote files in the same way as local files. When a user program invokes, say, OPEN ("/users/alice/.profile", READONLY), it cannot tell from the path name whether "users" or "alice" are local or remote directories.

To make naming remote files transparent to users and their programs, the NFS client must mount a remote file system on the local name space. NFS performs this operation by using a separate program, called the *mounter*. This program serves a similar function as the MOUNT call (described in Section 2.5.10); it grafts the remote file system—named by *host*:*path*, where *host* is a DNS name and *path* a path name—onto the local file name space. The mounter sends a remote procedure call to the file server *host* and asks for a *file handle*, a 32-byte name for the object identified by *path*. On receiving the reply, the NFS client marks the mount point in the local file system as a remote file system. It also remembers the file handle for *path* and the network address for the server.

To the NFS client a file handle is a 32-byte opaque name that identifies an object on a remote NFS server. An NFS client obtains file handles from the server when the client mounts a remote file system, or it looks up a file in a directory on the NFS server. In all subsequent remote procedure calls to the NFS server for that file, the NFS client includes the file handle. In many ways the file handle is similar to an inode number; it is not visible to applications, but it used as a name internal to NFS to name files.

To the NFS server a file handle is a structured name—containing a *file system identifier*, an *inode number*, and *a generation number*—which the server can use to locate the file. The file system identifier allows the server to identify the file system responsible for the file. The inode number (see page 58) allows the identified file system to locate the file on the disk.

One might wonder why the NFS designers didn't choose to put path names in file handles. To see why, consider the following scenario with two user programs running on different clients:

	Program 1 on client 1	Program 2 on client 2	Time
1	CHDIR ("dir1")		↓
2	*fd* ← OPEN ("f", READONLY)		
3		RENAME ("dir1", "dir2")	
4		RENAME ("dir3", "dir1")	
5	READ (*fd, buf, n*)		

RENAME (*source*, *destination*) changes the name of *source* to *destination*. The first rename operation (on line *3*) in program 2 renames "dir1" to "dir2", and the second one (on line *4*) renames "dir3" to "dir1". This scenario raises the following question: when program 1 invokes READ (line *5*) after the two rename operations have completed, does program 1 read data from "dir1/f", or "dir2/f"?

If the two programs were running on the same computer and sharing a local UNIX file system, program 1 would read "dir2/f", according to the UNIX specification. The goal is that NFS should provide the same behavior. If the NFS server were to put path names inside handles, then the READ call would result in a remote procedure call for the file "dir1/f". By putting the inode number in the handle the specification is met.

The file handle includes a generation number to handle scenarios such as the following almost correctly:

	Program 1 on client 1	Program 2 on client 2	Time
1		*fd* ← OPEN ("f", READONLY)	↓
2	UNLINK ("f")		
3	*fd* ← OPEN ("f", CREATE)		
4		READ (*fd, buf, n*)	

A program on a client 1 deletes a file "f" (line *2*) and creates a new file with the same name (line *3*), while another program on a client 2 already has opened the original file (on line *1*). If the two programs were running on the same computer and sharing a local UNIX file system, program 2 would read the old file on line *4*.

If the server should happen to reuse the inode of the old file for the new file, remote procedure calls from client 2 will get the new file, the one created by client 1, instead of the old file. The generation number allows NFS to avoid this incorrect behavior. When the server reuses an inode, it increases the generation number by one. In the example, client 1 and client 2 would receive different file handles, and client 2 will use the old handle. Increasing the generation number makes it always safe for the NFS server to recycle inodes immediately.

For this scenario, NFS does not provide identical semantics to a local UNIX file system because that would require that the server know which files are in use. With NFS, when client 2 uses the file handle, it will receive an error message: "stale file handle".

This case is one example of the NFS designers trading some UNIX semantics to obtain a simpler implementation.

File handles are usable across server failures, so that even if the server computer fails and restarts between a client program opening a file and then reading from the file, the server can identify the file using the information in the file handle. Making file handles (which include a file system identifier and a generation number) usable across server failures requires small changes to the server's on-disk file system: the NFS designers modified the super block to record the file system identifier and modified inodes to record the generation number for the inode. With this information recorded, after a reboot the NFS server will be able to process NFS requests that the server handed out before it failed.

4.5.2 The NFS Remote Procedure Calls

Table 4.1 shows the remote procedure calls used by NFS. The remote procedure calls are best explained by example. Suppose we have the following fragment of a user program:

```
fd ← OPEN ("f", READONLY)
READ (fd, buf, n)
CLOSE (fd)
```

Table 4.1 NFS Remote Procedure Calls

Remote Procedure Call	Returns
NULL ()	Do nothing.
LOOKUP (*dirfh, name*)	fh and file attributes
CREATE (*dirfh, name, attr*)	fh and file attributes
REMOVE (*dirfh, name*)	status
GETATTR (*fh*)	file attributes
SETATTR (*fh, attr*)	file attributes
READ (*fh, offset, count*)	file attributes and data
WRITE (*fh, offset, count, data*)	file attributes
RENAME (*dirfh, name, tofh, toname*)	status
LINK (*dirfh, name, tofh, toname*)	status
SYMLINK (*dirfh, name, string*)	status
READLINK (*fh*)	string
MKDIR (*dirfh, name, attr*)	fh and file attributes
RMDIR (*dirfh, name*)	status
READDIR (*dirfh, offset, count*)	directory entries
STATFS (*fh*)	file system information

Figure 4.11 shows the corresponding timing diagram where "f" is a remote file. The NFS client implements each file system operation using one or more remote procedure calls.

In response to the program's call to OPEN, the NFS client sends the following remote procedure call to the server:

LOOKUP (*dirfh*, "f")

From before the program runs, the client has a file handle for the current working directory's (*dirfh*). It obtained this handle as a result of a previous lookup or as a result of mounting the remote file system.

On receiving the LOOKUP request, the NFS server extracts the file system identifier and inode number from *dirfh*, and asks the identified file system to look up the inode number in *dirfh*. The identified file system uses the inode number in *dirfh* to locate the directory's inode. Now the NFS server searches the directory identified by the inode number for "f". If present, the server creates a handle for "f". The handle contains the file system identifier of the local file system, the inode number for "f", and the generation number stored in the inode of "f". The NFS server sends this file handle to the client.

On receiving the response, the client allocates the first unused entry in the program's file descriptor table, stores a reference to f's file handle in that entry, and returns the index for the entry (*fd*) to the user program.

Next, the program calls READ (*fd, buf, n*). The client sends the following remote procedure call to the NFS server:

READ (*fh*, 0, *n*)

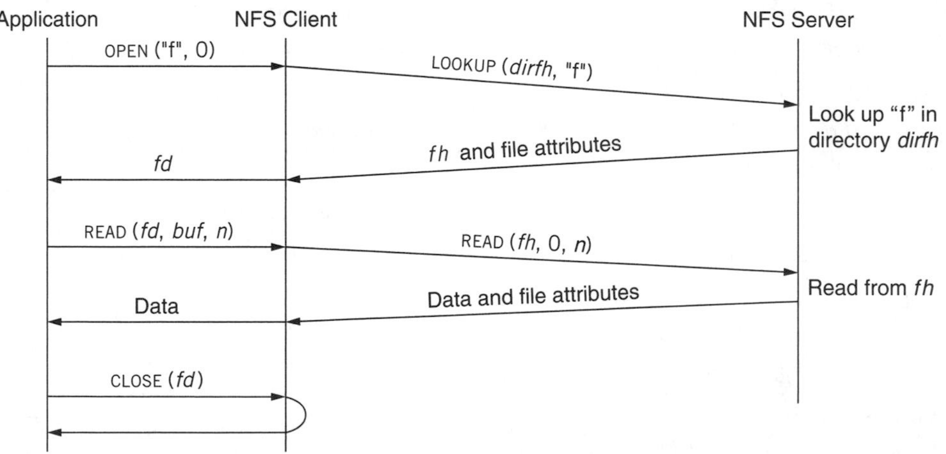

FIGURE 4.11

Example interaction between an NFS client and service. Since the NFS service is stateless, the client does not need to inform the service when the application calls CLOSE. Instead, it just deallocates *fd* and returns.

As with the directory file handle, the NFS server looks up the inode for *fh*. Then, the server reads the data and sends the data in a reply message to the client.

When the program calls CLOSE to tell the local file system that it is done with the file descriptor *fd*, NFS doesn't issue a CLOSE remote procedure call; the protocol doesn't have a CLOSE remote procedure call. Because the application didn't modify the file, the NFS client doesn't have to issue any remote procedure calls. As we shall see in Section 4.5.4, if a program modifies a file, the NFS client will issue remote procedure calls on a CLOSE system call to provide coherence for the file.

The NFS remote procedure calls are designed so that the server can be ***stateless***, that is, the server doesn't need to maintain any other state than the on-disk files. NFS achieves this property by making each remote procedure call contain all the information necessary to carry out that request. The server does not maintain any state about past remote procedure calls to process a new request. For example, the client, not the server, must keep track of the file cursor (see Section 2.3.2), and the client includes it as an argument in the READ remote procedure call. As another example, the file handle contains all information to find the inode on the server, as explained above.

This stateless property simplifies recovery from server failures: a client can just repeat a request until it receives a reply. In fact, the client cannot tell the difference between a server that failed and recovered, and a server that is slow. Because a client repeats a request until it receives a response, it can happen that the server executes a request twice. That is, NFS implements at-least-once semantics for remote procedure calls.

Since many requests are idempotent (e.g., LOOKUP, READ, etc.), that is not a problem, but for some requests it results in surprising behavior. Consider a user program that calls UNLINK on an existing file that is stored on a remote file system. The NFS client would send a REMOVE remote procedure call and the server would execute it, but it could happen that the network lost the reply. In that case, the client would resend the REMOVE request, the server would execute the request again, and the user program would receive an error saying that the file didn't exist!

Later implementations of NFS minimize this surprising behavior by avoiding executing remote procedure calls more than once when there are no server failures. In these implementations, each remote procedure call is tagged with a transaction number and the server maintains some "soft" state (it is lost if the server fails), namely, a reply cache. The reply cache is indexed by transaction identifier and records the response for the transaction identifier. When the server receives a request, it looks up the transaction identifier (ID) in the reply cache. If the ID is in the cache, the server returns the reply from the cache, without reexecuting the request. If the ID is not in the cache, the server processes the request.

If the server doesn't fail, a retry of a REMOVE request will receive the same response as the first attempt. If, however, the server fails and restarts between the first attempt and a retry, the request is executed twice. The designers opted to maintain the reply cache as soft state because storing it in non-volatile storage is expensive. Doing so would require that the reply cache be stored, for example, on a disk and would require a disk write for each remote procedure call to record the response. As explained in Section 6.1.8, disk writes are often a performance bottleneck and much more expensive than a remote procedure call.

Although the stateless property of NFS simplifies recovery, it makes it impossible to implement the UNIX file interface correctly because the UNIX specification requires maintaining state. Consider again the case where one program deletes a file that another program has open. The UNIX specification is that the file exists until the second program closes the file.

If the programs run on different clients, NFS cannot adhere to this specification because it would require that the server keep state. It would have to maintain a reference count per file, which would be incremented on an OPEN system call and decremented on a CLOSE system call, and persist across server failures. In addition, if a client would not respond to messages, the server would have to wait until the client becomes reachable again to decrement the reference count. Instead, NFS just does the easy but slightly wrong thing: remote procedure calls return an error "stale file handle" if a program on another client deletes a file that the first client has open.

NFS does not implement the UNIX specification faithfully because that simplifies the design of NFS. NFS preserves most of the UNIX semantics, and only in rarely encountered situations may users see different behavior. In practice, these situations are not a serious problem, and in return NFS gets by with simple recovery.

4.5.3 Extending the UNIX File System to Support NFS

To implement NFS as an extension of the UNIX file system while minimizing the number of changes required to the UNIX file system, the NFS designers split the file system program by introducing an interface that provides *vnodes*, virtual nodes (see Figure 4.12). A vnode is a structure in volatile memory that abstracts whether a file or directory is implemented by a local file system or a remote file system. This design allows many functions in the file system call layer to be implemented in terms of vnodes, without having to worry about whether a file or directory is local or remote. The interface has an additional advantage: a computer can easily support several, different local file systems.

When a file system call must perform an operation on a file (e.g., reading data), it invokes the corresponding procedure through the vnode interface. The vnode interface has procedures for looking up a file name in the contents of a directory vnode, reading from a vnode, writing to a vnode, closing a vnode, and so on. The local file system and NFS support their own implementation of these procedures.

By using the vnode interface, most of the code for file descriptor tables, current directory, name lookup, and the like, can be moved from the local file system module into the file system call layer with minimal effort. For example, with a few changes, the procedure PATHNAME_TO_INODE from Section 2.5 can be modified to be PATHNAME_TO_VNODE and be provided by the file system call layer.

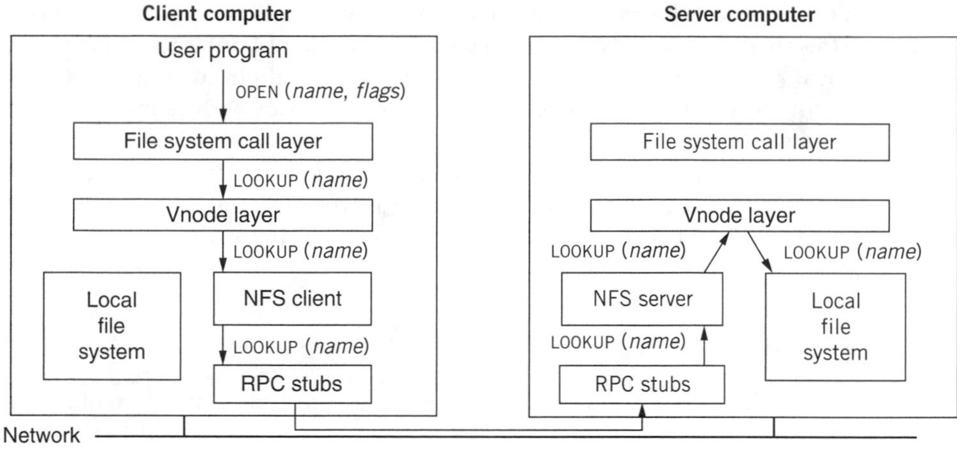

FIGURE 4.12

NFS implementation for the UNIX system

To illustrate the vnode design, we consider a user program that invokes OPEN for a file (see Figure 4.12). To open the file, the file system call layer invokes PATHNAME_TO_VNODE, passing the vnode for the current working directory and the path name for the file as arguments. PATHNAME_TO_VNODE will parse the path name, invoking LOOKUP in the vnode layer for each component in the path name. If the directory is a local directory, the vnode-layer LOOKUP invokes the LOOKUP procedure implemented by the local file system to obtain a vnode for the path name component. If the directory is a remote directory, LOOKUP invokes the LOOKUP procedure implemented by the NFS client.

The NFS client invokes the LOOKUP remote procedure call on the NFS server, passing as arguments the file handle of the directory and the path name's component. On receiving the lookup request, the NFS server extracts the file system identifier and inode number from the file handle for the directory to look up the directory's vnode and then invokes LOOKUP in the vnode layer, passing the path name's component as an argument. If the directory is implemented by the server's local file system, the vnode layer invokes the procedure LOOKUP implemented by the server's local file system, passing the path name's component as an argument. The local file system looks up the name and, if present, creates a vnode and returns the vnode to the NFS server. The NFS server sends a reply containing the vnode's file handle and some metadata for the vnode to the NFS client.

On receiving the reply, the NFS client creates a vnode, which contains the file handle, on the client computer and returns it to the file system call layer on the client machine. When the file system call layer has resolved the complete path name, it returns a file descriptor for the file to the user program.

To achieve usable performance, a typical NFS client maintains various caches. A client stores the vnode for every open file so that the client knows the file handles for open files. A client also caches recently used vnodes, their attributes, recently used blocks of those cached vnodes, and the mapping from path name to vnode. Caching reduces the latency of file system operations on remote files because for cached files a client can avoid the cost of remote procedure calls. In addition, because clients make fewer remote procedure calls, a single server can support more clients. If multiple clients cache the same file, however, NFS must ensure read/write coherence in some way.

4.5.4 Coherence

When programs share a local file in a UNIX system, the program calling READ observes the data from the most recent WRITE, even if this WRITE was performed by another program. This property is called read/write coherence (see Section 2.1.1.1). If the programs are running on different clients, caching complicates implementing these semantics correctly.

To illustrate the problem, consider a user program on one computer that writes a block of a file. The file system call layer on that computer might perform the update to the block in the cache, delaying the write to the server, just like the local UNIX file system delays a write to disk. If a program on another computer then reads the file from the server, it may not observe the change made on the first computer because that change may not have been propagated to the server yet. Because this behavior would be incorrect, NFS implements a form of read/write coherence.

NFS could guarantee read/write coherence for every operation, or just for certain operations. One option is to provide read/write coherence for only OPEN and CLOSE. That is, if an application OPENS a file, WRITES, and CLOSES the file on one client, and if later an application on a second client opens the same file, then the second application will observe the results of the writes by the first application. This option is called *close-to-open consistency*. Another option is to provide read/write coherence for every read and write. That is, if two applications on different clients have the same file open concurrently, then a READ of one observes the results of WRITES of the other.

Many NFS implementations provide close-to-open consistency because it allows for higher data rates for reading or writing a big file; a client can send several reads or write requests without having to wait for a response after each request. Figure 4.13 illustrates close-to-open semantics in more detail. If, as in case 1, a program on one client calls WRITE and then CLOSE, and then another client calls OPEN and READ, the NFS implementation will ensure that the READ will include the results of the WRITES by the first client. But, as in case 2, if two clients have the same file open, one client writes a block of the file, and then the other client invokes READ, READ may return the data either from before or after the last WRITE; the NFS implementation makes no guarantees in that case.

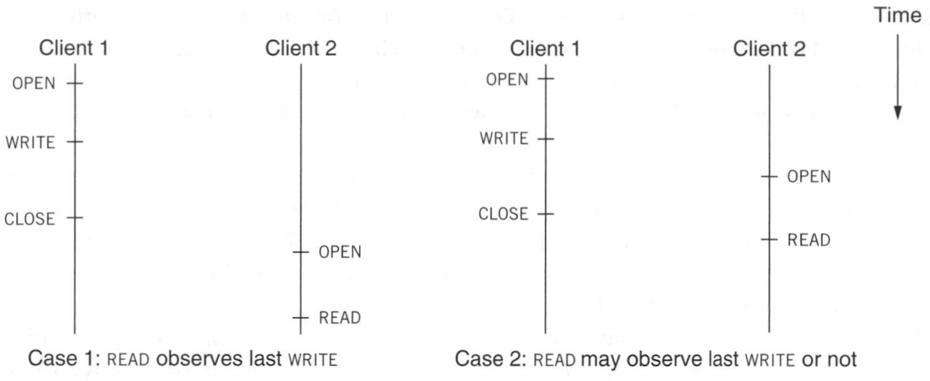

FIGURE 4.13

Two cases illustrating close-to-open consistency

NFS implementations provide close-to-open semantics as follows. The client stores with each data block in its cache the modification of the block's vnode at the time the client reads the block from the server. When a user program opens a file, the client sends a GETATTR request to fetch the last modification time of the file. The client reads a cached data block only if the block's modification time is the same as its vnode's modification time. If the modification times are not the same, the client removes the data block from its cache and fetches it from the server.

The client implements WRITE by modifying its local cached version, without incurring the overhead of remote procedure calls. Then, in the CLOSE call of Figure 4.11, the client, rather than simply returning, would first send any cached writes to the server and wait for an acknowledgment. This implementation is simple and provides decent performance. The client can perform READs and WRITEs at local memory speeds. By delaying sending the modified blocks until CLOSE, the client absorbs modifications that are overwritten (e.g., the application writes the same block multiple times) and aggregates WRITEs to the same block (e.g., WRITEs that modify different parts of the block).

By providing close-to-open semantics, most user programs written for a local UNIX file system will work correctly when their files are stored on NFS. For example, if a user edits a program on a personal workstation but prefers to compile on a faster compute machine, then NFS with close-to-open consistency works well, requiring no modifications to the editor and the compiler. After the editor has written out the modified file and the user starts the compiler on the compute machine, the compiler will observe the edits.

On the other hand, certain programs will not work correctly using NFS implementations that provide close-to-open consistency. For example, a multiclient database program that reads and writes records stored in a file over NFS will not work correctly because, as the second case in Figure 4.13 illustrates, close-to-open semantics doesn't specify the semantics when clients execute operations concurrently—for example, if client 2 opens the database file before client 1 closes it and client 3 opens the database file after client 1 closes it. If client 2 and 3 then read data from the file, client 2 may not see the data written by client 1, while client 3 will see the data written by client 1.

Furthermore, because NFS caches blocks (instead of whole files), the file may have blocks from different versions of the file intermixed. When a client fetches a file, it fetches only the inode and perhaps prefetches a few blocks. Subsequent READ RPCs may fetch blocks from a newer version of the file because another client may have written those blocks after this client opened the file.

To provide the correct semantics in this case requires more sophisticated machinery, which NFS implementations don't provide, because databases often have their own special-purpose solutions anyway, as we discuss in Chapters 9 [on-line] and 10 [on-line]. If the database program doesn't provide a special-purpose solution, then tough luck—one cannot run it over NFS.

4.5.5 NFS Version 3 and Beyond

NFS version 2 is being replaced by NFS version 3. Version 3 addresses a number of limitations in version 2, but the extensions do not significantly change the preceding description. For example, version 3 supports 64-bit numbers for recording file sizes and adds an asynchronous write (i.e., the server may acknowledge an asynchronous WRITE request as soon as it receives the request, before it has written the data to disk).

NFS version 4, which took a number of lessons from the Andrew File System [Suggestions for Further Reading 4.2.3], is a bigger change than version 3; in version 4 the server maintains some state. Version 4 also protects against intruders who can snoop and modify network traffic using techniques discussed in Chapter 11 [on-line]. Furthermore, it provides a more efficient scheme for providing close-to-open consistency, and it works well across the Internet, where the client and server may be connected using low-speed links.

The following references provide more details on NFS:

1. Russel Sandberg, David Goldberg, Steve Kleiman, Dan Walsh, and Bob Lyon. "Design and implementation of the Sun network file system", *Proceedings of the 1985 Summer Usenix Technical Conference*, June 1985, El Cerrito, CA, pages 119–130.

2. Chet Juszezak, "Improving the performance and correctness of an NFS server", *Proceedings of the 1989 Winter Usenix Technical Conference*, January 1989, Berkeley, CA, pages 53–63.

3. Brian Pawlowski, Chet Juszezak, Peter Staubach, Carl Smith, Diana Lebel, and David Hitz, "NFS Version 3 design and implementation", *Proceedings of the 1990 Summer Usenix Technical Conference*, June 1994, Boston, MA.

4. Brian Pawlowski, Spencer Shepler, Carl Beame, Brent Callaghan, Michael Eisler, David Noveck, David Robinson, and Robert Turlow, "The NFS Version 4 protocol", *Proceedings of Second International SANE Conference*, May 2000, Maastricht, The Netherlands.

EXERCISES

4.1 When modularity between a client and a service is enforced, there is no way for errors in the implementation of the service to propagate to its clients. True or False? Explain.

1995-1-1d

4.2 Chapter 1 discussed four general methods for coping with complexity: modularity, abstraction, hierarchy, and layering.

4.2a Which of those four methods does client/service use as its primary organizing scheme?

4.2b Which does remote procedure call use? Explain.

1996-1-1b,d

4.3 To client software, a notable difference between remote procedure call and ordinary local procedure call is:

A. None. That's the whole point of RPC!

B. There may be multiple returns from one RPC call.

C. There may be multiple calls for one RPC return.

D. Recursion doesn't work in RPC.

E. The runtime system may report a new type of error as a result of an RPC.

F. Arguments to RPCs must be scalars.

1998-2-4

4.4 Which of the following statements is true of the X Window System (see Sidebar 4.4)?

A. The X server is a trusted intermediary and attempts to enforce modularity between X clients in their use of the display resource.

B. An X client always waits for a response to a request before sending the next request to the X server.

C. When a program running on another computer displays its window on your local workstation, that *remote* computer is considered an X server.

2005-1-6

4.5 While browsing the Web, you click on a link that identifies an Internet host named `www.cslab.scholarly.edu`. Your browser asks your Domain Name System (DNS) name server, *M*, to find an Internet address for this domain name. Under what conditions is each of the following statements true of the name resolution process?

A. To answer your query, *M* must contact one of the root name servers.

B. If *M* answered a query for `www.cslab.scholarly.edu` in the past, then it can answer your query without asking any other name server.

C. M must contact one of the name servers for `cslab.scholarly.edu` to resolve the domain name.

D. If *M* has the current Internet address of a working name server for `scholarly.edu` cached, then that name server will be able to directly provide an answer.

E. If *M* has the current Internet address of a working name server for `cslab.scholarly.edu` cached, then that name server will be able to directly provide an answer.

4.6 For the same situation as in Exercise 4.5, which of the following is always true of the name resolution process, assuming that all name servers are configured correctly and no messages are lost?

A. If M had answered a query for the IP address corresponding to `www.cslab.scholarly.edu` at some time in the past, then it can respond to the current query without contacting any other name server.

B. If M has a valid IP address of a functioning name server for `cslab.scholarly.edu` in its cache, then M will get a response from that name server without any other name servers being contacted.

2000-2-5 and 2005-2-4

4.7 The Network File System (NFS) described in Section 4.5 allows a client machine to run operations on files that are stored at a remote server. For the version of NFS described there, decide if each of these assertions is true or false:

A. When the server responds to a client's WRITE call, all modifications required by that WRITE will have made it to the server's disk.

B. An NFS client might send multiple requests for the same operation to the NFS server.

C. When an NFS server crashes, after the operating system restarts and recovers the disk contents, the server must also run its own recovery procedure to make its state consistent with that of its clients.

2005-1-2

4.8 Assume that an NFS (described in Section 4.5) server contains a file `/a/b` and that an NFS client mounts the NFS server's root directory in the location `/x`, so that the client can now name the file as `/x/a/b`. Further assume that this is the only client and that the client executes the following two commands:

```
chdir /x/a
rm b
```

The REMOVE message from the client to the server gets through, and the server removes the file. Unfortunately, the response from the server to the client is lost and the client resends the message to remove the (now non-existent) file. The server receives the resent message. What happens next depends on the server implementation. Which of the following are correct statements?

A. If the server maintains an in-memory reply cache in which it records all operations it previously executed, and there are no server failures, the server will return "OK".

B. If the server maintains an in-memory reply cache but the server has failed, restarted, and its reply cache is empty, both of the following responses are possible: the server may return "file not found" or "OK".

C. If the server is stateless, it will return "file not found".

D. Because REMOVE is an idempotent operation, any server implementation will return "OK".

2006-2-2

Additional exercises relating to Chapter 4 can be found in the problem sets beginning on page 425.

CHAPTER

Enforcing Modularity with Virtualization

5

CHAPTER CONTENTS

Principles of Computer System Design: An Introduction

DOI: 10.1016/B978-0-12-374957-4.00013-X

OVERVIEW

The goal of the client/service organization is to limit the interactions between clients and services to messages. To ensure that there are no opportunities for hidden interactions, the previous chapter assumed that each client module and service module runs on a separate computer. Under that assumption, the network between the computers enforces modularity. This implementation reduces the opportunity for programming errors to propagate from one module to another, but it is also good for achieving security (because the service module can be penetrated only by sending messages) and fault tolerance (service modules can be separated geographically, which reduces the risk that a catastrophic failure such as an earthquake or a massive power failure affects all servers that implement the service).

The main disadvantage of using one computer per module is that it requires as many computers as modules. Since the modularity of a system and its applications shouldn't be dictated by the number of computers available, this requirement is undesirable. If the designer decides to split a system or application into n modules and would like to enforce modularity between them, the choice of n should not be constrained by the number of computers that happen to be in stock and easily obtained. Instead, the designer needs a way to run several modules on the same computer without resorting to soft modularity.

This chapter introduces *virtualization* as the primary approach to achieve this goal and presents three new abstractions (SEND and RECEIVE with *bounded buffers*, *virtual memory*, and *threads*) that correspond to virtualized versions of the three main abstractions (communication links, memory, and processors). The three new abstractions allow a designer to implement as many virtual computers as needed for running the desired *n* modules.

5.1 CLIENT/SERVER ORGANIZATION WITHIN A COMPUTER USING VIRTUALIZATION

To enforce modularity between modules running on the same computer, we create several *virtual* computers using one *physical* computer and execute each module (usually an application or a subsystem) in its own virtual computer.

This idea can be realized using a technique called *virtualization.* A program that virtualizes a physical object simulates the interface of the physical object, but it creates many virtual objects by *multiplexing* one physical instance, or it may provide one large virtual object by *aggregating* many physical instances, or implement a virtual object from a different kind of physical object using *emulation*. For the user of the simulated object, it provides the same behavior as a physical instance, but it isn't the physical instance, which is why it is called virtual. A primary goal of virtualization is to preserve an existing interface. That way, modules designed to use a physical instance of an object don't have to be modified to use a virtual instance. Figure 5.1 gives some examples of the three virtualization methods, which we will discuss in turn.

Hosting several Web sites on a single physical server is an example of virtualization involving multiplexing. If the aggregate peak load of the Web sites is less than what a

Virtualization Method	Physical Resource	Virtual Resource
multiplexing	server	Web site
multiplexing	processor	thread
multiplexing	real memory	virtual memory
multiplexing and emulation	real memory and disk	virtual memory with paging
multiplexing	wire or communication channel	virtual circuit
aggregation	communication channel	channel bonding
aggregation	disk	RAID
emulation	disk	RAM disk
emulation	Macintosh	virtual PC

FIGURE 5.1

Examples of virtualization.

single server computer can support, providers often prefer to use a single server to host several Web sites because it is less expensive than buying one server for each Web site.

The next three examples relate to threads and virtual memory, which we will overview in Section 5.1.1. Some of these usages don't rely on a single method of virtualization but combine several or use different methods to obtain different properties. For example, virtual memory with paging (described in Section 6.2) uses both multiplexing and aggregation.

A virtual circuit virtualizes a wire or communication channel using multiplexing. For example, it allows several phone conversations to take place over a single wire with a technique called time division multiplexing, as we will discuss in Chapter 7 [on-line]. Channel bonding aggregates several communication channels to provide a combined high data rate.

RAID (see Section 2.1.1.4) is an example of virtualization involving aggregation. In RAID, a number of disks are aggregated together in a clever way that provides an identical interface to the one of a single disk, but together the disks provide improved performance (by reading and writing disks concurrently) and durability (by writing information on more than one disk). A system administrator can replace a single disk with a RAID and take advantage of the RAID improvements without having to change the file system.

A RAM disk is an example of virtualization involving emulation. A RAM disk provides the same interface as a physical disk but stores blocks in memory instead of on a disk platter. RAM disks can therefore read and write blocks much faster than a physical disk but, because RAM is volatile, it provides little durability. Administrators can configure a file system to use a RAM disk instead of a physical disk without needing to modify the file system itself. For example, a system administrator may configure the file system to use RAM disk to store temporary files, which allows the file system to read and write temporary files fast. And since temporary files don't have to be stored durably, nothing is lost by storing them on a RAM disk.

A virtual PC is an example of virtualization using emulation. It allows the construction of a virtual personal computer out of a physical personal computer, perhaps of a different type (e.g., using a Macintosh to emulate a virtual PC). Virtual PCs can be useful to run several operating systems on a single computer, or simplify the testing and the development of a new operating system. Section 5.1.2 discusses this virtualization technique in more detail.

Designers are often tempted to tinker slightly with an interface rather than virtualizing it exactly, to improve it or to add a useful feature. Such tinkering can easily cross a line in which the original goal of not having to modify other modules that use the interface is lost. For example, the X Window System described in Sidebar 4.4 implements objects that could be thought of as virtual displays, but because the size of those objects can be changed on the fly and the program that draws on them should be prepared to redraw them on command, it is more appropriate to call them "windows".

Similarly, a file system (see Section 2.3.2) creates objects that store bits and thus has some similarity to a virtualized hard disk, but because files have names, are of adjustable length, allow controlled sharing, and can be organized into hierarchies, they are more appropriately thought of as a different memory abstraction.

The preceding examples suggest how we could implement the client/service organization within a single computer. Consider a computer on which we would like to run five modules: a text editor, an e-mail reader, a keyboard manager, the window service, and the file service. When a user works with the text editor, keyboard input should go to the editor. When the user moves the mouse from the editor window to the mail reader window, the next keyboard input should go to the mail reader. When the text editor saves a file, the file service must execute to store the file. If there are more modules than computers, some solution is needed for sharing a single computer.

The idea is to present each module with its own virtual computer. The power of this idea is that programmers can think of each module independently. From the programmer's perspective, every program module has a virtual computer to itself, which executes independently of the virtual computers of other modules. This idea enforces modularity because a virtual computer can contain a module's errors and no module can halt the progress of other modules.

The virtual computer design does not enforce modularity as well as running modules on physically separate computers because, for example, a power failure will knock out all virtual computers on the same physical computer. Also, once an attacker has broken into one virtual computer, the attacker may discover a way to exploit a flaw in the implementation of virtualization to break into other virtual computers. The primary modularity goal of employing virtual computers is to ensure that module failures due to accidental programming errors don't propagate from one virtual computer to another. Virtual computers can contribute to security goals but are better viewed as only one of several lines of defense.

5.1.1 Abstractions for Virtualizing Computers

The main challenge in implementing virtual computers is finding the right abstractions to build them. This chapter introduces three abstractions that correspond to virtualized versions of the main abstractions: SEND and RECEIVE with bounded buffers (virtualizes communication links), virtual memory (virtualizes memory), and threads (virtualizes processors).

These three abstractions are typically implemented by a program that is called the operating system (which was briefly discussed in Sidebar 2.4 but will be discussed in detail in this chapter). Using an operating system that provides the three abstractions, we can implement the client/service organization within a single computer (see Figure 5.2). For example, with this design the text editor running on one virtual computer can send a message over the virtual communication link to the file service, running on a different virtual computer, and ask it, for example, to save a file. In the figure each virtual computer has one virtual processor (implemented by a thread) and its own virtual memory with a virtual address space ranging from 0 to 2^n. To build an intuition for these abstractions and learn how they can be used to implement a virtual computer, we give a brief overview of them.

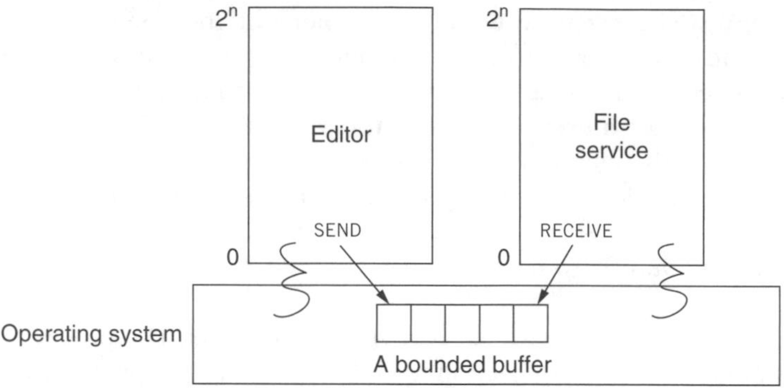

FIGURE 5.2

An operating system providing the editor and file service module each their own virtual computer. Each virtual computer has a thread that virtualizes the processor. Each virtual computer has a virtual memory that provides each module with the illusion that it has its own memory. To allow communication between virtual computers, the operating system provides SEND, RECEIVE, and a bounded buffer of messages.

5.1.1.1 Threads

The first step in virtualizing a computer is to virtualize the processor. To provide the editor module (shown in Figure 5.3) with a virtual processor, we create a *thread of execution*, or *thread* for short. A thread is an abstraction that encapsulates the execution state of an active computation. It encapsulates the state of a conceptual interpreter that executes the computation (see Section 2.1.2). The state of a thread consists of the variables internal to the interpreter (e.g., processor registers), which include

1. A reference to the next program step (e.g., a program counter)
2. References to the environment (e.g., a stack, a heap, and other current objects)

The thread abstraction encapsulates enough of the interpreter's state that one can stop a thread at any point in time, and later resume it. The ability to stop a thread and resume it later allows virtualization of the interpreter and provides a convenient way of multiplexing a physical processor. Threads are the most widely used implementation strategy to virtualize physical processors. In fact, this implementation strategy is so common that in the context of virtualizing physical processors the words "thread" and "virtual processor" have become synonyms in practice.

The next few paragraphs give a high-level overview of how threads can be used to virtualize physical processors. A user might type the name of the module that the user wants to run, or a user might select the name from a pull-down menu. The command line interpreter or the window system can then start the program as follows:

1. Load the program's text and data stored in the file system into memory.
2. Allocate a thread and start it at a specified address. Allocating a thread involves allocating a stack to allow the thread to make procedure calls, setting the SP register to the top of the stack, and setting the PC register to the starting address.

```
input ← OPEN (keyboard)          // open the keyboard device
file ← OPEN (argument)           // open the file that was passed an argument to the editor
do forever
    n ← READLINE (input, buf)    // read characters from the keyboard into buf
    APPLY (file, buf, n)         // apply them to the file being edited
```

FIGURE 5.3

Sketch of the program for the editor module.

A module may have one or several threads. A module with only *one* thread (and thus one processor) is common because then the programmer can think of it as executing a program serially: it starts at the beginning, computes (perhaps producing some output by performing a remote procedure call to a service), and then terminates. This simple structure follows the *principle of least astonishment* for programmers. Humans are better at understanding serial programs than at understanding programs that have several, concurrent threads, which can have surprising behavior.

Modules may have more than one thread by creating several threads. A module, for example, may create a thread per device that the module manages so that the module can operate the devices concurrently. Or a module may create several threads to overlap the latency of an expensive operation (e.g., waiting for a disk) by running the expensive operation in another thread. A module may allocate several threads to exploit several physical processors that run each thread concurrently. A service module may create several threads to process requests from different clients concurrently.

The thread abstraction is implemented by a *thread manager*. The thread manager's job is to multiplex the possibly many threads on the limited number of physical processors of the computer, and in such a way that a programming error in one thread cannot interfere with the execution of another thread. Since the thread encapsulates enough of the state so that one can stop a thread at any point in time, and later resume it, the thread manager can stop a thread and allocate the released physical processor to another thread by resuming that thread. Later the thread manager can resume the suspended thread again by reallocating a physical processor to that thread. In this way, the thread manager can multiplex many threads across a number of physical processors. The thread manager can ensure that no thread hogs a physical processor by forcing each thread to periodically give up its physical processor on a clock interrupt.

With the introduction of threads, it is helpful to refine the description of the interrupt mechanism described in Chapter 2. External events (e.g., a clock interrupt or a magnetic disk signals the completion of an I/O) interrupt a physical processor, but the event may have nothing to do with the thread running on the physical processor. On an interrupt, the processor invokes the interrupt handler and after returning from the handler continues running the thread that was running on the physical processor before the interrupt. If one processor should not be interrupted because it is already busy processing an interrupt, the next interrupt may interrupt another processor in the computer, allowing interrupts to be processed concurrently.

Some interrupts do pertain to the currently running thread. We shall refer to this class of interrupts as *exceptions*. The exception handler runs in the context of the interrupted thread; it can read and modify the interrupted thread's state. Exceptions often happen when a thread performs some operation that the hardware cannot complete (e.g., divide by zero). Many programming languages also have a notion of an exception; for example, a square root program may signal an exception if its caller hands it a negative argument. We shall see that because exception handlers run in the context of the interrupted thread, but interrupt handlers run in the context of the operating system, there are different restrictions on what the two kinds of handlers can safely do.

5.1.1.2 Virtual Memory

As described so far, all threads and handlers share the same physical memory. Each processor running a thread sends READ and WRITE requests across a bus along with an address identifying the memory location to be read or written. Sharing memory has benefits, but uncontrolled sharing makes it too easy to make a mistake. If several threads have their programs and data stored in the same physical memory, then the threads of each module have access to every other module's data. In fact, a simple programming error (e.g., the program computes the wrong address) can result in a STORE instruction overwriting another module's data or a JMP instruction executing procedures of another module. Thus, without a memory enforcement mechanism we have, at best, soft modularity. In addition, the physical memory and address space may be too small to fit the applications, requiring the applications to manage the memory carefully.

To enforce modularity, we must ensure that the threads of one module cannot overwrite the data of another module by accident. To do so, we give each module its own *virtual memory*, as Figure 5.2 illustrates. Virtual memory can provide each module with its own *virtual address space*, which has its own *virtual addresses*. That is, the arguments to JMP, LOAD, and STORE instructions are all virtual addresses, which a new hardware gadget (called a *virtual memory manager*) translates to physical addresses. If each module has its own virtual address space, then a module can name only its own physical memory and cannot store to the memory of another module. If a thread of a module by accident calculates an incorrect virtual address and stores to that virtual address, it will affect only that module.

With threads and virtual memory, we can create a virtual computer for each module. Each module has one or more threads that execute the code of the module. The threads of one module share a single virtual address memory that threads of other modules by default cannot touch.

5.1.1.3 Bounded Buffer

To allow client and service modules on virtual computers to communicate, we introduce SEND and RECEIVE with a *bounded buffer* of messages. A thread can invoke SEND, which attempts to insert the supplied message into a bounded buffer of messages. If the bounded buffer is full, the sending thread waits until there is space in the bounded buffer. A thread invokes RECEIVE to retrieve a message from the buffer; if there are no messages, the calling thread waits. Using SEND, RECEIVE, and bounded buffers, we can implement remote procedure calls and enforce strong modularity between modules on different virtual computers running on the same physical computer.

5.1.1.4 Operating System Interface

To make the abstractions concrete, this chapter develops a minimal operating system that provides the abstractions (see Table 5.1 for its interface). This minimal design exhibits many of the mechanisms that are found in existing operating systems, but to keep the explanation simple it doesn't describe any existing system. Existing systems have evolved over many years, incorporating new ideas as they came along. As a result, few existing systems provide an example of a clean, simple design. In addition, a complete operating system includes many services (such as a file system, a window system, etc.) that are not included in the minimal operating system described in this chapter.

Table 5.1 The Interface Developed in this Chapter

Abstraction	Procedure
Memory	CREATE_ADDRESS_SPACE DELETE_ADDRESS_SPACE ALLOCATE_BLOCK FREE_BLOCK MAP UNMAP
Interpreter	ALLOCATE_THREAD EXIT_THREAD DESTROY_THREAD YIELD AWAIT ADVANCE TICKET ACQUIRE RELEASE
Communication	ALLOCATE_BOUNDED_BUFFER DEALLOCATE_BOUNDED_BUFFER SEND RECEIVE

5.1.2 Emulation and Virtual Machines

The previous section described briefly three high-level abstractions to virtualize processors, memory, and links to enforce modularity. An alternative approach is to provide an interface that is identical to some physical hardware. In this approach, one can enforce modularity by providing each application with its own instance of the physical hardware.

This approach can be implemented using a technique called *emulation*. Emulation simulates some physical hardware so faithfully that the emulated hardware can run any software the physical hardware can. For example, Apple Inc. has used emulation successfully to move customers to new hardware designs. Apple used a program named Classic to emulate Motorola Inc.'s 68030 processor on the PowerPC processor and more recently used a program named Rosetta to emulate the PowerPC processor on Intel Inc.'s x86 processor. As another example, some processors include a microcode interpreter inside the processor to simulate instructions of other processors or instructions from older versions of the same processor. It is also standard practice for a vendor developing a new processor to start by writing an emulator for it and running the emulator on some already existing processor. This approach allows software development to begin before the chip for the new processor is manufactured, and when the chip does become available, the emulator acts as a kind of specification against which to debug the chip.

Emulation in software is typically slow because interpreting the instructions of the emulated machine in software has substantial overhead. Looking at the structure of an interpreter in Figure 2.5, it is easy to see that decoding the simulated instruction, performing its operation, and updating the state of the simulated processor can take tens of instructions on the processor that performs the emulation. As a result, emulation in software can cost a factor 10 in performance and a designer must work hard to do better.

A specialized approach to fast emulation is using ***virtual machines***. In this approach, a physical processor is used as much as possible to implement many virtual instances of itself. That is, virtual machines emulate many instances of a machine M using a physical machine M. This approach loses the portability of general emulation but provides better performance. The part of the operating system that provides virtual machines is often called a ***virtual machine monitor***. Section 5.8 of this chapter discusses virtual machines and virtual machine monitors in more detail. Internally, a virtual machine monitor typically uses bounded buffers, virtual memory, and threads, the main topics of this chapter.

5.1.3 Roadmap: Step-by-Step Virtualization

This chapter gradually develops the tools needed to provide a virtual computer. We start out assuming that there are more physical processors than threads and that the operating system can allocate each thread its own physical processor. We will even assume that each interrupt handler has its own physical processor, so when an interrupt occurs, the handler runs on that dedicated processor. Figure 5.4 shows a modified version of Figure 2.2, in which each thread has its own processor. Consider again the example that we would like to run the following five modules on a single computer: a text editor, an e-mail reader, a keyboard manager, the window service, and the file service. Processor 1, for example, might run the text editor thread. Processor 2 might run the e-mail reader thread. The window manager might have one thread per window, each running on a separate processor. Similarly, the file service might have several threads, each running on a separate processor. The LOAD and STORE instructions of threads refer to addresses that name memory locations or registers of the various controllers. That is, threads share the memories and controllers.

Given this setup, Section 5.2 shows how the client/server organization can be implemented in a computer with many processors and a single address space by allowing the threads of different modules to communicate through a bounded buffer. This implementation takes advantage of the fact that processors within a computer can interact with one another through a shared memory. That ability will prove useful to implement virtual communication links, but such unconstrained interaction through shared memory would drastically compromise modularity. For this reason, Section 5.3 will adjust this assumption to show how to provide and enforce walls between the memory regions used by different modules to restrict and control sharing of memory.

Sections 5.4, 5.5, and 5.6 of this chapter remove restrictions on the design presented in Sections 5.2 and 5.3. In Section 5.4 we will remove the restriction that processors must share one single, large address space, and provide each module with its own virtual memory, while still allowing controlled sharing. In Section 5.5 we remove the restriction that each thread must have its own physical processor while still ensuring that no thread can halt the progress of other threads involuntarily. Finally,

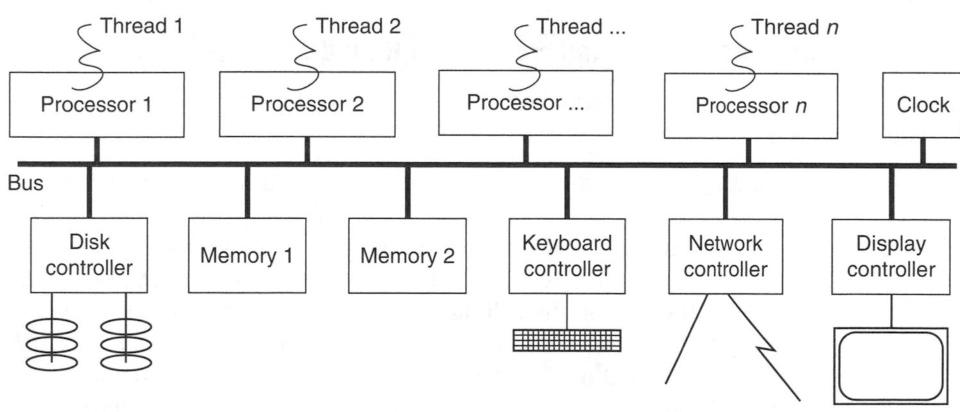

FIGURE 5.4

A computer with several hardware modules connected by a shared bus. Each thread of the software modules has its own processor allocated to it.

in Section 5.6 we remove the restriction that a thread must use a physical processor continuously to test if another thread has sent a message.

The operating system, thread manager, virtual memory manager, and SEND and RECEIVE with bounded buffers presented in this chapter are less complex than the designs found in contemporary computer systems. One reason is that most contemporary designs have evolved over time with changing technologies, while also allowing users to continue to run old programs. As an example of this evolution, Section 5.7 briefly describes the history of the Intel x86 processor, a widely used general-purpose processor design that has, over the years, provided increasing support for enforced modularity.

5.2 VIRTUAL LINKS USING SEND, RECEIVE, AND A BOUNDED BUFFER

Operating systems designers have developed many abstractions for virtual communication links. One popular abstraction is pipes [Suggestions for Further Reading 2.2.1 and 2.2.2], which allow two programs to communicate using procedures from the file system call interface. Because SEND and RECEIVE with a bounded buffer mirror a communication link directly, we describe them in more detail in this chapter. The implementation of SEND and RECEIVE with a bounded buffer also mirrors implementations of sockets, an interface for virtual links provided in operating systems such as UNIX and Microsoft Windows.

The main challenge in implementing SEND and RECEIVE with bounded buffers is that several threads, perhaps running in parallel on separate physical processors, may add and remove messages from the same bounded buffer concurrently. To ensure correctness, the implementation must coordinate these updates. This section will present bounded buffers in detail and introduce some techniques to coordinate concurrent actions.

5.2.1 An Interface for SEND and RECEIVE with Bounded Buffers

An operating system might provide the following interface for SEND and RECEIVE with bounded buffers:

- *buffer* ← ALLOCATE_BOUNDED_BUFFER (*n*): allocate a bounded buffer that can hold *n* messages.
- DEALLOCATE_BOUNDED_BUFFER (*buffer*): free the bounded buffer *buffer*.
- SEND (*buffer*, *message*): if there is room in the bounded buffer *buffer*, insert message in the buffer. If not, stop the calling thread and wait until there is room.
- *message* ← RECEIVE (*buffer*): if there is a message in the bounded buffer *buffer*, return the message to the calling thread. If there is no message in the bounded buffer, stop the calling thread and wait until another thread sends a message to buffer *buffer*.

SEND and RECEIVE with bounded buffers allow sending and receiving messages as described in Chapter 4. By building stubs that use these primitives, we can implement remote procedure calls between threads on the same physical computer in the same way as remote procedure calls between physical computers. That is, from the client's point of view in Figure 4.8, there is no difference between sending a message to a local virtual computer or to a remote physical computer. In both cases, if the client or service module fails because of a programming error, then the other module needs to provide a recovery strategy, but it doesn't necessarily fail.

5.2.2 Sequence Coordination with a Bounded Buffer

The implementation with bounded buffers requires coordination between sending and receiving threads because a thread may have to wait until buffer space is available or until a message arrives. Two quite different approaches to thread coordination have developed over the years by researchers in different fields. One approach, usually taken by operating system designers, assumes that the programmer is an all-knowing genius who makes no mistakes. The other approach, usually taken by database designers, assumes that the programmer is a mere mortal, so it provides strong automatic support for coordination correctness, but at some cost in flexibility.

The next couple of subsections exhibit the genius approach to coordination, not because it is the best way to tackle coordination problems, but rather to give some intuition about why it requires a coordination genius, and thus should be subcontracted to such a specialist whenever possible. In addition, to implement the database approach the designer of the automatic coordination support approach must use the genius approach. Chapter 9 [on-line] uses the concepts introduced in this chapter to implement the database approach for mere mortals.

The scenario is that we have two threads (a sending thread and a receiving thread) that share a buffer into which the sender puts messages and the receiver removes those messages. For clarity we will assume that the sending and receiving thread each have their own processor allocated to them; that is, for the rest of this section we can equate thread with processor, and thus threads can proceed concurrently at independent rates. As mentioned earlier, Section 5.5 will explore what happens when we eliminate that assumption.

The buffer is bounded, which means that it has a fixed size. To ensure that the buffer doesn't overflow, the sending thread should hold off putting messages into the buffer when the number of messages there reaches some predefined limit. When that happens, the sender must wait until the receiver has consumed some messages.

The problem of sharing a bounded buffer between two threads is an instance of the *producer and consumer problem*. For correct operation, the consumer and the producer must coordinate their activities. In our example, the constraint is that the producer must first add a message to the shared buffer before the consumer can remove it and that the producer must wait for the consumer to catch up when the buffer fills up. This kind of coordination is an example of *sequence coordination*: a coordination constraint among threads stating that, for correctness, an event in one thread must precede an event in another thread.

Figure 5.5 shows an implementation of SEND and RECEIVE using a bounded buffer. This implementation requires making some subtle assumptions, but before diving

```
1   shared structure buffer                          // A shared bounded buffer
2       message instance message[N]                  // With a maximum of N messages
3       integer in initially 0                       // Counts number of messages put in the buffer
4       integer out initially 0                      // Counts number of messages taken out of the buffer

5   procedure SEND (buffer reference p, message instance msg)
6       while p.in – p.out = N do nothing            // If buffer is full, wait for room
7       p.message [p.in modulo N] ← msg              // Put message in the buffer
8       p.in ← p.in + 1                              // Increment in

9   procedure RECEIVE (buffer reference p)
10      while p.in = p.out do nothing                // If buffer is empty, wait for message
11      msg ← p.message [p.out modulo N]             // Copy item out of buffer
12      p.out ← p.out + 1                            // Increment out
13      return msg                                   // Return message to receiver
```

FIGURE 5.5

An implementation of a SEND and RECEIVE using bounded buffers.

into these assumptions let's first consider how the program works. The two threads implement the sequence coordination constraint using N (the size of the shared bounded buffer) and the variables *in* (the number of items produced) and *out* (the number of items consumed). If the buffer contains items (i.e., *in* > *out* on line *10*), then the receiver can proceed to consume the items; otherwise, it loops until the sender has put some items in the buffer. Loops in which a thread is waiting for an event without giving up its processor are called *spin loops*.

To ensure that the sender waits when the buffer is full, the sender puts new items in the buffer only if *in* – *out* < N (line *6*); otherwise, it spins until the receiver made room in the buffer by consuming some items. This design ensures that the buffer does not overflow.

The correctness of this implementation relies on several assumptions:

1. The implementation assumes that there is one sending thread and one receiving thread and that only one thread updates each shared variable. In the program only the receiver thread updates *out*, and only the sender thread updates *in*. If several threads update the same shared variable (e.g., multiple sending threads update *in* or the receiving thread and the sending thread update a variable), then the updates to the shared variable must be coordinated, which this implementation doesn't do.

   This assumption exemplifies the principle that coordination is simplest when each shared variable has just one writer:

One-writer principle

If each variable has only one writer, coordination becomes easier.

That is, if you can, arrange your program so that two threads don't update the same shared variable. Following this principle also improves modularity because information flows in only one direction: from the single writer to the reader. In our implementation, *out* contains information that flows from the receiver thread to the sender, and *in* contains information that flows from the sender thread to the receiver. This restriction of information flow simplifies correctness arguments and, as we will see in Chapter 11 [on-line], can also enhance security.

A similar observation holds for the way the bounded buffer *buffer* is implemented. Because *messages* is a fixed-size array, the entries are written only by the sender thread. If the buffer had been implemented as a linked list, we might have a situation in which the sender and the receiver need to update a shared variable at the same time (e.g., the pointer to the head of the linked list) and then these updates would have to be coordinated.

2. The spin loops on lines *6* and *10* require the previously mentioned assumption that the sender and the receiver threads each run on a dedicated processor. When we remove that assumption in Section 5.5 we will have to do something about these spin loops.

3. This implementation assumes that the variables *in* and *out* are integers whose representation must be large enough that they will never overflow for the life of the buffer. Integers of width 64 or 96 bits would probably suffice for most applications. (An alternative way to remove this assumption is to make the implementation of the bounded buffer more complicated: perform all additions involving *in* and *out* modulo *N*, and reserve one additional slot in the buffer to distinguish a full buffer from an empty one.)

4. The implementation assumes that the shared memory provides read/write coherence (see Section 2.1.1.1) for *in* and *out*. That is, a LOAD of the variable *in* or *out* by one thread must be guaranteed to obtain the result of the most recent store to that variable by the other thread.

5. The implementation assumes before-or-after atomicity for the variables *in* and *out*. If these two variables fit in a 16- or 32-bit memory cell that can be read and written with a single LOAD or STORE, this assumption is likely to be true. But a 64- or 96-bit integer would probably require multiple memory cells. If they do, reading and writing *in* and *out* would require multiple LOADS or STORES, and additional measures will be necessary to make these multistep sequences atomic.

6. The implementation assumes that the result of executing a statement becomes visible to other threads in program order. If an optimizing compiler or processor reorders statements to achieve better performance, this program could work incorrectly. For example, if the compiler generates code that reads *p.in* once, holds it in a temporary register for use in lines *6* through *8*, and updates the memory copy of *p.in* immediately, then the receiver may read the contents of the *in*th entry of the shared buffer before the sender has copied its message into that entry.

The rest of this section explains what problems occur when assumptions *1* (the one-writer principle) and *5* (before-or-after atomicity of multistep LOAD and STORE sequences) don't hold and introduces techniques to ensure them. In Section 5.5 we will find out how to remove assumption *2* (more processors than threads). Throughout, we assume that assumptions *3*, *4*, and *6* always hold.

5.2.3 Race Conditions

To illustrate the importance of the six assumptions in guaranteeing the correctness of the program in Figure 5.5, let's remove two of those assumptions, one at a time, to see just what goes wrong. What we will find is that to deal with the removed assumptions we need additional mechanisms, mechanisms that Section 5.2.4 will introduce. This illustration reinforces the observation that concurrent programming needs the attention of specialists: all it takes is one subtle change to make a correct program wrong.

To remove the first assumption, let's allow several senders and receivers. This change will violate the one-writer principle, so we should not be surprised to find that it introduces errors. Multiple senders and receivers are common in practice. For example, consider a printer that is shared among many clients. The service managing the printer may receive requests from several clients. Each request adds a document to the shared buffer of to-be-printed documents. In this case, we have several senders (the threads adding jobs to the buffer) and one receiver (the printer).

As we will see, the errors that will manifest themselves are difficult to track down because they don't always show up. They appear only with a particular ordering of the instructions of the threads involved. Thus, concurrent programs are not only difficult to get right, but also difficult to debug when they are wrong.

The solution in Figure 5.5 doesn't work when several senders execute the code concurrently. To see why, let's assume N is 20 and that all entries in the buffer are empty (e.g., *out* is 0 and *in* is 0), and each thread is running on its own processor:

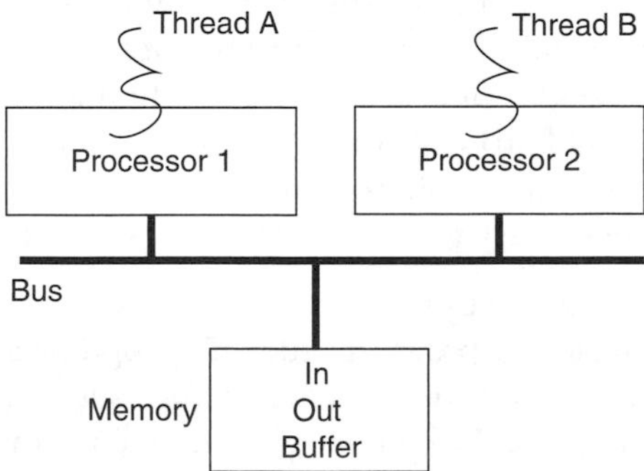

If two sending threads run concurrently—one on processor A and one on processor B—the threads issue instructions independently of each other, at their own pace. The processors may have different speeds and take interrupts at different times, or instructions may hit in the cache on one processor and miss on another, so there is no way to predict the relative timing of the LOAD and STORE instructions that the threads issue.

This scenario is an instance of asynchronous interpreters (described in Section 2.1.2). Thus, we should make no assumptions about the sequence in which the memory operations of the two threads execute. When analyzing the concurrent execution of two threads, both executing instructions *6* through *8* in Figure 5.5, we can assume they execute in some *serial* sequence (because the bus arbiter will order any memory operations that arrive at the bus at the same time). However, because the relative speeds of the threads are unpredictable, we can make no assumptions about the order in the sequence.

We represent the execution of instruction *6* by thread A as "*A6*". Using this representation, we see that one possible sequence might be as follows: *A6, A7, A8, B6, B7, B8*. In this case, the program works as expected. Suppose we just started, so variables *in* and *out* are both zero. Thread *A* performs all of its three instructions before thread *B* performs any of its three instructions. With this order, thread *A* inserts an item in entry 0 and increments *in* from 0 to 1. Thread *B* adds an item in entry 1 and increments *in* from 1 to 2.

Another possible, but undesirable, sequence is *A6, B6, B7, A7, A8, B8*, which corresponds to the following timing diagram:

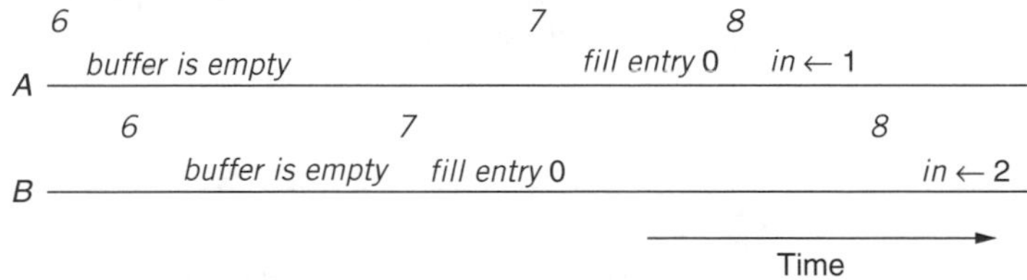

With this order, thread *A*, at *A6*, discovers that entry 0 of the buffer is free. Then, at *B6*, *B* also discovers that buffer entry 0 is free. At *B7*, *B* stores an item in entry 0 of *buffer*. Then, *A* proceeds: at *A7* it also stores an item in entry 0, overwriting *B*'s item. Then, both increment *in* (*A8* and *B8*), setting *in* first to 1 and then to 2. Thus, at the end of this order of instructions, one print job is lost (thread *B*'s job), and (because both threads incremented *in*) the receiver will find that entry 1 in the buffer was never filled in.

This type of error is called a *race condition* because it depends on the exact timing of two threads. Whether or not an error happens cannot be controlled. It is nasty, since some sequences deliver a correct result and some sequences deliver an incorrect result.

Worse, small timing changes between invocations might result in different behavior. If we notice that *B*'s print job was lost and we run it again to see what went wrong, we might get a correct result on the retry because the relative timing of the instructions has changed slightly. In particular, if we add instructions (e.g., for debugging) on the retry, it is almost guaranteed that the timing is changed (because the threads execute additional instructions) and we will observe a different behavior. Bugs that disappear when the debugger starts to close in on them are colloquially called "Heisenbugs" in a tongue-in-cheek pun on the Heisenberg uncertainty principle of quantum mechanics. Heisenbugs are difficult to reproduce, which makes debugging difficult.

Race conditions are the primary pitfall in writing concurrent programs and the main reason why developing concurrent programs should be left to specialists, despite the existence of tools to help identifying races (e.g., see Savage et al. [Suggestions for Further Reading 5.5.6]). Concurrent programming is subtle. In fact, with several senders the program of Figure 5.5 has a second race condition. Consider the statement *8* that the senders execute:

```
in ← in + 1
```

In reality, a thread executes this statement in three separate steps, which can be expressed as follows:

```
1 LOAD in, R0        // Load the value of in into a register
2 ADD R0, 1          // Increment
3 STORE R0, in       // Store result back to in
```

Consider two sending threads running simultaneously, threads *A* and *B*, respectively. The instructions of the threads might execute in the sequence *A1*, *A2*, *A3*, *B1*, *B2*, *B3*, which corresponds to the following timing diagram:

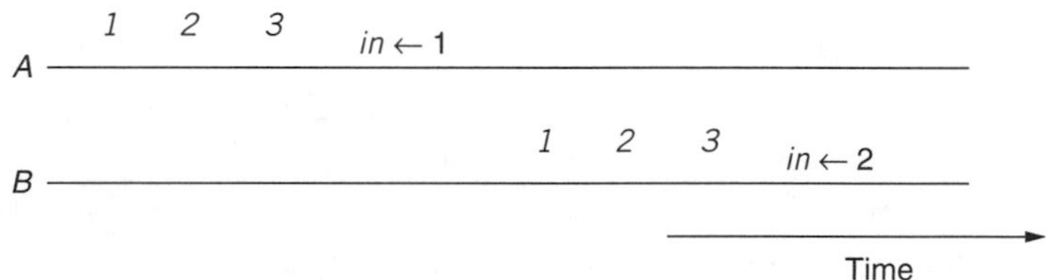

In this case *in* is incremented by two, as the programmer intended.

But now consider the execution sequence *A1*, *B1*, *A2*, *A3*, *B2*, *B3*, which corresponds to the following timing diagram:

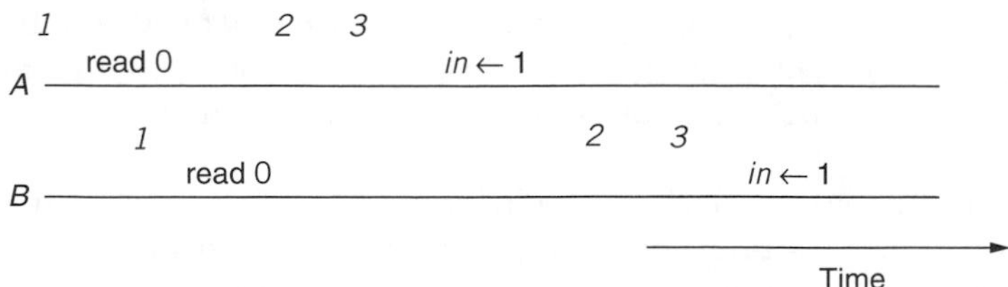

When the two threads finish, this ordering of memory references has increased *in* by only 1. At *A1*, thread *A* loads the R0 register of its thread with the value of *in*, which is 0. At *B1*, thread *B* does exactly the same thing, loading its thread's register R0 with the value 0. Then, at *A2*, thread A computes the new value in R0 and at *A3* updates *in* with the value 1. Next, at *B2* and *B3*, thread *B* does the same thing: it computes the new value in R0 and updates *in* with the value 1. Thus, *in* ends up containing 1 instead of the intended 2. Any time two threads update a shared variable concurrently (i.e., the one-writer principle is violated), a race condition is possible.

We caused this second race condition by allowing multiple senders. But the manipulation of the variables *in* and *out* also has a potential race even if there is only one sender and one receiver, and we remove assumption 5 (the before-or-after atomicity requirement). Let's assume that we want to make *in* and *out* of type **long integer** so that there is little risk of overflowing those two variables. In that case, *in* and *out* each span two memory cells instead of one, and updates to *in* and *out* are no longer atomic operations. That change creates yet another race.

If *in* is a long integer, then updating *in* would require two instructions:

```
1  STORE R0, in+1     // Update the least-significant word of in
2  STORE R1, in       // Update the most-significant word of in
```

To read *in* would also require two instructions:

```
3  LOAD in+1, R0      // Load the least-significant word of in into a register
4  LOAD in, R1        // Load the most-significant word of in into a register
```

If the sender executes instructions *1* and *2* at about the same time that the receiver executes instructions *3* and *4*, a race condition could manifest itself. Let's assume that two threads call SEND and RECEIVE $2^{32}-1$ times, and interleave their calls perfectly. At this point there are no messages in the buffer and *in* = *out* = $00000000FFFFFFFF_{hex}$ using big-endian notation.

Let's consider the scenario in which thread *A* has just added a message to the buffer, has read *in* into R0 and R1 (at instructions 3 and *4*), has computed the new value for *in* in the registers R0 and R1, and has executed instruction *1* to update *in* to memory. But before A executes instruction *2*, thread *B* adds a message:

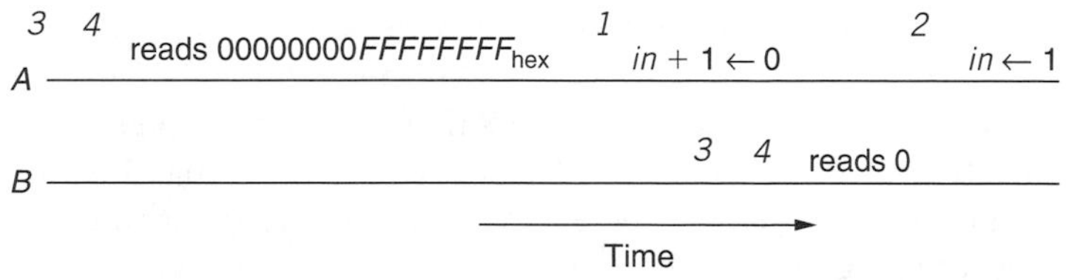

A: 3 4 reads $00000000FFFFFFFF_{hex}$ … 1 $in + 1 \leftarrow 0$ … 2 $in \leftarrow 1$

B: … 3 4 reads 0

Time →

In this case, the program works incorrectly because *A* has stored a message in entry 15 of the buffer ($00000000FFFFFFFF_{hex}$ **modulo** 20 = 15), *B* stores a message in entry 0, and *A* completes the update of *in*, which sets *in* to 0000000100000000_{hex}. *B*'s message in entry 0 will be lost because entry 0 will be overwritten by the next caller to SEND.

Race conditions are not uncommon in complex systems. Two notorious ones occurred in CTSS and in the Therac-25 machine. In CTSS, an early operating system, all running instances of a text editor used the same name for temporary files. At some point, two administrators were concurrently editing the file with the message of the day and a file containing passwords. The content of the two files ended up being exchanged (see Section 11.11.2 [on-line] for the details): when users logged into CTSS, it displayed the pass phrases of all other users as the message of the day.

The Therac-25 is a machine that delivers medical irradiation to human patients [Suggestions for Further Reading 1.9.5]. A race condition between a thread and the operator allowed an incorrect radiation intensity to be set: as a result, some patients died. The repairman could not reproduce the problem, since he typed more slowly than the more experienced operator of the machine.

Problem sets *4*, *5*, and *6* ask the reader to find race conditions in a few small, concurrent code fragments.

5.2.4 Locks and Before-or-After Actions

From the examples in the preceding section we can see that the program in Figure 5.5 was carefully written so that it didn't violate assumptions *1* and *5*. If we make slight modifications to the program or use the program in slightly different ways than it was intended to be used, we violate the assumptions and the program exhibits race conditions. We would like a technique by which a developer can systematically avoid race conditions. This section introduces a mechanism called a *lock*, with which a designer can make a multistep operation behave like a single-step operation. By using locks carefully, we can modify the program in Figure 5.5 so that it enforces assumptions *1* and *5*, and thus avoids the race conditions systematically.

A lock is a shared variable that acts as a flag to coordinate usage of other shared variables. To work with locks we introduce two new primitives: ACQUIRE and RELEASE, both of which take the name of a lock as an argument. A thread may ACQUIRE a lock, hold it for a while, and then RELEASE it. While a thread is holding a lock, other threads that attempt to acquire that same lock will wait until the first thread releases the lock. By surrounding multistep operations involving shared variables with ACQUIRE and RELEASE, the designer can make the multistep operation on shared variables behave like a single-step operation and avoid undesirable interleavings of multistep operations.

Figure 5.6 shows the code of Figure 5.5 with the addition of ACQUIRE and RELEASE invocations. The modified program uses only one lock (*buffer_lock*) because there is a single data structure that must protected. The lock guarantees that the program works correctly when there are several senders and receivers. It also guarantees correctness when *in* and *out* are long integers. That is, the two assumptions under which the program of Figure 5.5 is correct are now guaranteed by the program itself.

The ACQUIRE and RELEASE invocations make the reads and writes of the shared variables *p.in* and *p.out* behave like a single-step operation. The lock set by ACQUIRE and RELEASE ensures the test, and manipulation of the buffer is executed as one indivisible action; thus, no undesirable interleavings and races can happen. If two threads attempt to execute the multistep operation between ACQUIRE and RELEASE concurrently, one thread acquires the lock and finishes the complete multistep operation before the other thread starts on the operation. The ACQUIRE and RELEASE primitives have the effect of dynamically implementing the one-writer principle on those variables: they ensure there is only a single writer at any instant, but the identity of the writer can change.

It is important to keep in mind that when a thread acquires a lock, the shared variables that the lock is supposed to protect are not mechanically protected from access by other threads. Any thread can still read or write those variables without acquiring the lock. The lock variable merely acts as a flag, and for correct coordination all threads must honor an additional convention: they must not perform operations on shared variables unless they hold the lock. If any thread fails to honor that convention, there may be undesirable interleavings and races.

To ensure correctness in the presence of concurrent threads, a designer must identify *all* potential races and carefully insert invocations of ACQUIRE and RELEASE to prevent them. If the locking statements don't ensure that multistep operations on shared variables appear as single-step operations, then the program may have a race condition. For example, if in the SEND procedure of Figure 5.6 the programmer places the ACQUIRE and RELEASE statements around just the statements on lines *11* through

```
1   shared structure buffer                         // A shared bounded buffer
2       message instance message[N]                 // with a maximum of N messages
3       long integer in initially 0                 // Counts number of messages put in the buffer
4       long integer out initially 0                // Counts number of messages taken out of the buffer
5       lock instance buffer_lock initially UNLOCKED // Lock to order sender and receiver

6   procedure SEND (buffer reference p, message instance msg)
7       ACQUIRE (p.buffer_lock)
8       while p.in − p.out = N do                   // Wait until there is room in the buffer
9           RELEASE (p.buffer_lock)                 // While waiting release lock so that RECEIVE
10          ACQUIRE (p.buffer_lock)                 // can remove a message
11      p.message[p.in modulo N] ← msg              // Put message in the buffer
12      p.in ← p.in + 1                             // Increment in
13      RELEASE (p.buffer_lock)

14  procedure RECEIVE (buffer reference p)
15      ACQUIRE (p.buffer_lock)
16      while p.in = p.out do                       // Wait until there is a message to receive
17          RELEASE (p.buffer_lock)                 // While waiting release lock so that SEND
18          ACQUIRE (p.buffer_lock)                 // can add a message
19      msg ← p.message[p.out modulo N]             // Copy item out of buffer
20      p.out ← p.out + 1                           // Increment out
21      RELEASE (p.buffer_lock)
22      return msg
```

FIGURE 5.6

An implementation of SEND and RECEIVE that adds locks so that there can be multiple senders and receivers. The RELEASE and ACQUIRE on lines 9 and 10 are explained in Section 5.25.

12, then several race conditions may happen. If the lock doesn't protect the test of whether there's space in the buffer (line *8*), a buffer with only one space free could be appended to by multiple concurrent invocations to SEND. Also, before-or-after atomicity for *in* and *out* (assumption *5*) could be violated during the comparisons of *p.in* with *p.out*, so the race described in Section 5.2.3 could still occur. Programming with locks requires great attention to detail. Chapter 9 [on-line] will explore schemes that allow the designer to systematically ensure correctness for multistep operations involving shared variables.

A lock can be used to implement before-or-after atomicity. During the time that a thread holds a lock that protects one or more shared variables, it can perform a multistep operation on these shared variables. Because other threads that honor the lock protocol will not concurrently read or write any of the shared variables, from their point of view the multiple steps of the first thread appear to happen indivisibly: before the lock is acquired, none of the steps have occurred; after the lock is released all of them are complete. Any operation by a concurrent thread must happen either completely before or completely after the before-or-after atomic action.

The need for before-or-after atomicity has been realized in different contexts, and as a result that concept and before-or-after atomic actions are known by various names. The database literature uses the terms *isolation* and *isolated actions*; the operating system literature uses the terms *mutual exclusion* and *critical sections*; and the computer architecture literature uses the terms *atomicity* and *atomic actions*. Because Chapter 9 [on-line] introduces a second kind of atomicity, this text uses the qualified term "before-or-after atomicity" for precision as well as for its self-defining and mnemonic features.

In general, in the computer science community, a tremendous amount of work has been done on approaches to finding race conditions in programs and on approaches to avoid them in the first place. This text introduces the fundamental ideas in concurrent programming, but the interested reader is encouraged to explore the literature to learn more.

The usual implementation of ACQUIRE and RELEASE guarantees that only a single thread can acquire a given lock at any one time. This requirement is called the *single-acquire protocol*. If the programmer knows more details about how the protected shared variables will be used, a more relaxed protocol may be able to allow more concurrency. For example, Section 9.5.4 describes a multiple-reader, single-writer locking protocol.

In larger programs with many shared data structures, a programmer often uses several locks. For example, if each of the several data structures is used by different operations, then we might introduce a separate lock for each shared data structure. That way, the operations that use different shared data structures can proceed concurrently. If the program used just one lock to protect all of the data structures, then all operations would be serialized by the lock. On the other hand, using several locks raises the complexity of understanding a program by another notch, as we will see next.

Problem sets *4* and *5* explore several possible locations for ACQUIRE and RELEASE statements in an attempt to remove a race condition while still allowing for concurrent execution of some operations. Birrell's tutorial [Suggestions for Further Reading

5.3.1] provides a nice introduction on how to write concurrent programs with threads and locks.

5.2.5 Deadlock

A programmer must use locks with care, because it is easy to create other undesirable situations that are as bad as race conditions. For example, using locks, a programmer can create a *deadlock*, which is an undesirable interaction among a group of threads in which each thread is waiting for some other thread in the group to make progress.

Consider two threads, A and B, that both must acquire two locks, *L1* and *L2*, before they can proceed with their task:

Thread A	Thread B
ACQUIRE(*L1*)	ACQUIRE(*L2*)
ACQUIRE(*L2*)	ACQUIRE(*L1*)

This code fragment has a race condition that results in deadlock, as shown in the following timing diagram:

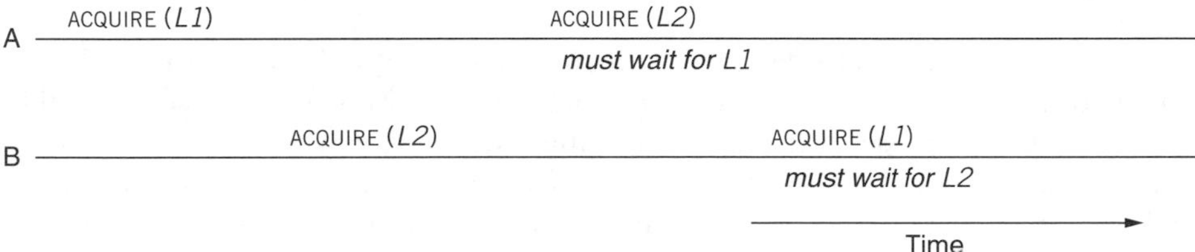

Thread A cannot make forward progress because thread B has acquired *L2*, and thread B cannot make forward progress because thread A has acquired *L1*. The threads are in a deadly embrace.

If we had modified the code so that both threads acquire the locks in the same order (*L1* and then *L2*, or vice versa), then no deadlock could have occurred. Again, small changes in the order of statements can result in good or bad behavior.

A convenient way to represent deadlocks is using a *wait-for* graph. The nodes in a wait-for graph are threads and resources such as locks. When a thread acquires a lock, it inserts a directed edge from the lock node to the thread node. When a thread must wait for a resource, it inserts another directed edge from the thread node to the resource node. As an example, the race condition with threads A, B, and locks *L1* and *L2* results in the following wait-for graph:

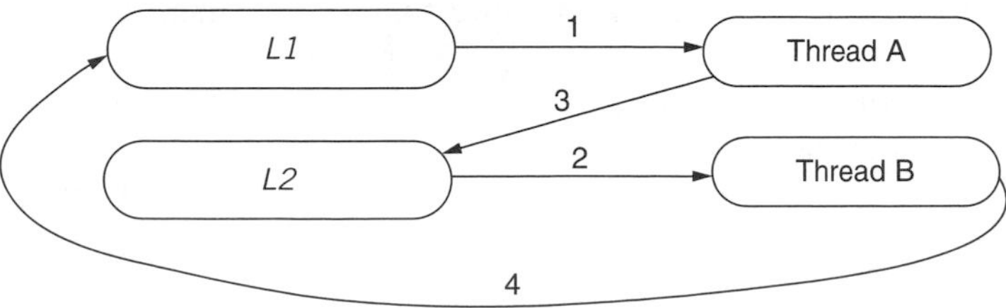

When thread A acquires lock *L1*, it inserts arrow 1. When thread B acquires lock *L2*, it inserts arrow 2. When thread A must wait for lock *L2*, it inserts arrow 3. When thread B attempts to acquire lock *L1* but must wait, it inserts arrow 4. When a thread must wait, we check if the wait-for graph contains a cycle. A cycle indicates deadlock: everyone is waiting for someone else to release a resource. In general, if, and only if, a wait-for graph contains a cycle, then threads are deadlocked.

When there are several locks, a good programming strategy to avoid deadlock is to enumerate all lock usages and ensure that all threads of the program acquire the locks in the same order. This rule will ensure there can be no cycles in the wait-for graph and thus no deadlocks. In our example, if thread B above did ACQUIRE(*L1*) before ACQUIRE (*L2*), the same order that thread A used, then there wouldn't have been a problem. In our example program, it is easy for the programmer to modify the program to ensure that locks are acquired in the same order because the ACQUIRE statements are shown next to each other and there are only two locks. In a real program, however, the four ACQUIRE statements may be buried deep inside two separate modules that threads A and B happen to call indirectly in different orders, and ensuring that all locks are acquired in a static global order requires careful thinking and design.

A deadlock doesn't always have to involve multiple locks. For example, if the sender forgets to release and acquire the lock on lines *9* and *10* of Figure 5.6, then a deadlock is also possible. If the buffer is full, the receiver will not get a chance to remove a message from the buffer because it cannot acquire the lock, which is being held by the sender. In this case, the sender is waiting on the receiver to change the value of *p.out* (in a wait-for graph, the resource is buffer space represented by the value of *p.out*), and the receiver is waiting on the sender to release the lock. Simple programming errors can lead to deadlocks.

A problem related to deadlock is *livelock*—an interaction among a group of threads in which each thread is repeatedly performing some operations but is never able to complete the whole sequence of operations. An example of livelock is given in Sidebar 5.2, which presents an algorithm to implement ACQUIRE and RELEASE.

5.2.6 Implementing ACQUIRE and RELEASE

A correct implementation of ACQUIRE and RELEASE must enforce the single-acquire protocol. Several threads may attempt to acquire the lock at the same time, but only one should succeed. This requirement makes the implementation of locks challenging. In essence, we must make sure that ACQUIRE itself is a before-or-after action.

To see what goes wrong if ACQUIRE is not a before-or-after action, consider the too-simple implementation of ACQUIRE as shown in Figure 5.7. This implementation is broken because it has a race condition. If two threads labeled A and B call

FAULTY_ACQUIRE at the same time, the threads may execute the statements in the order A5, B5, A6, B6, which corresponds to the following timing diagram:

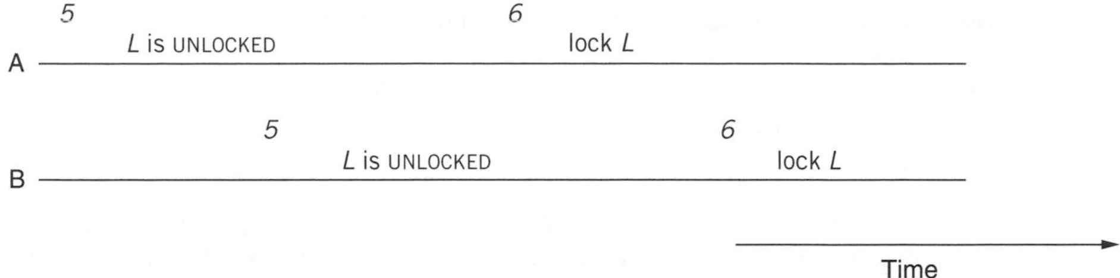

The result of this sequence of events is that both threads acquire the lock, which violates the single-acquire protocol.

The faulty ACQUIRE has a multistep operation on a shared variable (the lock), and we must ensure in some way that ACQUIRE itself is a before-or-after action. Once ACQUIRE is a before-or-after action, we can use it to turn arbitrary multistep operations on shared variables into before-or-after actions. This reduction is an example of a technique called *bootstrapping*, which resembles an inductive proof. Bootstrapping means that we look for a systematic way to reduce a general problem (e.g., making multistep operations on shared variables before-or-after actions) to some much-narrower particular version of the same problem (e.g., making an operation on a single shared lock a before-or-after action). We then solve the narrow problem using some specialized method that might work for only that case because it takes advantage of the specific situation. The general solution then consists of two parts: a method for solving the special case and a method for reducing the general problem to the special case. In the case of ACQUIRE, the solution for the specific problem is either building a special hardware instruction that is itself a before-or-after action or programming very carefully.

```
1   structure lock
2       integer state
3
4   procedure FAULTY_ACQUIRE (lock reference L)
5       while L.state = LOCKED do nothing      // spin until L is UNLOCKED
6       L.state ← LOCKED                       // the while test failed, got the lock
7
8   procedure RELEASE (lock reference L)
9       L.state ← UNLOCKED
```

FIGURE 5.7

Incorrect implementation of ACQUIRE. LOCKED and UNLOCKED are constants that have different values; for example, LOCKED is 1 and UNLOCKED is 0.

We first look at a solution involving a special instruction, *Read and Set Memory* (RSM). RSM performs the statements in the block **do atomic** as a before-or-after action:

```
1   procedure RSM (reference mem)     // RSM memory location mem
2       do atomic
3           r ← mem                   // Load value stored at mem into r
4           mem ← LOCKED              // Store LOCKED into memory location mem
5       return r
```

Most modern computers implement some version of the RSM procedure in hardware, as an extension to the memory abstraction. RSM is then often called *test-and-set*; see Sidebar 5.1. For the RSM instruction to be a before-or-after action, the bus arbiter that controls the bus connecting the processors to the memory must guarantee that the LOAD (line *3*) and STORE (line *4*) instruction execute as before-or-after actions—for example, by allowing the processor to read a value from a memory location and to write a new value into that same location in a single bus cycle. We have thus pushed the problem of providing a before-or-after action down to the bus arbiter, a piece of hardware whose precise function is turning bus operations into before-or-after

Sidebar 5.1 RSM, **Test-and-Set, and Avoiding Locks** RSM is often called "test-and-set" or "test-and-set-locked" for accidental reasons. An early version of the instruction tested the lock and performed the store only if the test showed that the lock was not set. The instruction also set a bit that the software could test to find out whether or not the lock had been set. Using this instruction, one can implement the body of ACQUIRE as follows:

```
while TEST_AND_SET (L) = LOCKED do nothing
```

This version appears to be shorter than the one shown in Figure 5.8, but the hardware performs a test that is redundant. Thus, later hardware designers removed the test from test-and-set, but the name stuck.

In addition to RSM, there are many other instructions, including "test-and-test-and-set" (which allows for a more efficient implementation of a spin lock) and COMPARE_AND_SWAP (*v1, m, v2*) (which compares, in a before-or-after action the content of a memory location *m* to the value *v1* and, if they are the same, stores *v2* in *m*). The "compare-and-swap" instruction can be used, for example, to implement a linked list in which threads can insert elements concurrently without having to use locks, avoiding the risk of spinning until other threads have completed their insert [see Suggestions for Further Reading 5.5.8 and 5.5.9]. Such implementations are called *non-blocking*.

The Linux kernel uses yet another form of coordination that avoids locks. It is called read-copy update and is tailored to data structures that are mostly read and infrequently updated [see Suggestions for Further Reading 5.5.7].

```
1   procedure ACQUIRE (lock reference L)
2       R1 ← RSM (L.state)                  // read and set lock L
3       while R1 = LOCKED do                // was it already locked?
4           R1 ← RSM(L.state)               // yes, do it again, till we see it wasn't
5
6   procedure RELEASE (lock reference L)
7       L.state ← UNLOCKED
```

FIGURE 5.8

ACQUIRE and RELEASE using RSM.

actions: the arbiter guarantees that if two requests arrive at the same time, one of those requests is executed completely before the other begins.

Using the RSM instruction, we can implement any other before-or-after action. It is the one essential before-or-after action from which we can bootstrap any other set of before-or-after actions. Using RSM, we can implement ACQUIRE and RELEASE as shown in Figure 5.8. This implementation follows the single-acquire protocol: if *L* is LOCKED, then one thread has the lock *L*; if *L* contains UNLOCKED, then no thread has acquired the lock *L*.

To see that the implementation is correct, let's assume that *L* is UNLOCKED. If some thread calls ACQUIRE (*L*), then after RSM, *L* is LOCKED and R1 contains UNLOCKED, so that thread has acquired the lock. The next thread that calls ACQUIRE (*L*) sees LOCKED in R1 after the RSM instruction, signaling that some other thread holds the lock. The thread that tried to acquire will spin until R1 contains UNLOCKED. When releasing a lock, no test is needed, so an ordinary STORE instruction can do the job without creating a race condition.

This implementation assumes that the shared memory provides read/write coherence. For example, if a manager thread sets *L* to UNLOCKED on line *7*, then we assume that the thread observes that store and falls out of the spinning loop on line *3* in ACQUIRE. Some memories provide more relaxed semantics than read/write coherence; in that case, additional mechanisms are needed to make this program work correctly.

With this implementation, even a single thread can deadlock itself by calling ACQUIRE twice on the same lock. With the first call to ACQUIRE, the thread obtains the lock. With the second call to ACQUIRE the thread deadlocks, since some thread (itself) already holds the lock. By storing the thread identifier of the lock's owner in *L* (instead of true or false), ACQUIRE could check for this problem and return an error.

Problem set *6* explores concurrency issues using a SET-AND-GET remote procedure call, which executes as a before-or-after action.

5.2.7 Implementing a Before-or-After Action Using the One-Writer Principle

The RSM instruction can also be implemented without extending the memory abstraction. In fact, one can implement RSM as a procedure in software using ordinary load and store instructions, but such implementations are complex. The key

Sidebar 5.2 Constructing a Before-or-After Action Without Special Instructions

In 1959, E. Dijkstra, a well-known Dutch programmer and researcher, posed to his colleagues the problem of providing a before-or-after action with ordinary read and write instructions as an amusing puzzle. Th. J. Dekker provided a solution for two threads, and Dijkstra generalized the idea into a solution for an arbitrary number of threads [Suggestions for Further Reading 5.5.2]. Subsequently, numerous researchers have looked for provable, efficient solutions. We present a simple implementation of RSM based on L. Lamport's solution. Lamport's solution, like other solutions, relies on the existence of a bus arbiter that guarantees that any single LOAD or STORE is a before-or-after action with respect to every other LOAD and STORE. Given this assumption, RSM can be implemented as follows:

```
shared boolean flag[N]                                // one boolean per thread

1   procedure RSM (lock reference L)                  // set lock L and return old value
2       do forever                                    // me is my index in flag
3           flag[me] ← TRUE                           // warn other threads
4           if ANYONE_ELSE_INTERESTED (me) then       // is another thread warning us?
5            flag[me] ← FALSE                         // yes, reset my warning, try again
6           else
7            R ← L.state                              // set R to value of lock
8            L.state ← LOCKED                         // and set the lock
9            flag[me] ← FALSE
10           return R
11
12  procedure ANYONE_ELSE_INTERESTED (me)             // is another thread updating L?
13      for i from 0 to N–1 do
14          if i ≠ me and flag[i] = TRUE then return TRUE
15      return FALSE
```

To guarantee that RSM is indeed a before-or-after action, we need to assume that each entry of the shared array is in its own memory cell, that the memory provides read/write coherence for memory cells, and that the instructions execute in program order, as we did for the sender and receiver in Figure 5.5.

Under these assumptions, RSM ensures that the shared variable *L* is never written by two threads at the same time. Each thread has a unique number, *me*. Before *me* is allowed to write *L*, it must express its interest in writing *L* by setting *me*'s entry in the boolean array *flag* (line *3*) and check that no other thread is interested in writing *L* (line *4*). If no other thread has expressed interest, then *me* acquires *L* (line *8*).

If two threads A and B call RSM at the same time, either A or B may acquire *L*, or both may retry, depending on how the shared memory system orders the accesses of A and B to the *flag*[i] array. There are three cases:

1. A sets *flag*[A], calls ANYONE_ELSE_INTERESTED, and reads flags at least as far as *flag*[B] before B sets *flag*[B]. In this case, A sees no other flags set and proceeds to acquire *L*;

(Sidebar continues)

B discovers A's flag and tries again. On its next try, B encounters no flags, but by the time B writes LOCKED to *L*, *L* is already set to LOCKED, so B's write will have no effect.

2. B sets *flag*[B], calls ANYONE_ELSE_INTERESTED, and reads flags at least as far as *flag*[A] before A sets *flag*[A]. In this case, B sees no other flags set and proceeds to acquire *L*;A discovers B's flag and tries again. On its next try, A encounters no flags, but by the time A writes *locked* to *L*, *L* is already set to *locked*, so A's write will have no effect.

3. A sets *flag*[A] and B sets *flag*[B] before either of them gets far enough through ANYONE_ELSE_INTERESTED to reach the other's flag location. In this case, both A and B reset their own *flag*[*i*] entries and try again. On the retry, all three cases are again possible.

The implementation of RSM has a livelock problem because the two threads A and B might end up in the final case (neither of them gets to update *L*), every time they retry. RSM could reduce the chance of livelock by inserting a random delay before retrying, a technique called *random backoff*. Chapter 7 [on-line] will refine the random backoff idea to make it applicable to a wider range of problems.

This implementation of RSM is not the most efficient one; it is linear in the number of threads because ANYONE_ELSE_INTERESTED reads all but one element of the array *flag*. More efficient versions of RSM exist, but even the best implementation [Suggestions for Further Reading 5.5.3] requires two loads and five stores (if there is no contention for *L*), which can be proven to be optimal under the given assumptions.

problem that our implementation without RSM of ACQUIRE has is that several threads are attempting to *modify* the same shared variable (*L* in our example). For two threads to read *L* concurrently is fine (the bus arbiter ensures that LOADs are before-or-after actions, and both threads will read the same value), but reading *and* modifying *L* is a multistep operation that must be performed as a before-or-after action. If not, this multistep operation can lead to a race condition in which the outcome may be a violation of the single-acquire protocol. This observation suggests an approach to implementing RSM based on the one-writer principle: ensure that only *one* thread modifies *L*.

Sidebar 5.2 describes a software solution that follows that approach. This software solution is complex compared to the hardware implementation of RSM. To ensure that only one thread writes *L*, the software solution requires an array with one entry per thread. Such an array must be allocated for each lock. Moreover, the number of memory accesses to acquire a lock is linear in the number of threads. Also, if threads are created dynamically, the software solution requires a more complex data structure than an array. Between the need for efficiency and the requirement for an array of unpredictable size, designers generally implement RSM as a hardware instruction that invokes a special bus cycle.

If one follows the *one-writer principle* carefully, one can write programs without locks (for example, as in Figure 5.5). This approach without locks can improve a program's performance because the expense of locks is avoided, but eliminating locks makes it more difficult to reason about the correctness.

The designers of the computer system for the space shuttle used many threads sharing many variables, and they deployed a systematic design approach to encourage a correct implementation. Designed in the late 1970s and early 1980s, the computers of the space shuttle were not efficient enough to follow the principled way of protecting all shared variables using locks. Understanding the risks of sharing variables among concurrent threads, however, the designers followed a rule that the program declaration for each unprotected shared variable must be accompanied by a comment, known as an *alibi*, explaining why no race conditions can occur even though that variable is unprotected. At each new release of the software, a team of engineers inspects all alibis and checks whether they still hold. Although this method has a high verification overhead, it helps discover many race conditions that otherwise might go undetected until too late. The use of alibis is an example of design for iteration.

5.2.8 Coordination between Synchronous Islands with Asynchronous Connections

As has been seen in this chapter, all implementations of before-or-after actions rely on bootstrapping from a properly functioning hardware arbiter. This reliance should catch the attention of hardware designers, who are aware that under certain conditions, it can be problematic (indeed, theoretically impossible) to implement a perfect arbiter. This section explains why and how hardware designers deal with this problem in practice. System designers need to be aware of how arbiters can fail, so that they know what questions to ask the designer of the hardware on which they rely.

The problem arises at the interface between asynchronous and synchronous components, when an arbiter that provides input to a synchronous subsystem is asked to choose between two asynchronous but closely spaced input signals. An asynchronous-input arbiter can enter a metastable state, with an output value somewhere between its two correct values or possibly oscillating between them at a high rate.* After applying asynchronous signals to an arbiter, one must therefore wait for the arbiter's output to settle. Although the probability that the output of the arbiter has not settled falls exponentially fast, for any given delay time some chance always remains that the arbiter has not settled yet, and a sample of its output may find it still changing. By waiting longer, one can reduce the probability of it not having settled to as small a figure as necessary for any particular application, but it is impossible to drive it to zero within a fixed time. Thus if the component that acquires the output of the arbiter is synchronous, when its clock ticks there is a chance that the component's

*Our colleague Andreas Reuter points out that the possibility that an arbiter may enter a metastable state has been of concern since antiquity: "How long halt ye between two opinions"?—*1 Kings* 18:21.

input (that is, the arbiter's output) is not ready. When that happens, the component may behave unpredictably, launching a chain of failure. Although the arbiter itself will certainly come to a decision at some point, not doing so before the clock ticks is known as *arbiter failure*.

Arbiter failure can be avoided in several ways:

- Synchronize the clocks of the two components. If the two processors, the arbiter, and the memory all operate with a common clock (more precisely, all of their interfaces are synchronous), arbiter design becomes straightforward. This technique is used, for example, to arbitrate access within some chips that have several processors.
- Design arbiters with multiple stages. Multiple stages do not eliminate the possibility of arbiter failure, but each additional stage multiplicatively reduces the probability of failure. The strategy is to provide enough stages that the probability of failure is so low that it can be neglected. With current technology, two or three stages are usually sufficient, and this technique is used in most interfaces between asynchronous and synchronous devices.
- Stop the clock of the synchronous component (thus effectively making it asynchronous) and wait for the arbiter's output to settle before restarting. In modern high-performance systems, clock distribution requires continuous ticks to provide signals for correcting phase errors, so one does not often encounter this technique in practice.
- Make all components asynchronous. The component that takes the output of the arbiter then simply waits until the arbiter reports that it has settled. A flurry of interest in asynchronous circuit design arose in the 1970s, but synchronous circuits proved to be easier to design and so won out. However, as clock speeds increase to the point that it is difficult to distribute clock even across a single chip, interest is reawakening.

Communication across a network link is nearly always asynchronous, communication between devices in the same box (for example, between a disk drive and a processor) is usually asynchronous, and as mentioned in the last bullet above, as advancing technology reduces gate delays, it is becoming challenging to maintain a common, fast-enough clock all the way across even a single chip. Thus, within-chip intercommunication is becoming more network-like, with synchronous islands connected by asynchronous links (see, for example, Suggestions for Further Reading 1.6.3).

As pointed out, arbiter failure is an issue only at the boundary between synchronous and asynchronous components. Over the years, that boundary has moved with changing technology. The authors are not aware of any current implementations of RSM () or their equivalents that cross a synchronous/asynchronous boundary (in other words, current multiprocessor practice is to use the method of the first bullet above). Thus, before-or-after atomicity based on RSM () is not at risk of arbiter failure. But that was not true in the past, and it may not be true again at some point in the future. The system designer thus needs to be aware of where arbiters are being used and verify that they are specified appropriately for the application.

5.3 ENFORCING MODULARITY IN MEMORY

The implementation of bounded buffers took advantage of the fact that all threads share the same physical memory (see Figure 5.4 on page 209), but sharing memory does not enforce modularity well. A program may calculate a shared address incorrectly and write to a memory location that logically belongs to another module. To enforce modularity, we must ensure that the threads of one module cannot overwrite the data of another module. This section introduces domains and a memory manager to enforce memory boundaries, assuming that the address space is very large (i.e., so large that we can consider it unlimited). In Section 5.4, we will remove that assumption.

5.3.1 Enforcing Modularity with Domains

To contain the memory references of a thread, we restrict the thread's references to a *domain*, a contiguous range of memory addresses. When a programmer calls ALLOCATE_THREAD, the programmer specifies a domain in which the thread is to run. The thread manager records a thread's domain.

To enforce the rule that a thread should refer only to memory within its domain, we add a domain register to each processor and introduce a special interpreter, a *memory manager*, that is typically implemented in hardware and placed between a processor and the bus (see Figure 5.9). A processor's domain register contains the

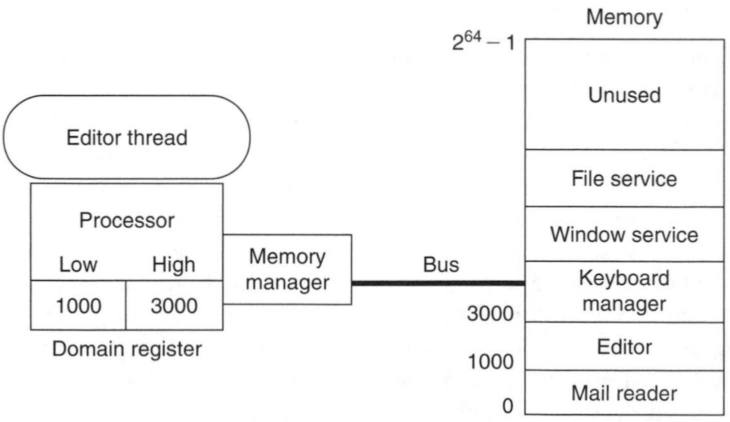

FIGURE 5.9

An editor thread running with its domain.

lowest (*low*) and highest address (*high*) that the currently running thread is allowed to use. ALLOCATE_THREAD loads the processor's domain register with the thread's domain.

The memory manager checks for each memory reference that the address is equal or higher than *low* and smaller than *high*. If it is, the memory manager issues the corresponding bus request. If not, it interrupts the processor, signaling a *memory reference exception*. The exception handler can then decide what to do. One option is to deliver an error message and destroy the thread.

This design ensures that a thread can make references only to addresses that are in its domain. Threads cannot overwrite or jump to memory locations of other threads.

This domain design achieves the main goal, but it lacks a number of desirable features:

1. A thread may need more than one domain. By using many domains, threads can control what memory they share and what memory they keep private. For example, a thread might allocate a domain for a bounded buffer and share that domain with another thread, but allocate private domains for the text of its program and private data structures.
2. A thread should be unable to change its own domain. That is, we must ensure that the thread cannot change the content of its processor's domain register directly or indirectly. If a thread can change the content of its processor's domain register, then the thread can make references to addresses that it shouldn't.

The rest of Section 5.3 adds these features.

5.3.2 Controlled Sharing Using Several Domains

To allow for sharing, we extend the design to allow each thread to have several domains and give each processor several domain registers, for the moment, as many as a thread needs. Now a designer can partition the memory of the programs shown in Figure 5.9 and control sharing. For example, a designer may split a client into four separate domains (see Figure 5.10): one domain containing the program text for the client thread, one domain containing the data for the client, one domain containing the stack of the client thread, and one domain containing the bounded message buffer. The designer may split a service in the same way. This setup allows both threads to use the shared bounded buffer domain, but restricts the other references of the threads to their private domains.

To manage this hardware design, we introduce a software component to the memory manager, which provides the following interface:

- *base_address* ← ALLOCATE_DOMAIN (*size*): Allocate a new domain of *size* bytes and return the base address of the domain.
- MAP_DOMAIN (*base_address*): Add the domain starting at address *base_address* to the calling thread's domains.

The memory manager can implement this interface by keeping a list of memory regions that are not in use, allocate *size* bytes of memory on an ALLOCATE_DOMAIN request, and maintain a *domain table* with allocated domains. An entry in the domain table records the *base_address* and *size*.

MAP_DOMAIN loads the domain's bounds from the domain table into a domain register of the thread's processor. If two or more threads map a domain, then that domain is shared among those threads.

We can improve the control mechanism by extending each domain register to record access permissions. In a typical design, a domain register might include three bits, which separately control permission to READ, WRITE, or EXECUTE (i.e., retrieve and use as an instruction) any of the bytes in the associated domain.

With these permissions, the designer can give the threads in Figure 5.10 EXECUTE and READ permissions to their text domains, and READ and WRITE permissions to their stack domains and the shared bounded buffer domain. This setup prevents a thread from taking instructions from its stack, which can help catch programming mistakes and also help avoid buffer overrun attacks (see Sidebar 11.4 [on-line]). Giving the program text only READ and EXECUTE permissions helps avoid the mistake of accidentally writing data into the text of the program.

The permissions also allow more controlled sharing: one thread can have access to a shared domain with only READ permission, whereas another thread can have READ and WRITE permissions.

To provide permissions, we modify the MAP_DOMAIN call as follows:

- MAP_DOMAIN (*base_address, permission*): loads the domain's bounds from the domain table into one of the calling thread's domain registers with permission *permission*.

To check permissions, the memory manager must know which permissions are needed for each memory reference. A LOAD instruction requires READ permission for its address, and thus the memory manager must check that the address is in a domain with READ access. A STORE instruction requires WRITE permission for its address, and

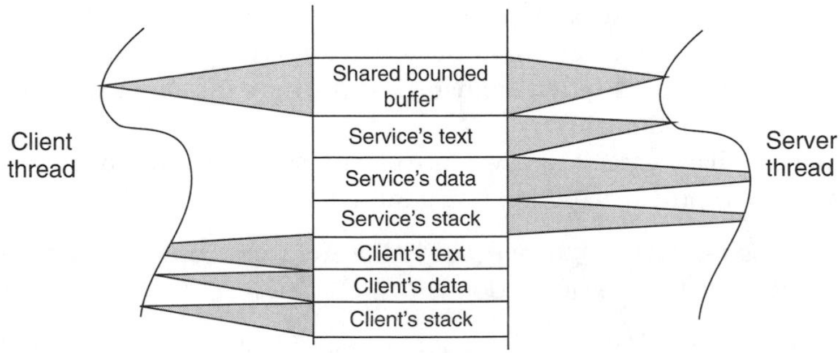

FIGURE 5.10

A client and service, each with three private domains and one shared domain.

thus the memory manager must check that the address is in a domain with WRITE access. To execute an instruction at the address in the PC requires EXECUTE permission. The domain holding instructions may also require READ permission because the program may have stored constants in the program text.

The pseudocode in Figure 5.11 details the check performed by the memory manager. Although we describe the function of the memory manager using pseudocode, in practice the memory manager is a hardware device that implements its function in digital circuitry. In addition, the memory manager is typically integrated with the processor so that the address checks run at the speed of the processor. As Section 5.3 develops, we will add more functions to the memory manager, some of which may be implemented in software as part of the operating system. Later, in Section 5.4.4, we discuss the trade-offs involved in implementing parts of the memory manager in software.

As shown in the figure, on a memory reference, the memory manager checks all the processor's domain registers. For each domain register, the memory manager calls CHECK_DOMAIN, which takes three arguments: the address the processor requested, a bit mask with the permissions needed by the current instruction, and the domain register. If *address* falls between *low* and *high* of the domain and if the permissions needed are a subset of permissions authorized for the domain, then CHECK_DOMAIN returns TRUE and the memory manager will issue the desired bus request. If *address* falls between *low* and *high* of the domain but the permissions needed aren't sufficient, then CHECK_DOMAIN interrupts the processor, indicating a memory reference exception as before. Now, however, it is useful to demultiplex the memory reference exception in two different categories: *illegal memory reference exception* and *permission error exception*. If *address* doesn't fall in any domain, the exception handler indicates an illegal memory reference exception. If the address falls in a domain, but the threads didn't have sufficient permissions, the exception handler indicates a permission error exception.

```
procedure LOOKUP_AND_CHECK (integer address, perm_needed)
    for each domain do                  // for each domain register of this processor
        if CHECK_DOMAIN (address, perm_needed, domain) return domain
    signal memory_exception

procedure CHECK_DOMAIN (integer address, perm_needed, domain) returns boolean
    if domain.low ≤ address and address < domain.high then
        if PERMITTED (perm_needed, domain.permission) then return TRUE
        else signal permission_exception
    return FALSE

procedure PERMITTED (perm_needed, perm_authorized) returns boolean
    if perm_needed ⊂ perm_authorized then return TRUE // is perm_needed a subset?
    else return FALSE              // permission violation
```

FIGURE 5.11

The memory manager's pseudocode for looking up an address and checking permissions.

The demultiplexing of memory reference exceptions can be implemented either in hardware or software. If implemented in hardware, the memory manager signals an illegal memory reference exception or a permission error exception to the processor. If implemented in software, the memory manager signals a memory reference exception, and the exception handler for memory reference exceptions demultiplexes it by calling either the illegal memory reference exception handler or the permission error exception handler. As we will see in Chapter 6 (see Section 6.2.2), we will want to refine the categories of memory exceptions further. In processors in the field, some of the demultiplexing is implemented in hardware with further demultiplexing implemented in software in the exception handler.

In practice, only a subset of the possible combinations of permissions are useful. The ones used are: READ permission, READ and WRITE permissions, READ and EXECUTE permissions, and READ, WRITE, and EXECUTE permissions. The READ, WRITE, and EXECUTE combination of permissions might be used for a domain that contains a program that generates instructions and then jumps to the generated instructions, so-called self-modifying programs. Supporting self-modifying programs is risky, however, because this also allows an adversary to write a new procedure as data into a domain (e.g., using a buffer overrun attack) and then execute that procedure. In practice, self-modifying programs have proven to be more trouble than they are worth, except to system crackers. A domain with only EXECUTE permission or with just WRITE and EXECUTE permissions isn't useful in practice.

If memory-mapped I/O (described in Section 2.3.1) is used, then domain registers can also control which devices a thread can use. For example, a keyboard manager thread may have access to a domain that corresponds to the registers of the keyboard controller. If none of the other threads has access to this domain, then only the keyboard manager thread has access to the keyboard device. Thus, the same technique that controls separation of memory ranges can also control access to devices.

The memory manager can implement security policies because it controls which threads have access to which parts of memory. It can deny or grant a thread's request for allocating a new domain or for sharing an existing domain. In the same way, it can control which threads have access to which devices. How to implement such security policies is the topic of Chapter 11 [on-line].

5.3.3 More Enforced Modularity with Kernel and User Mode

Domain registers restrict the addresses to which a thread can make reference, but we must also ensure that a thread cannot change its domains. That is, we need a mechanism to control changes to the *low*, *high*, and *permission* fields of a domain register. To complete the enforcement of domains, we modify the processor to prevent threads from overwriting the content of domain registers as follows:

- Add one bit to the processor indicating whether the processor is in *kernel mode* or *user mode*, and modify the processor as follows. Instructions can change the value of the processor's domain registers only in kernel mode, and instructions

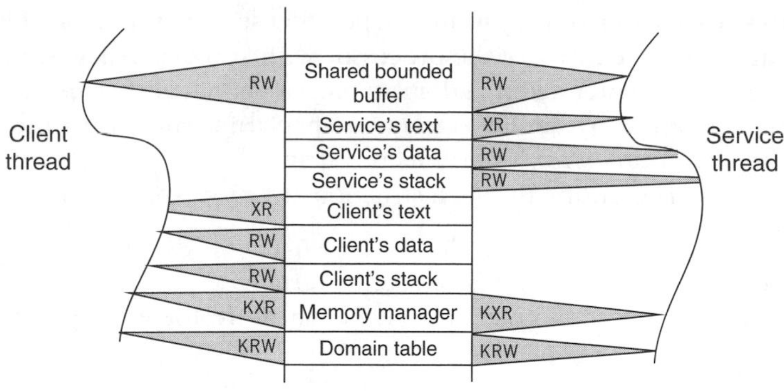

FIGURE 5.12

Threads with a kernel domain containing the memory manager and its domain table.

that attempt to change the domain register in user mode generate an *illegal instruction exception*. Similarly, instructions can change the mode bit only in kernel mode.

- Extend the set of permissions for a domain to include KERNEL-ONLY, and modify the processor to make it illegal for threads in user mode to reference addresses in a domain with KERNEL-ONLY permission. A thread in user mode that attempts to read or write memory with KERNEL-ONLY permission causes a permission error exception.
- Switch to kernel mode on an interrupt and on an exception so that the handler can process the interrupt (or exception) and invoke privileged instructions.

We can use the mechanisms as illustrated in Figure 5.12. Compared to Figure 5.10, each thread has two additional domains, which are marked K for KERNEL-ONLY. A thread must be in kernel mode to be able to make references to this domain. This domain contains the program text and data for the memory manager. These mechanisms ensure that a thread running in user mode cannot change its processor's domain registers; only when a thread executes in kernel mode can it change the processor domain registers. Furthermore, because the memory manager and its table are in kernel domains, a thread in user mode cannot change its domain information. We see that the kernel/user mode bit helps in enforcing modularity by restricting what threads in user mode can do.

5.3.4 Gates and Changing Modes

Because threads running in user mode cannot invoke procedures of the memory manager directly, a thread must have a way of changing from user mode to kernel mode and entering the memory manager in a controlled manner. If a thread could enter at an arbitrary address, it might create problems; for example, if a thread could enter a domain with kernel permission at the instruction that sets the user-mode bit to KERNEL, it might be able to gain control of the processor with kernel privileges. To avoid this problem, a thread may enter a kernel domain only at certain addresses, called *gates*.

We implement gates by adding one more special instruction to the processor, the ***supervisor call instruction*** (SVC), which specifies in a register the name for the intended gate. Upon executing the SVC instruction, the processor performs two operations as one action:

1. Change the processor mode from user to kernel.
2. Set the PC to an address predefined by the hardware, the entry point of the gate manager.

The gate manager now has control in kernel mode; it can call the appropriate procedures to serve the thread's request. Typically, gate names are numbers, and the gate manager has a table that records for each gate number the corresponding procedure. For example, the table might map gate 0 to ALLOCATE_DOMAIN, gate 1 to MAP_DOMAIN, gate 2 to ALLOCATE_THREAD, and so on.

Implementing SVC has a slight complication: the steps to enter the kernel must happen as a before-or-after action: they must all be executed *without* interruption. If the processor can be interrupted in the middle of these steps, a thread might end up in kernel mode but with the program counter still pointing to an address in one of its user-level domains. Now the thread is executing instructions from an application module in kernel mode. To avoid this potential problem, processors complete all steps of an SVC instructions before executing another instruction.

When the thread wants to return to user mode, it executes the following instructions:

1. Change mode from kernel to user.
2. Load the program counter from the top of the stack into the processor's PC.

Processors don't have to perform these steps as a before-or-after action. After step 1, it is fine for a processor to return to kernel mode, for example, to process an outstanding interrupt.

The return sequence assumes that a thread has pushed the return address on its stack before invoking SVC. If the thread hasn't done so, then the worst that can happen when the thread returns to user mode is that it resumes at some arbitrary address, which might cause the thread to fail (as with many other programming errors), but it cannot create a problem for a domain with KERNEL-ONLY permission because the thread cannot refer to that domain in user mode.

The difference between entering and leaving kernel mode is that on leaving, the value loaded in the program counter isn't a predefined value. Instead, the kernel sets it to the saved address.

Gates can also be used to handle interrupts and exceptions. If the processor encounters an interrupt, the processor enters a special gate for interrupts and the gate manager dispatches the interrupt to the appropriate handler, based on the source of the interrupt (clock interrupt, permission error, illegal memory reference, divide by zero, etc.). Some processors have a different gate for errors caused by exceptions (e.g., a permission error); others have one gate for interrupts (e.g., clock interrupt) and exceptions.

Problem set *9* explores in a minimal operating system the interactions between hardware and software for setting modes and handling interrupts.

5.3.5 Enforcing Modularity for Bounded Buffers

The implementation of SEND and RECEIVE in Figure 5.6 assumes that the sending and receiving threads share the bounded buffer, using, for example, a shared domain, as shown in Figure 5.12. This setup enforces a boundary between all domains of the threads, except for the domain containing the shared buffer. A thread can modify the shared buffer accidentally because both threads have write permissions to the shared domain. Thus, an error in one thread could indirectly affect the other thread; we would like to avoid that and enforce modularity for the bounded buffer.

We can protect the shared bounded buffer, too, by putting the buffer in a shared kernel domain (see Figure 5.13). Now the threads cannot directly write the shared buffer in user mode. The threads must transition to kernel mode to copy messages into the shared buffer. In this design, SEND and RECEIVE are supervisor calls. When a thread invokes SEND, it changes to kernel mode and copies the message from the sending thread's domain into the shared buffer. When the receiving thread invokes RECEIVE, it changes to kernel mode and copies a message from the shared buffer into the receiving's domain. As long as the program that is running in kernel mode is written carefully, this design provides stronger enforced modularity because threads in user mode have no direct access to a bounded buffer's messages.

This stronger enforced modularity comes at a performance cost for performing supervisor calls for SEND and RECEIVE. This cost can be significant because transitions between user mode and kernel mode can be expensive. The reason is that a processor typically maintains state in its pipeline and a cache as a speedup mechanism. This state

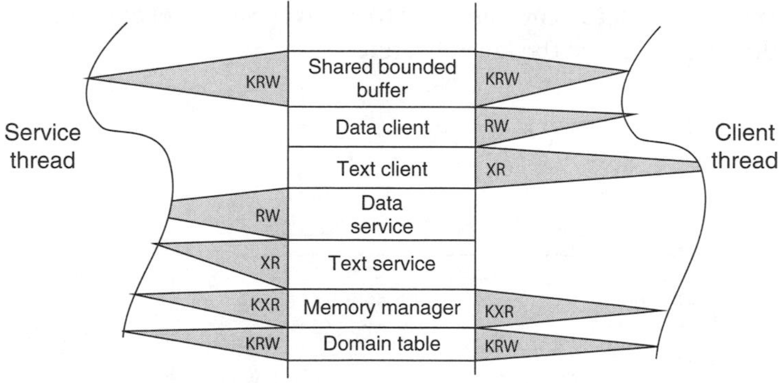

FIGURE 5.13

Threads with a kernel domain containing the shared buffer, the memory manager, and the domain table.

may have to be flushed or invalidated on a user-kernel mode transition because otherwise the processor may execute instructions that are still in the pipeline incorrectly.

Researchers have come up with techniques to reduce the performance cost by optimizing the kernel code paths for the SEND and RECEIVE supervisor calls, by having a combined call that sends and receives, by cleverly setting up domains to avoid the cost of copying large messages, by passing small arguments through processor registers, by choosing a suitable layout of data structures that reduces the cost of user-kernel mode transitions, and so on [Suggestions for Further Reading 6.2.1, 6.2.2, and 6.2.3]. Problem set 7 illustrates a lightweight remote procedure call implementation.

5.3.6 The Kernel

The collection of modules running in kernel mode is usually called the kernel program, or *kernel* for short. A question that arises is how the kernel and the first domain come into existence. Sidebar 5.3 details how a processor starts in kernel mode with domain checking disabled, how the kernel can then bootstrap the first domain, and how the kernel can create user-level domains.

The kernel is a trusted intermediary because it is the only program that can execute privileged instructions (such as storing to a processor's domain registers) and the application modules rely on the kernel to operate correctly. Because the kernel must be a trusted intermediary for the memory manager hardware, many designers also make the kernel the trusted intermediary for all other shared devices, such as the clock, display, and disk. Modules that manage these devices must then be part of the kernel program. In this design, the window manager module, network manager module, and file manager module run in kernel mode. This kernel design, in which most of the operating system runs in kernel mode, is called a *monolithic kernel* (see Figure 5.14).

In kernel mode, errors such as dividing by zero are fatal and halt the computer because these errors are typically caused by programming mistakes in the kernel program, from which there is no easy way to recover. Since kernel errors are fatal, we must program and structure the kernel carefully.

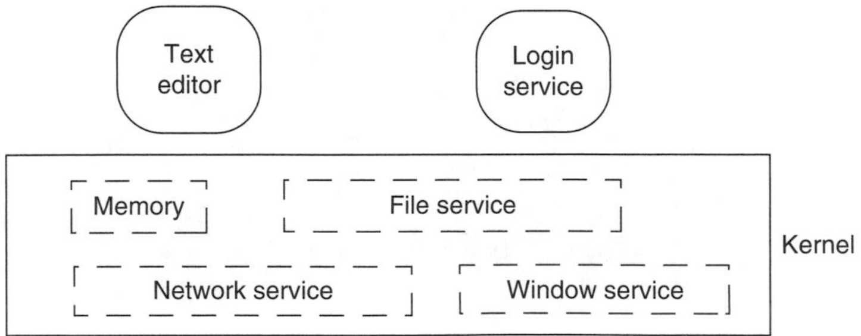

FIGURE 5.14

Monolithic organization: the kernel implements the operating system.

Sidebar 5.3 Bootstrapping an Operating System When the user switches on the power for the computer, the processor starts with all registers set to zero; thus, the user-mode bit is off. The first instruction the processor executes is the instruction at address 0 (the value of the pc register). Thus after a reset, the processor fetches its first instruction from address 0.

Address 0 typically corresponds to a read-only memory (ROM). This memory contains some initial code, the boot code, a rudimentary kernel program, which loads the full kernel program from a magnetic disk. The computer manufacturer burns into the read-only memory the boot program, after which the boot program cannot be changed. The boot program includes a rudimentary file system, which finds the kernel program (probably written by a software manufacturer) at a pre-agreed location on disk. The boot code reads the kernel into physical memory and jumps to the first instruction of the kernel.

Bootstrapping the kernel through a small boot program provides modularity. The hardware and software manufacturers can develop their products independently, and users can change kernels, for example, to upgrade to a newer version or to use a different kernel vendor, without having to modify their hardware.

Sometimes there are multiple layers of booting to handle additional constraints. For example, the first boot loader may be able to load only a single block, which can be too small to hold the rudimentary kernel program. In such cases, the boot code may load first an even simpler kernel program, which then loads the rudimentary kernel program, which then loads the kernel program.

Once it is running, the kernel allocates a thread for itself. This thread allocation involves allocating a domain for use as a stack so that it can invoke procedure calls, allowing the rest of the kernel to be written in a high-level language. It may also allocate a few other domains, for example, one for the domain table.

Once the kernel has initialized, it typically creates one or more threads to run non-kernel services. It allocates to each service one or more domains (e.g., one for program text, one for a stack, and one for data). The kernel typically preloads some of the domains with the program text and data of the non-kernel services. A common solution to locating the program text and data is to assume that the first non-kernel program, like the kernel program, is at a predefined address on the magnetic disk or part of the data of the kernel program.

Once thread is running in user mode, it can reenter the kernel using a gate for a kernel procedure. Using the kernel procedures, the user-level thread can create more threads, allocate domains for these threads, and, when done, exit.

Errors by threads in user mode (e.g., dividing by zero or using an address that is not in the thread's domains or violates permissions) cause an exception, which changes the processor to kernel mode. The exception handler can then clean up the thread.

We would like to keep the kernel small because the number of bugs in a program is at least proportional to the size of a program—and some even argue to the square of the size of program. In a monolithic kernel, if the programmer of the file manager module has made an error, the file manager module may overwrite kernel data structures unrelated to the file system, thus causing unrelated parts of the kernel to fail.

The *microkernel* architecture structures the operating system itself in a client/service style (see Figure 5.15). By applying the idea of enforced modularity to the operating system itself, we can avoid some of the major problems of a monolithic organization. In the microkernel architecture, system modules run in user mode in their own domain, as opposed to being part of a monolithic kernel. The microkernel itself implements a minimal set of abstractions, primarily domains to contain modules, threads to run programs, and virtual communication links to allow modules to send messages to one another. The kernel described in this chapter with its interface shown in Table 5.1 is an example of a microkernel.

In the microkernel organization, for example, the window service module runs in its own domain with access to the display, the file service module runs in its own domain with access to a disk extent, and the database service runs in its own domain with its own disk extent. Clients of the services communicate with them by invoking remote procedure calls, whose stubs in turn invoke the SEND and RECEIVE supervisor calls. An early, clean design for a microkernel is presented by Hansen [Suggestions for Further Reading 5.1.1].

A benefit of the microkernel organization is that errors are contained within a module, simplifying debugging. A programming error in the file service module affects only the file service module; no other module ever has its internal data structures unintentionally modified because of an error by the programmer of the file service module. If the file service fails, a programmer of the file service can focus on debugging the file service and rule out the other services immediately. In contrast with the monolithic kernel approach, it is difficult to attribute an error in the kernel to a particular module because the modules aren't isolated from each other and an error in one module may be caused by a flaw in another module.

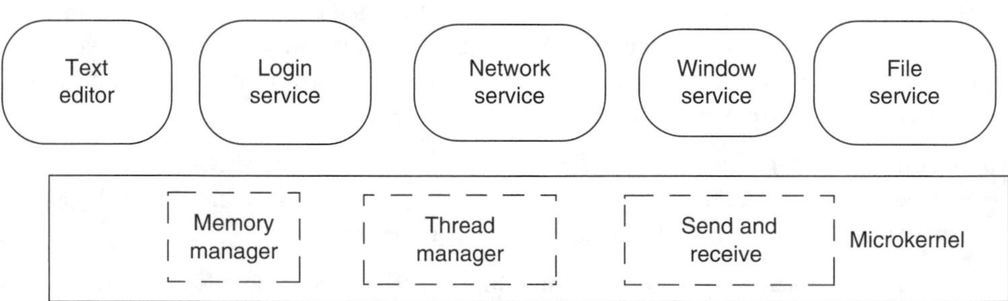

FIGURE 5.15

Microkernel organization: the operating system organized using the client/service model.

In addition, if the file service fails, the database service may be able to continue operating. Of course, if the file service module fails, its clients cannot operate, but they may be able to invoke a recovery procedure that repairs the damage and restarts the file service. In the monolithic kernel approach if the file service fails, the kernel usually fails too, and the entire operating system must reboot.

Few widely used operating systems implement the microkernel approach in its purest form. In fact, most widely used operating systems today have a mostly monolithic kernel. Many critical services run inside the kernel, and only a few run outside the kernel. For example, in the GNU/Linux operating system the file and the network service run in kernel mode, but the X Window System runs in user mode.

Monolithic operating systems dominate the field for several reasons. First, if a service (e.g., a file service) is critical to the functioning of the operating system, it doesn't matter much if it fails in user mode or in kernel mode; in either case, the system is unusable.

Second, some services are shared among many modules, and it can be easier to implement these services as part of the kernel program, which is already shared among all modules. For example, a cache of recently accessed file data is more effective when shared among all modules. Furthermore, this cache may need to coordinate its memory use with the memory manager, which is typically part of the kernel.

Third, the performance of some services is critical, and the overhead of SEND and RECEIVE supervisor calls may be too large to split subsystems into smaller modules and separate each module.

Fourth, monolithic systems can enjoy the ease of debugging microkernel systems if the monolithic kernel comes with good kernel debugging tools.

Fifth, it may be difficult to reorganize existing kernel programs. In particular, there is little incentive to change a kernel program that already works. If the system works and most of the errors have been eradicated, the debugging advantage of microkernels begins to evaporate, and the cost of SEND and RECEIVE supervisor calls begins to dominate.

In general, if one has the choice between a working system and a better designed, but new system, one doesn't want to switch over to the new system unless it is much better. One reason is the overhead of switching: learning the new design, reengineering the old system to use the new design, rediscovering undocumented assumptions, and discovering unrealized assumptions (large systems often work for reasons that weren't fully understood). Another reason is the uncertainty of the gain of switching. Until there is evidence from the field, the claims about the better design are speculative. In the case of operating systems, there is little experimental evidence that microkernel-based systems are more robust than existing monolithic kernels. A final reason is that there is an opportunity cost: one can spend time reengineering existing software, or one can spend time developing the existing software to address new needs. For these reasons, few systems have switched to a pure microkernel design. Instead many existing systems have stayed with monolithic kernels, perhaps running services that are not as performance critical as user-mode programs. Microkernel designs exist in more specialized areas, and research on microkernels continues to be active.

5.4 VIRTUALIZING MEMORY

To address one problem at a time, the previous section assumed that memory and its address space is very large, large enough to hold all domains. In practice, memory and address space are limited. Thus, when a programmer invokes ALLOCATE_DOMAIN, we would like the programmer to specify a reasonable size. To allow a program to grow its domain if the specified size turns out to be too small, we could offer the programmer an additional primitive GROW_DOMAIN.

Growing domains, however, creates memory management problems. For example, assume that program A allocates domain 1 and program 2 allocates domain 2, right after domain 1. Even if there is free memory after domain 2, program A cannot grow domain 1 because it would cross into domain 2. In this case, the only option left for program A is to allocate a new domain of the desired size, copy the contents of domain 1 into the new domain, change the addresses in the program that refer to addresses in domain 1 to instead refer to corresponding addresses in the new domain 2, and deallocate domain 1.

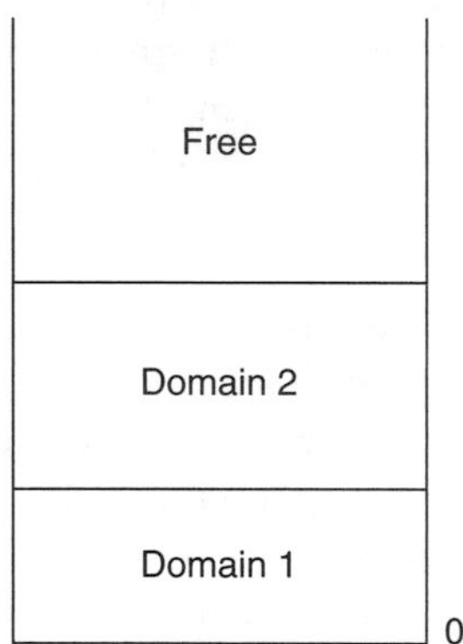

This memory management complicates writing programs and can make programs slow because of the memory copies. To reduce the programming burden of managing memory, most modern computer systems virtualize memory, a step that provides two features:

1. *Virtual addresses*. If programs address memory using virtual addresses and the memory manager translates the virtual addresses to physical addresses on the fly, then the memory manager can grow and move domains in memory behind the program's back.

2. *Virtual address spaces*. A single address space may not be large enough to hold all addresses of all applications at the same time. For example, a single large database program by itself may need all the address space available in the hardware. If we can create virtual address spaces, then we can give each program its own address space. This extension also allows a thread to have its program loaded at an address of its choosing (e.g., address 0).

A memory manager that virtualizes memory is called a *virtual memory manager*. The design we work out in this section replaces the domain manager but incorporates the main features of domains: controlled sharing and permissions. We describe the virtual memory design in two steps. For the first step, Sections 5.4.1 and 5.4.2 introduce virtual addresses and describe an efficient way to translate them. For the second step, Section 5.4.3 introduces virtual address spaces. Section 5.4.4 discusses the trade-offs of software and hardware aspects of implementing a virtual memory manager. Finally, the section concludes with an advanced virtual memory design.

5.4.1 Virtualizing Addresses

The virtual memory manager will deal with two types of addresses, so it is convenient to give them names. The threads issue *virtual addresses* when reading and writing to memory (see Figure 5.16). The memory manager translates each virtual address issued by the processor into a *physical address*, a bus address of a location in memory or a register on a controller of a device.

Translating addresses as they are being used provides design flexibility. One can design computers whose physical addresses have a different width than its virtual addresses. The memory manager can translate several virtual addresses to the same physical address, but perhaps with different permissions. The memory manager can allocate virtual addresses to a thread but postpone allocating physical memory until the thread makes a reference to one of the virtual addresses.

Virtualizing addresses exploits the design principle *decouple modules with indirection*. The virtual memory manager provides a layer of indirection between the processor and the memory system by translating the virtual addresses of program instructions into physical addresses, instead of having the program directly issue physical memory addresses. Because it controls the translation from the addresses issued by the program to the addresses understood by the memory system, the virtual memory manager can translate any particular virtual address to different physical memory addresses at different times. Thanks to the translation, the virtual memory manager can rearrange the data in the memory system without having to modify any application program.

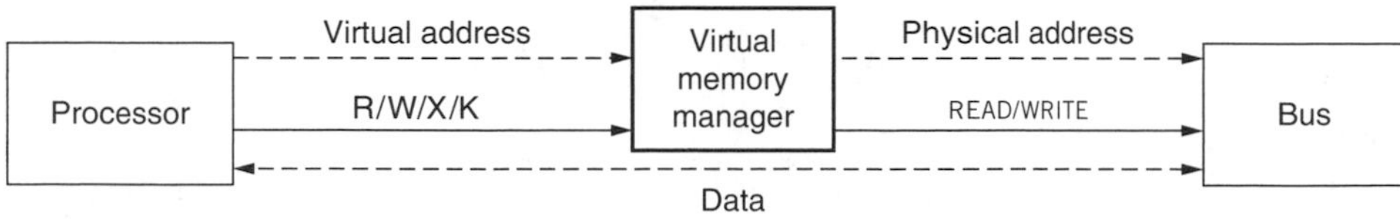

FIGURE 5.16

A virtual memory manager translating virtual addresses to physical addresses.

From a naming point of view, the virtual memory manager creates a name space of virtual addresses on top of a name space of physical addresses. The virtual memory manager's naming scheme translates virtual addresses into physical addresses.

Virtual memory has many uses. In this chapter, we focus on managing physical memory transparently. Later, in Section 6.2 of Chapter 6, we describe how virtual memory can also be used to transparently simulate a larger memory than the computer actually possesses.

To see how address translation can help memory management, consider a virtual memory manager with a virtual address space that is very large (e.g., 2^{64} bytes) but with a physical address space that is smaller. Let's assume that a thread has allocated two domains of size 100 bytes (see Figure 5.17a). The memory manager allocated the domains in physical memory contiguously, but in the virtual address space the domains are far away from each other. (ALLOCATE_DOMAIN returns a virtual address.) When a thread makes a reference to a virtual address, the virtual memory manager translates the address to the appropriate physical address.

Now consider the thread requesting to grow domain 1 from size 8 kilobytes to, say, 16 kilobytes. Without virtual addresses, the memory manager would deny this request because the domain cannot grow in physical memory without running into domain 2. With virtual addresses (see Figure 5.17b), however, the memory manager can grow the domain in the virtual address space, allocate the requested amount of physical memory, copy the content of domain 1 into the newly allocated physical memory, and update its mapping for domain 1. With virtual addresses, the application doesn't have to be aware that the memory manager moved the contents of its domain in order to grow it.

Even ignoring the cost of copying the content of a domain, introducing virtual addresses comes at a cost in complexity and performance. The memory manager must manage virtual addresses in addition to a physical address space. It must allocate

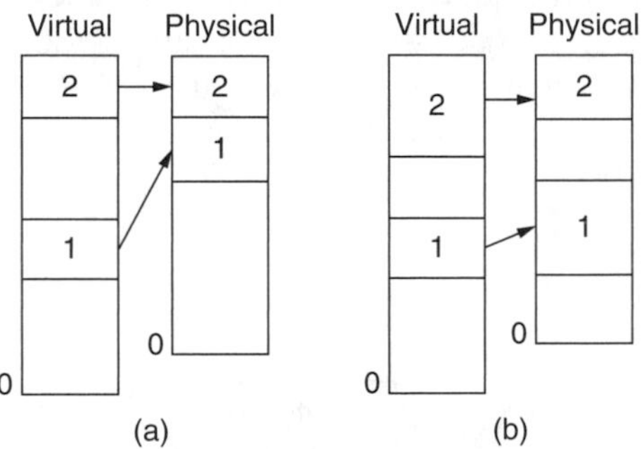

FIGURE 5.17

(a) A thread has allocated a domain 1 and 2; they are far apart in virtual memory but next to each other in physical memory. (b) In response to the thread's request to grow domain 1, the virtual memory manager transparently moved domain 1 in physical memory and adjusted the translation from virtual to physical addresses.

and deallocate them (if the virtual address space isn't large), it must set up translations between virtual and physical addresses, and so on. The translation happens on-the-fly, which may slow down memory references. The rest of this section investigates these issues and presents a plan that doesn't even require copying the complete content of a domain when growing the domain.

5.4.2 Translating Addresses Using a Page Map

A naïve way of translating virtual addresses into physical addresses is to maintain a map that for each virtual address records its corresponding physical address. Of course, the amount of memory required to maintain this map would be large. If each physical address is a word (8 bytes) and the address space has 2^{64} virtual addresses, then we might need 2^{72} bytes of physical memory just to store the mapping.

A more efficient way of translation is using a *page map*. The page map is an array of page map entries. Each entry translates a fixed-sized range of contiguous bytes of virtual addresses, called a *page*, to a range of physical addresses, called a *block*, which holds the page. For now, the memory manager maintains a single page map, so that all threads share the single virtual address space, as before.

With this organization, we can think of the memory that threads see as a set of contiguous pages. A virtual address then is a name overloaded with structure consisting of two parts: a page number and a byte offset within that page (see Figure 5.18). The page number uniquely identifies an entry in the page map, and thus a page, and the byte offset identifies a byte within that page. (If the processor provides word addressing instead of byte addressing, *offset* would specify the word within a page.) The size of a page, in bytes, is equal to the maximum number of different values that can be stored in the byte offset field of the virtual address. If the offset field is 12 bits wide, then a page contains 4,096 (2^{12}) bytes.

With this arrangement, the virtual memory manager records in the page map, for each page, the block of physical memory that contains that page. We can think of a *block* as the container of a page. Physical memory is then a contiguous set of blocks, holding pages, but the pages don't have to be contiguous in physical memory; that is, block 0 may hold page 100, block 1 may hold page 2, and so forth. The mapping between pages and the blocks that hold them can be arbitrary.

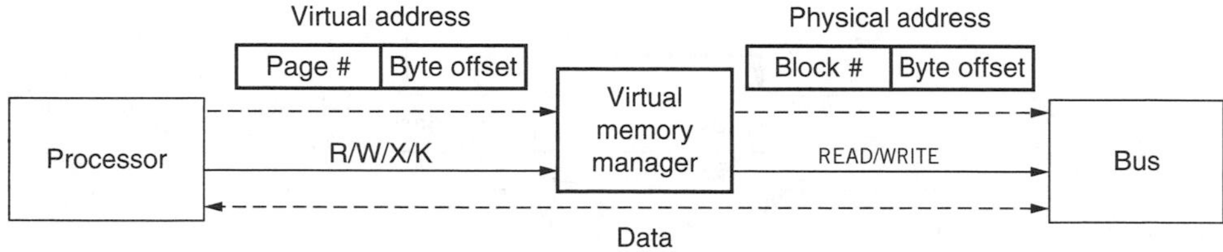

FIGURE 5.18

A virtual memory manager that translates virtual addresses by translating page numbers to block numbers.

The page map simplifies memory management because the memory manager can allocate a block anywhere in physical memory and insert the appropriate mapping into the page map, without having to copy domains in physical memory to coalesce free space.

A physical address can also be viewed as having two parts: a block number that uniquely identifies a block of memory and an offset that identifies a byte within that block. Translating a virtual address to a physical address is now a two-step process:

1. The virtual memory manager translates the page number of the virtual address to a block number that holds that page by means of some mapping from page numbers to block numbers.
2. The virtual memory manager computes the physical address by concatenating the block number with the byte offset from the original virtual address.

Several different representations are possible for the page map, each with its own set of trade-offs for translating addresses. The simplest implementation of a page map is an array implementation, often called a *page table*. It is suitable when most pages have an associated block. Figure 5.19 demonstrates the use of a page map implemented as a linear page table. The virtual memory manager resolves virtual addresses into physical addresses by taking the page number from the virtual address and using it as an index into the page table to find the corresponding block number. Then, the manager computes the physical address by concatenating the byte offset with the

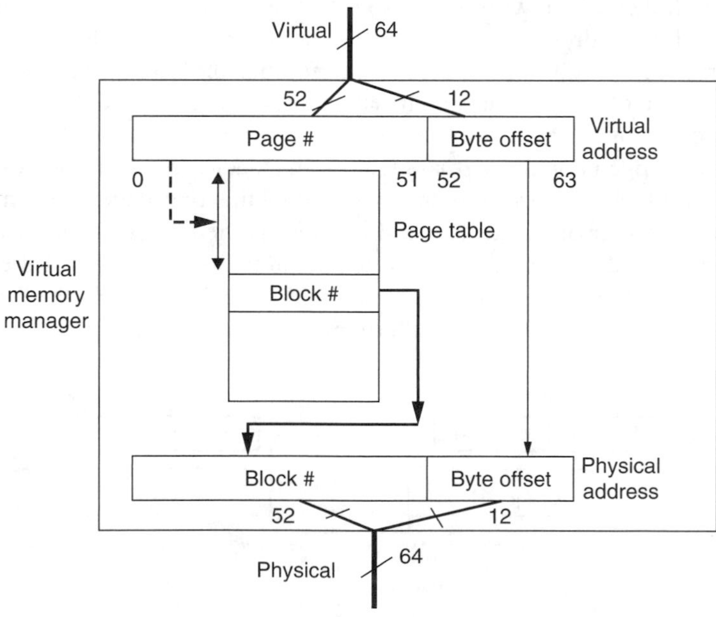

FIGURE 5.19

An implementation of a virtual memory manager using a page table.

block number found in the page-table entry. Finally, it sends this physical address to the physical memory.

If the page size is 2^{12} bytes and virtual addresses are 64 bits wide, then a linear page table is large ($2^{52} \times 52$ bits). Therefore, in practice, designers use a more efficient representation of a page map, such as a two-level one or an inverted one (i.e., indexed by physical address instead of virtual), but these designs are beyond the scope of this text.

To be able to perform the translation, the virtual memory manager must have a way of finding and storing the page table. In the usual implementation, the page table is stored in the same physical memory that holds the pages, and the *physical* address of the base of the page map is stored in a reserved processor register, typically named the *page-map address register*. To ensure that user-level threads cannot change translation directly and bypass enforced modularity, processor designs allow threads to write the page-map address register only in kernel mode and allow only the kernel to modify the page table directly.

Figure 5.20 shows an example of how a kernel could use the page map. The kernel has allocated a page map in physical memory at address 0. The page map provides modules with a contiguous universal address space, without forcing the kernel to allocate blocks of memory for a domain contiguously. In this example, block 100 contains page 12 and block 500 contains page 13. When a thread asks for a new domain or to grow an existing domain, the kernel can allocate any unused block and insert it in the page map. The level of indirection provided by the page map allows the kernel to do this transparently—the running threads are unaware.

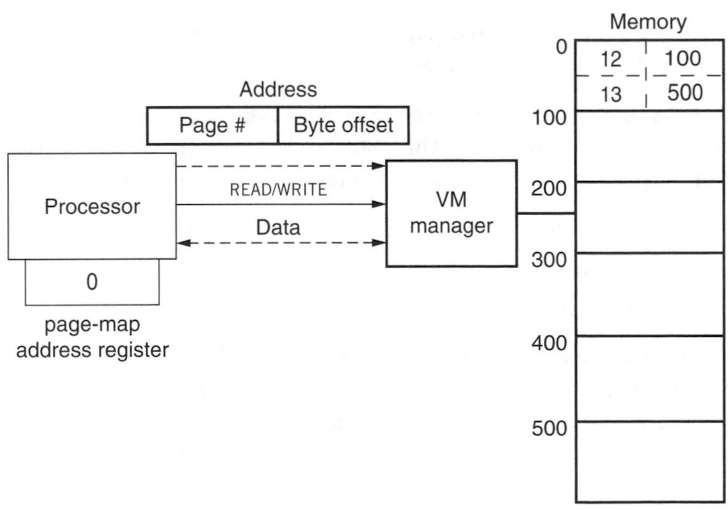

FIGURE 5.20

A virtual memory manager using a page table. The page table is located at physical address 0. It maps pages (e.g., 12) to blocks (e.g., 100).

5.4.3 Virtual Address Spaces

The design so far has assumed that all threads share a single virtual address space that is large enough that it can hold all active modules and their data. Many processors have a virtual address space that is too small to do that. For example, many processors use virtual addresses that are 32 bits wide and thus have only 2^{32} addresses, which represent 4 gigabytes of address space. This might be barely large enough to hold the most frequently used part of a large database, leaving little room for other modules. We can eliminate this assumption by virtualizing the physical address space.

5.4.3.1 Primitives for Virtual Address Spaces

A *virtual address space* provides each application with the illusion that it has a complete address space to itself. The virtual memory manager can implement a virtual address space by giving each virtual address space its own page map. A memory manager supporting multiple virtual address spaces may have the following interface:

- *id* ← CREATE_ADDRESS_SPACE (): create a new address space. This address space is empty, meaning that none of its virtual pages are mapped to real memory. CREATE_ADDRESS_SPACE returns an identifier for that address space.
- *block* ← ALLOCATE_BLOCK (): ask the memory manager for a block of memory. The manager attempts to allocate a block that is not in use. If there are no free blocks, the request fails. ALLOCATE_BLOCK returns the physical address of the block.
- MAP (*id, block, page_number, permission*): put a block into *id*'s address space. MAP maps the physical address *block* to virtual page *page_number* with permissions *permission*. The memory manager allocates an entry in the page map for address space *id*, mapping the virtual page *page_number* to block *block*, and setting the page's permissions to *permission*.
- UNMAP (*id, page_number*): remove the entry for *page_number* from the page map so that threads have no access to that page and its associated block. An instruction that refers to a page that has been deleted is an illegal instruction.
- FREE_BLOCK (*block*): add the block *block* to the list of free memory blocks.
- DELETE_ADDRESS_SPACE (*id*): destroy an address space. The memory manager frees the page map and its blocks of address space *id*.

Using this interface, a thread may allocate its own address space or share its address space with other threads. When a programmer calls ALLOCATE_THREAD, the programmer specifies the address space in which the thread is to run. In many operating systems, the word "*process*" is used for the combination of a single virtual address space shared by one or more threads, but not consistently (see Sidebar 5.4).

The virtual address space is a thread's domain, and the page map defines how it resides in physical memory. Thus the kernel doesn't have to maintain a separate domain table with domain registers. If a physical block doesn't appear in an address space's page map, then the thread cannot make a reference to that physical block.

If a physical block appears in an address space's page map, then the thread can make a reference to that physical block. If a physical block appears in two page maps, then threads in both address spaces can make references to that physical block, which allows sharing of memory.

The memory manager can support domain permissions by placing the permission bits in the page-map entries. For example, one address space may have a block mapped with READ and WRITE permissions, while another address space has only READ permissions for that block. This design allows us to remove the domain registers, while keeping the concept of domains.

Figure 5.21 illustrates the use of several address spaces. It depicts two threads, each with its own address space but sharing block 800. Threads A and B have block 800 mapped at page 12. (In principle, the threads could map block 800 at different virtual

Sidebar 5.4 Process, Thread, and Address Space The operating systems community uses the word "process" often, but over the years it has come up with enough variants on the concept that when you read or hear the word you need to guess its meaning from its context. In the UNIX system (see Section 2.5), a process may mean one thread in a private address space (as in the early version of that system), or a group of threads in a private address space (as in later versions), or a thread (or group of threads) in an address space that is partly or completely shared (as in later versions of UNIX that also allow processes to share memory). That range of meanings is so broad as to render the term less than useful, which is why this text uses process only in the context of the early version of the UNIX system and otherwise uses only the terms *thread* and *address space*, which are the two core concepts.

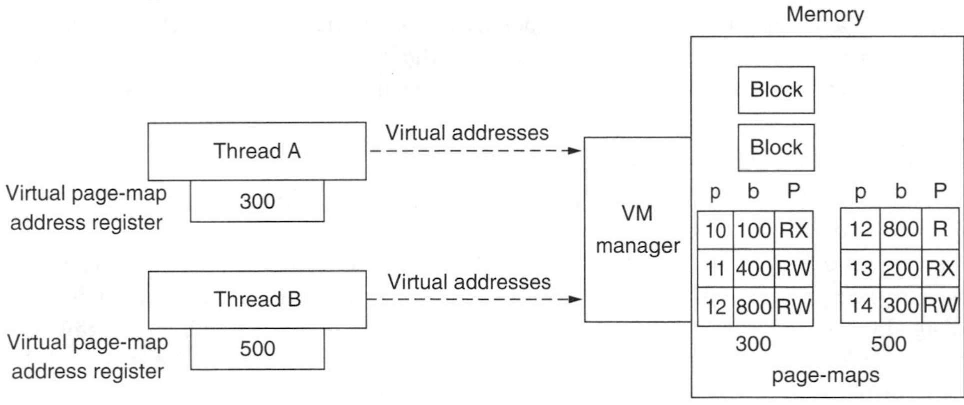

FIGURE 5.21

Each thread has its own page-map address register. Thread A runs with the page map stored at address 300, while B runs with the page map stored at address 500. The page map contains the translation from page (p) to block (b), and the permissions required (P).

addresses, but that complicates naming of the shared data in the block.) Thread A maps block 800 with READ permission, while thread B maps block 800 with READ and WRITE permissions. In addition to a shared block, each thread has two private blocks. Each thread has a block mapped with READ and EXECUTE permissions for, for example, its program text and a block mapped with READ and WRITE permissions for, for example, its stack.

To support virtual address spaces, the page-map address register of a processor holds the physical address of the page map of the running thread on the processor and translation works then as follows:

```
1  procedure TRANSLATE (integer virtual, perm_needed) returns physical_address
2      page ← virtual[0:41]                           // Extract page number
3      offset ← virtual[42:63]                        // Extract offset
4      page_table ← PMAR                              // Use the current page table
5      perm_page ← page_table[page].permissions       // Lookup permissions for page
6      if PERMITTED (perm_needed, perm_page) then
7          block ← page_table[page].address           // Index into page map
8          physical ← block + offset                  // Concatenate block and offset
9          return physical                            // Return physical address
10     else return error
```

Although usually implemented in hardware, in pseudocode form, we can view the linear page table as an array that is indexed by a page number and that stores the corresponding block number. Line *2* extracts the page number, *page*, by extracting the leftmost 42 bits. (As explained in Sidebar 4.3, this book uses the big-endian convention for numbering bits and begins numbering with zero.) Then, it extracts the *offset*, the 12 rightmost bits of the virtual address (line *3*). Line *4* reads the address from the active page map out of PMAR. Line *5* looks up the permissions for the page. If the permissions necessary for using *virtual* are a subset of the permissions for the page (line *6*), then TRANSLATE looks up the corresponding block number by using *page* as an index into *page_table* and computes the physical address by concatenating *block* with *offset* (lines *7* and *8*). Now the virtual memory manager issues the bus request for the translated physical address or interrupts the processor with an illegal memory reference exception.

5.4.3.2 The Kernel and Address Spaces

There are two options for setting up page maps for the kernel program. The first option is to have each address space include a mapping of the kernel into its address space. For example, the top half of the address space might contain the kernel, in which case the bottom half contains the user program. With this setup, switching from the user program to the kernel (and vice versa) doesn't require changing the processor's page-map address register; only the user-mode bit must be changed. To protect the kernel, the kernel sets the permissions for kernel pages to KERNEL-ONLY; in user mode, performing a STORE to kernel pages is an illegal instruction. An additional advantage of this design is that in kernel mode, it is easy for the kernel to read data structures of the user program because the user program and kernel share the same address space. A disadvantage of this design is that it reduces the available address space for user programs, which could be a problem in a legacy architecture that has small address spaces.

The second option is for the memory manager to give the kernel its own separate address space, which is inaccessible to user-level threads. To implement this option, we must extend the SVC instruction to switch the page-map address register to the kernel's page map when entering kernel mode. Similarly, when returning from kernel mode to user mode, the kernel must change the page-map address register to the page map of the thread that entered the gate.

The second option separates the kernel program and user programs completely, but the memory manager, which is part of the kernel, must be able to create new address spaces for user programs, and so on. The simple solution is to include the page tables of all user address spaces in the kernel address space. By modifying the page table for a user address space, the memory manager can modify that address space. Since a page table is smaller than the address space it defines, the second option wastes less address space than the first option.

If the kernel program and user programs have their own address spaces, the kernel cannot refer to data structures in user programs using kernel virtual addresses, since those virtual addresses refer to locations in the kernel address space. User programs must pass arguments to supervisor calls by value or the kernel must use a more involved method for copying data from a user address space to a kernel address space (and vice versa). For example, the kernel can compute the physical address for a user virtual address using the page table for that user address space, map the computed physical address into the kernel address space at an unused address, and then use that address.

5.4.3.3 Discussion

In the design with many virtual address spaces, virtual addresses are relative to an address space. This property has the advantage that programs don't have to be compiled to be position independent (see Sidebar 5.5). Every program can be stored at virtual address 0 and can use absolute addresses for making references to memory in its address space. In practice, this advantage is unimportant because it is not difficult for compiler designers to generate position-independent instructions.

A disadvantage of the design with many address spaces is that sharing can be confusing and less flexible. It can be confusing because a block to be shared can be mapped by threads into two different address spaces at different virtual addresses.

Sidebar 5.5 Position-Independent Programs Position-independent programs can be loaded at any memory address. To provide this feature, a compiler translating programs into processor instructions must generate relative, but not absolute, addresses. For example, when compiling a **for** loop, the compiler should use a jump instruction with an offset relative to the current PC to return to the top of a **for** loop rather than a jump instruction with an absolute address.

It can be less flexible because either threads share a complete address space or a designer must accept a restriction on sharing. Threads in different address spaces can share objects only at the granularity of a block: if two threads in different address spaces share an object, that object must be mapped at a page boundary, and holding the object requires allocating an integral number of pages and blocks. If the shared object is smaller than a page, then part of the address space and the block will be wasted. Section 5.4.5 describes an advanced design that doesn't have this restriction, but it is rarely used, since the waste isn't a big problem in practice.

5.4.4 Hardware versus Software and the Translation Look-Aside Buffer

An ongoing debate between hardware and software designers concerns what parts of the virtual memory manager should be implemented in hardware as part of the processor and what parts in software as part of the operating system, as well as what the interface between the hardware module and the software module should be.

There is no "right" answer because the designers must make a trade-off between performance and flexibility. Because address translation is in the critical path of processor instructions that use addresses, the memory manager is often implemented as a digital circuit that is part of the main processor so that it can run at the speed of the processor. A complete hardware implementation, however, reduces the opportunities for the operating system to exploit the translation between virtual and physical addresses. This trade-off must be made with care when implementing the memory manager and its page table.

The page table is usually stored in the same memory as the data, reachable over the bus. This design requires that the processor make an additional bus reference to memory each time it interprets an address: the processor must first translate the virtual address into a physical address, which requires reading an entry in the page map.

To avoid these additional bus references for translating virtual to physical addresses, the processor typically maintains a cache of entries of the page map in a smaller fast memory within the processor itself. The hope is that when the processor executes the next instruction, it will discover a previously cached entry that can translate the address, without making a bus reference to the larger memory. Only when the cache memory doesn't contain the appropriate entry must the processor retrieve an entry from memory. In practice, this design works well because most programs exhibit locality of reference. Thus, caching translation entries pays off, as we will see when we study caches in Chapter 6. Caching page table entries in the processor introduces new complexities: if a processor changes a page table entry, the cached versions must be updated too, or invalidated.

A final design issue is how to implement the cache memory of translations efficiently. A common approach is to use an associative memory instead of an indexed memory. By making the cache memory associative, any entry can store any translation. Furthermore, because the cache is much smaller than physical memory, an associative memory is feasible. In this design, the cache memory of translations is usually referred to as thc *translation look-aside buffer (TLB)*.

In the hardware design of Figure 5.19, the format of the page table is determined by the hardware. RISC processors typically don't fix the format of the page table in hardware but leave the choice of data structure to software. In these RISC designs, only the TLB is implemented in hardware. When a translation is not in the TLB, the processor generates a *TLB miss exception*. The handler for this interrupt looks up the mapping in a data structure implemented in software, inserts the translation in the TLB, and returns from the interrupt. With this design, the memory manager has complete freedom in choosing the data structure for the page map. If a module uses only a few pages, a designer may be able to save memory by storing the page map as a linked list or tree of pages. If, as is common, the union of virtual addresses is much larger than the physical memory, a designer may be able to save memory by inverting the page map and storing one entry per physical memory block; the contents of the entry identify the number of the page currently in the block.

In almost all designs of virtual addresses, the operating system manages the content of the page map in software. The hardware design may dictate the format of the table, but the kernel determines the values stored in the table entries and thus the mapping from virtual addresses to physical addresses. By allowing software to control the mapping, designers open up many uses of virtual addresses. One use is to manage physical memory efficiently, avoiding problems due to fragmentation. Another use is to extend physical memory by allowing pages to be stored on other devices, such as magnetic disks, as explained in Section 6.2.

5.4.5 Segments (Advanced Topic)

An address space per program (as in Figure 5.21) limits the way objects can be shared between threads. An alternative way is to use *segments*, which provide each object with a virtual address space starting at 0 and ending at the size of the object. In the segment approach, a large database program may have a segment for each table in a database (assuming the table isn't larger than a segment's address space). This allows threads to share memory at the granularity of objects instead of blocks, and in a flexible manner. A thread can share one object (segment) with one thread and another object (segment) with another thread.

To support segments, the processor must be modified because the addresses that programs use are really two numbers. The first identifies the segment number, and the second identifies the address within that segment. Unlike the model that has one virtual address space per program, where the programmer is unaware that the virtual address is implemented as a page number and an offset, in the segment model, the compiler and programmer must be aware that an address contains two parts. The programmer must specify which segment to use for an instruction, the compiler must put the generated code in the right segment, and so on. Problem set *11* explores segments with a simple operating system and a processor with minimal support for segments.

In the address space per program, a thread can do arithmetic on addresses because the program's address space is linear. In the segment model, a thread cannot do arithmetic on addresses in different segments because adding to a segment number yields a meaningless result; there is no notion of contiguity for segment numbers.

If two threads share an object, they typically use the same segment number for the object; otherwise naming shared objects becomes cumbersome too.

Segments can be implemented by reintroducing slightly modified domain registers. Each segment has its own domain register, but we add a *page_table* field to the domain register. This *page_table* field contains the physical address of the page table that should be used to translate virtual addresses of the segment. When domain registers are used in this way, the literature calls them *segment descriptors*. Using this implementation, the memory manager translates an address as follows: the memory manager uses the segment number to look up the segment descriptor and uses the *page_table* in the segment descriptor to translate the virtual address within the segment to a physical address.

Giving each object of an application its own segment potentially requires a large number of segment descriptors per processor. We can solve this problem by putting the segment descriptors in memory in a ***segment descriptor table*** and giving each processor a single register that points to the segment descriptor table.

An advantage of the segment model is that the designer doesn't have to predict the maximum size of objects that grow dynamically during computation. For example, as the stack of a running computation grows, the virtual memory manager can allocate more pages on demand and increase the length of the stack segment. In the address space per program model, the thread's stack may grow into another data structure in the virtual address space. Then either the virtual memory manager must raise an error, or the complete stack must be moved to a place in the address space that has a large enough range of unused contiguous addresses.

The programming model that goes with a segment per object can be a good match for new programs written in an object-oriented style: the methods of an object class can be in a segment with READ and EXECUTE permissions, the data objects of an instance of that class in a segment with READ and WRITE permissions, and so on. Porting an old program to the segment model can be easy if one stores the complete program, code, and data in a single segment, but this method loses much of the advantage of the segment model because the entire segment must have READ, WRITE, and EXECUTE permission. Restructuring an old program to take advantage of multiple segments can be challenging because addresses are not linear; the programmer must modify the old program to specify which segment to use. For example, upgrading a kernel program to take advantage of segments in its internal construction is disruptive. A number of processors and kernels tried but failed (see Section 5.7).

Although virtual memory systems supporting segments have advantages and have been influential (see, for example, the Multics virtual memory design [Suggestions for Further Reading 5.4.1]), most virtual memory systems today follow the address space per program approach instead of the segment approach. A few processors, such as the Intel x86 (see Section 5.7), have support for segments, but today's virtual memory systems don't exploit them. Virtual memory managers for the address space per program model tend to be less complex because sharing is not usually a primary requirement. Designers view an address space per program primarily as a method for achieving enforced modularity, rather than an approach to sharing. Although one can share pages between programs, that isn't the primary goal, but it is possible to do it in a limited way. Furthermore, porting an old application to the one address space per program model requires little effort at the outset: just allocate a complete address space for the application. If any sharing is necessary, it can be done later. In practice, sharing patterns tend to be simple, so no sophisticated support is necessary. Finally, today, address spaces are usually large enough that a program doesn't need an address space per object.

5.5 VIRTUALIZING PROCESSORS USING THREADS

In order to focus on one new idea at a time, the previous sections assumed that a separate processor was available to run each thread. Because there are usually not enough processors to go around, this section extends the thread manager to remove the assumption that each thread has its own processor. This extended thread manager shares a limited number of processors among a larger number of threads.

Sharing of processors introduces a new concern: if a thread hogs a processor, either accidentally or intentionally, it can slow down or even halt the progress of other threads, thereby compromising modularity. Because we have proposed that a primary requirement be to enforce modularity, one of the design challenges of the thread manager is to eliminate this concern.

This section starts with the design of a simple thread manager that does not avoid the hogging of a processor, and then moves to a design that does. It makes the design concrete by providing a pseudocode implementation of a thread manager. This implementation captures the essence of a thread manager. In practice, thread managers differ in many details and sometimes are much more complex than our example implementation.

5.5.1 Sharing a Processor Among Multiple Threads

Recall from Section 5.1.1 that a thread is an abstraction that encapsulates the state of a running module. A thread encapsulates enough state of the interpreter (e.g., a processor) that executes the thread that a thread manager can stop the thread and resume the thread later. A thread manager animates a thread by giving it a processor. This section explains how this ability to stop a thread and later resume it can be used to multiplex many threads over a limited number of physical processors.

To make the thread abstraction concrete, the thread manager might support this simple version of a THREAD_ALLOCATE procedure:

- *thread_id* ← ALLOCATE_THREAD (*starting_procedure, address_space_id*): allocate a new thread in address space *address_space_id*. The new thread is to begin with a call to the procedure specified in the argument *starting_procedure*. ALLOCATE_THREAD returns an identifier that names the just-created thread. If the thread manager cannot allocate a new thread (e.g., it doesn't have enough free memory to allocate a new stack), ALLOCATE_THREAD returns an error.

The thread manager implements ALLOCATE_THREAD as follows: it allocates a range of memory in *address_space_id* to be used as the stack for procedure calls, selects a processor, and sets the processor's PC to the address *starting_procedure* in *address_space_id* and the processor's SP to the bottom of the allocated stack.

Using ALLOCATE_THREAD, an application can create more threads than there are processors. Consider the applications running on the computer in Figure 5.4. These applications can have more threads than there are processors; for example, the file service might launch a new thread for each new client request. Starting a new module will also create additional threads. So the problem is to share a limited number of processors among potentially many threads.

We can solve this problem by observing that most threads spend much of their time waiting for events to happen. Most modules that run on the computer in Figure 5.4 call READ for input from the keyboard, the file system, or the network, and will wait by spinning until there is input. Instead of spinning, the thread could, while it is waiting, let another thread use its processor. If the consumer thread finds that it cannot proceed (because the buffer is empty), then it could release its processor, giving the keyboard manager (or any other thread) a chance to run.

This observation is the basic idea for virtualizing the processor: when a thread is waiting for an event, its processor can switch from that thread to another one by saving the state of the waiting thread and loading the state of a different thread. Since in most system designs many threads spend much of their life waiting for a condition to become true, this idea is general. For example, most of the other modules (the window manager, the mail reader, etc.) are consumers. They spend much of their existence waiting for input to arrive.

Over the years people have developed various labels for processor virtualization schemes, such as "time-sharing", "processor multiplexing", "multiprogramming", or "multitasking". For example, the word "time-sharing" was introduced in the 1950s to describe virtualization of a computer system so that it could be shared among several interactive human users. All these schemes boil down to the same idea: virtualizing the processor, which this section describes in detail.

To make the discussion more concrete, consider the implementation of SEND and RECEIVE with a bounded buffer in Figure 5.6. This spin-loop solution is appropriate if there is a processor for each thread, but it is inappropriate if there are fewer processors than threads. If there is just one processor and if the receiver started before the sender, then we have a major problem. The receiver thread executes its spinning loop, and the sender never gets a chance to run and add an item to the buffer.

A solution with thread switching is shown in Figure 5.22. Comparing this code with the code in Figure 5.6, we find that the only change is the addition of two calls to a procedure named YIELD (lines *10* and *20*). YIELD is an entry to the thread manager. When a thread invokes YIELD, the thread manager gives the calling thread's processor to some other thread. At some time in the future, the thread manager returns a processor to this thread by returning from the call to YIELD. In the case of the receiver, when the processor returns at line *21*, the receiving thread reacquires the lock again and tests *out* = *in*. If *out* is now less than *in*, there is at least one new item in the buffer, so the thread extracts an item from the buffer. If not, the thread releases the lock and calls YIELD again to allow another thread to run. A thread therefore alternates between two states, which we name RUNNING (executing on a processor) and RUNNABLE (ready to run but waiting for a processor to become available).

```
1   shared structure buffer              // A shared bounded buffer
2      message instance message[N]       // with a maximum of N messages
3      long integer in initially 0       // Counts number of messages put in the buffer
4      long integer out initially 0      // Counts number of messages taken out of the buffer
5      lock instance buffer_lock initially UNLOCKED // Lock to coordinate sender and receiver

6   procedure SEND (buffer reference p, message instance msg)
7      ACQUIRE (p.buffer_lock)
8      while p.in – p.out = N do         // Wait until there room in the buffer
9         RELEASE (p.buffer_lock)        // Release lock so that receiver can remove
10        YIELD ()                       // Let another thread use the processor
11        ACQUIRE (p.buffer_lock)        // Processor came back, maybe there is room
12                                       // Wait loop end, go back to test
13     p.message[p.in modulo N] ← msg    // Put message in the buffer
14     p.in ← p.in + 1                   // Increment in
15     RELEASE (p.buffer_lock)

16  procedure RECEIVE (buffer reference p)
17     ACQUIRE (p.buffer_lock)
18     while p.in = p.out do             // Wait until there is a message to receive
19        RELEASE (p.buffer_lock)        // Release lock so that sender can add
20        YIELD ()                       // Let another thread use the processor
21        ACQUIRE (p.buffer_lock)        // YIELD returned, maybe there is a message
22                                       // Wait loop end, go back to test
23     msg ← p.message[p.out modulo N]   // Copy item out of buffer
24     p.out ← p.out + 1                 // Increment out
25     RELEASE (p.buffer_lock)
26     return msg
```

FIGURE 5.22

An implementation of a virtual communication link for a system with more threads than processors.

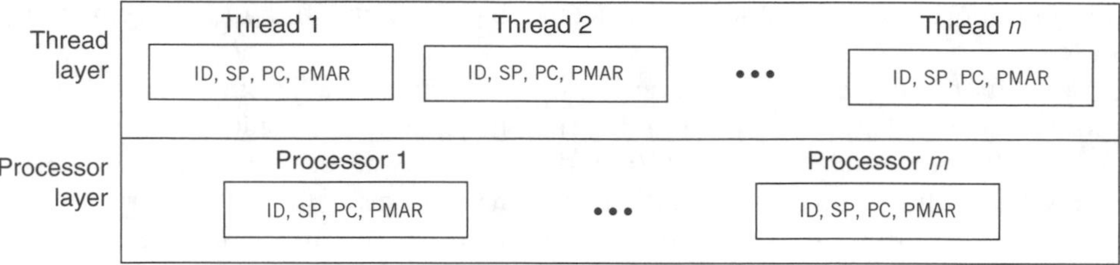

FIGURE 5.23

Multiplexing *m* processors among *n* threads ($n > m$).

The job of YIELD is to switch a processor from one thread to another. In its essence, YIELD is a simple three-step operation:

1. *Save* this thread's state so that it can resume later.
2. *Schedule* another thread to run on this processor.
3. *Dispatch* this processor to that thread.

The concrete problem that YIELD solves is multiplexing many threads over a potentially smaller number of processors (see Figure 5.23). Each processor typically has an identifier (ID), a stack pointer (SP), a program counter (PC), and a page-map address register (PMAR), pointing to the page map that defines the thread's address space. Processors may have additional state, such as floating point registers. Each thread has virtual versions of ID, SP, PC, and PMAR, and any additional state. YIELD must multiplex perhaps many threads in the thread layer over a limited number of processors in the processor layer.

YIELD implements the multiplexing as follows. When a thread running in the thread layer calls YIELD, YIELD enters the processor layer. The processor saves the state of the thread that is currently running. When that processor later exits from the processor layer, it runs a new thread, usually one that is different from the one it was running when it entered. This new thread may run in a different address space from the one used by the thread that called YIELD, or it may run in the same address space, depending on how the two threads were originally allocated.

Because the implementation of YIELD is specific to a processor and must load and save state that is often stored in processor registers (i.e., SP, PC, PMAR), YIELD is written in the instruction repertoire of the processor and can be thought of as a software extension of the processor. Programs using YIELD may be written in any programming language, but the implementation of YIELD itself is usually written in low-level processor-specific instructions. YIELD is typically a kernel procedure reached by a supervisor call.

Using this layering picture, we can also explain how interrupts and exceptions are multiplexed with threads. Interrupts invoke an interrupt handler, which always runs in the processor layer, even if the interrupt occurs while in the thread layer. On an interrupt, the interrupted processor runs the corresponding interrupt handler (e.g., when a clock interrupt occurs, it runs the clock handler) and then continues with the thread that the processor was running before the interrupt.

Exceptions happen in the thread layer. That is, the exception handler runs in the context of the interrupted thread; it has access to the interrupted thread's state and can invoke procedures on behalf of the interrupted thread.

As discussed in Sidebar 5.6, the literature is inconsistent both about the labels and about the distinction between the concepts of interrupts and exceptions. For purposes of this text, we define interrupts as events that may have no relation to the currently running thread, whereas exceptions are events that specifically pertain to the currently running thread. While both exceptions and interrupts are discovered by the processor, interrupts are handled by the processor layer, and exceptions are usually referred to a handler in the thread layer.

This difference places restrictions on what code can run in an interrupt handler: in general, an interrupt handler shouldn't invoke procedures (e.g., YIELD) of the thread layer that assume that the thread is running on the current processor because the interrupt may have nothing to do with the currently running thread. An interrupt handler can invoke an exception handler in the thread layer if the handler determines that this interrupt pertains to the thread running on the interrupted processor. The exception handler can then adjust the thread's environment. We will see an example of this case in Section 5.5.4 when the thread manager uses a clock interrupt to force the currently running thread to invoke YIELD.

Although the essence of multiplexing is simple, the code implementing YIELD is often among the most mysterious in an operating system. To dispel the mysteries, Section 5.5.2 develops a simple implementation of a thread manager that supports YIELD. Section 5.5.3 describes how this implementation can be extended to support creation and termination of threads. Section 5.5.4 explains how an operating system can enforce modularity among threads using interrupts and Section 5.5.5 adds enforcement of separate address spaces. Section 5.5.6 explains how systems use multiplexing recursively to implement several layers of processor virtualization.

Sidebar 5.6 Interrupts, Exceptions, Faults, Traps, and Signals The systems and architecture literature uses the words "interrupt" and "exception" inconsistently, and some authors use different words, such as "fault", "trap", "signal", and "sequence break". Some designers call a particular event an interrupt, while another designer calls the same event an exception or a signal. An operating system designer may label the handler for a hardware interrupt as an exception, trap, or fault handler. Terminology questions also arise because an interrupt handler in the operating system may invoke a thread's exception handler, which raises the question of whether the original event is an interrupt or an exception. The layered model helps answer this question: at the processor layer the event is an interrupt, and at the thread layer it is an exception.

5.5.2 Implementing YIELD

To keep the implementation of YIELD as simple as possible, let's temporarily restrict its implementation to a fixed number of threads, say, seven, and assume there are fewer than seven processors. (If there were seven or more processors and only seven threads, then processor virtualization would be unnecessary.) We further start by assuming that all seven threads run in the same address space, so we don't have to worry about saving and restoring a thread's PMAR. Finally, we will assume that the threads are already running. (Section 5.5.3 will remove the last assumption, explaining how threads are created and how the thread manager starts.)

With these assumptions we can implement YIELD as shown in Figure 5.24. The implementation of yield relies on four procedures: GET_THREAD_ID, ENTER_PROCESSOR_LAYER, EXIT_PROCESSOR_LAYER, and SCHEDULER. Each procedure has only a few lines of code, but they are subtle; we investigate them in detail.

As shown in the figure, the code for the procedures maintains two shared arrays: an array with one entry per processor, known as the *processor_table*, and an array with one entry per thread, known as the *thread_table*. The *processor_table* array records information for each processor. In this simple implementation, the information is just the identity of the thread that the processor is currently running. In later versions, we will need to keep track of more information. To be able to index into this table, a processor needs to know what its identity is, which is usually stored in a special register CPUID. That is, the procedure GET_THREAD_ID returns the identity of the thread running on processor CPUID (line *7*). The procedure GET_THREAD_ID virtualizes the register CPUID to create a virtual ID register for each thread, which records a thread's identity.

Entry *i* of *thread_table* holds the stack pointer for thread *i* (whenever thread *i* is not actually running on a processor) and records whether thread *i* is RUNNING (i.e., a processor is running thread *i*) or RUNNABLE (i.e., thread *i* is waiting to receive a processor). In a system with *n* processors, *n* threads can be in the RUNNING state at the same time.

With these data structures, the processor layer works as follows. Suppose that two processors, A and B, are busy running seven threads and that thread 0, which is running on processor A, calls YIELD. YIELD acquires *thread_table_lock* at line *9* so that the processor layer can implement switching threads as a before-or-after action. (The lock is needed because there is more than one processor, so different threads might try to invoke YIELD at the same time.) YIELD then calls ENTER_PROCESSOR_LAYER to release its processor.

The statement on line *14* records that the calling thread will no longer be running on the processor but that it is runnable. That is, if there are no other threads waiting to run, the processor layer can schedule thread 0 again.

Line *15* saves thread 0's stack pointer (held in processor A's SP register) into thread 0's entry in *thread_table*. The stack pointer is the only thread state that must be saved because the processor layer always suspends a thread in ENTER_PROCESSOR_LAYER; it is unnecessary to save and restore the program counter. We are assuming that all threads run in the same address space so PMAR doesn't have to be saved and restored either. Other processors or calling conventions (or if a thread may be resumed at a different address than in ENTER_PROCESSOR_LAYER) might require that ENTER_PROCESSOR_LAYER save

```
1   shared structure processor_table[7]
2       integer thread_id                        // identity of thread running on a processor
3   shared structure thread_table[7]
4       integer topstack                         // value of this thread's stack pointer
5       integer state                            // RUNNABLE OR RUNNING
6   shared lock instance thread_table_lock

7   procedure GET_THREAD_ID() return processor_table[CPUID].thread_id

8   procedure YIELD ()
9       ACQUIRE (thread_table_lock)
10      ENTER_PROCESSOR_LAYER (GET_THREAD_ID())
11      RELEASE (thread_table_lock)
12      return

13  procedure ENTER_PROCESSOR_LAYER (this_thread)
14      thread_table[this_thread].state ← RUNNABLE      // switch state to RUNNABLE
15      thread_table[this_thread].topstack ← SP         // store yielding's thread SP
16      SCHEDULER()
17      return

18  procedure SCHEDULER()
19      j = GET_THREAD_ID()
20      do                                              // schedule a RUNNABLE thread
21          j ← (j + 1) modulo 7
22      while thread_table[j].state ≠ RUNNABLE          // skip running threads
23      thread_table[j].state ← RUNNING                 // set state to RUNNING
24      processor_table[CPUID].thread_id ← j            // record that processor runs thread j
25      EXIT_PROCESSOR_LAYER (j)                        // dispatch this processor to thread j
26      return

27  // EXIT_PROCESSOR_LAYER returns from the new thread's invocation of
28  // ENTER_PROCESSOR_LAYER and returns control to the new thread's invocation of YIELD.
29  procedure EXIT_PROCESSOR_LAYER (new)
30      SP ← thread_table[new].topstack                 // dispatch: load SP of new thread
31      return
```

FIGURE 5.24

An implementation of YIELD. EXIT_PROCESSOR_LAYER will return to YIELD because EXIT_PROCESSOR_LAYER uses the SP that was saved in ENTER_PROCESS_LAYER. To make it easier to follow, the procedures have explicit **return** statements.

additional thread state. In that case, the *thread_table* entries must have additional fields, and ENTER_PROCESSOR_LAYER would save the additional state in the additional fields of the *thread_table* entries.

The part of the processor layer that chooses the next thread is called the *scheduler*. In our simple implementation, statements on lines *20* through *22* constitute the core of the scheduler. Processor A cycles through the thread table, skips threads that are already running on another processor, stops searching when it finds a runnable thread (let's say thread 6), and sets thread 6's state to RUNNING (line *23*) so that another processor doesn't again select thread 6. This implementation schedules threads in a ***round-robin*** fashion, but many other policies are possible; we discuss some others in Chapter 6 (Section 6.3).

This implementation of the processor layer assumes that the number of threads is more than (or at least equal to) the number of processors. Under this assumption, processor A will select and run a thread different from the one that called YIELD, unless the number of threads is the same as the number of processors, in which case processor A will cycle back to the thread that called YIELD because all the other threads are running on other processors. If there are fewer threads than processors, this implementation leaves processor A cycling forever through *thread_table* without giving up *thread_table_lock*, preventing any other thread from calling YIELD. We will fix this problem in Section 5.5.3, where we introduce a version of YIELD that supports the dynamic creation and termination of threads.

After selecting thread 6 to run, the processor records that thread 6 is running on this processor (line *24*), so that on the next call to ENTER_PROCESSOR_LAYER the processor knows which thread it is running. The processor leaves the processor layer by calling EXIT_PROCESSOR_LAYER, which dispatches processor A to thread 6. This part of the thread manager is often called the ***dispatcher***.

The procedure EXIT_PROCESSOR_LAYER loads the saved stack pointer of thread 6 into processor A's SP register (line *30*). (In implementations that have additional thread state that must be restored, these lines would need to be expanded.) Now processor A is running thread 6.

Because line *30* replaces SP with the value that thread 6 saved on line *15* when it last ran, the flow of control when the processor reaches the return on line *31* requires some thought. That return pops a return address off the stack. The return address is the address that thread 6 pushed on its stack when it called ENTER_PROCESSOR_LAYER at line *10*. Thus, the line *31* return actually goes to the caller of ENTER_PROCESSOR_LAYER, namely, YIELD, at line *11*. Line *12* pops the next return address off the stack, returning control to the program in thread 6 that originally called YIELD. The overall effect is that thread 0 called YIELD, but control returns to the instruction after the call to YIELD in thread 6.

This flow of control has the curious effect of abandoning two stack frames, the ones allocated on the calls to SCHEDULER and EXIT_PROCESSOR_LAYER. The original save of SP in thread 6 at line *15* actually accomplished two goals: (1) save the value of SP for future use when control returns to thread 6, and (2) mark a place that the processor layer thread can use as a stack when executing SCHEDULER and EXIT_PROCESSOR_LAYER. The reloading of SP at line *30* similarly accomplishes two goals: (1) restore the thread 6 stack and (2) abandon the processor layer stack, which is no longer needed. A more elaborate thread manager design, as we will see in Section 5.5.3, switches to a separate processor layer stack rather than borrowing space atop an existing thread layer stack.

To understand why this implementation of YIELD works, consider two threads: one running the SEND procedure of Figure 5.22 and one running the RECEIVE procedure. Furthermore, assume that the sender thread is thread 0, that the receiver thread is thread 6, and that the data and instructions of the procedures are located at address

1001 and up in memory. Finally, assume the following saved thread state for thread 0 and the following current state for processor A:

thread_table:

	Saved SP	State
0	100	RUNNABLE
	...	
6		

Processor A's *thread_id*: 6

Processor A's PC: 1009

Processor A's SP: 204

At some time in the past, thread 0 called YIELD and ENTER_PROCESSOR_LAYER stored the value of thread 0's stack pointer (100) into the thread table and went on to run some other thread. Processor A is currently running thread 6: A's entry in the *processor_table* array contains 6, A's SP register points to the top of the stack of thread 6, and A's PC register contains address 1009, which holds the first instruction of YIELD (see line *9*).

YIELD invokes the procedure ENTER_PROCESSOR_LAYER, following the procedure call convention of 4.1.1, which pushes some values on thread 6's stack—in particular, the return address (1011)—and change A's SP to 220 (204 + 16).* ENTER_PROCESSOR_LAYER knows that the current thread has index 6 by reading the processor's entry in the *processor_table* array. Line *15* saves thread 6's current top of stack (220) by storing processor A's SP into thread 6's entry into *thread_table*.

The statements at lines *19* through *22* choose which thread to run next, using a simple round-robin algorithm, and select thread 0. The scheduler invokes EXIT_PROCESSOR_LAYER to dispatch processor A to thread 0.

Line *30* loads the saved SP of thread 0 so that processor A can find the top of the stack at memory address 100. At the top of thread 0's stack will be the return address; this address will be 1011 (the line after the call to ENTER_PROCESSOR_LAYER into YIELD, line *11*), since thread 0 entered ENTER_PROCESSOR_LAYER from YIELD. Thread 0 releases *thread_table_lock* so that another thread can enter ENTER_PROCESSOR_LAYER and return from YIELD. Thread 0 returns from EXIT_PROCESSOR_LAYER following the procedure call convention, which pops off the return address from the top of the stack. The address that EXIT_PROCESSOR_LAYER uses is 1011 because EXIT_PROCESSOR_LAYER uses the SP saved by ENTER_PROCESSOR_LAYER and thus returns to YIELD at line *11*. YIELD releases the *thread_table_lock* and returns control to the program in thread 0 that originally called YIELD.

At this point, the thread switch has completed, and thread 0, rather than thread 6, is running on processor A; the state is as follows:

thread_table:

	Saved SP	State
0	100	RUNNING
	...	
6	220	RUNNABLE

Processor A's *thread_id*: 0

Processor A's PC: 1011

Processor A's SP: 72

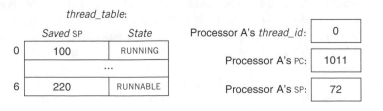

*The 16 bytes provide space to save R0, R1, one argument, and a return address.

At some time in the future, the thread manager will resume thread 6, at the instruction at address 1011.

From this example we can see that a thread always releases its processor by calling ENTER_PROCESSOR_LAYER and that the thread always resumes right after the call to ENTER_PROCESSOR_LAYER. This stylized flow of control in which a thread always releases its processor at the same point and resumes at that point is an example of what is sometimes called *co-routine*.

To ensure that the thread switch is atomic, the thread that invokes ENTER_PROCESSOR_LAYER acquires *thread_table_lock* and the thread that resumes using EXIT_PROCESSOR_LAYER releases *thread_table_lock* (line *11*). Because the scheduler is likely to choose a different thread to run from the one that called YIELD, the thread that releases the lock is most likely a different thread from the one that acquired the lock. In essence, the thread that releases the processor passes the lock along to the thread that next receives the processor.

Thread switching relies on a detailed understanding of the processor and the procedure call convention. In most systems, the implementation of thread switching is more complex than the implementation in Figure 5.24 because we made several assumptions that often don't hold in real systems: there is a fixed number of threads, all threads are runnable, and scheduling threads round-robin is an acceptable policy. In the next sections, we will eliminate some of these assumptions.

5.5.3 Creating and Terminating Threads

The example YIELD procedure supports only a fixed number of threads. A full-blown thread manager allows threads to be created and terminated on demand. To support a variable number of threads, we would need to modify the implementation of ALLOCATE_THREAD and extend the thread manager with the following procedures:

- EXIT_THREAD (): destroy and clean up the calling thread. When a thread is done with its job, it invokes EXIT_THREAD to release its state.
- DESTROY_THREAD (*id*): destroy the thread identified by *id*. In some cases, one thread may need to terminate another thread. For example, a user may have started a thread that turns out to have a programming error such as an endless loop, and thus the user wants to terminate it. For these cases, we might want to provide a procedure to destroy a thread.

For the most part, the implementation of these procedures is relatively straightforward, but there are a few subtle issues. For example, if threads can terminate, we have to fix the problem that the previous code required at least as many threads as processors. To get at these issues, we detail their implementation. First, we create a separate thread for each processor (which we will call a *processor-layer thread*, or *processor thread* for short), which runs the procedure SCHEDULER (see Figure 5.25). The way to think about this setup is that the SCHEDULER runs in the processor layer, and it virtualizes its processor. A processor thread per processor is necessary because a thread in the thread layer (a *thread-layer thread*) cannot deallocate its own stack since it cannot call a procedure (e.g., DEALLOCATE or YIELD) on a stack that it has released. Instead, we set it up so that the processor-layer thread cleans up thread-layer threads. When starting the operating system kernel (e.g., after turning the computer on), the kernel creates processor-layer threads as follows:

```
procedure RUN_PROCESSORS ()
    for each processor do
        allocate stack and set up a processor thread
        shutdown ← FALSE
        SCHEDULER ()
        deallocate processor thread stack
        halt processor
```

This procedure allocates a stack and sets up a processor thread for each processor. This thread runs the scheduler procedure until some procedure sets the global variable *shutdown* to TRUE. Then, the computer restarts or halts.

We first revisit YIELD with this setup, and we then see how this generalization supports thread creation and deletion. Using a separate processor thread, we find that switching a processor from one thread-layer thread to another actually requires two thread switches: one from the thread that is releasing its processor to the processor thread and one from the processor thread to the thread that is to receive the processor (see Figure 5.26). In more detail, let's suppose, as before, that thread 0 calls YIELD on processor A and that thread 6 is runnable and has called YIELD earlier. Thread 0 switches to the processor thread by invoking ENTER_PROCESSOR_LAYER (line *12*). The implementation of ENTER_PROCESSOR_LAYER is almost identical to ENTER_PROCESSOR_LAYER of Figure 5.24: it saves the stack pointer in the calling thread's *thread_table* entry, but it loads a new stack pointer from CPUID's *processor_table* entry. When ENTER_PROCESSOR_LAYER returns, it will switch to the processor thread and resume at line *24* (right after EXIT_PROCESSOR_LAYER).

The processor thread will cycle through the thread table until it hits thread 6, which is runnable. The SCHEDULER sets thread 6's state to RUNNING (line *21*), records that thread 6 will run on this processor (line *22*), and invokes EXIT_PROCESSOR_LAYER, to switch the processor to thread 6 (line *23*). EXIT_PROCESSOR_LAYER saves the scheduler's thread state into CPUID's entry in the *processor_table* and loads thread 6's state in the processor. Because line *37* of EXIT_PROCESSOR_LAYER has loaded SP, the **return** statement at line *38* acts like a return from the procedure that saved SP. That procedure was ENTER_PROCESSOR_LAYER at line *33*, so control passes to the caller of ENTER_PROCESSOR_LAYER, namely, YIELD, at line *13*. YIELD releases *thread_table_lock* and returns control to the program of thread 6 that originally called it.

With this setup of thread switching in place, we can return to creating and deallocating threads dynamically. To keep track of which *thread_table* entries are in use, we extend the set of possible states of each entry with the additional state FREE. Now we can implement ALLOCATE_THREAD as follows:

1. Allocate space in memory for a new stack.
2. Place on the new stack an empty frame containing just a return address and initialize that return address with the address of EXIT_THREAD.

```
1   shared structure processor_table[7] // each processor maintains the following information:
2       integer topstack                // value of stack pointer
3       byte reference stack            // preallocated stack for this processor
4       integer thread_id               // identity of thread currently running on this processor
5   shared structure thread_table[7]    // each thread maintains the following information:
6       integer topstack                // value of the stack pointer
7       integer state                   // RUNNABLE, RUNNING, or FREE
8       boolean kill_or_continue        // terminate this thread? initialized to CONTINUE
9       byte reference stack            // stack for this thread

10  procedure YIELD ()
11      ACQUIRE (thread_table_lock)
12      ENTER_PROCESSOR_LAYER (GET_THREAD_ID(), CPUID)      // See caption below!
13      RELEASE (thread_table_lock)
14      return
15
16  procedure SCHEDULER ()
17      while shutdown = FALSE do
18          ACQUIRE (thread_table_lock)
19          for i from 0 until 7 do
20              if thread_table[i].state = RUNNABLE then
21                  thread_table[i].state ← RUNNING
22                  processor_table[CPUID].thread_id ← i
23                  EXIT_PROCESSOR_LAYER (CPUID, i)
24                  if thread_table[i].kill_or_continue = KILL then
25                      thread_table[i].state ← FREE
26                      DEALLOCATE(thread_table[i].stack)
27                      thread_table[i].kill_or_continue = CONTINUE
28          RELEASE (thread_table_lock)
29      return                                          // Go shut down this processor

30  procedure ENTER_PROCESSOR_LAYER (tid, processor)
31      thread_table[tid].state ← RUNNABLE
32      thread_table[tid].topstack ← SP                 // save state: store yielding's thread SP
33      SP ← processor_table[processor].topstack        // dispatch: load SP of processor thread
34      return

35  procedure EXIT_PROCESSOR_LAYER (processor, tid) // transfers control to after line 14
36      processor_table[processor].topstack ← SP        // save state: store processor thread's SP
37      SP ← thread_table[tid].topstack                 // dispatch: load SP of thread
38      return
```

FIGURE 5.25

YIELD with support for dynamic thread creation and deletion. Control flow is not obvious because some of those procedures reload SP, which changes the place to which they return. To make it easier to follow, the procedures have explicit **return** statements. The procedure called on line *12* actually returns by passing control to line *24*, and the procedure called on line *23* actually returns by passing control to line *13*. Figure 5.26 shows the control flow graphically.

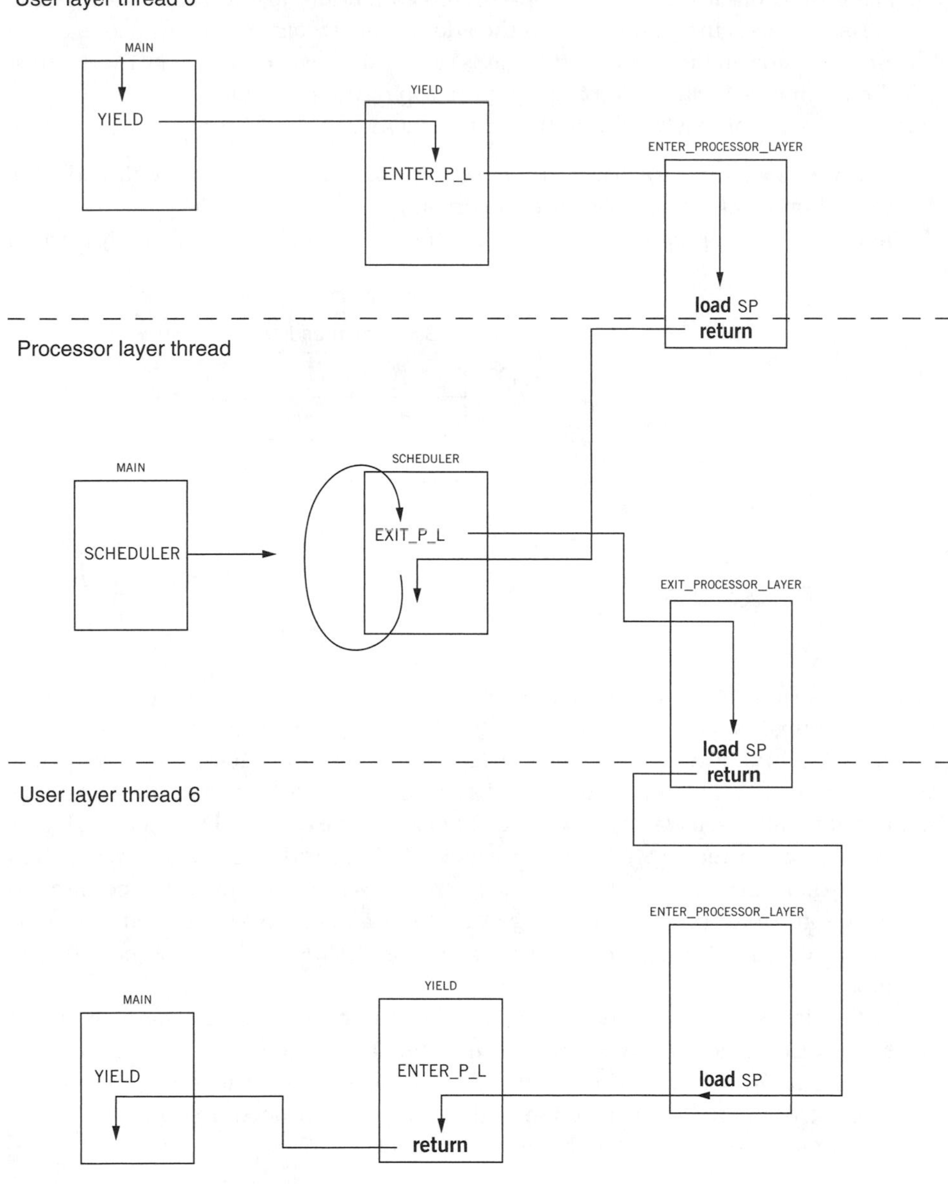

FIGURE 5.26

Control flow example when thread 0 yields to thread 6.

3. Place on the stack a second empty frame containing just a return address and initialize this return address with the address of *starting_procedure*.
4. Find an entry in the thread table that is FREE and initialize that entry for the new thread in the thread table by storing the top of the new stack.
5. Set the state of newly created thread to RUNNABLE.

If the thread manager cannot complete these steps (e.g., all entries in the thread table are in use), then THREAD_ALLOCATE returns an error.

To illustrate this implementation, consider the following state for a newly created thread 1:

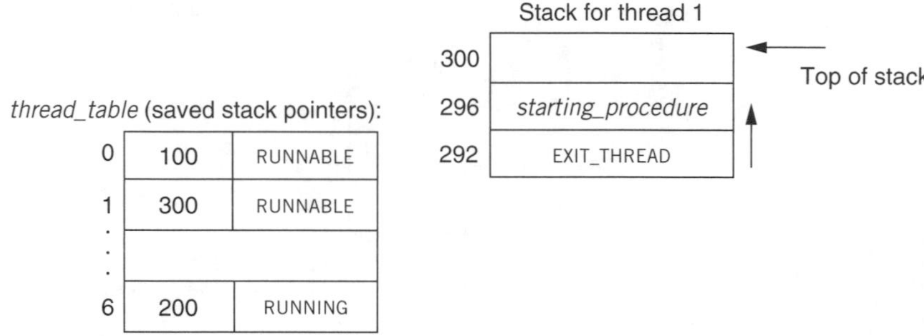

Thread 1's stack is located at address 292 and its saved stack pointer is 300. With this initial setup, it appears that EXIT_THREAD called the procedure STARTING_PROCEDURE, and thread 1 is about to return to this procedure. Thus, when SCHEDULER selects this thread, its return statement will go to the procedure *starting_procedure*. In detail, when the scheduler selects the new thread (1) as the next thread to execute, it sets its stack pointer to the top of the new stack (300) in EXIT_PROCESSOR_LAYER. When the processor returns from EXIT_PROCESSOR_LAYER, it will set its program counter to the address on top of the stack (*starting_procedure*), and start execution at that location. The procedure *starting_procedure* releases *thread_table_lock* and the new thread is running.

With this initial setup, when a thread finishes the procedure *starting_procedure*, it returns using the standard procedure return convention. Since the THREAD_CREATE procedure has put the address of the EXIT_THREAD procedure on the stack, this return transfers control to the first instruction of the EXIT_THREAD procedure.

The EXIT_THREAD procedure can be implemented as follows:

```
procedure EXIT_THREAD()
    ACQUIRE (thread_table_lock)
    thread_table[tid].kill_or_continue ← KILL
    ENTER_PROCESSOR_LAYER (GET_THREAD_ID (), CPUID)
```

EXIT_THREAD sets the *kill_or_continue* variable for thread and calls ENTER_PROCESSOR_LAYER, which switches the processor to the processor thread. The processor thread checks the variable *kill_or_continue* on line *24* to see if a thread is done, and, if so, it marks the thread entry as reusable (line *25*) and deallocates its stack (line *26*). Since no thread is using that stack, it is safe to deallocate it.

The implementation of DESTROY_THREAD is also a bit tricky because the target thread to be destroyed might be running on one of the processors. Thus, the calling thread cannot just free the target thread's stack; the processor running the target thread must do that. We can achieve that in an indirect way. DESTROY_THREAD just sets the *kill_or_continue* variable of the target thread to KILL and returns. When a thread invokes YIELD and enters the processor layer, the processor thread will check this variable and release the thread's resources. (Section 5.5.4 will show how to ensure that each thread running on a processor will call YIELD at least occasionally.)

The implementation described for allocating and deallocating threads is just one of many ways of handling the creation and destruction of threads. If one opens up the internals of half a dozen different thread packages, one will find half a dozen quite different ways to handle launching and terminating threads. The goal of this section was not to exhibit a complete catalog, but rather, by illustrating one example in detail, to dispel any mystery and expose the main issues that every implementation must address. Problem set *10* explores an implementation of a thread package in a trivial operating system for a single processor and two threads.

5.5.4 Enforcing Modularity with Threads: Preemptive Scheduling

The thread manager described so far switches to a new thread only when a thread calls YIELD. This scheduling policy, where a thread continues to run until it gives up its processor, is called *non-preemptive scheduling*. It can be problematic because the length of time a thread holds its processor is entirely under the control of the thread itself. If, for example, a programming error sends one thread into an endless loop, no other thread will ever be able to use that processor again. Non-preemptive scheduling might be acceptable for a single module that has several threads (e.g., a Web server that has several threads to increase performance) but not for several modules.

Some systems partially address this problem by having a gentlemen's agreement called *cooperative scheduling* (which in the literature sometimes is called *cooperative multitasking*): every thread is supposed to call YIELD periodically, for instance, once per 100 milliseconds. This solution is not robust because it relies on modules behaving well and not having any errors. If a programmer forgets to put in a YIELD, or if the program accidentally gets into an endless loop that does not include a YIELD, that processor will no longer participate in the gentlemen's agreement. If, as is common with cooperative multitasking designs, there is only a single processor, the processor may appear to freeze, since the other threads won't have an opportunity to make progress.

To enforce modularity among multiple threads, the operating system thread manager must ensure thread switching by using what is called *preemptive scheduling*. The thread manager must force a thread to give up its processor after, for example, 100 milliseconds. The thread manager can implement preemptive scheduling by setting the interval timer of a clock device. When the timer expires, the clock triggers an interrupt, switching to kernel mode in the processor layer. The clock interrupt handler can then invoke an exception handler, which runs in the thread layer and forces the currently running thread to yield. Thus, if a thread is in an endless loop, it receives 100 milliseconds to run on its turn, but it cannot stop other threads from getting at least some use of the processor, too.

Supporting preemptive scheduling requires some changes to the thread manager because in the implementation described so far an interrupt handler shouldn't invoke procedures in the thread layer at all, not even when the interrupt pertains to the currently running thread. To see why, consider a processor that invokes an interrupt handler that calls YIELD. If the interrupt happens right after the thread on that processor has acquired *thread_table_lock* in YIELD, then we will create a deadlock. The YIELD call in the handler will try to acquire *thread_table_lock* too, but it already has been acquired by the interrupted thread. That thread cannot continue and release the lock because it has been interrupted by the handler.

The problem is that we have concurrent activity within the processor layer (see Figure 5.23): the thread manager (i.e., YIELD) and the interrupt handler. The concurrent execution within the thread layer is coordinated with locks, but the processor needs its own mechanism. The processor may stop processing instructions of a thread at any time and switch to processing interrupt instructions. We are lacking a mechanism to turn the processor instruction stream and the interrupt instruction stream into separate before-or-after actions.

One solution to prevent the interrupt instruction stream from interfering with the processor instruction stream is to enable/disable interrupts. Disabling interrupts for a region greater than the region in which the *thread_table_lock* is set ensures that both streams are separate before-or-after actions. When a thread is about to acquire the *thread_table_lock*, it also disables interrupts on its processor. Now the processor will not switch to an interrupt handler when an interrupt arrives; interrupts are delayed until they are enabled again. After the thread has released the *thread_table_lock*, it is safe to reenable interrupts. Any pending interrupts will then execute immediately, but it is now safe since no thread on this processor can be inside the thread manager. This solution avoids the deadlock problem. For a more detailed description of the challenges and the solution in the Plan 9 operating system, see Suggestions for Further Reading 5.3.5.

Problem set *9* explores an implementation of a thread package with preemptive scheduling for a trivial operating system tailored to a single processor, which allows for other solutions to coordinating interrupts.

Preemptive scheduling is the mechanism that enforces modularity among threads because it isolates threads from one another's behavior, guaranteeing that no thread can halt the progress of other threads. The programmer can thus write a module as a standard computer program, execute it with its own thread, and not have to worry about any other modules in the system. Even though several programs are sharing the processors, programmers can consider each module independently and can think of each module as having a processor to itself. Furthermore, if a programming error causes a module to enter into an endless loop, another module that interacts with the user gets a chance to run at some point, thus allowing the user to destroy the ill-behaving thread by calling the THREAD_DESTROY procedure.

5.5.5 Enforcing Modularity with Threads and Address Spaces

Preemptive scheduling enforces modularity in the sense that one thread cannot stop the progress of another thread, but if all threads share a single address space, then they can modify each other's memory accidentally. That may be okay for threads that are working together on a common problem, but unrelated threads need to be protected from erroneous or malicious stores of one another. We can provide that protection by making the thread manager aware of the virtual address spaces of Section 5.4.

This awareness can be implemented by having the thread manager, when it switches a processor from one thread to another, also switch the address space. That is, ENTER_PROCESSOR_LAYER saves the contents of the processor's PMAR in the *thread_table* entry of the thread that is releasing the processor, and EXIT_PROCESSOR_LAYER loads the processor's PMAR with the value in the *thread_table* entry of the new thread.

Loading the PMAR adds one significant complication to the thread manager: starting at the instant that the processor loads a new value into the PMAR, the processor will translate virtual addresses using the new page table, so that it will take its next instruction from some location in the new virtual address space. As mentioned in Section 5.4.3.2, one way to deal with this complication is to map both the instructions and the data of the thread manager into the same set of virtual addresses in every virtual address space. Another possibility is to design hardware that can load the PMAR, SP, and PC as a single before-or-after action, thereby returning control to the thread in the new virtual address space at the saved location and with the saved stack pointer.

5.5.6 Layering Threads

Figure 5.23 and the program fragments in Figures 5.24 and 5.25 showed how to create several threads in the thread layer from one thread in the processor layer. In particular, Figure 5.25 explained how a processor thread in the processor layer can be used to dynamically create and delete threads in the thread layer. Many systems generalize this implementation to support interrupt handling and multiple layers of thread management, as shown in Figure 5.27.

To support interrupts, we can think of a processor as a hard-wired thread manager with two threads: (1) a processor thread (e.g., the thread that runs SCHEDULER in Figure 5.25) and (2) an interrupt thread that runs interrupt handlers in kernel mode. On an interrupt, a processor's hard-wired thread manager switches from a processor thread to an interrupt thread that runs an interrupt handler in kernel mode, which may invoke a thread-layer exception handler that calls YIELD.

The operating system thread layer uses the processor threads of the processor layer to implement a second layer of threads and gives each application module one

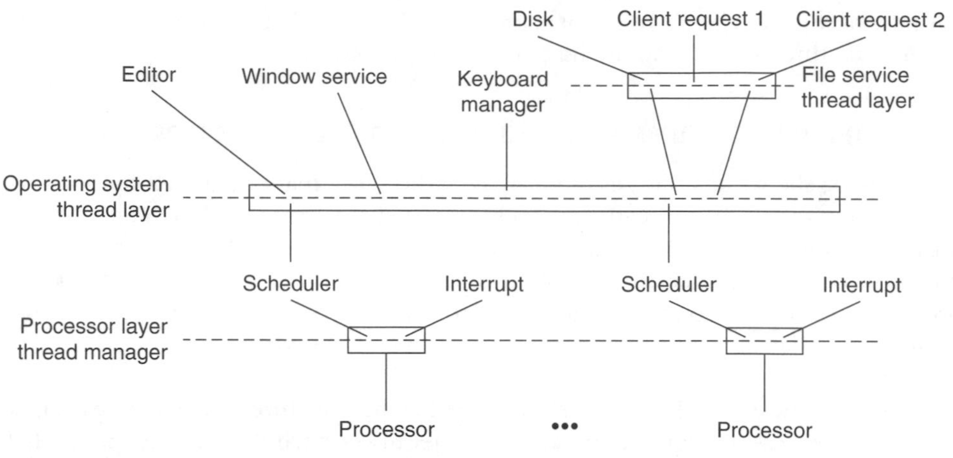

FIGURE 5.27

Thread managers applied recursively.

or more preemptively scheduled virtual processors. When the operating system thread manager switches to another thread, it may also have to load the chosen thread's page-map address into the page-map address register to switch to the address space of the chosen thread. The operating system thread manager runs in kernel mode.

Each application module in turn may implement, if it desires, its own, user-mode, third-layer thread manager using one or more virtual processors provided by the operating system layer. For example, some Web servers have an embedded Java interpreter to run Java programs, which may use several Java threads. To support threads at the Java level, the Java interpreter has its own thread manager. Typically, a third-layer thread manager uses non-preemptive scheduling because all threads belong to the same application module and don't have to be protected from each other.

Generalizing, we get the picture in Figure 5.27, where a number of threads at layer n can be used to implement higher-layer threads at layer $n + 1$. Each hardware processor at the lowest layer creates two threads: a processor thread and an interrupt thread. One layer up, the operating system uses the processor threads to provide one or more threads per module: one thread for the editor, one thread for the window manager, one thread for the keyboard manager, and several threads for the file service. One layer further up, the file service thread creates three application-level threads out of two operating system threads: one to wait for the disk and one for each of two client requests. At each layer, a thread manager switches one or more threads of layer $n - 1$ among several layer n threads.

Although the layering idea is simple in the abstract, in practice a number of issues must be carefully thought through—for example, if a thread blocks in a layer different than the layer where it was created and where its scheduler runs. Clark [Suggestions for Further Reading 5.3.3] and Anderson et al. [Suggestions for Further Reading 5.3.2] discuss some of the practical issues.

5.6 THREAD PRIMITIVES FOR SEQUENCE COORDINATION

The thread manager described in Section 5.5 allows processors to be shared among many threads. A thread can release its processor so that other threads get a chance to run, as the sender and receiver do using YIELD in Figure 5.22. When the sender or receiver is scheduled again, it retests the shared variables *in* and *out*. This mode of interaction, where a thread continually tests a shared variable, is called *polling*. Polling in software is usually undesirable because every time a thread discovers that the test for a shared variable fails, it has acquired and released its processor needlessly. If a system has many polling threads, then the thread manager spends much time performing unnecessary thread switches instead of running threads that have productive work to perform.

Ideally, a thread manager should schedule a thread only when the thread has useful work to perform. That is, we would prefer a way of waiting that avoids spinning on calls to YIELD. For example, a sender with a bounded buffer should be able to tell the thread manager not to run it until $in - out < N$. (That is, until the buffer has room.) One way to approach this goal is for a thread manager to support primitives for sequence coordination, which is what this section explores.

5.6.1 The Lost Notification Problem

To see what we need for the primitives for sequence coordination, consider an obvious, but incorrect, implementation of sender and receiver, as shown in Figure 5.28. This implementation uses a variable shared between the sender and receiver, and two new, but inadequate, primitives—WAIT and NOTIFY—that take as argument the name of the shared variable:

- WAIT (*event_name*) is a before-or-after action that sets this thread's state to WAITING, places *event_name* in the thread table entry for this thread, and yields its processor.
- NOTIFY (*event_name*) is a before-or-after action that looks in the thread table for a thread that is in the state WAITING for *event_name* and changes that thread to the RUNNABLE state.

To support this interface, the thread manager must add the WAITING state to the RUNNING and RUNNABLE state for threads in the thread table. When the scheduler runs (for example, when some thread invokes YIELD), it skips over any thread that is in the WAITING state.

The program in the figure uses these primitives as follows. A thread invokes WAIT to allow the thread manager to release the thread's processor until a call to NOTIFY (lines *15* and *25*). The thread that changes *in* invokes NOTIFY (line *15*) to tell the thread manager to give a processor to a receiver thread waiting on *nonempty* (line *22*), since now there is a message in the buffer (i.e., $out < in$). There is a similar call to NOTIFY by the thread that updates *out* (line *25*), to tell the thread manager to give a processor to a sending thread waiting on *room* (line *12*), since now there is room to add a message to the buffer. This implementation avoids needless thread switches because the waiting receiver thread receives a processor only if NOTIFY has been called.

```
1   shared structure buffer                      // A shared bounded buffer
2       message instance message[N]              // with a maximum of N messages
3       long integer in initially 0              // Counts number of messages put in the buffer
4       long integer out initially 0             // Counts number of messages taken out of the buffer
5       lock instance buffer_lock initially UNLOCKED // Lock to coordinate sender and receiver
6       event instance room                      // Event variable to wait until there is room in buffer
7       event instance notempty                  // Event variable to wait until the buffer is not empty

8   procedure SEND (buffer reference p, message instance msg)
9       ACQUIRE (p.buffer_lock)
10      while p.in − p.out = N do                        // Wait until there room in the buffer
11          RELEASE (p.buffer_lock)                      // Release lock so that receiver can remove
12          WAIT(p.room)                                 // Release processor
13          ACQUIRE (p.buffer_lock)
14      p.message[p.in modulo N] ← msg                   // Put message in the buffer
15      if p.in = p.out then NOTIFY(p.notempty)          // Signal thread that there is a message
16      p.in ← p.in + 1                                  // Increment in
17      RELEASE (p.buffer_lock)

18  procedure RECEIVE (buffer reference p)
19      ACQUIRE (p.buffer_lock)
20      while p.in = p.out do                            // Wait until there is a message to receive
21          RELEASE (p.buffer_lock)                      // Release lock so that sender can add
22          WAIT(p.notempty)                             // Release processor
23          ACQUIRE (p.buffer_lock)
24      msg ← p.message[p.out modulo N]                  // Copy item out of buffer
25      if p.in − p.out = N then NOTIFY(p.room)          // Signal thread that there is room now
26      p.out ← p.out + 1                                // Increment out
27      RELEASE (p.buffer_lock)
28      return msg
```

FIGURE 5.28

An implementation of a virtual communication link for a system with locks, NOTIFY, and WAIT.

Unfortunately, the use of WAIT and NOTIFY introduces a race condition. Let's assume that the buffer is empty (i.e., *in* = *out*) and a receiver and a sender run on separate processors. The following order of statements will result in a lost notification: *A20*, *A21*, *B9* through *B17*, and *A22*:

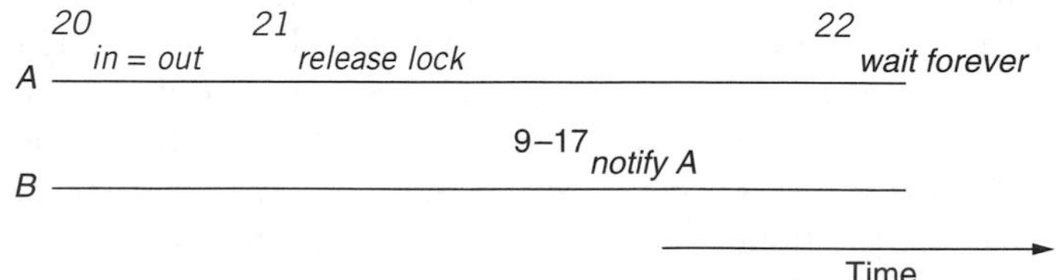

The receiver finds that *buffer* is empty (*A20*) and releases the lock (*A21*), but before the receiver executes *A22*, the sender executes *B9* through *B17*, which adds an item to the buffer and notifies the receiver. The notification is lost because the receiver hasn't called WAIT yet. Now the receiver executes WAIT (*A22*) and waits for a notification that will never come. The sender continues adding items to the buffer until the buffer is full and then calls WAIT. Now both the receiver and sender are waiting.

We could modify the program to call NOTIFY on each invocation of SEND, but that won't fix the problem. It will make it more unlikely that the notification will be lost, but it won't eliminate the possibility. The following ordering of statements could happen: the receiver executes *A20* and *A21*, then it is interrupted long enough for the sender to add N items, and then the receiver calls *A22*. With this ordering, the receiver misses all of the repeated notifications.

Swapping statements *21* and *22* will result in a lost notification too. Then the receiver would call WAIT while still holding the lock on *buffer_lock*. But the sender needs to be able to acquire *buffer_lock* in order to notify the receiver, so everything would come to a halt.

The problem is that we have three operations on the shared buffer state that must be turned into a before-or-after action: (1) testing if there is room in the shared buffer, and (2) if not, going to sleep until there is room and (3) releasing the shared lock so that another thread can make room. If these three operations are not a before-or-after action, then the risk of the lost notification problem arises.

The pseudocode that uses WAIT and NOTIFY illustrates a tension between modularity and locks. An observant reader might ask: if the problem is a race condition caused by having concurrent threads running multistep actions (e.g., the sender (1) tests for space and (2) calls WAIT, at the same time that the receiver (1) makes space and (2) calls NOTIFY), why don't we just make those steps into before-or-after actions by putting a lock around them? The problem is that the steps we would like to make into an atomic action are for the example of the sender (1) comparing *in* and *out* and (2) changing the thread table entry from RUNNING to WAITING. But the variables *in* and *out* are owned by the sender and receiver modules, whereas the thread table is owned by the thread manager module. These are not only separate modules, but the thread manager is probably in the kernel. So who should own the lock that creates the before-or-after action? We can't allow correctness of the kernel to depend on a user program properly setting and releasing a kernel lock, nor can we allow the correctness of the kernel to depend on a user lock being correctly implemented. The real problem here is that the lock needed to create the before-or-after action must protect an invariant that is a relation between a piece of application-owned state and a piece of system-owned state.

5.6.2 Avoiding the Lost Notification Problem with Eventcounts and Sequencers

Designers have identified various solutions to the problem of creating before-or-after actions to eliminate lost notifications. A general property of all these solutions is that they bring some additional thread state that characterizes the event for which the thread is waiting under protection of the thread table lock (i.e., *thread_table_lock*). By extending the semantics of WAIT and NOTIFY to include examining and modifying the variable *event_name*, it is possible to avoid lost notifications. We leave that solution as an exercise to the reader and instead offer simpler and more widely used solutions based on primitives other than WAIT and NOTIFY. Problem set *13* introduces a solution in which the additional thread state is held in what is called a *condition variable*, and Birrell's tutorial does a nice job of explaining how to program with threads and condition variables [Suggestions for Further Reading 5.3.1]. Sidebar 5.7 and problem set *12* describe a solution in which the additional thread state is a variable known as a *semaphore*. In this section we describe a solution (one that is intended to be particularly easy to reason about) in which the additional thread state is found in variables called *eventcounts* and *sequencers* [Suggestions for Further Reading 5.5.4]. In all of these solutions, the additional thread state must be shared between the application (e.g., SEND and RECEIVE) and the thread manager, so the semantics of WAIT/NOTIFY, condition variables, semaphores, eventcounts, and other similar solutions all contain non-obvious and sometimes quite subtle aspects. A good discussion of some of these subtle issues is provided by Lampson and Redell [Suggestions for Further Reading 5.5.5].

Eventcounts and sequencers are variables that are shared among the sender, the receiver, and the thread manager. They are manipulated using the following interface:

- AWAIT (*eventcount, value*) is a before-or-after action that compares eventcount to value. If *eventcount* exceeds *value*, AWAIT returns to its caller. If *eventcount* is less than or equal to *value*, AWAIT changes the state of the calling thread to WAITING, places *value* and the name of *eventcount* in this thread's entry in the thread table, and yields its processor.

- ADVANCE (*eventcount*) is a before-or-after action that increments *eventcount* by one and then searches the thread table for threads that are waiting on this eventcount. For each one it finds, if *eventcount* now exceeds the value for which that thread is waiting, ADVANCE changes that thread's state to RUNNABLE.

- TICKET (*sequencer*) is a before-or-after action that returns a non-negative value that increases by one on each call. Two threads concurrently calling TICKET on the same *sequencer* receive different values, and the ordering of the values returned corresponds to the time ordering of the execution of TICKET.

- READ (*eventcount* or *sequencer*) is a before-or-after action that returns to the caller the current value of the variable. Having an explicit READ procedure ensures before-or-after atomicity for eventcounts and sequencers whose value may grow to be larger than a memory cell.

To implement this interface, the scheduler skips over any thread that is in the WAITING state.

To understand these primitives, consider first the implementation of a bounded buffer for a single sender and receiver. Using eventcounts, we can rewrite the implementation of the bounded buffer from Figure 5.6 as shown in Figure 5.29. SEND waits until there is space in the buffer. Because AWAIT implements the waiting operation, the code in Figure 5.29 does not need the **while** loop that waits for success in Figure 5.6. Once there is space, the sender adds the message to the buffer and increments *in* using

Sidebar 5.7 Avoiding the Lost Notification Problem with Semaphores Semaphores are counters with special semantics for sequence coordination. A semaphore supports two operations:

- DOWN (*semaphore*): if *semaphore* > 0 decrement *semaphore* and return otherwise, wait until another thread increases *semaphore* and then try to decrement again.

- UP (*semaphore*): increment *semaphore*, wake up all threads waiting on *semaphore*, and return.

Semaphores are inspired by the ones that the railroad system uses to coordinate the use of a shared track. If a semaphore is down, trains must stop until the current train on the track leaves the track and raises the semaphore. If a semaphore can take on only the values 0 and 1 (sometimes called a binary semaphore), then UP and DOWN operate similar to a railroad semaphore. Semaphores were introduced in computer systems by the Dutch programmer Edgar Dijkstra (see also Sidebar 5.2), who called the DOWN operation P ("pakken", for grabbing in Dutch) and the UP operation V ("verhogen", for raising in Dutch) [Suggestions for Further Reading 5.5.1].

The implementation of DOWN and UP must be before-or-after actions to avoid the lost notification problem. This property can be realized in the same way as the eventcount operations:

```
structure semaphore
    integer count

procedure UP (semaphore reference sem)
    ACQUIRE (thread_table_lock)
    sem.count ← sem.count + 1
    for i from 0 to 6 do  // wakeup all threads waiting on this semaphore
        if thread_table[i].state = WAITING and thread_table[i].sem = sem then
            thread_table[i].state ← RUNNABLE
    RELEASE (thread_table_lock)
procedure DOWN (semaphore reference sem)
    ACQUIRE (thread_table_lock)
    id ← GET_THREAD_ID()
    thread_table[id].sem ← sem  // record the semaphore ID is waiting on
    while sem.count < 1 do       // give up the processor when sem < 1
        thread_table[id].state ← WAITING
        ENTER_PROCESSOR_LAYER (id, CPUID)
    sem.count ← sem.count − 1
    RELEASE (thread_table_lock)
```

Using semaphores, one can implement SEND and RECEIVE with a bounded buffer without lost notifications (see problem set *12*).

```
shared structure buffer
    message instance message[N]
    eventcount instance in initially 0
    eventcount instance out initially 0

procedure SEND (buffer reference p, message instance msg)
    AWAIT (p.out, p.in − N)                       // Wait until there is space in buffer
    p.message[READ(p.in) modulo N] ← msg          // Copy message into buffer
    ADVANCE (p.in)                                // Increment in and alert receiver

procedure RECEIVE (buffer reference p)
    AWAIT (p.in, p.out)                           // Wait till something in buffer
    msg ← p.message[READ(p.out) modulo N]         // Copy message out of buffer
    ADVANCE (p.out)                               // Increment out and Alert sender
    return msg
```

FIGURE 5.29

An implementation of a virtual communication link for a single sender and receiver using eventcounts.

ADVANCE, which may change the receiver's state to RUNNABLE. Because AWAIT and ADVANCE operations are before-or-after actions, the lost notification problem cannot occur.

Again, because AWAIT implements the waiting operation, the receiver implementation is also simple. RECEIVE waits until there is a message in the buffer. If so, the receiver extracts the message from the buffer and increments *out* using ADVANCE, which may change the sender's state to RUNNABLE.

Figure 5.30 shows the implementation for the case of multiple senders with a single receiver. To ensure that several senders don't try to write into the same location within the buffer, we need to coordinate their actions. We can use the TICKET primitive to solve this problem, which requires changes only to SEND. The main difference between Figure 5.30 and Figure 5.29 is that the senders must obtain a ticket to serialize their operations. SEND obtains a ticket from the sequencer *sender* (line *7*). TICKET operates likes the "take a number" machine in a bakery or post office. The returned tickets create an ordering of senders and tell each sender its position in the order. Each sender thread then waits until its turn comes up by invoking AWAIT, passing as arguments the eventcount *sent* and the value of its TICKET (*t*) (line *8*). When *sent* reaches the number on the ticket of a sender thread, that sender thread proceeds to the next step, which is to wait until there is space in the buffer (line *9*), and only then does it add its item to its entry in *buffer*. Because TICKET is a before-or-after action, no two threads will get the same number. Again, because AWAIT and ADVANCE operations are before-or-after actions, the lost notification problem cannot happen.

Again, this solution doesn't use a **while** loop that waits for the success in Figure 5.6. With multiple senders, it is slightly tricky to see why this is correct. AWAIT guarantees that *eventcount* exceeded *value* at some instant after AWAIT was called, but if there are other, concurrent, threads that may increment *value*, by the time AWAIT's caller gets control back, *eventcount* may no longer exceed *value*. The proper view is that a

```
shared structure buffer
    message instance message[N]
    eventcount instance in initially 0
    eventcount instance out initially 0
    sequencer instance sender

procedure SEND (buffer reference p, message instance msg)
    t ← TICKET (p.sender)                       // Allocate a buffer slot
    AWAIT (p.in, t)                              // Wait till previous slots are filled
    AWAIT (p.out, READ(p.in) – N)                // Wait till there is space in buffer
    p.message[READ(p.in) modulo N] ← msg         // Copy message into buffer
    ADVANCE (p.in)                               // Increment in and alert receiver
```

FIGURE 5.30

An implementation of a virtual communication link for several senders using eventcounts.

return from AWAIT is a hint that the condition AWAIT was waiting for was true and it may still be true, but the program that called AWAIT must check again to be sure.

The issue seems to arise when there are multiple senders. Suppose the buffer is full (say *in* and *out* are 10) and there are two sending threads that are both waiting for a slot to become empty. The first one of those sending threads that runs will absorb the buffer entry and change *in* to 11. The second sending thread will find that *in* is 11 but *out* is also 11, so from its point of view, AWAIT returned with $in = out$. Yet it doesn't recheck the condition. Closer inspection of the code reveals that this case can never arise because the second sender is actually waiting its turn on the ticket returned by the sequencer *sender*, not waiting for $in < out$. There is never a case in which two senders are waiting for the same condition to become true. If the program had used a different way of coordinating the senders, it might have required a retest of the condition when AWAIT returns. This is another example of why programming with concurrent threads requires great care.

If the implementation must also work with multiple receivers, then a similar sequencer is needed in RECEIVE to allow the receivers to serialize themselves.

With these additional primitives for sequence coordination, we can describe the life of a thread as a state machine with four states (see Figure 5.31). The thread manager

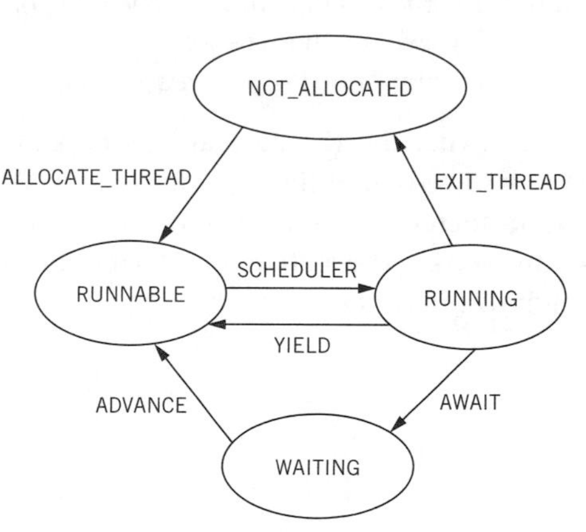

FIGURE 5.31

Thread state diagram. In any of the three states RUNNABLE, WAITING, or RUNNING, a call to DESTROY_THREAD sets a flag that causes the scheduler to force the state to NOT_ALLOCATED the next time that thread would have entered the RUNNING state.

creates a thread in the RUNNABLE state. The thread manager schedules one of the runnable threads and dispatches a processor to it; that thread changes to the RUNNING state. By calling YIELD, the thread reenters the RUNNABLE state, and the manager can select another thread and dispatch to it. Alternatively, a thread can change from the RUNNING state to the NOT_ALLOCATED state by calling EXIT_THREAD. Or a running thread can enter the WAITING state by calling AWAIT when it cannot proceed until some event occurs. Another thread, by calling ADVANCE, can make the waiting thread enter the RUNNABLE state again.

These primitives provide new opportunities for a programmer to create deadlocks. For example, thread A may call AWAIT on an eventcount that it expects thread B to ADVANCE, but thread B may be AWAITing an eventcount that only thread A is in a position to ADVANCE. Eventcounts and tickets can eliminate lost notifications, but the primitives that manipulate them must still be used with care. The last few questions of problem set *11* explore the problem of lost notifications by comparing a simple Web service implemented using NOTIFY and ADVANCE.

5.6.3 Implementing AWAIT, ADVANCE, TICKET, and READ (Advanced Topic)

To implement AWAIT, ADVANCE, TICKET, and READ we extend the thread manager as follows. YIELD doesn't require any modifications to support AWAIT and ADVANCE, but we must extend the *thread_table* to record, for threads in the WAITING state, a reference to the eventcount on which it is waiting:

```
shared structure thread_table[7]
    integer topstack                          // value of the stack pointer
    integer state                             // WAITING, RUNNABLE, TERMINATE, NOT_ALLOCATED
    eventcount reference event                // if waiting, the eventcount we are waiting on
    long integer value                        // if waiting, what value are we waiting for
shared lock instance thread_table_lock        // lock to protect entries of thread_table
```

The field *event* is a reference to an eventcount so that the thread manager and the calling thread can share it. This sharing is the key to resolving the tension mentioned earlier: it allows a calling thread variable to be protected by the thread manager lock.

We implement AWAIT by testing the eventcount, setting the state to WAITING if the test fails, and calling ENTER_PROCESSOR_LAYER to switch to the processor thread:

```
structure eventcount
    long integer count

procedure AWAIT (eventcount reference event, value)
    ACQUIRE (thread_table_lock)
    id ← GET_THREAD_ID ()
    thread_table[id].event ← event
    thread_table[id].value ← value
    if event.count ≤ value then thread_table[id].state ← WAITING
    ENTER_PROCESSOR_LAYER (id, CPUID)
    RELEASE (thread_table_lock)
```

This implementation of AWAIT releases its processor unless eventcount *event* exceeds value in a before-or-after action. As before, the thread data structures are protected by the lock *thread_table_lock*. In particular, the lock ensures that the line *8* comparison of *event* with *value* and the potential change of state from RUNNING to WAITING are two steps of a before-or-after action that must occur either completely before or completely after any concurrent call to ADVANCE that might change the value of *event* or the state of this thread. The lock thus prevents lost notifications.

ENTER_PROCESSOR_LAYER in AWAIT causes control to switch from this thread to the processor thread, which may give the processor away. The thread that calls ENTER_PROCESSOR_LAYER passes the lock it acquired to the processor thread, which passes it to the next thread to run on this processor. Thus, no other thread can modify the thread state while the thread that invoked AWAIT holds *thread_table_lock*. A return from that call to ENTER_PROCESSOR_LAYER means that some other thread called AWAIT or YIELD and the processor thread has decided it is appropriate to assign a processor to this thread again. The thread will return to line *10*, release *thread_table_lock*, and return to the caller of AWAIT.

The ADVANCE procedure increments the eventcount *event*, finds all threads that are waiting on *count* and whose *value* is less than *count's*, and changes their state to RUNNABLE:

```
1  procedure ADVANCE (eventcount reference event)
2     ACQUIRE (thread_table_lock)
3     event.count ← event.count + 1
4     for i from 0 until 7 do
5        if thread_table[i].state = WAITING and thread_table[i].event = event and
6                                  event.count > thread_table[i].value then
7           thread_table[i].state ← RUNNABLE
8     RELEASE (thread_table_lock)
```

The key in the implementation of ADVANCE is that it uses *thread_table_lock* to make ADVANCE a before-or-after action. In particular, the line *6* comparison of *event.count* with *thread*[*i*].*value* and the line 7 change of *state* to RUNNABLE of the thread that called AWAIT are now two steps of a before-or-after action. No thread calling AWAIT can interfere with a thread that is in ADVANCE. Similarly, no thread calling ADVANCE can interfere with a thread that is in AWAIT. This setup avoids races between AWAIT and ADVANCE, and thus the lost notification problem.

ADVANCE just makes a thread runnable; it doesn't call ENTER_PROCESSOR_LAYER to release its processor. The runnable thread won't run until some other thread (perhaps the caller of ADVANCE) calls YIELD or AWAIT, or until the scheduler preemptively releases a processor.

We implement a sequencer and the TICKET operation as follows:

```
structure sequencer
   long integer ticket

procedure TICKET (sequencer reference s)
   ACQUIRE (thread_table_lock)
   t ← s.ticket
   s.ticket ← t + 1
   RELEASE (thread_table_lock)
   return t
```

For completeness, the implementation of READ of an eventcount is as follows:

```
procedure READ (eventcount reference event)
    ACQUIRE (thread_table_lock)
    e ← event.count
    RELEASE (thread_table_lock)
    return e
```

To ensure that READ provides before-or-after atomicity, READ is implemented as a before-or-after action using locks. The implementation of READ of a sequencer is similar.

Recall that in Figure 5.8, ACQUIRE itself is implemented with a spin loop, polling the lock continuously instead of releasing the processor. Given that ACQUIRE and RELEASE are used to protect only short sequences of instructions, a spinning implementation is acceptable. Furthermore, inside the thread manager we must use a spinning lock because if ACQUIRE (*thread_table_lock*) were to call AWAIT to wait until the lock is unlocked, then the thread manager would be calling itself, but it isn't designed to be recursive. In particular, it does not have a base case that could stop recursion.

5.6.4 Polling, Interrupts, and Sequence Coordination

Some threads must interact with external devices. For example, the keyboard manager must be able to interact with the keyboard controller on the keyboard, which is a separate, special-purpose processor. As we shall see, this interaction is just another example of sequence coordination.

The keyboard controller is a special-purpose processor, which runs a single program that gathers key strokes. In the terminology of this chapter, we can think of the keyboard controller as a single, hard-wired thread running with its own dedicated processor. When the user presses a key, the keyboard controller thread raises a signal line long enough to set a flip-flop, a digital circuit that can store one bit that the keyboard manager can read. The controller thread then lowers the signal line until next time (i.e., until the next keystroke). The flip-flop shared between the controller and the manager allows them to coordinate their activities.

In fact, using the shared flip-flop, the keyboard manager can run a wait-for-input loop similar to the one in the receiver:

```
while FLIP_FLOP = 0 do
    YIELD ()
```

In this case, the keyboard controller sets the flip-flop and the keyboard manager reads the flip-flip and tests it. If the flip-flop is not set, it reads 0, and the manager yields. If it is set, it falls out of the loop. As a side-effect of reading the flip-flop, it is reset to 0, thus providing a kind of coordination lock.

Here we have another example of polling. In polling, a thread keeps checking whether another (perhaps hardware) thread needs attention. In our example, the keyboard manager runs every time the scheduler offers it a chance, to see if any new keys have been pressed. The keyboard manager thread is continually in a RUNNABLE state, and whenever the scheduler selects it to run, the thread checks the flip-flop.

Polling has several disadvantages, especially if it is done by a program. If it is difficult to predict the time until the event will occur, then there is no good choice for how often a thread should poll. If the polling thread executes infrequently (e.g., because the processors are busy executing other threads), then it might take a long time before a device receives attention. In this case, the computer system might appear to be unresponsive; for example, if a user must wait a long time before the computer processes the user's keyboard input, the user has a bad interactive experience. On the other hand, if the scheduler selects the polling thread frequently (e.g., faster than users can type), the thread wastes processor cycles, since often there will be no input available. Finally, some devices might require that a processor executes their managers by a certain deadline because otherwise the device won't operate correctly. For example, the keyboard controller may have only a single keystroke register available to communicate with the keyboard manager. If the user types a second keystroke before the keyboard manager gets a chance to run and absorb the first one, the first keystroke may be lost.

These disadvantages are similar to the disadvantages of not having explicit primitives for sequence coordination. Without AWAIT and ADVANCE, the thread scheduler doesn't know when the receiver thread must run; therefore, the receiver thread may make unnecessary, repeated calls to YIELD. This situation with the keyboard manager is similar; ideally, when the controller has input that needs to be processed, it should be able to alert the scheduler that the keyboard manager thread should run. We would like to program the keyboard manager and keyboard controller as a sender and a receiver using the primitives for sequence coordination, much as in Figure 5.30, except we could use a solution that works for a single sender and a single receiver. Unfortunately, the controller cannot invoke procedures such as AWAIT and ADVANCE directly; it shares only a single flip-flop with the processors.

The trick is to move the polling loop down into the hardware by using interrupts. The keyboard manager enables interrupts by setting a processor's interrupt control register to ON, indicating to that processor that it must take interrupts from the keyboard controller. Then, to check for an interrupt, the processor polls the shared flip-flop at the beginning of every instruction cycle. When the processor finds that the shared flip-flop has changed, instead of proceeding to the next instruction, the processor executes the interrupt handler. In other words, interrupts are actually implemented as a polling loop inside a processor. A processor may support multiple interrupts by providing multiple shared flip-flops and a map that associates a different interrupt handler with each flip-flop.

A simple interrupt handler for the keyboard device calls ADVANCE, the call that the keyboard controller is unable make directly, and then returns. The interrupted thread continues operation without realizing that anything happened. But the next time any thread calls YIELD or AWAIT, the thread manager can notice that the keyboard manager thread has become runnable. When it runs, the keyboard manager can then copy the keystrokes from the device, translate them to a character representation, put them in a shared buffer, (e.g., for the receiver), and wait for the next keystroke.

Because the interrupt handler gains control of a processor within one instruction time, it can be used to meet deadlines. For example, the interrupt handler for the keyboard device could copy the user's keystrokes to a buffer owned by the keyboard manager immediately, instead of waiting until the keyboard manager gets a chance to run. This way the keyboard device is immediately ready for the user's next keystroke. To meet such deadlines, interrupt handlers are usually more elaborate than a single call to ADVANCE. It is common to place modest-sized chunks of code in an interrupt handler to move data out of the device buffers (e.g., keystrokes out of the keyboard device) or immediately restart an I/O device that has turned itself off.

Putting code in an interrupt handler must be done with great care. An interrupt handler must be cautious in reading or writing shared variables because it may be invoked between any pair of instructions. Therefore, the handler cannot be sure of the state of the thread currently running on the processor or on other processors.

Since interrupt handlers are not threads managed by the operating system thread manager, the interrupt handlers and the operating system thread manager must be carefully programmed. For example, the thread manager should call ACQUIRE and RELEASE on the *thread_table_lock* with interrupts disabled because otherwise a deadlock might occur, as we saw in Section 5.5.4. As another example, an interrupt handler should never call AWAIT because AWAIT may release its processor to the surprise of the interrupted thread—the interrupted thread may be a thread that has nothing to do with the interrupt but just happened to be running on the processor when the interrupt occurred. On the other hand, an interrupt handler can invoke ADVANCE without causing any problems.

The restrictions on exception handlers that process errors caused by the currently running thread (e.g., a divide-by-zero error) are less severe because the handler runs on behalf of the thread currently running on the processor. So, in that case, the handler can call YIELD or AWAIT.

5.7 CASE STUDY: EVOLUTION OF ENFORCED MODULARITY IN THE INTEL X86

The previous sections introduced the main ideas for enforcing modularity within a computer using a simple processor. This section presents a case study of how the popular Intel x86 processor provides support for enforced modularity and how commonly used operating systems use this support. The next section provides a case study of enforcing modularity at the processor level using virtual machines.

The Intel x86 processor architecture is currently the most widely used architecture for microprocessors of personal computers, laptops, and servers. The x86 architecture started without any support for enforced modularity. As the robustness of software on personal computers, laptops, and servers has become important, the Intel designers have added support for enforcing modularity. The Intel designers didn't get it right on the first try. The evolution of x86 architecture to include enforced modularity provides some good examples of the rapid improvement in technology and challenges of designing complex systems, including market pressure.

5.7.1 The Early Designs: No Support for Enforced Modularity

In 1971 Intel produced its first microprocessor, the 4004, intended for calculators and implemented in 2,250 transistors. The 4004 is a 4-bit processor (i.e., the word size is 4 bits and the processor computes with 4-bit wide operands) and can address as much as 4 kilobytes of program memory and 640 bytes of data memory. The 4004 provides a stack that can store only three stack frames, no interrupts, and no support for enforcing modularity. Hardware support for the missing features was well known in 1971, but there is little need for them in a calculator.

The follow-on processor, the 8080 (1974), was Intel's first microprocessor that was used in a personal computer, namely, the Altair, produced by MITS. Unlike the 4004, the 8080 is a general-purpose microprocessor. The 8080 has 5,000 transistors: an 8-bit processor that can address up to 64 kilobytes of memory (16-bit addresses), without support for enforcing modularity. Bill Gates and Paul Allen of Microsoft fame developed a program that could run BASIC applications on the Altair. Since the Altair couldn't run more than a single, simple program at one time, there was still no need for enforcing modularity.

The 8080 was followed by the 8086 in 1978, with 29,000 transistors. The 8086 is a 16-bit processor but with 20-bit bus addresses, allowing access to 1 megabyte of memory. To make a 20-bit address out of a 16-bit address register, the 8086 has four 16-bit wide segment descriptors. The 8086 combines the value in the segment descriptors and the 16-bit address in an operand as follows: (16-bit segment descriptor $\times$ 16) + 16-bit address, producing a 20-bit value. The segment descriptor can be viewed as a memory address to which the 16-bit address in the operand field of the instruction is added.

The primary purpose of these segments is to extend physical memory, as opposed to providing enforced modularity. Using the four segment descriptors, a program can refer to a total of 256 kilobytes of memory at one time. If a program needs to address other memory, the programmer must save one of the segment descriptors and load it with a new value. Thus, writing programs for the 8086 that use more than 256 kilobytes of memory is inconvenient because the programmer must keep track of segment descriptors and where segment data is located.

Although the 8086 has a different instruction repertoire from the 8080, programs for the 8080 could run on the 8086 unmodified using a translator provided by Intel. As we will see, backwards compatibility is a recurring theme in the evolution of the Intel processor architecture and one key to Intel's success.

The 8088 (1979) was put together hastily in response to IBM's request for a processor for its personal computer. The 8088 is identical to the 8086, except that it has an 8-bit data bus, which made the processor less expensive. Most devices at that time had an 8-bit interface anyway. Microsoft supplied the operating system, named Microsoft Disk Operating System (MS-DOS), for the IBM PC. Microsoft first licensed the operating system from Seattle Computer Products and then acquired it shortly before the release of the PC for $50,000. The IBM PC was a commercial success and started the rise of Intel and Microsoft.

The IBM PC reserved the first 640 kilobytes of the 1-megabyte physical address space for programs and the top 360 kilobytes for input and output. The designers assumed that no programs on a personal computer needed more than 640 kilobytes of memory. To keep the price and complexity down, neither 8088 nor MS-DOS had any support for enforcing modularity.

5.7.2 Enforcing Modularity Using Segmentation

Because the IBM PC was inexpensive, it became widely used; more and more new software was developed for it, and the existing software became richer in features. In addition, users wanted to run several programs at the same time; that is, they wanted to easily switch from one program to another without having to exit a program and start it again later. These developments posed three new design goals for Intel and Microsoft: larger address spaces to run more complex programs, running several programs at once, and enforcing modularity between them. Unfortunately, the last goal conflicts with backwards compatibility because existing programs took full advantage of having direct access to physical memory.

Intel's first attempt to achieve some of these goals was the 80286* (1982), a 16-bit processor that can address up to 16 megabytes of memory (24-bit physical addresses) and has 134,000 transistors. The 80286 has two modes, named *real* and *protected*: in real mode old 8086 programs can run; in protected mode new programs can take advantage of enforced modularity through a change in the interpretation of segment descriptors. In protected mode the segment descriptors don't define the base address of a segment (as in real mode); rather, they select a segment descriptor out of a table of segment descriptors. This application of the design principle *decouple modules with indirection* allows a protected-mode program to refer to 2^{14} segments. Furthermore, the low 2 bits of a segment selector are reserved for permission bits; 2 bits supports four protection levels so that operating systems designers can exploit several protection rings†. In practice, protection rings are of limited usefulness, and operating system designers use only two rings (user and

*In 1982 Intel also introduced the 80186 and 80188, but these 6-mHz processors were used mostly as embedded processors instead of processors for personal computing. One of the major contributions of the 80186 is the reduction in the number of chips required because it included a DMA controller, an interrupt controller, and a timer.

†Michael D. Schroeder and Jerome H. Saltzer. A hardware architecture for implementing protection rings. *Communications of the ACM* 15, 3 (March 1972), pages 157–170.

kernel) to ensure, for example, that user-level programs cannot access kernel-only segments.

Although Intel sold 15 million 80286s, it achieved the three goals only partially. First, 24 bits was small compared to the 32 bits of address space offered by competing processors. Second, although it is easy to go from real to protected mode, there was no easy way (other than exploiting an unrelated feature in the design of the processor) to switch from protected mode back to real. This restriction meant that an operating system could not easily switch between old and new programs. Third, it took years after the introduction of the 80286 to develop an operating system, OS/2, that could take advantage of the segmentation provided by the 80286. OS/2 was jointly created by Microsoft and IBM, for the purpose of taking advantage of all the protected-mode features of the 80286. But when Microsoft grew concerned about the project, it disowned OS/2, gave it to IBM, and focused instead on Windows 2.0. Most buyers didn't wait for IBM and Microsoft to get their operating system acts together and instead simply treated the 80286-based PC as a faster 8086 PC that could use more memory.

Overlapping with the 80286, Intel invested over 100 person-years in the design of a full-featured segment-based processor architecture known as the i432. This processor was a ground-up design to enforce modularity and support object-oriented programming. The segment-based architecture included direct support for capabilities, a protection technique for access control (see Chapter 11 [on-line]). The resulting implementation was so complex that it didn't fit on a single chip and it ran slower than the 80286. It was eventually abandoned, not because it enforced modularity, but because it was overly complex, slow, and lacked backward compatibility with the x86 processor architectures.

5.7.3 Page-Based Virtual Address Spaces

Under market pressure from Motorola, which was selling a 32-bit processor with support for page-based virtual memory, Intel scratched the i432 and followed the 80286 with the 80386 in 1985. The 80386 has 270,000 transistors and addresses the main shortcomings of the 80286, while still being backwards compatible with it. The 80386 is a 32-bit processor, which can refer to up to 4 gigabytes of memory (32-bit addresses) and supports 32-bit external data and address busses. Compared with the two real and protected modes of the 80286, the 80386 provides an additional mode, called virtual real mode, which allows several real-mode programs to run at the same time in virtual environments fully protected from one another. The 80386 design also allows a single segment to grow to 2^{32} bytes, the maximum size of physical memory. Within a segment, the 80386 designers added support for virtual memory using paging with a separate page table for each segment. Operating system designers can choose to use virtual memory with segments, or pages, or both.

This design allows several old programs to run in virtual real mode, each in its own paged address space. This design also allows old programs to have access to more memory than on the 80286, without being forced to use multiple segments. Furthermore, because the 80386 segmentation was backwards compatible with the 80286, 80286 programs and the Windows 2.0 successor (Windows 3.0) could use the larger segments without any modification. For these reasons, the 80386 was a big hit immediately, but it took a while until 32-bit operating systems were available. GNU/Linux, a widely-used open-source UNIX-based system came out in 1991, and Microsoft's Windows 3.1 and IBM's OS/2 2.0 in 1992. All of these systems incorporated the enforced modularity ideas, pioneered in the time-sharing systems of the 1960s and 1970s.

5.7.4 Summary: More Evolution

After 1985, the Intel processor architecture was extended with new instructions, but the core instruction repertoire remained the same. The main changes occurred under the hood. Intel and other companies figured out how to implement processors that provide the complex x86 instruction repertoire—some instructions are 1 byte, and others can be up to 17 bytes long, which is why the literature calls the x86 a Complex Instruction Set Computer, or CISC, while still running as fast as processor architectures designed from scratch with a RISC instruction repertoire. This effort has paid off in terms of performance but has required a large number of transistors to achieve it.

Figure 5.32 shows the growth of Intel processors in terms of transistors over the period 1970–2008*. The *y*-axis is on a logarithmic scale, and the straight line suggests that the growth has been approximately exponential. The Pentium was originally designated the 80586, but Intel redesignated the 80586 the "Pentium" in order to secure a trademark. This growth is a nice example of *d(technology)/dt* in action (see Sidebar 1.6).

The growth in software is also large. Figure 5.33 shows the growth of the Linux kernel in terms of lines of code during the period 1991–2008†. In this graph, the *y*-axis is on a linear scale. As can be seen, the growth in terms of lines of code has been large, and what is shown is just the kernel. A large contributor to this growth is device drivers for new hardware devices.

The success of the x86 illustrates the importance of a specific instance of the *unyielding foundations rule*: provide backwards compatibility. If one must change an interface, keep the old interface around or simulate the old version of the interface using the new version of the interface, so that clients keep working without modifications. It is typically much less work to develop a simulation layer that provides backwards compatibility than to reimplement all of the clients from scratch.

For processors, backwards compatibility is particularly important because legacy software is a big factor in the success of a processor architecture. The reason is that

*Source: Intel Web page (http://www.intel.com/pressroom/kits/quickreffam.htm).

†The sum of number of lines in all C files (source and include) in a kernel release.

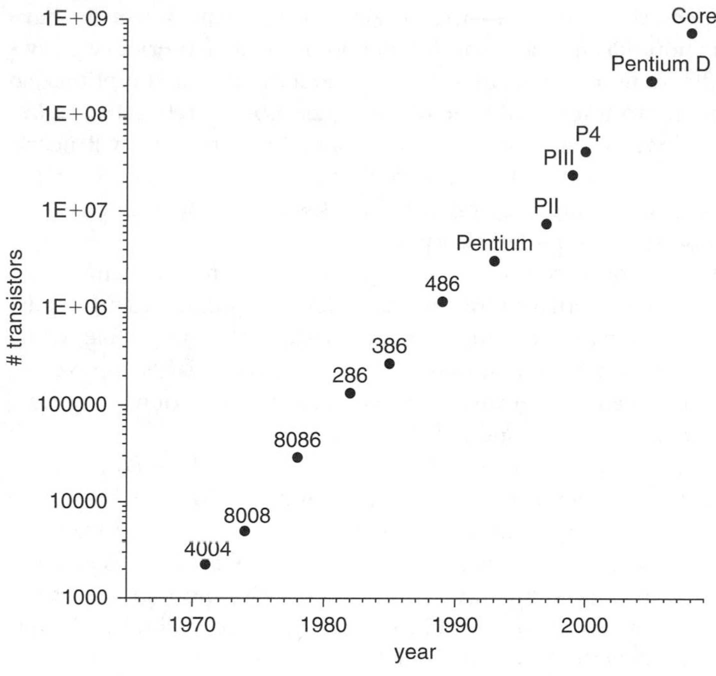

FIGURE 5.32

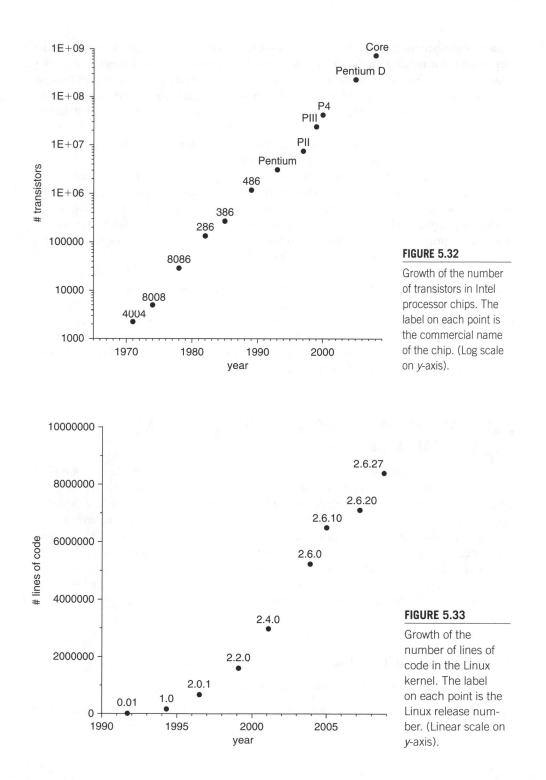

Growth of the number of transistors in Intel processor chips. The label on each point is the commercial name of the chip. (Log scale on *y*-axis).

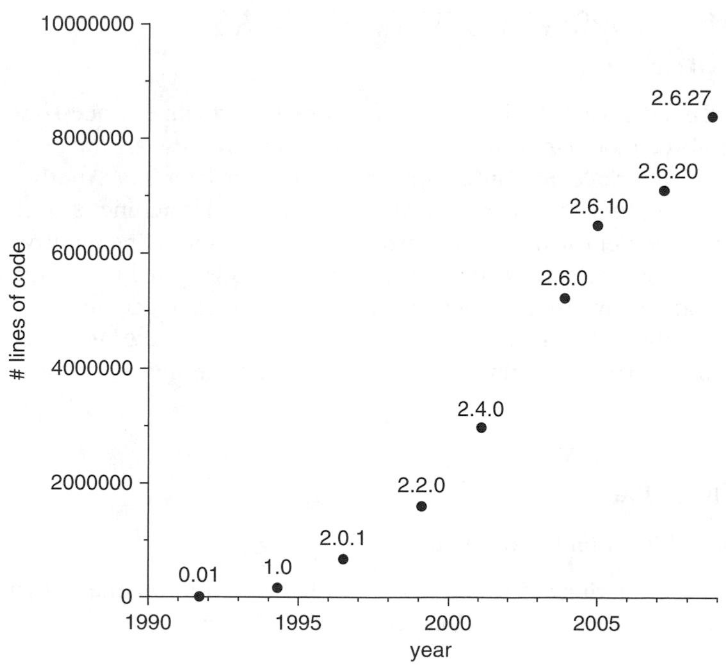

FIGURE 5.33

Growth of the number of lines of code in the Linux kernel. The label on each point is the Linux release number. (Linear scale on *y*-axis).

legacy software is expensive to modify—the original programmers usually have departed (or forgotten about it) and have not documented it well. Experience shows that even minor modifications risk violating some undocumented assumptions, so it is necessary for someone to understand the old program completely, which takes almost as much effort as writing a completely new one. So customers will nearly always choose the architecture that allows them to continue to run legacy software unchanged. Because the x86 architecture provided backwards compatibility, it was able to survive the competition from RISC processors.

Today we see the legacy software scenario being played out in the change from 32-bit virtual addresses to 64-bit virtual addresses. Intel's Itanium architecture is gradually disappearing beneath the waves because it is not backwards compatible, while competitor Advanced Micro Devices (AMD)'s 64-bit Athlon is backwards compatible with the billion or so x86 processors currently in the field. At the time of writing, Intel is abandoning the Itanium architecture and following AMD.

Backwards compatibility can also backfire. For example, Xerox decided it looked more promising to create a PC-clone rather than to commercialize a workstation that Xerox developed in its research lab, which had a mouse, a window manager, and a WYSIWYG editor [Suggestions for Further Reading 1.3.3]. Steve Jobs saw the prototype and developed an equivalent—the Apple Macintosh. The benefits of the Macintosh were so great compared to PCs that customers were willing to buy it. (The later evolution of the Macintosh is a different, less successful story.)

5.8 APPLICATION: ENFORCING MODULARITY USING VIRTUAL MACHINES

This chapter has introduced several high-level abstractions to virtualize processors, memory, and links to enforce modularity. Applications interact with these abstractions through a supervisor-call interface, and interrupt and exception handlers. Another approach uses *virtual machines*. In this approach, a real physical machine is used as much as possible to implement many virtual instances of itself (including its privileged instructions, such as loading and storing to the page-map address register). That is, virtual machines emulate many instances of a machine A using a real machine A. The software that implements the virtual machines is known as a *virtual machine monitor*. This section discusses virtual machines and virtual machine monitors in more detail.

5.8.1 Virtual Machine Uses

A virtual machine is useful in a number of situations:

- To run several *guest* operating systems side by side. For example, on one virtual Intel x86 machine, one can run the GNU/Linux operating system, and on another one can run the Windows/XP operating system. If the virtual machine monitor implements the Intel x86 faithfully (i.e., instructions, state, protection levels, page tables), then one can run GNU/Linux, Windows/XP, and their applications on top of the monitor without modifications.

- To contain errors in a guest operating system. Because the guest runs inside a virtual machine, errors in the guest operating system cannot affect the operating systems software on other virtual machines. This feature is handy for debugging a new operating system or for containing an operating system that is flaky but important for certain applications.
- To simplify development of operating systems. The virtual machine monitor can virtualize the physical hardware to provide a simpler interface, which may simplify the development of an operating system. For example, the virtual machine monitor may turn a multiprocessor computer into a few uniprocessor computers to allow the guest operating system to be written for a uniprocessor, which simplifies coordination.

5.8.2 Implementing Virtual Machines

Virtual machine monitors can be implemented in two ways. First, one can run the monitor directly on hardware in kernel mode, with the guest operating systems in user mode. Second, one can run the monitor as an application in user mode on top of a *host* operating system. The latter may be less complex to implement because the monitor can take advantage of the abstractions provided by the host operating systems, but it is only possible if the host operating system forwards all the events that monitor needs to perform its job. For simplicity, we assume the first approach (see Figure 5.34); the issues are the same in either case.

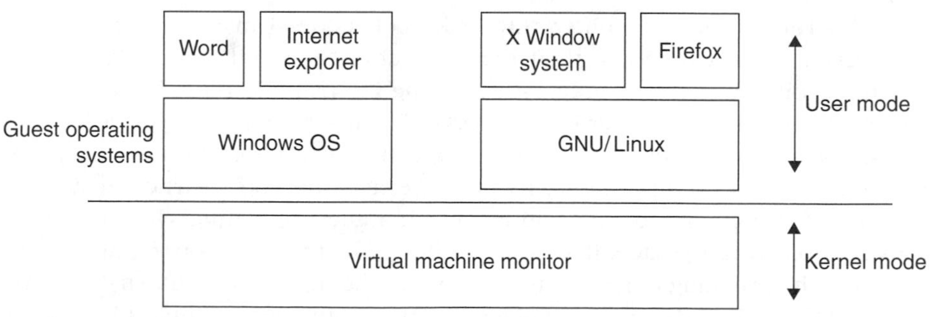

FIGURE 5.34

A virtual machine monitor providing two virtual machines, each running a different guest operating with its own applications.

To implement virtual machine, the virtual machine monitor must provide three primary functions:

1. *Virtualizing the computer*. For example, if a guest operating system stores a new value into the page-map address register, then the monitor must make the guest operating system believe that it can do so, even though the guest is running in user mode.
2. *Dispatch events*. For example, the monitor must forward interrupts, exceptions, and supervisor calls invoked by the applications to the appropriate guest operating systems.
3. *Allocate resources*. For example, the monitor must divide physical memory among the guest operating systems.

Virtualizing the computer is easy if all instructions are *virtualizable*. That is, all the instructions that allow a guest to tell the difference between running on the physical and running on a virtual machine must result in an exception to the monitor so that the monitor can emulate the intended behavior. In addition, the exception must leave enough information for the exception handler to emulate the instruction and restart the guest operating system as if it has executed the instruction.

Consider instructions that load the page-map address register. These instructions behave differently in user mode and kernel mode. In user mode, these instructions result in an illegal instruction exception (because they are privileged), and in kernel mode the hardware performs them. If a guest operating system invokes such an instruction, for example, to switch to another application on the guest, the monitor must emulate that instruction faithfully so that the application will run with the right page-map. Thus, a requirement for such an instruction is that it results in an exception so that the monitor receives control, that it leaves enough information around that the monitor can emulate it, and that the monitor can restart the guest as if it executed the instruction. That is, the guest should not be able to tell that the monitor emulated the instruction.

If an instruction behaves differently in kernel mode than in user mode and doesn't result in an exception, then the instruction is called *non-virtualizable*. For example, on the Intel x86 processor enabling interrupts is done by setting the interrupt-enable bit in a register called EFLAGS. This instruction behaves differently in user mode and in kernel mode. In user mode, the instruction does not have any effect (i.e., the processor just ignores it), but in kernel mode, the instruction sets the bit in the EFLAGS register and allows interrupts. If a guest operating system invokes this instruction in user space, it will do nothing, but the guest operating system assumes that it is running in kernel mode and that the instruction will enable interrupts. This instruction is an example of a non-virtualizable instruction, and handling instructions like these requires a more sophisticated plan, which is beyond the scope of this text. The paper by Adams and Agesen explains it well [Suggestions for Further Reading 5.6.4].

Allocating resources well among the guest operating systems is more challenging than the usual scheduling problem. For example, the monitor must guess which blocks of physical memory are not in use so that it can use those blocks for other guests; the monitor cannot directly inspect the guest's list of free memory blocks. The paper by Waldspurger introduces a nice trick for addressing this problem [Suggestions for Further Reading 5.6.3]. As another example, the monitor must guess when a guest operating system has no work to do; the monitor cannot directly observe that the guest is in its idle loop. The literature on virtual machines contains schemes to address these challenges.

5.8.3 Virtualizing Example

To make concrete what the implementation challenges of these functions are, consider a guest operating system that implements its own page tables, mapping virtual addresses to physical addresses. Let's assume that this guest operating system runs on the processor developed in this text. The goal of the virtual machine monitor is to run several guest operating system by virtualizing the example processor used in this book (see Section 2.1.2), extended with the instructions documented in this chapter.

To allow each guest operating system to address all physical memory, but not other guests' physical memory, the virtual machine monitor must guard the guest's physical addresses. One way to do so is to virtualize addresses recursively. That is, the guest and virtual machine translate application virtual addresses to virtual machine addresses; the monitor translates machine virtual addresses to physical addresses. One challenge in designing the monitor is to maintain this mapping from application virtual to virtual machine to physical addresses. The general plan is for the monitor to emulate loads and stores to the page-map address register, and keep its own translation map per virtual machine, which we will refer to as the machine map.

The monitor can deduce which virtual machine memory a guest is using and the mappings from virtual to machine addresses when the guest invokes a store instruction to the page-map address register. Because this instruction is privileged, the processor will generate an illegal-instruction exception and transfer control to the monitor. The argument to the store instruction contains the machine address of a page map. The monitor can read that memory and see which virtual machine memory the guest is planning to use and what the guest's mappings from virtual to machine are (including the permissions).

For each machine page (including the one that holds the guest page map), the monitor can allocate a physical page and record in the machine map the translation from virtual to machine to physical address, together with its permissions. Equipped with this information, the monitor can construct a new page map that maps the guest's virtual addresses to physical addresses and install that new map in the real page-map address register (which will succeed since the monitor is running in kernel mode). Thus, although there are two layers of page maps (virtual to machine and machine to physical), the translation performed by the physical processor is only one level: it translates application virtual addresses directly to physical addresses, using the new page map set up by the monitor. To support this double translation plan efficiently, Intel and AMD have added additional hardware support.

As the final step, the monitor can resume the guest operating system at the instruction after the store to the page-map addresses register, providing the illusion to the guest that it updated the page-map address register directly. Now the guest and the applications can continue execution.

If the guest changes its page map (e.g., it switches to one of its other applications), the monitor will learn about this event because the store to the page-map address register will result in an exception (because the instruction is privileged) and invoke an exception handler in the monitor. The exception handler emulates this instruction by updating the physical page-map address register as above and resumes the guest.

If the monitor wants to switch to another guest OS, it can just switch the page-map address register to the new guest's page map, like a switch between applications.

If the application addresses a page that is not part of its address space, the hardware will generate a missing-page exception, which will invoke an exception handler in the monitor. Then, the exception handler in the monitor can invoke the exception handler of the appropriate guest. The guest exception handler now believes it received the missing-page exception directly from the processor, and it can take appropriate action.

A reader interested in learning more about this topic might find the readings on virtual machines useful [Suggestions for Further Reading 5.6].

EXERCISES

5.1 Chapter 1 discussed four general methods for coping with complexity: modularity, abstraction, hierarchy, and layering.

5.1a Which of those four methods does virtual memory use as its primary organizing scheme?

5.1b Which does a microkernel use? Explain.

1996–1–1c,e

5.2 Alyssa is trying to organize her notes on virtual memory systems, and it occurred to her that virtual memory systems can usefully be analyzed as naming systems. She went through Chapter 3 and made a list of some technical terms about naming systems; that list is on the right, below. She then listed some mechanisms found in virtual memory systems on the left. But she isn't sure which naming concept goes with which mechanism. Help Alyssa out by telling her which letters on the right apply to each numbered mechanism on the left.

1. page map	**a.** Search path
2. virtual address	**b.** Naming network
3. physical address	**c.** Context reference
4. a TLB entry	**d.** Object
5. the page-map address register	**e.** Name
	f. Context
	g. None of the above

1994–2–4

5.3 The Modest Mini Corporation's best-selling computer allows at most two users to run at a time. Its only addressing architecture feature is a single page map, which creates a simple linear address space for the processor. The time-sharing system for this computer loads the page map with a set of memory block addresses before running a user; to switch to the other user, it reloads the entire page map with a new set of memory block addresses. Normally, the set of memory blocks belonging to one user has no overlap with the set of memory blocks belonging to the other user, except that memory block 19 is always assigned as page 3 in every user's address space, providing a "communication region".

5.3a Protection and privacy are obviously a problem with a completely public communication area, but is there any *other* difficulty in using the communication region for any of the following types of data?

A. The character string name of the payroll file
B. An integer representing the number of names in the current payroll file
C. The virtual memory address, within the communication region, of another data item
D. The virtual memory address of a program that lies outside the communication region
E. A small program that is designed to remain within the communication region and execute there

1980–2–4a

5.3b Ben Bitdiddle has decided that programming with page 3 always preassigned is a nuisance. He has therefore proposed that a call to the system be added that reassigns the communication region to a different page of the calling user's address space, while not affecting the other users. What effect would this proposal have on your answers to 5.3a?

1980–2–4b

5.4 One advantage of a microkernel over a monolithic kernel is that it reduces the load on the translation look-aside buffer, and thereby increases its hit rate and its consequent effect on performance. True or False? Explain.

1994-1-3a

5.5 Louis writes a multithreaded program, which produces an incorrect answer some of the time, but always completes. He suspects a race condition. Which of the following are strategies that can reduce, and with luck eliminate, race conditions in Louis's program?

A. Separate a multithreaded program into multiple single-threaded programs, run each thread in its own address space, and share data between them via a communication link that uses SEND and RECEIVE.

B. Apply the one-writer rule.

C. Ensure that for each shared variable v, it is protected by some lock l_v.

D. Ensure that all locks are acquired in the same order.

2006-1-4

5.6 Which of the following statements about operating system kernels are true?

A. Preemptive scheduling allows the kernel's thread manager to run applications in a way that helps avoid fate sharing.

B. The kernel serves as a trusted intermediary between programs running on the same computer.

C. In an operating system that provides virtual memory, the kernel must be invoked to resolve every memory reference.

D. When a kernel switches a processor from one application to another, the target application sets the page-map address register appropriately after it is running in user space.

2007-1-4

5.7 Two threads, A and B, execute a procedure named GLORP but always at different times (that is, only one of the threads calls the procedure at a given time). GLORP contains the following code:

```
procedure GLORP ()
    ACQUIRE (lock_a)
        ACQUIRE (lock_b)
        ...
        RELEASE (lock_b)
    RELEASE (lock_a)
    ...
    ACQUIRE (lock_b)
        ACQUIRE (lock_a)
        ...
        RELEASE (lock_a)
    RELEASE (lock_b)
```

5.7a Assuming that no other code in other procedures ever acquires more than one lock at a time, can there be a deadlock? (If yes, give an example; if not, argue why not.)

1995–1–3a

5.7b Now, assuming that the two threads can be in the code fragment above at the same time, can the program deadlock? (If yes, give an example; if not, argue why not.)

1995–1–3b

5.8 Consider three threads, concurrently executing the three programs shown here. The variables x, y, and z are integers with initial value 0.

Thread 1:	Thread 2:	Thread 3:
for *i* **from** 1 **to** 100 **do**	**for** *i* **from** 1 **to** 100 **do**	**for** *i* **from** 1 **to** 100 **do**
ACQUIRE (*A*)	ACQUIRE (*B*)	ACQUIRE (*A*)
ACQUIRE (*B*)	ACQUIRE (*C*)	ACQUIRE (*C*)
$x \leftarrow x + 1$	$y \leftarrow z + 1$	$z \leftarrow x + 1$
RELEASE (*B*)	RELEASE (*C*)	RELEASE (*C*)
RELEASE (*A*)	RELEASE (*B*)	RELEASE (*A*)

5.8a Can executing these three threads concurrently produce a deadlock? (If yes, give an example; if not, argue why not.)

1993–1–5a

5.8b Does your answer change if the order of the release operations in each thread is reversed? (If they can deadlock, give an example; if not, argue why not.)

1993–1–5b

Additional exercises relating to Chapter 5 can be found in the problem sets beginning on page 425.

CHAPTER

Performance

6

CHAPTER CONTENTS

Principles of Computer System Design: An Introduction

DOI: 10.1016/B978-0-12-374957-4.00014-1

OVERVIEW

The specification of a computer system typically includes explicit (or implicit) performance goals. For example, the specification may indicate how many concurrent users the system should be able to support. Typically, the simplest design fails to meet these goals because the design has a *bottleneck*, a stage in the computer system that takes longer to perform its task than any of the other stages. To overcome bottlenecks, the system designer faces the task of creating a design that performs well, yet is simple and modular.

This chapter describes techniques to avoid or hide performance bottlenecks. Section 6.1 presents ways to identify bottlenecks and the general approaches to handle them, including exploiting workload properties, concurrent execution of operations, speculation, and batching. Section 6.2 examines specific versions of the general techniques to attack the common problem of implementing multilevel memory systems efficiently. Section 6.3 presents scheduling algorithms for services to choose which request to process first, if there are several waiting for service.

6.1 DESIGNING FOR PERFORMANCE

Performance bottlenecks show up in computer systems for two reasons. First, limits imposed by physics, technology, or economics restrict the rate of improvement in some dimensions of technology, while other dimensions improve rapidly. An obvious class of limits are the physical ones. The speed of light limits how fast signals travel from one end of a chip to the other, how many memory elements can be within a given latency from the processor, and how fast a network message can travel in the Internet. Many other physical limits appear in computer systems, such as power and heat dissipation.

These limits force a designer to make trade-offs. For example, by shrinking a chip, a designer can make the chip faster, but it also reduces the area from which heat can be dissipated. Worse, the power dissipation increases as the designer speeds up the chip. A related trade-off is between the speed of a laptop and its power consumption. A designer wants to minimize a laptop's power consumption so that the battery lasts longer, yet customers want laptops with fast processors and large, bright screens.

Physical limits are only a subset of the limits a designer faces; there are also algorithmic, reliability, and economic limits. More limits mean more trade-offs and a higher risk of bottlenecks.

The second reason bottlenecks surface in computer systems is that several clients may share a device. If a device is busy serving one client, other clients must wait until the device becomes available. This property forces the system designer to answer questions such as which client should receive the device first. Should the device first perform the request that requires little work, perhaps at the cost of delaying the request that requires a lot of work? The designer would like to devise a scheduling plan that doesn't starve some clients in favor of others, provides low turnaround time for each individual client request, and has little overhead so that it can serve many clients. As we will see, it is impossible to maximize all of these goals simultaneously, and thus a designer must make trade-offs. Trade-offs may favor one class of requests over another and may result in bottlenecks for the unfavored classes of requests.

Designing for performance creates two major challenges in computer systems. First, one must consider the benefits of optimization in the context of technology improvements. Some bottlenecks are intrinsic ones; they require careful thinking to ensure that the system runs faster than the performance of the slowest stage. Some bottlenecks are technology dependent; time may eliminate these, as technology improves. Unfortunately, it is sometimes difficult to decide whether or not a bottleneck is intrinsic. Not uncommonly, a performance optimization for the next product release is irrelevant by the time the product ships because technology improvements have removed the bottleneck completely. This phenomenon is so common in computer design that it has led to formulation of the design hint: *when in doubt use brute force*. Sidebar 6.1 discusses this hint.

Sidebar 6.1 Design Hint: When in Doubt use Brute Force This chapter describes a few design hints that help a designer resolve trade-offs in the face of limits. These design hints are hints because they often guide the designer in the right direction, but sometimes they don't. In this book we cover only a few, but the interested reader should digest *Hints for computer system design* by B. Lampson, which presents many more practical guidelines in the form of hints [Suggestions for Further Reading 1.5.4].

The design hint "when in doubt use brute force" is a direct corollary of the *d(technology)/dt* curve (see Section 1.4). Given computing technology's historical rate of improvement, it is typically wiser to choose simple algorithms that are well understood rather than complex, badly characterized algorithms. By the time the complex algorithm is fully understood, implemented, and debugged, new hardware might be able to execute the simple algorithm fast enough. Thompson and Ritchie used a fixed-size table of processes in the UNIX system and searched the table linearly because a table was simple to implement and the number of processes was small. With Joe Condon, Thompson also built the Belle chess machine that relied mostly on special-purpose hardware to search many positions per second rather than on sophisticated algorithms. Belle won the world computer chess championships several times in the late 1970s and early 1980s and achieved an ELO rating of 2250. (ELO is a numerical rating systems used by the World Chess Federation (FIDI) to rank chess players; a rating of 2250 makes one a strong competitive player.) Later, as technology marched on, programs that performed brute-force searching algorithms on an off-the-shelf PC conquered the world computer chess championships. As of August 2005, the Hydra supercomputer (64 PCs, each with a chess coprocessor) is estimated by its creators to have an ELO rating of 3200, which is better than the best human player.

A second challenge in designing for performance is maintaining the simplicity of the design. For example, if the design uses different devices with approximately the same high-level function but radically different performance, a challenge is to abstract devices such that they can be used through a simple uniform interface. In this chapter, we see how a clever implementation of the READ and WRITE interface for memory can transparently extend the effective size of RAM to the size of a magnetic disk.

6.1.1 Performance Metrics

To understand bottlenecks more fully, recall that computer systems are organized in modules to achieve the benefits of modularity and that to process a request, the request may be handed from one module to another. For example, a camera may generate a continuous stream of requests containing video frames and send them to a service that digitizes each frame. The digitizing service in turn may send its output to a file service that stores the frames on a magnetic disk.

By describing this application in a client/service style, we can obtain some insights about important performance metrics. It is immediately clear that in a computer system such as this one, four metrics are of importance: the capacity of the service, its utilization, the time clients must wait for request to complete, and throughput, the rate at which services can handle requests. We will discuss each metric in turn.

6.1.1.1 Capacity, Utilization, Overhead, and Useful Work

Every service has some *capacity*, a consistent measure of a service's size or amount of resources. *Utilization* is the percentage of capacity of a resource that is used for some given workload of requests. A simple measure of processor capacity is cycles. For example, the processor might be utilized 10% for the duration of some workload, which means that 90% of its processor cycles are unused. For a magnetic disk, the capacity is usually measured in sectors. If a disk is utilized 80%, then 80% of its sectors are used to store data.

In a layered system, each layer may have a different view of the capacity and utilization of the underlying resources. For example, a processor may be 95% utilized but delivering only 70% of its cycles to the application because the operating system uses 25%. Each layer considers what the layers below it do to be *overhead* in time and space, and what the layers above it do to be *useful work*. In the processor example, from the application point of view, the 25% of cycles used by the operating system is overhead and the 70% is useful work. In the disk example, if 10% of the disk is used for storing file system data structures, then from the application point of view that 10% used by the file system is overhead and only 90% is useful capacity.

6.1.1.2 Latency

Latency is the delay between a change at the input to a system and the corresponding change at its output. From the client/service perspective, the latency of a request is the time from issuing the request until the time the response is received from the service.

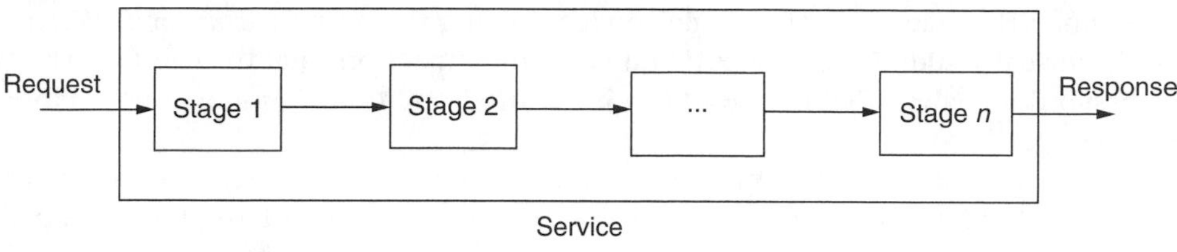

FIGURE 6.1

A simple service composed of several stages.

This latency has several components: the latency of sending a message to the service, the latency of processing the request, and the latency of sending a response back.

If a task, such as asking a service to perform a request, is a sequence of subtasks, we can think of the complete task as traversing stages of a pipeline, where each stage of the pipeline performs a subtask (see Figure 6.1). In our example, the first stage in the pipeline is sending the request, the second stage is the service digitizing the frame, the third stage is the file service storing the frame, and the final stage is sending a response back to the client.

With this pipeline model in mind, it is easy to see that latency of a pipeline with stages A and B is greater than or equal to the sum of the latencies for each stage in the pipeline:

$$latency_{A+B} \geq latency_A + latency_B$$

It is possibly greater because passing a request from one stage to another might add some latency. For example, if the stages correspond to different services, perhaps running on different computers connected by a network, then the overhead of passing requests from one stage to another may add enough latency that it cannot be ignored.

If the stages are of a single service, that additional latency is typically small (e.g., the overhead of invoking a procedure) and can usually be ignored for first-order analysis of performance. Thus, in this case, to predict the latency of a service that isn't running yet but is expected to perform two functions, A and B, with known latencies, a designer can approximate the joint latency of A and B by adding the latency of A and the latency of B.

6.1.1.3 Throughput

Throughput is a measure of the rate of useful work done by a service for some given workload of requests. In the camera example, the throughput we might care about is how many frames per second the system can process because it may determine what quality camera we want to buy.

The throughput of a system with pipelined stages is less than or equal to the minimum of the throughput for each stage:

$$throughput_{A+B} \leq minimum(throughput_A,\ throughput_B)$$

Again, if the stages are of a single service, passing the request from one stage to another usually adds little overhead and has little impact on total throughput. Thus, for first-order analysis that overhead can be ignored, and the relation is usually close to equality.

Consider a computer system with two stages: one that is able to process data at a rate of 1,000 kilobytes per second and a second one at a rate of 100 kilobytes per second. If the fast stage generates one byte of output for each byte of input, the overall throughput must be less than or equal to 100 kilobytes per second. If there is negligible overhead in passing requests between the two stages, then the throughput of the system is equal to the throughput of the bottleneck stage, 100 kilobytes per second. In this case, the utilization of stage 1 is 10% and that of stage 2 is 100%.

When a stage processes requests serially, the throughput and the latency of a stage are directly related. The average number of requests a stage handles is inversely proportional to the average time to process a single request:

$$throughput = \frac{1}{latency}$$

If all stages process requests serially, the average throughput of the complete pipeline is inversely proportional to the average time a request spends in the pipeline. In these pipelines, reducing latency improves throughput, and the other way around.

When a stage processes requests concurrently, as we will see later in this chapter, there is *no* direct relationship between latency and throughput. For stages that process requests concurrently, an increase in throughput may *not* lead to a decrease in latency. A useful analogy is pipes through which water flows with a constant velocity. One can have several parallel pipes (or one fatter pipe), which improves throughput but doesn't change latency.

6.1.2 A Systems Approach to Designing for Performance

To gauge how much improvement we can hope for in reducing a bottleneck, we must identify and determine the performance of the slowest and the next-slowest bottleneck. To improve the throughput of a system in which all stages have equal throughput requires improving *all* stages. On the other hand, improving the stage that has a throughput that is 10 times lower than any other stage's throughput may result in a factor of 10 improvement in the throughput of the whole system. We might determine these bottlenecks by measurements or by using simple analytical calculations based on the performance characteristics of each bottleneck. In principle, the performance of any issue in a computer system can be explained, but sometimes it may require substantial digging to find the explanation; see, for example, the study by Perl and Sites on Windows NT's performance [Suggestions for Further Reading 6.4.1].

One should approach performance optimization from a systems point of view. This observation may sound trivial, but many person-years of work have disappeared in optimizing individual stages that resulted in small overall performance improvements. The reason that engineers are tempted to fine-tune a single stage is that optimizations result in some measurable benefits. An individual engineer can design an optimization (e.g., replacing a slow algorithm with a faster algorithm, removing unnecessary expensive operations, reorganizing the code to have a fast path, etc.), implement it, and measure it, and can usually observe some performance improvement in that stage. This improvement stimulates the design of another optimization, which results in new benefits, and so on. Once one gets into this cycle, it is difficult to keep the *law of diminishing returns* in mind and realize that further improvements may result in little benefit to the system as a whole.

Since optimizing individual stages typically runs into the law of diminishing returns, an approach that focuses on overall performance is preferred. The iterative approach articulated in Section 1.5.2 achieves this goal because at each iteration the designer must consider whether or not the next iteration is worth performing. If the next iteration identifies a bottleneck that, if removed, shows diminished returns, the designer can stop. If the final performance is good enough, the designer's job is done. If the final performance doesn't meet the target, the designer may have to rethink the whole design or revisit the design specification.

The iterative approach for designing for performance has the following steps:

1. Measure the system to find out whether or not a performance enhancement is needed. If performance is a problem, identify which aspect of performance (throughput or latency) is the problem. For multistage pipelines in which stages process requests concurrently, there is no direct relationship between latency and throughput, so improving latency and improving throughput might require different techniques.

2. Measure again, this time to identify the performance bottleneck. The bottleneck may not be in the place the designer expected and may shift from one design iteration to another.

3. Predict the impact of the proposed performance enhancement with a simple back-of-the-envelope model. (We introduce a few simple models in this chapter.) This prediction includes determining where the next bottleneck will be. A quick way to determine the next bottleneck is to unrealistically assume that the planned performance enhancement will remove the current bottleneck and result in a stage with zero latency and infinite throughput. Under this assumption, determine the next bottleneck and calculate its performance. This calculation will result in one of two conclusions:

   a. Removing the current bottleneck doesn't improve system performance significantly. In this case, stop iterating, and reconsider the whole design or revisit the requirements. Perhaps the designer can adjust the interfaces between stages with the goal of tolerating costly operations. We will discuss several approaches in the next sections.

   b. Removing the current bottleneck is likely to improve the system performance. In this case, focus attention on the bottleneck stage. Consider brute-force methods of relieving the bottleneck stage (e.g., add more memory). Taking advantage of the $\frac{d(technology)}{dt}$ curve may be less expensive than being clever. If brute-force methods won't relieve the bottleneck, be smart. For example, try to exploit properties of the workload or find better algorithms.

4. Measure the new implementation to verify that the change has the predicted impact. If not, revisit steps 1–3 and determine what went wrong.

5. Iterate. Repeat steps 1–5 until the performance meets the required level.

The rest of this chapter introduces various systems approaches to reducing latency and increasing throughput, as well as simple performance models to predict the resulting performance.

6.1.3 Reducing Latency by Exploiting Workload Properties

Reducing latency is difficult because the designer often runs into physical, algorithmic, and economic limits. For example, sending a message from a client on the east coast of the United States to a service on the west coast is dominated by the speed of light. Looking up an item in a hash table cannot go faster than the best algorithm for implementing hash tables. Building a very large memory that has uniform low latency is economically infeasible.

Once a designer has run into such limits, the common approach is to reduce the latency of some requests, perhaps even at the cost of increasing the latency for other requests. A designer may observe that certain requests are more common than other requests, and use that observation to improve the performance of the frequent operations by splitting the staged pipeline into a *fast path* for the frequent requests and a *slow path* for other requests (see Figure 6.2). For example, a service might remember the results of frequently asked requests so that when it receives a repeat of a recently handled request, it can return the remembered result immediately without having to recompute it. In practice, exploiting non-uniformity in applications

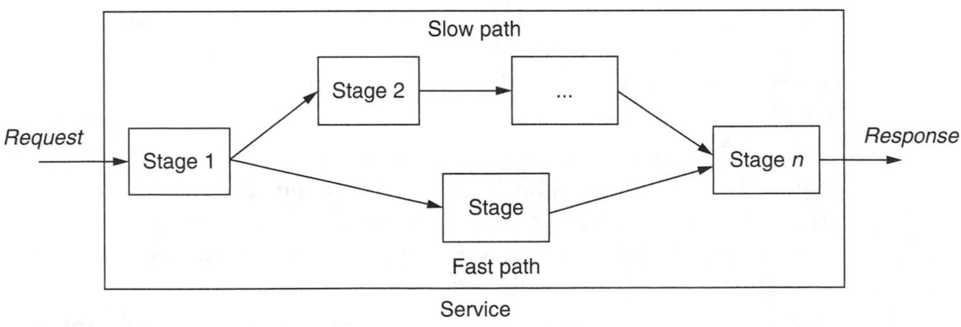

FIGURE 6.2

A simple service with a slow and fast path.

> **Sidebar 6.2 Design Hint: Optimize for the Common Case** A cache (see Section 2.1.1.3) is the most common example of optimizing for the most frequent cases. We saw caches in the case study of the Domain Name System (in Section 4.4). As another example, consider a Web browser. Most Web browsers maintain a cache of recently accessed Web pages. This cache is indexed by the name of the Web page (e.g., http://www.Scholarly.edu) and returns the page for that name. If the user asks to view the same page again, then the cache can return the cached copy of the page immediately (a fast path); only the first access requires a trip to the service (a slow path). In addition to improving the user's interactive experience, the cache helps reduce the load on services and the load on the network. Because caches are so effective, many applications use several of them. For example, in addition to caching Web pages, many Web browsers have a cache to store the results of looking up names, such as "www.Scholarly.edu", so that the next request to "www.Scholarly.edu" doesn't require a DNS lookup.
>
> The design of multilevel memory in Section 6.2 is another example of how well a designer can exploit non-uniformity in a workload. Because applications have locality of reference, one can build large and fast memory systems out of a combination of a small but fast memory and a large but slow memory.

works so well that it has led to the design hint *optimize for the common case* (see Sidebar 6.2).

To evaluate the performance of systems with a fast and slow path, designers typically compute the average latency. If we know the latency of the fast and slow paths, and the frequency with which the system will take the fast path, then the average latency is:

$$AverageLatency = Frequency_{fast} \times Latency_{fast} + Frequency_{slow} \times Latency_{slow} \quad (6.1)$$

Whether introducing a fast path is worth the effort is dependent on the relative difference in latency between the fast and slow path, and the frequency with which the system can use the fast path, which is dependent on the workload. In addition, one might be able to change the design so that the fast path becomes faster at the cost of a slower slow path. If the frequency of taking the fast path is low, then introducing a fast path (and perhaps optimizing it at the cost of the slow path) is likely not worth the complexity. In practice, as we will see in Section 6.2, many workloads don't have a uniform distribution of requests, and introducing a fast path works well.

6.1.4 Reducing Latency using Concurrency

Another way to reduce latency that may require some intellectual effort but that can be effective is to parallelize a stage. We take the processing that a stage must do for a single request and divide that processing up into subtasks that can be performed concurrently. Then, whenever several processors are available they can be assigned to run those subtasks in parallel. The method can be applied either within a multiprocessor system or (if the subtasks aren't too entangled) with completely separate computers.

If the processing parallelizes perfectly (i.e., each subtask can run without any coordination with other subtasks and each subtask requires the same amount of work), then this plan can, in principle, speed up the processing by a factor n, where n is the number of subtasks executing in parallel. In practice, the speedup is usually less than n because there is overhead in parallelizing a computation—the subtasks need to communicate with each other, for example, to exchange intermediate results; because the subtasks do not require an equal amount of work; because the computation cannot be executed completely in parallel, so some fraction of the computation must be executed sequentially; or because the subtasks interfere with each other (e.g., they contend for a shared resource such as a lock, a shared memory, or a shared communication network).

Consider the processing that a search engine needs to perform in order to respond to a user search query. An early version of Google's search engine—described in more detail in Suggestions for Further Reading 3.2.4—parallelized this processing as follows. The search engine splits the index of the Web up in n pieces, each piece stored on a separate machine. When a front end receives a user query, it sends a copy of the query to each of the n machines. Each machine runs the query against its part of the index and sends the results back to the front end. The front end accumulates the results from the n machines, chooses a good order in which to display them, generates a Web page, and sends it to the user. This plan can give good speedup if the index is large and each of the n machines must perform a substantial, similar amount of computation. It is unlikely to achieve a full speedup of a factor n because there is parallelization overhead (to send the query to the n machines, receive n partial results, and merge them); because the amount of work is not balanced perfectly across the n machines and the front end must wait until the slowest responds; and because the work done by the front end in farming out the query and merging hasn't been parallelized.

Although parallelizing can improve performance, several challenges must be overcome. First, many applications are difficult to parallelize. Applications such as search have exploitable parallelism, but other computations don't split easily into n mostly independent pieces. Second, developing parallel applications is difficult because the programmer must manage the concurrency and coordinate the activities of the different subtasks. As we saw in Chapter 5, it is easy to get this wrong and introduce race conditions and deadlocks. Systems have been developed to make development of parallel applications easier, but they are often limited to a particular domain. The paper by Dean and Ghemawat [Suggestions for Further Reading 6.4.3] provides an example of how the programming and management effort can be minimized for certain stylized applications running in parallel on hundreds of machines. In general, however, programmers must often struggle with threads and locks, or explicit message passing, to obtain concurrency.

Because of these two challenges in parallelizing applications, designers traditionally have preferred to rely on continuous technology improvements to reduce application latency. However, physical and engineering limitations (primarily the problem of heat dissipation) are now leading processor manufacturers away from making processors faster and toward placing several (and soon, probably, several hundred or even several thousand, as some are predicting [Suggestions for Further Reading 1.6.4]) processors on a single chip. This development means that improving performance by using concurrency will inevitably increase in importance.

6.1.5 Improving Throughput: Concurrency

If the designer cannot reduce the latency of a request because of limits, an alternative approach is to *hide* the latency of a request by overlapping it with other requests. This approach doesn't improve the latency of an individual request, but it can improve system throughput. Because hiding latency is often much easier to achieve than improving latency, it has led to the hint: ***instead of reducing latency, hide it*** (see Sidebar 6.3). This section discusses how one can introduce concurrency in a multistage pipeline to increase throughput.

To overlap requests, we give each stage in the pipeline its own thread of computation so that it can compute concurrently, operating much like an assembly line (see Figure 6.3). If a stage has completed its task and has handed off the request to the next stage, then the stage can start processing the second request while the next stage processes the first request. In this fashion, the pipeline can work on several requests concurrently.

An implementation of this approach has two challenges. First, some stages of the pipeline may operate more slowly than other stage. As a result, one stage might not be able to hand off the request to the next stage because that next stage is still working on a previous request. As a result, a queue of requests may build up, while other stages might be idle. To ensure that a queue between two stages doesn't grow without bound, the stages are often coupled using a bounded buffer. We will discuss queuing in more detail in Section 6.1.6.

The second challenge is that several requests must be available. One natural source of multiple requests is if the system has several clients, each generating a request. A single client can also be a source of multiple requests if the client operates asynchronously. When an asynchronous client issues a request, rather than waiting for the response, it continues computing, perhaps issuing more requests. The main challenge

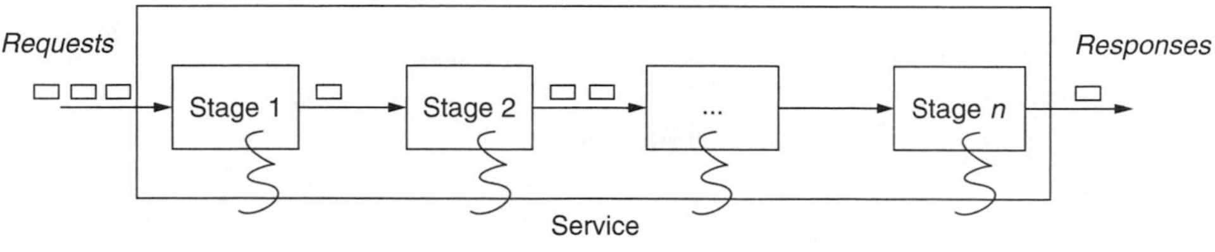

FIGURE 6.3

A simple service composed of several stages, with each stage operating concurrently using threads.

> **Sidebar 6.3 Design Hint: Instead of Reducing Latency, Hide it** Latency is often not under the control of the designer but rather is imposed on the designer by physical properties such as the speed of light. Consider sending a message from the east coast of the United States to the west coast at the speed of light. This takes about 20 milliseconds (see Section 7.1 [online]); in the same time, a processor can execute millions of instructions. Worse, each new generation of processors gets faster every year, but the speed of light doesn't improve. As David Clark, a network researcher, put it succinctly: "One cannot bribe God." The speed of light shows up as an intrinsic barrier in many places of computer design, even when the distances are short. For example, dies are so large that for a signal to travel from one end of a chip to another is a bottleneck that limits the clock speed of a chip.
>
> When a designer is faced with such intrinsic limits, the only option is to design systems that hide latency and try to exploit performance dimensions that do follow d(technology)/dt. For example, transmission rates for data networks have improved dramatically, and so if a designer can organize the system such that communication can be overlapped with useful computation and many network requests can be batched into a large request, then the large request can be transferred efficiently. Many Web browsers use this strategy: while a large transfer runs in the background, users can continue browsing Web pages, hiding the latency of the transfer.

in issuing multiple requests asynchronously is that the client must then match the responses with the outstanding requests.

Once the system is organized to have many requests in flight concurrently, a designer may be able to improve throughput further by using *interleaving*. The idea is to make n instances of the bottleneck stage and run those n instances concurrently (see Figure 6.4). Stage 1 feeds the first request to instance 1, the second request to instance 2, and so on. If the throughput of a single instance is t, then the throughput using interleaving is $n \times t$, assuming enough requests are available to run all instances

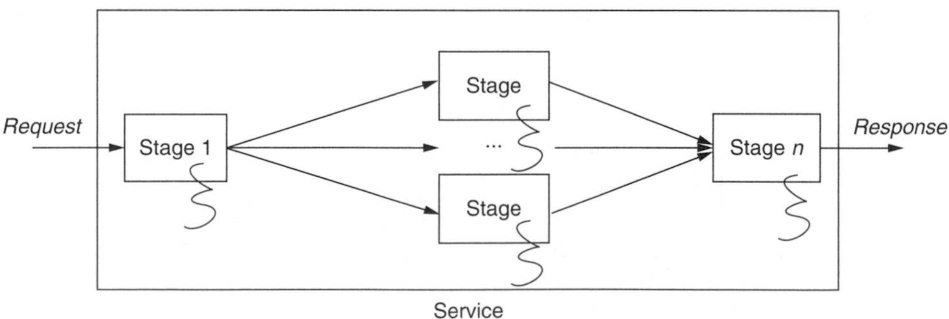

FIGURE 6.4

Interleaving requests.

concurrently at full speed and the requests don't interfere with each other. The cost of interleaving is additional copies of the bottleneck stage.

RAID (see Section 2.1.1.4) interleaves several disks to achieve a high aggregate disk throughput. RAID 0 stripes the data across the disks: it stores block 0 on disk 0, block 1 on disk 1, and so on. If requests arrive for blocks on different disks, the RAID controller can serve those requests concurrently, improving throughput. In a similar style one can interleave memory chips to improve throughput. If the current instruction is stored in memory chip 0 and the next one is in memory chip 1, the processor can retrieve them concurrently. The cost of this design is the additional disks and memory chips, but often systems already have several memory chips or disks, in which case the added cost of interleaving can be small in comparison with the performance benefit.

6.1.6 Queuing and Overload

If a stage in Figure 6.3 operates at its capacity (e.g., all physical processors are running threads), then a new request must wait until the stage becomes available; a queue of requests builds up waiting for the busy stage, while other stages may run idle. For example, the thread manager of Section 5.5 maintains a table of threads, which records whether a thread is runnable; a runnable thread must wait until a processor is available to run it. The stage that runs with an input queue while other stages are running idle is a bottleneck.

Using queuing theory* we can estimate the time that a request spends waiting in a queue for its turn to be processed (e.g., the time a thread spends in the ready queue). In queuing theory, the time that it takes to process a request (e.g., the time from when a thread starts running on the processor until it yields) is called the *service time*. The simplest queuing theory model assumes that requests (e.g., a thread entering the ready queue) arrive according to a random, memoryless process and have independent, exponentially distributed service times. In that case, a well-known queuing theory result tells us that the average queuing delay, measured in units of the average service time and including the service time of this request, will be $1/(1-\rho)$, where ρ is the service utilization. Thus, as the utilization approaches 1, the queuing delay will grow without bound.

This same phenomenon applies to the delays for threads waiting for a processor and to the delays that customers experience in supermarket checkout lines. Any time the demand for a service comes from many statistically independent sources, there will be fluctuations in the arrival of load and thus in the length of the queue at the bottleneck stage and the time spent waiting for service. The rate of arrival of requests for service is known as the *offered load*. Whenever the offered load is greater than the capacity of a service for some duration, the service is said to be *overloaded* for that time period.

*The textbook by Jain is an excellent source to learn about queuing theory and how to reason about performance in computer systems [Suggestions for Further Reading 1.1.2].

In some constrained cases, where the designer can plan the system so that the capacity just matches the offered load of requests, it is possible to calculate the degree of concurrency necessary to achieve high throughput and the maximum length of the queue needed between stages. For example, suppose we have a processor that performs one instruction per nanosecond using a memory that takes 10 nanoseconds to respond. To avoid having the processor wait for the memory, it must make a memory request 10 instructions in advance of the instruction that needs it. If every instruction makes a request of memory, then by the time the memory responds, the processor will have issued 9 more. To avoid being a bottleneck, the memory therefore must be prepared to serve 10 requests concurrently.

If half of the instructions make a request of memory, then on average there will be five outstanding requests. Thus, a memory that can serve five requests concurrently would have enough capacity to keep up. To calculate the maximum length of the queue needed for this case depends on the application's pattern of memory references. For example, if every second instruction makes a memory request, a fixed-size queue of size five is sufficient to ensure that the queue never overflows. If the processor performs five instructions that make memory references followed by five that don't, then a fixed-size queue of size five will work, but the queue length will vary in length and the throughput will be different. If the requests arrive randomly, the queue can grow, in principle, without limit. If we were to use a memory that can handle 10 requests concurrently for this random pattern of memory references, then the memory would be utilized at 50% of capacity, and the average queue length would be $(1/(1-0.5) = 2$. With this configuration, the processor observes latencies for some memory requests of 20 or more instruction cycles, and it is running much slower than the designer expected. This example illustrates that a designer must understand non-uniform patterns in the references to memory and exploit them to achieve good performance.

In many computer systems, the designer cannot plan the offered load that precisely, and thus stages will experience periods of overload. For example, an application may have several threads that become runnable all at the same time and there may not be enough processors available to run them. In such cases, at least occasional overload is inevitable. The significance of overload depends critically on how long it lasts. If the duration is comparable to the service time, then a queue is simply an orderly way to delay some requests for service until a later time when the offered load drops below the capacity of the service. Put another way, a queue handles short bursts of too much demand by time-averaging with adjacent periods when there is excess capacity.

If overload persists over long periods of time, the system designer has only two choices:

1. *Increase the capacity of the system*. If the system must meet the offered load, one approach is to design a system that has less overhead so that it can perform more useful work or purchase a better computer system with higher capacity. In computer systems, it is typically less expensive to buy the next generation of

the computer system that has higher capacity because of technology improvements than trying to squeeze the last ounce out of the implementation through complex algorithms.

2. *Shed load.* If purchasing a computer system with higher capacity isn't an option and system performance cannot be improved, the preferred method is to shed load by reducing or limiting the offered load until the load is less than the capacity of the system.

One approach to control the offered load is to use a bounded buffer (see Figure 5.5) between stages. When the bounded buffer ahead of the bottleneck stage is full, then the stage before it must wait until the bounded buffer empties a slot. Because the previous stage is waiting, its bounded buffer may fill up too, which may cause the stage before it to wait, and so on. The bottleneck may be pushed all the way back to the beginning of the pipeline. If this happens, the system cannot accept any more input, and what happens next depends on how the system is used.

If the source of the load needs the results of the output to generate the next request, then the load will be self-managing. This model of use applies to some interactive systems, in which the users cannot type the next command until the previous one finishes. This same idea will be used in Chapter 7 [on-line] in the implementation of self-pacing network protocols.

If the source of the load decides not to make the request at all, then the offered load decreases. If the source, however, simply holds on to the request and resubmits it later, then the offered load doesn't decrease, but some requests are just deferred, perhaps to a time when the system isn't overloaded.

A crude approach to limiting a source is to put a *quota* on how many requests a source may have outstanding. For example, some systems enforce a rule that an application may not create more than some fixed number of active threads at the same time and may not have more than some fixed number of open files. If a source has reached its quota for a given service, the system denies the next request, limiting the offered load on the system.

An alternative to limiting the offered load is reducing it when a stage becomes overloaded. We will see one example of this approach in Section 6.2. If the address spaces of a number of applications cannot fit in memory, the virtual memory manager can swap out a complete address space of one or more applications so that the remaining applications fit in memory. When the offered load decreases to normal levels, the virtual memory manager can swap in some of the applications that were swapped out.

6.1.7 Fighting Bottlenecks

If the designer cannot remove a bottleneck with the techniques described above, it may be possible instead to fight the bottleneck using one or more of three different techniques: batching, dallying, and speculation.

6.1.7.1 Batching

Batching is performing several requests as a group to avoid the setup overhead of doing them one at a time. Opportunities for batching arise naturally at a bottleneck stage, which may have a queue of requests waiting to be processed. For example, if a stage has several requests to send to the next stage, the stage can combine all of the messages into a single message and send that one message to the next stage. This use of batching divides the overhead of an expensive operation (e.g., sending a message) over the several messages. More generally, batching works well when processing a request has a fixed delay (e.g., transmitting the request) and a variable delay (e.g., performing the operation specified in the request). Without batching, processing n requests takes $n \times (f + v)$, where f is the fixed delay and v is the variable delay. With batching, processing n requests takes $f + n \times v$.

Once a stage performs batching, the potential arises for additional performance wins. Batching may create opportunities for the stage to avoid work. If two or more write requests in a batch are for the same disk block, then the stage can perform just the last one.

Batching may also provide opportunities to improve latency by *reordering* the processing of requests. As we will see in Section 6.3.4, if a disk controller receives a batch of requests, it can schedule them in an order that reduces the movement of the disk arm, reducing the total latency for the batch of requests.

6.1.7.2 Dallying

Dallying is delaying a request on the chance that the operation won't be needed, or to create more opportunities for batching. For example, a stage may delay a request that overwrites a disk block in the hope that a second one will come along for the same block. If a second one comes along, the stage can delete the first request and perform just the second one. As applied to writes, this benefit is sometimes called *write absorption*.

Dallying also increases the opportunities for batching. It purposely increases the latency of some requests in the hope that more requests will come along that can be combined with the delayed requests to form a batch. In this case, dallying increases the latency of some requests to improve the average latency of all requests.

A key design question in dallying is to decide how long to wait. There is no generic answer to this question. The costs and benefits of dallying are application and system specific.

6.1.7.3 Speculation

Speculation is performing an operation in advance of receiving a request on the chance that it will be requested. The goal is that the results can be delivered with less latency and perhaps with less setup overhead. Speculation can achieve this goal in two different ways. First, speculation can perform operations using otherwise idle resources. In this case, even if the speculation is wrong, performing the additional operations has no downside. Second, speculation can use a busy resource to do an operation that has a long lead time so that the result of the operation can be available without waiting if it turns out to be needed. In this case, speculation might increase the delay and overhead of other requests without benefit because the prediction that the results may be needed might turn out to be wrong.

Speculating may sound bewildering because how can a computer system predict the input of an operation if it hasn't received the request yet, and how can it predict if the result of the operation will be useful in the future? Fortunately, many applications have request patterns that a system designer can exploit to predict an input. In some cases, the input value is evident; for example, a future instruction may add register 5 to register 9, and these register values may be available now. In some cases, the input values can be predicted accurately; for example, a program that asks to read byte n is likely to want to read bytes $n + 1$, $n + 2$, and so on, too. Similarly, for many applications a system can predict what results will be useful in the future. If a program performs instruction n, it will likely soon need the result of instruction $n + 1$; only when the instruction n is a JMP will the prediction be wrong.

Sometimes a system can use speculation even if the system cannot predict accurately what the input to an operation is or whether the result will be useful. For example, if an input has only two values, then the system might create a new thread and have the main thread run with one input value and the second thread with the other input value. Later, when the system knows the value of the input, it terminates the thread that is computing with the wrong value and undoes any changes that thread might have made. This use of speculation becomes challenging when it involves shared state that is updated by different thread, but using techniques presented in Chapter 9 [on-line] it is possible to undo the operations of a thread, even when shared state is involved.

Speculation creates more opportunities for batching and dallying. If the system speculates that a read request for block n will be followed by read requests for blocks $n + 1$ through $n + 8$, then the system can batch those read requests. If a write request might soon be followed by another write request, the system can dally for a while to see if any others come in and, if so, batch all the writes together.

Key design questions associated with speculation are when to speculate and how much. Speculation can increase the load on later stages. If this increase in load results in a load higher than the capacity of a later stage, then requests must wait and latency will increase. Also, any work done that turns out to be not useful is overhead, and performing this unnecessary work may slow down other requests. There is no generic answer to this design question; instead, a designer must evaluate the benefits and cost of speculation in the context of the system.

6.1.7.4 Challenges with Batching, Dallying, and Speculation

Batching, dallying, and speculation introduce complexity because they introduce concurrency. The designer must coordinate incoming requests with the requests that are batched, dallied, or speculated. Furthermore, if the requested operations share variables, the designer must coordinate the references to these variables. Since coordination is difficult to get right, a designer must use these performance-enhancing techniques with discipline. There is always the risk that by the time the designer has worked out the concurrency problems and the system has made it through the system tests, technology improvements will have made the extra complexity unnecessary. Problem set *14* explores several performance-enhancing techniques and their challenges with a simple multithreaded service.

6.1.8 An Example: The I/O Bottleneck

We illustrate design for performance using batching, dallying, and speculation through a case study involving a magnetic disk such as was described in Sidebar 2.2. The performance problem with disks is that they are made of mechanical components. As a result, reading and writing data to a magnetic disk is slow compared to devices that have no mechanical components, such as RAM chips. The disk is therefore a bottleneck in many applications. This bottleneck is usually referred to as the *I/O bottleneck*.

Recall from Sidebar 2.2 that the performance of reading and writing a disk block is determined by (1) the time to move the head to the appropriate track (the seek latency); (2) plus the time to wait until the requested sector rotates under the disk head (the rotational latency); (3) plus the time to transfer the data from the disk to the computer (the transfer latency).

The I/O bottleneck is getting worse over time. Seek latency and rotational latency are not improving as fast as processor performance. Thus, from the perspective of programs running on ever faster processors, I/O is getting slower over time. This problem is an example of problems due to incommensurate rates of technology improvement. Following the *incommensurate scaling rule* of Chapter 1, applications and systems have been redesigned several times over the last few decades to cope with the I/O bottleneck.

To build some intuition for the I/O bottleneck, consider a typical disk of the last decade. The average seek latency (the time to move the head over one-third of the disk) is about 8 milliseconds. The disks spin at 7,200 rotations per minute, which is one rotation every 8.33 milliseconds. On average, the disk has to wait a half rotation for the desired block to be under the disk head; thus, the average rotational latency is 4.17 milliseconds.

Bits read from a disk encounter two potential transfer rate limits, either of which may become the bottleneck. The first limit is mechanical: the rate at which bits spin under the disk heads on their way to a buffer. The second limit is electrical: the rate at which the I/O channel or I/O bus can transfer the contents of the buffer to the computer. A typical modern 400-gigabyte disk has 16,383 cylinders, or about 24 megabytes per cylinder. That disk would probably have 8 two-sided platters and thus 16 read/write heads, so there would be 24/16 = 1.5 megabytes per track. When rotating at 7,200 revolutions per minute (120 revolutions per second), the bits will go by a head at 120 × 1.5 = 180 megabytes per second. The I/O channel speed depends on which standard bus connects the disk to the computer. For the Integrated Device Electronics (IDE) bus, 66 megabytes per second is a common number in practice; for the Serial ATA 3 bus the limit is 3 gigabytes per second. Thus, the IDE bus would be the bottleneck at 66 megabytes per second; with a Serial ATA 3 bus, the disk mechanics would be the bottleneck at 180 megabytes per second.

Using such a disk and I/O standard, reading a 4-kilobyte block chosen at random takes:

average seek time + average rotation latency + transmission of 4 kilobytes
= 8 + 4.17 + (4 / (180 × 1024)) × 1000 milliseconds
= 8 + 4.17 + 0.02 milliseconds
= 12.19 milliseconds

The throughput for reading randomly chosen blocks one by one is:

= 1000/12.19 × 4 kilobytes per second
= 328 kilobytes per second

The main opportunity to handle the I/O bottleneck is to drive the disk at the transfer rate (180 megabytes per second) instead of the rate of seeks and rotations (327 kilobytes per second). This strategy is an example of hiding latency (moving the disk arm) by exploiting throughput (the high transfer rate between computer and disk).

Consider the following prototypical program, which processes a large input file sequentially and produces an output file sequentially:

```
1   in ← OPEN ("in", READ)                  // open "in" for reading
2   out ← OPEN ("out", WRITE)               // open "out" for reading
3
4   while not ENDOFFILE (in) do
5       block ← READ (in, 4096)             // read 4 kilobyte block from in
6       block ← COMPUTE (block)             // compute for 1 millisecond
7       WRITE (out, block, 4096)            // write 4 kilobyte block to out
8   CLOSE (in)
9   CLOSE (out)
```

If we think of this application as a pipeline, then there are the following stages: (1) the file system, which reads data from a disk in response to a READ (line 5); (2) the application, which computes new data using the data read (line 6); and (3) the file system, which writes the new data to the disk (line 7).

If the application is organized naively, without batching, dallying, and speculation, the average time to go around the loop is equal to the latency of the three stages. The latencies of the two file system stages are dominated by the latency of the disk operations, and thus we can approximate the average latency of the loop as follows:

reading 4 kilobytes + 1 millisecond of computation + writing 4 kilobytes
= 12.19 + 1 + 12.19 milliseconds
= 25.38 milliseconds

In practice, the latency might be lower because this calculation assumes that each disk access involves an average seek time, but if the file system has allocated the blocks near each other on the disk, the disk might have to perform only a short seek.

How can we improve the performance of this program? The program reads the file only once, and thus a cache cannot improve the latency of reading a block. The only alternative is to hide the latency of read and write operations. The simplest optimization is to overlap the reading and writing of blocks with the computation on line 6. Let's start with reading.

When the application READs a block, the file system can speculate that the application will read a few blocks following the requested block. This speculation can improve performance for our application if we combine it with two further optimizations. First, we modify the file system to lay out the blocks of a file contiguously. Second, we modify the file system to prefetch an entire track of data on each read. Our prototypical application is perfect for prefetching, since the whole data set is read sequentially.

These optimizations eliminate rotational delay before reading can start. An entire track can be read in:

average seek time + 1 rotational delay
= 8 + 8.33 milliseconds
= 16.33 milliseconds

With 1.5 megabytes (1,536 kilobytes) per track, the file system issues one read request per 384 (1536/4) loop iterations, and we have the following timing diagram:

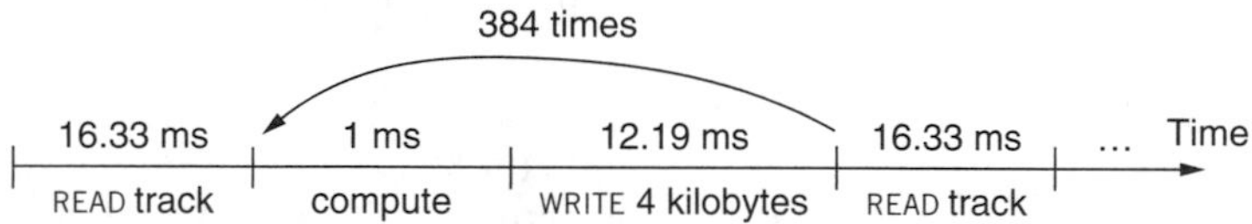

The average time for 384 iterations is:

= reading 1536 kilobytes + 384 × (1 millisecond of computation + writing 4 kilobytes)
= 16.33 + 384 × (1 + 12.19) milliseconds
= 16.33 + 5065 milliseconds
= 5081 milliseconds

Thus, the average time for a loop iteration is 5081/384 = 13.23 milliseconds, a substantial improvement over 25.38 milliseconds.

We can improve the performance of writing blocks by dallying and batching write requests. We modify WRITE to use a buffer of blocks in RAM (see Figure 6.5). The WRITE call stores the updated block into this buffer and returns immediately, and the application thread can continue. When the buffers fill up, the file system can batch the blocks in the buffer and combine them into a single disk request, which the disk can process in parallel with the processor running the application. Batching allows the disk controller to execute writes to adjacent sectors with no rotational delay. Because blocks are written contiguously in our example, the file system may take 384 contiguous writes and batch them together to form a complete track write. These optimizations result in the following timing diagram:

This optimization reduces the average time around the loop:

$= (16.33 + 384 + 16.33)/384$ milliseconds
$= 1.09$ milliseconds

If we modify the file system to prefetch the next track before the application calls the 385th READ, we can overlap computation and I/O completely. If we modify the file system to read the next track after it has processed, say, half of the last track read, then we obtain the following timing diagram for each block of 384 loop iterations, other than the first one:

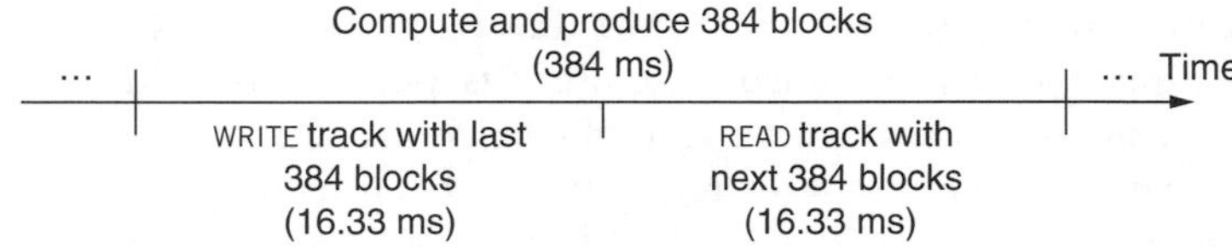

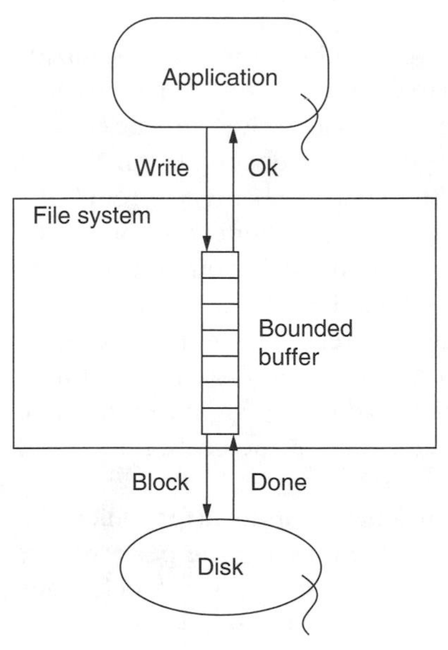

FIGURE 6.5

Using a buffer to delay writes.

Now the system overlaps computation with I/O completely, the average time around the loop is 1 millisecond, and the application is now bottlenecked by computation, rather than by I/O.

The optimizations take advantage of the facts that the application processes the input file sequentially and that the file system allocates blocks for the output contiguously on disk. However, even for applications that process blocks not in the order in which they are laid out on the disk, these optimizations can be beneficial. The file system, for example, can reorder the disk requests for a batch in the order of their track number, thereby minimizing disk arm movement, and thus improving performance for the whole batch of requests. (To understand what a good algorithm is for disk scheduling, we need to think more broadly about scheduling requests in computer systems, which is the topic of Section 6.3.)

The analysis assumes a simple performance model for the disk; for a more in-depth discussion of the performance of disks, see Suggestions for Further Reading 6.3.1. The analysis also assumes a single disk; using several disks can offer opportunities for improving performance. For example, RAIDs have several disks (see Section 2.1.1.4), which allows the file system to interleave read and write requests instead of serving them one by one, providing additional opportunities for increasing performance. Finally, practical, alternative storage technologies are emerging, which change the trade-offs. For example, designing a high performance storage system with Flash disks provides new opportunities and new challenges (see, for example, Suggestions for Further Reading 6.3.4).

A buffer without write-through can provide substantial performance improvements but can lose on reliability. If the computer system fails before the file system has written out data to the disk, some data is lost. The basic problem is how long to delay before forcing the data to the disk. The longer the file system delays writes, the larger the opportunity for higher performance will be, but the greater the probability that data will be lost if, for example, the power fails and the volatile RAM resets.

There are at least four choices as to when the WRITE request to the disk can be issued:

- Before WRITE returns to the caller (write-through).
- On an explicit *force* request from the user (user-controlled write).
- When the file is closed (another kind of user-controlled write).
- When a certain number of write requests have been accumulated or when some fixed time has passed since the last write request. This option can be a bad idea if one needs to control the order of writes.

A buffer without write-through also introduces some other complexities, mostly related to reliability in the face of system failures. First, if the file system batches several write requests in a single disk request, then the disk may write the blocks in an order different from the order issued by the file system to reduce seek time. Thus, the disk may not reflect a consistent state if the system crashes halfway through the batched write request. Second, the disk controller may also use a buffer without write-through. The file system may think the data has been stored reliably on disk when, in fact, the disk controller is caching it. We shall see systematic ways of controlling the problem caused by caches without write-through in Chapter 9 [on-line]; a nice application of these systematic ways to design a high-performance and robust file system is given by Ganger and Patt [Suggestions for Further Reading 6.3.3]. In general, here we have a good example that increased performance comes at the cost of increased complexity, as illustrated by Figure 1.1.

The prototypical application represents one particular workload for which the techniques described above improve performance well. Improving the performance of the prototypical application is challenging because it doesn't reuse a block. Many applications read and write a block multiple times, and in that case additional techniques are available to improve performance. In particular, in that case it is worthwhile for the file system to maintain a cache of recently read blocks in RAM. If an application reads a block that is already in the cache, then the file system doesn't have to perform any disk operations.

Introducing a cache leads to additional coordination constraints. The file system may have to coordinate WRITE and READ operations with outstanding disk requests. For example: a READ operation may force the removal of a modified block from the cache to make space for the block to be read. But the file system cannot throw out a modified block until it has been written it to the disk, so the file system must wait until the write request of the modified block has completed before proceeding with the READ operation.

Understanding for what workloads a cache works well, learning how to design a cache (e.g., which block to throw out to make space for a new block), and analyzing a cache's performance benefits are sophisticated topics, which we discuss next. Problem set *16* explores these issues, as well as topics related to scheduling, in the context of a simple high-performance video server.

6.2 MULTILEVEL MEMORIES

The previous section described how to address the I/O bottleneck by using two types of digital memory devices: a RAM chip and a magnetic disk, which have different capacities, costs, and speeds. A system designer would like to have a single memory device that is both as large and as fast as the application requires, and that at the same time is affordable. Unfortunately, application requirements often exceed one or another of these three parameters—a memory device that is both fast enough and large enough is usually too expensive—so the designer must make some trade-offs. The usual trade-off is to use more than one memory device, for example, one that is fast but expensive (and thus necessarily too small), and another that is large and cheap (but slower than desired). But fitting an application into such an environment adds the complexity of deciding which parts of the application should use the small, fast memory and which parts the large, slow one. It may also increase maintenance effort if the memory configuration changes.

One might think that improvements in technology may eventually make a brute-force solution economical—someday the designer can just buy a memory that is both large and fast enough. But there are two problems with that thought: one practical and one intrinsic. The practical problem is that historically the increase in memory size has been matched by an equal increase in problem sizes. That is, the data that people want to manipulate has grown along with memory technology.

The intrinsic problem is that memory has a trade-off between latency and size. This trade-off becomes clear when we consider the underlying physics. Even if one has an unlimited budget to throw at the design problem, the speed of light interferes. To see why, imagine a processor that occupies a single point in space, with memory clustered around it in a sphere, using the densest packing that physics allows. With this packing, some of the memory cells will end up located quite near the processor, so the latency (that is, the time required for access to those cells, which requires a propagation of a signal at the speed of light from the processor to the bit and back) will be short. But because only a few memory cells can fit in the space near the processor, most memory cells will be farther away, and they will necessarily have a larger latency. Put another way, for any specified minimum latency requirement, there will be some memory size for which at least some cells must exceed that latency, based on speed-of-light considerations alone. Moreover, the geometry of spheres (the volume of a shell of radius r grows with the square of r) dictates that there must be more high-latency cells than low-latency ones.

In practical engineering terms, available technologies also exhibit analogous packing problems. For example, the latency of a memory array on the same chip as the processor (where it is usually called an L1 cache) is less than the latency of a separate memory chip (which is usually called an L2 cache), which in turn is less than the latency of a much larger memory implemented as a collection of memory chips on a separate card. The result is that the designer is usually forced to deal with a composite memory system in which different component memories have different parameters of latency, capacity, and cost. The challenge then becomes that of achieving overall maximum performance by deciding which data items to store in the fastest memory device, which can be relegated to the slower devices, and deciding if and when to move data items from one memory device to another.

6.2.1 Memory Characterization

Different memory devices are characterized not just by dimensions of capacity, latency, and cost, but also by cell size and throughput. In more detail, these dimensions are:

- *Capacity*, measured in bits or bytes. For example, a RAM chip may have a capacity from a few to tens of megabytes, whereas magnetic disks have capacities measured in scores or hundreds of gigabytes.

- *Average random latency*, measured in seconds or processor clock cycles, for a memory cell chosen at random. For example, the average latency of RAM is measured in nanoseconds, which might correspond to hundreds of processor clock cycles. (On closer examination, RAM READ latency is actually more complicated—see Sidebar 6.4.) Magnetic disks have an average latency measured in milliseconds, which corresponds to millions of processor clock cycles. In addition, magnetic disks, because of their mechanical components, usually have a much wider variance in their latency than does RAM.

- *Cost*, measured in some currency per storage unit. The cost of RAM is typically measured in cents per megabyte, while the cost of magnetic disks is measured in dollars per gigabyte.

- *Cell size,* measured as the number of bits or bytes transferred in or out of the device by a single READ or WRITE operation. For example, the cell size of RAM is typically a few bytes, perhaps 4, 8, or 16. The cell size of a magnetic disk is typically 512 bytes or more.

Sidebar 6.4 RAM Latency Performance analysis sometimes requires a better model of random access memory latency for READ operations. Most random access memory devices actually have two latency parameters of interest: *cycle time* and *access time*. The distinction arises because the physical memory device may need time to recover from one access before it can handle the next one. For example, some memory READ mechanisms are destructive: to READ a bit out, the memory device literally smashes the bit and examines the resulting debris to determine the value that the bit had. Once it determines that value, the memory device writes the bit back so that its value can again be available for future READs. This write-back operation typically cannot be overlapped with an immediately following READ operation. Thus, the *cycle time* of the memory device is the minimum time that must pass between issuance of one READ request and issuance of the next one. However, the result of the READ may be available for delivery to the processor well before the cycle time is complete. The time from issuance of the READ to delivery of the response to the processor is known as the *access time* of the memory device. The following figure illustrates.

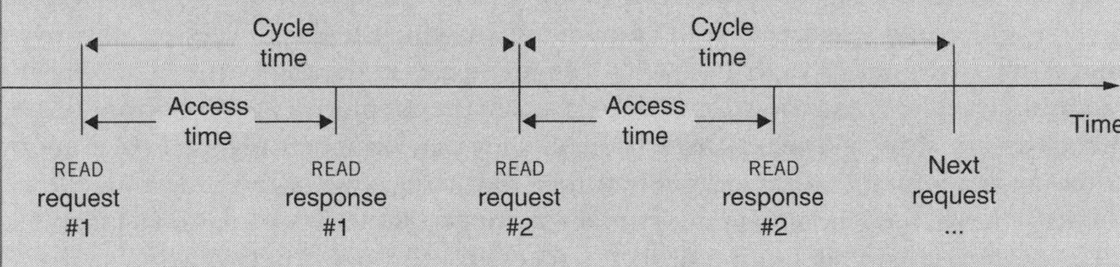

- *Throughput*, measured in bits per second. RAM can typically transfer data at rates measured in gigabytes per second, while magnetic disks transfer at the rate of hundreds of megabytes per second.

The differences between RAM and magnetic disks along these dimensions are orders of magnitude in all cases. RAM is typically about five orders of magnitude faster than magnetic disk and two orders of magnitude more expensive. Many, but not all, of the dimensions have been improving rapidly. For example, the capacity of magnetic disks has doubled, and cost has fallen by a factor of 2 every year for the last two decades, while the average latency has improved by only a factor of 2 in that same 20 years. Latency has not improved much because it involves mechanical operations as opposed to all-electronic ones, as described in Sidebar 2.2. This incommensurate rate of technology improvement makes effective memory management a challenge to implement well.

6.2.2 Multilevel Memory Management using Virtual Memory

Because larger latency and larger capacity usually go hand in hand, it is customary and useful to describe the various available memory devices as belonging to different levels, with the fastest, smallest device being at the highest level and slower, larger

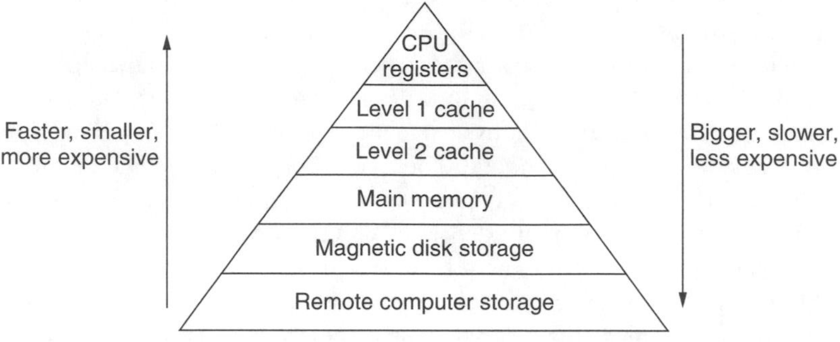

FIGURE 6.6

A multilevel memory pyramid.

devices being at lower levels. A memory system constructed of devices from more than one level is called a *multilevel memory*. Figure 6.6 shows a popular way of depicting the multiple levels, using a pyramid, in which higher levels are narrower, suggesting that their capacity is smaller. The memories in the top of the hierarchy are fast and expensive, and they are therefore small; the memories at the bottom of the hierarchy are slow and inexpensive; and so they can be much bigger. In a modern computer system, an information item can be in the registers of the processor, the L1 cache memory, the L2 cache memory, main memory, a RAM disk cache, on a magnetic disk, or even on another computer that is accessible through a network.

Two quite different ways can be used to manage a multilevel memory. One way is to leave it to each application programmer to decide in which memory to place data items and when to move them. The second way is automatic management: a subsystem independent of any application program observes the pattern of memory references being made by the program. With that pattern in mind, the automatic memory management subsystem decides where to place data items and when to move them from one memory device to another.

Most modern memory management is automatic because (1) there exist automatic algorithms that have good performance on average and (2) automatic memory management relieves the programmer of the need to conform the program to specifics of the memory system such as the capacities of the various levels. Without automatic memory management, the application program explicitly allocates memory space within each level and moves data items from one memory level to another. Such programs become dependent on the particular hardware configuration for which they were written, which makes them difficult to write, to maintain, or to move to a different computer. If someone adds more memory to one of the levels, the program will probably have to be modified to take advantage of it. If some memory is removed, the program may stop working.

As Chapter 2 described, there are two commonly encountered memory interfaces: an interface to small-cell memory to which threads refer using READ and WRITE operations, and an interface to large-cell memory to which threads refer using GET and

PUT operations. These two interfaces correspond roughly to the levels of a multilevel memory; higher levels typically have small cells and use the READ/WRITE interface, while lower levels typically have large cells and use the GET/PUT interface.

One opportunity in the design of an automatically managed multilevel memory system is to combine it with a virtual memory manager in such a way that the small-cell READ/WRITE interface appears to the application program to apply to the entire memory system. This creates what is sometimes called a *one-level store*, an idea first introduced in the Atlas system.* Put another way, this scheme virtualizes the entire memory system around the small-cell READ/WRITE interface, thus hiding from the application programmer the GET/PUT interface as well as the specifics of latency, capacity, cost, cell size, and throughput of the component memory devices. The programmer instead sees a single memory system that appears to have a large capacity, a uniform cell size, a modest average cost per bit, and a latency and throughput that depend on the memory access patterns of the application.

Just as with virtualization of addresses, virtualization of the READ/WRITE memory interface further exploits the design principle *decouple modules with indirection*. In this case, indirection allows the virtual memory manager to translate any particular virtual address not only to different physical memory addresses at different times but also to addresses in a different memory level. With the support of the virtual memory manager, a *multilevel memory manager* can then rearrange the data among the memory levels without having to modify any application program. By adding one more feature, the *indirection exception*, this rearrangement can become completely automatic. An indirection exception is a memory reference exception that indicates that memory manager cannot translate a particular virtual address. The exception handler examines the virtual address and may bind or rebind that value before resuming the interrupted thread.

With these techniques, the virtual memory manager not only can contain errors and enforce modularity, but it also can help make it appear to the program that there is a single, uniform, large memory. The multilevel memory management feature can be slipped in underneath the application program *transparently*, which means that the application program does not need to be modified.

Virtualization of widely used interfaces creates an opportunity to transparently add features and thus evolve a system. Since by definition many modules use a widely used interface, the transparent addition of features beneath such an interface can have a wide impact, without having to change the clients of the interface. The memory interface is an example of such a widely used interface. In addition to implementing single-level stores, here are several other ways in which systems designers have used a virtual memory manager with indirection exceptions:

- *Memory-mapped files*. When an application opens a file, the virtual memory manager can map files into an application's address space, which allows the application to read and write portions of a file as if they were located in RAM. Memory-mapped files extend the idea of a single-level store to include files.

*T. Kilburn, D.B.J. Edwards, M.J. Lanigan, and F.H. Sumner. One-level storage system. *IRE Transactions on Electronic Computers, EC-11*, 2 (April 1962), pages 223–235.

- *Copy-on-write*. If two threads are working on the same data concurrently, then the data can be stored once in memory by mapping the pages that hold the data with only READ permissions. If one of the threads attempts to write a shared page, the virtual memory hardware will interrupt the processor with a permission exception. The handler can demultiplex this exception as an indirection exception of the type copy-on-write. In response to the indirection exception, the virtual memory manager transparently makes a copy of the page and maps the copy with READ and WRITE permissions in the address space of the threads that wants to write the page. With this technique, only changed pages must be copied.
- *On-demand zero-filled pages*. When an application starts, a large part of its address space must be filled with zeros—for instance, the parts of the address space that aren't preinitialized with instructions or initial data values. Instead of allocating zero-filled pages in RAM or on disk, the virtual memory manager can map those pages without READ and WRITE permissions. When the application refers to one of those pages, the virtual memory hardware will interrupt the processor with a memory reference exception. The exception handler can demultiplex this exception as an indirection exception of the type zero-fill. In response to this zero-fill exception, the virtual memory manager allocates a page dynamically and fills it with zeros. This technique can save storage in RAM or on disk because the parts of the address space that the application doesn't use will not take up space.
- *One zero-filled page*. Some designers implement zero-filled pages with a copy-on-write exception. The virtual memory manager allocates just one page filled with zeros and maps that one page in all page-map entries for pages that should contain all zeros, but granting only READ permission. Then, if a thread writes to this read-only zero-filled page, the exception handler will demultiplex this indirect exception as a copy-on-write exception, and the virtual memory manager will make a copy and update that thread's page table to have WRITE permission for the copy.
- *Virtual shared memory*. Several threads running on different computers can share a single address space. When a thread refers to a page that isn't in its local RAM, the virtual memory manager can fetch the page over the network from a remote computer's RAM. The remote virtual memory manager unmaps the page and sends the content of the page back. The Apollo DOMAIN system (mentioned in Suggestions for Further Reading 3.2.1) used this idea to make a collection of distributed computers look like one computer. Li and Hudak use this idea to run parallel applications on a collection of workstations with shared virtual memory [Suggestions for Further Reading 10.1.8].

The virtual memory design for the Mach operating system [Suggestions for Further Reading 6.1.3] provides an example design that supports many of these features and that is used by some current operating systems.

The remainder of this section focuses on building large virtual memories using automatic multilevel memory management. To do so, a designer must address some challenging problems, but, once it is designed, application programmers do not have to worry about memory management. Except for embedded devices (e.g., a computer acting as the controller of a microwave oven), nearly all modern computer systems use virtual memory to contain errors, enforce modularity, and manage multiple memory levels.

6.2.3 Adding Multilevel Memory Management to a Virtual Memory

Suppose for the moment that we have two memory devices, one that has a READ/WRITE interface, such as a RAM, and the second that has a GET/PUT interface, such as a magnetic disk. If the processor is already equipped with a virtual memory manager such as the one illustrated in Figure 5.20, it is straightforward to add multilevel memory management to create a one-level store.

The basic idea is that at any instant, only some of the pages listed in the page map are actually in RAM (because the RAM has limited capacity) and the rest are on the disk. To support this idea, we add to each entry of the page map a single bit, called the *resident* bit, in the column identified as *r?* in Figure 6.7. If the resident bit of a page is TRUE, that means that the page is in a block of RAM and the physical address in the page map identifies that block. If the resident bit of a page is FALSE, that means that the page is not currently in any block of RAM; it is instead on some block on the disk.

In the example, pages 10 and 12 are in RAM, while page 11 is only on the disk. Thus, references to pages 10 and 12 can proceed as usual, but if the program tries to refer to page 11, for example, with a LOAD instruction, the virtual memory manager must take some action because the processor can't refer to the disk with READ/WRITE operations. The action it takes is to alert the multilevel memory manager that it needs

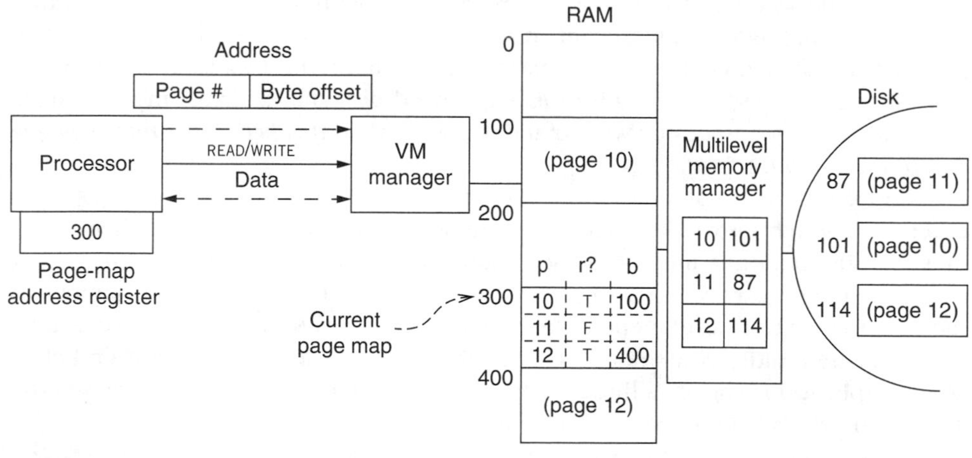

FIGURE 6.7

Integrating a virtual memory manager with a multilevel memory manager. The virtual memory manager is typically implemented in hardware, while the multilevel memory manager is typically implemented in software as part of the operating system.

```
7.1    if resident of page_table[page] = FALSE then      // check if page is resident
7.2        signal MISSING_PAGE (page)                    // no, signal a missing-page exception
7.3    else
7.4        block ← page_table[page].address              // Index into page map
8          physical ← block + offset                     // Concatenate block and offset
9          return physical                               // return physical address
```

FIGURE 6.8

Replacement for lines *7–9* of procedure TRANSLATE of Chapter 5, to implement a multilevel memory.

to use the GET/PUT interface of the disk to copy that page from the disk block into some block in the RAM where the processor can directly refer to it. For this purpose, the multilevel memory manager (at least conceptually) maintains a second, parallel map that translates page numbers to disk block addresses. In practice, real implementations may merge the two maps.

The pseudocode of Figure 6.8 (which replaces lines *7–9* of the version of the TRANSLATE procedure of Section 5.4.3.1) illustrates the integration. When a program makes a reference to a virtual memory address, the virtual memory manager invokes TRANSLATE, which (after performing the usual domain and permission checks) looks up the page number in the page map. If the requested address is in a page that is resident in memory, the manager proceeds as it did in Chapter 5, translating the virtual address to a physical address in the RAM. If the page is not resident, the manager signals that the page is missing.

The pseudocode of Figure 6.8 describes the operation of the virtual memory manager as a procedure, but to maintain adequate performance a virtual memory manager is nearly always implemented in hardware because it must translate every virtual address the processor issues. With this page-based design, the virtual memory manager interrupts the processor with an indirect exception that is called a *missing-page exception* or a *page fault*.

The exception handler examines the value in the program counter register to determine which instruction caused the missing-page exception, and it then examines that instruction in memory to see what address that instruction issued. Next, it calls SEND (see Figure 5.30) with a request containing the missing page number to the port for the multilevel memory manager. SEND invokes ADVANCE, which wakes up a thread of the multilevel memory manager. Then, the handler invokes AWAIT on behalf of the application program's thread (i.e., with the stack of the thread that caused the exception). The AWAIT procedure yields the processor.

The multilevel memory manager receives the request and copies pages between RAM blocks and disk blocks as they are needed. For each missing-page exception, the multilevel memory manager first looks up that page in its parallel page map to determine the address of the disk block that holds the page. Next, it locates an unused block in RAM. With these two parameters, it issues a GET for the disk block that holds the page, writing the result into the unused RAM block. The multilevel memory manager then informs the virtual memory manager about the presence of the page in RAM by writing the block number in the virtual memory manager's page map and changing the resident bit to TRUE, and makes the thread that experienced the missing-page exception runnable by calling ADVANCE.

When that thread next runs, it backs up the program counter found in its return point so that after the return to user mode the application program will reexecute the instruction that encountered the missing page. Since that page is now resident in RAM and the multilevel memory manager has updated the mappings of the virtual memory manager, this time the TRANSLATE function will be able to translate the virtual address to a physical address.

If all blocks in RAM are occupied with pages, the multilevel memory manager must select some page from RAM and remove it to make space for the missing page. The page selected for removal is known colloquially as the *victim*, and the algorithm that the multilevel memory manager uses to select a victim is called the *page-removal policy*. A bad choice (for example, systematically selecting for removal the page that will be needed by the next memory access) could cause the multilevel memory system to run at the rate that pages can be retrieved from the disk, rather than the rate that words can be retrieved from RAM. In practice, a selection algorithm that exploits a property of most programs known as *locality* can allow those programs to run with only occasional missing-page exceptions. The locality property is discussed in Section 6.2.5, and several different page removal policies are discussed in Section 6.2.6.

If the selected page was modified while it was in RAM, the multilevel memory manager must PUT the modified page back to the disk before issuing a GET for the new page. Thus, in the worst case, a missing-page exception results in two accesses to the disk: one to PUT a modified page back to the disk and one to GET the page requested by the missing-page exception handler. In the best case, the page in RAM has not been modified since being read from disk, so it is identical to the disk copy. In this case, the multilevel memory manager can simply adjust the virtual memory page-map entry to show that this page is no longer resident, and the number of disk accesses needed is just the one to GET the missing page. This scheme maintains a copy of *every* virtual memory page on the disk, whether or not that page is also resident in RAM, so the disk must be larger than the RAM and the effective virtual memory capacity is equal to the space allocated for virtual memory on the disk.

A concern about this scheme is that it introduces what sometimes are called *implicit I/Os*. The multilevel memory manager performs I/O operations beyond the ones performed by the application (which are then called *explicit I/Os*). Given that a disk is often an I/O bottleneck (see Section 6.1.8), these implicit I/Os may risk slowing down the application. Problem set *15* explores some of the issues related to implicit I/Os in the context of a page-based and an object-based single-level store.

To mitigate the I/O bottleneck for missing-page exceptions, a designer can exploit concurrency by implementing the multilevel memory manager with multiple threads. When a missing-page exception occurs, the next available multilevel memory manager thread can start to work on that missing page. The thread begins a GET operation and waits for the GET to complete. Meanwhile, the thread manager can assign the processor to some other thread. When the GET completes, an interrupt notifies the multilevel memory manager thread and it completes processing of the missing-page exception. With this organization, the multilevel memory manager can overlap the handling of a missing-page exception with the computation of other threads, and it can handle multiple missing-page exceptions concurrently.

A quite different, less modular organization is used in many older systems: integrate the multilevel memory manager with the virtual memory manager in the kernel, with the goal of reducing the number of instructions required to handle a missing-page exception, and thus improving performance. Typically, when integrated, the multilevel memory manager runs in the application thread in the kernel, thus reducing the number of threads and avoiding the cost of context switches. Most such systems were designed decades ago when instruction count was a major concern.

Comparing these two organizations, one benefit of the modularity of a separate multilevel memory manager is that several multilevel memory managers can easily coexist. For example, one multilevel memory manager that reads and writes blocks to a magnetic disk to provide applications with the illusion of a large memory may

Sidebar 6.5 Design Hint: Separate Mechanism from Policy If a module needs to make a policy decision, it is better to leave the policy decision to the clients of the module so that they can make a decision that meets their goals. If the interface between the mechanism and policy module is well defined, then this split allows the schedule policies to be changed without having to change the implementation of the mechanism. For example, one could replace the page-removal policy without having to change the mechanism for handling missing-page exceptions. Furthermore, when porting the missing-page exception mechanism to another processor, the missing-page handler may have to be rewritten, but the policy module may require no modifications.

Of course, if a change in policy requires changes to the interface between the mechanism and policy modules, then both modules must be replaced. Thus, the success of following the hint is limited by how well the interface between the mechanism and policy module is designed. The potential downsides of separating mechanism and policy are a loss in performance due to control transfers between the mechanism and policy module, and increased complexity if flexibility is unneeded. For example, if one policy is always the right one, then separating policy and mechanism may just be unnecessary complexity.

In the case of multilevel memory management, separating the missing-page mechanism from the page replacement policy is mostly for ease of porting because the least recently used page-replacement policy (discussed in Section 6.2.5) works well in practice for most applications.

coexist with another multilevel memory manager that provides memory-mapped files. These different multilevel memory managers can be implemented as separate modules, as opposed to being integrated together with the virtual memory manager. Separating the multilevel memory manager from the virtual memory manager is an example of the design hint *separate mechanism from policy*, discussed in Sidebar 6.5. The Mach virtual memory system is an example of a modern, modular design [Suggestions for Further Reading 6.1.3].

If the multilevel managers are implemented as separate modules from the virtual memory manager, then the designer has the choice of running the multilevel manager modules in kernel mode or as separate applications in user mode. For the same reasons that many deployed systems are monolithic kernel systems (see Section 5.3.6), designers often choose to run the multilevel manager modules in kernel mode. In a few systems, the multilevel managers run as separate user applications with their own address spaces.

One question that requires some careful thought is what to do if a multilevel memory manager encounters a missing-page exception in its own procedures or data. In principle, there is no problem with recursive missing-page exceptions as long as the recursion bottoms out. To ensure that the recursion does bottom out, it is necessary to make sure that some essential set of pages (for example, the pages containing the instructions and tables of the interrupt handler and the kernel thread manager) is never selected for removal from RAM. The usual method is to add a mark to the page-map entries for those essential pages saying, in effect, "Don't remove this page." Pages so marked are commonly said to be *wired down*.

6.2.4 Analyzing Multilevel Memory Systems

Multilevel memories are common engineering practice. From the processor perspective, stored instructions and data traverse some pyramid of memory devices such as the one that was illustrated in Figure 6.6. But when analyzing or constructing a multilevel memory, we do so by analyzing each adjacent pair of levels individually as a two-level memory system, and then stacking the several two-level memory systems. (One reason for doing it this way is that it seems to work. Another is that no one has yet figured out a more satisfactory way to analyze or manage a three- or more-level memory as a single system.)

Devices that function as the fast level in a two-level memory system are called *primary devices*, and devices that function as the slow level are called *secondary devices*. In virtual memory systems, the primary device is usually some form of RAM; the secondary device can be either a slower RAM or a magnetic disk. Web browsers typically use the local disk as a cache that holds pages of remote Web services. In this case, the primary device is a magnetic disk; the remote service is the secondary device, which may itself use magnetic disks for storage. The multilevel memory management algorithms described in the remainder of this section apply to both of these different configurations, and many others.

A cache and a virtual memory are two similar kinds of multilevel memory managers. They are so similar, in fact, that the only difference between them is in the name space they provide for memory cells:

- The user of a *cache* identifies memory cells using the name space of the secondary memory device.
- The user of a *virtual memory* identifies memory cells using the name space of the primary memory device.

Apart from that difference, designers of virtual memories and caches choose policies for multilevel memory management from the same range of possibilities.

The pyramid of Figure 6.6 is typically implemented with the highest level explicitly managed by the application, a cache design at some levels and a virtual memory design at other levels. For example, a multilevel memory system that includes all six levels of the figure might be organized something like the following:

1. At the highest level, the registers of the processor are the primary device, and the rest of the memory system is the secondary device. The application program (as constructed by the compiler code generator) explicitly loads and stores the registers to and from the rest of the memory system.

2. When the processor issues a READ or WRITE to the rest of the memory system, it provides as an argument a name from the main memory name space, but this name goes to a primary memory device located on the same chip as the processor. Since the name is from the lower level main memory name space, this level of memory is being managed as a cache, commonly known as a "level 1 cache" or "L1 cache".

3. If the named cell is not found in the level 1 cache, a multilevel memory manager looks in its secondary memory, an off-chip memory device, but again using the name from the main memory name space. The off-chip memory is thus another example of a cache, this one known as a "level 2 cache" or "L2 cache".

4. The level 2 cache is now the primary device, and if the named memory cell is not found there, the next lower multilevel manager (the one that manages the level 2/main memory pair) looks in its secondary device—the main memory—still using the name from the main memory name space.

5. At the next level, the main memory is the primary device. If an addressed cell is not in main memory, a virtual memory manager invokes the next lower level multilevel memory manager (the one described in Section 6.2.3, that manages movement between main and disk memory) but still using the name from the main memory name space. The multilevel memory manager translates this name to a disk block address.

6. The sequence may continue down another layer; if the disk block is not found on the (primary) local disk, yet another multilevel memory manager may retrieve it from some remote (secondary) system. In some systems, this last memory pair is managed as a cache, and in others as a virtual memory.

It should be apparent that the above example is just one of a vast range of possibilities open to the multilevel memory designer.

6.2.5 Locality of Reference and Working Sets

It is not obvious that an automatically managed multilevel memory system should perform well. The basic requirement for acceptable performance is that all information items stored in the memory must not have equal frequency of use. If every item is used with equal frequency, then a multilevel memory cannot have good performance, since the overall memory will operate at approximately the speed of the slowest memory component. To illustrate this effect, consider a two-level memory system. The average latency of a two-level memory is:

$$AverageLatency = R_{hit} \times Latency_{primary} + R_{miss} \times Latency_{secondary} \tag{6.2}$$

The term R_{hit} (known as the *hit ratio*) is the frequency with which items are found in the primary device, and R_{miss} is $(1 - R_{hit})$. This formula is a direct application of Equation 6.1, (in Section 6.1) which gives the average performance of a system with a fast and slow path. Here the fast path is a reference to the primary device, while the slow path is a reference to the secondary device.

If accesses to every cell of the primary and secondary devices were of equal frequency, then the average latency would be proportional to the number of cells of each device:

$$AverageLatency = \frac{S_{primary}}{S_{primary} + S_{secondary}} \times T_{primary} + \frac{S_{secondary}}{S_{primary} + S_{secondary}} \times T_{secondary} \tag{6.3}$$

where S is the capacity of a memory device and T is its average latency. In a multilevel memory, it is typical that $T_{primary} \ll T_{secondary}$ and $S_{secondary} \gg S_{primary}$ (as, for example, with RAM for primary memory and magnetic disk for secondary memory), in which case the first term is much smaller than the second, the coefficient of the second term approaches 1, and $AverageLatency \approx T_{secondary}$. Thus, if accesses to every cell of primary and secondary are equally likely, a multilevel memory doesn't provide any performance benefit.

On the other hand, if the frequency of use of some stored items is significantly higher than the frequency of use of other stored items, even for a short time, automatically managed multilevel memory becomes feasible. For example, if, somehow, 99% of accesses were directed to the faster memory and only 1% to the slower memory, then the average latency would be:

$$AverageLatency = 0.99 \times T_{primary} + 0.01 \times T_{secondary} \tag{6.4}$$

Thus if the primary device is L2 cache with 1 nanosecond latency and the secondary device is main memory with 10 nanoseconds latency, the average latency becomes 0.99 + 0.10 = 1.09 nanoseconds, which makes the composite memory, with a capacity equal to that of the main memory, nearly as fast as the L2 cache. For a second example, if the primary device is main memory with 10 nanoseconds latency and the secondary device is magnetic disk with average latency of 10 milliseconds, the average latency of the multilevel memory is

$$0.99 \times 10 \text{ nanoseconds} + 0.01 \times 10 \text{ milliseconds} = 100.0099 \text{ microseconds}$$

That latency is substantially larger than the 10 nanosecond primary memory latency, but it is also much smaller than the 10 millisecond secondary memory latency. In essence, a multilevel memory just exploits the design hint *optimize for the common case*.

Most applications are not so well behaved that one can identify a static set of information that is both small enough to fit in the primary device and for which reference is so concentrated that it is the target of 99% of all memory references. However, in many situations most memory references are to a small set of addresses for significant periods of time. As the application progresses, the area of concentration of access shifts, but its size still typically remains small. This concentration of access into a small but shifting locality is what makes an automatically managed multilevel memory system feasible. An application that exhibits such a concentration of accesses is said to have *locality of reference*.

Analyzing the situation, we can think of a running application as generating a stream of virtual addresses, known as the *reference string*. A reference string can exhibit locality of reference in two ways:

- *Temporal locality*: the reference string contains several closely spaced references to the same address.
- *Spatial locality*: the reference string contains several closely spaced references to adjacent addresses.

An automatically managed multilevel memory system can exploit temporal locality by keeping in the primary device those memory cells that appeared in the reference string recently—thus applying speculation. It can exploit spatial locality by moving into the primary device memory cells that are adjacent to those that have recently appeared in the reference string—a combination of speculation and batching (because issuing a GET to a secondary device can retrieve a large block of data that can occupy many adjacent memory cells in the primary device).

There are endless ways in which applications exhibit locality of reference:

- Programs are written as a sequence of instructions. Most of the time, the next instruction is stored in the memory cell that is physically adjacent to the previous instruction, thus creating spatial locality. In addition, applications frequently execute a loop, which means there will be repeated references to the same instructions, creating temporal locality. Between loops, conditional tests, and jumps, it is common to see many instruction references directed to a small subset of all the instructions of an application for an extended time. In addition, depending on the conditional structure, large parts of an application program may not be exercised at all.

- Data structures are typically organized so that a reference to one component of the structure makes references to physically nearby components more likely. Arrays are an example; reference to the first element is likely to be followed shortly by reference to the second. Similarly, if an application retrieves one field of a record, it will likely soon retrieve another field of the same record. Each of these examples creates spatial locality.
- Information processing applications typically process files sequentially. For example, a bank audit program may examine accounts one by one in physical storage order (creating spatial locality) and may perform multiple operations on each account (creating temporal locality).

Although most applications naturally exhibit a significant amount of locality of reference, to a certain extent the concept also embodies an element of self-fulfilling prophecy. Application programmers are usually aware that multilevel memory management is widely used, so they try to write programs that exhibit good locality of reference in the expectation of better performance.

If we look at an application that exhibits locality of reference, in a short time the application refers to only a subset of the total collection of memory cells. The set of references of an application in a given interval Δt is called its *working set*. In one such interval, the application may execute a procedure or loop that operates on a group of related data items, causing most references to go to the text of the procedure and that group of data items. Then, the application might call another procedure, causing most references to go to the text and related data items of that procedure. The working set of an application thus grows, shrinks, and shifts with time.

If at some instant the current working set of an application is entirely stored in the primary memory device, the application will make no references to the secondary device. On the other hand, if the current working set of an application is larger than the primary device, the application (or at least the multilevel memory manager) will have to make at least some references to the secondary device, and it will therefore run more slowly. An application whose working set is much larger than the primary device is likely to cause repeated movement of data back and forth between the primary and secondary devices, a phenomenon called *thrashing*. A design goal is to avoid, or at least minimize, thrashing.

6.2.6 Multilevel Memory Management Policies

Equipped with the concepts of locality of reference and working set, we can now examine the behavior of some common multilevel memory management policies, algorithms that choose which stored objects to place in the primary device, which to place in the secondary device, and when to move a stored object from one device to the other. To make the discussion concrete, we will analyze multilevel memory management policies in the context of a virtual memory system with two levels: RAM (the primary device) and a magnetic disk (the secondary device), in which the stored objects are pages of uniform size. However, it is important to keep in mind that the same analysis applies to any multilevel memory system, whether organized as a cache or a virtual memory, with uniform or variable-sized objects, and any variety of primary and secondary devices.

Each level of a multilevel memory system can be characterized by four items:

- *The string of references directed to that level.* In a virtual memory system, the reference string seen by the primary device is the sequence of page numbers extracted from virtual addresses of both instructions and data, in the order that the application makes references to them. The reference string seen by the secondary device is the sequence of page numbers that were misses in the primary device. The secondary device reference string is thus a shortened version of the primary device reference string.
- *The bring-in policy for that level.* In a virtual memory system, the usual bring-in policy for the primary device is *on-demand*: whenever a page is used, bring it to the primary device if it is not already there. The only remaining policy decision is whether or not to bring along some adjacent pages. In a two-level memory system there is no need for a bring-in policy for the secondary device.
- *The removal policy for that level.* In the primary device of a virtual memory system, this policy chooses a page to evict (the victim) to make room for a new page. Again, in a two-level memory system there is no need for a removal policy for the secondary device.
- *The capacity of the level.* In a virtual memory system, the capacity of the primary level is the number of primary memory blocks, and the capacity of the secondary level is the number of secondary memory blocks. Since the secondary memory normally contains a copy of every page, the capacity of the multilevel memory system is equal to the capacity of the secondary device.

The goal of a multilevel memory system is to have the primary device serve as many references in its reference string as possible, thereby minimizing the number of references in the secondary device reference string. In the example of the multilevel memory manager, this goal means to minimize the number of missing-page exceptions. One might expect that increasing the capacity of the primary device would guarantee a reduction (or at least not an increase) in the number of missing-page exceptions. Surprisingly, this expectation is not always true. As an example, consider the *first-in, first-out (FIFO) page-removal policy*, in which the page selected for removal is the one that has been in the primary device the longest. (That is, the first page that was brought in will be the first page to be removed. This policy is attractive because it is easy to implement by managing the pages of the primary device as a circular buffer.) If the reference string is 0 1 2 3 0 1 4 0 1 2 3 4, and the primary device starts empty, then a primary device with a capacity of three pages will experience nine missing-page exceptions, while a primary device with a capacity of four pages will experience ten missing-page exceptions, as shown in Tables 6.1 and 6.2:

Table 6.1 FIFO Page-Removal Policy with a Three-Page Primary Device

Time	1	2	3	4	5	6	7	8	9	10	11	12	
Reference string	**0**	**1**	**2**	**3**	**0**	**1**	**4**	**0**	**1**	**2**	**3**	**4**	
Primary device contents	-	0	0	0	3	3	3	4	4	4	4	4	Pages brought in
	-	-	1	1	1	0	0	0	0	0	2	2	
	-	-	-	2	2	2	1	1	1	1	1	3	
Remove	-	-	-	0	1	2	3	-	-	0	1	-	
Bring in	0	1	2	3	0	1	4	-	-	2	3	-	9

Table 6.2 FIFO Page-Removal Policy with a Four-Page Primary Device

Time	1	2	3	4	5	6	7	8	9	10	11	12	
Reference string	**0**	**1**	**2**	**3**	**0**	**1**	**4**	**0**	**1**	**2**	**3**	**4**	
Primary device contents	-	0	0	0	0	0	0	4	4	4	4	3	Pages brought in
	-	-	1	1	1	1	1	1	0	0	0	0	
	-	-	-	2	2	2	2	2	2	1	1	1	
	-	-	-	-	3	3	3	3	3	3	2	2	
Remove	-	-	-	-	-	-	0	1	2	3	4	0	
Bring in	0	1	2	3	-	-	4	0	1	2	3	4	10

This unexpected increase of missing-page exception numbers with a larger primary device capacity is called *Belady's anomaly*, named after the author of the paper that first reported it. Belady's anomaly is not commonly encountered in practice, but it suggests that when comparing page-removal policies, what appears to be a better policy might actually be worse with a different primary device capacity. As we shall see, one way to simplify analysis is to avoid policies that can exhibit Belady's anomaly.

The objective of a multilevel memory management policy is to select for removal the page that will minimize the number of missing-page exceptions in the future. If we knew the future reference string, we could look ahead to see which pages are about to be touched. The optimal policy would always choose for removal the page not needed for the longest time. Unfortunately, this policy is unrealizable because it requires predicting the future. However, if we run a program and keep track of its reference string, afterwards we can review that reference string to determine how many missing-page exceptions would have occurred if we had used that optimal policy. That result can then be compared with the policy that was actually used to determine how close it is to the optimal one. This unrealizable policy is known as the *optimal (OPT) page-removal policy*. Tables 6.3 and 6.4 show the result of the OPT page-removal policy applied to the same reference string as before.

Table 6.3 The OPT Page-Removal Policy with a Three-Page Primary Device

Time	1	2	3	4	5	6	7	8	9	10	11	12	
Reference string	**0**	**1**	**2**	**3**	**0**	**1**	**4**	**0**	**1**	**2**	**3**	**4**	
Primary	–	0	0	0	0	0	0	0	0	0	2	3	Pages brought in
device	–	–	1	1	1	1	1	1	1	1	1	1	
contents	–	–	–	2	3	3	3	4	4	4	4	4	
Remove	–	–	–	2	–	–	3	–	–	0	2	–	
Bring in	0	1	2	3	–	–	4	–	–	2	3	–	7

Table 6.4 The OPT Page-Removal Policy with a Four-Page Primary Device

Time	1	2	3	4	5	6	7	8	9	10	11	12	
Reference string	**0**	**1**	**2**	**3**	**0**	**1**	**4**	**0**	**1**	**2**	**3**	**4**	
Primary	–	0	0	0	0	0	0	0	0	0	0	3	Pages brought in
device	–	–	1	1	1	1	1	1	1	1	1	1	
contents	–	–	–	2	2	2	2	2	2	2	2	2	
	–	–	–	–	3	3	3	4	4	4	4	4	
Remove	–	–	–	–	–	–	3	–	–	–	0	–	
Bring in	0	1	2	3	–	–	4	–	–	–	3	–	6

It is apparent from the number of pages brought in that, at least for this reference string, the OPT policy is better than FIFO. In addition, at least for this reference string, the OPT policy gets better when the primary device capacity is larger.

The design goal thus becomes to devise page-removal algorithms that (1) avoid Belady's anomaly, (2) have hit ratios not much worse than the optimal policy, and (3) are mechanically easy to implement.

Some easy-to-implement page-removal policies have an average performance on a wide class of applications that is close enough to the optimal policy to be effective. A popular one is the *least-recently-used (LRU) page-removal policy.* LRU is based on the observation that, more often than not, the recent past is a fairly good predictor of the immediate future. The LRU prediction is that the longer the time since a page has been used, the less likely it will be needed again soon. So LRU selects as its victim the page in the primary device that has not been used for the longest time (that is, the "least-recently-used" page). Let's see how LRU fares when it tackles our example reference string:

Table 6.5 The LRU Page-Removal Policy with a Three-Page Primary Device

Time	**1**	**2**	**3**	**4**	**5**	**6**	**7**	**8**	**9**	**10**	**11**	**12**	
Reference string	**0**	**1**	**2**	**3**	**0**	**1**	**4**	**0**	**1**	**2**	**3**	**4**	
Primary device contents	-	0	0	0	0	0	0	0	0	0	0	3	Pages brought in
	-	-	1	1	2	1	1	1	1	1	1	1	
	-	-	-	2	3	3	3	4	4	4	2	2	
Remove	-	-	-	1	-	2	3	-	-	4	0	1	
Bring in	0	1	2	3	-	1	4	-	-	2	3	4	9

Table 6.6 The LRU Page-Removal Policy with a Four-Page Primary Device

Time	**1**	**2**	**3**	**4**	**5**	**6**	**7**	**8**	**9**	**10**	**11**	**12**	
Reference string	**0**	**1**	**2**	**3**	**0**	**1**	**4**	**0**	**1**	**2**	**3**	**4**	
Primary device contents	-	0	0	0	0	0	0	0	0	0	0	0	Pages brought in
	-	-	1	1	1	1	1	1	1	1	1	1	
	-	-	-	2	2	2	2	4	2	2	2	2	
	-	-	-	-	3	3	3	3	4	4	4	3	
Remove	-	-	-	-	-	-	2	-	-	-	4	0	
Bring in	0	1	2	3	-	-	4	-	-	-	3	4	8

For this reference string, LRU is better than FIFO for a primary memory device of size 4 but not as good as the OPT policy. And for both LRU and the OPT policy the number of page movements is monotonically non-decreasing with primary device size; these two algorithms avoid Belady's anomaly, for a non-obvious reason that will be explained in Section 6.2.7.

Most useful algorithms require that the new page be the only page that moves in and that only one page move out. Algorithms that have this property are called *demand algorithms.* FIFO, LRU, and some algorithms that implement the OPT policy are demand algorithms. If any other page moves in to primary memory, the algorithm is said to use *prepaging*, one of the topics of Section 6.2.9.

As seen above, LRU is not as good as the OPT policy. Because it looks at history rather than the future, it sometimes throws out exactly the wrong page (the page movement at reference #11 in the four-page memory provides an example). For a more extreme example, a program that runs from top to bottom through a virtual memory that is larger than the primary device will always evict exactly the wrong page. Consider a primary device with capacity of four pages that is part of a virtual memory that contains five pages being managed with LRU (the letter "F" means that this reference causes a missing-page exception):

Reference string	0	1	2	3	4	0	1	2	3	4	0	1	2
4-page primary device	F	F	F	F	F	F	F	F	F	F	F	F	F

If the application repeatedly cycles through the virtual memory from one end to the other, each reference to a page will result in a page movement. If we start with an empty primary device, references to page 0 through 3 will result in page movements. The reference to page 4 will also result in a page movement, in which LRU will remove page 0, since page 0 has been used least recently. The next reference, to page 0, will also result in a page movement, which leads LRU to remove page 1, since it has been used least recently. As a consequence, the next reference, to page 1, will result in a page movement, replacing page 2, and so on. In short, every access to a page will result in a page movement.

For such an application, a *most-recently-used (MRU) page-removal policy* would be better. MRU chooses as the victim the most recently used page.

Let's see how MRU fares on the contrived example that gave LRU so much trouble:

Reference string	0	1	2	3	4	0	1	2	3	4	0	1	2
4-page primary memory	F	F	F	F	F				F				F

The initial references to pages 0 through 3 result in page movements that fill the empty primary device. The first reference to page 4 will also result in a page movement, replacing page 3, since page 3 has been used most recently. The next reference, to page 0, will *not* result in a missing-page exception since page 0 is still in the primary device. Similarly, the succeeding references to page 1 and 2 will not result in page movements. The second reference to page 3 will result in a page movement, replacing page 2, but then there will be three references that do not require page movements. Thus, with the MRU page-removal policy, our contrived application will experience fewer missing-page exceptions than with the LRU page-removal policy: once in steady state, MRU will result in one page movement per loop iteration.

In practice, however, LRU is surprisingly robust because past references frequently are a reasonable predictor of future references; examples in which MRU does better are uncommon. A secondary reason why LRU works well is that programmers assume that the multilevel memory system uses LRU or some close approximation as the removal policy and they design their programs to work well under that policy.

6.2.7 Comparative Analysis of Different Policies

Once an overall system architecture that includes a multilevel memory system has been laid out, the designer needs to decide two things that will affect performance:

- How large the primary memory device should be
- Which page removal policy to use

These two decisions can be—and in practice often are—supported by an analysis that begins by instrumenting a hardware processor or an emulator of a processor to maintain a trace of the reference string of a running program. After collecting several such traces of typical programs that are to be run on the system under design, these traces can then be used to simulate the operation of a multilevel memory with various primary device sizes and page-removal policies. The usual measure of a multilevel memory's performance is the hit ratio because it is a pure number whose value depends only on the size of the primary device and the page-removal policy. Given the hit ratio and the latency of the primary and secondary memory devices, one can immediately estimate the performance of the multilevel memory system by using Equation 6.2.

In the early 1970s, a team of researchers at the IBM Corporation developed a rapid way of doing such simulations to calculate hit ratios for one class of page-removal policies. If we look more carefully at the "primary device contents" rows of Tables 6.3 and 6.4, we notice that at all times the optimal policy keeps in the three-page memory a subset of the pages that it keeps in the four-page memory. But in FIFO Tables 6.1 and 6.2, at times 8, 9, 11, and 12, this *subset property* does not hold. This difference is no accident; it is the key to understanding how to avoid Belady's anomaly and how to rapidly analyze a reference string to see how a particular policy will perform for any primary device size.

If a page-removal policy can somehow maintain this subset property at all times and for every possible primary device capacity, then a larger primary device can never have more missing-page exceptions than a smaller one. Moreover, if we consider a primary device of capacity n pages and a primary device of capacity $n + 1$ pages, the subset property ensures that the larger primary device contains exactly one page that is not in the smaller primary device. Repeating this argument for every possible primary device size n, we see that the subset property creates a total ordering of all the pages of the multilevel memory system. For example, suppose a memory of size 1 contains page A. A memory of size 2 must also contain page A, plus one other page, perhaps B. A memory of size 3 must then contain pages A and B plus one other page, perhaps C. Thus, the subset property creates the total ordering $\{A, B, C\}$. This total ordering is independent of the actual capacity chosen for the primary memory device.

The IBM research team called this ordering a "stack" (in a use of that word that has no connection with push-down stacks), and page-removal policies that maintain the subset property have since become known as *stack algorithms*. Although requiring the subset property constrains the range of algorithms, there are still several different, interesting, and practical algorithms in the class. In particular, the OPT policy, LRU, and MRU all turn out to be stack algorithms. When a stack algorithm is in use, the virtual memory system keeps just the pages from the front of the ordering in the primary device; it relegates the remaining pages to the secondary device. As a consequence, if $m < n$, the set of pages in a primary device of capacity m is always a subset of the set of pages in a primary device of capacity n. Thus a larger memory will always be able to satisfy all of the requests that a smaller memory could—and with luck some additional requests. Put another way, the total ordering ensures that if a particular reference hits in a primary memory of size n, it will also hit in every memory larger than n. When a

Table 6.7 Simulation of the LRU Page-Removal Policy for Several Primary Device Sizes

Time	1	2	3	4	5	6	7	8	9	10	11	12	
Reference string	**0**	**1**	**2**	**3**	**0**	**1**	**4**	**0**	**1**	**2**	**3**	**4**	
Stack	0	1	2	3	0	1	4	0	1	2	3	4	
contents	-	0	1	2	3	0	1	4	0	1	2	3	Number of
after reference	-	-	0	1	2	3	0	1	4	0	1	2	moves in
	-	-	-	0	1	2	3	3	3	4	0	1	
	-	-	-	-	-	-	2	2	2	3	4	0	
Size 1 in/out	0/-	1/0	2/1	3/2	0/3	1/0	4/1	0/4	1/0	2/1	3/2	4/3	12
Size 2 in/out	0/-	1/-	2/0	3/1	0/2	1/3	4/0	0/1	1/4	2/0	3/1	4/2	12
Size 3 in/out	0/-	1/-	2/-	3/0	0/1	1/2	4/3	-/-	-/-	2/4	3/0	4/1	10
Size 4 in/out	0/-	1/-	2/-	3/-	-/-	-/-	4/2	-/-	-/-	2/3	3/4	4/0	8
Size 5 in/out	0/-	1/-	2/-	3/-	-/-	-/-	4/-	-/-	-/-	-/-	-/-	-/-	5

stack algorithm is in use, the hit ratio in the primary device is thus guaranteed to be a non-decreasing function of increasing capacity. Belady's anomaly cannot arise.

The more interesting feature of the total ordering and the subset property is that for a given page-removal policy an analyst can perform a simulation of all possible primary memory sizes, with a single pass through a given reference string, by computing the total ordering associated with that policy. At each reference, some page moves to the top of the ordering, and the pages that were above it either move down or stay in their same place, as dictated by the page-removal policy. The simulation notes, for each primary memory device size of interest, whether or not these movements within the total ordering also correspond to movements between the primary and secondary memory devices. By counting those movements, when it reaches the end of the reference string the simulation can directly calculate the hit ratio for each potential primary memory size. Table 6.7 shows the result of this kind of simulation for the LRU policy when it runs with the reference string used in the previous examples. In this table, the "size n in/out" rows indicate which pages, if any, the LRU policy will choose to bring into and remove from primary memory in order to satisfy the reference above. Note that at every instant of time, the "stack contents after reference" are in order by time since last usage, which is exactly what intuition predicts for the LRU policy.

In contrast, when analyzing a non-stack algorithm such as FIFO, one would have to perform a complete simulation of the reference string for each different primary device capacity of interest and construct a separate table such as the one above for each memory size. It is instructive to try to create a similar table for FIFO.

In addition, since the reference string is available, its future is known, and the analyst can, with another simulation pass (running backward through the reference string), learn how the optimal page-removal policy would have performed on that same string for every memory size of interest. The analyst can then compare the OPT result with various realizable page-removal candidate policies.

Table 6.8 The Optimal Page-Removal Policy for All Primary Memory Sizes

Time	**1**	**2**	**3**	**4**	**5**	**6**	**7**	**8**	**9**	**10**	**11**	**12**	
Reference string	**0**	**1**	**2**	**3**	**0**	**1**	**4**	**0**	**1**	**2**	**3**	**4**	
Stack contents after reference	0	1	2	3	0	1	4	0	1	2	3	4	Number of pages removed
	-	0	0	0	3	0	0	4	0	0	0	0	
	-	-	1	1	1	3	1	1	4	4	4	3	
	-	-	-	2	2	2	3	3	3	3	2	2	
	-	-	-	-	-	-	2	2	2	1	1	1	
Size 1 victim	-	0	1	2	3	0	1	4	0	1	2	3	11
Size 2 victim	-	-	1	2	-	3	1	-	1	2	3	4	10
Size 3 victim	-	-	-	2	-	-	4	-	-	2	3	-	7
Size 4 victim	-	-	-	-	-	-	4	-	-	2	-	-	6
Size 5 victim	-	-	-	-	-	-	-	-	-	-	-	-	5

Sidebar 6.6 OPT is a Stack Algorithm and Optimal To see that OPT is a stack algorithm, consider the following description of OPT, in terms of a total ordering:

1. Start with an empty primary device and an empty set that will become a total ordering. As each successive page is touched, note its depth d in the total ordering (if it is not yet in the ordering, set d to infinity) and move it to the front of the total ordering.
2. Then, move the page that was at the front down in the ordering. Move it down until it follows all pages already in the ordering that will be touched before this page is needed again, or to depth d, whichever comes first. This step requires knowing the future.
3. If $d > m$ (where m is the size of the primary memory device), step 1 will require moving a page from the secondary device to the primary device, and step 2 will require moving a page from the primary device to the secondary device.

The result is that, if the algorithm removes a page from primary memory, it will always choose the page that will not be needed for the longest time in the future. Since the total ordering of all pages is independent of the capacity of the primary device, OPT is a stack algorithm. Therefore, for a particular reference string, the set of pages in a primary device of capacity m is always a subset of the set of pages in a primary device of capacity $m + 1$. Table 6.8 illustrates this subset property.

Proof that the optimal page removal policy minimizes page movements, and that it can be implemented as an on-demand stack algorithm, is non-trivial. Table 6.8 illustrates that the statement is correct for the reference string of the previous examples. Sidebar 6.6 provides the intuition of why OPT is a stack algorithm and optimal. The interested reader can find a detailed line of reasoning in the 1970 paper by the IBM researchers [Suggestions for Further Reading 6.1.2] who introduced stack algorithms and explained in depth how to use them in simulations.

6.2.8 Other Page-Removal Algorithms

Any algorithm based on the LRU policy requires updating recency-of-usage information on every memory reference, whether or not a page moves between the primary and secondary devices. For example, in a virtual memory system every instruction and data reference of the running program causes such an update. But manipulating the representation of this usage information may itself require several memory references, which escalates the cost of the original reference. For this reason, most multilevel memory designers look for algorithms that have approximately the same effect but are less costly to implement. One elegant approximation to LRU is the *clock page-removal algorithm.*

The clock algorithm is based on a modest hardware extension in which the virtual memory manager (implemented in the hardware of the processor) sets to TRUE a bit, called the *referenced* bit, in the page table entry for a page whenever the processor makes a reference that uses that page table entry. If at some point in time the multilevel memory manager clears the referenced bit for every page to FALSE, and then the application runs for a while, a survey of the referenced bits will reveal which pages that application used. The clock algorithm consists of a systematic survey of the referenced bits.

Suppose the physical block numbers of the primary device are arranged in numerical order in a ring (i.e., the highest block number is followed by block number 0), as illustrated in Figure 6.9. All referenced bits are initially set to FALSE, and the system begins running. A little later, in Figure 6.9, we find that the pages residing in blocks 0, 1, 2, 4, 6, and 7 have their referenced bits set to TRUE, indicating that some program touched them. Then, some program causes a missing-page exception, and the system invokes the clock algorithm to decide which resident page to evict in order to make room for the missing page. The clock algorithm maintains a pointer much like a clock arm (which is why it is called the clock algorithm). When the virtual memory system needs a free page, the algorithm begins moving the pointer clockwise, surveying the referenced bits as it goes:

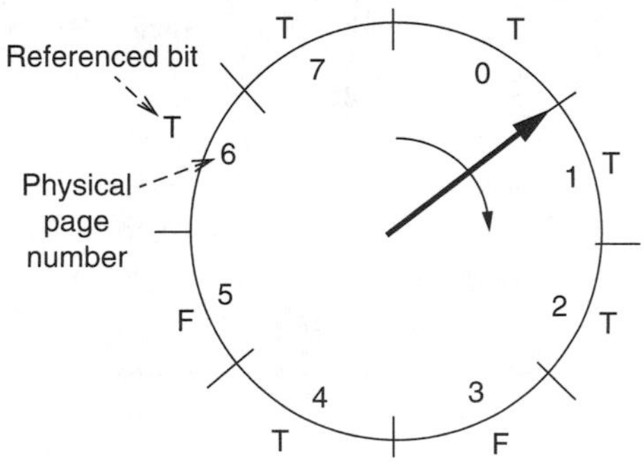

FIGURE 6.9

Example operation of the clock page-removal policy.

1. If the clock arm comes to a block for which the referenced bit is TRUE, the algorithm sets the referenced bit to FALSE and moves the arm ahead to the next block. Thus,

the meaning of the referenced bit becomes "The processor has touched the page residing in this block since the last pass of the clock arm."

2. If the clock arm comes to a block for which the referenced bit is FALSE, that means that the page residing in this block has not been touched since the last pass of the clock arm. This page is thus a good candidate for removal, since it has been used less recently than any page that has its referenced bit set to TRUE. The algorithm chooses this page for eviction and leaves the arm pointing to this block for the next execution of the algorithm.

The clock algorithm thus removes the page residing in the first block that it encounters that has a FALSE referenced bit. If there are no such pages (that is, every block in the primary device has been touched since the previous pass of the clock arm), the clock will move all the way around once, resetting referenced bits as it goes, but at the end of that round it will come again to the first block it examined, which now has a FALSE referenced bit, so it chooses the page in that block. If the clock algorithm were run starting in the state depicted in Figure 6.9, it would choose to remove the page in block 3, since that is the first block in the clockwise direction that has a FALSE referenced bit.

The clock algorithm has a number of nice properties. Space overhead is small: just one extra bit per block of the primary device. The extra time spent per page reference is small: forcing a single bit to TRUE. Typically, the clock algorithm has to scan only a small fraction of the primary device blocks to find a page with a FALSE referenced bit. Finally, the algorithm can be run incrementally and speculatively. For example, if the designer of the virtual memory system wants to keep the number of free blocks above some threshold, it can run the policy ahead of demand, removing pages that haven't been used recently, and stop moving the arm as soon as it has met the threshold.

The clock algorithm provides only a rough approximation to LRU. Rather than strictly determining which page has been used least recently, it simply divides pages into two categories: (1) those used since the last sweep and (2) those not used since the last sweep. It then chooses as its victim the first page that the arm happens to encounter in the second category. This page has been used less recently than any of the pages in the first category, but is probably not the least-recently-used page. What seems like the worst-case scenario for the clock algorithm would be when all pages have their referenced bit set to TRUE; then the clock algorithm has no information on which to decide which pages have recently been used. On the other hand, if every page in the primary device has been used since the last sweep, there probably isn't a much better way of choosing a page to remove.

In multilevel memory systems that are completely implemented in hardware, even the clock algorithm may involve too much complexity, so designers resort to yet simpler policies. For example, some processors use a *random removal policy* for the translation look-aside buffer described in Chapter 5. Random removal can be quite effective in this application because

- its implementation requires minimal state to implement.
- if the look-aside buffer is large enough to hold the current working set of translations, the chance that a randomly chosen victim turns out to be a translation that is about to be needed is relatively small.
- the penalty for removing the wrong translation is also quite small—just one extra reference to a slightly slower random access memory.

Alternatively, some processor cache managers use a completely stateless policy called *direct mapping* in which the page chosen for eviction is the one located in block n modulo m, where n is the secondary device block number of the missing page and m is the number of blocks in the primary device. If the compiler optimizer is aware that the processor uses a direct mapping policy, and it knows the size of the primary device, it can minimize the number of cache misses by carefully positioning instructions and data in the secondary device.

When page-removal policies are implemented in software, designers can use methods that maintain more state. One popular software policy is least-frequently-used, which tracks how often a page is used. Complete coverage of page-removal polices is beyond the scope of this book. The reader is encouraged to explore the large literature on this topic.

6.2.9 Other Aspects of Multilevel Memory Management

Page-removal policies are only one aspect of multilevel memory management. The designer of a multilevel memory manager must also provide a bring-in policy that is appropriate for the system load and, for some systems, may include measures to counter thrashing.

The bring-in policy of all of the paging systems described so far is that pages are moved to the primary device only when the application attempts to use them; such systems are called *demand paging* systems. The alternative method is known as *prepaging*. In a prepaging system, the multilevel memory manager makes a prediction about which pages might be needed and brings them in before the application demands them. By moving pages that are likely to be used before they are actually requested, the multilevel memory manager may be able to satisfy a future reference immediately instead of having to wait for the page to be retrieved from a slower memory. For example, when someone launches a new application or restarts one that hasn't been used for a while, none of its pages may be in the primary device. To avoid the delay that would occur from bringing in a large number of pages one at a time, the multilevel memory manager might choose to prepage as a single batch all of the pages that constitute the program text of the application, or all of the data pages that the application used on a previous execution.

Both demand paging and prepaging make use of speculation to improve performance. Demand paging speculates that the application will touch other bytes on the page just brought in. Prepaging speculates that the application will use the prepaged pages.

A problem that arises in a multiple-application system is that the working sets of the various applications may not all simultaneously fit in the primary device. When that is case, the multilevel memory manager may have to resort to more drastic measures to avoid thrashing. One such drastic measure is *swapping*. When an application encounters a long wait, the multilevel memory manager moves all of its pages out of the primary device in a batch. A batch of writes to the disk can usually be scheduled to go faster than a series of single-block writes (Section 6.3.4 discusses this opportunity). In addition, swapping an application completely out immediately provides space for the other applications, so when they encounter a missing-page exception there is no need to wait to move some page out. However, to do swapping, the multilevel memory manager must be able to quickly identify which pages in primary memory are being used by the application being swapped out, and which of those pages are shared with other applications and therefore should not be swapped out.

Swapping is usually combined with prepaging. When a swapped-out application is restarted, the multilevel memory manager prepages the previous working set of that application, in the hope of later reducing the number of missing-page exceptions. This strategy speculates that when the program restarts, it will need the same pages that it was using before it was swapped out.

The trade-offs involved in swapping and prepaging are formidable, and they resist modeling analysis because reasonably accurate models of application program behavior are difficult to obtain. Fortunately, technology improvements have made these techniques less important for a large class of systems. However, they continue to be applicable to specialized systems that require the utmost in performance.

6.3 SCHEDULING

When a stage is temporarily overloaded in Figure 6.3, a queue of requests builds up. An important policy decision is to determine which requests from the queue to perform first. For example, if the disk has a queue of disk requests, in which order should the disk manager schedule them to minimize latency? For another example, should a stage schedule requests in the order they are received? That policy may result in high throughput, but perhaps in high average latency for individual requests because one client's expensive request may delay several inexpensive requests from other clients. These questions are all examples of the general question of how to schedule resources. This section provides an introduction to systematic answers to this general question. This introduction is sufficient to tackle resource scheduling problems that we encounter in later chapters but scratches only the surface of the literature on scheduling.

Because the technology underlying resources improves rapidly in computer systems, some scheduling decisions become irrelevant over time. For example, in the 1960s and 1970s when several users shared a single computer and the processor was a performance bottleneck, scheduling the processor among users was important. With the arrival of personal computers and the increase in processing power, processor scheduling became mostly irrelevant because it is no longer a performance bottleneck in most situations, and any reasonable policy is good enough. On the other hand, with massive Internet services handling millions of paying customers, the issue of scheduling has increased in importance. The Internet exposes Web sites to extreme variations in load, which can result in more requests than a server can handle at an instant of time, and the service must make a choice in which order to handle the queued requests.

6.3.1 Scheduling Resources

Computer systems make scheduling decisions at different levels of abstraction. At a high level of abstraction, a Web site selling goods might allocate more memory and processor time to a user who always buys goods than to a user who never buys goods but just browses the catalog. At a lower level of abstraction, a bus arbiter must decide to which processor's memory reference to allocate a shared bus.

Although in these examples allocation decisions are made at different levels of abstraction, the scheduling problem is similar. From the perspective of scheduling, a computer system is a collection of entities that require the use of a set of resources, and *scheduling* is the set of policies and dispatch mechanisms to allocate resources to entities. Examples of entities include threads, address spaces, users, clients, services, and requests. Examples of resources include processor time, physical memory space, disk space, network capacity, and I/O-bus time. Policies to assign resources to entities include dividing the resources equally among the entities, giving one entity priority over another entity, and providing some minimum guarantee by performing admission control on the number of entities. The *scheduler* is the component that implements a policy.

Designing the right policy is difficult because there are usually gaps between the high-level goal and the available policy, between the chosen policy and mechanism to dispatch, and between the chosen mechanism and its actual implementation. We discuss each of these challenges in turn.

The desired scheduling policy might incorporate elements of the environment in which the computer system is used but that are difficult to capture in a computer system. For example, how can a Web site identify a high-value customer (that is, one who is likely to make a large purchase)? The high-value user might never have bought before at this site, or it may be difficult to associate an anonymous catalog-browsing request with a particular previous customer. Even if we could identify the request with a particular customer, the request may traverse several modules of the Web site, some of which may have no notion of users. For example, the database that contains information about prices and goods might be unable to prioritize requests from an important customer.

If we can construct the right policy, then there is the challenge of identifying the mechanism to implement the policy. One module might implement a scheduling policy, but because another module is not aware of it, the policy is ineffective. For example, we might desire to give the text editor high priority to provide a good interactive experience to users. We can easily change the thread scheduler to give the thread running the editor higher priority than any other runnable thread. However, how does the bus arbiter, shared file service, or disk scheduler know that a memory, file, or disk request on behalf of the editor should have higher priority than other disk or memory requests? Worse, the disk scheduler is likely to delay operations to batch disk requests to achieve high throughput, but this decision may result in bad interactive performance for the text editor because its requests are delayed.

The final challenge is getting the actual implementation of the mechanism right. Sidebar 6.7 on receive livelock provides an example of how easy it is for two schedulers to interact badly. It illustrates that to design a computer system that doesn't collapse under overload is a challenge and requires that a designer carefully think through all implementation decisions.

The list of challenges in designing and implementing schedulers is formidable, but fortunately sophisticated schedulers are often not a requirement for computer systems. Airlines use sophisticated and complex scheduling algorithms because they deal with genuinely expensive and scarce resources (such as airplanes, landing slots, and fuel) and situations in which the peak load can be far larger than usual load (e.g., travel around family holidays). Usually, in a computer system few resources are truly scarce, and simple policies, mechanisms, and implementations suffice.

The rest of Section 6.3 introduces some common goals for a scheduler in a computer system, describes some basic policies to achieve these goals, and presents a case study of scheduling a disk arm. Along the way, the section points out a few scheduling pitfalls, such as receive livelock and priority inversion.

6.3.2 Scheduling Metrics

To appreciate possible goals for a scheduler, consider the thread scheduler from the previous chapter. It chooses a thread from a set of runnable threads. In the implementation of the thread manager in Figure 5.24, the scheduler picks the threads in the order in which they appear in the thread table. This scheduling policy is one of many possible policies.

By slightly restructuring the thread scheduler, it could implement different policies easily. A more general implementation of the thread manager would follow the design hint *separate mechanism from policy* (see Sidebar 6.5). This implementation would separate the dispatch mechanism (the mechanisms for suspending and resuming a thread) from scheduling policy (selecting which thread to run next) by putting them into their own procedures, so that a designer can change the policy without having to change the dispatch mechanism.

A designer may want to change the policy because there is no one single best scheduling policy. "Best" might mean different things in different situations. For example, there is tension between achieving good overall efficiency and providing good service to individual requests. From the system's perspective, the two important measures for "best" are throughput and utilization. With a good scheduler, throughput grows linearly with offered load until throughput hits the capacity of the system. A good scheduler will also ensure that a system doesn't collapse under overload conditions. Finally, a good scheduler is efficient: it doesn't consume many resources itself. A scheduler that needs 90% of the processor's time to do its job is not of much value.

Applications achieve high throughput by being immediately scheduled when a request arrives and processing it to completion, without being rescheduled.

Sidebar 6.7 Receive Livelock When a system is temporarily overloaded, it is important to have an effective response to the overload situation. The response doesn't have to be perfect, but it must ensure that the system doesn't collapse. For example, suppose that a Web news server can handle 1,000 requests per second, but a short time ago there was a big earthquake in Los Angeles and requests are arriving at the rate 10,000 per second. The goal is to successfully serve (perhaps a random) 10% of the load, but if the designer isn't careful, the server may end up serving 0%. The problem is called *receive livelock*, and it can arise if the server spends too much of its time saying "I'm too busy" and as a result never gets a chance to serve any of the requests. Consider the following simple interrupt-driven Web service with a bounded buffer:

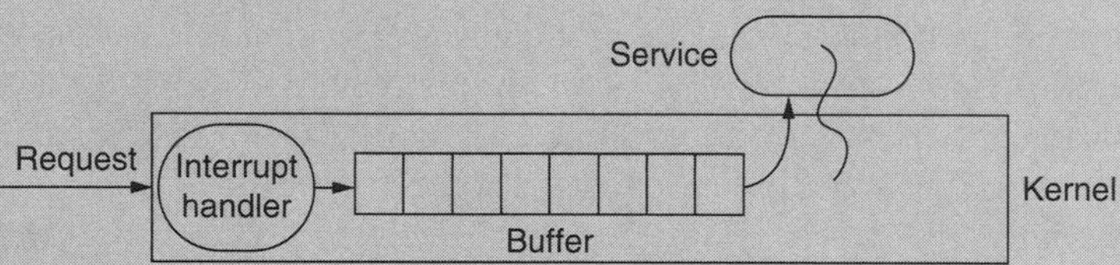

When a request arrives on the network device, the device generates an interrupt, which causes the interrupt handler to run. The interrupt handler copies the request from the device into a bounded buffer and reenables interrupts so that it can receive the next request. The service has a single thread, which consumes requests from the bounded buffer. When the service is overloaded and requests arrive faster than the service can process them, then the system as described reaches a state where it serves no requests at all because it experiences receive livelock.

Consider what happens when requests arrive much faster than the service can process them. While the service thread is processing a request, the processor receives an interrupt from the network device and the interrupt handler runs. The interrupt handler copies the request into the buffer, notifies the service thread, and returns, reenabling interrupts. As soon as the handler reenables interrupts, the arrival of another request may interrupt the processor again, invoking the interrupt handler. The interrupt handler goes through the same sequence as before until the buffer fills up; then it has no other choice than to discard the request and return from the interrupt, reenabling interrupts. If the network device has another request available, it will interrupt the processor immediately again; the interrupt handler will throw the request away and return. This sequence of events continues indefinitely as long as requests arrive faster than the time for the interrupt handler to run. We have receive livelock: the service never runs, and as a result the number of requests processed by the service per second drops to zero; to users the Web site appears to be down!

The problem here is that the processor's internal scheduler interacts badly with the thread scheduler. Conceptually, the processor schedules the main thread and the

(*Sidebar continues*)

interrupt thread, and the thread manager schedules the main processor thread among the service thread and any other threads. The processor scheduler gives absolute priority to the interrupt thread, scheduling it as soon as an interrupt arrives; the main thread never gets a chance to run the thread manager, and as a result the service thread never receives the processor. This problem occurs when some processing must be performed *outside* of the interrupt handler. One could contemplate moving all processing into interrupt handlers. This approach has its own problems (as discussed in Section 5.6.4) and negates the modularity advantages of using threads. However, once the problem is stated as a scheduling problem, a solution is available.

The solution [Suggestions for Further Reading 6.4.2] is to modify the scheduling policy so that the service thread gets a chance to run when requests are available in the bounded buffer. This policy can be implemented with a slight modification to the interrupt handler. If the bounded buffer fills up, the interrupt handler should not reenable interrupts as it returns. When the service thread has drained the bounded buffer, say, to only half full, it should reenable interrupts. This policy ensures that the network device doesn't discard requests unless the buffer is full (i.e., there is an overload situation) and sees that the service thread gets a chance to process requests, avoiding livelock.

It is still possible that requests may be discarded. If the network device receives a request but it cannot generate an interrupt, the device has no other choice than to discard the next request. This situation is unavoidable: if the network can generate a higher load than the capacity of the service, the device must shed load. The good news is that under overload the system will at least process some requests rather than none at all.

For example, any time a thread scheduler starts a thread, but then preempts it to run another thread, it is delaying the preempted thread. Thus, for an application to achieve high throughput, a scheduler must minimize the number of preemptions and the number of scheduling decisions. Unfortunately, this system-level goal may conflict with the needs of individual threads.

Each individual request wants good service, which typically means good response: it starts soon and completes quickly. There are several ways of measuring a request's response:

- *Turnaround time*. The length of time from when a request arrives at a service until it completes.
- *Response time*. The length of time from when a request arrives at a service until it starts producing output. For interactive requests, this measure is typically more useful than turnaround time. For example, many Web browsers optimize for this metric. Typically, a browser displays an incomplete Web page as soon as the browser receives parts of it (e.g., the text) and fills in the remainder later (e.g., images).

- *Waiting time*. The length of time from when a request arrives at a service until the service starts processing the request. This measure is better than turnaround time, since it captures how long the thread must wait even though it is ready to execute. The ideal waiting time is zero seconds.

More sophisticated measures are also possible by combining the performance of all requests using some of these measures and some way of combining. For example, one can compute *average waiting time* as the average of waiting times of all requests. Similarly, one can calculate the sum of the waiting times, the variance in response time, and so on.

In an interactive computer system, many requests are on behalf of a human user sitting in front of a display. Therefore, the perception of the user is another measure of the goodness of the service that a request receives. For example, an interactive user may tend to perceive a high variance in response time to be more annoying than a high mean. On the other hand, a response time that is faster than the human reaction time may not improve the perception of goodness.

Sometimes a designer desires a scheduler that provides some degree of *fairness*, which means that each request obtains an equal share of the shared service. A scheduler that starves a request to serve other requests is an unfair scheduler. An unfair scheduler is not necessarily a bad scheduler; it may have higher throughput and better response time than a fair scheduler.

It is easy to convince oneself that designing a scheduler that optimizes for fairness, throughput, and response time all at the same time is an impossible task. As a result, there are many different scheduling algorithms; each one of them optimizes along different dimensions.

6.3.3 Scheduling Policies

To illustrate some basic scheduling algorithms, we present a number of them in the context of a thread manager. The objective is to share the processor efficiently among multiple threads. For example, when one thread is blocked waiting for I/O, we would like to run a different, runnable thread on the processor. These threads might be running different programs on a shared computer, or a number of threads that cooperate to implement a high-performance Web service on a dedicated computer.

Since threads typically go through a cycle of running and waiting (e.g., waiting for user input, a client request, or completion of disk request), it is useful to model a thread as a series of *jobs*. Each job corresponds to one burst of activity.

We survey a few different algorithms to schedule these jobs. Many textbooks, lecture notes, and papers explore these algorithms in more detail, and our description is based on this literature. Although the algorithms are described in the context of a thread manager for a single processor, the algorithms are generic and apply to other contexts as well. For example, they work equally well for multiprocessors and have the same pros and cons, but they are harder to illustrate when several jobs run concurrently. The algorithms also apply to disk-arm scheduling, which we shall discuss in Section 6.3.4.

6.3.3.1 First-Come, First-Served

At a busy post office, customers may be asked to take a ticket with a number as they walk in and wait until the number on their ticket is called. Typically, the post office allocates the numbers in strict increasing order and calls the numbers in that order. This policy is called a *first-come, first-served (FCFS) scheduler* and some thread managers use it too.

A thread manager can implement the first-come, first-served policy by organizing the ready list as a first-in, first-out queue. The manager simply runs the first job on the queue until it finishes; then the manager runs the next job, which is now the first job, and so on. When a job becomes ready, the scheduler simply adds it to the end of the queue.

To illustrate and analyze the behavior of a scheduling policy, the literature uses sequences of job arrivals, in which each job has a specific amount of work. We adopt one particular sequence, which illustrates the differences between the scheduling algorithms that we cover. This sequence is the following:

Job	Arrival Time	Amount of Work
A	0	3
B	1	5
C	3	2

Given a specific sequence, one can draw a timeline that depicts when the thread manager dispatches jobs. For the above sequence and the first-come, first-served policy this timeline is as follows:

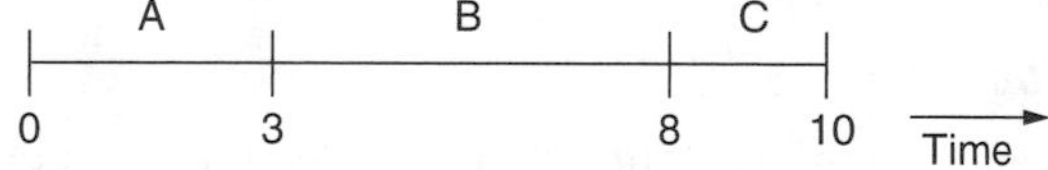

Given this timeline, one can fill out a table that includes finish time and waiting times, and make some observations about a policy. For the above timeline and the first-come, first-served policy this table is as follows:

Job	Arrival Time	Amount of Work	Start Time	Finish Time	Waiting Time Till Job Starts	Wait Time Till Job is Done
A	0	3	0	3	0	3
B	1	5	3	8	2	7
C	3	2	8	10	5	7
	Total waiting				7	

From the table we can see that for the given job sequence, the first-come, first-served policy favors the long jobs A and B. Job C waits 5 seconds to start a job that takes 2 seconds. Relative to the amount of work, job C is punished the most.

Because first-come, first-served can favor long jobs over short jobs, a system can get into an undesirable state. Consider what happens if we have a system with one thread that periodically waits for I/O but mostly computes and several threads that perform mostly I/O operations. Suppose the scheduler runs the I/O-bound threads first. They will all quickly finish their jobs and go start their I/O operations, leaving the scheduler to run the processor-bound thread. After a while, the I/O-bound threads will finish their I/O and queue up behind the processor-bound thread, leaving all the I/O devices idle. When the processor-bound thread finishes its job, it initiates its I/O operation, allowing the scheduler to run the I/O-bound threads.

As before, the I/O-bound threads will quickly finish computation and initiate an I/O operation. Now we have the processor sitting idle, while all the threads are waiting for their I/O operations to complete. Since the processor-bound thread started its I/O first, it will likely finish first, grabbing the processor and making all the other threads wait before they can run. The system will continue this way, alternating between periods when the processor is busy and all the I/O devices are idle with periods when the processor is idle and all the threads are doing I/O in a convoy, which is why the literature sometimes refers to this case as a *convoy effect*. The main opportunity for having threads is missed, since in this convoy scenario the system never overlaps computation with I/O.

This scenario is unlikely to materialize in practice because workloads are unlikely to have exactly the right mix of computing and I/O threads that would produce a sequence of scheduling decisions that lead to a situation where I/O isn't overlapped at all with computation. Nevertheless, it has inspired researchers to think about policies other than first-come, first-served.

6.3.3.2 Shortest-Job-First

The undesirable scenario with the first-come first-served policy suggests another scheduler: a *shortest-job-first scheduler*. Whenever the time comes to dispatch a job, the scheduler chooses the job that has the shortest expected running time. Shortest-job-first requires that the scheduler has a prediction of the running time of a job before running it. In the general case, it is difficult to make predictions of the running time of a job, but in practice there are special cases that can work.

Let's assume we know the running time of a job beforehand and see how a shortest-job-first scheduler performs on the example sequence:

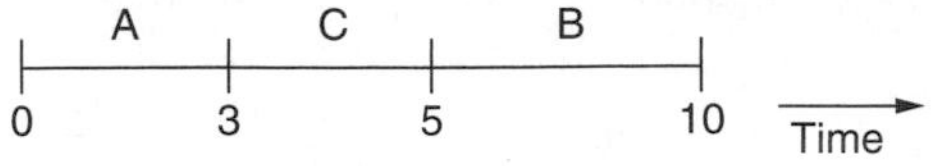

A C B
0 3 5 10 Time

As we can see, job C runs before job B because when the scheduler runs after job A completes, it picks C instead of B, since job C has just entered the system and needs less time than job B. Here is the complete table for the shortest-job-first policy:

Job	Arrival Time	Amount of Work	Start Time	Finish Time	Waiting Time Till Job Starts	Waiting Time Till Job is Done
A	0	3	0	3	0	3
B	1	5	5	10	4	9
C	3	2	3	5	0	2
	Total waiting				4	

Job B's waiting time has increased, but relative to the amount of work it has to do, it has to wait less than job C did under the first-come, first-served policy. The *total* amount of waiting time for the shortest-job-first policy decreased compared to the first-come, first-served policy (4 versus 7).

The shortest-job-first policy has one implementation challenge: how do we know the amount of work a job has to do? In some cases, we may be able to decide before running the job whether or not this is a short job. For example, if we have two requests for reading different sectors on the disk and the disk arm is close to one of them, then the request that requires moving the arm to the closer track is the shorter job.

If we cannot decide without executing a job whether or not the job is short, we can make some forward progress by assuming that jobs fall in different classes: a thread that is interactive has mostly short jobs, while a thread that is computationally intensive is likely to have mostly long jobs. This suggests that if we track the past behavior of a thread, then we might be able to predict its future behavior. For example, if a thread just completed a short job, we might predict that its next job also will be short. We can make this idea more precise by basing our prediction on all past jobs of a given thread. One way of doing so is using an *Exponentially Weighted Moving Average (EWMA)* (see Sidebar 7.6 [on-line]). Of course, past behavior may be a weak indicator of future behavior.

A disadvantage of the shortest-job-first policy versus the first-come first-served policy is that shortest-job-first may lead to *starvation*. Several threads that consist entirely of short jobs and that together present a load large enough to use up the available processors may prevent a long job from ever being run. In practice, as we will see in Sections 6.3.3.4 and 6.3.4, the shortest-job-first policy can be combined with other policies to avoid starvation.

6.3.3.3 Round-Robin

One of the issues with shortest job first is identifying which jobs are short and which are long. One approach is to make all jobs short by breaking long jobs up into a number of smaller jobs using preemptive scheduling. A preemptive scheduling policy stops a job after a certain amount of time so that the scheduler can pick another job, resuming the preempted one at some time later. As we discussed in Chapter 5, preemptive scheduling also has the benefit that it enforces modularity; a programming error cannot cause a job to never release the processor.

A simple preemptive scheduling policy is *round-robin scheduling*. A round-robin scheduler maintains a queue of runnable jobs as before. It selects the first job from this queue, as in the first-come first-serve policy, but stops the job after some period of time, and selects a new job. Some time later the scheduler will select the stopped job again and run it again for no longer than the fixed period of time, and so on, until the job completes.

Round-robin can be implemented as follows. Before running the job, the round-robin scheduler sets a timer with a fixed time value, called a *quantum*. When the timer expires, it causes an interrupt and the interrupt handler calls YIELD. This call gives control back to the scheduler, which moves the job to the end of the queue and selects a new job from the front of the queue. The quantum should be long enough that most short jobs complete without being interrupted, and it should be short enough that most long jobs do get interrupted so that short jobs can get to run sooner.

Let's look at how a round-robin scheduler with a quantum of 1 second performs on the example sequence:

A B A B C A B C B B
0 1 2 3 4 5 6 7 8 9 10 Time

At time 0, only A is in the queue of runnable jobs, so the scheduler selects it. At time 1, B is in the queue so the scheduler selects B and appends A to the end of the queue, since it is not done. At time 2, A is at the front, so the scheduler selects A and appends B to the end of the queue. At time 3, the scheduler appends C to the end of the queue after B. Then, the scheduler selects B, since it is at the front of the queue, and appends A after C. At time 4, the scheduler appends B to the end of the queue and selects C to run. At time 5, the scheduler appends C to the end of the queue and selects A. At time 6, A is done, and the scheduler selects B, and so on.

This timeline results in the following table:

Job	Arrival Time	Amount of Work	Start Time	Finish Time	Waiting Time Till Job Starts	Waiting Time Till Job is Done
A	0	3	0	6	0	6
B	1	5	1	10	1	9
C	3	2	5	8	2	5
	Total waiting				3	

As can been seen in this example, compared to first-come, first-served and shortest-job-first, round-robin results in the worst performance to complete an individual job, measured in total time elapsed since start. This is not surprising because a round-robin scheduler forces long jobs to stop after a quantum of time.

Round-robin, however, has the shortest total waiting time because with round-robin jobs start earlier: every job runs no longer than a quantum before it is stopped and the scheduler selects another job.

Round-robin favors jobs that run for less than a quantum at the expense of jobs that are more than a quantum long, since the scheduler will stop a long job after one quantum and run the short one before returning the processor to the long one. Round-robin is found in many computer systems because many computer systems are interactive, have short jobs, and a quick response provides a good user experience.

6.3.3.4 Priority Scheduling

Some jobs are more important than others. For example, a system thread that performs minor housekeeping chores such as garbage collecting unused temporary files might be given lower priority than a thread that runs a user program. In addition, if a thread has been blocked for a long time, it might be better to give it higher priority over threads that have run recently.

A scheduler can implement such policies using a *priority scheduling policy*, which assigns each job a priority number.The dispatcher selects the job with the highest priority number. The scheduler must have some rule to break ties, but it doesn't matter much what the rule is, as long as it doesn't consistenly favor one job over another.

A scheduler can assign priority numbers in many different ways. The scheduler could use a predefined assignment (e.g., systems jobs have priority 1, and user jobs have priority 0) or the priority could be computed using a policy function provided by the system designer. Or the scheduler could compute priorities *dynamically*. For example, if a thread has been waiting to run for a long time, the scheduler could temporarily boost the priority number of the thread's job. This approach can be used, for example, to avoid the starvation problem of the shortest-job-first policy.

A priority scheduler may be preemptive or non-preemptive. In the preemptive version, when a high-priority job enters while a low-priority job is running, the scheduler may preempt the low-priority job and start the high-priority job immediately. For example, an interrupt may notify a high-priority thread. When the interrupt handler calls NOTIFY, a preemptive thread manager may run the scheduler, which may interrupt some other processor that is running a low-priority job. The non-preemptive version would not do any rescheduling or preemption at interrupt time, so the low-priority job would run to completion; when it calls AWAIT, the scheduler will switch to the newly runnable high-priority job.

As we make schedulers more sophisticated, we have to be on the alert for surprising interactions among different schedulers. For example, if a thread manager that provides priorities isn't carefully designed, it is possible that the highest priority thread obtains the least amount of processor time. Sidebar 6.8, which explains priority inversion, describes this pitfall.

Sidebar 6.8 Priority Inversion Priority inversion is a common pitfall in designing a scheduler with priorities. Consider a thread manager that implements a preemptive, priority scheduling policy. Let's assume we have three threads, T_1, T_2, and T_3, and threads T_1 and T_3 share a lock *l* that serializes references to a shared resource. Thread T_1 has a low priority (1), thread T_2 has a medium priority (2), and thread T_3 has a high priority (3).

The following timing diagram shows a sequence of events that causes the high-priority thread T_3 to be delayed indefinitely while the medium priority thread T_2 receives the processor continuously.

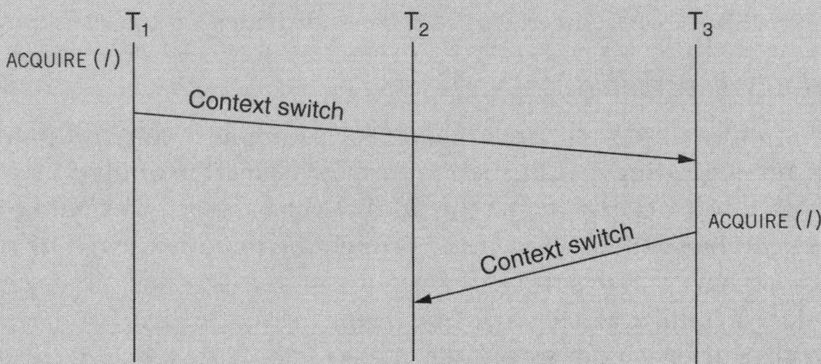

Let's assume that T_2 and T_3 are not runnable; for example, they are waiting for an I/O operation to complete. The scheduler will schedule T_1, and T_1 acquires lock *l*. Now the I/O operation completes, and the I/O interrupt handler notifies T_2 and T_3. The scheduler chooses T_3 because it has the highest priority. T_3 runs for a short time until it tries to acquire lock *l*, but because T_1 already holds that lock, T_3 must wait. Because T_2 is runnable and has higher priority than T_1, the thread scheduler will select T_2. T_2 can compute indefinitely; when T_2's time quantum runs out, the scheduler will find two threads runnable: T_1 and T_2. It will select T_2 because T_2 has a higher priority than T_1. As long as T_2 doesn't call WAIT, T_2 will keep the processor. As long as T_2 is runnable, the scheduler won't run T_1, and thus T_1 will not be able to release the lock and T_3, the high priority thread, will wait indefinitely. This undesirable phenomenon is known as *priority inversion*.

The solution to this specific example is simple. When T_3 blocks on acquiring lock *l*, it should temporarily lend its priority to the holder of the lock (sometimes called *priority inheritance*)—in this case, T_1. With this solution, T_1 will run instead of T_2, and as soon as T_1 releases the lock its priority will return to its normal low value and T_3 will run. In essence, this example is one of interacting schedulers. The thread manager schedules the processor and locks schedule references to shared resources. A challenge in designing computer systems is recognizing schedulers and understanding the interactions between them.

(Sidebar continues)

The problem and solution have been "discovered" by researchers in the real-time system, database, and operating system communities, and are well documented by now. Nevertheless, it is easy to fall into the priority inversion pitfall. For example, in July 1997 the Mars Pathfinder spacecraft experienced total systems resets on Mars, which resulted in loss of experimental data collected. The software engineers traced the cause of the resets to a priority inversion problem*.

*Mike Jones. What really happened on Mars? *Risks Forum 19,* 49 (December 1997). The Web page http://research.microsoft.com/~mbj/Mars_Pathfinder/Mars_Pathfinder.html includes additional information, including a follow-up by Glenn Reeves, who led the software team for the Mars Pathfinder.

6.3.3.5 Real-Time Schedulers

Certain applications have *real-time* constraints; they require delivery of results before a specified deadline. A chemical process controller, for instance, might have a valve that must be opened every 10 seconds because otherwise a container overflows. Such applications employ *real-time schedulers* to guarantee that jobs complete by the stated deadline.

For some systems, such as a chemical plant, a nuclear reactor, or a hospital intensive-care unit, missing a deadline might result in disaster. Such systems require a *hard real-time scheduler.* For these schedulers, designers must carefully determine the amount of resources each job takes and design the complete system to ensure that all jobs can be handled in a timely manner, even in the worst case. Determining the amount of resources necessary and the time that a job takes, however, is difficult. For example, a system with a cache might sometimes run a job fast (when the job's references hit in the cache) and sometimes slow (when the job's references miss in the cache). Therefore, designers of hard real-time systems make the time a job takes as predictable as possible, either by turning off performance-enhancing techniques (e.g., caches) or by assuming the worst case performance. Typically, designers turn off interrupts and poll devices so that they can carefully control when to interact with a device. These techniques combined increase the likelihood that the designer can estimate when jobs will arrive and for how long they will run. Once the amount of resources and time required for each job are estimated, the designer of a hard real-time system can compute the schedule for executing all jobs.

For other systems, such as a digital music system, missing a deadline occasionally might be just a minor annoyance; such systems can use a *soft real-time scheduler.* A soft real-time scheduler attempts to meet all deadlines but doesn't guarantee it; it may miss a deadline. If, for example, multiple jobs arrive simultaneously, all have 1 second of work, and all have a deadline in 1 second, all jobs except one will miss their deadlines. The goal of a soft real-time scheduler is to avoid missing deadlines but to accept that it might happen when there is more work than there is time before the deadline to do the work.

One popular heuristic for avoiding missing deadlines is the *earliest-deadline-first scheduler*, which keeps the queue of jobs sorted by deadline. The dispatcher runs the first job on the queue, which is always the one with the closest deadline. Most students and faculty follow this policy: work first on the homework or paper that has the earliest deadline. This scheduling policy minimizes the total (summed) lateness of all the jobs.

For soft real-time schedulers that have a given set of jobs that must execute at periodic intervals, we can develop scheduling algorithms instead of just heuristics. Systems with periodic jobs are quite common. For example, a digital video recorder must process a picture frame every 1/30th of a second to make the output look like a movie.

To develop a scheduler for such a system, the total amount of work to be done by the periodic jobs must be less than the capacity of the system. Consider a system with n periodic jobs i that happen with a period of P_i seconds and that each requires C_i seconds. The load of such a system can be handled only if:

$$\left(\sum_{i=1}^{n} \frac{C_i}{P_i}\right) \leq 1$$

If the total amount of work exceeds the system's capacity at any time, then the system will miss a deadline. If the total amount of work is less than the capacity, the system may still miss a deadline occasionally because for some short interval of time the total amount of work to be done is greater than the capacity of the system. For example, a periodic interrupt may arrive at the same time that a periodic task must run. Thus, the condition stated is a necessary condition but not a sufficient one.

A good algorithm for dynamically scheduling periodic jobs is the *rate monotonic scheduler*. In the design phase of the system, the designer assigns each job a priority that is proportional to the frequency of the occurrence of that job. For example, a job that needs to run every 100 milliseconds receives a priority 10, and a job that needs to run every 200 milliseconds receives a priority 5. At runtime, the scheduler always runs the highest priority job, preempting a running job if necessary.

6.3.4 Case Study: Scheduling the Disk Arm

Much work has been done on thread scheduling, but since processors are no longer a usual performance bottleneck, thread scheduling has become less important. As explained in Section 6.1, however, disk arm scheduling is important because the mechanical disk arm creates an I/O bottleneck. The typical goal of a disk arm scheduler is to optimize overall throughput as opposed to the delay for each individual request.

When a disk controller receives a batch of disk requests from the file system, it must decide the order in which to process these requests. At first glance, it might appear that first-come first-served is a fine choice for scheduling the requests, but unfortunately that choice is a bad one.

To see why, recall from Section 6.1 that if the controller moves the disk arm, it reduces the transfer rate of the disk because seeking from one track to another takes time. However, the time required to do a seek depends on how many tracks the arm must cross. A simple, but adequate, model is that a seek from one track to another track that is n tracks away takes $n \times t$ seconds, where t is roughly constant.

Consider a disk controller that is on track 0 and receives four requests that require seeks to the tracks 0 (the innermost track), 90, 5, and 100 (outermost track). If the disk controller performs the four requests in the order in which it received them (first-come first-served), then it will seek first to track 0, then to 90, back to 5, and then forward to 100, for a total seek latency of $270t$:

Request	Movement	Time
Seek 1	$0 \rightarrow 0$	$0t$
Seek 2	$0 \rightarrow 90$	$90t$
Seek 3	$90 \rightarrow 5$	$85t$
Seek 4	$5 \rightarrow 100$	$95t$
Total		$270t$

A much better algorithm is to sort the requests by track number and process them in the sorted order. The total seek latency for that algorithm is $100t$:

Request	Movement	Time
Seek 1	$0 \rightarrow 0$	$0t$
Seek 2	$0 \rightarrow 5$	$5t$
Seek 3	$5 \rightarrow 90$	$85t$
Seek 4	$90 \rightarrow 100$	$10t$
Total		$100t$

In practice, disk scheduling algorithms are more complex because new requests arrive while the disk controller is working on a set of requests. For example, if the disk controller is working on requests in the order of track number (0, 5, 90, and 100), it finishes 5, and receives a new request for track 1, which request should it perform next? It can go back and perform 1, or it can keep going and perform 90 and 100. The first choice is an algorithm that is called shortest seek first; the second choice is called the *elevator algorithm*, named after the algorithm that many elevators execute to transport people from floor to floor in buildings. With shortest-seek-first, the total seek time is $108t$:

Request	Movement	Time
Seek 1	$0 \rightarrow 0$	$0t$
Seek 2	$0 \rightarrow 5$	$5t$
Seek 3	$5 \rightarrow 1$	$4t$
Seek 4	$1 \rightarrow 90$	$89t$
Seek 5	$90 \rightarrow 100$	$10t$
Total		$108t$

With the elevator algorithm, the total seek latency is $199t$:

Request	Movement	Time
Seek 1	$0 \rightarrow 0$	$0t$
Seek 2	$0 \rightarrow 5$	$5t$
Seek 3	$5 \rightarrow 90$	$85t$
Seek 4	$90 \rightarrow 100$	$10t$
Seek 5	$100 \rightarrow 1$	$99t$
Total		$199t$

Many disk controllers use a combination of the shortest-seek-first algorithm and the elevator algorithm. When processing requests, for a while they use the shortest-seek algorithm to choose requests, minimizing seek time, but then switch to the elevator algorithm to avoid starving requests for more distant tracks. For example, if the controller performs the request for track 1 first, starts seeking into the direction of 90, but at track 5 another request for track 1 comes in, then shortest-seek-first would go back to track 1. Since this sequence of events may repeat forever, the disk controller may never serve the request for tracks 90 and 100. By bounding the time that disk controllers perform shortest-seek-first and then switching to the elevator algorithm, requests for the distant tracks will also be served. This method is fine for disk systems, since the primary objective is to maximize total throughput, and thus delaying one request over another is acceptable. In a building, however, people do not want to have long delays, and therefore for buildings the elevator algorithm is better.

EXERCISES

6.1 Suppose a processor has a clock rate of 100 megahertz. The time required to retrieve a word from the cache is 1 nanosecond, and the time required to retrieve a word not in the cache is 101 nanoseconds.

6.1a Determine the hit rate needed such that the average memory latency equals the processor cycle time.

1988–1–4a

6.1b Keeping the same memory devices but considering processors with a higher clock rate, what is the maximum useful clock rate such that the average memory latency equals the processor cycle time, and to what hit rate does it correspond?

1988–1–4b

6.2 A particular program uses 100 data objects, each 10^5 bytes long. The objects are contiguously allocated in a two-level memory system using the LRU page replacement policy with a fast memory of 10^6 bytes and a page size of 10^3 bytes. The program always makes 1,000 accesses to randomly selected bytes in one object, then moves on to another randomly selected object (with probability 0.01 it could be the same object), makes 1,000 accesses to randomly selected bytes there, and so on.

6.2a Ignoring any memory accesses that might be needed for fetching instructions, if the program runs long enough to reach an equilibrium state, what will the hit ratio be?

1987–1–5a

6.2b Will the hit ratio go up or down if the page size is changed from 10^3 words to 10^4 words, with all other memory parameters unchanged?

1987–1–5b

6.3 OutTel corporation has been delivering j786 microprocessors to the computer industry for some time, and Metoo systems has decided to get into the act by building a microprocessor called the "clone786+", which differs from the j786 by providing twice as many processor registers. Metoo has simulated many programs and concluded that this one change reduces the number of loads and stores to memory by an average of 30%, and thus should improve performance, assuming of course that all programs—including its popular microkernel operating system—are recompiled to take advantage of the extra registers. Why might Metoo find the performance improvement to be less than their simulations predict? If there is more than one reason, which one is likely to reduce performance the most?

1994–1–6

6.4 Mike R. Kernel is designing the OutTel P97 computer system, which currently has one page table in hardware. The first tests with this design show excellent performance with one application, but with multiple applications, performance is awful. Suggest three design changes to Mike's system that would improve performance with multiple applications, and explain your choices briefly. You cannot change processor speed, but any other aspect of the system is fair game.

1996–1–3

6.5 Ben Bitdiddle gets really excited about remote procedure call and implements an RPC package himself. His implementation starts a new service thread for each arriving request. The thread performs the operation specified in the request, sends a reply, and terminates. After measuring the RPC performance, Ben decides that it needs some improvement, so Ben comes up with a brute-force solution: he buys a much faster network. The transit time of the new network is half as large as it was before. Ben measures the performance of small RPCs (meaning that each RPC message contains only a few bytes of data) on the new network. To his surprise, the performance is barely improved. What might be the reason that his RPCs are not twice as fast?

1995–1–5c

6.6 Why might increasing the page size of a virtual memory system increase performance? Why might increasing the page size of a virtual memory system decrease performance?

1993–2–4a

6.7 Ben Bitdiddle and Louis Reasoner are examining a 3.5-inch magnetic disk that spins at 7,500 RPM, with an average seek time of 6.5 milliseconds and a data transfer rate of 10 megabytes per second. Sectors contain 512 bytes of user data.

6.7a On average, how long does it take to read a block of eight contiguous sectors when the starting sector is chosen at random?

6.7b Suppose that the operating system maintains a one-megabyte cache in RAM to hold disk sectors. The latency of this cache is 25 nanoseconds, and for block transfers the data transfer rate from the cache to a different location in RAM is 160 megabytes per second. Explain how these two specifications can simultaneously be true.

6.7c Give a formula that tells the expected time to read 100 randomly chosen disk sectors, assuming that the hit ratio of the disk block cache is h.

6.7d Ben's workstation has 256 megabytes of RAM. To increase the cache hit ratio, Ben reconfigures the disk sector cache to be much larger than one megabyte. To his surprise he discovers that many of his applications now run slower rather than faster. What has Ben probably overlooked?

6.7e Louis has disassembled the disk unit to see how it works. Remembering that the centrifuge in the biology lab runs at 36,000 RPM, he has come up with a bright idea on how to reduce the rotational latency of the disk. He suggests speeding it up to

96,000 RPM. He calculates that the rotation time will now be 625 microseconds. Ben says this idea is crazy. Explain Ben's concern.

1994-3-1

6.8 Ben Bitdiddle has proposed the simple neat and robust file system (SNARFS).* Ben's system has no on-disk data structures other than the disk blocks themselves, which are ***self-describing***. Each 4-kilobyte disk block starts with the following 24 bytes of information:

- *fid* (File-ID): a 64-bit number that uniquely defines a file. A *fid* of zero implies that the disk block is free.
- *sn* (Sequence Number): a 64-bit number that identifies which block of a file this disk block contains.
- *t* (Time): The time this block was last updated.

In addition, the first block of a file contains the file name (string), version number, and the *fid* of its parent directory. The rest of the first block is filled with data. Setting the directory *fid* to zero marks the entire file free.

Directories are just files. Each directory should contain only the *fid* of its parent directory. However, as a "hint" directories may also include a table giving the mapping from name to *fid* and the mapping from *fid* to blocks for some of the files in the directory.

To allow fast access, three in-memory (virtual memory) structures are created each time the system is booted:

- MAP: an in-memory hash table that associates a (*fid*, *sn*) pair with the disk block containing that block of that file
- FREE: a free list that represents all of the free blocks on disk in a compact manner
- RECYCLE: a list of blocks that are available for reuse but have not yet been written with a *fid* of 0

6.8a Each read or write of a disk block results in one disk I/O. What is the minimum number of disk I/Os required in SNARFS to create a new file containing 2 kilobytes of data in an existing directory? If the system crashes (i.e., the contents of virtual memory are lost) after these I/Os are completed, the file should be present in the appropriate directory after recovery.

6.8b Ben argues that the in-memory structures can easily be rebuilt after a crash. Explain what actions are required to rebuild MAP, FREE, and RECYCLE at boot time.

1995-3-4a...c

6.9 Ben Bitdiddle has written a "style checker" intended to uncover writing problems in technical papers. The program picks up one sentence at a time, computes intensely for a while to parse it into nouns, verbs, and the like, and then looks up

*Credit for developing *Ex.* 6.8 goes to William J. Dally.

the resulting pattern in an enormous database of linguistic rules. The database was so large that it was necessary to place it on a remote service and do the lookup with a remote procedure call.

Ben is distressed to find that the RPCs have such a long latency that his style checker runs much more slowly than he hoped. He wonders if adding multiple threads to the client could speed up his program.

6.9a Ben's checker is running on a single-processor workstation. Explain how multiple client threads could reduce the time to analyze a technical paper.

6.9b Ben implements a multithreaded style checker and runs a series of experiments with various numbers of threads. He finds that performance does indeed improve when he adds a second thread and again when he adds a third. But he finds that as he adds more and more threads the additional performance improvement diminishes, and finally adding more threads leads to reduced performance. Give an explanation for this behavior.

6.9c Suggest a way of improving the style checker's performance without introducing threads. (Ben is allowed to change only the client.)

1994–1–4a...c

6.10 Threads in a new multithreaded Web browser periodically query a nearby World Wide Web server to retrieve documents. On average, a browser's thread performs a query every N instructions. Each request to the server incurs an average round-trip time of T milliseconds before the answer returns.

6.10a For $N = 2{,}000$ instructions and $T = 1$ millisecond, what is the smallest number of such threads that would be required to keep a single 100 million instructions every second (MIPS) processor 100% busy? Assume that the context switch between threads is instantaneous and that the scheduler is optimal.

6.10b But context switches are not instantaneous. Assume that a context switch takes C instructions to perform. Recompute the answer to 6.10a for $C = 500$ instructions.

6.10c What property of the application threads might cause the answers of parts 6.10a and 6.10b to be incorrect? That is, why might more threads be required to keep the processor running the browser busy?

6.10d What property of the actual computer system might make the answers of 6.10a and 6.10b gross overestimates?

1995–1–4a...d

6.11 What are the advantages of using the clock algorithm as compared with implementing LRU directly?

A. Only a single bit per object or page is required.

B. Clock is more efficient to execute.

C. The first object or page to be purged is the most recently used one.

2001–1–4

6.12 Louis Reasoner found the mention of prepaging systems in Section 6.2.9 to be so intriguing that he has devised a version of OPT that uses prepaging. Here is a description of Louis's prepage-OPT:

- Knowing the reference string, create a total ordering of the pages in which each page is in the order in which the application will next make reference to it. Then, prepage the front of the stack into the primary memory.
- After each page reference, rearrange the ordering so that every page is again in the order in which the application will next make reference to it. Thus, in contrast with LRU, which maintains an ordering since most recent use, prepage-OPT maintains an ordering of next use.

To do this rearrangement requires moving exactly one page, the one that was just touched, down in the ordering to the depth d where it will next be used. All of the pages that were above depth d move up one position. A page that will never be used again is assigned a depth of infinity and moves to the bottom of the stack. This rearrangement scheme ensures that the first page of the ordering is always the page that will be used next.

- If $d > m$ (where m is the size of the primary memory device), the operation of the second bullet will result in a page being moved from the secondary memory to the primary memory. Since the reference string has not yet demanded this page, this movement anticipates a future need, another example of prepaging.

6.11a Is prepage-OPT a stack algorithm? Why or why not?

6.11b For the reference string in the example of Table 6.3, develop a version of that table (or of Table 6.8 if that is more appropriate) that shows what page movements occur with prepage-OPT for each memory size. Assume that the first step of the run is to preload the primary memory with pages from the front of the ordering.

6.11c Is prepage-OPT better or worse than demand-OPT?

2006-0-1

Additional exercises relating to Chapter 6 can be found in the problem sets beginning on page 425.

About Part II

Part II of this textbook continues a main theme of Part I—enforcing modularity—by introducing still stronger forms of modularity. Part I introduces the client/service model and virtualization, both of which help prevent accidental errors in one module from propagating to another. Part II introduces stronger forms of modularity that can help protect against component and system failures, as well as malicious attacks. Part II explores communication networks, constructing reliable systems from unreliable components, creating all-or-nothing and before-or-after transactions, and implementing security. In doing so, Part II also introduces additional design principles to guide a designer who needs to build computer systems that have stronger modularity. Following is a brief summary of the topics of those [on-line] chapters and supplementary materials. In addition, the Table of Contents for Part I lists the sections of the Part II chapters.

Chapter 7 [on-line]: ***Networks.*** By running clients and services on different computers that are connected by a network, one can build computer systems that exploit geographic separation to tolerate failures and construct systems that can enable information sharing across geographic distances. This chapter approaches the network as a case study of a system and digs deeply into how networks are organized internally and how they work. After a discussion that offers insight into why networks are built the way they are, it introduces a three-layer model, followed by a major section on each layer. A discussion of congestion control helps bring together the complete picture of interaction among the layers. The chapter ends with a short collection of war stories about network design flaws.

Chapter 8 [on-line]: ***Fault tolerance.*** This chapter introduces the basic techniques to build computer systems that, despite component failures, continue to provide service. It offers a systematic development of design principles and techniques for creating reliable systems from unreliable components, based on modularity and on generalization of some of the techniques used in the design of networks. The chapter ends with a case study of fault tolerance in memory systems and a set of war stories about fault tolerant systems that failed to be fault tolerant. This chapter is an unusual feature for an introductory text—this material, if it appears at all in a curriculum, is usually left to graduate elective courses—yet some degree of fault tolerance is a requirement for almost all computer systems.

Chapter 9 [on-line]: ***Atomicity.*** This chapter deals with the problem of making flawless updates to data in the presence of concurrent threads and despite system failures. It expands on concepts introduced in Chapter 5, taking a cross-cutting approach to atomicity—making actions atomic with respect to failures and also with respect to concurrent actions—that recognizes that atomicity is a form of modularity that plays a fundamental role in operating systems, database management, and processor design. The chapter begins by laying the groundwork for intuition about how a designer achieves atomicity, and then it introduces an easy-to-understand atomicity scheme.

This basis sets the stage for straightforward explanations of instruction renaming, transactional memory, logs, and two-phase locking. Once an intuition is established about how to systematically achieve atomicity, the chapter goes on to show how database systems use logs to create all-or-nothing actions and automatic lock management to ensure before-or-after atomicity of concurrent actions. Finally, the chapter explores methods of obtaining agreement among geographically separated workers about whether or not to commit an atomic action. The chapter ends with case studies of atomicity in processor design and management of disk storage.

Chapter 10 [on-line]: ***Consistency.*** This chapter discusses a variety of requirements that show up when data is replicated for performance, availability, or durability: cache coherence, replica management for extended durability, and reconciliation of usually disconnected databases (e.g., "hotsync" of a personal digital assistant or cell phone with a desktop computer). The chapter introduces the reader to the requirements and the basic mechanisms used to meet those requirements. Sometimes these topics are identified with the label "distributed systems".

Chapter 11 [on-line]: ***Security.*** Earlier chapters gradually introduced more powerful and far-reaching methods of enforcing modularity. This chapter cranks up the enforcement level to maximum strength by introducing the techniques of ensuring that modularity is enforced even in the face of adversaries who behave malevolently. It starts with design principles and a security model, and it then applies that model both to enforcement of internal modular boundaries (traditionally called "protection") and to network security. An advanced topics section explains cryptographic techniques, which are the basis for most network security. A case study of the Secure Socket Layer (SSL) protocol and a set of war stories of protection system failures illustrate the range and subtlety of considerations involved in achieving security.

Suggestions for further reading. The suggested reading list in Part II is, apart from updates, the same as the one in this book.

Problem sets. The Part II collection of problem sets includes both the Part I problem sets and many additional problem sets for the Part II chapters.

Glossary. The on-line Glossary is identical to the one in this book. In addition to its primary purpose of supporting this textbook, the on-line Glossary also can serve as a reference source that workers in other specialties may find useful in coordinating their terminology with that of the field of systems.

Comprehensive Index. The on-line Index of Concepts provides page numbers for both Part I and Part II in a single alphabetic list.

APPENDIX

The Binary Classification Trade-off

A *binary classification trade-off* arises when we wish to classify a set of things into two categories (call them *In* and *Out*), but we do not have a direct way of doing the classifying. On the other hand, there is a *proxy* for those things that is relatively easy to classify. The problem is that the proxy is only approximate. Because it is only approximate, there are four classification outcomes:

- *True positive:* The proxy classifies things as *In* that should be *In*.
- *True negative:* The proxy classifies things as *Out* that should be *Out*.
- *False negative:* The proxy classifies things as *Out* that should be *In*.
- *False positive:* The proxy classifies things as *In* that should be *Out*.

The trade-off is that it may be possible to reduce the frequency of one of the false outcomes by adjusting some parameter of the proxy, but that adjustment will probably increase the frequency of the other false outcome*.

A common example is an e-mail spam filter, which is a proxy for the division between wanted e-mail and spam. The filter correctly classifies e-mail most of the time, but it occasionally misclassifies a wanted message as spam, with the undesirable outcome that you may never see that message. It may also misclassify some spam as wanted e-mail, with the undesirable outcome that the spam clutters up your mailbox. The trade-off appears when someone tries to adjust the spam filter. If the filter becomes more aggressive, more wanted e-mail is likely to end up misclassified as spam. If the spam filter becomes less aggressive, more spam is likely to end up in your mailbox.

Reducing both undesirable outcomes simultaneously usually requires discovering a better proxy, but a better one may be hard to find or may not exist at all.

Representations: One can conveniently represent a binary classification trade-off with a 2 × 2 matrix such as the one on the next page by answering two questions: (1) What are the real categories? and (2) What are the proxy categories? The example describes a smoke detector. The real categories are {fire, no fire}. The proxy categories are {smoke detector signals, smoke detector is quiet}. A too-sensitive smoke detector

*In some areas, such as computer security and biometrics, the words "acceptance" and "rejection" replace "positive" and "negative", respectively.

		Real categories	
		fire	no fire
Proxy categories	detector signals	TA: fire extinguished	FA: false alarm
	detector quiet	FR: house burns down	TR: all quiet

may signal more false alarms, but an insensitive one may miss more real fires. When someone replaces the labels with numbers of actual events, this representation is called a *confusion matrix*.

A Venn diagram, such as the one below, can be another useful representation of a binary classification trade-off. Take, for example, document retrieval (e.g., a Google search) The real categories are wanted and unwanted documents. The proxy is a query, for which the categories are that the query matches or the query misses.

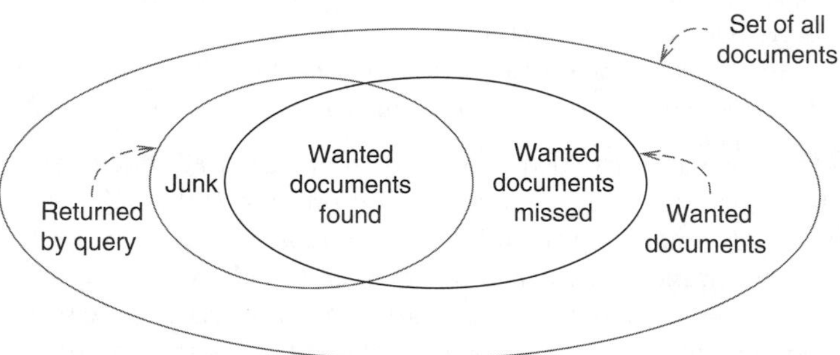

Measures: Sometimes one can identify the true categorizations and compare them with the proxy classifications. When that is possible, it can be useful to calculate ratios to measure proxy quality. Unfortunately, there are too many possible ratios. The confusion matrix contains four numbers, which may be used singly or may be added up to use as either a numerator or a denominator in 14 ways, so it is possible to calculate $14 \times 13 = 182$ different ratios. Not all of these ratios are interesting, but one can usually find at least one ratio among the 182 that seems to support his or her position in a debate.

Nine of these ratios are popular enough to have names, although three of the nine are just complements of other named ratios. The information retrieval community uses one set of labels for these ratios, whereas the medical and bioinformatics communities use another, with other communities developing their own nomenclature. As will be seen, all of the labels can be confusing.

Suppose that there is a population of $In + Out = N$ items and that we have run the classifier and counted the number of true and false positives and negatives. Here are the nine ratios:

1. *Prevalance*: The fraction of the population that is *In*.

$$Prevalance = In/N$$

2. *Efficiency*, *Accuracy*, or *Hit Rate*: The fraction of the population the proxy classifies correctly.

$$Efficiency = (True\,Positives + True\,Negatives)/N$$

3. *Precision* (information retrieval) or *Positive Predictive Value* (medical): The fraction of things that the proxy classifies as *In* that are actually *In*.

$$Precision = (True\,Positives)/(True\,Positives + False\,Positives)$$

4. *Recall* (information retrieval), *Sensitivity* (medical), or *True acceptance rate* (biometrics): The fraction of things in the population that are *In* that the proxy classifies as *In*.

$$Recall = (True\,Positives)/In$$

5. *Specificity* (medical) or *True rejection rate* (biometrics): The fraction of things in the population that are *Out* that the proxy classifies as *Out*.

$$Specificity = (True\,Negatives)/Out$$

6. *Negative Predictive Value*: The fraction of things that the proxy classifies as *Out* that are actually *Out*.

$$Negative\,Predictive\,Value = \frac{True\,Negatives}{True\,Negatives + False\,Negatives}$$

7. *Misclassification Rate* or *Miss Rate*: The fraction of the population the proxy classifies wrong.

$$Miss\,Rate = (False\,Negatives + False\,Positives)/N = (1 - Efficiency)$$

8. *False Acceptance Rate*: The fraction of *Out* items that are falsely classified as *In*.

$$Fasle\ Acceptance\,Rate = (False\,Positives)/Out = (1 - Specificity)$$

9. *False Rejection Rate*: The fraction of *In* items that are falsely classified as *Out*.

$$Fasle\,Rejection\,Rate = (False\,Negatives)/In = (1 - Sensitivity)$$

Suggestions for Further Reading

TABLE OF CONTENTS

INTRODUCTION

The hardware technology that underlies computer systems has improved so rapidly and continuously for more than four decades that the ground rules for system design are constantly subject to change. It takes many years for knowledge and experience to be compiled, digested, and presented in the form of a book, so books about computer systems often seem dated or obsolete by the time they appear in print. Even though some underlying principles are unchanging, the rapid obsolescence of details acts to discourage prospective book authors, and as a result some important ideas are never documented in books. For this reason, an essential part of the study of computer systems is found in current—and, frequently, older—technical papers, professional journal articles, research reports, and occasional, unpublished memoranda that circulate among active workers in the field.

Despite that caveat, there are a few books, relatively recent additions to the literature in computer systems, that are worth having on the shelf. Until the mid-1980s, the books that existed were for the most part commissioned by textbook publishers to fill a market, and they tended to emphasize the mechanical aspects of systems rather than insight into their design. Starting around 1985, however, several very good books started to appear, when professional system designers became inspired to capture their insights. The appearance of these books also suggests that the concepts involved in computer system design are finally beginning to stabilize a bit. (Or it may just be that computer system technology is beginning to shorten the latencies involved in book publishing.)

The heart of the computer systems literature is found in published papers. Two of the best sources are Association for Computing Machinery (ACM) publications: the journal *ACM Transactions on Computer Systems (TOCS)* and the bi-annual series of conference proceedings, the *ACM Symposium on Operating Systems Principles (SOSP)*. The best papers of each SOSP are published in a following issue of TOCS, and the rest—in recent years all—of the papers of each symposium appear in a special edition of *Operating Systems Review*, an ACM special interest group quarterly that publishes an extra issue in symposium years. Three other regular symposia are also worth following: the *European Conference on Computer Systems (EuroSys)*, the *USENIX Symposium on Operating Systems Design and Implementation (OSDI)*, and the USENIX *Symposium on Networked Systems Design and Implementation (NSDI)*. These sources are not the only ones—worthwhile papers about computer systems appear in many other journals, conferences, and workshops. Complete copies of most of the papers listed here, including many of the older ones, can be found on the World Wide Web by an on-line search for an author's last name and a few words of the paper title. Even papers whose primary listing requires a subscription are often posted elsewhere as open resources.

The following pages contain suggestions for further reading about computer systems, both papers and books. The list makes no pretensions of being complete. Instead, the suggestions have been selected from a vast literature to emphasize the best available thinking, best illustrations of problems, and most interesting case studies of computer systems. The readings have been reviewed for obsolescence, but it is often the case that a good idea is still best described by a paper from some time ago, where the idea was developed in a context that no longer seems very interesting. Sometimes that early context is much simpler than today's systems, thus making it easier to see how the idea works. Often, an early author was the first on the scene, so it was necessary to describe things more completely than do modern authors who usually assume significant familiarity with the surroundings and with all of the predecessor systems. Thus the older readings included here provide a very useful complement to current works.

By its nature, the study of the engineering of computer systems overlaps with other areas of computer science, particularly computer architecture, programming languages, databases, information retrieval, security, and data communications. Each of those areas has an extensive literature of its own, and it is often not obvious where to draw the boundary lines. As a general rule, this reading list tries to provide only first-level guidance on where to start in those related areas.

One thing the reader must watch for is that the terminology of the computer systems field is not agreed upon, so the literature is often confusing even to the professional. In addition, the quality level of the literature is quite variable, ranging from the literate through the readable to the barely comprehensible. Although the selections here try to avoid that last category, the reader must still be prepared for some papers, however important in their content, that do not explain their subject as well as they could.

In the material that follows, each citation is accompanied by a comment suggesting why that paper is worth reading—its importance, interest, and relation to other readings. When a single paper serves more than one area of interest, cross-references appear rather than repeating the citation.

1 Systems

As mentioned above, a few wonderful and several really good books about computer systems have recently begun to appear. Here are the must-have items for the reference shelf of the computer systems designer. In addition to these books, the later groupings of readings by topic include other books, generally of narrower interest.

1.1 Wonderful Books About Systems

1.1.1 David A. Patterson and John L. Hennessy. *Computer Architecture: A Quantitative Approach*. Morgan Kaufman, fourth edition, 2007. ISBN: 978-0-12-370490-0. 704 + various pages (paperback). The cover gives the authors' names in the opposite order.

This book provides a spectacular tour-de-force that explores much of the design space of current computer architecture. One of the best features is that each area includes a discussion of misguided ideas and their pitfalls. Even though the subject matter gets very sophisticated, the book is always very readable. The book is opinionated (with a strong bias toward RISC architecture), but nevertheless this is a definitive work on computer organization from the system perspective.

1.1.2 Raj Jain. *The Art of Computer Systems Performance Analysis*. John Wiley & Sons, 1991. ISBN: 978-0-471-50336-1. 720 pages.

Much work on performance analysis of computer systems originates in academic settings and focuses on analysis that is mathematically tractable rather than on measurements that matter. This book is at the other end of the spectrum. It is written by someone with extensive industrial experience but an academic flair for explaining things. If you have a real performance analysis problem, it will tell you how to tackle it, how to avoid measuring the wrong thing, and how to step by other pitfalls.

1.1.3 Frederick P. Brooks Jr. *The Mythical Man-Month: Essays on Software Engineering*. Addison-Wesley, 20th Anniversary edition, 1995. ISBN: 978-0-201-83595-3 (paperback). 336 pages.

Well-written and full of insights, this reading is by far the most significant one on the subject of controlling system development. This is where you learn why adding more staff to a project that is behind schedule will delay it further. Although a few of the chapters are now a bit dated, much of the material here is timeless. Trouble in system development is also timeless, as evidenced by continual reports of failures of large system projects. Most successful system designers have a copy of this book on their bookshelf, and some claim to reread it at least once a year. Most of the 1995 edition is identical to the first, 1974, edition; the newer edition adds Brooks' *No Silver Bullets* paper (which is well worth reading) and some summarizing chapters.

1.1.4 Lawrence Lessig. *Code and Other Laws of Cyberspace, Version 2.0*. Basic Books, 2006. ISBN: 978-0-465-03914-28 (paperback). 432 pages; 978-0-465-03913-5 (paperback). 320 pages. Also available on-line at `http://codev2.cc/`

This book is an updated version of an explanation by a brilliant teacher of constitutional law of exactly how law, custom, market forces, and architecture together regulate things. In addition to providing a vocabulary to discuss many of the legal issues surrounding technology and the Internet, a central theme of this book is that because technology raises issues that were foreseen neither by law nor custom, the default is that it will be regulated entirely by market forces and architecture, neither of which is subject to the careful and deliberative thought that characterize the development of law and custom. If you have any interest in the effect of technology on intellectual property, privacy, or free speech, this book is required reading.

1.1.5 Jim [N.] Gray and Andreas Reuter. *Transaction Processing: Concepts and Techniques*. Morgan Kaufmann, San Mateo, California, 1993 (Look for the low-bulk paper edition, which became available with the third printing in 1994). ISBN: 978-1-55860-190-1. 1,070 pages.

All aspects of fault tolerance, atomicity, coordination, recovery, rollback, logs, locks, transactions, and engineering trade-offs for performance are pulled together in this comprehensive book. This is the definitive work on transactions. Though not intended for beginners, given the high quality of its explanations, this complex material is surprisingly accessible. The glossary of terms is excellent, whereas the historical notes are good as far as they go, but are somewhat database-centric and should not be taken as the final word.

1.1.6 Alan F. Westin. *Privacy and Freedom*. Atheneum Press, 1967. 487 pages. (Out of print.)

If you have any interest in privacy, track down a copy of this book in a library or used-book store. It is the comprehensive treatment, by a constitutional lawyer, of what privacy is, why it matters, and its position in the U.S. legal framework.

1.1.7 Ross Anderson. *Security Engineering: A Guide to Building Dependable Distributed Systems*. John Wiley & Sons, second edition, 2008. ISBN: 978-0-470-06852-6. 1,040 pages.

This book is remarkable for the range of system security problems it considers, from taxi mileage recorders to nuclear command and control systems. It provides great depth on the mechanics, assuming that the reader already has a high-level picture. The book is sometimes quick in its explanations; the reader must be quite knowledgeable about systems. One of its strengths is that most of the discussions of how to do it are immediately followed by a section titled "What goes wrong", exploring misimplementations, fallacies, and other modes of failure. The first edition is available on-line.

1.2 Really Good Books About Systems

1.2.1 Andrew S. Tanenbaum. *Modern Operating Systems*. Prentice-Hall, third edition, 2008. ISBN: 978-0-13-600663-3 (hardcover). 952 pages.

This book provides a thorough tutorial introduction to the world of operating systems but with a tendency to emphasize the mechanics. Insight into why things are designed the way they are is there, but in many cases requires teasing out. Nevertheless, as a starting point, it is filled with street knowledge that is needed to get into the rest of the literature. It includes useful case studies of GNU/Linux, Windows Vista, and Symbian OS, an operating system for mobile phones.

1.2.2 Thomas P. Hughes. *Rescuing Prometheus*. Vintage reprint (paperback), originally published in 1998. ISBN: 978-0679739388. 372 pages.

A retired professor of history and sociology explains the stories behind the management of four large-scale, one-of-a-kind system projects: the Sage air defense system, the Atlas rocket, the Arpanet (predecessor of the Internet), and the design phase of the Big Dig (Boston Central Artery/Tunnel). The thesis of the book is that such projects, in addition to unique engineering, also had to develop a different kind of management style that can adapt continuously to change, is loosely coupled with distributed control, and can identify a consensus among many players.

1.2.3 Henry Petroski. *Design Paradigms: Case Histories of Error and Judgment in Engineering*. Cambridge University Press, 1994. ISBN: 978-0-521-46108-5 (hardcover), 978-0-521-46649-3 (paperback). 221 pages.

This remarkable book explores how the mindset of the designers (in the examples, civil engineers) allowed them to make what in retrospect were massive design errors. The failures analyzed range from the transportation of columns in Rome through the 1982 collapse of the walkway in the Kansas City Hyatt Regency Hotel, with a number of famous bridge collapses in between. Petroski analyzes particularly well how a failure of a scaled-up design often reveals that the original design worked correctly, but for a different reason than originally thought. There is no mention of computer systems in this book, but it contains many lessons for computer system designers.

1.2.4 Bruce Schneier. *Applied Cryptography*. John Wiley and Sons, second edition, 1996. ISBN: 978-0-471-12845-8 (hardcover), 978-0-471-11709-4 (paperback). 784 pages.

Here is everything you might want to know about cryptography and cryptographic protocols, including a well-balanced perspective on what works and what doesn't. This book saves the need to read and sort through the thousand or so technical papers on the subject. Protocols, techniques, algorithms, real-world considerations, and source code can all be found here. In addition to being competent, it is also entertainingly written and very articulate. Be aware that a number of minor errors have been reported in this book; if you are implementing code, it would be a good idea to verify the details by consulting reading *1.3.13*.

1.2.5 Radia Perlman. *Interconnections, second edition: Bridges, Routers, Switches, and Internetworking Protocols*. Addison-Wesley, 1999. ISBN: 978-0-201-63448-8. 560 pages.

This book presents everything you could possibly want to know about how the network layer actually works. The style is engagingly informal, but the content is absolutely first-class, and every possible variation is explored. The previous edition was simply titled *Interconnections: bridges and routers*.

1.2.6 Larry L. Peterson and Bruce S. Davie. *Computer Networks: A Systems Approach*. Morgan Kaufman, fourth edition, 2007. ISBN: 978-0-12-370548-8. 848 pages.

This book provides a systems perspective on computer networks. It represents a good balance of why networks are they way they are and a discussion of the important protocols in use. It follows a layering model but presents fundamental concepts independent of layering. In this way, the book provides a good discussion of timeless ideas as well as current embodiments of those ideas.

1.3 Good Books on Related Subjects Deserving Space on the Systems Bookshelf

There are several other good books that many computer system professionals insist on having on their bookshelves. They don't appear in one of the previous categories because their central focus is not on systems or because the purpose of the book is somewhat narrower.

1.3.1 Thomas H. Cormen, Charles E. Leiserson, Ronald L. Rivest, and Clifford Stein. *Introduction to Algorithms*. McGraw-Hill, second edition, 2001. 1,184 pages. ISBN: 978-0-07-297054-8 (hardcover); 978-0-262-53196-2 (M.I.T. Press paperback, not sold in U.S.A.)

1.3.2 Nancy A. Lynch. *Distributed Algorithms*. Morgan Kaufman, 1996. 872 pages ISBN: 978-1-55860-348-6.

Occasionally, a system designer needs an algorithm. Cormen et al. and Lynch's books are the place to find that algorithm, together with the analysis necessary to decide whether or not it is appropriate for the application. In a reading list on theory, these two books would almost certainly be in one of the highest categories, but for a systems list they are better identified as supplementary.

1.3.3 Douglas K. Smith and Robert C. Alexander. *Fumbling the Future*. William Morrow and Company, 1988. ISBN: 978-0-688-06959-9 (hardcover), 978-1-58348266-7 (iuniverse paperback reprint). 274 pages.

The history of computing is littered with companies that attempted to add general-purpose computer systems to an existing business—for examples, Ford, Philco, Zenith, RCA, General Electric, Honeywell, A. T. & T., and Xerox. None has succeeded, perhaps because when the going gets tough the option of walking away from this business is too attractive. This book documents how Xerox managed to snatch defeat from the jaws of victory by inventing the personal computer, then abandoning it.

1.3.4 Marshall Kirk McKusick, Keith Bostic, and Michael J. Karels. *The Design and Implementation of the 4.4BSD Operating System.* Addison-Wesley, second edition, 1996. ISBN: 978-0-201-54979-9. 606 pages.

This book provides a complete picture of the design and implementation of the Berkeley version of the UNIX® operating system. It is well-written and full of detail. The 1989 first edition, describing 4.3BSD, is still useful.

1.3.5 Katie Hafner and John Markoff. *Cyberpunk: Outlaws and Hackers on the Computer Frontier*. Simon & Schuster (Touchstone), 1991, updated June 1995. ISBN: 978-0-671-68322-1 (hardcover), 978-0-684-81862-7 (paperback). 368 pages.

This book is a very readable, yet thorough, account of the scene at the ethical edges of cyberspace: the exploits of Kevin Mitnick, Hans Hubner, and Robert Tappan Morris. It serves as an example of a view from the media, but an unusually well-informed view.

1.3.6 Deborah G. Johnson and Helen Nissenbaum. *Computers, Ethics & Social Values*. Prentice-Hall, 1995. ISBN: 978-0-13-103110-4 (paperback). 714 pages.

A computer system designer is likely to consider reading a treatise on ethics to be a terribly boring way to spend the afternoon, and some of the papers in this extensive collection do match that stereotype. However, among the many scenarios, case studies, and other reprints in this volume are a large number of interesting and thoughtful papers about the human consequences of computer system design. This collection is a good place to acquire the basic readings concerning privacy, risks, computer abuse, and software ownership as well as professional ethics in computer system design.

1.3.7 Carliss Y. Baldwin and Kim B. Clark. *Design Rules: Volume 1, The Power of Modularity*. M.I.T. Press, 2000. ISBN: 978-0-262-02466-2. 471 pages.

This book focuses wholely on modularity (as used by the authors, this term merges modularity, abstraction, and hierarchy) and offers an interesting representation of interconnections to illustrate the power of modularity and of clean, abstract interfaces. The work uses these same concepts to interpret several decades of developments in the computer industry. The authors, from the Harvard Business School, develop a model of the several ways in which modularity operates by providing design options and making substitution easy. By the end of the book, most readers will have seen more than they wanted to know, but there are some ideas here that are worth at least a quick reading. (Despite the "Volume 1" in the title, there does not yet seem to be a Volume 2.)

1.3.8 Andrew S. Tanenbaum. *Computer Networks*. Prentice-Hall, fourth edition, 2003. ISBN: 978-0-13-066102-9. 813 pages.

This book provides a thorough tutorial introduction to the world of networks. Like the same author's book on operating systems (see reading *1.2.1*), this one also tends to emphasize the mechanics. But again it is a storehouse of up-to-date street knowledge, this time about computer communications, that is needed to get into (or perhaps avoid the need to consult) the rest of the literature. The book includes a selective and thoughtfully annotated bibliography on computer networks. An abbreviated version of this same material, sufficient for many readers, appears as a chapter of the operating systems book.

1.3.9 David L. Mills. *Computer Network Time Synchronization: The Network Time Protocol*. CRC Press/Taylor & Francis, 2006. ISBN: 978-0849358050. 286 pages.

A comprehensive but very readable explanation of the Network Time Protocol (NTP), an under-the-covers protocol of which most users are unaware: NTP coordinates multiple timekeepers and distributes current date and time information to both clients and servers.

1.3.10 Robert G. Gallager. *Principles of Digital Communication*. Cambridge University Press, 2008. ISBN: 978-0-521-87907-1. 422 pages.

This intense textbook focuses on the theory that underlies the link layer of data communication networks. It is not for casual browsing or for those easily intimidated by mathematics, but its an excellent reference source for analysis.

1.3.11 Daniel P. Siewiorek and Robert S. Swarz. *Reliable Computer Systems: Design and Evaluation*. A. K. Peters Ltd., third edition, 1998. ISBN: 978-1-56881-092-8. 927 pages.

This is probably the best comprehensive treatment of reliability that is available, with well-explained theory and reprints of several case studies from recent literature. Its only defect is a slight "academic" bias in that little judgment is expressed on alternative methods, and some examples are without warning of systems that were never really deployed. The first, 1982, edition, with the title *The Theory and Practice of Reliable System Design*, contains an almost completely different (and much older) set of case studies.

1.3.12 Bruce Schneier. *Secrets & Lies/Digital Security in a Networked World*. John Wiley & Sons, 2000. ISBN: 978-0-471-25311-2 (hardcover), 978-0-471-45380-2 (paperback). 432 pages.

This overview of security from a systems perspective provides much motivation, many good war stories (though without citations), and a high-level outline of how one achieves a secure system. Being an overview, it provides no specific guidance on the mechanics, other than to rely on people who know what they are doing. This is excellent book particularly for the manager who wants to go beyond the buzzwords and get an idea of what achieving computer system security involves.

1.3.13 A[lfred] J. Menezes, Paul C. Oorschot, and Scott A. Vanstone. *Handbook of Applied Cryptography*. CRC Press, 1997. ISBN: 978-08493-8523-0. 816 pages.

This book is exactly what its title claims: a very complete handbook on putting cryptography to work. It lacks the background and perspective of Reading 1.2.4, and it is extremely technical, which makes parts of it inaccessible to less mathematically inclined readers. But its precise definitions and careful explanations make this by far the best reference book available on the subject.

1.3.14 Johannes A. Buchman. *Introduction to Cryptography*. Springer, second edition, 2004. ISBN: 978-0-387-21156-56 (hardcover). 335 pages.

Buchman provides a nice, concise introduction to number theory for cryptography.

1.3.15 Simson Garfinkel and Gene [Eugene H.] Spafford. *Practical Unix and Internet Security*. O'Reilly & Associates, Sebastopol, California, third edition, 2003. ISBN: 978-59600323-4 (paperback). 986 pages.

This is a really comprehensive guide to how to run a network-attached UNIX system with some confidence that it is relatively safe against casual intruders. In addition to providing practical information for a system manager, it incidentally gives the reader quite a bit of insight into the style of thinking and design needed to provide security.

1.3.16 Simson Garfinkel. *PGP: Pretty Good Privacy*. O'Reilly & Associates, Sebastopol, California, 1995. ISBN: 978-1-56592-098-9 (paperback). 430 pages.

Nominally a user's guide to the PGP encryption package developed by Phil Zimmermann, this book starts out with six very readable overview chapters on the subject of encryption, its history, and the political and licensing environment that surrounds encryption systems. Even the later chapters, which give details on how to use PGP, are filled with interesting tidbits and advice applicable to all encryption uses.

1.3.17 Warwick Ford and Michael S. Baum. *Secure Electronic Commerce: Building the Infrastructure for Digital Signatures and Encryption*. Prentice-Hall, second edition, 2000. ISBN: 978-0-13-027276-8. 640 pages.

Although the title implies more generality, this book is about public key infrastructure: certificate authorities, certificates, and their legal status in practice. The authors are a technologist (Ford) and a lawyer (Baum). The book provides very thorough coverage and is a good way to learn a lot about the subject. Because the status of this topic changes rapidly, however, it should be considered a snapshot rather than the latest word.

1.4 Ways of Thinking About Systems

Quite a few books try to generalize the study of systems. They tend to be so abstract, however, that it is hard to see how they apply to anything, so none of them are listed here. Instead, here are five old but surprisingly relevant papers that illustrate ways to think about systems. The areas touched are allometry, aerodynamics, hierarchy, ecology, and economics.

1.4.1 J[ohn] B[urdon] S[anderson] Haldane (1892–1964). On being the right size. In *Possible Worlds and Other Essays*, pages 20–28. Harper and Brothers Publishers, 1928. Also published by Chatto & Windus, London, 1927, and recently reprinted in John Maynard Smith, editor, *On Being the Right Size and Other Essays*, Oxford University Press, 1985. ISBN: 0-19-286045-3 (paperback), pages 1–8.

This is the classic paper that explains why a mouse the size of an elephant would collapse if it tried to stand up. It provides lessons on how to think about incommensurate scaling in all kinds of systems.

1.4.2 Alexander Graham Bell (1847–1922). The tetrahedral principle in kite structure. *National Geographic Magazine 14*, 6 (June 1903), pages 219–251.

This classic paper demonstrates that arguments based on scale can be quite subtle. This paper—written at a time when physicists were still debating the theoretical possibility of building airplanes—describes the obvious scale argument against heavier-than-air craft and then demonstrates that one can increase the scale of an airfoil in different ways and that the obvious scale argument does not apply to all those ways. (This paper is a rare example of unreviewed vanity publication of an interesting engineering result. The *National Geographic* was—and still is—a Bell family publication.)

1.4.3 Herbert A. Simon (1916-2001). The architecture of complexity. *Proceedings of the American Philosophical Society 106*, 6 (December 1962), pages 467–482. Republished as Chapter 4, pages 84–118, of *The Sciences of the Artificial*, M.I.T. Press, Cambridge, Massachusetts, 1969. ISBN: 0-262-191051-6 (hardcover); 0-262-69023-3 (paperback).

This paper is a tour-de-force of how hierarchy is an organizing tool for complex systems. The examples are breathtaking in their range and scope—from watchmaking and biology through political empires. The style of thinking shown in this paper suggests that it is not surprising that Simon later received the 1978 Nobel Prize in economics.

1.4.4 LaMont C[ook] Cole (1916–1978). Man's effect on nature. *The Explorer: Bulletin of the Cleveland Museum of Natural History 11*, 3 (Fall 1969), pages 10–16.

This brief article looks at the Earth as an ecological system in which the actions of humans lead both to surprises and to propagation of effects. It describes a classic example of the propagation of effects: attempts to eliminate malaria in North Borneo led to an increase in the plague and roofs caving in.

1.4.5 Garrett [James] Hardin (1915–). The tragedy of the commons. *Science 162*, 3859 (December 13, 1968), pages 1243–1248. Extensions of "the tragedy of the commons". *Science 280*, 5364 (May 1, 1998), pages 682–683.

This seminal paper explores a property of certain economic situations in which Adam Smith's "invisible hand" works against everyone's interest. It is interesting for its insight into how to predict things about otherwise hard-to-model systems. In revisiting the subject 30 years later, Hardin suggested that the adjective "unmanaged" should be placed in front of "commons". Rightly or wrongly, the Internet is often described as a system to which the tragedy of the (unmanaged) commons applies.

1.5 Wisdom About System Design

Before reading anything else on this topic, one should absorb the book by Brooks, *The Mythical Man-Month*, reading *1.1.3*, and the essay by Simon, "The architecture of complexity", reading *1.4.3*. The case studies on control of complexity in Section 1.9 also are filled with wisdom.

1.5.1 Richard P. Gabriel. Worse is better. Excerpt from LISP: good news, bad news, how to win BIG, *AI Expert 6*, 6 (June 1991), pages 33–35.

This paper explains why doing the thing expediently sometimes works out to be a better idea than doing the thing right.

1.5.2 Henry Petroski. Engineering: History and failure. *American Scientist 80*, 6 (November–December 1992), pages 523–526.

Petroski provides insight along the lines that one primary way that engineering makes progress is by making mistakes, studying them, and trying again. Petroski also visits this theme in two books, the most recent being reading *1.2.3*.

1.5.3 Fernando J. Corbató. On building systems that will fail. *Communications of the ACM 34*, 9 (September 1991), pages 72–81. (Reprinted in the book by Johnson and Nissenbaum, reading *1.3.6*.)

The central idea in this 1991 Turing Award Lecture is that all ambitious systems will have failures, but those that were designed with that expectation are more likely to eventually succeed.

1.5.4 Butler W. Lampson. Hints for computer system design. *Proceedings of the Ninth ACM Symposium on Operating Systems Principles*, in *Operating Systems Review 17*, 5 (October 1983), pages 33–48. Later republished, but with less satisfactory copy editing, in *IEEE Software 1*, 1 (January 1984), pages 11–28.

This encapsulation of insights is expressed as principles that seem to apply to more than one case. It is worth reading by all system designers.

1.5.5 Jon Bentley. The back of the envelope—programming pearls. *Communications of the ACM 27*, 3 (March 1984), pages 180–184.

One of the most important tools of a system designer is the ability to make rough but quick estimates of how big, how long, how fast, or how expensive a design will be. This brief note extols the concept and gives several examples.

1.5.6 Jeffrey C. Mogul. Emergent (mis)behavior vs. complex software systems. *Proceedings of the First European Conference on Computer Systems* (EuroSys 2006, Leuven, Belgium), pages 293–304. ACM Press, 2006, ISBN: 1-59593-322-0. Also in *Operating Systems Review 40*, 4 (October 2006).

This paper explores in depth the concept of emergent properties described in Chapter 1, providing a nice collection of examples and tying together issues and problems that arise throughout computer and network system design. It also suggests a taxonomy of emergent properties, lays out suggestions for future research, and includes a comprehensive and useful bibliography.

1.5.7 Pamela Samuelson, editor. Intellectual property for an information age. *Communications of the ACM 44*, 2 (February 2001), pages 67–103.

This work is a special section comprising several papers about the challenges of intellectual property in a digital world. Each of the individual articles is written by a member of a new generation of specialists who understand both technology and law well enough to contribute some thoughtful insights to both domains.

1.5.8 Mark R. Chassin and Elise C. Becher. The wrong patient. *Annals of Internal Medicine 136* (June 2002), pages 826–833.

This paper is a good example, first, of how complex systems fail for complex reasons and second, of the value of the "keep digging" principle. The case study presented here centers on a medical system failure in which the wrong patient was operated on. Rather than just identifying the most obvious reason, the case study concludes that there were a dozen or more opportunities in which the error that led to the failure should have been detected and corrected, but for various reasons all of those opportunities were missed.

1.5.9 P[hillip] J. Plauger. Chocolate. *Embedded Systems Programming* 7, 3 (March 1994), pages 81–84.

This paper provides a remarkable insight based on the observation that many failures in a bakery can be remedied by putting more chocolate into the mixture. The author manages, with only a modest stretch, to convert this observation into a more general technique of keeping recovery simple, so that it is likely to succeed.

1.6 Changing Technology and its Impact on Systems

1.6.1 Gordon E. Moore. Cramming more components onto integrated circuits. *Electronics 38*, 8 (April 19, 1965), pages 114–117. Reprinted in *Proceedings of the IEEE 86*, 1 (January 1998), pages 82-85.

This paper defined what we now call Moore's law. The phenomena Moore describes have driven the rate of technology improvement for more than four decades. This paper articulates why and displays the first graph to plot Moore's law, based on five data points.

1.6.2 John L. Hennessy and Norman P. Jouppi. Computer technology and architecture: An evolving interaction. *IEEE Computer 24*, 9 (September 1991), pages 19-29.

Although some of the technology examples are a bit of out of date, the systems thinking and the paper's insights remain relevant.

1.6.3 Ajanta Chakraborty and Mark R. Greenstreet. Efficient self-timed interfaces for crossing clock domains. *Proceedings of the Ninth International Symposium on Asynchronous Circuits and Systems*, IEEE Computer Society (May 2003), pages 78-88. ISBN: 0-7695-1898-2.

This paper addresses the challenge of having a fast, global clock on a chip by organizing the resources on a chip as a number of synchronous islands connected by asynchronous links. This design may pose problems for constructing perfect arbiters (see Section 5.2.8).

1.6.4 Anant Agarwal and Markus Levy. The KILL Rule for multicore. *44th ACM/IEEE Conference on Design Automation* (June 2007), pages 750-753. ISBN: 978-1-59593-627-1.

This short paper looks ahead to multiprocessor chips that contain not just four or eight, but thousands of processors. It articulates a rule for power-efficient designs: Kill If Less than Linear. For example, the designer should increase the chip area devoted to a resource such as a cache only if for every 1% increase in area there is at least a 1% increase in chip performance. This rule focuses attention on those design elements that make most effective use of the chip area and from back-of-the-envelope calculations favors increasing processor count (which the paper assumes to provide linear improvement) over other alternatives.

1.6.5 Stephen P. Walborn et al. Quantum erasure. *American Scientist 91*, 4 (July-August 2003), pages 336-343.

This paper was written by physicists and requires a prerequisite of undergraduate-level modern physics, but it manages to avoid getting into graduate-level quantum mechanics. The strength of the article is its clear identification of what is reasonably well understood and what is still a mystery about these phenomena. That identification seems to be of considerable value both to students of physics, who may be inspired to tackle the parts that are not understood, and to students of cryptography, because knowing what aspects of quantum cryptography are still mysteries may be important in deciding how much reliance to place on it.

1.7 Dramatic Visions

Once in a while a paper comes along that either has a dramatic vision of what future systems might do or takes a sweeping new look at some aspect of systems design that had previously been considered to be settled. The ideas found in the papers listed in reading sections 1.7 and 1.8 often become part of the standard baggage of all future writers in the area, but the reprises rarely do justice to the originals, which are worth reading if only to see how the mind of a visionary (or revisionist) works.

1.7.1 Vannevar Bush. As we may think. *Atlantic Monthly 176*, 1 (July 1945), pages 101–108. Reprinted in Adele J. Goldberg, *A History of Personal Workstations*, Addison-Wesley, 1988, pages 237–247 and also in Irene Greif, ed., *Computer-Supported Cooperative Work: A Book of Readings*, Morgan Kaufman, 1988. ISBN: 0-934613-57-5.

Bush looked at the (mostly analog) computers of 1945 and foresaw that they would someday be used as information engines to augment the human intellect.

1.7.2 John G. Kemeny, with comments by Robert M. Fano and Gilbert W. King. A library for 2000 A.D. In Martin Greenberger, editor, *Management and the Computer of the Future*, M.I.T. Press and John Wiley, 1962, pages 134–178. (Out of print.)

It has taken 40 years for technology to advance far enough to make it possible to implement Kemeny's vision of how the library might evolve when computers are used in its support. Unfortunately, the engineering that is required still hasn't been done, so the vision has not yet been realized, but Google has stated a similar vision and is making progress in realizing it; see reading *3.2.4*.

1.7.3 [Alan C. Kay, with the] Learning Research Group. *Personal Dynamic Media*. Xerox Palo Alto Research Center Systems Software Laboratory Technical Report SSL-76-1 (undated, circa March 1976).

Alan Kay was imagining laptop computers and how they might be used long before most people had figured out that desktop computers might be a good idea. He gave many inspiring talks on the subject, but he rarely paused long enough to write anything down. Fortunately, his colleagues captured some of his thoughts in this technical report. An edited version of this report, with some pictures accidentally omitted, appeared in a journal in the year following this technical report: Alan [C.] Kay and Adele Goldberg. Personal dynamic media. *IEEE Computer 10*, 3 (March 1977), pages 31–41. This paper was reprinted with omitted pictures restored in Adele J. Goldberg, *A history of personal workstations*, Addison-Wesley, 1988, pages 254–263. ISBN: 0-201-11259-0.

1.7.4 Doug[las] C. Engelbart. *Augmenting Human Intellect: A Conceptual Framework*. Research Report AFOSR-3223, Stanford Research Institute, Menlo Park, California, October 1962. Reprinted in Irene Greif, ed., *Computer-Supported Cooperative Work: A Book of Readings*, Morgan Kaufman, 1988. ISBN: 0-934613-57-5.

In the early 1960s Engelbart saw that computer systems would someday be useful in myriad ways as personal tools. Unfortunately, the technology of his time, multimillion-dollar mainframes, was far too expensive to make his vision practical. Today's personal computers and engineering workstations have now incorporated many of his ideas.

1.7.5 F[ernando] J. Corbató and V[ictor] A. Vyssotsky. Introduction and overview of the Multics system. *AFIPS 1965 Fall Joint Computer Conference 27*, part I (1965), pages 185–196.

Working from a few primitive examples of time-sharing systems, Corbató and his associates escalated the vision to an all-encompassing computer utility. This paper is the first in a set of six about Multics in the same proceedings, pages 185–247.

1.8 Sweeping New Looks

1.8.1 Jack B. Dennis and Earl C. Van Horne. Programming semantics for multiprogrammed computations. *Communications of the ACM 9*, 3 (March 1966), pages 143–155.

This paper set the ground rules for thinking about concurrent activities, both the vocabulary and the semantics.

1.8.2 J. S. Liptay. Structural aspects of the System/360 model 85: II. The cache. *IBM Systems Journal* 7, 1 (1968), pages 15–21.

The idea of a cache, look-aside, or slave memory had been suggested independently by Francis Lee and Maurice Wilkes some time around 1963, but it was not until the advent of LSI technology that it became feasible to actually build one in hardware. As a result, no one had seriously explored the design space options until the designers of the IBM System/360 model 85 had to come up with a real implementation. Once this paper appeared, a cache became a requirement for most later computer architectures.

1.8.3 Claude E. Shannon. The communication theory of secrecy systems. *Bell System Technical Journal 28*, 4 (October 1949), pages 656–715.

This paper provides the underpinnings of the theory of cryptography, in terms of information theory.

1.8.4 Whitfield Diffie and Martin E. Hellman. Privacy and authentication: An introduction to cryptography. *Proceedings of the IEEE 67*, 3 (March 1979), pages 397-427.

This is the first technically competent paper on cryptography since Shannon in the unclassified literature, and it launched modern unclassified study. It includes a complete and scholarly bibliography.

1.8.5 Whitfield Diffie and Martin E. Hellman. New directions in cryptography. *IEEE Transactions on Information Theory IT-22*, 6 (November 1976), pages 644-654.

Diffie and Hellman were the second inventors of public key cryptography (the first inventor, James H. Ellis, was working on classified projects for the British Government Communications Headquarters at the time, in 1970, and was not able to publish his work until 1987). This is the paper that introduced the idea to the unclassified world.

1.8.6 Charles T. Davies, Jr. Data processing spheres of control. *IBM Systems Journal 17*, 2 (1978), pages 179-198. Charles T. Davies, Jr. Recovery semantics for a DB/DC system. *1973 ACM National Conference 28* (August 1973), pages 136-141.

This pair of papers—vague but thought-provoking—gives a high-level discussion of "spheres of control", a notion closely related to atomicity. Everyone who writes about transactions mentions that they found these two papers inspiring.

1.8.7 Butler W. Lampson and Howard Sturgis. Crash recovery in a distributed data storage system. Working paper, Xerox Palo Alto Research Center, November 1976 and April 1979. (Never published)

Jim Gray called the 1976 version of this paper "an underground classic". The 1979 version presents the first good definition of models of failure. Both describe algorithms for coordinating distributed updates; they are sufficiently different that both are worth reading.

1.8.8 Leonard Kleinrock. *Communication Nets: Stochastic Message Flow and Delay*. McGraw-Hill, 1964. Republished by Dover, 2007. ISBN: 0-486-45880-6. 224 pages.

1.8.9 Paul Baran, S. Boehm, and J. W. Smith. *On Distributed Communications*. A series of 11 memoranda of the RAND Corporation, Santa Monica, California, August 1964.

Since the growth in the Internet's popularity, there has been considerable discussion about who first thought of packet switching. It appears that Leonard Kleinrock, working in 1961 on his M.I.T. Ph.D. thesis on more effective ways of using wired networks, and Paul Baran and his colleagues at Rand, working in 1961 on survivable communications, independently proposed the idea of packet switching at about the same time; both wrote internal memoranda in 1961 describing their ideas. Neither one actually used the words "packet switching", however; that was left to Donald Davies of the National Physical Laboratory, who coined that label several years later.

1.8.10 Lawrence G. Roberts and Barry D. Wessler. Computer network development to achieve resource sharing. *AFIPS Spring Joint Computer Conference 36* (May 1970), pages 543–549.

This paper and four others presented at the same conference session (pages 543–597) represent the first public description of the ARPANET, the first successful packet-switching network and the prototype for the Internet. Two years later, *AFIPS Spring Joint Computer Conference 40* (1972), pages 243–298, presented five additional, closely related papers. The discussion of priority concerning reading *1.8.8* and reading *1.8.9* is somewhat academic; it was Roberts's sponsorship of the ARPANET that demonstrated the workability of packet switching.

1.8.11 V[inton G.] Cerf et al. Delay-Tolerant Networking Architecture. *Request for Comments RFC 4838*, Internet Engineering Task Force (April 1997).

This document describes an architecture that evolved from a vision for an Interplanetary Internet, an Internet-like network for interplanetary distances. This document introduces several interesting ideas and highlights some assumptions that people make in designing networks without realizing it. NASA performed its first successful tests of a prototype implementation of a delay-tolerant network.

1.8.12 Jim Gray et al. *Terascale Sneakernet. Using Inexpensive Disks for Backup, Archiving, and Data Exchange*. Microsoft Technical Report MS-TR-02-54 (May 2002). `http://arxiv.org/pdf/cs/0208011`

Sneakernet is a generic term for transporting data by physically delivering a storage device rather than sending it over a wire. Sneakernets are attractive when data volume is so large that electronic transport will take a long time or be too expensive, and the latency until the first byte arrives is less important. Early sneakernets exchanged programs and data using floppy disks. More recently, people have exchanged data by burning CDs and carrying them. This paper proposes to build a sneakernet by sending hard disks, encapsulated in a small, low-cost computer called a storage brick. This approach allows one to transfer by mail terabytes of data across the planet in a few days. By virtue of including a computer and operating system, it minimizes compatibility problems that arise when transferring the data to another computer.

Several other papers listed under specific topics also provide sweeping new looks or have changed the way people think about systems: Simon, The architecture of complexity, reading *1.4.3*; Thompson, Reflections on trusting trust, reading *11.3.3*;

Lampson, Hints for computer system design, reading *1.5.4*; and Creasy's VM/370 paper, reading *5.6.1*.

1.9 Keeping Big Systems Under Control

1.9.1 F[ernando] J. Corbató and C[harles] T. Clingen. A managerial view of the Multics system development. In Peter Wegner, *Research Directions in Software Technology*, M.I.T. Press, Cambridge, Massachusetts, 1979, pages 139–158. ISBN: 0-262-23096-8.

1.9.2 W[illiam A.] Wulf, R[oy] Levin, and C. Pierson. Overview of the Hydra operating system development. *Proceedings of the Fifth ACM Symposium on Operating Systems Principles*, in *Operating Systems Review 9*, 5 (November 1975), pages 122–131.

1.9.3 Thomas R. Horsley and William C. Lynch. Pilot: A software engineering case study. *Fourth International Conference on Software Engineering* (September 1979), pages 94–99.

These three papers are early descriptions of the challenges of managing and developing large systems. They are still relevant and easy to read, and provide complementary insights.

1.9.4 Effy Oz. When professional standards are lax: The CONFIRM failure and its lessons. *Communications of the ACM 37*, 10 (October 1994), pages 30–36.

CONFIRM is an airline/hotel/rental-car reservation system that never saw the light of day despite four years of work and an investment of more than $100M. It is one of many computer system developments that went out of control and finally were discarded without ever having been placed in service. One sees news reports of software disasters of similar magnitude a few times each year. It is difficult to obtain solid facts about system development failures because no one wants to accept the blame, especially when lawsuits are pending. This paper suffers from a shortage of facts and an oversimplistic recommendation that better ethics are all that are needed to solve the problem. (It seems likely that the ethics and management problems simply delayed recognition of the inevitable.) Nevertheless, it provides a sobering view of how badly things can go wrong.

1.9.5 Nancy G. Leveson and Clark S. Turner. An investigation of the Therac-25 accidents. *Computer 26*, 7 (July 1993), pages 18–41. (Reprinted in reading *1.3.6*.)

This is another sobering view of how badly things can go wrong. In this case, the software controller for a high-energy medical device was inadequately designed; the device was placed in service, and lethal injuries ensued. This paper manages to inquire quite deeply into the source of the problems. Unfortunately, similar mistakes have been made since; see, for example, United States Nuclear Regulatory Commission Information Notice 2001-8s1 (June 2001), which describes radiation therapy overexposures in Panama.

1.9.6 Joe Morgenstern. City perils: The fifty-nine-story crisis. *The New Yorker 71*, 14 (May 29, 1995), pages 45–53.

This article discusses how an engineer responded to the realization that a skyscraper he had designed was in danger of collapsing in a hurricane.

1.9.7 Eric S. Raymond. The cathedral and the bazaar. In *The Cathedral and The Bazaar: Musings on Linux and Open Source by an Accidental Revolutionary*, pages 19–64. O'Reilly Media Inc., 2001. ISBN: 978–0596001087, 241 pages.

The book is based on a white paper of the same title that compares two styles of software development: the Cathedral model, which is used mostly by commercial software companies and some open-source projects such as the BSD operating system; and the Bazaar model, which is exemplified by development of the GNU/Linux operating system. The work argues that the Bazaar model leads to better software because the openness and independence of Bazaar allow anyone to become a participant and to look at anything in the system that seems of interest: "Given enough eyeballs, all bugs are shallow".

1.9.8 Philip M Boffey. Investigators agree N.Y. blackout of 1977 could have been avoided. *Science 201*, 4360 (September 15, 1978), pages 994-996.

This is a fascinating description of how the electrical generation and distribution system of New York's Consolidated Edison fell apart when two supposedly tolerable faults occurred in close succession, recovery mechanisms did not work as expected, attempts to recover manually got bogged down by the system's complexity, and finally things cascaded out of control.

2 Elements of Computer System Organization

To learn more about the basic abstractions of memory and interpreters, the book *Computer Architecture* by Patterson and Hennessy (reading 1.1.1) is one of the best sources. Further information about the third basic abstraction, communication links, can be found in readings section 7.

2.1 Naming Systems

2.1.1 Bruce [G.] Lindsay. Object naming and catalog management for a distributed database manager. *Proceedings of the Second International Conference on Distributed Computing Systems*, Paris, France (April 1981), pages 31–40. Also IBM San Jose Research Laboratory Technical Report RJ2914 (August 1980). 17 pages.

This paper, a tutorial treatment of names as used in database systems, begins with a better-than-average statement of requirements and then demonstrates how those requirements were met in the R* distributed database management system.

2.1.2 Yogen K. Dalal and Robert S. Printis. 48-bit absolute Internet and Ethernet host numbers. *Proceedings of the Seventh Data Communications Symposium*,

Mexico City, Mexico, (October 1981), pages 240-245. Also Xerox Office Products Division Technical Report OPD-T8101 (July 1981), 14 pages.

This paper describes how hardware addresses are handled in the Ethernet local area network.

2.1.3 Theodor Holm Nelson. *Literary Machines, Ed. 87.1*. Project Xanadu, San Antonio, Texas, 1987. ISBN: 0-89347-056-2 (paperback). Various pagings.

Project Xanadu is an ambitious vision of a future in which books are replaced by information organized in the form of a naming network, in the form that today is called "hypertext". The book, being somewhat non-linear, is a primitive example of what Nelson advocates.

2.2 The UNIX® System

The following readings and the book by Marshall McKusick et al., reading *1.3.4*, are excellent sources on the UNIX system to follow up the case study in Section 2.5. A good, compact summary of its main features can be found in Tanenbaum's operating systems book [reading 1.2.1], which also covers Linux.

2.2.1 Dennis M. Ritchie and Ken [L.] Thompson. The UNIX time-sharing system. *Bell System Technical Journal 57*, 6, part 2 (1978), pages 1905–1930.

This paper describes an influential operating system with very low-key, but carefully chosen and hard-to-discover, objectives. The system provides a hierarchical catalog structure and succeeds in keeping naming completely distinct from file management. An earlier version of this paper appeared in the *Communications of the ACM 17*, 7 (July, 1974), pages 365-375, after being presented at the *Fourth ACM Symposium on Operating Systems Principles*. The UNIX system evolved rapidly between 1973 and 1978, so the *BSTJ* version, though harder to find, contains significant additions, both in insight and in technical content.

2.2.2 John Lions. *Lions' Commentary on UNIX 6th Edition with Source Code*. Peer-to-peer communications, 1977. ISBN: 978-1-57398-013-7, 254 pages.

This book contains the source code for UNIX Version 6, with comments to explain how it works. Although Version 6 is old, the book remains an excellent starting point for understanding how the system works from the inside, because both the source code and the comments are short and succinct. For decades, this book was part of the underground literature from which designers learned about the UNIX system, but now it is available to the public.

3 The Design of Naming Schemes

Almost any system has a naming plan, and many of the interesting naming plans can be found in papers that describe a larger system. Any reader interested in naming should study the Domain Name System, reading *4.3*, and the topic of Section 4.4.

3.1 Addressing Architectures

Several early sources still contain some of the most accessible explanations of designs that incorporate advanced naming features directly in hardware.

3.1.1 Jack B. Dennis. Segmentation and the design of multiprogrammed computer systems. *Journal of the ACM 12*, 4 (October 1965), pages 589–602.

This is the original paper outlining the advantages of providing naming support in hardware architecture.

3.1.2 R[obert] S. Fabry. Capability-based addressing. *Communications of the ACM 17*, 7 (July 1974), pages 403–412.

This is the first comprehensive treatment of capabilities, a mechanism introduced to enforce modularity but actually more of a naming feature.

3.1.3 Elliott I. Organick. *Computer System Organization, The B5700/B6700 Series*. Academic Press, 1973. ISBN: 0–12–528250–8. 132 pages.

The Burroughs Descriptor system explained in this book is apparently the only example of a hardware-supported naming system actually implemented before the advent of microprogramming.

3.1.4 Elliott I. Organick. *The Multics System: an Examination of its Structure*. M.I.T. Press, Cambridge, Massachusetts, 1972. ISBN: 0–262–15012–3. 392 pages.

This book explores every detail and ramification of the extensive naming mechanisms of Multics, both in the addressing architecture and in the file system.

3.1.5 R[oger] M. Needham and A[ndrew] D. Birrell. The CAP filing system. *Proceedings of the Sixth ACM Symposium on Operating Systems Principles*, in *Operating Systems Review 11*, 5 (November 1977), pages 11–16.

The CAP file system is one of the few implemented examples of a genuine naming network.

3.2 Examples

3.2.1 Paul J. Leach, Bernard L. Stumpf, James A. Hamilton, and Paul H. Levine. UIDs as internal names in a distributed file system. In *ACM SIGACT–SIGOPS Symposium on Principles of Distributed Computing*, Ottawa, Ontario (August 18–20, 1982), pages 34–41.

The Apollo DOMAIN system supports a different model for distributed function. It provides a shared primary memory called the Single Level Store, which extends transparently across the network. It is also one of the few systems to make substantial use of unstructured unique identifiers from a compact set as object names. This paper focuses on this latter issue.

3.2.2 Rob Pike et al. Plan 9 from Bell Labs. *Computing Systems 8*, 3 (Summer 1995), pages 221–254. An earlier version by Rob Pike, Dave Presotto, Ken Thompson, and Howard Trickey appeared in *Proceedings of the Summer 1990 UKUUG Conference* (1990), London, pages 1-9.

This paper describes a distributed operating system that takes the UNIX system idea that every resource is a file one step further by using it also for network and window system interactions. It also extends the file idea to a distributed system by defining a single file system protocol for access to all resources, whether they are local or remote. Processes can mount any remote resources into their name space, and to the user these remote resources behave just like local resources. This design makes users perceive the system as an easy-to-use time-sharing system that behaves like a single powerful computer, instead of a collection of separate computers.

3.2.3 Tim Berners-Lee et al. The World Wide Web. *Communications of the ACM 37*, 8 (August 1994), pages 76-82.

Many of the publications about the World Wide Web are available only on the Web, with a good starting point being the home page of the World Wide Web Consortium at `<http://w3c.org/>`.

3.2.4 Sergey Brin and Lawrence Page. The anatomy of a large-scale hypertextual web search engine. *Proceedings of the 7th WWW Conference*, Brisbane, Australia (April 1998). Also in *Computer Networks 30* (1998), pages 107-117.

This paper describes an early version of Google's search engine. It also introduces the idea of page rank to sort the results to a query in order of importance. Search is a dominant way in which users "name" Web pages.

3.2.5 Bryan Ford et al. Persistent personal names for globally connected mobile devices. *Proceedings of the Seventh USENIX Symposium on Operating Systems Design and Implementation* (November 2006), pages 233-248.

This paper describes a naming system for personal devices. Each device is a root of its own naming network and can use short, convenient names for other devices belonging to the same user or belonging to people in the user's social network. The implementation of the naming system allows devices to be disconnected from the Internet and resolve names of devices that are reachable. The first five pages lay out the basic naming plan. Later sections explain security properties and a security-based implementation, which involves material of Chapter 11 [on-line].

4 Enforcing Modularity with Clients and Services

Many systems are organized in a client/service style. A system that provides a good case study is the Network File System (see Section 4.5). The following papers provide some other examples.

4.1 Remote Procedure Call

4.1.1 Andrew D. Birrell and Bruce Jay Nelson. Implementing remote procedure calls. *ACM Transactions on Computer Systems 2*, 1 (February 1984), pages 39–59.

A well-written paper that shows first, the simplicity of the basic idea, second, the complexity required to deal with real implementations, and third, the refinements needed for high effectiveness.

4.1.2 Andrew Birrell, Greg Nelson, Susan Owicki, and Edward Wobber. Network objects. *Proceedings of the Fourteenth ACM Symposium on Operating Systems Principles*, in *Operating Systems Review 27*, 5 (December 1993), pages 217–230.

This paper describes a programming language for distributed applications based on remote procedure calls, which hide most "distributedness" from the programmer.

4.1.3 Ann Wollrath, Roger Riggs, and Jim Waldo. A distributed object model for the Java™ system. *Computing Systems 9*, 4 (1996), pages 265–290. Originally published in *Proceedings of the Second USENIX Conference on Object-Oriented Technologies Volume 2* (1996).

This paper presents a remote procedure call system for the Java programming language. It provides a clear description of how an RPC system can be integrated with an object-oriented programming language and the new exception types RPC introduces.

4.2 Client/Service Systems

4.2.1 Daniel Swinehart, Gene McDaniel, and David [R.] Boggs. WFS: A simple shared file system for a distributed environment. *Proceedings of the Seventh ACM Symposium on Operating Systems Principles*, in *Operating Systems Review 13*, 5 (December 1979), pages 9–17.

This early version of a remote file system opens the door to the topic of distribution of function across connected cooperating computers. The authors' specific goal was to keep things simple; thus, the relationship between mechanism and goal is much clearer than in more modern, but more elaborate, systems.

4.2.2 Robert Scheifler and James Gettys. The X Window System. *ACM Transactions on Graphics 5*, 2 (April 1986), pages 79–109.

The X Window System is the window system of choice on practically every engineering workstation in the world. It provides a good example of using the client/service model to achieve modularity. One of the main contributions of the X Window System is that it remedied a defect that had crept into the UNIX system when displays replaced typewriters: the display and keyboard were the only hardware-dependent parts of the UNIX application programming interface. The X Window System allowed display-oriented UNIX applications to be completely independent of the underlying hardware. In addition, the X Window System interposes an efficient network connection between the application and the display, allowing configuration flexibility in a distributed system.

4.2.3 John H. Howard et al. Scale and performance in a distributed file system. *ACM Transactions on Computer Systems 6*, 1 (February 1988), pages 51–81.

This paper describes experience with a prototype of the Andrew network file system for a campus network and shows how the experience motivated changes in the design. The Andrew file system had strong influence on version 4 of NFS.

4.3 Domain Name System (DNS)

The domain name system is one of the most interesting distributed systems in operation. It is not only a building block in many distributed applications, but is itself an interesting case study, offering many insights for anyone wanting to build a distributed system or a naming system.

4.3.1 Paul V. Mockapetris and Kevin J. Dunlap. Development of the Domain Name System. *Proceedings of the SIGCOMM 1988 Symposium*, pages 123–133. Also published in *ACM Computer Communications Review 18*, 4 (August 1988), pages 123–133, and republished in *ACM Computer Communications Review 25*, 1 (January 1995), pages 112–122.

4.3.2 Paul [V.] Mockapetris. Domain names—Concepts and facilities. *Request for Comments RFC 1034*, Internet Engineering Task Force (November 1987).

4.3.3 Paul [V.] Mockapetris. Domain names—Implementation and specification. *Request for Comments RFC 1035*, Internet Engineering Task Force (November 1987).

These three documents explain the DNS protocol.

4.3.4 Paul Vixie. DNS Complexity. *ACM Queue 5*, 3 (April 2007), pages 24–29.

This paper uncovers many of the complexities of how DNS, described in the case study in Section 4.4, works in practice. The protocol for DNS is simple, and no complete, precise specification of the system exists. The author argues that the current descriptive specification of DNS is an advantage because it allows various implementations to evolve to include new features as needed. The paper describes many of these features and shows that DNS is one of the most interesting distributed systems in use today.

5 Enforcing Modularity with Virtualization

5.1 Kernels

The readings on the UNIX system (see readings section 2.2) are a good starting point for studying kernels.

5.1.1 Per Brinch Hansen. The nucleus of a multiprogramming system. *Communications of the ACM 13*, 4 (April 1970), pages 238–241.

The RC-4000 was the first, and may still be the best explained, system to use messages as the primary concurrency coordination mechanism. It is also what would today be called a microkernel design.

5.1.2 M. Frans Kaashoek et al. Application performance and flexibility on exokernel systems. In *Proceedings of the Sixteenth ACM Symposium on Operating Systems Principles*, in *Operating Systems Review 31*, 5 (December 1997), pages 52–65.

The exokernel provides an extreme version of separation of policy from mechanism, sacrificing abstraction to expose (within protection constraints) all possible aspects of the physical environment to the next higher layer, giving that higher layer maximum flexibility in creating abstractions for its preferred programming environment, or tailored to its preferred application.

5.2 Type Extension as a Modularity Enforcement Tool

5.2.1 Butler W. Lampson and Howard E. Sturgis. Reflections on an operating system design. *Communications of the ACM 19*, 5 (May 1976), pages 251–265.

An operating system named CAL, designed at the University of California at Berkeley, appears to be the first system to make explicit use of types in the interface to the operating system. In addition to introducing this idea, Lampson and Sturgis also give good insight into the pros and cons of various design decisions. Documented late, the system was actually implemented in 1969.

5.2.2 Michael D. Schroeder, David D. Clark, and Jerome H. Saltzer. The Multics kernel design project. *Proceedings of the Sixth ACM Symposium on Operating Systems Principles*, in *Operating Systems Review 11*, 5 (November 1977), pages 43–56.

This paper addresses a wide range of issues encountered in applying type extension (as well as microkernel thinking, though it wasn't called that at the time) to Multics in order to simplify its internal organization and reduce the size of its trusted base. Many of these ideas were explored in even more depth in Philippe Janson's Ph.D. Thesis, *Using Type Extension to Organize Virtual Memory Mechanisms*, M.I.T. Department of Electrical Engineering and Computer Science, August 1976. That thesis is also available as M.I.T. Laboratory for Computer Science Technical Report TR-167, September 1976.

5.2.3 Galen C. Hunt and James R. Larus. Singularity: Rethinking the software stack. *Operating Systems Review 41*, 2 (April 2007), pages 37–49.

Singularity is an operating system that uses type-safe languages to enforce modularity between different software modules, instead of relying on virtual-memory hardware. The kernel and all applications are written in a strongly typed programming language with automatic garbage collection. They run in a single address space and are isolated from each other by the language runtime. They can interact with each other only through communication channels that carry type-checked messages.

5.3 Virtual Processors: Threads

5.3.1 Andrew D. Birrell. *An introduction to programming with threads*. Digital Equipment Corporation Systems Research Center Technical Report #35, January 1989. 33 pages. (Also appears as Chapter 4 of Greg Nelson, editor, *Systems Programming with Modula-3*, Prentice-Hall, 1991, pages 88–118.) A version for the C# programming language appeared as Microsoft Research Report MSR-TR-2005-68.

This is an excellent tutorial, explaining the fundamental issues clearly and going on to show the subtleties involved in exploiting threads correctly and effectively.

5.3.2 Thomas E. Anderson et al. Scheduler activations: Effective kernel support for the user-level management of parallelism. *ACM Transactions on Computer Systems 10*, 1 (February 1992), pages 53–79. Originally published in *Proceedings of the Thirteenth ACM Symposium on Operating Systems Principles*, in *Operating Systems Review 25*, 5 (December 1991), pages 95–109.

The distinction between user threads and kernel threads comes to the fore in this paper, which offers a way of getting the advantages of both by having the right kind of user/kernel thread interface. The paper also revisits the idea of a virtual processor, but in a multiprocessor context.

5.3.3 David D. Clark. The structuring of systems using upcalls. *Proceedings of the Tenth ACM Symposium on Operating Systems Principles*, in *Operating Systems Review 19*, 5 (December 1985), pages 171–180.

Attempts to impose modular structure by strict layering sometimes manage to overlook the essence of what structure is most appropriate. This paper describes a rather different intermodule organization that seems to be especially effective when dealing with network implementations.

5.3.4 Jerome H. Saltzer. *Traffic Control in a Multiplexed Computer System*. Ph.D. Thesis, Massachusetts Institute of Technology, Department of Electrical Engineering, June 1966. Also available as Project MAC Technical Report TR-30, 1966.

This work describes what is probably the first systematic virtual processor design and thread package, the multiprocessor multiplexing scheme used in the Multics system. It defines the coordination primitives BLOCK and WAKEUP, which are examples of binary semaphores assigned one per thread.

5.3.5 Rob Pike et al. Processor sleep and wakeup on a shared-memory multiprocessor. *Proceedings of the EurOpen Conference* (1991), pages 161–166.

This well-written paper does an excellent job of explaining how difficult it is to get preemptive multiplexing, handling interrupts, and implementing coordination primitives correct on shared-memory multiprocessor.

5.4 Virtual Memory

There are few examples of papers that describe a simple, clean design. The older papers (some can be found in reading section 3.1) get bogged down in technology constraints; the more recent papers (some of the them can be found in reading section 6.1 on multilevel memory management) often get bogged down in performance optimizations. The case study on the evolution of enforcing modularity with the Intel x86 (see Section 5.7 of Chapter 5) describes virtual memory support in the most widely used processor and shows how it evolved over time.

5.4.1 A[ndre] Bensoussan, C[harles] T. Clingen, and R[obert] C. Daley. The Multics virtual memory: Concepts and design. *Communications of the ACM 15*, 5 (May 1972), pages 308–318.

This is a good description of a system that pioneered the use of high-powered addressing architectures to support a sophisticated virtual memory system, including memory-mapped files. The design was constrained and shaped by the available hardware technology (0.3 MIPS processor with an 18-bit address space), but the paper is a classic and easy to read.

5.5 Coordination

Every modern textbook covers the topic of coordination but typically brushes past the subtleties and also typically gives the various mechanisms more emphasis than they deserve. These readings either explain the issues much more carefully or extend the basic concepts in various directions.

5.5.1 E[dsger] W. Dijkstra. Co-operating sequential processes. In F. Genuys, editor, *Programming Languages*, NATO Advanced Study Institute, Villard-de-Lans, 1966. Academic Press, 1968, pages 43–112.

This paper introduces semaphores, the synchronizing primitive most often used in academic exercises, and is notable for its very careful, step-by-step development of the requirements for mutual exclusion and its implementation. Many modern treatments ignore the subtleties discussed here as if they were obvious. They aren't, and if you want to understand synchronization you should read this paper.

5.5.2 E[dsger] W. Dijkstra. Solution of a problem in concurrent programming control. *Communications of the ACM 8*, 9 (September 1965), page 569.

In this very brief paper, Dijkstra first reports Dekker's observation that multiprocessor locks can be implemented entirely in software, relying on the hardware to guarantee only that read and write operations have before-or-after atomicity.

5.5.3 Leslie Lamport. A fast mutual exclusion algorithm. *ACM Transactions on Computer Systems 5*, 1 (February 1987), pages 1–11.

This paper presents a fast version of a software-only implementation of locks and gives an argument as to why this version is optimal.

5.5.4 David P. Reed and Rajendra K. Kanodia. Synchronization with eventcounts and sequencers. *Communications of the ACM 22*, 2 (February 1979), pages 115–123.

This paper introduces an extremely simple coordination system that uses less powerful primitives for sequencing than for mutual exclusion; a consequence is simple correctness arguments.

5.5.5 Butler W. Lampson and David D. Redell. Experience with processes and monitors in Mesa. *Communications of the ACM 23*, 2 (February 1980), pages 105–117.

This is a nice discussion of the pitfalls involved in integrating concurrent activity coordination into a programming language.

5.5.6 Stefan Savage et al. Eraser: A dynamic data race detector for multi-threaded programs. *ACM Transactions on Computer Systems 15*, 4 (November 1997), pages 391–411. Also in the *Proceedings of the Sixteenth ACM Symposium on Operating Systems Principles* (October 1997).

This paper describes an interesting strategy for locating certain classes of locking mistakes: instrument the program by patching its binary data references; then watch those data references to see if the program violates the locking protocol.

5.5.7 Paul E. McKenney et al. Read-copy update. *Proceedings of the Ottawa Linux Symposium*, 2002, pages 338–367.

This paper observes that locks can be an expensive mechanism for before-or-after atomicity for data structures that are mostly read and infrequently modified. The authors propose a new technique, read-copy update (RCU), which improves performance and scalability. The Linux kernel uses this mechanism for many of its data structures that processors mostly read.

5.5.8 Maurice Herlihy. Wait-free synchronization. *ACM Transactions on Programming Languages and Systems* 11, 1 (January 1991), pages 124–149.

This paper introduces the goal of wait-free synchronization, now often called non-blocking coordination, and gives non-blocking, concurrent implementations of common data structures such as sets, lists, and queues.

5.5.9 Timothy L. Harris. A pragmatic implementation of non-blocking linked lists. *Proceedings of the fifteenth International Symposium on Distributed Computing*, (October 2001), pages 300–314.

This paper describes a practical implementation of a linked list in which threads can insert concurrently without blocking.

See also reading *5.1.1*, by Brinch Hansen, which uses messages as a coordination technique, and reading *5.3.1* by Birrell, which describes a complete set of coordination primitives for programming with threads.

5.6 Virtualization

5.6.1 Robert J. Creasy. The origin of the VM/370 time-sharing system. *IBM Journal of Research and Development 25*, 5 (1981), pages 483–490.

This paper is an insightful retrospective about a mid-1960s project to virtualize the IBM 360 computer architecture and the development that led to VM/370, which in the 1970s became a popular virtual machine system. At the time, the unusual feature of VM/370 was its creation of a strict, by-the-book, hardware virtual machine, thus providing the ability to run any system/370 program in a controlled environment. Because it was a pioneer project, the author explained things particularly well, thus providing a good introduction to the concepts and problems in implementing virtual machines.

5.6.2 Edouard Bugnion et al. Disco: running commodity operating systems on scalable multiprocessors. *ACM Transactions on Computer Systems 15*, 14 (November 1997), pages 412–447.

This paper brought virtual machines back as a mainstream way of building systems.

5.6.3 Carl Waldspurger. Memory resource management in VMware ESX server. *Proceedings of the Fifth USENIX Symposium on Operating Systems Design and Implementation* (December 2002), pages 181–194.

This well-written paper introduces a nice trick (a balloon driver) to decide how much physical memory to give to guest operating systems.

5.6.4 Keith Adams and Ole Agesen. A comparison of software and hardware techniques for x86 virtualization. *Proceedings of the Twelfth Symposium on Architectural Support for Programming Languages and Operating Systems* (October 2006). ISBN: 1-59593-451-0. Also in *Operating Systems Review 40*, 5 (December 2006), pages 2–13.

This paper describes how one can virtualize the Intel x86 instruction set to build a high-performance virtual machine. It compares two implementation strategies: one that uses software techniques, such as binary rewriting, to virtualize the instruction set, and one that uses recent hardware additions to the x86 processor to make virtualizing easier. The comparison provides insights about implementing modern virtual machines and operating system support in modern x86 processors.

Also see the paper on the secure virtual machine monitor for the VAX machine, reading *11.3.5*.

6 Performance

6.1 Multilevel Memory Management

An excellent discussion of memory hierarchies, with special attention paid to the design space for caches, can be found in Chapter 5 of the book by Patterson and Hennessy, reading *1.1.1*. A lighter-weight treatment focused more on virtual memory, and including a discussion of stack algorithms, can be found in Chapter 3 of Tanenbaum's computer systems book, reading *1.2.1*.

6.1.1 R[obert] A. Frieburghouse. Register allocation via usage counts. *Communications of the ACM 17*, 11 (November 1974), pages 638–642.

This paper shows that compiler code generators must do multilevel memory management and that they have the same problems as do caches and paging systems.

6.1.2 R[ichard] L. Mattson, J. Gecsei, D[onald] R. Slutz, and I[rving] L. Traiger. Evaluation techniques for storage hierarchies. *IBM Systems Journal 9*, 2 (1970), pages 78–117.

The original reference on stack algorithms and their analysis, this paper is well written and presents considerably more in-depth observations than the brief summaries that appear in modern textbooks.

6.1.3 Richard Rashid et al. Machine-independent virtual memory management for paged uniprocessor and multiprocessor architectures. *IEEE Transactions on Computers 37*, 8 (August 1988), pages 896-908. Originally published in *Proceedings of the Second International Conference on Architectural Support for Programming Languages and Operating Systems* (November 1987), pages 31-39.

This paper describes a design for a sophisticated virtual memory system that has been adopted by several operating systems, including several BSD operating systems and Apple's OS X. The system supports large, sparse virtual address spaces, copy-on-write copying of pages, and memory-mapped files.

6.1.4 Ted Kaehler and Glenn Krasner. LOOM: Large object-oriented memory for Smalltalk-80 systems. In Glenn Krasner, editor, *Smalltalk-80: Bits of History, Words of Advice*. Addison-Wesley, 1983, pages 251–271. ISBN: 0-201-11669-3.

This paper describes the memory-management system used in Smalltalk, an interactive programming system for desktop computers. A coherent virtual memory language support system provides for lots of small objects while taking into account address space allocation, multilevel memory management, and naming in an integrated way.

The paper on the Woodstock File System, by Swinehart et al., reading *4.2.1*, describes a file system that is organized as a multilevel memory management system. Also see reading *10.1.8* for an interesting application (shared virtual memory) using multilevel memory management.

6.2 Remote Procedure Call

6.2.1 Michael D. Schroeder and Michael Burrows. Performance of Firefly RPC. *ACM Transactions on Computer Systems 8*, 1 (February 1990), pages 1–17. Originally published in *Proceedings of the Twelfth ACM Symposium on Operating Systems Principles*, in *Operating Systems Review 23*, 5 (December 1989), pages 102–113.

As a complement to the abstract discussion of remote procedure call in reading *4.1.1*, this paper gives a concrete, blow-by-blow accounting of the steps required in a particular implementation and then compares this accounting with overall time measurements. In addition to providing insight into the intrinsic costs of remote procedures, this work demonstrates that it is possible to do bottom-up performance analysis that correlates well with top-down measurements.

6.2.2 Brian N. Bershad, Thomas E. Anderson, Edward D. Lazowska, and Henry M. Levy. Lightweight remote procedure call. *ACM Transactions on Computer Systems 8*, 1 (February 1990), pages 37–55. Originally published in *Proceedings of the Twelfth ACM Symposium on Operating Systems Principles*, in *Operating Systems Review 23*, 5 (December 1989), pages 102–113.

6.2.3 Jochen Liedtke. Improving IPC by kernel design. *Proceedings of the Fourteenth ACM Symposium on Operating Systems Principles*, in *Operating Systems Review 27*, 5 (December 1993), pages 175–187.

These two papers develop techniques to allow local kernel-based client/service modularity to look just like remote client/service modularity to the application designer, while at the same time capturing the performance advantage that can come from being local.

6.3 Storage

6.3.1 Chris Ruemmler and John Wilkes. An introduction to disk drive modeling. *Computer 27*, 3 (March 1994), pages 17–28.

This paper is really two papers in one. The first five pages provide a wonderfully accessible explanation of how disk drives and controllers actually work. The rest of the paper, of interest primarily to performance modeling specialists, explores the problem of accurately simulating a complex disk drive, with measurement data to show the size of errors that arise from various modeling simplifications (or oversimplifications).

6.3.2 Marshall K. McKusick, William N. Joy, Samuel J. Leffler, and Robert S. Fabry. A fast file system for UNIX. *ACM Transactions on Computer Systems 2*, 3 (August 1984), pages 181–197.

The "fast file system" nicely demonstrates the trade-offs between performance and complexity in adding several well-known performance enhancement techniques, such as multiple block sizes and sector allocation based on adjacency, to a file system that was originally designed as the epitome of simplicity.

6.3.3 Gregory R. Ganger and Yale N. Patt. Metadata update performance in file systems. *Proceedings of the First USENIX Symposium on Operating Systems Design and Implementation* (November 1994), pages 49–60.

This paper is an application to file systems of some recovery and consistency concepts originally developed for database systems. It describes a few simple rules (e.g., an inode should be written to the disk after writing the disk blocks to which it points) that allow a system designer to implement a file system that is high performance and always keeps its on-disk data structures consistent in the presence of failures. As applications perform file operations, the rules create dependencies between data blocks in the write-behind cache. A disk driver that knows about these dependencies can write the cached blocks to disk in an order that maintains consistency of on-disk data structures despite system crashes.

6.3.4 Andrew Birrell et al. A design for high-performance flash disks. *ACM Operating Systems Review 41*, 2 (April 2007), pages 88–93. (Also appeared as Microsoft Corporation technical report TR-2005-176.)

Flash (non-volatile) electronic memory organized to appear as a disk has emerged as a more expensive but very low-latency alternative to magnetic disks for durable storage. This short paper describes, in an easy-to-understand way, the challenges associated with building a high-performance file system using flash disks and proposes a design to address the challenges. This paper is a good start for readers who want to explore flash-based storage systems.

6.4 Other Performance-Related Topics

6.4.1 Sharon E. Perl and Richard L. Sites. Studies of Windows NT performance using dynamic execution traces. *Proceedings of the Second USENIX Symposium on Operating Systems Design and Implementation* (October 1996). Also in *Operating System Review 30*, SI (October 1996), pages 169–184.

This paper shows by example that any performance issue in computer systems can be explained. The authors created a tool to collect complete traces of instructions executed by the Windows NT operating system and applications. The authors conclude that pin bandwidth limits the achievable execution speed of applications and that locks inside the operating system can limit applications to scale to more than a moderate number of processors. The paper also discusses the impact of cache-coherence hardware (see Chapter 10 [on-line]) on application performance. All of these issues are increasingly important for multiprocessors on a single chip.

6.4.2 Jeffrey C. Mogul and K. K. Ramakrishnan. Eliminating receive livelock in an interrupt-driven kernel. *Transactions on Computer Systems 15*, 3 (August 1997), pages 217–252.

This paper introduces the problem of receive livelock (described in Sidebar 6.7) and presents a solution. Receive livelock is a possible undesirable situation when a system is temporarily overloaded. It can arise if the server spends too much of its time saying "I'm too busy" and as a result has no time left to serve any of the requests.

6.4.3 Jeffrey Dean and Sanjay Ghemawat. MapReduce: Simplified data processing on large clusters. *Proceedings of the Sixth USENIX Symposium on Operating Systems Design and Implementation* (December 2004), pages 137–150. Also in *Communications of the ACM 51*, 1 (January 2008), pages 1–10.

This paper is a case study of aggregating arrays (reaching into the thousands) of computers to perform parallel computations on large data sets (e.g., all the pages of the Web). It uses a model that applies when a composition of two serial functions (Map and Reduce) has no side-effects on the data sets. The charm of MapReduce is that for computations that fit the model, the runtime uses concurrency but hides it completely from the programmer. The runtime partitions the input data set, executes the functions in parallel on different parts of the data set, and handles the failures of individual computers.

7 The Network as a System and as a System Component

Proceedings of the IEEE 66, 11 (November 1978), a special issue of that journal devoted to packet switching, contains several papers mentioned under various topics here. Collectively, they provide an extensive early bibliography on computer communications.

7.1 Networks

The book by Perlman on bridges and routers, reading *1.2.5*, explains how the network layer really works.

7.1.1 David D. Clark, Kenneth T. Pogran, and David P. Reed. An introduction to local area networks. *Proceedings of the IEEE 66*, 11 (November 1978), pages 1497–1517.

This basic tutorial on local area network communications characterizes the various modular components of a local area network, both interface and protocols, gives specific examples, and explains how local area networks relate to larger, interconnected networks. The specific examples are now out of date, but the rest of the material is timeless.

7.1.2 Robert M. Metcalfe and David R. Boggs. Ethernet: Distributed packet switching for local computer networks. *Communications of the ACM 19*, 7 (July 1976), pages 395–404.

This paper provides the design of what has proven to be the most popular local area network technology.

7.2 Protocols

7.2.1 Louis Pouzin and Hubert Zimmerman. A tutorial on protocols. *Proceedings of the IEEE 66*, 11 (November 1978), pages 1346–1370.

This paper is well written and provides perspective along with the details. The fact that it was written a long time ago turns out to be its major appeal. Because networks were not widely understood at the time, it was necessary to fully explain all of the assumptions and offer extensive analogies. This paper does an excellent job of both, and as a consequence it provides a useful complement to modern texts. While reading this paper, anyone familiar with current network technology will frequently exclaim, "So that's why the Internet works that way."

7.2.2 Vinton G. Cerf and Peter T. Kirstein. Issues in packet-network interconnection. *Proceedings of the IEEE 66*, 11 (November 1978), pages 1386–1408.

At the time this paper was written, an emerging problem was the interconnection of independently administered data communication networks. This paper explores the issues in both breadth and depth, a combination that more recent papers do not provide.

7.2.3 David D. Clark and David L. Tennenhouse. Architectural considerations for a new generation of protocols. *ACM SIGCOMM '91 Conference: Communications Architectures and Protocols*, in *Computer Communication Review 20*, 4 (September 1990), pages 200–208.

This paper captures 20 years of experience in protocol design and implementation and lays out the requirements for the next few rounds of protocol design. The basic observation is that the performance requirements of future high-speed networks and applications will require that the layers used for protocol description not constrain implementations to be similarly layered. This paper is required reading for anyone who is developing a new protocol or protocol suite.

7.2.4 Danny Cohen. On holy wars and a plea for peace. *IEEE Computer 14*, 10 (October 1981), pages 48–54.

This is an entertaining discussion of big-endian and little-endian arguments in protocol design.

7.2.5 Danny Cohen. Flow control for real-time communication. *Computer Communication Review 10*, 1–2 (January/April 1980), pages 41–47.

This brief item is the source of the "servant's dilemma", a parable that provides helpful insight into why flow control decisions must involve the application.

7.2.6 Geoff Huston. Anatomy: A look inside network address translators. *The Internet Protocol Journal* 7, 3 (September 2004), pages 2–32.

Network address translators (NATs) break down the universal connectivity property of the Internet: when NATs are in use, one can no longer assume that every computer in the Internet can communicate with every other computer in the Internet. This paper discusses the motivation for NATs, how they work, and in what ways they create havoc for some Internet applications.

7.2.7 Van Jacobson. Congestion avoidance and control. *Proceedings of the Symposium on Communications Architectures and Protocols* (SIGCOMM '88), pages 314-329. Also in *Computer Communication Review 18*, 4 (August 1988).

Sidebar 7.9 gives a simplified description of the congestion avoidance and control mechanism of TCP, the most commonly used transport protocol in the Internet. This paper explains those mechanisms in full detail. They are surprisingly simple but have proven to be effective.

7.2.8 Jordan Ritter. Why Gnutella can't scale. No, really. Unpublished grey literature. <http://www.darkridge.com/~jpr5/doc/gnutella.html>

This paper offers a simple performance model to explain why the Gnutella protocol (see problem set *20*) cannot support large networks of Gnutella peers. The problem is incommensurate scaling of its bandwidth requirements.

7.2.9 David B. Johnson. Scalable support for transparent mobile host internetworking. *Wireless Networks 1*, 3 (1995), pages 311-321.

Addressing a laptop computer that is connected to a network by a radio link and that can move from place to place without disrupting network connections can be a challenge. This paper proposes a systematic approach based on maintaining a tunnel between the laptop computer's current location and an agent located at its usual home location. Variations of this paper (based on the author's 1993 Ph.D. Thesis at Carnegie-Mellon University and available as CMU Computer Science Technical Report CS-93-128) have appeared in several 1993 and 1994 workshops and conferences, as well as in the book *Mobile Computing*, Tomasz Imielinski and Henry F. Korth, editors, Kluwer Academic Publishers, c. 1996. ISBN: 079239697-9.

One popular protocol, remote procedure call, is covered in depth in reading *4.1.1* by Birrell and Nelson, as well as Section 10.3 of Tanenbaum's *Modern Operating Systems*, reading *1.2.1*.

7.3 Organization for Communication

7.3.1 Leonard Kleinrock. Principles and lessons in packet communications. *Proceedings of the IEEE 66*, 11 (November 1978), pages 1320-1329.

7.3.2 Lawrence G. Roberts. The evolution of packet switching. *Proceedings of the IEEE 66*, 11 (November 1978), pages 1307-1313.

These two papers discuss experience with the ARPANET. Anyone faced with the need to design a network should look over these two papers, which focus on lessons learned and the sources of surprise.

7.3.3 J[erome] H. Saltzer, D[avid]. P. Reed, and D[avid]. D. Clark. End-to-end arguments in system design. *ACM Transactions on Computer Systems 2*, 4 (November 1984), pages 277-288. An earlier version appears in the *Proceedings* *of the Second International Conference on Distributed Computing Systems* (April 1981), pages 504–512.

This paper proposes a design rationale for deciding which functions belong in which layers of a layered network implementation. It is one of the few papers available that provides a system design principle.

7.3.4 Leonard Kleinrock. The latency/bandwidth trade-off in gigabit networks. *IEEE Communications Magazine 30*, 4 (April 1992), pages 36–40.

Technology has made gigabit/second data rates economically feasible over long distances. But long distances and high data rates conspire to change some fundamental properties of a packet network—latency becomes the dominant factor that limits applications. This paper provides a very good explanation of the problem.

7.4 Practical Aspects

For the complete word on the Internet protocols, check out the following series of books.

7.4.1 W. Richard Stevens. *TCP/IP illustrated*. Addison-Wesley; v. 1, 1994, ISBN: 0-201-63346-9, 576 pages; v. 2 (with co-author Gary R. Wright,) 1995, ISBN: 0-201-63354-x, 1174 pages.; v. 3, 1996, ISBN: 0-201-63495-3, 328 pages. *Volume 1: The Protocols. Volume 2: The Implementation. Volume 3: TCP for Transactions, HTTP, NNTP, and the UNIX® Domain Protocols.*

These three volumes will tell you more than you wanted to know about how TCP/IP is implemented, using the network implementation of the Berkeley System Distribution for reference. The word "illustrated" refers more to computer printouts—listings of packet traces and programs—than to diagrams. If you want to know how some aspect of the Internet protocol suite is actually implemented, this is the place to look—though it does not often explain why particular implementation choices were made.

8 Fault Tolerance: Reliable Systems from Unreliable Components

A plan for some degree of fault tolerance shows up in many systems. For an example of fault tolerance in distributed file systems, see the paper on Coda by Kistler and Satyanarayanan, reading *10.1.2*. See also the paper on RAID by Katz et al., reading *10.2.2*.

8.1 Fault Tolerance

Chapter 3 of the book by Gray and Reuter, reading *1.1.5*, provides a bedrock text on this subject.

8.1.1 Jim [N.] Gray and Daniel P. Siewiorek. High-availability computer systems. *Computer 24*, 9 (September 1991), pages 39–48.

This is a very nice, easy-to-read overview of how high availability can be achieved.

8.1.2 Daniel P. Siewiorek. Architecture of fault-tolerant computers. *Computer 17*, 8 (August 1984), pages 9–18.

This paper provides an excellent taxonomy, as well as a good overview of several architectural approaches to designing computers that continue running even when a single hardware component fails.

8.2 Software Errors

8.2.1 Dawson Engler et al. Bugs as deviant behavior: A general approach to inferring errors in systems code. *Proceedings of the Eighteenth ACM Symposium on Operating Systems Principles*, 2001, in *Operating Systems Review 35*, 5 (December 2001), pages 57–72.

This paper describes a method for finding possible programming faults in large systems by looking for inconsistencies. For example, if in most cases an invocation of a certain function is preceded by disabling interrupts but in a few cases it is not, there is a good chance that a programming fault is present. The paper uses this insight to create a tool for finding potential faults in large systems.

8.2.2 Michael M. Swift et al. Recovering device drivers. *Proceedings of the Sixth Symposium on Operating Systems Design and Implementation* (December 2004), pages 1–16.

This paper observes that software faults in device drivers often lead to fatal errors that cause operating systems to fail and thus require a reboot. It then describes how virtual memory techniques can be used to enforce modularity between device drivers and the rest of the operating system kernel, and how the operating system can recover device drivers when they fail, reducing the number of reboots.

8.3 Disk Failures

8.3.1 Bianca Schroeder and Garth A. Gibson. Disk failures in the real world: What does an MTTF of 1,000,000 hours mean to you? *Proceedings of the Fifth USENIX Conference on File and Storage Technologies* (2007), pages 1–16.

As explained in Section 8.2, it is not uncommon that data sheets for disk drives specify MTTFs of one hundred years or more, many times the actual observed lifetimes of those drives in the field. This paper looks at disk replacement data for 100,000 disk drives and discusses what MTTF means for those disk drives.

8.3.2 Eduardo Pinheiro, Wolf-Dietrich Weber, and Luiz Andre Barroso. Failure trends in a large disk drive population. *Proceedings of the Fifth USENIX Conference on File and Storage Technologies* (2007), pages 17–28.

Recently, outfits such as Google have deployed large enough numbers of off-the-shelf disk drives for a long enough time that they can make their own evaluations of disk drive failure rates and lifetimes, for comparison with the a priori reliability models of the disk vendors. This paper reports data collected from such observations. It analyzes the correlation between failures and several parameters that are generally believed to impact the lifetime of disk and finds some surprises. For example, it reports that temperature is less correlated with disk drive failure than was previously reported, as long as the temperature is within a certain range and stable.

9 Atomicity: All-or-Nothing and Before-or-After

9.1 Atomicity, Coordination, and Recovery

The best source on this topic is reading *1.1.5*, but Gray and Reuter's thousand-page book can be a bit overwhelming.

9.1.1 Warren A. Montgomery. *Robust Concurrency Control for a Distributed Information System*. Ph.D. Thesis, Massachusetts Institute of Technology, Department of Electrical Engineering and Computer Science, December 1978. Also available as M.I.T. Laboratory for Computer Science Technical Report TR-207, January 1979. 197 pages.

This work describes alternative strategies that maximize concurrent activity while achieving atomicity: maintaining multiple values for some variables, atomic broadcast of messages to achieve proper sequence.

9.1.2 D. B. Lomet. Process structuring, synchronization, and recovery using atomic actions. *Proceedings of an ACM Conference on Language Design for Reliable Software* (March 1977), pages 128–137. Published as *ACM SIGPLAN Notices 12*, 3 (March 1977); *Operating Systems Review 11*, 2 (April 1977); and *Software Engineering Notes 2*, 2 (March 1977).

This is one of the first attempts to link atomicity to both recovery and coordination. It is written from a language, rather than an implementation, perspective.

9.2 Databases

9.2.1 Jim [N.] Gray et al. The recovery manager of the system R database manager. *ACM Computing Surveys 13*, 2 (June 1981), pages 223–242.

This paper is a case study of a sophisticated, real, high-performance logging and locking system. It is one of the most interesting case studies of its type because it shows the number of different, interacting mechanisms needed to construct a system that performs well.

9.2.2 C. Mohan et al. ARIES: A transaction recovery method supporting fine-granularity locking and partial rollbacks using write-ahead logging. *ACM Transactions on Database Systems 17*, 1 (1992), pages 94-162.

This paper describes all the intricate design details of a fully featured, commercial-quality database transaction system that uses write-ahead logging.

9.2.3 C. Mohan, Bruce Lindsey, and Ron Obermarck. transaction management in the R* distributed database management system. *ACM Transactions on Database Systems (TODS) 11*, 4 (December 1986), pages 378–396.

This paper deals with transaction management for distributed databases, and introduces two new protocols (Presumed Abort and Presumed Commit) that optimize two-phase commit (see Section 9.6), resulting in fewer messages and log writes. Presumed Abort is optimized for transactions that perform only read operations, and Presumed Commit is optimized for transactions with updates that involve several distributed databases.

9.2.4 Tom Barclay, Jim Gray, and Don Slutz. Microsoft TerraServer: A spatial data warehouse. *Microsoft Technical Report MS-TR-99-29*. June 1999.

The authors report on building a popular Web site that hosts aerial, satellite, and topographic images of Earth using a off-the-shelf components, including a standard database system for storing the terabytes of data.

9.2.5 Ben Vandiver et al. Tolerating byzantine faults in transaction processing systems using commit barrier scheduling. *Proceedings of the Twenty-first ACM Symposium on Operating Systems Principles*, in *Operating Systems Review 41*, 6 (December 2005), pages 59–79.

This paper describes a replication scheme for handling Byzantine faults in database systems. It issues queries and updates to multiple replicas of unmodified, off-the-shelf database systems, and it compares their responses, thus creating a single database that is Byzantine fault tolerant (see Section 8.6 for the definition of Byzantine).

9.3 Atomicity-Related Topics

9.3.1 Mendel Rosenblum and John K. Ousterhout. The design and implementation of a log-structured file system. *ACM Transactions on Computer Systems 10*, 1 (February 1992), pages 26–52. Originally published in *Proceedings of the Thirteenth ACM Symposium on Operating Systems Principles*, in *Operating Systems Review 25*, 5 (December 1991), pages 1–15.

Although it has long been suggested that one could in principle store the contents of a file system on disk in the form of a finite log, this design is one of the few that demonstrates the full implications of that design strategy. The paper also presents a fine example of how to approach a system problem by carefully defining the objective, measuring previous systems to obtain a benchmark, and then comparing performance as well as functional aspects that cannot be measured.

9.3.2 H. T. Kung and John T. Robinson. On optimistic methods for concurrency control. *ACM Transactions on Database Systems 9*, 4 (June 1981), pages 213–226.

This early paper introduced the idea of using optimistic approaches to controlling updates to shared data. An optimistic scheme is one in which a transaction proceeds in the hope that its updates are not conflicting with concurrent updates of another transaction. At commit time, the transaction checks to see if the hope was justified. If so, the transaction commits. If not, the transaction aborts and tries again. Applications that use a database in which contention for particular records is infrequent may run more efficiently with this optimistic scheme than with a scheme that always acquires locks to coordinate updates.

See also the paper by Lampson and Sturgis, reading *1.8.7* and the paper by Ganger and Patt, reading *6.3.3*.

10 Consistency and Durable Storage

10.1 Consistency

10.1.1 J. R. Goodman. Using cache memory to reduce processor-memory traffic. *Proceedings of the 10th Annual International Symposium on Computer Architecture*, pages 124–132 (1983).

The paper that introduced a protocol for cache-coherent shared memory using snoopy caches. The paper also sparked much research in more scalable designs for cache-coherent shared memory.

10.1.2 James J. Kistler and M[ahadarev] Satyanarayanan. Disconnected operation in the Coda file system. *Proceedings of the Thirteenth ACM Symposium on Operating Systems Principles*, in *Operating Systems Review 25*, 5 (December 1991), pages 213–225.

Coda is a variation of the Andrew File System (AFS) that provides extra fault tolerance features. It is notable for using the same underlying mechanism to deal both with accidental disconnection due to network partition and the intentional disconnection associated with portable computers. This paper is very well written.

10.1.3 Jim Gray et al. The dangers of replication and a solution. *Proceedings of the 1996 ACM SIGMOD International Conference on Management of Data*, in *ACM SIGMOD Record 25*, 2 (June 1996), pages 173–182.

This paper describes the challenges for replication protocols in situations where the replicas are stored on mobile computers that are frequently disconnected. The paper argues that trying to provide transactional semantics for an optimistic replication protocol in this setting is unstable because there will be too many reconciliation conflicts. It proposes a new two-tier protocol for reconciling disconnected replicas that addresses this problem.

10.1.4 Leslie Lamport. Paxos made simple. Distributed computing (column), *ACM SIGACT News 32*, 4 (Whole Number 121, December 2001), pages 51–58.

This paper describes an intricate protocol, Paxos, in a simple way. The Paxos protocol allows several computers to agree on a value (e.g., the list of available computers in a replicated service) in the face of network and computer failures. It is an important building block in building fault tolerant services.

10.1.5 Fred Schneider. Implementing fault-tolerant services using the state machine approach: A tutorial. *ACM Computing Surveys 22*, 4 (1990), pages 299–319.

This paper provides a clear description of one of the most popular approaches for building fault tolerant services, the replicated-state machine approach.

10.1.6 Leslie Lamport. Time, clocks, and the ordering of events in a distributed system. *Communications of the ACM 21*, 7 (1978), pages 558–565.

This paper introduces an idea that is now known as Lamport clocks. A Lamport clock provides a global, logical clock for a distributed system that respects the physical clocks of the computers comprising the distributed system and the communication between them. The paper also introduces the idea of replicated state machines.

10.1.7 David K. Gifford. Weighted voting for replicated data. *Proceedings of the Seventh ACM Symposium on Operating Systems Principles*, in *Operating Systems Review 13*, 5 (December 1979), pages 150–162. Also available as Xerox Palo Alto Research Center Technical Report CSL-79-14 (September 1979).

The work discusses a replicated data algorithm that allows the trade-off between reliability and performance to be adjusted by assigning weights to each data copy and requiring transactions to collect a quorum of those weights before reading or writing.

10.1.8 Kai Li and Paul Hudak. Memory coherence in shared virtual memory systems. *ACM Transactions on Computer Systems* 7, 4 (November 1989), pages 321–359.

This paper describes a method to create a shared virtual memory across several separated computers that can communicate only with messages. It uses hardware support for virtual memory to cause the results of a write to a page to be observed by readers of that page on other computers. The goal is to allow programmers to write parallel applications on a distributed computer system in shared-memory style instead of a message-passing style.

10.1.9 Sanjay Ghemawat, Howard Gobioff, and Shun-Tak Leung. The Google file system. *Proceedings of the Nineteenth ACM Symposium on Operating Systems Principles* (October 2003), pages 29–43. Also in *Operating Systems Review 37*, 5 (December 2003).

This paper introduces a file system used in many of Google's applications. It aggregates the disks of thousands of computers in a cluster into a single storage system with a simple file system interface. Its design is optimized for large files and replicates files for fault tolerance. The Google File System is used in the storage back-end of many of Google's applications, including search.

10.1.10 F[ay] Chang et al. Bigtable: A distributed storage system for structured data. *ACM Transactions on Computer Systems 26*, 2 article 4 (2008), pages 1–26.

This paper describes a database-like system for storing petabytes of structured data on thousands of commodity servers.

10.2 Durable Storage

10.2.1 Raymond A. Lorie. The long-term preservation of digital information. *Proceedings of the First ACM/IEEE Joint Conference on Digital Libraries* (2001), pages 346–352.

This is a thoughtful discussion of the problems of archiving digital information despite medium and technology obsolescence.

10.2.2 Randy H. Katz, Garth A. Gibson, and David A. Patterson. Disk system architectures for high performance computing. *Proceedings of the IEEE* 77, 12 (December 1989), pages 1842–1857.

The first part of this reference paper on Redundant Arrays of Independent Disks (RAID) reviews disk technology; the important material is the catalog of six varieties of RAID organization.

10.2.3 Petros Maniatis et al. LOCKSS: A Peer-to-peer digital preservation system *ACM Transactions on Computer Systems 23*, 1 (February 2005), pages 2–50.

This paper describes a peer-to-peer system for preserving access to journals and other archival information published on the Web. Its design is based on the mantra "lots of copies keep stuff safe" (LOCKSS). A large number of persistent Web caches keep copies and cooperate to detect and repair damage to their copies using a new voting scheme.

10.2.4 A[lan J.] Demers et al. Epidemic algorithms for replicated database maintenance. *Proceedings of the Sixth Symposium on Principles of Distributed Computing* (August 1987), pages 1–12. Also in *Operating Systems Review 22*, 1 (January 1988), pages 8–32.

This paper describes an epidemic protocol to update data that is replicated on many machines. The essence of an epidemic protocol is that each computer periodically gossips with some other, randomly chosen computer and exchanges information; multiple computers thus learn about all updates in a viral fashion. Epidemic protocols can be simple and robust, yet can spread updates relatively quickly.

10.3 Reconciliation

10.3.1 Douglas B. Terry et al. Managing update conflicts in Bayou, a weakly connected replicated storage system. In *Proceedings of the 15th Symposium on Operating Systems Principles* (December 1995), in *Operating Systems Review 29*, 5 (December 1995), pages 172–183.

This paper introduces a replication scheme for computers that share data but are not always connected. For example, each computer may have a copy of a calendar, which it can update optimistically. Bayou will propagate these updates, detect conflicts, and attempt to resolve conflicts, if possible.

10.3.2 Trevor Jim, Benjamin C. Pierce, and Jérôme Vouillon. How to build a file synchronizer. (A widely circulated piece of grey literature—dated February 22, 2002 but never published.)

This paper describes the nuts and bolts of Unison, a tool that efficiently synchronizes the files stored on two computers. Unison is targeted to users who have their files stored in several places (e.g., on a server at work, a laptop to carry while traveling, and a desktop at home) and would like to have all the files on the different computers be the same.

11 Information Security

11.1 Privacy

The fundamental book about privacy is reading *1.1.6* by Alan Westin.

11.1.1 Arthur R. Miller. *The Assault on Privacy*. University of Michigan Press, Ann Arbor, Michigan, 1971. ISBN: 0-47265500-0. 333 pages. (Out of print.)

This book articulately spells out the potential effect of computerized data-gathering systems on privacy, and of possible approaches to improving legal protection. Part of the latter is now out of date because of advances in legislation, but most of this book is still of much interest.

11.1.2 Daniel J. Weitzner et al. Information accountability. *Communications of the ACM 51*, 6 (June 2008), pages 82–87.

The paper suggests that in the modern world Westin's definition covers only a subset of privacy. See Sidebar 11.1 for a discussion of the paper's proposed extended definition.

11.2 Protection Architectures

11.2.1 Jerome H. Saltzer and Michael D. Schroeder. The protection of information in computer systems. *Proceedings of the IEEE 63*, 9 (September 1975), pages 1278–1308.

After 30 years, this paper (an early version of the current Chapter 11) still provides an effective treatment of protection mechanics in multiuser systems. Its emphasis on protection inside a single system, rather than between systems connected to a network, is one of its chief shortcomings, along with antique examples and omission of newer techniques of certification such as authentication logic.

11.2.2 R[oger] M. Needham. Protection systems and protection implementations. *AFIPS Fall Joint Conference 41*, Part I (December 1972), pages 571–578.

This paper is probably as clear an explanation of capability systems as one is likely to find. For another important paper on capabilities, see Fabry, reading *3.1.2*.

11.3 Certification, Trusted Computer Systems, and Security Kernels

11.3.1 Butler [W.] Lampson, Martín Abadi, Michael Burrows, and Edward Wobber. Authentication in distributed systems: Theory and practice. *ACM Transactions on Computer Systems 10*, 4 (November 1992), pages 265–310.

This paper, one of a series on a logic that can be used to reason systematically about authentication, provides a relatively complete explication of the theory and shows how to apply it to the protocols of a distributed system.

11.3.2 Edward Wobber, Martín Abadi, Michael Burrows, and Butler W. Lampson. Authentication in the Taos operating system. *Proceedings of the Fourteenth ACM Symposium on Operating Systems Principles*, in *Operating Systems Review 27*, 5 (December 1993), pages 256–269.

This paper applies the authentication logic developed in reading *11.3.1* to an experimental operating system. In addition to providing a concrete example, the explanation of the authentication logic itself is a little more accessible than that in the other paper.

11.3.3 Ken L. Thompson. Reflections on trusting trust. *Communications of the ACM 27*, 8 (August 1984), pages 761–763.

Anyone seriously interested in developing trusted computer systems should think hard about the implications for verification that this paper raises. Thompson demonstrates the ease with which a compiler expert can insert undetectable Trojan Horses into a system. Reading 11.3.4 describes a way to detect a Trojan horse. [The original idea that Thompson describes came from a paper whose identity he could not recall at the time, and which is credited with a footnote asking for help locating it. The paper was a technical report of the United States Air Force Electronic Systems Division at Hanscom Air Force Base. Paul A. Karger and Roger R. Schell. *Multics Security Evaluation: Vulnerability Analysis. ESD-TR-74-193, Volume II* (June 1974), page 52.]

11.3.4 David A. Wheeler. Countering trusting trust through diverse double-Compiling. *Proceedings of the 21st Annual Computer Security Applications Conference* (2005), pages 28–40.

This paper proposes a solution that the author calls "diverse double compiling", to detect the attack discussed in Thompson's paper on trusting trust (see reading *11.3.3*). The idea is to recompile a new, untrusted compiler's source code twice: first, using a trusted compiler, and second, using the result of this compilation. If the resulting binary for the compiler is bit-for-bit identical with the untrusted compiler's original binary, then the source code accurately represents the untrusted binary, which is the first step in developing trust in the new compiler.

11.3.5 Paul A. Karger et al. A VMM security kernel for the VAX architecture. *1990 IEEE Computer Society Symposium on Security and Privacy* (May 1990), pages 2–19.

In the 1970's, the U.S. Department of Defense undertook a research effort to create trusted computer systems for defense purposes and in the process created a large body of literature on the subject. This paper distills most of the relevant ideas from that literature into a single, readable case study, and it also provides pointers to other key papers for those seeking more details on these ideas.

11.3.6 David D. Clark and David. R. Wilson. A Comparison of commercial and military computer security policies. *1987 IEEE Symposium on Security and Privacy* (April 1987), pages 184–194.

This thought-provoking paper outlines the requirements for security policy in commercial settings and argues that the lattice model is often not applicable. It suggests that these applications require a more object-oriented model in which data may be modified only by trusted programs.

11.3.7 Jaap-Henk Hoepman and Bart Jacobs. Increased security through open source. *Communications of the ACM 50*, 1 (January 2007), pages 79–83.

It has long been argued that the open design principle (see Section 11.1.4) is important to designing secure systems. This paper extends that argument by making the case that the availability of source code for a system is important in ensuring the security of its implementation.

See also reading *1.3.15* by Garfinkel and Spafford, reading *5.2.1* by Lampson and Sturgis, and reading *5.2.2* by Schroeder, Clark, and Saltzer.

11.4 Authentication

11.4.1 Robert [H.] Morris and Ken [L.] Thompson. Password security: A case history. *Communications of the ACM 22*, 11 (November 1979), pages 594–597.

This paper is a model of how to explain something in an accessible way. With a minimum of jargon and an historical development designed to simplify things for the reader, it describes the UNIX password security mechanism.

11.4.2 Frank Stajano and Ross J. Anderson. The resurrecting duckling: Security issues for ad-hoc wireless networks. *Security Protocols Workshop 1999*, pages 172–194.

This paper discusses the problem of how a new device (e.g., a surveillance camera) can establish a secure relationship with the remote controller of the device's owner, instead of its neighbor's or adversary's. The paper's solution is that a device will recognize as its owner the first principal that sends it an authentication key. As soon as the device receives a key, its status changes from newborn to imprinted, and it stays faithful to that key until its death. The paper illustrates the problem and solution, using a vivid analogy of how ducklings authenticate their mother (see Sidebar 11.5).

11.4.3 David Mazières. *Self-certifying File System*. Ph.D. Thesis, Massachusetts Institute of Technology Department of Electrical Engineering and Computer Science (May 2000).

This thesis proposes a design for a cross-administrative domain file system that separates the file system from the security mechanism using an idea called self-certifying path names. Self-certifying names can be found in several other systems.

See also Sidebar 11.6 on Kerberos and reading *3.2.5*, which uses cryptographic techniques to secure a personal naming system.

11.5 Cryptographic Techniques

The fundamental books about cryptography applied to computer systems are reading *1.2.4*, by Bruce Schneier, and reading *1.3.13*, by Alfred Menezes et al. In light of these two books, the first few papers from the 1970's listed below are primarily of historical interest. There is also a good, more elementary, treatment of cryptography in the book by Simson Garfinkel, reading *1.3.15*. Note that all of these books and papers focus on the application of cryptography, not on crypto-mathematics, which is a distinct area of specialization not covered in this reading list. An accessible crypto-mathematics reference is reading *1.3.14*.

11.5.1 R[onald] L. Rivest, A[di] Shamir, and L[en] Adleman. A method for obtaining digital signatures and public-key cryptosystems. *Communications of the ACM 21*, 2 (February 1978), pages 120–126.

This paper was the first to suggest a possibly workable public key system.

11.5.2 Whitfield Diffie and Martin E. Hellman. Exhaustive cryptanalysis of the NBS Data Encryption Standard. *Computer 10*, 6 (June 1977), pages 74-84.

This is the unofficial analysis of how to break the DES by brute force—by building special-purpose chips and arraying them in parallel. Twenty-five years later, brute force still seems to be the only promising attack on DES, but the intervening improvements in hardware technology make special chips unnecessary—an array of personal computers on the Internet can do the job. The Advanced Encryption Standard (AES) is DES's successor (see Section 11.9.3.1).

11.5.3 Ross J. Anderson. Why cryptosystems fail. *Communications of the ACM 37*, 11 (November 1994), pages 32–40.

Anderson presents a very nice analysis of what goes wrong in real-world cryptosystems—secure modules don't necessary lead to secure systems—and the applicability of systems thinking in their design. He points out that merely doing the best possible design isn't enough; a feedback loop that corrects errors in the design following experience in the field is an equally important component that is sometimes forgotten.

11.5.4 David Wagner and Bruce Schneier. Analysis of the SSL 3.0 protocol. *Proceedings of the Second USENIX Workshop on Electronic Commerce, Volume 2* (November 1996), pages 29–40.

This paper is useful not only because it provides a careful analysis of the security of the subject protocol, but it also explains how the protocol works in a form that is more accessible than the protocol specification documents. The originally published version was almost immediately revised with corrections. The revised version is available on the World Wide Web at `<http://www.counterpane.com/ssl.html>`.

11.5.5 M[ihir] Bellare, R[an] Canetti, and H[ugo] Krawczyk. Keying hash functions for message authentication. *Proceedings of the 16th International Cryptography Conference* (August 1996), pages 1–15. (Also see H. Krawczyk, M. Bellare, and R. Canetti, HMAC: Keyed-hashing for message authentication, *Request For Comments RFC 2104*, Internet Engineering Task Force (February 1997).

This paper and the RFC introduce and define HMAC, a hash function used in widely deployed protocols.

11.5.6 David Chaum. Untraceable electronic mail, return addresses, and digital pseudonyms. *Communications of the ACM 24*, 2 (February 1981), pages 84–88.

This paper introduces a system design, named mixnet, that allows a sender of a message to hide its true identity from a receiver but still allow the receiver to respond.

11.6 Adversaries (The Dark Side)

Section 11.11 on war stories gives a wide range of examples of how adversaries can break a system's security. This section lists a few papers that provide a longer and more detailed descriptions of attacks. This is a fast-moving area; as soon as designers fend off new attacks, adversaries try to find new attacks. This arms race is reflected in some of the following readings, and although some of the attacks described have become ineffective (or will over time), these papers provide valuable insights. The proceedings of *Usenix Security* and *Computer and Communication Security* often contain papers explaining current attacks, and conferences run by the so-called "black hat" community document the "progress" on the dark side.

11.6.1 Eugene Spafford, Crisis and aftermath. *Communications of the ACM 32*, 6 (June 1989), pages 678–687.

This paper documents how the Morris worm works. It was one of the first worms, as well as one of the most sophisticated.

11.6.2 Jonathan Pincus and Brandon Baker. Beyond stack smashing: Recent advances in exploiting buffer overruns. *IEEE Security and Privacy 2*, 4 (August 2004), pages 20–27.

This paper describes how buffer overrun attacks have evolved since the Morris worm.

11.6.3 Abhishek Kumar, Vern Paxson, and Nicholas Weaver. Exploiting underlying structure for detailed reconstruction of an Internet scale event. *Proceedings of the ACM Internet Measurement Conference* (October 2005), pages 351–364.

This paper describes the Witty worm and how the authors were able to track down its source. The work contains many interesting nuggets of information.

11.6.4 Vern Paxson. An analysis of using reflectors for distributed denial-of-service attacks. *Computer Communications Review 31*, 3 (July 2001), pages 38–47.

This paper describes how an adversary can trick a large set of Internet servers to send their combined replies to a victim and in that way launch a denial-of-service attack on the victim. It speculates on several possible directions for defending against such attacks.

11.6.5 Chris Kanich et al. Spamalytics: An empirical analysis of spam marketing conversion. *Proceedings of the ACM Conference on Computer and Communications Security (CCS)* (October 2008), pages 3–14.

This paper describes the infrastructure that spammers use to send unsolicited e-mail and tries to establish what the financial reward system is for spammers. This paper has its shortcomings, but it is one of the few papers that tries to understand the economics behind spam.

11.6.6 Tom Jagatic, Nathaniel Johnson, Markus Jakobsson, and Filippo Menczer. Social phishing. *Communications of the ACM 50*, 10 (October 2007), pages 94–100.

This study investigates the success rate of individual phishing attacks.

Problem Sets

TABLE OF CONTENTS

INTRODUCTION

These problem sets seek to make the student think carefully about how to apply the concepts of the text to new problems. These problems are derived from examinations given over the years while teaching the material in this textbook. Many of the problems are multiple choice with several right answers. The reader should try to identify *all* right options.

Some significant and interesting system concepts that are not mentioned in the main text, and therefore at first read seem to be missing from the book, are actually to be found within the exercises and problem sets. Definitions and discussion of these concepts can be found in the text of the exercise or problem set in which they appear. Here is a list of concepts that the exercises and problem sets introduce:

- *action graph* (Problem set *36*)
- *ad hoc wireless network* (Problem sets *19* and *21*)
- *bang-bang protocol* (Exercise *7.13*)
- *blast protocol* (Exercise *7.25*)
- *commutative cryptographic transformation* (Exercise *11.4*)
- *condition variable* (Problem set *13*)
- *consistent hashing* (Problem set *23*)
- *convergent encryption* (Problem set *48*)
- *cookie* (Problem set *45*)
- *delayed authentication* (Exercise *11.9*)
- *delegation forwarding* (Exercise *2.1*)
- *event variable* (Problem set *11*)

- *fast start* (Exercise *7.12*)
- *flooding* (Problem set *20*)
- *follow-me forwarding* (Exercise *2.1*)
- *Information Management System atomicity* (Exercise *9.5*)
- *mobile host* (Exercise *7.24*)
- *lightweight remote procedure call* (Problem set *7*)
- *multiple register set processor* (Problem set *9*)
- *object-oriented virtual memory* (Problem set *15*)
- *overlay network* (Problem set *20*)
- *pacing* (Exercise *7.16*)
- *peer-to-peer network* (Problem set *20*)
- *RAID 5,* with rotating parity (Exercise *8.8*)
- *restartable atomic region* (Problem set *9*)
- *self-describing storage* (Exercise *6.8*)
- *serializability* (Problem set *36*)
- *timed capability* (Exercise *11.7*)

Exercises for Chapter 7 and above are in on-line chapters, and problem sets numbered 17 and higher are in the on-line book of problem sets.

Some of these problem sets span the topics of several different chapters. A parenthetical note at the beginning of each set indicates the primary chapters that it involves. Following each exercise or problem set question is an identifier of the form "*1978-3-14*". This identifier reports the year, examination number, and problem number of the examination in which some version of that problem first appeared. For those problem sets not developed by one of the authors, a credit line appears in a footnote on the first page of the problem set.

1 Bigger Files*

(Chapter 2)

For his many past sins on previous exams, Ben Bitdiddle is assigned to spend eternity maintaining a PDP-11 running version 7 of the UNIX® operating system. Recently, one of his user's database applications failed after reaching the file size limit of 1,082,201,088 bytes (approximately 1 gigabyte). In an effort to solve the problem, he upgraded the computer with an old 4-gigabyte (2^{32} byte) drive; the disk controller hardware supports 32-bit sector addresses, and can address disks up to 2 terabytes in size. Unfortunately, Ben is disappointed to find the file size limit unchanged after installing the new disk.

In this question, the term *block number* refers to the block pointers stored in inodes. There are 512 bytes in a block. In addition, Ben's version 7 UNIX system has a file system that has been expanded from the one described in Section 2.5: its inodes

*Credit for developing this problem set goes to Lewis D. Girod.

are designed to support larger disks. Each inode contains 13 block numbers of 4 bytes each; the first 10 block numbers point to the first 10 blocks of the file, and the remaining 3 are used for the rest of the file. The 11th block number points to an indirect block, containing 128 block numbers, the 12th block number points to a double-indirect block, containing 128 indirect block numbers, and the 13th block number points to a triple-indirect block, containing 128 double-indirect block numbers. Finally, the inode contains a four-byte file size field.

Q 1.1 Which of the following adjustments will allow files larger than the current 1-gigabyte limit to be stored?

- **A.** Increase just the file size field in the inode from a 32-bit to a 64-bit value.
- **B.** Increase just the number of bytes per block from 512 to 2048 bytes.
- **C.** Reformat the disk to increase the number of inodes allocated in the inode table.
- **D.** Replace one of the direct block numbers in each inode with an additional triple-indirect block number.

2008-1-5

Ben observes that there are 52 bytes allocated to block numbers in each inode (13 block numbers at 4 bytes each), and 512 bytes allocated to block numbers in each indirect block (128 block numbers at 4 bytes each). He figures that he can keep the total space allocated to block numbers the same, but change the size of each block number, to increase the maximum supported file size. While the number of block numbers in inodes and indirect blocks will change, Ben keeps exactly one indirect, one double-indirect and one triple-indirect block number in each inode.

Q 1.2 Which of the following adjustments (without any of the modifications in the previous question), will allow files larger than the current approximately 1-gigabyte limit to be stored?

- **A.** Increasing the size of a block number from 4 bytes to 5 bytes.
- **B.** Decreasing the size of a block number from 4 bytes to 3 bytes.
- **C.** Decreasing the size of a block number from 4 bytes to 2 bytes.

2008-1-6

2 Ben's Stickr*

(Chapter 4)

Ben is in charge of system design for Stickr, a new Web site for posting pictures of bumper stickers and tagging them. Luckily for him, Alyssa had recently implemented

*Credit for developing this problem set goes to Samuel R. Madden.

a Triplet Storage System (TSS), which stores and retrieves arbitrary triples of the form {*subject, relationship, object*} according to the following specification:

procedure FIND (*subject, relationship, object, start, count*)
// returns OK + array of matching triples

procedure INSERT (*subject, relationship, object*)
// adds the triple to the TSS if it is not already there and returns OK

procedure DELETE (*subject, relationship, object*)
// removes the triple if it exists, returning TRUE, FALSE otherwise

Ben comes up with the following design:

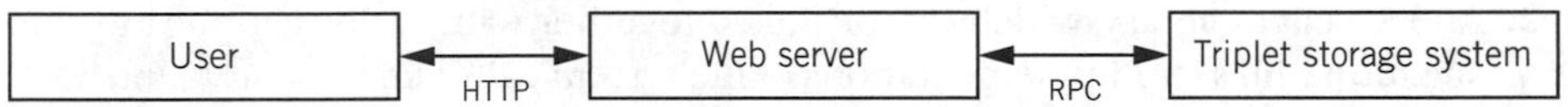

As shown in the figure, Ben uses an RPC interface to allow the Web server to interact with the triplet storage system. Ben chooses *at-least-once* RPC semantics. Assume that the triplet storage system never crashes, but the network between the Web server and triplet storage system is unreliable and may drop messages.

Q 2.1 Suppose that only a single thread on Ben's Web server is using the triplet storage system and that this thread issues just one RPC at a time. What types of incorrect behavior can the Web server observe?

A. The FIND RPC stub on the Web server sometimes returns no results, even though matching triples exist in the triplet storage system.
B. The INSERT RPC stub on the Web server sometimes returns OK without inserting the triple into the storage system.
C. The DELETE RPC stub on the Web server sometimes returns FALSE when it actually deleted a triple.
D. The FIND RPC stub on the Web server sometimes returns triples that have been deleted.

Q 2.2 Suppose Ben switches to *at-most-once* RPC; if no reply is received after some time, the RPC stub on the Web server gives up and returns a "timer expired" error code. Assume again that only a single thread on Ben's Web server is using the triple storage system and that this thread issues just one RPC at a time. What types of incorrect behavior can the Web server observe?

A. Assuming it does not time out, the FIND RPC stub on the Web server can sometimes return no results when matching triples exist in the storage system.
B. Assuming it does not time out, the INSERT RPC stub on the Web server can sometimes return OK without inserting the triple into the storage system.
C. Assuming it does not time out, the DELETE RPC stub on the Web server can sometimes return FALSE when it actually deleted a triple.
D. Assuming it does not time out, the FIND RPC stub on the Web server can sometimes return triples that have been deleted.

2007–1–5/6

3 Jill's File System for Dummies*

(Chapter 4)

Mystified by the complexity of NFS, Moon Microsystems guru Jill Boy decides to implement a simple alternative she calls File System for Dummies, or FSD. She implements FSD in two pieces:

1. An FSD server, implemented as a simple user application, which responds to FSD requests. Each request corresponds exactly to a UNIX file system call (e.g., READ, WRITE, OPEN, CLOSE, or CREATE) and returns just the information returned by that call (status, integer file descriptor, data, etc.).
2. An FSD client library, which can be linked together with various applications to substitute Jill's FSD implementations of file system calls like OPEN, READ, and WRITE for their UNIX counterparts. To avoid confusion, let's refer to Jill's FSD versions of these procedures as FSD_OPEN, and so on.

Jill's client library uses the standard UNIX calls to access local files but uses names of the form

```
/fsd/hostname/apath
```

to refer to the file whose absolute path name is /apath on the host named hostname. Her library procedures recognize operations involving remote files e.g.,

```
FSD_OPEN("/fsd/cse.pedantic.edu/foobar", READ_ONLY)
```

and translates them to RPC requests to the appropriate host, using the file name on that host e.g.,

```
RPC("/fsd/cse.pedantic.edu/foobar", "OPEN", "/foobar", READ_ONLY).
```

The RPC call causes the corresponding UNIX call e.g.,

```
OPEN("/foobar", READ_ONLY)
```

to be executed on the remote host and the results (e.g., a file descriptor) to be returned as the result of the RPC call. Jill's server code catches errors in the processing of each request and returns ERROR from the RPC call on remote errors.

Figure 1 describes pseudocode for Version 1 of Jill's FSD client library. The RPC calls in the code relay simple RPC commands to the server, using *exactly-once* semantics. Note that no data caching is done by either the server or the client library.

Q 3.1 What does the above code indicate via an empty string ("") in an entry of handle to host table?

A. An unused entry of the table.
B. An open file on the client host machine.
C. An end-of-file condition on an open file.
D. An error condition.

*Credit for developing this problem set goes to Stephen A. Ward.

```
// Map FSD handles to host names, remote handles:
string handle_to_host_table[1000]                // initialized to UNUSED
integer handle_to_rhandle_table[1000]            // handle translation table

procedure FSD_OPEN (string name, integer mode)
    integer handle ← FIND_UNUSED_HANDLE ()
    if name begins with "/fsd/" then
        host ← EXTRACT_HOST_NAME (name)
        filename ← EXTRACT_REMOTE_FILENAME (name)  // returns remote file handle or ERROR
        rhandle ← RPC (host, "OPEN", filename, mode)
    else
        host ← ""
        rhandle ← OPEN (name, mode)
    if rhandle ← ERROR then return ERROR
    handle_to_rhandle_table[handle] ← rhandle
    handle_to_host_table[handle] ← host
    return handle

procedure FSD_READ (integer handle, string buffer, integer nbytes)
    host ← handle_to_host_table[handle]
    rhandle ← handle_to_rhandle_table[handle]
    if host ← "" then return READ (rhandle, buffer, nbytes)
    // The following call sets "result" to the return value from
    // the read(...) on the remote host, and copies data read into buffer:
    result, buffer ← RPC (host, "READ", rhandle, nbytes)
    return result

procedure FSD_CLOSE (integer handle)
    host ← handle_to_host_table[handle]
    rhandle ← handle_to_rhandle_table[handle]
    handle_to_rhandle_table[handle] ← UNUSED
    if host ← "" then return CLOSE (rhandle)
    else return RPC (host, "CLOSE", rhandle)
```

FIGURE 1

Pseudocode for FSD client library, Version 1

Mini Malcode, an intern assigned to Jill, proposes that the above code be simplified by eliminating the *handle_to_rhandle_table* and simply returning the untranslated handles returned by OPEN on the remote or local machines. Mini implements her simplified client library, making appropriate changes to each FSD call, and tries it on several test programs.

Q 3.2 Which of the following test programs will continue to work after Mini's simplification?

A. A program that reads a single, local file.
B. A program that reads a single remote file.
C. A program that reads and writes many local files.
D. A program that reads and writes several files from a single remote FSD server.
E. A program that reads many files from different remote FSD servers.
F. A program that reads several local files as well as several files from a single remote FSD server.

Jill rejects Mini's suggestions, insisting on the Version 1 code shown above. Marketing asks her for a comparison between FSD and NFS (see Section 4.5).

Q 3.3 Complete the following table comparing NFS to FSD by circling yes or no under each of NFS and FSD for each statement:

Statement	NFS	FSD
Remote handles include inode numbers	Yes/No	Yes/No
Read and write calls are idempotent	Yes/No	Yes/No
Can continue reading an open file after deletion (e.g., by program on remote host)	Yes/No	Yes/No
Requires mounting remote file systems prior to use	Yes/No	Yes/No

Convinced by Moon's networking experts that a much simpler RPC package promising *at-least-once* rather than *exactly-once* semantics will save money, Jill substitutes the simpler RPC framework and tries it out. Although the new (Version 2) FSD works most of the time, Jill finds that an `FSD_READ` sometimes returns the wrong data; she asks you to help. You trace the problem to multiple executions of a single RPC request by the server and are considering

- A response cache on the client, sufficient to detect identical requests and returning a cached result for duplicates without resending the request to the server.
- A response cache on the server, sufficient to detect identical requests and returning a cached result for duplicates without reexecuting them.
- A monotonically increasing *sequence number* (nonce) added to each RPC request, making otherwise identical requests distinct.

Q 3.4 Which of the following changes would you suggest to address the problem introduced by the *at-least-once* RPC semantics?

A. Response cache on each client.
B. Response cache on server.
C. Sequence numbers in RPC requests.
D. Response cache on client AND sequence numbers.
E. Response cache on server AND sequence numbers.
F. Response caches on both client and server.

2007-2-7...10

4 EZ-Park*

(Chapter 5 in Chapter 4 setting)

Finding a parking spot at Pedantic University is as hard as it gets. Ben Bitdiddle, deciding that a little technology can help, sets about to design the EZ-Park client/server

*Credit for developing this problem set goes to Hari Balakrishnan.

system. He gets a machine to run an EZ-Park server in his dorm room. He manages to convince Pedantic University parking to equip each car with a tiny computer running EZ-Park client software. EZ-Park clients communicate with the server using remote procedure calls (RPCs). A client makes requests to Ben's server both to find an available spot (when the car's driver is looking for one) and to relinquish a spot (when the car's driver is leaving a spot). A car driver uses a parking spot if, and only if, EZ-Park allocates it to him or her.

In Ben's initial design, the server software runs in one address space and spawns a new thread for each client request. The server has two procedures: FIND_SPOT () and RELINQUISH_SPOT (). Each of these threads is spawned in response to the corresponding RPC request sent by a client. The server threads use a shared array, *available*[], of size NSPOTS (the total number of parking spots). *available*[*j*] is set to TRUE if spot *j* is free, and FALSE otherwise; it is initialized to TRUE, and there are no cars parked to begin with. The NSPOTS parking spots are numbered from 0 through NSPOTS - 1. *numcars* is a global variable that counts the total number of cars parked; it is initialized to 0.

Ben implements the following pseudocode to run on the server. Each FIND_SPOT () thread enters a **while** loop that terminates only when the car is allocated a spot:

```
procedure FIND_SPOT ()                  // Called when a client car arrives
    while TRUE do
        for i ← 0 to NSPOTS do
            if available[i] = TRUE then
                available[i] ← FALSE
                numcars ← numcars + 1
                return i     // Client gets spot i

procedure RELINQUISH_SPOT (spot)        // Called when a client car leaves
    available[spot] ← TRUE
    numcars ← numcars − 1
```

Ben's intended correct behavior for his server (the "correctness specification") is as follows:

A. FIND_SPOT () allocates any given spot in [0, . . . , NSPOTS − 1] to at most one car at a time, even when cars are concurrently sending requests to the server requesting spots.
B. *numcars* must correctly maintain the number of parked cars.
C. If at any time (1) spots are available and no parked car ever leaves in the future, (2) there are no outstanding FIND_SPOT () requests, and (3) exactly one client makes a FIND_SPOT request, then the client should get a spot.

Ben runs the server and finds that when there are no concurrent requests, EZ-Park works correctly. However, when he deploys the system, he finds that sometimes multiple cars are assigned the same spot, leading to collisions! His system does not meet the correctness specification when there are concurrent requests.

Make the following assumptions:

1. The statements to update *numcars* are *not* atomic; each involves multiple instructions.
2. The server runs on a single processor with a preemptive thread scheduler.
3. The network delivers RPC messages reliably, and there are no network, server, or client failures.
4. Cars arrive and leave at random.
5. ACQUIRE and RELEASE are as defined in chapter 5.

Q 4.1 Which of these statements is true about the problems with Ben's design?

A. There is a race condition in accesses to *available*[], which may violate one of the correctness specifications when two FIND_SPOT () threads run.

B. There is a race condition in accesses to *available*[], which may violate correctness specification A when one FIND_SPOT () thread and one RELINQUISH_SPOT () thread runs.

C. There is a race condition in accesses to *numcars*, which may violate one of the correctness specifications when more than one thread updates *numcars*.

D. There is no race condition as long as the average time between client requests to find a spot is larger than the average processing delay for a request.

Ben enlists Alyssa's help to fix the problem with his server, and she tells him that he needs to set some locks. She suggests adding calls to ACQUIRE and RELEASE as follows:

```
1    procedure FIND_SPOT ()              // Called when a client car wants a spot
2        while TRUE do
!→           ACQUIRE (avail_lock)
3                for i ← 0 to NSPOTS do
4                    if available[i] = TRUE then
5                        available[i] ← FALSE
6                        numcars ← numcars + 1
!→                       RELEASE (avail_lock)
7                        return i  // Allocate spot i to this client
!→                   RELEASE (avail_lock)

8    procedure RELINQUISH_SPOT (spot)        // Called when a client car is leaving spot
!→       ACQUIRE (avail_lock)
9        available[spot] ← TRUE
10       numcars ← numcars − 1
!→       RELEASE (avail_lock)
```

Q 4.2 Does Alyssa's code solve the problem? Why or why not?

Q 4.3 Ben can't see any good reason for the RELEASE (*avail_lock*) that Alyssa placed after line 7, so he removes it. Does the program still meet its specifications? Why or why not?

Hoping to reduce competition for *avail_lock*, Ben rewrites the program as follows:

```
    procedure FIND_SPOT ()                    // Called when a client car wants a spot
        while TRUE do
            for i ← 0 to NSPOTS do
!→              ACQUIRE (avail_lock)
                if available[i] = TRUE then
                    available[i] ← FALSE
                    numcars ← numcars + 1
!→                  RELEASE (avail_lock)
                    return i        // Allocate spot i to this client
!→              else RELEASE (avail_lock)

    procedure RELINQUISH_SPOT (spot)          // Called when a client car is leaving spot
!→      ACQUIRE (avail_lock)
        available[spot] ← TRUE
        numcars ← numcars − 1
!→      RELEASE (avail_lock)
```

Q 4.4 Does that program meet the specifications?

Now that Ben feels he understands locks better, he tries one more time, hoping that by shortening the code he can really speed things up:

```
    procedure FIND_SPOT ()                  // Called when a client car wants a spot
        while TRUE do
!→          ACQUIRE (avail_lock)
            for i ← 0 to NSPOTS do
                if available[i] = TRUE then
                    available[i] ← FALSE
                    numcars ← numcars + 1
                    return i // Allocate spot i to this client

    procedure RELINQUISH_SPOT (spot)        // Called when a client car is leaving spot
        available[spot] ← TRUE
        numcars ← numcars − 1
!→      RELEASE (avail_lock)
```

Q 4.5 Does Ben's slimmed-down program meet the specifications?

Ben now decides to combat parking at a truly crowded location: Pedantic's stadium, where there are always cars looking for spots! He updates NSPOTS and deploys the system during the first home game of the football season. Many clients complain that his server is slow or unresponsive.

Q 4.6 If a client invokes the FIND_SPOT () RPC when the parking lot is full, how quickly will it get a response, assuming that multiple cars may be making requests?

A. The client will not get a response until at least one car relinquishes a spot.
B. The client may never get a response even when other cars relinquish their spots.

Alyssa tells Ben to add a client-side timer to his RPC system that expires if the server does not respond within 4 seconds. Upon a timer expiration, the car's driver may retry the request, or instead choose to leave the stadium to watch the game on TV. Alyssa warns Ben that this change may cause the system to violate the correctness specification.

Q 4.7 When Ben adds the timer to his client, he finds some surprises. Which of the following statements is true of Ben's implementation?

A. The server may be running multiple active threads on behalf of the same client car at any given time.
B. The server may assign the same spot to two cars making requests.
C. *numcars* may be smaller than the actual number of cars parked in the parking lot.
D. *numcars* may be larger than the actual number of cars parked in the parking lot.

Q 4.8 Alyssa thinks that the operating system running Ben's server may be spending a fair amount of time switching between threads when many RPC requests are being processed concurrently. Which of these statements about the work required to perform the switch is correct? Notation: PC = program counter; SP = stack pointer; PMAR = page-map address register. Assume that the operating system behaves according to the description in Chapter 5.

A. On any thread switch, the operating system saves the values of the PMAR, PC, SP, and several registers.
B. On any thread switch, the operating system saves the values of the PC, SP, and several registers.
C. On any thread switch between two RELINQUISH_SPOT () threads, the operating system saves *only* the value of the PC, since RELINQUISH_SPOT () has no return value.
D. The number of instructions required to switch from one thread to another is proportional to the number of bytes currently on the thread's stack.

5 Goomble*

(Chapter 5)

Observing that U.S. legal restrictions have curtailed the booming on-line gambling industry, a group of laid-off programmers has launched a new venture called Goomble. Goomble's Web server allows customers to establish an account, deposit funds using a credit card, and then play the Goomble game by clicking a button labeled **I FEEL LUCKY**. Every such button click debits their account by $1, until it reaches zero.

Goomble lawyers have successfully defended their game against legal challenges by arguing that there's no gambling involved: the Goomble "service" is entirely deterministic.

The initial implementation of the Goomble server uses a single thread, which causes all customer requests to be executed in some serial order. Each click on the **I FEEL LUCKY** button results in a procedure call to LUCKY (*account*), where *account*

*Credit for developing this problem set goes to Stephen A. Ward.

refers to a data structure representing the user's Goomble account. Among other data, the account structure includes an unsigned 32-bit integer *balance*, representing the customer's current balance in dollars.
The LUCKY procedure is coded as follows:

```
1    procedure LUCKY (account)
2        if account.balance > 0 then
3            account.balance ← account.balance -1
```

The Goomble software quality control expert, Nellie Nervous, inspects the single-threaded Goomble server code to check for race conditions.

Q 5.1 Should Nellie find any potential race conditions? Why or why not?

2007-1-8

The success of the Goomble site quickly swamps their single-threaded server, limiting Goomble's profits. Goomble hires a server performance expert, Threads Galore, to improve server throughput.

Threads modifies the server as follows: Each **I FEEL LUCKY** click request spawns a new thread, which calls LUCKY (*account*) and then exits. All other requests (e.g., setting up an account, depositing, etc.) are served by a single thread. Threads argues that the bulk of the server traffic consists of player's clicking **I FEEL LUCKY**, so that his solution addresses the main performance problem.

Unfortunately, Nellie doesn't have time to inspect the multithreaded version of the server. She is busy with development of a follow-on product: the Goomba, which simultaneously cleans out your bank account and washes your kitchen floor.

Q 5.2 Suppose Nellie had inspected Goomble's multithreaded server. Should she have found any potential race conditions? Why or why not?

2007-1-9

Willie Windfall, a compulsive Goomble player, has two computers and plays Goomble simultaneously on both (using the same Goomble account). He has mortgaged his house, depleted his retirement fund and the money saved for his kid's education, and his Goomble account is nearly at zero. One morning, clicking furiously on **I FEEL LUCKY** buttons on both screens, he notices that his Goomble balance has jumped to something over four billion dollars.

Q 5.3. Explain a possible source of Willie's good fortune. Give a simple scenario involving two threads, T1 and T2, with interleaved execution of lines *2* and *3* in calls to LUCKY (*account*), detailing the timing that could result in a huge *account.balance*. The first step of the scenario is already filled in; fill as many subsequent steps as needed.

1. **T1 evaluates** "if *account.balance* > 0", **finds statement is true**
2.
3.
4.

2007-1-10

Word of Willie's big win spreads rapidly, and Goomble billionaires proliferate. In a state of panic, the Goomble board calls you in as a consultant to review three possible fixes to the server code to prevent further "gifts" to Goomble customers. Each of the following proposals involves adding a lock (either global or specific to an account) to rule out the unfortunate race:

Proposal 1

```
procedure LUCKY (account)
    ACQUIRE (global_lock);
    if account.balance > 0 then
        account.balance ← account.balance - 1;
    RELEASE (global_lock)
```

Proposal 2

```
procedure LUCKY (account)
    ACQUIRE (account.lock)
    temp ← account.balance
    RELEASE (account.lock)
    if temp > 0 then
        ACQUIRE (account.lock);
        account.balance ← account.balance - 1;
        RELEASE (account.lock);
```

Proposal 3

```
procedure LUCKY (account)
    ACQUIRE (account.lock);
    if account.balance > 0 then
        account.balance ← account.balance - 1
    RELEASE (account.lock);
```

Q 5.4 Which of the three proposals have race conditions?

2007-1-11

Q 5.5 Which proposal would you recommend deploying, considering both correctness and performance goals?

2007-1-12

6 Course Swap*

(Chapter 5 in Chapter 4 setting)

The Subliminal Sciences Department, in order to reduce the department head's workload, has installed a Web server to help assign lecturers to classes for the

*Credit for developing this problem set goes to Robert T. Morris.

Fall teaching term. There happen to be exactly as many courses as lecturers, and department policy is that every lecturer teach exactly one course and every course have exactly one lecturer. For each lecturer in the department, the server stores the name of the course currently assigned to that lecturer. The server's Web interface supports one request: to swap the courses assigned to a pair of lecturers.

Version One of the server's code looks like this:

```
// CODE VERSION ONE
    assignments[]        // an associative array of course names indexed by lecturer

    procedure SERVER ()
        do forever
            m ← wait for a request message
            value ← m.FUNCTION (m.arguments, ...) // execute function in request message
            send value to m.sender

    procedure EXCHANGE (lecturer1, lecturer2)
        temp ← assignments[lecturer1]
        assignments[lecturer1] ← assignments[lecturer2]
        assignments[lecturer2] ← temp
        return "OK"
```

Because there is only one application thread on the server, the server can handle only one request at a time. Requests comprise a function, and its arguments (in this case EXCHANGE (*lecturer1*, *lecturer2*)), which is executed by the *m*.FUNCTION (*m.arguments*, ...) call in the SERVER () procedure.

For all following questions, assume that there are no lost messages and no crashes. The operating system buffers incoming messages. When the server program asks for a message of a particular type (e.g., a request), the operating system gives it the oldest buffered message of that type.

Assume that network transmission times never exceed a fraction of a second and that computation also takes a fraction of a second. There are no concurrent operations other than those explicitly mentioned or implied by the pseudocode, and no other activity on the server computers.

Suppose the server starts out with the following assignments:

```
assignments["Herodotus"] = "Steganography"
assignments["Augustine"] = "Numerology"
```

Q 6.1 Lecturers Herodotus and Augustine decide they wish to swap lectures, so that Herodotus teaches Numerology and Augustine teaches Steganography. They each send an EXCHANGE ("Herodotus", "Augustine") request to the server at the same time.

If you look a moment later at the server, which, if any, of the following states are possible?

A.

```
assignments["Herodotus"] = "Numerology"
assignments["Augustine"] = "Steganography"
```

B.

```
assignments["Herodotus"] = "Steganography"
assignments["Augustine"] = "Numerology"
```

C.

```
assignments["Herodotus"] = "Steganography"
assignments["Augustine"] = "Steganography"
```

D.

```
assignments["Herodotus"] = "Numerology"
assignments["Augustine"] = "Numerology"
```

The Department of Dialectic decides it wants its own lecturer assignment server. Initially, it installs a completely independent server from that of the Subliminal Sciences Department, with the same rules (an equal number of lecturers and courses, with a one-to-one matching). Later, the two departments decide that they wish to allow their lecturers to teach courses in either department, so they extend the server software in the following way. Lecturers can send either server a CROSSEXCHANGE request, asking to swap courses between a lecturer in that server's department and a lecturer in the other server's department. In order to implement CROSSEXCHANGE, the servers can send each other SET-AND-GET requests, which set a lecturer's course and return the lecturer's previous course. Here's Version Two of the server code, for both departments:

```
// CODE VERSION TWO
procedure SERVER ()             // same as in Version One
procedure EXCHANGE ()           // same as in Version One

procedure CROSSEXCHANGE (local-lecturer, remote-lecturer)
    temp1 ← assignments[local-lecturer]
    send {SET-AND-GET, remote-lecturer, temp1} to the other server
    temp2 ← wait for response to SET-AND-GET
    assignments[local-lecturer] ← temp2
    return "OK"

procedure SET-AND-GET (lecturer, course) {
    old ← assignments[lecturer]
    assignments[lecturer] ← course
    return old
```

Suppose the starting state on the Subliminal Sciences server is:

```
assignments["Herodotus"] = "Steganography"
assignments["Augustine"] = "Numerology"
```

And on the Department of Dialectic server:

```
assignments["Socrates"] = "Epistemology"
assignments["Descartes"] = "Reductionism"
```

Q 6.2 At the same time, lecturer Herodotus sends a CROSSEXCHANGE ("Herodotus", "Socrates") request to the Subliminal Sciences server, and lecturer Descartes sends a CROSSEXCHANGE ("Descartes", "Augustine") request to the Department of Dialectic server. If you look a minute later at the Subliminal Sciences server, which, if any, of the following states are possible?

A.

```
assignments["Herodotus"] = "Steganography"
assignments["Augustine"] = "Numerology"
```

B.

```
assignments["Herodotus"] = "Epistemology"
assignments["Augustine"] = "Reductionism"
```

C.

```
assignments["Herodotus"] = "Epistemology"
assignments["Augustine"] = "Numerology"
```

In a quest to increase performance, the two departments make their servers multithreaded: each server serves each request in a separate thread. Thus, if multiple requests arrive at roughly the same time, the server may process them in parallel. Each server has multiple processors. Here's the threaded server code, Version Three:

```
// CODE VERSION THREE
procedure EXCHANGE ()                // same as in Version Two
procedure CROSSEXCHANGE ()           // same as in Version Two
procedure SET-AND-GET ()             // same as in Version Two

procedure SERVER ()
    do forever
        m ← wait for a request message
        ALLOCATE_THREAD (DOIT, m)    // create a new thread that runs DOIT (m)

procedure DOIT (m)
    value ← m.FUNCTION(m.arguments, ...)
    send value to m.sender
    EXIT ()                          // terminate this thread
```

Q 6.3 With the same starting state as the previous question, but with the new version of the code, lecturer Herodotus sends a CROSSEXCHANGE ("Herodotus", "Socrates") request to the Subliminal Sciences server, and lecturer Descartes sends a CROSSEXCHANGE ("Descartes","Augustine") request to the Department of Dialectic server, at the same time. If you look a minute later at the Subliminal Sciences server, which, if any, of the following states are possible?

A.

assignments["Herodotus"] = "Steganography"
assignments["Augustine"] = "Numerology"

B.

assignments["Herodotus"] = "Epistemology"
assignments["Augustine"] = "Reductionism"

C.

assignments["Herodotus"] = "Epistemology"
assignments["Augustine"] = "Numerology"

An alert student notes that Version Three may be subject to race conditions. He changes the code to have one lock per lecturer, stored in an array called *locks*[]. He changes EXCHANGE CROSSEXCHANGE, and SET-AND-GET to ACQUIRE locks on the lecturer(s) they affect. Here is the result, Version Four:

```
// CODE VERSION FOUR
procedure SERVER ()              // same as in Version Three
procedure DOIT ()                // same as in Version Three

procedure EXCHANGE (lecturer1, lecturer2)
    ACQUIRE (locks[lecturer1])
    ACQUIRE (locks[lecturer2])
    temp ← assignments[lecturer1]
    assignments[lecturer1] ← assignments[lecturer2]
    assignments[lecturer2] ← temp
    RELEASE (locks[lecturer1])
    RELEASE (locks[lecturer2])
    return "OK"

procedure CROSSEXCHANGE (local-lecturer, remote-lecturer)
    ACQUIRE (locks[local-lecturer])
    temp1 ← assignments[local-lecturer]
    send SET-AND-GET, remote-lecturer, temp1 to other server
    temp2 ← wait for response to SET-AND-GET
    assignments[local-lecturer] ← temp2
    RELEASE (locks[local-lecturer])
    return "OK"

procedure SET-AND-GET (lecturer, course)
    ACQUIRE (locks[lecturer])
    old ← assignments[lecturer]
    assignments[lecturer] ← course
    RELEASE (locks[lecturer])
    return old
```

Q 6.4 This code is subject to deadlock. Why?

Q 6.5 For each of the following situations, indicate whether deadlock can occur. In each situation, there is no activity other than that mentioned.

A. Client A sends EXCHANGE ("Herodotus", "Augustine") at the same time that client B sends EXCHANGE ("Herodotus", "Augustine"), both to the Subliminal Sciences server.

B. Client A sends EXCHANGE ("Herodotus", "Augustine") at the same time that client B sends EXCHANGE ("Augustine", "Herodotus"), both to the Subliminal Sciences server.

C. Client A sends CROSSEXCHANGE ("Augustine", "Socrates") to the Subliminal Sciences server at the same time that client B sends CROSSEXCHANGE ("Descartes", "Herodotus") to the Department of Dialectic server.

D. Client A sends CROSSEXCHANGE ("Augustine", "Socrates") to the Subliminal Sciences server at the same time that client B sends CROSSEXCHANGE ("Socrates", "Augustine") to the Department of Dialectic server.

E. Client A sends CROSSEXCHANGE ("Augustine", "Socrates") to the Subliminal Sciences server at the same time that client B sends CROSSEXCHANGE ("Descartes", "Augustine") to the Department of Dialectic server.

7 Banking on Local Remote Procedure Call

(Chapter 5)

The bank president has asked Ben Bitdiddle to add enforced modularity to a large banking application. Ben splits the program into two pieces: a client and a service. He wants to use remote procedure calls to communicate between the client and service, which both run on the same physical machine with one processor. Ben explores an implementation, which the literature calls *lightweight remote procedure call* (LRPC). Ben's version of LRPC uses user-level gates. User gates can be bootstrapped using two kernel gates—one gate that registers the name of a user gate and a second gate that performs the actual transfer:

- REGISTER_GATE (*stack*, *address*). It registers address *address* as an entry point, to be executed on the stack *stack*. The kernel stores these addresses in an internal table.
- TRANSFER_TO_GATE (*address*). It transfers control to address *address*. A client uses this call to transfer control to a service. The kernel must first check if *address* is an address that is registered as a gate. If so, the kernel transfers control; otherwise it returns an error to the caller.

We assume that a client and service each run in their own virtual address space. On initialization, the service registers an entry point with REGISTER_GATE and allocates a block, at address *transfer*. Both the client and service map the transfer block in each address space with READ and WRITE permissions. The client and service use this shared transfer page to communicate the arguments to and results of a remote procedure call. The client and service each start with one thread. There are no user programs other than the client and service running on the machine.

The following pseudocode summarizes the initialization:

Service

```
procedure INIT_SERVICE ()
    REGISTER_GATE (STACK, receive)
    ALLOCATE_BLOCK (transfer)
    MAP (my_id, transfer, shared_server)
    while TRUE do YIELD ()
```

Client

```
procedure INIT_CLIENT ()
    MAP (my_id, transfer, shared_client)
```

When a client performs an LRPC, the client copies the arguments of the LRPC into the transfer page. Then, it calls TRANSFER_TO_GATE to transfer control to the service address space at the registered address *receive*. The client thread, which is now in the service's address space, performs the requested operation (the code for the procedure at the address *receive* is not shown because it is not important for the questions). On returning from the requested operation, the procedure at the address *receive* writes the result parameters in the transfer block and transfers control back to the client's address space to the procedure RETURN_LRPC. Once back in the client address space in RETURN_LRPC, the client copies the results back to the caller. The following pseudocode summarizes the implementation of LRPC:

```
procedure LRPC (id, request)
    COPY (request, shared_client)
    TRANSFER_TO_GATE (receive)
    return

procedure RETURN_LRPC()
    COPY (shared_client, reply)
    return (reply)
```

Now that we know how to use the procedures REGISTER_GATE and TRANSFER_TO_GATE, let's turn our attention to the implementation of TRANSFER_TO_GATE (*entrypoint* is the internal kernel table recording gate information):

```
1    procedure TRANSFER_TO_GATE (address)
2        if id exists such that entrypoint[id].entry = address then
3            R1 ← USER_TO_KERNEL (entrypoint [id].stack)
4            R2 ← address
5            STORE R2, R1          // put address on service's stack
6            SP ← entrypoint[id].stack    // set SP to service stack
7            SUB 4, SP             // adjust stack
8            PMAR ← entrypoint[id].pmar // set page map address
9            USER ← ON             // switch to user mode
10           return                // returns to address
11       else
12           return (ERROR)
```

The procedure checks whether or not the service has registered *address* as an entry point (line *2*). Lines *4*–*7* push the entry address on the service's stack and set the register SP to point to the service's stack. To be able to do so, the kernel must translate the address for the stack in the service address space into an address in the kernel address space so that the kernel can write the stack (line *3*). Finally, the procedure stores the page-map address register for the service into PMAR (line *8*), sets the user-mode bit to ON (line *9*), and invokes the gate's procedure by returning from TRANSFER_TO_GATE (line *10*), which loads *address* from the service's stack into PC.

The implementation of this procedure is tricky because its switches address spaces, and thus the implementation must be careful to ensure that it is referring to the appropriate variable in the appropriate address space. For example, after line *8* TRANSFER_TO_GATE runs the next instruction (line *9*) in the service's address space. This works only if the kernel is mapped in both the client and service's address space at the same address.

Q 7.1 The procedure INIT_SERVICE calls YIELD. In which address space or address spaces is the code that implements the supervisor call YIELD located?

Q 7.2 For LRPC to work correctly, must the two virtual addresses *transfer* have the same value in the client and service address space?

Q 7.3 During the execution of the procedure located at address *receive* how many threads are running or are in a call to YIELD in the service address space?

Q 7.4 How many supervisor calls could the client perform in the procedure LRPC?

Q 7.5 Ben's goal is to enforce modularity. Which of the following statements are true statements about Ben's LRPC implementation?

- **A.** The client thread cannot transfer control to any address in the server address space.
- **B.** The client thread cannot overwrite any physical memory that is mapped in the server's address space.
- **C.** After the client has invoked TRANSFER_TO_GATE in LRPC, the server is guaranteed to invoke RETURN_LRPC.
- **D.** The procedure LRPC ought to be modified to check the response message and process only valid responses.

Q 7.6 Assume that REGISTER_GATE and TRANSFER_TO_GATE are also used by other programs. Which of the following statements is true about the implementations of REGISTER_GATE and TRANSFER_TO_GATE?

- **A.** The kernel might use an invalid address when writing the value *address* on the stack passed in by a user program.
- **B.** A user program might use an invalid address when entering the service address space.
- **C.** The kernel transfers control to the server address space with the user-mode bit switched OFF.
- **D.** The kernel enters the server address space only at the registered address entry *address*.

Ben modifies the client to have multiple threads of execution. If one client thread calls the server and the procedure at address *receive* calls YIELD, another client thread can run on the processor.

Q 7.7 Which of the following statements is true about the implementation of LRPC with multiple threads?

- **A.** On a single-processor machine, there can be race conditions when multiple client threads call LRPC, even if the kernel schedules the threads non-preemptively.
- **B.** On a single-processor machine, there can be race conditions when multiple clients threads call LRPC and the kernel schedules the threads preemptively.
- **C.** On multiprocessor computer, there can be race conditions when multiple client threads call LRPC.
- **D.** It is impossible to have multiple threads if the computer doesn't have multiple physical processors.

2004-1-4…10

8 The Bitdiddler*

(Chapter 5)

Ben Bitdiddle is designing a file system for a new handheld computer, the Bitdiddler, which is designed to be especially simple for, as he likes to say, "people who are just average, like me."

In keeping with his theme of simplicity and ease of use for average people, Ben decides to design a file system without directories. The disk is physically partitioned into three regions: an inode list, a free list, and a collection of 4K data blocks, much like the UNIX file system. Unlike in the UNIX file system, each inode contains the name of the file it corresponds to, as well as a bit indicating whether or not the inode is in use. Like the UNIX file system, the inode also contains a list of blocks that compose the file, as well as metadata about the file, including permission bits, its length in bytes, and modification and creation timestamps. The free list is a bitmap, with one bit per data block indicating whether that block is free or in use. There are no indirect blocks in Ben's file system. The following figure illustrates the basic layout of the Bitdiddler file system:

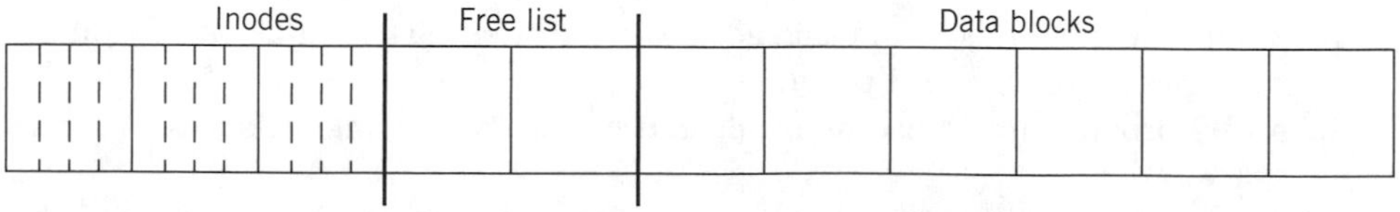

*Credit for developing this problem set goes to Samuel R. Madden.

The file system provides six primary calls: CREATE, OPEN, READ, WRITE, CLOSE, and UNLINK. Ben implements all six correctly and in a straightforward way, as shown below. All updates to the disk are synchronous; that is, when a call to write a block of data to the disk returns, that block is definitely installed on the disk. Individual block writes are atomic.

```
procedure CREATE (filename)
    scan all non-free inodes to ensure filename is not a duplicate (return ERROR if
    duplicate)
    find a free inode in the inode list
    update the inode with 0 data blocks, mark it as in use, write it to disk
    update the free list to indicate the inode is in use, write free list to disk

procedure OPEN (filename)            // returns a file handle
    scan non-free inodes looking for filename
    if found, allocate and return a file handle fh that refers to that inode

procedure WRITE (fh, buf, len)
    look in file handle fh to determine inode of the file, read inode from disk
    if there is free space in last block of file, write to it
    determine number of new blocks needed, n
    for i ← 1 to n
        use free list to find a free block b
        update free list to show b is in use, write free list to disk
        add b to inode, write inode to disk
        write appropriate data for block b to disk

procedure READ (fh, buf, len)
    look in file handle fh to determine inode of the file, read inode from disk
    read len bytes of data from the current location in file into buf

procedure CLOSE (fh)
    remove fh from the file handle table

procedure UNLINK (filename)
    scan non-free inodes looking for filename, mark that inode as free
    write inode to disk
    mark data blocks used by file as free in free list
    write modified free list blocks to disk
```

Ben writes the following simple application for the Bitdiddler:

```
CREATE (filename)
fh ← OPEN (filename)
WRITE (fh, app_data, LENGTH (app_data))        // app_data is some data to be written
CLOSE (fh)
```

Q 8.1 Ben notices that if he pulls the batteries out of the Bitdiddler while running his application and then replaces the batteries and reboots the machine, the file his application created exists but contains unexpected data that he didn't write into the file. Which of the following are possible explanations for this behavior? (Assume that the disk controller never writes partial blocks.)

A. The free list entry for a data page allocated by the call to WRITE was written to disk, but neither the inode nor the data page itself was written.

B. The inode allocated to Ben's application previously contained a (since deleted) file with the same name. If the system crashed during the call to CREATE, it may cause the old file to reappear with its previous contents.

C. The free list entry for a data page allocated by the call to WRITE as well as a new copy of the inode were written to disk, but the data page itself was not.

D. The free list entry for a data page allocated by the call to WRITE as well as the data page itself were written to disk, but the new inode was not.

Q 8.2 Ben decides to fix inconsistencies in the Bitdiddler's file system by scanning its data structures on disk every time the Bitdiddler starts up. Which of the following inconsistencies can be identified using this approach (without modifying the Bitdiddler implementation)?

A. In-use blocks that are also on the free list.

B. Unused blocks that are not on the free list.

C. In-use blocks that contain data from previously unlinked files.

D. Blocks used in multiple files.

2007-3-6 & 7

9 Ben's Kernel

(Chapter 5)

Ben develops an operating system for a simple computer. The operating system has a kernel that provides virtual address spaces, threads, and output to a console.

Each application has its own user-level address space and uses one thread. The kernel program runs in the kernel address space but doesn't have its own thread. (The kernel program is described in more detail below.)

The computer has one processor, a memory, a timer chip (which will be introduced later), a console device, and a bus connecting the devices. The processor has a user-mode bit and is a ***multiple register set*** design, which means that it has two sets of program counter (PC), stack pointer (SP), and page-map address registers (PMAR). One set is for user space (the user-mode bit is set to ON): *upc*, *usp*, and *upmar*. The other set is for kernel space (the user-mode bit is set to OFF): *kpc*, *ksp*, and *kpmar*. Only programs in kernel mode are allowed to store to *upmar*, *kpc*, *ksp*, and *kpmar*—storing a value in these registers is an illegal instruction in user mode.

The processor switches from user to kernel mode when one of three events occurs: an application issues an illegal instruction, an application issues a supervisor call instruction (with the SVC instruction), or the processor receives an interrupt in user mode. The processor switches from user to kernel mode by setting the user-mode bit OFF. When that happens, the processor continues operation but using the current values in the *kpc*, *ksp*, and *kpmar*. The user program counter, stack pointer, and page-map address values remain in *upc*, *usp*, and *upmar*, respectively.

To return from kernel to user space, a kernel program executes the RTI instruction, which sets the user-mode bit to ON, causing the processor to use *upc*, *usp*, and *upmar*. The *kpc*, *ksp*, and *kpmar* values remain unchanged, awaiting the next SVC. In addition to these registers, the processor has four general-purpose registers: *ur0*, *ur1*, *kr0*, and *kr1*. The *ur0* and *ur1* pair are active in user mode. The *kr0* and *kr1* pair are active in kernel mode.

Ben runs two user applications. Each executes the following set of programs:

```
integer t initially 1                  // initial value for shared variable t
procedure MAIN ()
   do forever
      t ← t + t
         PRINT (t)
         YIELD ()
procedure YIELD
      SVC 0
```

PRINT prints the value of *t* on the output console. The output console is an output-only device and generates no interrupts.

The kernel runs each program in its own user-level address space. Each user address space has one thread (with its own stack), which is managed by the kernel:

```
integer currentthread          // index for the current user thread

structure thread[2]            // Storage place for thread state when not running
   integer sp                  // user stack pointer
   integer pc                  // user program counter
   integer pmar                // user page-map address register
   integer r0                  // user register 0
   integer r1                  // user register 1

procedure DOYIELD ()
   thread[currentthread].sp ← usp                          // save registers
   thread[currentthread].pc ← upc
   thread[currentthread].pmar ← upmar
   thread[currentthread].r0 ← ur0
   thread[currentthread].r1 ← ur1
   currentthread ← (currentthread + 1) modulo 2            // select new thread
   usp ← thread[currentthread].sp                          // restore registers
   upc ← thread[currentthread].pc
   upmar ← thread[currentthread].pmar
   ur0 ← thread[currentthread].r0
   ur1 ← thread[currentthread].r1
```

For simplicity, this non-preemptive thread manager is tailored for just the two user threads that are running on Ben's kernel. The system starts by executing the procedure KERNEL. Here is its code:

```
procedure KERNEL ()
    CREATE_THREAD (MAIN)                // Set up Ben's two threads
    CREATE_THREAD (MAIN)                //
    usp ← thread[1].sp                  // initialize user registers for thread 1
    upc ← thread[1].pc
    upmar ← thread[1].pmar
    ur0 ← thread[1].r0
    ur1 ← thread[1].r1
    do forever
        RTI                             // Run a user thread until it issues an SVC
        n ← ???                         // See question Q 9.1
        if n = 0 then DOYIELD()
```

Since the kernel passes control to the user with the RTI instruction, when the user executes an SVC, the processor continues execution in the kernel at the instruction following the RTI.

Ben's operating system sets up three page maps, one for each user program, and one for the kernel program. Ben has carefully set up the page maps so that the three address spaces don't share any physical memory.

Q 9.1 Describe how the supervisor obtains the value of *n*, which is the identifier for the SVC that the calling program has invoked.

Q 9.2 How can the current address space be switched?

A. By the kernel writing the *kpmar* register.
B. By the kernel writing the *upmar* register.
C. By the processor changing the user-mode bit.
D. By the application writing the *kpmar* or *upmar* registers.
E. By DOYIELD saving and restoring *upmar*.

Q 9.3 Ben runs the system for a while, watching it print several results, and then halts the processor to examine its state. He finds that it is in the kernel, where it is just about to execute the RTI instruction. In which procedure(s) could the user-level thread resume when the kernel executes that RTI instruction?

A. In the procedure KERNEL.
B. In the procedure MAIN.
C. In the procedure YIELD.
D. In the procedure DOYIELD.

Q 9.4 In Ben's design, what mechanisms play a role in enforcing modularity?

A. Separate address spaces because wild writes from one application cannot modify the data of the other application.
B. User-mode bit because it disallows user programs to write to upmar and kpmar.
C. The kernel because it forces threads to give up the processor.
D. The application because it has few lines of code.

Ben reads about the timer chip in his hardware manual and decides to modify the kernel to take advantage of it. At initialization time, the kernel starts the timer chip, which will generate an interrupt every 100 milliseconds. (Ben's computer has no other sources of interrupts.) Note that the interrupt-enable bit is OFF when executing in the kernel address space; the processor checks for interrupts only before executing a user-mode instruction. Thus, whenever the timer chip generates an interrupt while the processor is in kernel mode, the interrupt will be delayed until the processor returns to user mode. An interrupt in user mode causes an SVC -1 instruction to be inserted in the instruction stream. Finally, Ben modifies the kernel by replacing the **do forever** loop and adding an interrupt handler, as follows:

```
do forever
    RTI                          // Run a user thread until it issues an SVC
    n ← ???                      // Assume answer to question Q 9.1
    if n = 1 then DOINTERRUPT ()
    if n = 0 then DOYIELD ()

procedure DOINTERRUPT ()
    DOYIELD ()
```

Do not make any assumption about the speed of the processor.

Q 9.5 Ben again runs the system for a while, watching it print several results, and then he halts the processor to examine its state. Once again, he finds that it is in the kernel, where it is just about to execute the RTI instruction. In which procedure(s) could the user-level thread resume after the kernel executes the RTI instruction?

A. In the procedure DOINTERRUPT.
B. In the procedure KERNEL.
C. In the procedure MAIN.
D. In the procedure YIELD.
E. In the procedure DOYIELD.

Q 9.6 In Ben's second design, what mechanisms play a role in enforcing modularity?

A. Separate address spaces because wild writes from one application cannot modify the data of the other application.
B. User-mode bit because it disallows user programs to write to *upmar* and *kpmar*.
C. The timer chip because it, in conjunction with the kernel, forces threads to give up the processor.
D. The application because it has few lines of code.

Ben modifies the two user programs to share the variable *t*, by mapping *t* in the virtual address space of both user programs at the same place in physical memory. Now both threads read and write the same *t*.

Note that registers are not shared between threads: the scheduler saves and restores the registers on a thread switch. Ben's simple compiler translates the critical region of code:

$$t \leftarrow t + t$$

into the processor instructions:

```
100   LOAD t, r0        // read t into register 0
104   LOAD t, r1        // read t into register 1
108   ADD r1, r0        // add registers 0 and 1, leave result in register 0
112   STORE r0, t       // store register 0 into t
```

The numbers in the leftmost column in this code are the virtual addresses where the instructions are stored in both virtual address spaces. Ben's processor executes the individual instructions atomically.

Q 9.7 What values can the applications print (don't worry about overflows)?

A. Some odd number.
B. Some even number other than a power of two.
C. Some power of two.
D. 1

In a conference proceedings, Ben reads about an idea called *restartable atomic regions** and implements them. If a thread is interrupted in a critical region, the thread manager restarts the thread at the beginning of the critical region when it resumes the thread. Ben recodes the interrupt handler as follows:

```
procedure DOINTERRUPT ()
    if upc ≥ 100 and upc ≤ 112 then  // Were we in the critical region?
        upc ← 100                    // yes, restart critical region when resumed!
    DOYIELD ()
```

The processor increments the program counter after interpreting an instruction and before processing interrupts.

Q 9.8 Now, what values can the applications print (don't worry about overflows)?

A. Some odd number.
B. Some even number other than a power of two.
C. Some power of two.
D. 1

---

*Brian N. Bershad, David D. Redell, and John R. Ellis. Fast mutual exclusion for uniprocessors. *Proceedings of the Fifth International Conference on Architectural Support for Programming Languages and Operating Systems* (October 1992), pages 223–233.

Q 9.9 Can a second thread enter the region from virtual addresses 100 through 112 while the first thread is in it (i.e., the first thread's *upc* contains a value in the range 100 through 112)?

A. Yes, because while the first thread is in the region, an interrupt may cause the processor to switch to the second thread and the second thread might enter the region.

B. Yes, because the processor doesn't execute the first three lines of code in DOINTERRUPT atomically.

C. Yes, because the processor doesn't execute DOYIELD atomically.

D. Yes, because MAIN calls YIELD.

Ben is exploring if he can put just any code in a restartable atomic region. He creates a restartable atomic region that contains three instructions, which swap the content of two variables *a* and *b* using a temporary *x*:

```
100   x ← a
104   a ← b
108   b ← x
```

Ben also modifies DOINTERRUPT, replacing 112 with 108:

```
procedure DOINTERRUPT ()
    if upc ≥ 100 and upc ≤ 108 then        // Were we in the critical region?
        upc ← 100;                         // yes, restart critical region when resumed!
    DOYIELD ()
```

Variables *a* and *b* start out with the values $a = 1$ and $b = 2$, and the timer chip is running.

Q 9.10 What are some possible outcomes if a thread executes this restartable atomic region and variables *a*, *b*, and *x* are not shared?

A. $a = 2$ and $b = 1$

B. $a = 1$ and $b = 2$

C. $a = 2$ and $b = 2$

D. $a = 1$ and $b = 1$

2003–1–5...13

10 A Picokernel-Based Stock-Ticker System

(Chapter 5)

Ben Bitdiddle decides to design a computer system based on a new kernel architecture he calls *picokernels* and on a new hardware platform called *simplePC*. Ben has paid attention to Section 1.1 and is going for extreme simplicity. The simplePC platform contains one simple processor, a page-based virtual memory manager (which translates the virtual addresses issued by the processor), a memory module, and an input and output device. The processor has two special registers, a program counter (PC) and a stack pointer (SP). The SP points to the value on the top of the stack.

The calling convention for the simplePC processor uses a simple stack model:

- A call to a procedure pushes the address of the instruction after the call onto the stack and then jumps to the procedure.
- Return from a procedure pops the address from the top of the stack and jumps.

Programs on the simplePC don't use local variables. Arguments to procedures are passed in registers, which are *not* saved and restored automatically. Therefore, the only values on the stack are return addresses.

Ben develops a simple stock-ticker system to track the stocks of the start-up he joined. The program reads a message containing a single integer from the input device and prints it on the output device:

```
101. boolean input_available

1.   procedure READ_INPUT ()
2.       do forever
3.           while input_available = FALSE do nothing // idle loop
4.           PRINT_MSG(quote)
5.           input_available ← FALSE

200. boolean output_done
201. structure output_buffer at 71FFF2hex        // hardware address of output buffer
202.     integer quote

12.  procedure PRINT_MSG (m)
13.      output_buffer.quote ← m
14.      while output_done = FALSE do nothing  // idle loop
15.      output_done ← FALSE

17.  procedure MAIN ()
18.      READ_INPUT ()
19.      halt                                     // shutdown computer
```

In addition to the MAIN program, the program contains two procedures: READ_INPUT and PRINT_MSG. The procedure READ_INPUT spin-waits until *input_available* is set to TRUE by the input device (the stock reader). When the input device receives a stock quote, it places the quote value into *msg* and sets *input_available* to TRUE.

The procedure PRINT_MSG prints the message on an output device (a terminal in this case); it writes the value stored in the message to the device and waits until it is printed; the output device sets *output_done* to TRUE when it finishes printing.

The numbers on each line correspond to addresses as issued by the processor to read and write instructions and data. Assume that each line of pseudocode compiles into one machine instruction and that there is an implicit **return** at the end of each procedure.

Q 10.1 What do these numbers mentioned on each line of the program represent?

A. Virtual addresses.
B. Physical addresses.
C. Page numbers.
D. Offsets in a virtual page.

Ben runs the program directly on simplePC, starting in MAIN, and at some point he observes the following values on the stack (remember, only the stock-ticker program is running):

```
stack
19
5     ← stack pointer
```

Q 10.2 What is the meaning of the value 5 on the stack?

A. The return address for the next return instruction.
B. The return address for the previous return instruction.
C. The current value of PC.
D. The current value of SP.

Q 10.3 Which procedure is being executed by the processor?

A. READ_INPUT
B. PRINT_MSG
C. MAIN

Q 10.4 PRINT_MSG writes a value to *quote*, which is stored at the address $71FFF2_{hex}$, with the expectation that the value will end up on the terminal. What technique is used to make this work?

A. Memory-mapped I/O.
B. Sequential I/O.
C. Streams.
D. Remote procedure call.

Ben wants to run multiple instances of his stock-ticker program on the simplePC platform so that he can obtain more frequent updates to track more accurately his current net worth. Ben buys another input and output device for the system, hooks them up, and he implements a trivial thread manager:

```
300. integer threadtable[2];          // stores stack pointers of threads.
                                      // first slot is threadtable[0]
302. integer current_thread initially 0;

21.   procedure YIELD ()
22.       threadtable[current_thread] ← SP  // move value of SP into table
23.       current_thread ← (current_thread + 1) modulo 2
24.       SP ← threadtable[current_thread]  // load value from table into SP
25.       return
```

Each thread reads from and writes to its own device and has its own stack. Ben also modifies READ_INPUT:

```
100. integer msg[2]                                       // CHANGED to use array
102. boolean input_available[2]                           // CHANGED to use array
30.   procedure READ_INPUT ()
31.       do forever
32.           while input_available[current_thread] = FALSE do        // CHANGED
33.           YIELD ()                                    // CHANGED
34.           continue                                    // CHANGED
35.       PRINT_MSG (msg[current_thread])                 // CHANGED to use array
36.       input_available[current_thread] ← FALSE         // CHANGED to use array
```

Ben powers up the simplePC platform and starts each thread running in MAIN. The two threads switch back and forth correctly. Ben stops the program temporarily and observes the following stacks:

```
stack of thread 0                        stack of thread 1
        19                                       19
        36 ← stack pointer                       34 ← stack pointer
```

Q 10.5 Thread 0 was running (i.e., *current_thread* = 0). Which instruction will the processor be running after thread 0 executes the **return** instruction in YIELD the next time?

A. 34. **continue**
B. 19. **halt**
C. 35. PRINT_MSG (*msg*[*current_thread*]);
D. 36. *input_available*[*current_thread*] ← FALSE;

and which thread will be running?

Q 10.6 What address values can be on the stack of each thread?

A. Addresses of any instruction.
B. Addresses to which called procedures return.
C. Addresses of any data location.
D. Addresses of instructions and data locations.

Ben observes that each thread in the stock-ticker program spends most of its time polling its input variable. He introduces an explicit procedure that the devices can use to notify the threads. He also rearranges the code for modularity:

```
400. integer state[2];

40.  procedure SCHEDULE_AND_DISPATCH ()
41.      threadtable[current_thread] ← SP
42.      while (what should go here?) do        // See question Q 10.7.
43.          current_thread ← (current_thread + 1) modulo 2
45.      SP ← threadtable[current_thread];
46.      return

50.  procedure YIELD()
51.      state[current_thread] ← WAITING
52.      SCHEDULE_AND_DISPATCH ()
53.      return

60.  procedure NOTIFY (n)
61.      state[n] ← RUNNABLE
62.      return
```

When the input device receives a new stock quote, the device interrupts the processor and saves the PC of the currently running thread on the currently running thread's stack. Then the processor runs the interrupt procedure. When the interrupt handler returns, it pops the return address from the current stack, returning control to a thread. The pseudocode for the interrupt handler is:

```
procedure DEVICE (n)                                   // interrupt for input device n
    push current thread's PC on stack pointed to by SP;
    while input_available[n] = TRUE do nothing;        // wait until read_input is done
                                                       // with the last input
    msg[n] ← stock quote
    input_available[n] ← TRUE
    NOTIFY (n)                                         // notify thread n
    return                                             // i.e., pop PC
```

During the execution of the interrupt handler, interrupts are disabled. Thus, an interrupt handler and the procedures that it calls (e.g., NOTIFY) cannot be interrupted. Interrupts are reenabled when DEVICE returns.

Using the new thread manager, answer the following questions:

Q 10.7 What expression should be evaluated in the **while** at address 42 to ensure correct operation of the thread package?

A. *state*[*current_thread*] = WAITING
B. *state*[*current_thread*] = RUNNABLE
C. *threadtable*[*current_thread*] = SP
D. FALSE

Q 10.8 Assume thread 0 is running and thread 1 is not running (i.e., it has called YIELD). What event or events need to happen before thread 1 will run?

A. Thread 0 calls YIELD.
B. The interrupt procedure for input device 1 calls NOTIFY.
C. The interrupt procedure for input device 0 calls NOTIFY.
D. No events are necessary.

Q 10.9 What values can be on the stack of each thread?

A. Addresses of any instruction except those in the device driver interrupt procedure.
B. Addresses of all instructions, including those in the device driver interrupt procedure.
C. Addresses to which procedures return.
D. Addresses of instructions and data locations.

Q 10.10 Under which scenario can thread 0 deadlock?

A. When device 0 interrupts thread 0 just before the first instruction of YIELD.
B. When device 0 interrupts just after thread 0 completed the first instruction of YIELD.
C. When device 0 interrupts thread 0 between instructions 35 and 36 in the READ_INPUT procedure on page 454.
D. When device 0 interrupts when the processor is executing SCHEDULE_AND_DISPATCH and thread 0 is in the WAITING state.

2000–1–7...16

11 Ben's Web Service

(Chapter 5)

Ben Bitdiddle is so excited about Amazing Computer Company's plans for a new segment-based computer architecture that he takes the job the company offered him.

Amazing Computer Company has observed that using one address space per program puts the text, data, stack, and system libraries in the same address space. For example, a Web server has the program text (i.e., the binary instructions) for the Web server, its internal data structures such as its cache of recently-accessed Web pages, the stack, and a system library for sending and receiving messages all in a single address space. Amazing Computer Company wants to explore how to enforce modularity even further by separating the text, data, stack, and system library using a new memory system.

The Amazing Computer Company has asked every designer in the company to come up with a design to enforce modularity further. In a dusty book about the PDP-11/70, Ben finds a description of a hardware gadget that sits between the processor and the physical memory, translating virtual addresses to physical addresses. The PDP-11/70 used that gadget to allow each program to have its own address space, starting at address 0.

The PDP-11/70 did this through having one segment per program. Conceptually, each segment is a variable-sized, linear array of bytes starting at virtual address 0. Ben bases his memory system on the PDP-11/70's scheme with the intention of implementing hard modularity. Ben defines a segment through a segment descriptor:

```
structure segmentDescriptor
    physicalAddress physAddr
    integer length
```

The *physAddr* field records the address in physical memory where the segment is located. The *length* field records the length of the segment in bytes.

Ben's processor has addresses consisting of 34 bits: 18 bits to identify a segment and 16 bits to identify the byte within the segment:

segment_id	*index*
18 bits	16 bits

A virtual address that addresses a byte outside a segment (i.e., an *index* greater than the *length* of the segment) is illegal.

Ben's memory system stores the segment descriptors in a table, *segmentTable*, which has one entry for each segment:

```
structure segmentDescriptor
        segmentTable[NSEGMENT]
```

The segment table is indexed by *segment_id*. It is shared among all programs and stored at physical address 0.

The processor used by Ben's computer is a simple RISC processor, which reads and writes memory using LOAD and STORE instructions. The LOAD and STORE instructions take a virtual address as their argument. Ben's computer has enough memory that all programs fit in physical memory.

Ben ports a compiler that translates a source program to generate machine instructions for his processor. The compiler translates into a position-independent machine code: JUMP instructions specify an offset relative to the current value of the program counter. To make a call into another segment, it supports the LONGJUMP instruction, which takes a virtual address and jumps to it.

Ben's memory system translates a virtual address to a physical address with TRANSLATE:

```
procedure TRANSLATE (addr)
    segment_id ← addr[0:17]
    segment ← segmentTable[segment_id]
    index ← addr[18:33]
    if index < segment.length then return segment.physAddr + index
    ...                  // What should the program do here? (see Q 11.4, below)
```

After successfully computing the physical address, Ben's memory management unit retrieves the addressed data from physical memory and delivers it to the processor (on a LOAD instruction) or stores the data in physical memory (on a STORE instruction).

Q 11.1 What is the maximum sensible value of NSEGMENT?

Q 11.2 Given the structure of a virtual address, what is the maximum size of a segment in bytes?

Q 11.3 How many bits wide must a physical address be?

Q 11.4 The missing code on line *6* should

A. signal the processor that the instruction that issued the memory reference has caused an illegal address fault
B. signal the processor that it should change to user mode
C. **return** *index*
D. signal the processor that the instruction that issues the memory reference is an interrupt handler

Ben modifies his Web server to enforce modularity between the different parts of the server. He allocates the text of the program in segment 1, a cache for recently used Web pages in segment 2, the stack in segment 3, and the system library in segment 4. Segment 4 contains the text of the library program but no variables (i.e., the library program doesn't store variables in its own segment).

Q 11.5 To translate the Web server the compiler has to do which of the following?

A. Compute the physical address for each virtual address.
B. Include the appropriate segment ID in the virtual address used by a LOAD instruction.
C. Generate LONGJUMP instructions for calls to procedures located in different segments.
D. Include the appropriate segment ID in the virtual address used by a STORE instruction.

Ben runs the segment-based implementation of his Web server and to his surprise observes that errors in the Web server program can cause the text of the system library to be overwritten. He studies his design and realizes that the design is bad.

Q 11.6 What aspect of Ben's design is bad and can cause the observed behavior?

A. A STORE instruction can overwrite the segment ID of an address.
B. A LONGJMP instruction in the Web server program may jump to an address in the library segment that is not the start of a procedure.
C. It doesn't allow for paging of infrequently used memory to a secondary storage device.
D. The web server program may get into an endless loop.

Q 11.7 Which of the following extensions of Ben's design would address each of the preceding problems?

A. The processor should have a protected user-mode bit, and there should be a separate segment table for kernel and user programs.

B. Each segment descriptor should have a protection bit, which specifies whether the processor can write or only read from this segment.

C. The LONGJMP instruction should be changed so that it can transfer control only to designated entry points of a segment.

D. Segments should all be the same size, just like pages in page-based virtual memory systems.

E. Change the operating system to use a preemptive scheduler.

The system library for Ben's Web server contains code to send and receive messages. A separate program, the network manager, manages the network card that sends and receives messages. The Web server and the network manager each have one thread of execution. Ben wants to understand why he needs eventcounts for sequence coordination of the network manager and the Web server, so he decides to implement the coordination twice, once using eventcounts and the second time using event variables.

Here are Ben's two versions of the Web server:

Web server using eventcounts

```
eventcount inCnt
integer doneCnt

procedure SERVE ()
do forever
    AWAIT (inCnt, doneCnt);
    DO_REQUEST ();
    doneCnt ← doneCnt + 1;
```

Web server using events

```
event input
integer inCnt
integer doneCnt

procedure SERVE ()
do forever
    while inCnt ≤ doneCnt do        //A
        WAITEVENT (Input);          //B
    DO_REQUEST ();                  //C
```

Both versions use a thread manager as described in Chapter 5, except for the changes to support eventcounts or events. The eventcount version is exactly the one described in Chapter 5. The AWAIT procedure has semantics for eventcounts: when the Web server thread calls AWAIT, the thread manager puts the calling thread into the WAITING state unless *inCnt* exceeds *doneCnt*.

The event-based version is almost identical to the eventcount one but has a few changes. An *event variable* is a list of threads waiting for the event. The procedure WAITEVENT puts the current executing thread on the list for the event, records that the current thread is in the WAITING state, and releases the processor by calling YIELD.

In both versions, when the Web server has completed processing a packet, it increases *doneCnt*.

The two corresponding versions of the code for handling each packet arrival in the network manager are:

Network manager using eventcounts

```
ADVANCE (inCnt)
```

Network manager using events

```
inCnt ← inCnt + 1       //D
NOTIFYEVENT (input)     //E
```

The ADVANCE procedure wakes up the Web server thread if it is already asleep. The NOTIFYEVENT procedure removes all threads from the list of the event and puts them into the READY state. The shared variables are stored in a segment shared between the network manager and the Web server.

Ben is a bit worried about writing code that involves coordinating multiple activities, so he decides to test the code carefully. He buys a computer with one processor to run both the Web server and the network manager using a preemptive thread scheduler. Ben ensures that the two threads (the Web server and the network manager) never run inside the thread manager at the same time by turning off interrupts when the processor is running the thread manager's code (which includes ADVANCE, AWAIT, NOTIFYEVENT, and WAITEVENT).

To test the code, Ben changes the thread manager to preempt threads frequently (i.e., each thread runs with a short time slice). Ben runs the old code with event-counts and the program behaves as expected, but the new code using events has the problem that the Web server sometimes delays processing a packet until the next packet arrives.

Q 11.8 The program steps that might be causing the problem are marked with letters in the code of the event-based solution above. Using those letters, give a sequence of steps that creates the problem. (Some steps might have to appear more than once, and some might not be necessary to create the problem.)

2002-1-4...11

12 A Bounded Buffer with Semaphores

(Chapter 5)

Using semaphores, DOWN and UP (see Sidebar 5.7), Ben implements an in-kernel bounded buffer as shown in the pseudocode below. The kernel maintains an array of *port_infos*. Each *port_info* contains a bounded buffer. The content of the message structure is not important for this problem, other than that it has a field *dest_port*, which specifies the destination port. When a message arrives from the network, it generates an interrupt, and the network interrupt handler (INTERRUPT) puts the message in the bounded buffer of the port specified in the message. If there is no space in that bounded buffer, the interrupt handler throws the message away. A thread consumes a message by calling RECEIVE_MESSAGE, which removes a message from the bounded buffer of the port it is receiving from.

To coordinate the interrupt handler and a thread calling RECEIVE_MESSAGE, the implementation uses a semaphore. For each port, the kernel keeps a semaphore *n* that counts the number of messages in the port's bounded buffer. If *n* reaches 0, the thread calling DOWN in RECEIVE_MESSAGE will enter the WAITING state. When INTERRUPT adds a message to the buffer, it calls UP on *n*, which will wake up the thread (i.e., set the thread's state to RUNNABLE).

```
structure port_info
    semaphore instance n initially 0
    message instance buffer[NMSG]                    // an array of messages
    long integer in initially 0
    long integer out initially 0

procedure INTERRUPT (message instance m, port_info reference port)
    // an interrupt announcing the arrival of message m
    if port.in – port.out ≥ NMSG then                // is there space?
        return                                       // No, ignore message
    port.buffer[port.in modulo NMSG] ← m
    port.in ← port.in + 1
    UP (port.in)

procedure RECEIVE_MESSAGE (port_info reference port)
1   ...                                              // another line of code will go here
    DOWN (port.in)
    m ← port.buffer[port.in modulo NMSG]
    port.out ← port.out + 1
    return m
```

The kernel schedules threads preemptively.

Q 12.1 Assume that there are no concurrent invocations of INTERRUPT and that there are no concurrent invocations of RECEIVE_MESSAGE on the same port. Which of the following statements is true about the implementation of INTERRUPT and RECEIVE_MESSAGE?

A. There are no race conditions between two threads that invoke RECEIVE_MESSAGE concurrently on different ports.

B. The complete execution of UP in INTERRUPT will not be interleaved between the statements labeled *15* and *16* in DOWN in Sidebar 5.7.

C. Because DOWN and UP are atomic, the processor instructions necessary for the subtracting of *sem* in DOWN and adding to *sem* in UP will not be interleaved incorrectly.

D. Because *in* and *out* may be shared between the interrupt handler running INTERRUPT and a thread calling RECEIVE_MESSAGE on the same port, it is possible for INTERRUPT to throw away a message, even though there is space in the bounded buffer.

Alyssa claims that semaphores can also be used to make operations atomic. She proposes the following addition to a *port_info* structure:

```
semaphore instance mutex initially ????          // see question below
```

and adds the following line to RECEIVE_MESSAGE, on line 1 in the pseudocode above:

```
DOWN(port.mutex)                                 // enter atomic section
```

Alyssa argues that these changes allow threads to concurrently invoke RECEIVE on the same port without race conditions, even if the kernel schedules threads preemptively.

Q 12.2 To what value can *mutex* be initialized (by replacing ???? with a number in the *semaphore* declaration) to avoid race conditions and deadlocks when multiple threads call RECEIVE_MESSAGE on the same port?

A. 0
B. 1
C. 2
D. −1

2006-1-11&12

13 The Single-Chip NC*

(Chapter 5)

Ben Bitdiddle plans to create a revolution in computing with his just-developed $15 single-chip Network Computer, NC. In the NC network system, the network interface thread calls the procedure MESSAGE_ARRIVED when a message arrives. The procedure WAIT_FOR_MESSAGE can be called by a thread to wait for a message. To coordinate the sequences in which threads execute, Ben deploys another commonly used coordination primitive: ***condition variables***.

Part of the code in the NC is as follows:

```
lock instance m
boolean message_here
condition instance message_present

procedure MESSAGE_ARRIVED ()
    message_here ← TRUE
    NOTIFY_CONDITION (message_present) // notify threads waiting on this condition

procedure WAIT_FOR_MESSAGE ()
    ACQUIRE (m)
    while not message_here do
        WAIT_CONDITION (message_present, m);        // release m and wait
     RELEASE (m)
```

The procedures ACQUIRE and RELEASE are the ones described in Chapter 5. NOTIFY_CONDITION (*condition*) atomically wakes up all threads waiting for *condition* to become TRUE. WAIT_CONDITION (*condition, lock*) does several things atomically: it tests *condition*; if TRUE it returns; otherwise it puts the calling thread on the waiting queue for *condition* and releases *lock*. When NOTIFY_CONDITION wakens a thread, that thread becomes

*Credit for developing this problem set goes to David K. Gifford.

runnable, and when the scheduler runs that thread, WAIT_CONDITION reacquires *lock* (waiting, if necessary, until it is available) before returning to its caller.

Assume there are no errors in the implementation of condition variables.

Q 13.1 It is possible that WAIT_FOR_MESSAGE will wait forever even if a message arrives while it is spinning in the **while** loop. Give an execution ordering of the above statements that would cause this problem. Your answer should be a simple list such as 1, 2, 3, 4.

Q 13.2 Write new version(s) of MESSAGE_ARRIVED and/or WAIT_FOR_MESSAGE to fix this problem.

1998-1-3a/b

14 Toastac-25*

(Chapters 5 and 7 [on-line])

Louis P. Hacker bought a used Therac-25 (the medical irradiation machine that was involved in several fatal accidents—see Suggestions for Further Reading 1.9.5) for $14.99 at a yard sale. After some slight modifications, he has hooked it up to his home network as a computer-controllable turbo-toaster, which can toast one slice in under 2 milliseconds. He decides to use RPC to control the Toastac-25. Each toasting request starts a new thread on the server, which cooks the toast, returns an acknowledgment (or perhaps a helpful error code, such as "Malfunction 54"), and exits. Each server thread runs the following procedure:

```
procedure SERVER () {
    ACQUIRE (message_buffer_lock)
    DECODE (message)
    ACQUIRE (accelerator_buffer_lock)
    RELEASE (message_buffer_lock)
    COOK_TOAST ()
    ACQUIRE (message_buffer_lock)
    message ← "ack"
    SEND (message)
    RELEASE (accelerator_buffer_lock)
    RELEASE (message_buffer_lock)
```

Q 14.1 To his surprise, the toaster stops cooking toast the first time it is heavily used! What has gone wrong?

- **A.** Two server threads might deadlock because one has *message_buffer_lock* and wants *accelerator_buffer_lock*, while the other has *accelerator_buffer_lock* and wants *message_buffer_lock*.
- **B.** Two server threads might deadlock because one has *accelerator_buffer_lock* and *message_buffer_lock*.
- **C.** Toastac-25 deadlocks because COOK_TOAST is not an atomic operation.
- **D.** Insufficient locking allows inappropriate interleaving of server threads.

---

*Credit for developing this problem set goes to Eddie Kohler.

Once Louis fixes the multithreaded server, the Toastac gets more use than ever. However, when the Toastac has many simultaneous requests (i.e., there are many threads), he notices that the system performance degrades badly—much more than he expected. Performance analysis shows that competition for locks is not the problem.

Q 14.2 What is probably going wrong?

- **A.** The Toastac system spends all its time context switching between threads.
- **B.** The Toastac system spends all its time waiting for requests to arrive.
- **C.** The Toastac gets hot, and therefore cooking toast takes longer.
- **D.** The Toastac system spends all its time releasing locks.

Q 14.3 An upgrade to a supercomputer fixes that problem, but it's too late—Louis is obsessed with performance. He switches from RPC to an asynchronous protocol, which groups several requests into a single message if they are made within 2 milliseconds of one another. On his network, which has a very high transit time, he notices that this speeds up some workloads far more than others. Describe a workload that is sped up and a workload that is not sped up. (An example of a possible workload would be one request every 10 milliseconds.)

Q 14.4 As a design engineering consultant, you are called in to critique Louis's decision to move from RPC to asynchronous client/service. How do you feel about his decision? Remember that the Toastac software sometimes fails with a "Malfunction 54" instead of toasting properly.

1996-1-5c/d & 1999-1-12/13

15 BOOZE: Ben's Object-Oriented Zoned Environment

(Chapters 5 and 6)

Ben Bitdiddle writes a large number of object-oriented programs. Objects come in different sizes, but pages come in a fixed size. Ben is inspired to redesign his page-based virtual memory system (PAGE) into an object memory system. PAGE is a page-based virtual memory system like the one described in Chapter 5 with the extensions for multilevel memory systems from Chapter 6. BOOZE is Ben's *object-based virtual memory* system.* Of course, he can run his programs on either system.

Each BOOZE object has a unique ID called a UID. A UID has three fields: a disk address for the disk block that contains the object; an offset within that disk block where the object starts; and the size of the object.

```
structure uid
    integer blocknr          // disk address for disk block
    integer offset           // offset within block blocknr
    integer size             // size of object
```

*Ben chose this name after reading a paper by Ted Kaehler, "Virtual memory for an object-oriented Language" [Suggestions for Further Reading 6.1.4]. In that paper, Kaehler describes a memory management system called the Object-Oriented Zoned Environment, with the acronym OOZE.

Applications running on BOOZE and PAGE have similar structure. The only difference is that on PAGE, program refer to objects by their virtual address, while on BOOZE programs refer to objects by UIDs.

The two levels of memory in BOOZE and PAGE are main memory and disk. The disk is a linear array of fixed-size blocks of 4 kilobytes. A disk block is addressed by its block number. In *both* systems, the transfer unit between the disk and main memory is a 4-kilobyte block. Objects don't cross disk block boundaries, are smaller than 4 kilobytes, and cannot change size. The page size in PAGE is equal to the disk block size; therefore, when an application refers to an object, PAGE will bring in all objects on the same page.

BOOZE keeps an object map in main memory. The object map contains entries that map a UID to the memory address of the corresponding object.

```
structure mapentry
    uid instance UID
    integer addr
```

On all references to an object, BOOZE translates a UID to an address in main memory. BOOZE uses the following procedure (implemented partly in hardware and partly in software) for translation:

```
procedure ObjectToAddress(UID) returns address
    addr ← isPresent(UID)                 // is UID present in object map?
    if addr ≥ 0 then return addr           // UID is present, return addr
    addr ← FindFreeSpace(UID.size)         // allocate space to hold object
    ReadObject(addr, UID)                  // read object from disk & store at addr
    EnterIntoMap(UID, addr)                // enter UID in object map
    return addr                            // return memory address of object
```

isPresent looks up *UID* in the object map; if present, it returns the address of the corresponding object; otherwise, it returns 1. FindFreeSpace allocates free space for the object; it might evict another object to make space available for this one. ReadObject reads the *page* that contains the object, and then copies the *object* to the allocated address.

Q 15.1 What does *addr* in the *mapentry* data structure denote?

A. The memory address at which the object map is located.

B. The disk address at which to find a given object.

C. The memory address at which to find a given object that is *currently* resident in memory.

D. The memory address at which a given non-resident object *would have to be loaded*, when an access is made to it.

Q 15.2 In what way is BOOZE better than PAGE?

A. Applications running on BOOZE generally use less main memory because BOOZE stores only objects that are in use.
B. Applications running on BOOZE generally run faster because UIDs are smaller than virtual addresses.
C. Applications running on BOOZE generally run faster because BOOZE transfers objects from disk to main memory instead of complete pages.
D. Applications running on BOOZE generally run faster because typical applications will exhibit better locality of reference.

When FINDFREESPACE cannot find enough space to hold the object, it needs to write one or more objects back to the disk to create free space. FINDFREESPACE uses WRITEOBJECT to write an object to the disk.

Ben is figuring out how to implement WRITEOBJECT. He is considering the following options:

1.
```
procedure WRITEOBJECT (addr, UID)
    WRITE(addr, UID.blocknr, 4096)
```

2.
```
procedure WRITEOBJECT(addr, UID)
    READ(buffer, UID.blocknr, 4096)
    COPY(addr, buffer + UID.offset, UID.size)
    WRITE(buffer, UID.blocknr, 4096)
```

READ (*mem_addr*, *disk_addr*, 4096) and WRITE (*mem_addr*, *disk_addr*, 4096) read and write a 4-kilobyte page from/to the disk. COPY (*source*, *destination*, *size*) copies *size* bytes from a source address to a destination address in main memory.

Q 15.3 Which implementation should Ben use?

A. Implementation 2, since implementation 1 is incorrect.
B. Implementation 1, since it is more efficient than implementation 2.
C. Implementation 1, since it is easier to understand.
D. Implementation 2, since it will result in better locality of reference.

Ben now turns his attention to optimizing the performance of BOOZE. In particular, he wants to reduce the number of writes to the disk.

Q 15.4 Which of the following techniques will reduce the number of writes without losing correctness?

A. Prefetching objects on a read.
B. Delaying writes to disk until the application finishes its computation.
C. Writing to disk only objects that have been modified.
D. Delaying a write of an object to disk until it is accessed again.

Ben decides that he wants even better performance, so he decides to modify FINDFREESPACE. When FINDFREESPACE has to evict an object, it now tries not to write an object modified in the last 30 seconds (in the belief that it may be used again soon). Ben does this by setting the *dirty* flag when the object is modified. Every 30 seconds, BOOZE calls a procedure WRITE_BEHIND that walks through the object map and writes out all objects that are dirty. After an object has been written, WRITE_BEHIND clears its *dirty* flag. When FINDFREESPACE needs to evict an object to make space for another, clean objects are the *only* candidates for replacement.

When running his applications on the latest version of BOOZE, Ben observes once in a while that BOOZE runs out of physical memory when calling OBJECTTOADDRESS for a new object.

Q 15.5 Which of these strategies avoids the above problem?

A. When FINDFREESPACE cannot find any clean objects, it calls WRITE_BEHIND and then tries to find clean objects again.

B. BOOZE could call WRITE_BEHIND every second instead of every 30 seconds.

C. When FINDFREESPACE cannot find any clean objects, it picks *one* dirty object, writes the block containing the object to the disk, clears the *dirty* flag, and then uses that address for the new object.

D. All of the above strategies.

1999–1–7...11

16 OutOfMoney.com

(Chapter 6, with a bit of Chapter 4)

OutOfMoney.com has decided it needs a real product, so it is laying off most of its Marketing Department. To replace the marketing folks, and on the advice of a senior computer expert, OutOfMoney.com hires a crew of 16-year-olds. The 16-year-olds get together and decide to design and implement a video service that serves MPEG-1 video, so that they can watch Britney Spears on their computers in living color.

Since time to market is crucial, Mark Bitdiddle—Ben's 16-year-old kid brother, who is working for OutOfMoney—surfs the Web to find some code from which they can start. Mark finds some code that looks relevant, and he modifies it for OutOfMoney's video service:

```
procedure SERVICE ()
    do forever
        request ← RECEIVE_MESSAGE ()
        file ← GET_FILE_FROM_DISK (request)
        REPLY (file)
```

The SERVICE procedure waits for a message from a client to arrive on the network. The message contains a *request* for a particular file. The procedure GET_FILE_FROM_DISK reads the file from disk into the memory location *file*. The procedure REPLY sends the file from memory in a message back to the client.

(In the pseudocode, undeclared variables are local variables of the procedure in which they are used, and the variables are thus stored on the stack or in registers.)

Mark and his 16-year-old buddies also write code for a network driver to SEND and RECEIVE network packets, a simple file system to PUT and GET files on a disk, and a loader for booting a machine. They run their code on the bare hardware of an off-the-shelf personal computer with one disk, one processor (a Pentium III), and one network interface card (1 gigabit per second Ethernet). After the machine has booted, it starts one thread running SERVICE.

The disk has an average seek time of 5 milliseconds, a complete rotation takes 6 milliseconds, and its throughput is 10 megabytes per second when no seeks are required.

All files are 1 gigabyte (roughly a half hour of MPEG-1 video). The file system in which the files are stored has no cache, and it allocates data for a file in 8-kilobyte chunks. It pays no attention to file layout when allocating a chunk; as a result, disk blocks of the same file can be all over the disk. A 1-gigabyte file contains 131,072 8-kilobyte blocks.

Q 16.1 Assuming that the disk is the main bottleneck, how long does the service take to serve a file?

Mark is shocked about the performance. Ben suggests that they should add a cache. Mark, impressed by Ben's knowledge, follows his advice and adds a 1-gigabyte cache, which can hold one file completely:

```
cache [1073741824]                         // 1-gigabyte cache

procedure SERVICE ()
    do forever
        request ← RECEIVE_MESSAGE ()
        file ← LOOK_IN_CACHE (request)
        if file = NULL then
            file ← GET_FILE_FROM_DISK (request)
            ADD_TO_CACHE (request, file)
        REPLY (file)
```

The procedure LOOK_IN_CACHE checks whether the file specified in the request is present in the cache and returns it if present. The procedure ADD_TO_CACHE copies a file to the cache.

Q 16.2 Mark tests the code by asking once for every video stored. Assuming that the disk is the main bottleneck (serving a file from the cache takes 0 milliseconds), what now is the average time for the service to serve a file?

Mark is happy that the test actually returns every video. He reports back to the only person left in the Marketing Department that the prototype is ready to be evaluated. To keep the investors happy, the marketing person decides to use the prototype to run OutOfMoney's Web site. The one-person Marketing Department loads the machine up with videos and launches the new Web site with a big PR campaign, blowing their remaining funding.

Seconds after they launch the Web site, OutOfMoney's support organization (also staffed by 16-year-olds) receives e-mail from unhappy users saying that the service is not responding to their requests. The support department measures the load on the service CPU and also the service disk. They observe that the CPU load is low and the disk load is high.

Q 16.3 What is the most likely reason for this observation?

A. The cache is too large.
B. The hit ratio for the cache is low.
C. The hit ratio for the cache is high.
D. The CPU is not fast enough.

The support department beeps Mark, who runs to his brother Ben for help. Ben suggests using the example thread package of Chapter 5. Mark augments the code to use the thread package and after the system boots, it starts 100 threads, each running SERVICE:

```
for i from 1 to 100 do CREATE_THREAD (SERVICE)
```

In addition, mark modifies RECEIVE_MESSAGE and GET_FILE_FROM_DISK to release the processor by calling YIELD when waiting for a new message to arrive or waiting for the disk to complete a disk read. In no other place does his code release the processor. The implementation of the thread package is non-preemptive.

To take advantage of the threaded implementation, Mark modifies the code to read blocks of a file instead of complete files. He also runs to the store and buys some more memory so he can increase the cache size to 4 gigabytes. Here is his latest effort:

```
cache [4 × 1073741824]          // The 4-gigabyte cache, shared by all threads.

procedure SERVICE ()
    do forever
        request ← RECEIVE_MESSAGE ()
        file ← NULL
        for k from 1 to 131072 do
            block ← LOOK_IN_CACHE (request, k)
            if block = NULL then
                block ← GET_BLOCK_FROM_DISK (request, k)
                ADD_TO_CACHE (request, block, k)
            file ← file + block       // + concatenates strings
        REPLY (file)
```

The procedure LOOK_IN_CACHE (*request*, *k*) checks whether block *k* of the file specified in *request* is present; if the block is present, it returns it. The procedure

GET_BLOCK_FROM_DISK reads block *k* of the file specified in *request* from the disk into memory. The procedure ADD_TO_CACHE adds block *k* from the file specified in *request* to the cache.

Mark loads up the service with one video. He retrieves the video successfully. Happy with this result, Mark sends many requests for the single video in parallel to the service. He observes no disk activity.

Q 16.4 Based on the information so far, what is the most likely explanation why Mark observes no disk activity?

Happy with the progress, Mark makes the service ready for running in production mode. He is worried that he may have to modify the code to deal with concurrency—his past experience has suggested to him that he needs an education, so he is reading Chapter 5. He considers protecting ADD_TO_CACHE with a lock:

```
lock instance cachelock                                    // A lock for the cache

procedure SERVICE ()
    do forever
        request ← RECEIVE_MESSAGE ()
        file ← NULL
        for k from 1 to 131072 do
            block ← LOOK_IN_CACHE (request, k)
            if block = NULL then
                block ← GET_BLOCK_FROM_DISK (request, k)
                ACQUIRE (cachelock)                        // use the lock
                ADD_TO_CACHE (request, block, k)
                RELEASE (cachelock)                        // here, too
            file ← file + block
        REPLY (file)
```

Q 16.5 Ben argues that these modifications are not useful. Is Ben right?

Mark doesn't like thinking, so he upgrades OutOfMoney's Web site to use the multi-threaded code with locks. When the upgraded Web site goes live, Mark observes that most users watch the same three videos, while a few are watching other videos.

Q 16.6 Mark observes a hit-ratio of 90% for blocks in the cache. Assuming that the disk is the main bottleneck (serving blocks from the cache takes 0 milliseconds), what is the average time for SERVICE to serve a single movie?

Q 16.7 Mark loads a new Britney Spears video onto the service and observes operation as the first users start to view it. It is so popular that no users are viewing any other video. Mark sees that the first batch of viewers all start watching the video at about the same time. He observes that the service threads all read block 0 at about the same time, then all read block 1 at about the same time, and so on. For this workload what is a good cache replacement policy?

A. Least-recently used.
B. Most-recently used.
C. First-in, first-out.
D. Last-in, first-out.
E. The replacement policy doesn't matter for this workload.

The Marketing Department is extremely happy with the progress. Ben raises another round of money by selling his BMW and launches another PR campaign. The number of users dramatically increases. Unfortunately, under high load the machine stops serving requests and has to be restarted. As a result, some users have to restart their videos from the beginning, and they call up the support department to complain. The problem appears to be some interaction between the network driver and the service threads. The driver and service threads share a fixed-sized input buffer that can hold 1,000 request messages. If the buffer is full and a message arrives, the driver drops the message. When the card receives data from the network, it issues an interrupt to the processor. This interrupt causes the network driver to run immediately on the stack of the currently running thread. The code for the driver and RECEIVE_MESSAGE is as follows:

```
buffer[1000]
lock instance bufferlock

procedure DRIVER ()
    message ← READ_FROM_INTERFACE ()
    ACQUIRE (bufferlock)
    if SPACE_IN_BUFFER () then ADD_TO_BUFFER (message)
    else DISCARD_MESSAGE (message)
    RELEASE (bufferlock)

procedure RECEIVE_MESSAGE ()
    while BUFFER_IS_EMPTY () do YIELD ()
    ACQUIRE (bufferlock)
    message ← REMOVE_FROM_BUFFER ()
    RELEASE (bufferlock)
    return message

procedure INTERRUPT ()
    DRIVER ()
```

Q 16.8 Which of the following could happen under high load?

A. Deadlock when an arriving message interrupts DRIVER.
B. Deadlock when an arriving message interrupts a thread that is in RECEIVE_MESSAGE.
C. Deadlock when an arriving message interrupts a thread that is in REMOVE_FROM_BUFFER.
D. RECEIVE_MESSAGE misses a call to YIELD when the buffer is not empty, because it can be interrupted between the BUFFER_IS_EMPTY test and the call to YIELD.

Q 16.9 What fixes should Mark implement?

A. Delete all the code dealing with locks.
B. DRIVER should run as a separate thread, to be awakened by the interrupt.
C. INTERRUPT and DRIVER should use an eventcount for sequence coordination.
D. DRIVER shouldn't drop packets when the buffer is full.

Mark eliminates the deadlock problems and, to attract more users, announces the availability of a new Britney Spears video. The news spreads rapidly, and an enormous number of requests for this one video start hitting the service. Mark measures the throughput of the service as more and more clients ask for the video. The resulting graph is plotted below. The throughput first increases while the number of clients increases, then reaches a maximum value, and finally drops off.

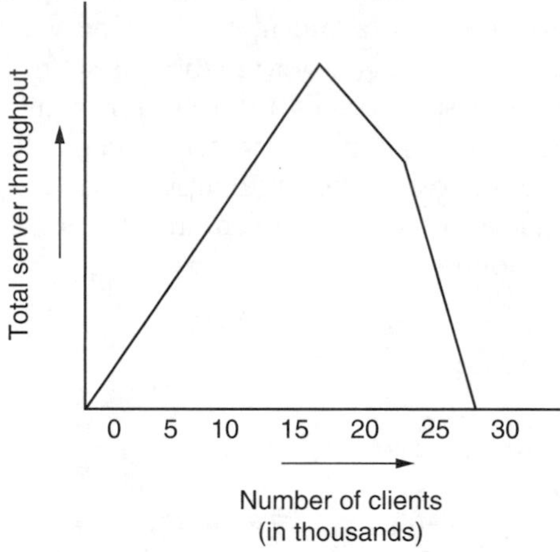

Q 16.10 Why does the throughput decrease with a large number of clients?

A. The processor spends most of its time taking interrupts.
B. The processor spends most of its time updating the cache.
C. The processor spends most of its time waiting for the disk accesses to complete.
D. The processor spends most of its time removing messages from the buffer.

2001-1-6...15

Glossary

Abort Upon deciding that an all-or-nothing action cannot or should not commit, to undo all of the changes previously made by that all-or-nothing action. After aborting, the state of the system, as viewed by anyone above the layer that implements the all-or-nothing action, is as if the all-or-nothing action never existed. Compare with *commit*. [Ch. 9]

Absolute path name In a naming hierarchy, a path name that a name resolver resolves by using a universal context known as the *root* context. [Ch. 2]

Abstraction The separation of the interface specification of a module from its internal implementation so that one can understand and make use of that module with no need to know how it is implemented internally. [Ch. 1]

Access control list (ACL) A list of principals authorized to have access to some object. [Ch. 11]

Acknowledgment (ACK) A status report from the recipient of a communication to the originator. Depending on the protocol, an acknowledgment may imply or explicitly state any of several things—for example, that the communication was received, that its checksum verified correctly, that delivery to a higher level was successful, or that buffer space is available for another communication. Compare with *negative acknowledgment*. [Ch. 2]

Action An operation performed by an interpreter. Examples include a microcode step, a machine instruction, a higher-level language instruction, a procedure invocation, a shell command line, a response to a gesture at a graphical interface, or a database update. [Ch. 9]

Active fault A fault that is currently causing an error. Compare with *latent fault*. [Ch. 8]

Adaptive routing A method for setting up forwarding tables so that they change automatically when links are added to and deleted from the network or when congestion makes a path less desirable. Compare with *static routing*. [Ch. 7]

Address A name that is overloaded with information useful for locating the named object. In a computer system, an address is usually of fixed length and resolved by hardware into a physical location by mapping to geometric coordinates. Examples of addresses include the names for a byte of memory and for a disk track. Also see *network address*. [Ch. 2]

Address resolution protocol (ARP) A protocol used when a broadcast network is a component of a packet-forwarding network. The protocol dynamically constructs tables that map station identifiers of the broadcast network to network attachment point identifiers of the packet-forwarding network. [Ch. 7]

Address space The name space of a location-addressed memory, usually a set of contiguous integers (0, 1, 2,...). [Ch. 2]

Adversary An entity that intentionally tries to defeat the security measures of a computer system. The entity may be malicious, out for profit, or just a hacker. A friendly adversary is one that tests the security of a computer system. [Ch. 11]

Advertise In a network-layer routing protocol, for a participant to tell other participants which network addresses it knows how to reach. [Ch. 7]

Alias One of multiple names that map to the same value; another term for *synonym*. (Beware: some operating systems define *alias* to mean an *indirect name*.) [Ch. 2]

All-or-nothing atomicity A property of a multistep action that if an anticipated failure occurs during the steps of the action, the effect of the action from the point of view of its invoker is either never to have started or else to have been accomplished completely. Compare with *before-or-after atomicity* and *atomic*. [Ch. 9]

Any-to-any connection A desirable property of a communication network, that any node be able to communicate with any other. [Ch. 7]

Archive A record, usually kept in the form of a log, of old data values, for auditing, recovery from application mistakes, or historical interest. [Ch. 9]

Asynchronous (From Greek roots meaning "not timed") 1. Describes concurrent activities that are not coordinated by a common clock and thus may make progress at different rates. For example, multiple processors are usually asynchronous, and I/O operations are typically performed by an I/O channel processor that is asynchronous with respect to the processor that initiated the I/O. [Ch. 2] 2. In a communication network, describes a communication link over which data is sent in frames whose timing relative to other frames is unpredictable and whose lengths may not be uniform. Compare with *isochronous*. [Ch. 7]

At-least-once A protocol assurance that the intended operation or message delivery was performed at least one time. It may have been performed several times. [Ch. 4]

At-most-once A protocol assurance that the intended operation or message delivery was performed no more than one time. It may not have been performed at all. [Ch. 4]

Atomic (adj.); Atomicity (n.) A property of a multistep action that there be no evidence that it is composite above the layer that implements it. An atomic action can be before-or-after, which means that its effect is as if it occurred either completely before or completely after any other before-or-after action. An atomic action can also be all-or-nothing, which means that if an anticipated failure occurs during the action, the effect of the action as seen by higher layers is either never to have started or else to have completed successfully. An atomic action that is *both* all-or-nothing and before-or-after is known as a *transaction*. [Ch. 9]

Atomic storage Cell storage for which a multicell PUT can have only two possible outcomes: (1) it stores all data successfully, or (2) it does not change the previous data at all. In consequence, either a concurrent thread or (following a failure) a later thread doing a GET will always read either all old data or all new data. Computer architectures in which multicell PUTs are not atomic are said to be subject to *write tearing*. [Ch. 9]

Authentication Verifying the identity of a principal or the authenticity of a message. [Ch. 11]

Authentication tag A cryptographically computed string, associated with a message, that allows a receiver to verify the authenticity of the message. [Ch. 11]

Automatic rate adaptation A technique by which a sender automatically adjusts the rate at which it introduces packets into a network to match the maximum rate that the narrowest bottleneck can handle. [Ch. 7]

Authorization A decision made by an authority to grant a principal permission to perform some operation, such as reading certain information. [Ch. 11]

Availability A measure of the time that a system was actually usable, as a fraction of the time that it was intended to be usable. Compare with its complement, *down time*. [Ch. 8]

Backup copy Of a set of replicas that is not written or updated synchronously, one that is written later. Compare with *primary copy* and *mirror*. [Ch. 10]

Backward error correction A technique for correcting errors in which the source of the data or control signal applies enough redundancy to allow errors to be detected and, if an error does occur, that source is asked to redo the calculation or repeat the transmission. Compare with *forward error correction*. [Ch. 8]

Bad-news diode An undesirable tendency of people in organizations that design and implement systems: good news, for example, that a module is ready for delivery ahead of schedule, tends to be passed immediately throughout the organization, but bad news, for example, that a module did not pass its acceptance tests, tends to be held locally until either the problem can be fixed or it cannot be concealed any longer. [Ch. 1]

Bandwidth A measure of analog spectrum space for a communication channel. The bandwidth, the acceptable signal power, and the noise level of a channel together determine the maximum possible data rate for that channel. In digital systems, this term is so often misused as a synonym for maximum data rate that it has now entered the vocabulary of digital designers with that additional meaning. Analog engineers, however, still cringe at that usage. [Ch. 7]

Batching A technique to improve performance by combining several operations into a single operation to reduce setup overhead. [Ch. 6]

Before-or-after atomicity A property of concurrent actions: Concurrent actions are before-or-after actions if their effect from the point of view of their invokers is the same as if the actions occurred either completely before or completely after one another. One consequence is that concurrent before-or-after software actions cannot discover the composite nature of one another (that is, one action cannot tell that another has multiple steps). A consequence in the case of hardware is that concurrent before-or-after WRITES to the same memory cell will be performed in some order, so there is no danger that the cell will end up containing, for example, the OR of several WRITE values. The database literature uses the words "isolation" and "serializable", the operating system literature uses the words "mutual exclusion" and "critical section", and the computer architecture literature uses the unqualified word "atomicity" for this concept. [Ch. 5] Compare with *all-or-nothing atomicity* and *atomic*. [Ch. 9]

Best-effort contract The promise given by a forwarding network when it accepts a packet: it will use its best effort to deliver the packet, but the time to delivery is not fixed, the order of delivery relative to other packets sent to the same destination is unpredictable, and the packet may be duplicated or lost. [Ch. 7]

Binding (n.); Bind (v.) As used in naming, a mapping from a specified name to a particular value in a specified context. When a binding exists, the name is said to be *bound*. Binding may occur at any time up to and including the instant that a name is resolved. The term is also used more generally, meaning to choose a specific lower-layer implementation for some higher-layer feature. [Ch. 2]

Bit error rate In a digital transmission system, the rate at which bits that have incorrect values arrive at the receiver, expressed as a fraction of the bits transmitted, for example, one in 10^{10}. [Ch. 7]

Bit stuffing The technique of inserting a bit pattern as a marker in a stream of bits and then inserting bits elsewhere in the stream to ensure that payload data never matches the marker bit pattern. [Ch. 7]

Blind write An update to a data value *X* by a transaction that did not previously read *X*. [Ch. 9]

Bootstrapping A systematic approach to solving a general problem, consisting of a method for reducing the general problem to a specialized instance of the same problem and a method for solving the specialized instance. [Ch. 5]

Bottleneck The stage in a multistage pipeline that takes longer to perform its task than any of the other stages. [Ch. 6]

Broadcast To send a packet that is intended to be received by many (ideally, all) of the stations of a broadcast link (link-layer broadcast), or all the destination addresses of a network (network-layer broadcast). [Ch. 7]

Burst A batch of related bits that is irregular in size and timing relative to other such batches. Bursts of data are the usual content of messages and the usual payload of packets. One can also have bursts of noise and bursts of packets. [Ch. 7]

Byzantine fault A fault that generates inconsistent errors (perhaps maliciously) that can confuse or disrupt fault tolerance or security mechanisms. [Ch. 8]

Cache A performance-enhancing module that remembers the result of an expensive computation on the chance that the result may soon be needed again. [Ch. 2]

Cache coherence Read/write coherence for a multilevel memory system that has a cache. It is a specification that the cache provide strict consistency at its interface. [Ch. 10]

Capability In a computer system, an unforgeable ticket, which when presented is taken as incontestable proof that the presenter is authorized to have access to the object named in the ticket. [Ch. 11]

Capacity Any consistent measure of the size or amount of a resource. [Ch. 6]

Cell storage Storage in which a WRITE or PUT operates by overwriting, thus destroying previously stored information. Many physical storage devices, including magnetic disk and CMOS random access memory, implement cell storage. Compare with *journal storage*. [Ch. 9]

Certificate A message that attests the binding of a principal identifier to a cryptographic key. [Ch. 11]

Certificate authority (CA) A principal that issues and signs certificates. [Ch. 11]

Certify To check the accuracy, correctness, and completeness of a security mechanism. [Ch. 11]

Checkpoint 1. (n.) Information written to non-volatile storage that is intended to speed up recovery from a crash. 2. (v.) To write a checkpoint. [Ch. 9]

Checksum A stylized error-detection code in which the data is unchanged from its uncoded form and additional, redundant data is placed in a distinct, separately architected field. [Ch. 7]

Cipher Synonym for a *cryptographic transformation*. [Ch. 11]

Ciphertext The result of encryption. Compare with *plaintext*. [Ch. 11]

Circuit switch A device with many electrical circuits coming in to it that can connect any circuit to any other circuit; it may be able to perform many such connections simultaneously. Historically, telephone systems were constructed of circuit switches. [Ch. 7]

Cleartext Synonym for *plaintext*. [Ch. 11]

Client A module that initiates actions, such as sending a request to a service. [Ch. 4] At the end-to-end layer of a network, the end that initiates actions. Compare with *service*. [Ch. 7]

Client/service organization An organization that enforces modularity among modules of a computer system by limiting the interaction among the modules to messages. [Ch. 4]

Close-to-open consistency A consistency model for file operations. When a thread opens a file and performs several write operations, all of the modifications will be visible to concurrent threads only after the first thread closes the file. [Ch. 2]

Closure In a programming language, an object that consists of a reference to the text of a procedure and a reference to the context in which the program interpreter is to resolve the variables of the procedure. [Ch. 2]

Coherence See *read/write coherence* or *cache coherence*.

Collision 1. In naming, a particular kind of name conflict in which an algorithmic name generator accidentally generates the same name more than once in what is intended to be a unique identifier name space. [Ch. 3] 2. In networks, an event when two stations attempt to send a message over the same physical medium at the same time. See also *Ethernet*. [Ch. 7]

Commit To renounce the ability to abandon an all-or-nothing action unilaterally. One usually commits an all-or-nothing action before making its results available to concurrent or later all-or-nothing actions. Before committing, the all-or-nothing action can be abandoned and one can pretend that it had never been undertaken. After committing, the all-or-nothing action must be able to complete. A committed all-or-nothing action cannot be abandoned; if it can be determined precisely how far its results have propagated, it may be possible to reverse some or all of its effects by compensation. Commitment also usually includes an expectation that the results preserve any appropriate invariants and will be durable to the extent that the application requires those properties. Compare with *compensate* and *abort*. [Ch. 9]

Communication link A data communication path between physically separated components. [Ch. 2]

Compensate (adj.); Compensation (n.) To perform an action that reverses the effect of some previously committed action. Compensation is intrinsically application dependent; it is easier to reverse an incorrect accounting entry than it is to undrill an unwanted hole. [Ch. 9]

Complexity A loosely defined notion that a system has so many components, interconnections, and irregularities that it is difficult to understand, implement, and maintain. [Ch. 1]

Confidentiality Limiting information access to authorized principals. *Secrecy* is a synonym. [Ch. 11]

Confinement Allowing a potentially untrusted program to have access to data, while ensuring that the program cannot release information. [Ch. 11]

Congestion Overload of a resource that persists for significantly longer than the average service time of the resource. (Since significance is in the eye of the beholder, the concept is not a precise one.) [Ch. 7]

Congestion collapse When an increase in offered load causes a catastrophic decrease in useful work accomplished. [Ch. 7]

Connection A communication path that requires maintaining state between successive messages. See *set up* and *tear down*. [Ch. 7]

Connectionless Describes a communication path that does not require coordinated state and can be used without set up or tear down. See *connection*. [Ch. 7]

Consensus Agreement at separated sites on a data value despite communication failures. [Ch. 10]

Consistency A particular constraint on the memory model of a storage system that allows concurrency and uses replicas: that all readers see the same result. Also used in some professional literature as a synonym for *coherence*. [Ch. 10]

Constraint An application-defined invariant on a set of data values or externally visible actions. Example: a requirement that the balances of all the accounts of a bank sum to zero, or a requirement that a majority of the copies of a set of data be identical. [Ch. 10]

Context One of the inputs required by a name-mapping algorithm in order to resolve a name. A common form for a context is a set of name-to-value bindings. [Ch. 2]

Context reference The name of a context. [Ch. 2]

Continuous operation An availability goal, that a system be capable of running indefinitely. The primary requirement of continuous operation is that it must be possible to perform repair and maintenance without stopping the system. [Ch. 8]

Control point An entity that can adjust the capacity of a limited resource or change the load that a source offers. [Ch. 7]

Cooperative scheduling A style of thread scheduling in which each thread on its own initiative releases the processor periodically to allow other threads to run. [Ch. 5]

Covert channel In a flow-control security system, a way of leaking information into or out of a secure area. For example, a program with access to a secret might touch several shared but normally unused virtual memory pages in a pattern to bring them into real memory; a conspirator outside the secure area may be able to detect the pattern by measuring the time required to read those same shared pages. [Ch. 11]

Cryptographic hash function A cryptographic function that maps messages to short values in such a way that it is difficult to (1) reconstruct a message from its hash value; and (2) construct two different messages having the same value. [Ch. 11]

Cryptographic key The easily changeable component of a key-driven cryptographic transformation. A cryptographic key is a string of bits. The bits may be generated randomly, or they may be a transformed version of a password. The cryptographic key, or at least part of it, usually must be kept secret, while all other components of the transformation can be made public. [Ch. 11]

Cryptographic transformation Mathematical transformation used as a building block for implementing security primitives. Such building blocks include functions for implementing encryption and decryption, creating and verifying authentication tags, cryptographic hashes, and pseudorandom number generators. [Ch. 11]

Cryptography A discipline of theoretical computer science that specializes in the study of cryptographic transformations and protocols. [Ch. 11]

Cut-through A forwarding technique in which transmission of a packet or frame on an outgoing link begins while the packet or frame is still being received on the incoming link. [Ch. 7]

Dallying A technique to improve performance by delaying a request on the chance that the operation won't be needed, or to create more opportunities for batching. [Ch. 6]

Dangling reference Use of a name that has outlived the binding of that name. [Ch. 3]

Data integrity Authenticity of the apparent content of a message or file. [Ch. 11] In a network, a transport protocol assurance that the data delivered to the recipient is identical to the original data the sender provided. Compare with *origin authenticity*. [Ch. 7]

Data rate The rate, usually measured in bits per second, at which bits are sent over a communication link. When talking of the data rate of an asynchronous communication link, the term is often used to mean the maximum data rate that the link allows. [Ch. 7]

Deadlock Undesirable interaction among a group of threads in which each thread is waiting for some other thread in the group to make progress. [Ch. 5]

Decay Unintended loss of stored state with the passage of time. [Ch. 2]

Decay set A set of storage blocks, words, tracks, or other physical groupings, in which all members of the set may spontaneously fail together, but independently of any other decay set. [Ch. 8]

Decrypt To perform a reverse cryptographic transformation on a previously encrypted message to obtain the plaintext. Compare with *encrypt*. [Ch. 11]

Default context reference A context reference chosen by the name resolver rather than specified as part of the name or by the object that used the name. Compare with *explicit context reference*. [Ch. 2]

Demand paging A class of page-movement algorithm that moves pages into the primary device only at the instant that they are used. Compare with *prepaging*. [Ch. 6]

Destination The network attachment point to which the payload of a packet is to be delivered. Sometimes used as shorthand for *destination address*. [Ch. 7]

Destination address An identifier of the destination of a packet, usually carried as a field in the header of the packet. [Ch. 7]

Detectable error An error or class of errors for which a reliable detection plan can be devised. An error that is not detectable usually leads to a failure, unless some mechanism that is intended to mask some other error accidentally happens to mask the undetectable error. Compare with *maskable error* and *tolerated error*. [Ch. 8]

Digital signature An authentication tag computed with public-key cryptography. [Ch. 11]

Directory In a file system, an object consisting of a table of bindings between symbolic file names and some description (e.g., a file number or a file map) of the corresponding file. Other terms used for this concept include *catalog* and *folder*. A directory is an example of a context. [Ch. 2]

Discretionary access control A property of an access control system. In a discretionary access control system, the owner of an object has the authority to decide which principals have access to that object. Compare with *non-discretionary access control*. [Ch. 11]

Do action (n.) Term used in some systems for a *redo action*. [Ch. 9]

Domain A range of addresses to which a thread has access. It is the abstraction that enforces modularity within a memory, separating modules and allowing for controlled sharing. [Ch. 5]

Down time A measure of the time that a system was not usable, as a fraction of the time that it was intended to be usable. Compare with its complement, *availability*. [Ch. 8]

Duplex Describes a link or connection between two stations that can be used in both directions. Compare with *simplex*, *half-duplex*, and *full-duplex*. [Ch. 7]

Duplicate suppression A transport protocol mechanism for achieving at-most-once delivery assurance, by identifying and discarding extra copies of packets or messages. [Ch. 7]

Durability A property of a storage medium that, once written, it can be read for as long as the application requires. Compare with *stability* and *persistence*, terms that have different technical definitions as explained in Sidebar 2.1. [Ch. 2]

Durable storage Storage with the property that it (ideally) is decay-free, so it never fails to return on a GET the data that was stored by a previously successful PUT. Since that ideal is impossibly strict, in practice, storage is considered durable when the probability of failure is sufficiently low that the application can tolerate it. Durability is thus an application-defined specification of how long the results of an action, once completed, must be preserved. Durable is distinct from *non-volatile*, which describes storage that maintains its memory while the power is off, but may still have an intolerable probability of decay. The term *persistent* is sometimes used as a synonym for durable, as explained in Sidebar 2.1, but to minimize confusion this text avoids that usage. [Ch. 8]

Dynamic scope An example of a default context, used to resolve names of program variables in some programming languages. The name resolver searches backward in the call stack for a binding, starting with the stack frame of the procedure that used the name, then the stack frame of its caller, then the caller's caller, and so on. Compare with *static scope*. [Ch. 2]

Earliest deadline first scheduling policy A scheduling policy for real-time systems that gives priority to the thread with the earliest deadline. [Ch. 6]

Early drop A predictive strategy for managing an overloaded resource: the system refuses service to some customers before the queue is full. [Ch. 7]

Emergent property A property of an assemblage of components that would not be predicted by examining the components individually. Emergent properties are a surprise when first encountered. [Ch. 1]

Emulation Faithfully simulating some physical hardware so that the simulated hardware can run any software that the physical hardware can. [Ch. 5]

Encrypt To perform a cryptographic transformation on a message with the objective of achieving confidentiality. The cryptographic transformation is usually key-driven. Compare with the inverse operation, *decrypt*, which can recover the original message. [Ch. 11]

End-to-end Describes communication between network attachment points, as contrasted with communication between points within the network or across a single link. [Ch. 7]

End-to-end layer The communication system layer that manages end-to-end communications. [Ch. 7]

Enforced modularity Modularity that prevents accidental errors from propagating from one module to another. Compare with *soft modularity*. [Ch. 4]

Enumerate To generate a list of all the names that can currently be resolved (that is, that have bindings) in a particular context. [Ch. 2]

Environment 1. In a discussion of systems, everything surrounding a system that is not viewed as part of that system. The distinction between a system and its environment is a choice based on the purpose, ease of description, and minimization of interconnections. [Ch. 1] 2. In an interpreter, the state on which the interpreter should perform the actions directed by program instructions. [Ch. 2]

Environment reference The component of an interpreter that tells the interpreter where to find its environment. [Ch. 2]

Erasure An error in a string of bits, bytes, or groups of bits in which an identified bit, byte, or group of bits is missing or has indeterminate value. [Ch. 8]

Ergodic A property of some time-dependent probabilistic processes: that the (usually easier to measure) ensemble average of some parameter measured over a set of elements subject to the process is the same as the time average of that parameter of any single element of the ensemble. [Ch. 8]

Error Informally, a label for an incorrect data value or control signal caused by an active fault. If there is a complete formal specification for the internal design of a module, an error is a violation of some assertion or invariant of the specification. An error in a module is not identical to a failure of that module, but if an error is not masked, it may lead to a failure of the module. [Ch. 8]

Error containment Limiting how far the effects of an error propagate. A module is normally designed to contain errors in such a way that the effects of an error appear in a predictable way at the module's interface. [Ch. 8]

Error correction A scheme to set to the correct value a data value or control signal that is in error. Compare with *error detection*. [Ch. 8]

Error-correction code A method of encoding stored or transmitted data with a modest amount of redundancy, in such a way that any errors during storage or transmission will, with high probability, lead to a decoding that is identical to the original data. See also the general definition of *error correction*. Compare with *error-detection code*. [Ch. 7]

Error detection A scheme to discover that a data value or control signal is in error. Compare with *error correction*. [Ch. 8]

Error-detection code A method of encoding stored or transmitted data with a small amount of redundancy, in such a way that any errors during storage or transmission will, with high probability, lead to a decoding that is obviously wrong. See also the general definition of *error detection*. Compare with *error-correction code* and *checksum*. [Ch. 7]

Ethernet A widely used broadcast network in which all participants share a common wire and can hear one another transmit. Ethernet is characterized by a transmit protocol in which a station wishing to send data first listens to ensure that no one else is sending, and then continues to monitor the network during its own transmission to see if some other station has tried to transmit at the same time, an error known as a *collision*. This protocol is named *Carrier Sense Multiple Access with Collision Detection*, abbreviated CSMA/CD. [Ch. 7]

Eventcount A special type of shared variable used for sequence coordination. It supports two primary operations: AWAIT and ADVANCE. An eventcount is a counter that is incremented atomically, using ADVANCE, while other threads wait for the counter to reach a certain value using AWAIT. Eventcounts are often used in combination with sequencers. [Ch. 5]

Eventual consistency A requirement that at some unspecified time following an update to a collection of data, if there are no more updates, the memory model for that collection will hold. [Ch. 10]

Exactly-once A protocol assurance that the intended operation or message delivery was performed both at-least-once and at-most-once. [Ch. 4]

Exception An interrupt event that pertains to the thread that a processor is currently running. [Ch. 5]

Explicit context reference For a name or an object, an associated reference to the context in which that name, or all names contained in that object, are to be resolved. Compare with *default context reference.* [Ch. 2]

Explicitness A property of a message in a security protocol: if a message is explicit, then the message contains all the information necessary for a receiver to reliably determine that the message is part of a particular run of the protocol with a specific function and set of participants. [Ch. 11]

Exponential backoff An adaptive procedure used to set a timer, for example, to wait for congestion to dissipate. Each time the timer setting proves to be too small, the action doubles (or, more generally, multiplies by a constant greater than one) the length of its next timer setting. The intent is to obtain a suitable timer value as quickly as possible. See also *exponential random backoff*. [Ch. 7]

Exponential random backoff A form of *exponential backoff* in which an action that repeatedly encounters interference repeatedly doubles (or, more generally, multiplies by a constant greater than one) the size of an interval from which it randomly chooses its next delay before retrying. The intent is that by randomly changing the timing relative to other, interfering actions, the interference will not recur. [Ch. 9]

Export In naming, to provide a name for an object that other objects can use. [Ch. 2]

Fail-fast Describes a system or module design that contains detected errors by reporting at its interface that its output may be incorrect. Compare with *fail-stop*. [Ch. 8]

Fail-safe Describes a system design that detects incorrect data values or control signals and forces them to values that, even if not correct, are known to allow the system to continue operating safely. [Ch. 8]

Fail-secure Describes an application of fail-safe design to information protection: a failure is guaranteed not to allow unauthorized access to protected information. In early work on fault tolerance, this term was also occasionally used as a synonym for *fail-fast*. [Ch. 8]

Fail-soft Describes a design in which the system specification allows errors to be masked by degrading performance or disabling some functions in a predictable manner. [Ch. 8]

Fail-stop Describes a system or module design that contains detected errors by stopping the system or module as soon as possible. Compare with *fail-fast*, which does not require other modules to take additional action, such as setting a timer, to detect the failure. [Ch. 8]

Fail-vote Describes an *N*-modular redundancy system with a majority voter. [Ch. 8]

Failure The outcome when a component or system does not produce the intended result at its interface. Compare with *fault*. [Ch. 8]

Failure tolerance A measure of a system's ability to mask active faults and continue operating correctly. A typical measure counts the number of contained components that can fail without causing the system to fail. [Ch. 8]

Fault A defect in materials, design, or implementation that may (or may not) cause an error and lead to a failure. Compare with *failure*. [Ch. 8]

Fault avoidance A strategy to design and implement a component with a probability of faults that is so low that it can be neglected. When applied to software, fault avoidance is sometimes called *valid construction*. [Ch. 8]

Fault tolerance A set of techniques that involve noticing active faults and lower-level subsystem failures and masking them, rather than allowing the resulting errors to propagate. [Ch. 8]

File A popular memory abstraction to durably store and retrieve data. A typical interface for a file consists of procedures to OPEN the file, to READ and WRITE regions of the file, and to CLOSE the file. [Ch. 2]

Fingerprint Another term for a *witness*. [Ch. 10]

First-come, first-served (FCFS) scheduling policy A scheduling policy in which requests are processed in the order in which they arrive. [Ch. 6]

First-in, first-out (FIFO) policy A particular page-removal policy for a multilevel memory system. FIFO chooses to remove the page that has been in the primary device the longest. [Ch. 6]

Flow control 1. In networks, an end-to-end protocol between a fast sender and a slow recipient, a mechanism that limits the sender's data rate so that the recipient does not receive data faster than it can handle. [Ch. 7] 2. In security, a system that allows untrusted programs to work with sensitive data but confines all program outputs to prevent unauthorized disclosure. [Ch. 11]

Force (v.) When output may be buffered, to ensure that a previous output value has actually been written to durable storage or sent as a message. Caches that are not write-through usually have a feature that allows the invoker to force some or all of their contents to the secondary storage medium. [Ch. 9]

Forward error correction A technique for controlling errors in which enough redundancy to correct anticipated errors is applied before an error occurs. Forward error correction is particularly applicable when the original source of the data value or control signal will not be available to recalculate or resend it. Compare with *backward error correction*. [Ch. 8]

Forward secrecy A property of a security protocol. A protocol has forward secrecy if information, such as an encryption key, deduced from a previous transcript, doesn't allow an adversary to decrypt future messages. [Ch. 11]

Forwarding table A table that tells the network layer which link to use to forward a packet, based on its destination address. [Ch. 7]

Fragment 1. (v.) In network protocols, to divide the payload of a packet so that it can fit into smaller packets for carriage across a link with a small maximum transmission unit. 2. (n.) The resulting pieces of payload. [Ch. 7]

Frame 1. (n.) The unit of transmission in the link layer. Compare with *packet, segment,* and *message*. 2. (v.) To delimit the beginning and end of a bit, byte, frame (n.), packet, segment, or message within a stream. [Ch. 7]

Freshness A property of a message in a security protocol: if the message is fresh, it is assured not to be a replay. [Ch. 11]

Full-duplex Describes a duplex link or connection between two stations that can be used in both directions at the same time. Compare with *simplex*, *duplex*, and *half-duplex*. [Ch. 7]

Gate A predefined protected entry point into a domain. [Ch. 5]

Generated name A name created algorithmically, rather than chosen by a person. [Ch. 3]

Global name In a layered naming scheme, a name that is bound only in the outermost context layer and thus has the same meaning to all users. [Ch. 2]

Half-duplex Describes a duplex link or connection between two stations that can be used in only one direction at a time. Compare with *simplex*, *duplex*, and *full-duplex*. [Ch. 7]

Hamming distance In an encoding system, the number of bits in an element of a code that would have to change to transform it into a different element of the code. The Hamming distance of a code is the minimum Hamming distance between any pair of elements of the code. [Ch. 8]

Hard real-time scheduling policy A real-time scheduler in which missing a deadline may result in a disaster. [Ch. 6]

Hash function A function that algorithmically derives a relatively short, fixed-length string of bits from an arbitrarily large block of data. The resulting short string is known as a *hash*. See also *cryptographic hash function*. [Ch. 3]

Header Information that a protocol layer adds to the front of a packet. [Ch. 7]

Hierarchical routing A routing system that takes advantage of hierarchically assigned network destination addresses to reduce the size of its routing tables. [Ch. 7]

Hierarchy A technique of organizing systems that contain many components: group small numbers of components into self-contained and stable subsystems that then become components of larger self-contained and stable subsystems, and so on. [Ch. 1]

Hit ratio In a multilevel memory, the fraction of references satisfied by the primary memory device. [Ch. 6]

Hop limit A network-layer protocol field that acts as a safety net to prevent packets from endlessly circulating in a network that has inconsistent forwarding tables. [Ch. 7]

Hot swap To replace modules in a system while the system continues to provide service. [Ch. 8]

Idempotent Describes an action that can be interrupted and restarted from the beginning any number of times and still produce the same result as if the action had run to completion without interruption. The essential feature of an idempotent action is that if there is any question about whether or not it completed, it is safe to do it again. "Idempotent" is correctly pronounced with the accent on the second syllable, not on the first and third. [Ch. 4]

Identifier A synonym for *name*, sometimes used to avoid an implication that the name might be meaningful to a person rather than to a machine. [Ch. 3]

Illegal instruction An instruction that an interpreter is not equipped to execute because it is not in the interpreter's instruction repertoire or it has an out-of-range operand (for example, an attempt to divide by zero). An illegal instruction typically causes an interrupt. [Ch. 2]

Incommensurate scaling A property of most systems, that as the system grows (or shrinks) in size, not all parts grow (or shrink) at the same rate, thus stressing the system design. [Ch. 1]

Incremental backup A backup copy that contains only data that has changed since making the previous backup copy. [Ch. 10]

Indirect name A name that is bound to another name in the same name space. "Symbolic link", "soft link", and "shortcut" are other words used for this concept. Some operating systems also define the term *alias* to have this meaning rather than its more general meaning of synonym. [Ch. 2]

Indirection Decoupling a connection from one object to another by interposing a name with the goal of delaying the choice of (or allowing a later change about) which object the name refers to. Indirection makes it possible to delay the choice of or change which object is used without the need to change the object that uses it. Using a name is sometimes described as "inserting a level of indirection". [Ch. 1]

Install In a system that uses logs to achieve all-or-nothing atomicity, to write data to cell storage. [Ch. 9]

Instruction reference A characteristic component of an interpreter: the place from which it will take its next instruction. [Ch. 2]

Intended load The amount of a shared resource that a set of users would attempt to utilize if the resource had unlimited capacity. In systems that have no provision for congestion control, the intended load is equal to the offered load. The goal of congestion control is to make the offered load smaller than the intended load. Compare with *offered load*. [Ch. 7]

Interleaving A technique to improve performance by distributing apparently sequential requests to several instances of a device, so that the requests may actually be processed concurrently. [Ch. 6]

Intermittent fault A persistent fault that is active only occasionally. Compare with *transient fault*. [Ch. 8]

International Organization for Standardization (ISO) An international non-governmental body that sets many technical and manufacturing standards, including the (frequently ignored) Open Systems Interconnect (OSI) reference model for data communication networks. The short name ISO is not an acronym; it is the Greek word for "equal", chosen to be the same in all languages and always spelled in all capital letters. [Ch. 7]

Interpreter The abstraction that models the active mechanism performing computations. An interpreter comprises three components: an instruction reference, a context reference, and an instruction repertoire. [Ch. 2]

Interrupt An event that causes an interpreter to transfer control to the first instruction of a different procedure, an interrupt handler, instead of executing the next instruction. [Ch. 2]

Invalidate In a cache, to mark "do not use" or completely remove a cache entry because some event has occurred that may make the value associated with that entry incorrect. [Ch. 10]

Isochronous (From Greek roots meaning "equal" and "time") Describes a communication link over which data is sent in frames whose length is fixed in advance and whose timing relative to other frames is precisely predictable. Compare with *asynchronous*. [Ch. 7]

Jitter In real-time applications, variability in the delivery times of successive data elements. [Ch. 7]

Job The unit of granularity on which threads are scheduled. A job corresponds to the burst of activity of a thread between two idle periods. [Ch. 6]

Journal storage Storage in which a WRITE or PUT appends a new value, rather than overwriting a previously stored value. Compare with *cell storage*. [Ch. 9]

Kernel A trusted intermediary that virtualizes resources for mutually distrustful modules running on the same computer. Kernel modules typically run with kernel mode enabled. [Ch. 5]

Kernel mode A feature of a processor that, when set, allows threads to use special processor features (e.g., the page-map address register) that are disallowed to threads that run with kernel mode disabled. Compare with *user mode*. [Ch. 5]

Key-based cryptographic transformation A cryptographic transformation for which successfully meeting the cryptographic goals depends on the secrecy of some component of the transformation. That component is called a cryptographic key, and a usual design is to make that key a small, modular, separable, and easily changeable component. [Ch. 11]

Key distribution center (KDC) A principal that authenticates other principals to one another and also provides one or more temporary cryptographic keys for communication between other principals. [Ch. 11]

Latency The delay between a change at the input to a system and the corresponding change at its output. [Ch. 2] As used in reliability, the time between when a fault becomes active and when the module in which the fault occurred either fails or detects the resulting error. [Ch. 8]

Latent fault A fault that is not currently causing an error. Compare with *active fault*. [Ch. 8]

Layering A technique of organizing systems in which the designer builds on an interface that is already complete (a lower layer) to create a different complete interface (an upper layer). [Ch. 1]

Least-recently-used (LRU) Policy A popular page-removal policy for a multilevel memory system. LRU chooses to remove the page that has not been used the longest. [Ch. 6]

Lexical scope Another term for *static scope*. [Ch. 2]

Limited name space A name space in which a limited number of names can be expressed and therefore names must be allocated, deallocated, and reused. [Ch. 3]

Link 1. (n.) Another term for a *synonym* (usually called a hard link) or an *indirect name* (usually called a soft or symbolic link). 2. (v.) Another term for *bind*. [Ch. 2]. 3. (n.) In data communication, a communication path between two points. [Ch. 7]

Link layer The communication system layer that moves data directly from one physical point to another. [Ch. 7]

List system A design for an access control system in which each protected object is associated with a list of authorized principals. [Ch. 11]

Livelock An undesirable interaction among a group of threads in which each thread begins a sequence of actions, discovers that it cannot complete the sequence because actions of other threads have interfered, and begins again, endlessly. [Ch. 5]

Locality of reference A property of most programs that memory references tend to be clustered in both time and address space. [Ch. 6]

Lock A flag associated with a data object, set by a thread to warn concurrent threads that the object is in use and that it may be a mistake for other threads to read or write it. Locks are one technique used to achieve before-or-after atomicity. [Ch. 5]

Lock point In a system that provides before-or-after atomicity by locking, the first instant in a before-or-after action when every lock that will ever be in its lock set has been acquired. [Ch. 9]

Lock set The collection of all locks acquired during the execution of a before-or-after action. [Ch. 9]

Lock-step protocol In networking, any transport protocol that requires acknowledgment of the previously sent message, segment, packet, or frame before sending another message, segment, packet, or frame to the same destination. Sometimes called a *stop and wait* protocol. Compare with *pipeline*. [Ch. 7]

Log 1. (n.) A specialized use of journal storage to maintain an append-only record of some application activity. Logs are used to implement all-or-nothing actions, for performance enhancement, for archiving, and for reconciliation. 2. (v.) To append a record to a log. [Ch. 9]

Logical copy A replica that is organized in a form determined by a higher layer. An example is a replica of a file system that is made by copying one file at a time. Analogous to logical locking. Compare with *physical copy*. [Ch. 10]

Logical locking Locking of higher-layer data objects such as records or fields of a database. Compare with *physical locking*. [Ch. 9]

Manchester code A particular type of phase encoding in which each bit is represented by two bits of opposite value. [Ch. 7]

Margin The amount by which a specification is better than necessary for correct operation. The purpose of designing with margins is to mask some errors. [Ch. 8]

Mark point 1. (adj.) An atomicity-assuring discipline in which each newly created action n must wait to begin reading shared data objects until action $(n - 1)$ has marked all of the variables it intends to modify. 2. (n.) The instant at which an action has marked all of the variables it intends to modify. [Ch. 9]

Marshal/unmarshal To marshal is to transform the internal representation of one or more pieces of data into a form that is more suitable for transmission or storage. The opposite action, to unmarshal, is to parse marshaled data into its constituent data pieces and transform those pieces into a suitable internal representation. [Ch. 4]

Maskable error An error or class of errors that is detectable and for which a systematic recovery strategy can in principle be devised. Compare with *detectable error* and *tolerated error*. [Ch. 8]

Masking As used in reliability, containing an error within a module in such a way that the module meets its specifications as if the error had not occurred. [Ch. 8]

Master In a multiple-site replication scheme, the site to which updates are directed. Compare with *slave*. [Ch. 10]

Maximum transmission unit (MTU) A limit on the size of a packet, imposed to control the time commitment involved in transmitting the packet, to control the amount of loss if congestion causes the packet to be discarded, and to keep low the probability of a transmission error. [Ch. 7]

Mean time between failures (MTBF) The sum of MTTF and MTTR for the same component or system. [Ch. 8]

Mean time to failure (MTTF) The expected time that a component or system will operate continuously without failing. "Time" is sometimes measured in cycles of operation. [Ch. 8]

Mean time to repair (MTTR) The expected time to replace or repair a component or system that has failed. The term is sometimes written as "mean time to restore service", but it is still abbreviated MTTR. [Ch. 8]

Mediation Before a service performs a requested operation, determining which principal is associated with the request and whether the principal is authorized to request the operation. [Ch. 11]

Memory The abstraction for remembering data values, using READ and WRITE operations. The WRITE operation specifies a value to be remembered and a name by which that value can be recalled in the future. See also *storage*. [Ch. 2]

Memoryless A property of some time-dependent probabilistic processes, that the probability of what happens next does not depend on what has happened before. [Ch. 8]

Memory manager A device located between a processor and memory that translates virtual to physical addresses and checks that memory references by the thread running on the processor are in the thread's domain(s). [Ch. 5]

Memory-mapped I/O An interface that allows an interpreter to communicate with an I/O module using LOAD and STORE instructions that have ordinary memory addresses. [Ch. 2]

Message The unit of communication at the application level. The length of a message is determined by the application that sends it. Since a network may have a maximum size for its unit of transmission, the end-to-end layer divides a message into one or more segments, each of which is carried in a separate packet. Compare with *frame* (n.), *segment*, and *packet*. [Ch. 7]

Message authentication The verification of the integrity of the origin and the data of a message. [Ch. 11]

Message authentication code (MAC) An authentication tag computed with shared-secret cryptography. MAC is sometimes used as a verb in security jargon, as in "Just to be careful, let's MAC the address field of that message." [Ch. 11]

Metadata Information about an object that is not part of the object itself. Examples are the name of the object, the identity of its owner, the date it was last modified, and the location in which it is stored. [Ch. 3]

Microkernel A kernel organization in which most operating system components run in separate, user-mode address spaces. [Ch. 5]

Mirror (n.) One of a set of replicas that is created or updated synchronously. Compare with *primary copy* and *backup copy*. Sometimes used as a verb, as in "Let's mirror that data by making three replicas." [Ch. 8]

Missing-page exception The event when an addressed page is not present in the primary device and the virtual memory manager has to move the page in from a secondary device. The literature also uses the term *page fault*. [Ch. 6]

Modular sharing Sharing of an object without the need to know details of the implementation of the shared object. With respect to naming, modular sharing is sharing without the need to know the names that the shared object uses to refer to its components. [Ch. 3]

Module A system component that can be separately designed, implemented, managed, and replaced. [Ch. 1]

Monolithic kernel A kernel organization in which most operating system procedures run in a single, kernel-mode address space. [Ch. 5]

Most-recently-used (MRU) policy A page-removal policy for a multilevel memory system. MRU chooses for removal the most recently used page in the primary device. [Ch. 6]

MTU discovery A procedure that systematically discovers the smallest maximum transmission unit along the path between two network attachment points. [Ch. 7]

Multihomed Describes a single physical interface between the network layer and the end-to-end layer that is associated with more than one network attachment point, each with its own network-layer address. [Ch. 7]

Multilevel memory Memory built out of two or more different memory devices that have significantly different latencies and cost per bit. [Ch. 6]

Multiple lookup A name-mapping algorithm that tries several contexts in sequence, looking for the first one that can successfully resolve a presented name. [Ch. 2]

Multiplexing Sharing a communication link among several, usually independent, simultaneous communications. The term is also used in layered protocol design when several different higher-layer protocols share the same lower-layer protocol. [Ch. 7]

Multipoint Describes communication that involves more than two parties. A multipoint link is a single physical medium that connects several parties. A multipoint protocol coordinates the activities of three or more participants. [Ch. 7]

$N + 1$ redundancy When a load can be handled by sharing it among N equivalent modules, the technique of installing $N + 1$ or more of the modules, so that if one fails the remaining modules can continue to handle the full load while the one that failed is being repaired. [Ch. 8]

N-modular redundancy (NMR) A redundancy technique that involves supplying identical inputs to N equivalent modules and connecting the outputs to one or more voters. [Ch. 8]

N-version programming The software version of N-modular redundancy. N different teams each independently write a program from its specifications. The programs then run in parallel, and voters compare their outputs. [Ch. 8]

Name A designator or an identifier of an object or value. A name is an element of a name space. [Ch. 2]

Name conflict An occurrence when, for some reason, it seems necessary to bind the same name to two different values at the same time in the same context. Usually, a result of encountering a preexisting name in a naming scheme that does not provide modular sharing. When names are algorithmically generated, name conflicts are called *collisions*. [Ch. 3]

Name-mapping algorithm See *naming scheme.* [Ch. 2]

Name space The set of all possible names of a particular naming scheme. A name space is defined by a set of symbols from some alphabet together with a set of syntax rules that define which names are members of the name space. [Ch. 2]

Name-to-key binding A binding between a principal identifier and a cryptographic key. [Ch. 11]

Naming hierarchy A naming network that is constrained to a tree-structured form. The root used for interpretation of absolute path names (which in a naming hierarchy are sometimes called "tree names") is normally the base of the tree. [Ch. 2]

Naming network A naming scheme in which contexts are named objects and any context may contain a binding for any other context, as well as for any non-context object. An object in a naming network is identified by a multicomponent path name that traces a path through the naming network from some starting point, which may be either a default context or a root. [Ch. 2]

Naming scheme A particular combination of a name space, a universe of values (which may include physical objects) that can be named, and a name-mapping algorithm that provides a partial mapping from the name space to the universe of values. [Ch. 2]

Negative acknowledgment (NAK or NACK) A status report from a recipient to a sender asserting that some previous communication was not received or was received incorrectly. The usual reason for sending a negative acknowledgment is to avoid the delay that would be incurred by waiting for a timer to expire. Compare with *acknowledgment*. [Ch. 7]

Network A communication system that interconnects more than two things. [Ch. 7]

Network address In a network, the identifier of the source or destination of a packet. [Ch. 7]

Network attachment point The place at which the network layer accepts or delivers payload data to and from the end-to-end layer. Each network attachment point has an identifier, its *address*, that is unique within that network. A network attachment point is sometimes called an *access point*, and in ISO terminology, a *Network Services Access Point* (NSAP). [Ch. 7]

Network layer The communication system layer that forwards data through intermediate links to carry it to its intended destination. [Ch. 7]

Non-discretionary access control A property of an access control system. In a non-discretionary access control system, some principal other than the owner has the authority to decide which principals have to access the object. Compare with *discretionary access control*. [Ch. 11]

Non-preemptive scheduling A scheduling policy in which threads run until they explicitly yield or wait. [Ch. 5]

Non-volatile memory A kind of memory that does not require a continuous source of power, so it retains its content when its power supply is off. The phrase "stable storage" is a common synonym. Compare with *volatile memory*. [Ch. 2]

Nonce A unique identifier that should never be reused. [Ch. 7]

Object As used in naming, any software or hardware structure that can have a distinct name. [Ch. 2]

Offered load The amount of a shared service that a set of users attempt to utilize. *Presented load* is an occasionally encountered synonym. [Ch. 6]

Opaque name In a modular system, a name that, from the point of view of the current module, carries no overloading that the module knows how to interpret. [Ch. 3]

Operating system A collection of programs that provide services such as abstraction and management of hardware devices and features such as libraries of commonly needed procedures, all of which are intended to make it easier to write application programs. [Ch. 2]

Optimal (OPT) page-removal policy An unrealizable page-removal policy for a multilevel memory system. The optimal policy removes from primary memory the page that will not be used for the longest time. Because identifying that page requires knowing the future, the optimal policy is not implementable in practice. Its utility is that after any particular reference string has been observed, one can then simulate the operation of that reference string with the optimal policy, to compare the number of missing-page exceptions with the number obtained when using other, realizable policies. [Ch. 6]

Optimistic concurrency control A concurrency control scheme that allows concurrent threads to proceed even though a risk exists that they will interfere with each other, with the plan of detecting whether there actually is interference and, if necessary, forcing one of the threads to abort and retry. Optimistic concurrency control is an effective technique in situations where interference is possible but not likely. Compare with *pessimistic concurrency control*. [Ch. 9]

Origin authenticity Authenticity of the claimed origin of a message. Compare with *data integrity*. [Ch. 11]

Overload When offered load exceeds the capacity of a service for a specified period of time. [Ch. 6]

Overloaded name A name that does more than simply identify an object; it also carries other information, such as the type of the object, the date it was modified, or how to locate it. Overloading is commonly encountered when a system has not made suitable provision to handle metadata. Contrast with *pure name*. [Ch. 3]

Packet The unit of transmission of the network layer. A packet consists of a segment of payload data, accompanied by guidance information that allows the network to forward it to the network attachment point that is intended to receive the data carried in the packet. Compare with *frame* (n.), *segment,* and *message*. [Ch. 7]

Packet forwarding In the network layer, upon receiving a packet that is not destined for the local end layer, to send it out again along some link with the intention of moving the packet closer to its destination. [Ch. 7]

Packet switch A specialized computer that forwards packets in a data communication network. Sometimes called a *packet forwarder* or, if it also implements an adaptive routing algorithm, a *router*. [Ch. 7]

Page In a page-based virtual memory system, the unit of translation between virtual addresses and physical addresses. [Ch. 5]

Page fault See *missing-page exception*.

Page map Data structure employed by the virtual memory manager to map virtual addresses to physical addresses. [Ch. 5]

Page-map address register A processor register maintained by the thread manager. It contains a pointer to the page map used by the currently active thread, and it can be changed only when the processor is in kernel mode. [Ch. 5]

Page-removal policy A policy for deciding which page to move from the primary to the secondary device to make a space to bring in a new page. [Ch. 6]

Page table A particular form of a page map, in which the map is organized as an array indexed by page number. [Ch. 5]

Pair-and-compare A method for constructing fail-fast modules from modules that do not have that property, by connecting the inputs of two replicas of the module together and connecting their outputs to a comparator. When one repairs a failed pair-and-compare module by replacing the entire two-replica module with a spare, rather than identifying and replacing the replica that failed, the method is called *pair-and-spare*. [Ch. 8]

Pair-and-spare See *pair-and-compare*.

Parallel transmission A scheme for increasing the data rate between two modules by sending data over several parallel lines that are coordinated by the same clock. [Ch. 7]

Partition To divide a job up and assign it to different physical devices, with the intent that a failure of one device does not prevent the entire job from being done. [Ch. 8]

Password A secret character string used to authenticate the claimed identity of an individual. [Ch. 11]

Path name A name with internal structure that traces a path through a naming network. Any prefix of a path name can be thought of as the explicit context reference to use for resolution of the remainder of the path name. See also *absolute path name* and *relative path name*. [Ch. 2]

Path selection In a network-layer routing protocol, when a participant updates its own routing information with new information learned from an exchange with its neighbors. [Ch. 7]

Payload In a layered description of a communication system, the data that a higher layer has asked a lower layer to send; used to distinguish that data from the headers and trailers that the lower layer adds. (This term seems to have been borrowed from the transportation industry, where it is used frequently in aerospace applications.) [Ch. 7]

Pending A state of an all-or-nothing action, when that action has not yet either committed or aborted. Also used to describe the value of a variable that was set or changed by a still-pending all-or-nothing action. [Ch. 9]

Persistence A property of an active agent such as an interpreter that, when it detects it has failed, it keeps trying until it succeeds. Compare with *stability* and *durability*, terms that have different technical definitions as explained in Sidebar 2.1. The adjective "persistent" is used in some contexts as a synonym for stable and sometimes also in the sense of immutable. [Ch. 2]

Persistent fault A fault that cannot be masked by retry. Compare with *transient fault* and *intermittent fault*. [Ch. 8]

Persistent sender A transport protocol participant that, by sending the same message repeatedly, tries to ensure that at least one copy of the message gets delivered. [Ch. 7]

Pessimistic concurrency control A concurrency control scheme that forces a thread to wait if there is any chance that by proceeding it may interfere with another, concurrent, thread. Pessimistic concurrency control is an effective technique in situations where interference between concurrent threads has a high probability. Compare with *optimistic concurrency control*. [Ch. 9]

Phase encoding A method of encoding data for digital transmission in which at least one level transition is associated with each transmitted bit, to simplify framing and recovery of the sender's clock. [Ch. 7]

Physical address An address that is translated geometrically to read or write data stored on a device. Compare with *virtual address*. [Ch. 5]

Physical copy A replica that is organized in a form determined by a lower layer. An example is a replica of a disk that is made by copying it sector by sector. Analogous to *physical locking*. Compare with *logical copy*. [Ch. 10]

Physical locking Locking of lower-layer data objects, typically chunks of data whose extent is determined by the physical layout of a storage medium. Examples of such chunks are disk sectors or even an entire disk. Compare with *logical locking*. [Ch. 9]

Piggybacking In an end-to-end protocol, a technique for reducing the number of packets sent back and forth by including acknowledgments and other protocol state information in the header of the next packet that goes to the other end. [Ch. 7]

Pipeline In networking, a transport protocol design that allows sending a packet before receiving an acknowledgment of the packet previously sent to the same destination. Contrast with *lock-step protocol.* [Ch. 7]

Plaintext The result of decryption. Also sometimes used to describe data that has not been encrypted, as in "The mistake was sending that message as plaintext." Compare with *ciphertext*. [Ch. 11]

Point-to-point Describes a communication link between two stations, as contrasted with a broadcast or multipoint link. [Ch. 7]

Polling A style of interaction between threads or between a processor and a device in which one periodically checks whether the other needs attention. [Ch. 5]

Port In an end-to-end transport protocol, the multiplexing identifier that tells which of several end-to-end applications or application instances should receive the payload. [Ch. 7]

Preemptive scheduling A scheduling policy in which a thread manager can interrupt and reschedule a running thread at any time. [Ch. 5]

Prepaging An optimization for a multilevel memory manager in which the manager predicts which pages might be needed and brings them into the primary memory before the application demands them. Compare with *demand algorithm*. [Ch. 6]

Prepared In a layered or multiple-site all-or-nothing action, a state of a component action that has announced that it can, on command, either commit or abort. Having reached this state, it awaits a decision from the higher-layer coordinator of the action. [Ch. 9]

Presentation protocol A protocol that translates semantics and data of the network to match those of the local programming environment. [Ch. 7]

Presented load See *offered load*.

Preventive maintenance Active intervention intended to increase the mean time to failure of a module or system and thus improve its reliability and availability. [Ch. 8]

Primary copy Of a set of replicas that are not written or updated synchronously, the one that is considered authoritative and, usually, written or updated first. Compare with *mirror* and *backup copy*. [Ch. 10]

Primary device In a multilevel memory system, the memory device that is faster and usually more expensive and thus smaller. Compare with *secondary device*. [Ch. 6]

Principal The representation inside a computer system of an agent (a person, a computer, a thread) that makes requests to the security system. A principal is the entity in a computer system to which authorizations are granted; thus, it is the unit of accountability and responsibility in a computer system. [Ch. 11]

Priority scheduling policy A scheduling policy in which some jobs have priority over other jobs. [Ch. 6]

Privacy A socially defined ability of an individual (or organization) to determine if, when, and to whom personal (or organizational) information is to be released and also what limitations should apply to use of released information. [Ch. 11]

Private key In public-key cryptography, the cryptographic key that must be kept secret. Compare with *public key*. [Ch. 11]

Processing delay In a communication network, that component of the overall delay contributed by computation that takes place in various protocol layers. [Ch. 7]

Program counter A processor register that holds the reference to the current or next instruction that the processor is to execute. [Ch. 2]

Progress A desirable guarantee provided by an atomicity-assuring mechanism: that, despite potential interference from concurrency, some useful work will be done. An example of such a guarantee is that the atomicity-assuring mechanism will not abort at least one member of the set of concurrent actions. In practice, lack of a progress guarantee can sometimes be repaired by using exponential random backoff. In formal analysis of systems, progress is one component of a property known as "liveness". Progress is an assurance that the system will move toward some specified goal, whereas liveness is an assurance that the system will eventually reach that goal. [Ch. 9]

Propagation delay In a communication network, the component of overall delay contributed by the velocity of propagation of the physical medium used for communication. [Ch. 7]

Propagation of effects A property of most systems: a change in one part of the system causes effects in areas of the system that are far removed from the changed part. A good system design tends to minimize propagation of effects. [Ch. 1]

Protection 1. Synonym for *security*. 2. Sometimes used in a narrower sense to denote mechanisms and techniques that control the access of executing programs to information. [Ch. 11]

Protection group A principal that is shared by more than one user. [Ch. 11]

Protocol An agreement between two communicating parties, for example, on the messages and the format of data that they intend to exchange. [Ch. 7]

Public key In public-key cryptography, the key that can be published (i.e., the one that doesn't have to be kept secret). Compare with *private key*. [Ch. 11]

Public-key cryptography A key-based cryptographic transformation that can provide both confidentiality and authenticity of messages without the need to share a secret between sender and recipient. Public-key systems use two cryptographic keys, one of which must be kept secret, but does not need to be shared. [Ch. 11]

Publish/subscribe A communication style using a trusted intermediary. Clients push or pull messages to or from an intermediary. The intermediary determines who actually receives a message and if a message should be fanned out to multiple recipients. [Ch. 4]

Pure name A name that is not overloaded in any way. The only operations that apply to a pure name are COMPARE, RESOLVE, BIND, and UNBIND. Contrast with *overloaded name*. [Ch. 3]

Purging A technique used in some N-modular redundancy designs, in which the voter ignores the output of any replica that, at some time in the past, disagreed with several others. [Ch. 8]

Qualified name A name that includes an explicit context reference. [Ch. 2]

Quench (n.) An administrative message sent by a packet forwarder to another forwarder or to an end-to-end-layer sender asking that the forwarder or sender stop sending data or reduce its rate of sending data. [Ch. 7]

Queuing delay In a communication network, the component of overall delay that is caused by waiting for a resource such as a link to become available. [Ch. 7]

Quorum A partial set of replicas intended to improve availability. One defines a read quorum and a write quorum that intersect, with the goal that for correctness it is sufficient to read from a read quorum and write to a write quorum. [Ch. 10]

Race condition A timing-dependent error in thread coordination that may result in threads computing incorrect results (for example, multiple threads simultaneously try to update a shared variable that they should have updated one at a time). [Ch. 5]

RAID An acronym for Redundant Array of Independent (or Inexpensive) Disks, a set of techniques that use a controller and multiple disk drives configured to improve some combination of storage performance or durability. A RAID system usually has an interface that is electrically and programmatically identical to a single disk, thus allowing it to transparently replace a single disk. [Ch. 2]

Random access memory A memory device for which the latency for memory cells chosen at random is approximately the same as the latency obtained by choosing cells in the pattern best suited for that memory device. [Ch. 2]

Random drop A strategy for managing an overloaded resource: the system refuses service to a queue member chosen at random. [Ch. 7]

Random early detection (RED) A combination of random drop and early drop. [Ch. 7]

Rate monotonic scheduling policy A policy that schedules periodic jobs for a real-time system. Each job receives in advance a priority that is proportional to the frequency of the occurrence of that job. The scheduler always runs the highest priority job, preempting a running job, if necessary. [Ch. 6]

Read and set memory (RSM) A hardware or software function used primarily for implementing locks. RSM loads a value from a memory location into a register and stores another value in the same memory location. The important property of RSM is that no other loads and stores by concurrent threads can come between the load and the store of an RSM. RSM is nearly always implemented as a hardware instruction. [Ch. 5]

Read/write coherence A property of a memory, that a READ always returns the result of the most recent WRITE. [Ch. 2]

Ready/acknowledge protocol A data transmission protocol in which each transmission is framed by a ready signal from the sender and an acknowledge signal from the receiver. [Ch. 7]

Real time 1. (adj.) Describes a system that requires delivery of results before some deadline. 2. (n.) The wall-clock sequence that an all-seeing observer would associate with a series of actions. [Ch. 6]

Real-time scheduling policy A scheduler that attempts to schedule jobs in such a way that all jobs complete before their deadlines. [Ch. 6]

Reassembly Reconstructing a message by arranging, in correct order, the segments it was divided into for transmission. [Ch. 7]

Reconciliation A procedure that compares replicas that are intended to be identical and repairs any differences. [Ch. 10]

Recursive name resolution A method of resolving path names. The least significant component of the path name is looked up in the context named by the remainder of the path name, which must thus be resolved first. [Ch. 2]

Redo action An application-specified action that, when executed during failure recovery, produces the effect of some committed component action whose effect may have been lost in the failure. (Some systems call this a "do action". Compare with *undo action.*) [Ch. 9]

Redundancy Extra information added to detect or correct errors in data or control signals. [Ch. 8]

Reference (n.) Use of a name by an object to refer to another object. In grammatical English, the corresponding verb is "to refer to". In computer jargon, the non-standard verb "to reference" appears frequently, and the coined verb "dereference" is a synonym for *resolve*. [Ch. 2]

Reference string The string of addresses issued by a thread during its execution (typically, the string of the virtual addresses issued by a thread's execution of LOAD and STORE instructions; it may also include the addresses of the instructions themselves). [Ch. 6]

Relative path name A path name that the name resolver resolves in a default context provided by the environment. [Ch. 2]

Reliability A statistical measure, the probability that a system is still operating at time t, given that it was operating at some earlier time t_0. [Ch. 8]

Reliable delivery A transport protocol assurance: it provides both at-least-once delivery and data integrity. [Ch. 7]

Remote procedure call (RPC) A stylized form of client/service interaction in which each request is followed by a response. Usually, remote procedure call systems also provide marshaling and unmarshaling of the request and the response data. The word "procedure" in "remote procedure call" is misleading, since RPC semantics are different from those of an ordinary procedure call: for example, RPC specifically allows for clients and the service to fail independently. [Ch. 4]

Repair An active intervention to fix or replace a module that has been identified as failing, preferably before the system of which it is a part fails. [Ch. 8]

Repertoire The set of operations or actions an interpreter is prepared to perform. The repertoire of a general-purpose processor is its instruction set. [Ch. 2]

Replica 1. One of several identical modules that, when presented with the same inputs, is expected to produce the same output. 2. One of several identical copies of a set of data. [Ch. 8]

Replicated state machine A method of performing an update to a set of replicas that involves sending the update request to each replica and performing it independently at each replica. [Ch. 10]

Replication The technique of using multiple replicas to achieve fault tolerance. [Ch. 8]

Repudiate To disown an apparently authenticated message. [Ch. 11]

Request The message sent from a client to a service. [Ch. 4]

Resolve To perform a name-mapping algorithm from a name to the corresponding value. [Ch. 2]

Response The message sent from a service to a client in response to a previous request. [Ch. 4]

Roll-forward recovery A write-ahead log protocol with the additional requirement that the application log its outcome record *before* it performs any install actions. If there is a failure before the all-or-nothing action passes its commit point, the recovery procedure does not need to undo anything; if there is a failure after commit, the recovery procedure can use the log record to ensure that cell storage installs are not lost. Also known as *redo logging*. Compare with *rollback recovery*. [Ch. 9]

Rollback recovery Also known as *undo logging*. A write-ahead log protocol with the additional requirement that the application perform all install actions *before* logging an outcome record. If there is a failure before the all-or-nothing action commits, a recovery procedure can use the log record to undo the partially completed all-or-nothing action. Compare with *roll-forward recovery*. [Ch. 9]

Root The context used for the interpretation of absolute path names. The name for the root is usually bound to a constant value (typically, a well-known name of a lower layer), and that binding is normally built in to the name resolver at design time. [Ch. 2]

Round-robin scheduling A preemptive scheduling policy in which a thread runs for some maximum time before the next one is scheduled. When all threads have run, the scheduler starts again with the first thread. [Ch. 6]

Round-trip time In a network, the time between sending a packet and receiving the corresponding response or acknowledgment. Round-trip time comprises two (possibly different) network transit times and the time required for the correspondent to process the packet and prepare a response. [Ch. 7]

Router A packet forwarder that also participates in a routing algorithm. [Ch. 7]

Routing algorithm An algorithm intended to construct consistent, efficient forwarding tables. A routing algorithm can be either *centralized*, which means that one node calculates the forwarding tables for the entire network, or *decentralized*, which means that many participants perform the algorithm concurrently. [Ch. 7]

Scheduler The part of the thread manager that implements the policy for deciding which thread to run. Policies can be preemptive or non-preemptive. [Ch. 5]

Scope In a layered naming scheme, the set of contexts in which a particular name is bound to the same value. [Ch. 2]

Search As used in naming, a synonym for *multiple lookup*. This usage of the term is a highly constrained form of the more general definition of search as used in information retrieval and full-text search systems: to locate all instances of records that match a given query. [Ch. 2]

Search path A default context reference that consists of the identifiers of the contexts to be used in a multiple lookup name resolution. The word "path" as used here has no connection with its use in *path name*, and the word "search" has only a distant connection with the concept of key word search. [Ch. 2]

Secondary device In a multilevel memory system, the memory device that is larger but also usually slower. Compare with *primary device*. [Ch. 6]

Secrecy Synonym for *confidentiality*. [Ch. 11]

Secure area A physical space or a virtual address space in which confidential information can be safely confined. [Ch. 11]

Secure channel A communication channel that can safely send information from one secure area to another. The channel may provide confidentiality or authenticity or, more commonly, both. [Ch. 11]

Security The protection of information and information systems against unauthorized access or modification of information, whether in storage, processing, or transit, and against denial of service to authorized users. [Ch. 11]

Security protocol A message protocol designed to achieve some security objective (e.g., authenticating a sender). Designers of security protocols must assume that some of the communicating parties are adversaries. [Ch. 11]

Segment 1. A numbered block of contiguously addressed virtual memory, the block having a range of memory addresses starting with address zero and ending at some specified size. Programs written for a segment-based virtual memory issue addresses that are really two numbers: the first identifies the segment number, and the second identifies the address within that segment. The memory manager must translate the segment number to determine where in real memory the segment is located. The second address may also require translation using a page map. [Ch. 5] 2. In a communication network, the data that the end-to-end layer gives to the network layer for forwarding across the network. A segment is the payload of a packet. Compare with *frame* (n.), *message*, and *packet*. [Ch. 7]

Self-pacing A property of some transmission protocols. A self-pacing protocol automatically adjusts its transmission rate to match the bottleneck data rate of the network over which it is operating. [Ch. 7]

Semaphore A special type of shared variable for sequence coordination among several concurrent threads. A semaphore supports two atomic operations: DOWN and UP. If the semaphore's value is larger than zero, DOWN decrements the semaphore and returns to its caller; otherwise, DOWN releases its processor until another thread increases the semaphore using UP. When control returns to the thread that originally issued the DOWN operation, that thread retries the DOWN operation. [Ch. 5]

Sequence coordination A coordination constraint among threads: for correctness, a certain event in one thread must precede some other certain event in another thread. [Ch. 5]

Sequencer A special type of shared variable used for sequence coordination. The primary operation on a sequencer is TICKET, which operates likes the "take a number" machine in a bakery or post office: two threads concurrently calling TICKET on the same sequencer receive different values, and the ordering of the values returned corresponds to the time ordering of the execution of TICKET. [Ch. 5]

Serial transmission A scheme for increasing the data rate between two modules by sending a series of self-clocking bits over a single transmission line with infrequent or no acknowledgments. [Ch. 7]

Serializable A property of before-or-after actions, that even if several operate concurrently, the result is the same as if they had acted one at a time, in some sequential (in other words, serial) order. [Ch. 9]

Server A module that implements a service. More than one server might implement the same service, or collaborate to implement a fault tolerant version of the service such that even if a server fails, the service is still available. [Ch. 4]

Service A module that responds to actions initiated by clients. [Ch. 4] At the end-to-end layer of a network, the end that responds to actions initiated by the other end. Compare with *client*. [Ch. 7]

Set up The steps required to allocate storage space for and initialize the state of a connection. [Ch. 7]

Shadow copy A working copy of an object that an all-or-nothing action creates so that it can make several changes to the object while the original remains unmodified. When the all-or-nothing action has made all of the changes, it then carefully exchanges the working copy with the original, thus preserving the appearance that all of the changes occurred atomically. Depending on the implementation, either the original or the working copy may be identified as the "shadow" copy, but the technique is the same in either case. [Ch. 9]

Shared-secret cryptography A key-based cryptographic transformation in which the cryptographic key for transforming can be easily determined from the key for the reverse transformation, and vice versa. In most shared-secret systems, the keys for a transformation and its reverse transformation are identical. [Ch. 11]

Shared-secret key The key used by a shared-secret cryptography system. [Ch. 11]

Sharing Allowing an object to be used by more than one other object without requiring multiple copies of the first object. [Ch. 2]

Sign To generate an authentication tag by transforming a message so that a receiver can use the tag to verify that the message is authentic. The word "sign" is usually restricted to public-key authentication systems. The corresponding description for shared-secret authentication systems is "generate a MAC". [Ch. 11]

Simple locking A locking protocol for creating before-or-after actions requiring that no data be read or written before reaching the lock point. For the atomic action to also be all-or-nothing, a further requirement is that no locks be released before commit (or abort). Compare with *two-phase locking*. [Ch. 9]

Simple serialization An atomicity protocol requiring that each newly created atomic action must wait to begin execution until all previously started atomic actions are no longer pending. [Ch. 9]

Simplex Describes a link between two stations that can be used in only one direction. Compare with *duplex*, *half-duplex*, and *full-duplex*. [Ch. 7]

Single-acquire protocol A simple protocol for locking: a thread can acquire a lock only if some other thread has not already acquired it. [Ch. 5]

Single-event upset A synonym for *transient fault*. [Ch. 8]

Slave In a multiple-site replication scheme, a site that takes update requests from only the master site. Compare with *master.* [Ch. 10]

Sliding window In flow control, a technique in which the receiver sends an additional window allocation before it has fully consumed the data from the previous allocation, intending that the new allocation arrive at the sender in time to keep data flowing smoothly, taking into account the transit time of the network. [Ch. 7]

Snoopy cache In a multiprocessor system with a bus and a cache in each processor, a cache design in which the cache actively monitors traffic on the bus to watch for events that invalidate cache entries. [Ch. 10]

Soft modularity Modularity defined by convention but not enforced by physical constraints. Compare with *enforced modularity*. [Ch. 4]

Soft real-time scheduler A real-time scheduler in which missing a deadline occasionally is acceptable. [Ch. 6]

Soft state State of a running program that the program can easily reconstruct if it becomes necessary to abruptly terminate and restart the program. [Ch. 8]

Source The network attachment point that originated the payload of a packet. Sometimes used as shorthand for *source address*. [Ch. 7]

Source address An identifier of the source of a packet, usually carried as a field in the header of the packet. [Ch. 7]

Spatial locality A kind of locality of reference in which the reference string contains clusters of references to adjacent or nearby addresses. [Ch. 6]

Speaks for A phrase used to express delegation relationships between principals. "A speaks for B" means that B has delegated some authority to A. [Ch. 11]

Speculation A technique to improve performance by performing an operation in advance of receiving a request on the chance that it will be requested. The hope is that the result can be delivered with less latency and with less setup overhead. Examples include demand paging with larger pages than strictly necessary, prepaging, prefetching, and writing dirty pages before the primary device space is needed. [Ch. 6]

Spin loop A situation in which a thread waits for an event to happen without releasing the processor. [Ch. 5]

Stability A property of an object that, once it has a value, it maintains that value indefinitely. Compare with *durability* and *persistence*, terms that have different technical definitions, as explained in Sidebar 2.1. [Ch. 2]

Stable binding A binding that is guaranteed to map a name to the same value for the lifetime of the name space. One of the features of a unique identifier name space. [Ch. 2]

Stack algorithm A class of page-removal algorithms in which the set of pages in a primary device of size m is always a subset of the set of pages in a primary device of size n, if m is smaller than n. Stack algorithms have the property that increasing the size of the memory is guaranteed not to result in increased numbers of missing-page exceptions. [Ch. 6]

Starvation An undesirable situation in which several threads are competing for a shared resource and because of adverse scheduling one or more of the threads never receives a share of the resource. [Ch. 6]

Static routing A method for setting up forwarding tables in which, once calculated, they do not automatically change in response to changes in network topology and load. Compare with *adaptive routing*. [Ch. 7]

Static scope An example of an explicit context, used to resolve names of program variables in some programming languages. The name resolver searches for a binding starting with the procedure that used the name, then in the procedure in which the first procedure was defined, and so on. Sometimes called *lexical scope*. Compare with *dynamic scope*. [Ch. 2]

Station A device that can send or receive data over a communication link. [Ch. 7]

Stop and wait A synonym for *lock step.* [Ch. 7]

Storage Another term for memory. Memory devices that are non-volatile and are read and written in large blocks are traditionally called storage devices, but there are enough exceptions that in practice the words "memory" and "storage" should be treated as synonyms. [Ch. 2]

Store and forward A forwarding network organization in which transport-layer messages are buffered in a non-volatile memory such as magnetic disk, with the goal that they never be lost. Many authors use this term for any forwarding network. [Ch. 7]

Stream A sequence of data bits or messages that an application intends to flow between two attachment points of a network. It also usually intends that the data of a stream be delivered in the order in which it was sent, and that there be no duplication or omission of data. [Ch. 7]

Strict consistency An interface requirement that temporary violation of a data invariant during an update never be visible outside of the action doing the update. One feature of the read/write coherence memory model is strict consistency. Sometimes called *strong consistency*. [Ch. 10]

Stub A procedure that hides from the caller that the callee is not invoked with the ordinary procedure call conventions. The stub may marshal the arguments into a message and send the message to a service, where another stub unmarshals the message and invokes the callee. [Ch. 4]

Supermodule A set of replicated modules interconnected in such a way that it acts like a single module. [Ch. 8]

Supervisor call instruction (SVC) A processor instruction issued by user modules to pass control of the processor to the kernel. [Ch. 5]

Swapping A feature of some virtual memory systems in which a multilevel memory manager removes a complete address space from a primary device and moves in a complete new one. [Ch. 6]

Synonym One of multiple names that map to the same value. Compare with *alias,* a term that usually, but not always, has the same meaning. [Ch. 2]

System A set of interconnected components that has an expected behavior observed at the interface with its environment. Contrast with *environment*. [Ch. 1]

Tail drop A strategy for managing an overloaded resource: the system refuses service to the queue entry that arrived most recently. [Ch. 7]

Tear down The steps required to reset the state of a connection and deallocate the space that was used for storage of that state. [Ch. 7]

Temporal locality A kind of locality of reference in which the reference string contains closely spaced references to the same address. [Ch. 6]

Thrashing An undesirable situation in which the primary device is too small to run a thread or a group of threads, leading to frequent missing-page exceptions. [Ch. 6]

Thread An abstraction that encapsulates the state of a running module. This abstraction encapsulates enough of the state of the interpreter that executes the module so that one can stop a thread at any point in time and later resume it. The ability to stop a thread and resume it later allows virtualization of the interpreter. [Ch. 5]

Thread manager A module that implements the thread abstraction. It typically provides calls for creating a thread, destroying it, allowing the thread to yield, and coordinating with other threads. [Ch. 5]

Threat A potential security violation from either a planned attack by an adversary or an unintended mistake by a legitimate user. [Ch. 11]

Throughput A measure of the rate of useful work done by a service for a given workload. [Ch. 6]

Ticket system A security system in which each principal maintains a list of capabilities, one for each object to which the principal is authorized to have access. [Ch. 11]

Tolerated error An error or class of errors that is both detectable and maskable, and for which a systematic recovery procedure has been implemented. Compare with *detectable error*, *maskable error*, and *untolerated error.* [Ch. 8]

Tombstone A piece of data that will probably never be used again but cannot be discarded because there is still a small chance that it will be needed. [Ch. 7]

Trailer Information that a protocol layer adds to the end of a packet. [Ch. 7]

Transaction A multistep action that is both atomic in the face of failure and atomic in the face of concurrency. That is, it is both all-or-nothing and before-or-after. [Ch. 9]

Transactional memory A memory model in which multiple references to primary memory are both all-or-nothing and before-or-after. [Ch. 9]

Transient fault A fault that is temporary and for which retry of the putatively failed component has a high probability of finding that it is okay. Sometimes called a *single-event upset*. Compare with *persistent fault* and *intermittent fault*. [Ch. 8]

Transit time In a forwarding network, the total delay time required for a packet to go from its source to its destination. In other contexts, this kind of delay is sometimes called *latency*. [Ch. 7]

Transmission delay In a communication network, the component of overall delay contributed by the time spent sending a frame at the available data rate. [Ch. 7]

Transport protocol An end-to-end protocol that moves data between two attachment points of a network while providing a particular set of specified assurances. It can be thought of as a prepackaged set of improvements on the best-effort specification of the network layer. [Ch. 7]

Triple-modular redundancy (TMR) N-modular redundancy with $N = 3$. [Ch. 8]

Trusted computing base (TCB) That part of a system that must work properly to make the overall system secure. [Ch. 11]

Trusted intermediary A service that acts as the trusted third party on behalf of multiple, perhaps distrustful, clients. It enforces modularity, thereby allowing multiple distrustful clients to share resources in a controlled manner. [Ch. 4]

Two generals dilemma An intrinsic problem that no finite protocol can guarantee to simultaneously coordinate state values at two places that are linked by an unreliable communication network. [Ch. 9]

Two-phase commit A protocol that creates a higher-layer transaction out of separate, lower-layer transactions. The protocol first goes through a preparation (sometimes called voting) phase, at the end of which each lower-layer transaction reports either that it cannot perform its part or that it is prepared to either commit or abort. It then enters a commitment phase in which the higher-layer transaction, acting as a coordinator, makes a final decision—thus the name two-phase. Two-phase commit has no connection with the similar-sounding term *two-phase locking*. [Ch. 9]

Two-phase locking A locking protocol for before-or-after atomicity that requires that no locks be released until all locks have been acquired (that is, there must be a lock point). For the atomic action to also be all-or-nothing, a further requirement is that no locks for objects to be written be released until the action commits. Compare with *simple locking*. Two-phase locking has no connection with the similar-sounding term *two-phase commit*. [Ch. 9]

Undo action An application-specified action that, when executed during failure recovery or an abort procedure, reverses the effect of some previously performed, but not yet committed, component action. The goal is that neither the original action nor its reversal be visible above the layer that implements the action. Compare with *redo* and *compensate*. [Ch. 9]

Unique identifier name space A name space in which each name, once it is bound to a value, can never be reused for a different value. A unique identifier name space thus provides a stable binding. In a billing system, customer account numbers usually constitute a unique identifier name space. [Ch. 2]

Universal name space A name space of a naming scheme that has only one context. A universal name space has the property that no matter who uses a name it has the same binding. Computer file systems typically provide a universal name space for absolute path names. [Ch. 2]

Universe of values The set of all possible values that can be named by a particular naming scheme. [Ch. 2]

Unlimited name space A name space in which names never have to be reused. [Ch. 3]

Untolerated error An error or class of errors that is undetectable, unmaskable, or unmasked and therefore can be expected to lead to a failure. Compare with *detectable error*, *maskable error*, and *tolerated error.* [Ch. 8]

User-dependent binding A binding for which a name used by a shared object resolves to different values, depending on the identity of the user of the shared object. [Ch. 2]

User mode A feature of a processor that, when set, disallows the use of certain processor features (e.g., changing the page-map address register). Compare with *kernel mode*. [Ch. 5]

Utilization The percentage of capacity used for a given workload. [Ch. 6]

Value The thing to which a name is bound. A value may be a real, physical object, or it may be another name either from the original name space or from a different name space. [Ch. 2]

Valid construction The term used by software designers for *fault avoidance*. [Ch. 8]

Version history The set of all values for an object or variable that have ever existed, stored in journal storage. [Ch. 9]

Virtual address An address that must be translated to a physical address before using it to refer to memory. Compare with *physical address*. [Ch. 5]

Virtual circuit A connection intended to carry a stream through a forwarding network, in some ways simulating an electrical circuit. [Ch. 7]

Virtual machine A method of emulation in which, to maximize performance, a physical processor is used as much as possible to implement virtual instances of itself. [Ch. 5]

Virtual machine monitor The software that implements virtual machines. [Ch. 5]

Virtualization A technique that simulates the interface of a physical object, in some cases creating several virtual objects using one physical instance, in others creating one large virtual object by aggregating several smaller physical instances, and in yet other cases creating a virtual object from a different kind of physical object. [Ch. 5]

Virtual memory manager A memory manager that implements virtual addresses, resolving them to physical addresses by using, for example, a page map. [Ch. 5]

Volatile memory A kind of memory in which the mechanism of retaining information actively consumes energy. When one disconnects the power source, it forgets its information content. Compare with *non-volatile memory*. [Ch. 2]

Voter A device used in some NMR designs to compare the output of several nominally identical replicas that all have the same input. [Ch. 8]

Well-known name (or address) A name or address that has been advertised so widely that one can depend on it not changing for the lifetime of the value to which it is bound. In the United States, the emergency telephone number "911" is a well-known name. In some file system designs, sector or block number 1 of every storage device is reserved as a place to store device data, making "1" a well-known address in that context. [Ch. 2]

Window In flow control, the quantity of data that the receiving side of a transport protocol is prepared to accept from the sending side. [Ch. 7]

Witness A (usually cryptographically strong) hash value that attests to the content of a file. Another widely used term for this concept is *fingerprint*. [Ch. 10]

Working directory In a file system, a directory used as a default context, for resolution of relative path names. [Ch. 2]

Working set The set of all addresses to which a thread refers in the interval Δt. If the application exhibits locality of reference, this set of addresses will be small compared to the maximum number of possible addresses during Δt. [Ch. 6]

Write-ahead-log (WAL) protocol A recovery protocol that requires appending a log record in journal storage before installing the corresponding data in cell storage. [Ch. 9]

Write tearing See *atomic storage.*

Write-through A property of a cache: a write operation updates the value in both the primary device and the secondary device before acknowledging completion of the write. (A cache without the write-through property is sometimes called a *write-behind cache*.) [Ch. 6]

Index of Concepts

Design principles and hints appear in *underlined italics*. Procedure names appear in SMALL CAPS. Page numbers in **bold face** are in the Glossary. Page numbers that are greyed out are in a section that is [on-line].

E

N

O

Q

R

S